Chicorel Bibliography to the Performing Arts: Books and Periodicals

VOLUME 3A

Chicorel Index Series
VOLUME 3A
First Edition

CHICOREL BIBLIOGRAPHY TO THE PERFORMING ARTS

Edited by   MARIETTA CHICOREL

CHICOREL LIBRARY PUBLISHING CORP.
330 West 58th Street, New York, N.Y. 10019

Chicorel index series, v. 1–.
New York, Chicorel Library Pub. Corp. 1970–
v. 27cm

1. Drama–Indexes. I. Title: Chicorel Theater index to plays in anthologies, periodicals, discs, and tapes (v.1–3,6,7,8–). II. Chicorel index to poetry in collections, on discs and tapes (v. 4;5–). III. Title: Theater index to plays in anthologies, periodicals, discs and tapes.
Notes: Edited by Marietta Chicorel and others.

X5781.C485   016.80882

Chicorel Index Series Publications

Volume 1 Chicorel Theatre Index to Plays in Anthologies, Periodicals, Discs & Tapes.
Edited by Marietta Chicorel.
Lists approximately 10,000 entries. Indexes and analyzes plays in over 550 collections in print, and in current periodicals.

Indexes Plays, Playwrights, Editors, and Play Collections in Anthologies, Single Author Collections, Text Books, and Plays in books of Criticism and Essays. The scope includes International Plays from Antiquity to the Current Scene.

All bibliographic information is in one single alphabet, supplemented by separate Indexes in back of the book. 572p. 1970.

Volume 2 Chicorel Theater Index to Plays in Anthologies, Periodicals, Discs & Tapes.
Edited by Marietta Chicorel.
Lists approximately 10,000 new entries, plus 1,000 starred entries new in print since Volume 1. Indexes and analyzes current periodicals, as well.

Simplified single alphabet dictionary arrangement plus lists of Anthologies indexed, Authors/Playwrights, Editors, Play Titles, and Periodicals included. 502p. 1971.

Volume 3 Chicorel Theater Index to Plays in Anthologies, Periodicals, Discs & Tapes.
Edited by Marietta Chicorel.
Indexes and analyzes approximately 9600 entries to plays and collections, periodicals and discs in the English language published in England.

Scope: Worldwide drama of all nations and all time. 1972.

Volume 3A Chicorel Bibliography to the Performing Arts
A buying guide that comprises more than 8,000 entries arranged under more than 300 subject headings such as Actors, Black Drama, Drama, Tape Recorders and Recording, Staging, Play Production, Costume, Design, Lighting, Stereophonic Sound Systems, Finance, Shakespeare, Theater, and more. It also contains a list of periodicals, as well as a group of out of print classics. 1972.

Volume 4 Chicorel Index To Poetry On Discs & Tapes: Poetry-On-Media·
Locates recorded poetry by title, first-line, poet, reader/actor, director on approximately 500 recorded media read in English; over 20,000 entries. 1972.

Volume 5A Chicorel Index To Poetry In Collections: Poetry-In-Print
Locates poetry now in print in over 1,000 anthologies and single works by title, first-line, author, editor, collection title. Lists all bibliographic elements, incl. translator and subject descriptors. 1972.

Volume 5B
Chicorel Index to Poetry in Collections: Poetry-in-Print. Second Part completes Vol. 5A. 1971.

Volume 6 Chicorel Index to Poetry
A retrospective volume covering o.p. titles for approximately the last 6 years. 1972.

Volume 7 Chicorel Theater Index to Plays in Anthologies, Periodicals, Discs & Tapes: Plays on Discs and Tapes.
Locates, analyzes and indexes plays and performers on over 1200 recorded media; includes U.S. and foreign productions. Indexes discs, tapes, and video play performances. One single alphabetical arrangement includes approximately 12,000 entries by Play Title, Album Title, Playwright, Actors, and Director.

Scope is International, from antiquity to the Present. Includes translations and productions in the original languages as well.

Contents

8

9

11

12

13

14

15

16

Foreword

The Chicorel Bibliography to the Performing Arts, a self-contained volume that forms part of the Chicorel Index Series, is intended as a basic bibliographical resource used by people interested in all aspects of the performing arts, including history and practice.

This volume answers the need expressed by theater critics, playwrights, producers, departmental chairmen, librarians, students and researchers for an up-to-date, comprehensive and well organized Bibliography to the Performing Arts. The scope of the Chicorel Bibliography is international with emphasis on the English language and covering significant historical periods. Of the many potential users of the bibliography the following may find it of special use: secondary school and library supervisors; English speech and communications instructors; television, educational and commercial film producers; theatrical producers; playwrights; critics; and anyone concerned with communications media and the performing arts.

For ease in using, the organization of the Chicorel Bibliography to the Performing Arts is alphabetical by author within each subject category. There are approximately 275 subject headings with more than 9,000 entries. As new publications become available, supplementary volumes will be issued. The subject categories are subdivided where this appears helpful. To assist the user the running-heads consist of the main subject headings with which the sub-headings on any given page relate. For example: Dance — Education and Dance — History have the same running head, DANCE, on the pages that list books relating to either subdivision. The contents pages of this volume should be consulted in order to determine the subdivisions into which a particular subject has been divided and arranged.

The purpose of this bibliography is to fill the gap in the tools presently available to the researcher in these various areas as well as those of interest to the layman and the investor or director of commercial and amateur performances in almost every medium of creative endeavor.

Subject coverage includes appropriate titles that are important to each of the libraries mentioned and those that are significant for professionals and for the instructional staff through university and graduate school.

The scope is historical as well as providing up-to-date sources of current trends and practice. This facilitates the locating of almost any specific background in the histroy of the performing arts and its current availability. The volume's comprehensive subject arrangement makes it easy to use. Future supplements are planned.

Additional special features include a unique Table of Contents that represents in fact a prototype vertical file arrangement; further, a list of publisher addresses with telephone numbers for ease in ordering. Greatest care was taken to achieve accuracy, but some errors will creep in. This publisher is not legally responsible for errors which may have occurred, and will appreciate your advice in correcting them.

We wish to gratefully acknowledge the enthusiastic response and encouragement we have already received from the users of the Series and especially wish to thank those people whose suggestions have led to its increased usefulness. Your continued suggestions as the users of these volumes are warmly appreciated.

Marietta Chicorel
Editor-in-Chief

New York City
August, 1972

Acknowledgment of Thanks

The Editors wish to thank the following for their invaluable assistance:

Celeste Ashley, *Stanford University Library*

Mariella Bednar, *Flushing, New York*

Arthur Mandelbaum, *New York City*

Herbert Meadow, *New York City*

Norman Roth, *New York City*

Richard Samuelson, *Fiorello H. LaGuardia Community College Library, N.Y.C.*

Judy Serebnick, *New York City*

Lois Zimmerman, *New York City*

Martin Zimmerman, *New York City*

MAIN LISTING SECTION

ACTING

Albright, Hardie. Acting: The Creative Process. 1967. $10.60 Hdbd. $7.95 text ed. Dickenson Publ. Co., CA.

Albright, Harry D. Working up a Part. 2nd ed. 1959. $5.50 pa. (3-00472). Houghton Mifflin, NY.

Ben Auram, R. Act & the Image. $3.25 text ed. Odyssey Pr., NY.

Benedetti, Robert L. Actor at Work. (Speech & Drama Ser). 1970. ref. ed. $6.50 Hdbd. (ISBN 0-13-003657-9). Prentice-Hall.

Bernhardt, Sarah. Art of the Theater. facsimile ed. Stenning, H. J., tr. (Select Bibliographies Reprint Ser). 1924. $10.00 Hdbd. (ISBN 0-8369-5038-0). Bks for Libraries, NY.

Bernhardt, Sarah. Art of the Theatre. 1924. $12.50 Hdbd. Benjamin Blom, NY.

Blunt, J. Composite Art of Acting. 1966. $8.50 Hdbd. (31115). Macmillan Co., NY.

Brown, Andrew. Drama. 1962. $3.50 Hdbd. (ISBN 0-668-00979-9); $0.95 pa. (ISBN 0-668-00984-5). Arc Bks, NY.

Brown, Gilmor & Garwood, Alice. General Principles of Play Direction. 1936. $2.75 Hdbd. Samuel French, NY.

Cartmell, Van H. Amateur Theater: A Guide for Actor & Director. 1961. $4.95 Hdbd. Van Nostrand Reinhold, NY.

Cartmell, Van H. Amateur Theatre: A Guide for Actor & Director. 1968. (1961) $1.50 pa. (900840, Paperbooks). Funk & Wagnalls, NY.

Chekhov, Michael. To the Actor. 1953. $5.95 Hdbd. (ISBN 0-06-010755-3). Harper & Row, NY.

Cohen, Robert S. Acting Professionally. 1971. price "n.g." (ISBN 0-87484-191-7); $1.95 pa. (ISBN 0-87484-190-9). Natl Pr., CA.

Cole, Toby & Chinoy, Helen K., eds. Actors on Acting: Theories, Techniques, & Practices of the World's Great Actors, Told in Their Own Words. rev. ed. 1970. $8.95 Hdbd. Crown Publ., NY.

Collier, Gaylan J. Assignments in Acting. 1966. $7.50 pa. (ISBN 0-06-041328-X, Harper & Row, NY.

Crawford, Lane. Acting. 1930. $12.50 Hdbd. Benjamin Blom, NY.

Diderot, Dennis. The Paradox of Acting. Incl. Masks of Faces: Archer William. 1957. $1.65 pa. (ISBN 0-8090-0504-2). Hill & Wang, NY.

Dolman, John. Art of Acting. 1949. $14.75 Hdbd. (ISBN 0-8371-3832-9). Greenwood Pr., CT.

Dolman, John, Jr. Art of Play Production. rev. ed. 1946. $9.50 Hdbd. (ISBN 0-06-041680-7). Harper & Row, NY.

Duerr, Edwin. Length & Depth of Acting. 1962. $13.95 Hdbd. (ISBN 0-03-026075-2); $9.95 text ed. (ISBN 0-03-011025-4). Holt, Rinehart & Winston, NY.

Duerr, Edwin. Radio & Television Acting. (1950). $29.50 Hdbd. (ISBN 0-8371-5580-0). Greenwood Pr., CT.

Dunn, Charles W., ed. Actors' Analects. (Studies in Oriental Culture Ser). 1970. $12.00 Hdbd. (ISBN 0-231-03391-5). Columbia Univ Pr., NY.

Engel, Johann. Practical Illustrations of Rhetorical Gesture & Action. Siddons, Henry, ed. 1968. $17.50 Hdbd. Benjamin Blom, NY.

Eustis, Morton. Players at Work. 1937. $8.75 Hdbd. Benjamin Blom, NY.

Eustis, Morton. Players at Work: Acting According to the Actors. (Essay Index Reprint Ser). 1937. $7.00 Hdbd. (ISBN 0-8369-0432-X). Bks for Libraries, NY.

Foote, Samuel. Treatise on the Passions. 1747. $6.75 Hdbd. Benjamin Blom, NY.

Franklin, Miriam A. Rehearsal: The Principles & Practice of Acting for the Stage. 4th ed. 1963. $8.75 pa. (ISBN 0-13-771568-4). Prentice Hall, NY.

Funke, Lewis & Booth, John E., eds. Actors Talk About Acting. 1967. $1.25 pa. Avon Books, NY.

Grotowski, Jerzy. Toward a Poor Theatre. 1970. $2.45 pa. Simon & Schuster, NY.

Grotowski, Jerzy. Toward a Poor Theatre. 1970. $6.50 Hdbd. (20392). Simon & Schuster, NY.

Guthrie, Tyrone. Tyrone Guthrie on Acting. 1971. $8.95 Hdbd. (ISBN 0-670-73832-8, Studio). Viking Pr., NY.

Hammerton, J. A., ed. Actor's Art. 1897. $10.75 Hdbd. Benjamin Blom, NY.

Harris, Julie & Tarshis, Barry. Julie Harris Talks to Young Actors. (Jr. Hi.). 1971. $4.95 Hdbd. (ISBN 0-688-30020-0); $4.95 Hdbd. (ISBN 0-688-35020-8). Lothrop, Lee & Shepard Co., NY.

Held, Jack P. Improvisational Acting: A Handbook of Exercises for the Student Actor. 1971. $3.35 text ed.; $2.50 pa. Wadsworth Publ. Co., CA.

Herman, Lewis & Herman, Marguerite. Foreign Dialects. $8.50 Hdbd. Theatre Arts Books, NY.

Hethmon, Robert H., ed. Strasberg at the Actors Studio. 1965. $5.75 Hdbd. (ISBN 0-670-67792-2). Viking Pr., NY.

Hethmon, Robert H., ed. Strasberg at the Actors Studio. $1.95 pa. (ISBN 0-670-00228-3). Viking Pr., NY.

Hill, John. Actor. 1750. $18.50 Hdbd. Benjamin Blom, NY.

Hill, John. Actor. 1755. $17.50 Hdbd. Benjamin Blom, NY.

Irving, Henry. Drama: Addresses. 1893. $6.75 Hdbd. Benjamin Blom, NY.

Joels, Merrill E. How to Get into Show Business. rev. ed. (Communication Arts Books Ser). Orig. Title: Acting Is a Business. 1969. $5.95 Hdbd. (ISBN 0-8038-3004-1). Hastings House Publ., NY.

Johnson, Albert & Johnson, Bertha. Drama for Junior High, with Selected

Scenes. 1971. $6.95 Hdbd. (ISBN 0-498-07587-7). A. S. Barnes, NY.

Kahan, Stanley. Actor's Workbook. $6.50 pa. (ISBN 0-15-500500-6). Harcourt-Brace & World, NY.

Kahan, Stanley. Introduction to Acting. 1962. text ed. $7.95 Hdbd. (ISBN 0-15-541550-6). Harcourt, Brace & World, NY.

King, Nancy. Theatre Movement: The Actor & His Space. 1971. $7.50 text ed. (ISBN 0-910482-28-4). Drama Book Shop, NY.

Kline, Peter. Scenes to Perform. Kozelka, Paul, ed. (Theatre Student Ser). Hi-Sch. 1969. $6.96 Hdbd. Rosen, Richards, Pr., NY.

Kline, Peter & Meadors, Nancy. Physical Movement for the Theatre. (Theatre Student Ser). 1971. lib. bdg. $10.50 Hdbd. (ISBN 0-8239-0235-8). Rosen, Richards, Pr., NY.

Laban, Rudolf. Mastery of Movement. 2nd ed. $8.00 Hdbd. DBS Publ., NY.

Lewes, George H. On Actors & the Art of Acting. 1968. (1957). $10.75 Hdbd. Greenwood Pr., CT.

Lewis, Robert. Method-or Madness. 1958. $3.50 Hdbd. French.

Lochrer, Robert. Mienenspiel und Maske in der Griechischen Tragoedie. 1927. $8.00 pa. Johnson Reprint Corp., NY.

Logan, Olive S. Mimic World. 1968. $12.50 Hdbd. Benjamin Blom, NY.

Luc, Jean. Paradox of Acting. Pollock,

Walter H., tr. 1883. $12.50 Hdbd. (ISBN 0-8337-4241-8). Burt Franklin, NY.

McGaw, Charles J. Acting Is Believing. 2nd ed. (Rinehart Editions). 1966. $6.95 text ed. (ISBN 0-03-057295-9). Holt, Rinehart & Winston, NY.

Machlin, Evangeline. Speech for the Stage. 1966. $6.75 Hdbd. Theatre Arts Books, NY.

Mackay, Edward & Mackay, Alice. Elementary Principles of Acting. 1934. $2.50 Hdbd. Samuel French, NY.

MacKenzie, Frances. Amateur Actor. $3.00 Hdbd. Theatre Arts Books, NY.

Moore, Dick. Opportunities in Acting. (Hi-Sch.). $3.75 text ed. (VGM); $1.95 pa. (V101). Univ. Publ. & Dist. Corp., NY.

Moore, Sonia. Stanislavski System. $0.75 pa. Pocket Books, Inc., NY.

Moore, Sonia. Stanislavski System: The Professional Training of an Actor. rev. ed. Orig. Title: Stanislavski Method. 1965. $1.25 pa. (ISBN 0-670-0118-X). Viking Pr., NY.

Nutall, Kenneth. Your Book of Acting. $3.25 Hdbd. Transatlantic Arts, NY.

Ommanney, Katharine A. Stage & the School. 3rd ed. 1960. $7.96 text ed. (ISBN 0-07-047669-1). McGraw-Hill, NY.

Ormsbee, Helen. Backstage with Actors. (Essay Index Reprint Ser). $11.75 Hdbd. (ISBN 0-8369-1934-3). Books for Libraries, NY.

Ormsbee, Helen. Backstage with Actors. 1938. $10.75 Hdbd. Benjamin Blom, NY.

Oxenford, Lyn. Design for Movement. 1954. $2.95 Hdbd. Theatre Arts Books, NY.

Pate, Michael. Film Actor. 1969. $9.50 Hdbd. (ISBN 0-498-06941-9). A. S. Barnes, NJ.

Pudovkin, V. Film Technique & Acting. $3.95 Hdbd Wehman Bros., NJ.

Pudovkin, V. I. Film Techniques & Film Acting. 1959. $3.75 Hdbd. Crown Publ., NY.

Rawson, Ruth. Acting. (Theatre Student Ser). 1969. $6.96 Hdbd. (ISBN 0-8239-0151-3). Rosen, Richards, Pr., NY.

Redgrave, Michael. Mask or Face. $4.15 Hdbd. Theatre Arts Books, NY.

Roose-Evans, James. Directing a Play. 1968. $6.95 Hdbd. Theatre Arts Books, NY.

Rosenstein, Sophie, et al. Modern Acting: A Manual. 1936. $2.00 Hdbd. Samuel French, NY.

Sand, Maurice, pseud. History of the Harlequinade, 2 Vols. 1968. $25.00 Hdbd. Benjamin Blom, NY.

Schreck, Everett M. Principles & Styles of Acting. (Speech & Drama). 1970. $8.95 text ed. (ISBN 0-201-06765-X). Addison-Wesley, MA.

Selden, Samuel. First Steps in Acting. 2nd ed. $5.50 text ed. (ISBN 0-390-79360-4). Appleton-Century-Crofts, NY.

Seyler, Athene & Haggard, Stephen. Craft of Comedy. $2.75 Hdbd. Theatre Arts Books, NY.

Stanislavski, Constantin. Creating a Role. Popper, Hermine I., ed. Hapgood, Elizabeth R., tr. 1961. $4.45 Hdbd. Theatre Arts Books, NY.

Stanislavski, Constantin. Actor Prepares. $4.45 Hdbd. Theatre Arts Books, NY.

Stanislavski, Constantin. Actor's Handbook. Hapgood, Elizabeth R., tr. 1963. $1.95 pa. (9). Theatre Arts Books, NY.

Stanislavski, Constantin. Building a Character. $4.95 Hdbd. Theatre Arts Books, NY.

Stanislavski, Constantin. Stanislavski's Legacy. rev. ed. Hapgood, Elizabeth R., tr. 1968. $5.50 Hdbd. $2.45 pa. Theatre Arts Books, NY.

Stanislavsky, Constantia. Stanislavsky on the Art of the Stage. 1962. $4.50 Hdbd. (ISBN 0-8090-8830-4, Drama); $1.65 pa. (ISBN 0-8090-0532-8). Hill & Wang, NY.

Steinbeck, Muriel. On Stage. 1970. $10.50 Hdbd. (ISBN 0-392-00147-0). Sportshelf & Soccer Assoc., NY.

Strickland, Francis C. Technique of Acting. 1956. text ed. $7.95 (ISBN 0-07-062190-X). McGraw-Hill, NY.

White, Edwin C. & Battye, Marguerite. Acting & Stage Movement. 1963. $0.95 pa. (ISBN 0-668-01054-1). Arc Books, Inc., NY.

Wilson, Garff B. History of American Acting. 1966. $7.95 Hdbd. (ISBN 0-253-13770-5). Indiana Univ. Pr., IN.

ACTING EDUCATION

Boleslavsky, Richard. Acting: The First Six Lessons. $3.25 Hdbd. Theatre Arts Books, NY.

Bourne, John. Teach Yourself Amateur Acting. $2.50 Hdbd. (ISBN 0-486-21426-5). Dover Publ., NY.

Cole, Toby. Acting: A Handbook of the Stanislavski Method. 1955. $3.95 Hdbd. Crown Publ., NY.

Courtney, Richard. Teaching Drama. 2nd ed. 1965. $3.75 Hdbd. International Publ. Serv., NY.

Dow, Marguerite R. Magic Mask: A Basic Textbook of Theatre Arts. Hi-Sch. 1968. $5.00 text ed. St. Martin's Pr., NY.

Hayman, Ronald. Techniques of Acting. 1971. $4.95 Hdbd. Holt-Rinehart & Winston, NY.

Kester, Katharine. Problem-Projects in Acting. 1937. $2.00 Hdbd. Samuel French, NY.

Lewis, Mary K. Acting for Children. 1969. $5.95 Hdbd. John Day Co., NY.

Moore, Sonia. Training an Actor: The Stanislavski System in Class. 1968. $2.45 pa. (ISBN 0-670-00249-6). Viking Pr., NY.

Moore, Sonia. Training an Actor, the Stanislavski System in Class. 1968.

$5.75 Hdbd. (ISBN 0-670-72391-6). Viking Pr., NY.

Olfson, Lewy. You Can Act. Rodegast, Roland, tr. (Elem.) 1971. $2.95 Hdbd. (ISBN 0-8069-7016-2); PLB $3.39 Hdbd. (ISBN 0-8069-7017-0). Sterling Publ. Co., NY.

ACTING FOR TELEVISION

Duerr, Edwin. Radio & Television Acting. (1950). $29.50 Hdbd. (ISBN 0-8371-5580-0). Greenwood Pr., CT.

Kingson, Walter K. & Cowgill, Rome. Television Acting & Directing: A Handbook. (Rinehart Editions). 1965. $8.95 pa. (ISBN 0-03-049810-4). Holt, Rinehart & Winston, NY.

Pate, Michael. Film Actor. 1969. $9.50 Hdbd. (ISBN 0-498-069141-9). A. S. Barnes & Co., NJ.

ACTORS AND ACTRESSES

Adams, William D. Dictionary of the Drama Vol. 1, A-G, 1965. (1904) $28.50 Hdbd. Burt Franklin, NY.

Angelou, Maya. I Know Why the Caged Bird Sings. 1970. $5.95 Hdbd. Random House, NY.

Bancroft, Marie & Bancroft, Squire. Bancrofts: Recollections of Sixty Years. 1909. $12.50 Hdbd. Benjamin Blom, NY.

Barrymore, Ethel. Memories: An Autobiography. 1968. (1955) $10.50 Hdbd. Kraus Reprint Co., NY.

Barrymore, John. Confessions of an Actor. 1926. $9.75 Hdbd. Benjamin Blom, NY.

Benjamin, Lewis S. Stage Favorites of the Eighteenth Century. facs. ed. (Essay Index Reprint Ser). 1928. $8.50 Hdbd. (ISBN 0-8369-0060-X). Books for Libraries, NY.

Bennett, Joan & Kibbee, Lois. Bennett Playbill. 1970. $6.95 Hdbd. (ISBN 0-03-081840-0). Holt, Rinehart & Winston, NY.

Bernardi, Jack. My Father the Actor. 1971. $6.50 Hdbd. (ISBN 0-393-07457-9). W. W. Norton, NY.

Bernhardt, Sarah. Art of the Theater, facsimile ed. Stenning, H. J., tr. (Select Bibliographies Reprint Ser). 1924. $10.00 Hdbd. (ISBN 0-8369-5038-0). Books for Libraries, NY.

Bernhardt, Sarah. Art of the Theatre. 1924. $12.50 Hdbd. Benjamin Blom, NY.

Bernhardt, Sarah. Memories of My Life, Being My Personal Professional, Social Recollections As a Woman & Artist. 1968. (1907) $6.50 Hdbd. (ISBN 0-403-00111-0). Scholarly Pr., MI.

Best, Marc. Those Endearing Young Charms: Child Performers of the Screen. $10.00 Hdbd. (ISBN 0-498-07729-2). A. S. Barnes & Co., NJ.

Boaden, James. Life of Mrs. Jordan, 2 Vols. 1831. $27.50 Hdbd. Benjamin Blom, NY.

Bradbrook, Muriel. Rise of the Common Player: A Study of Actor & Society in Shakespeare's England. 1962. $8.50 Hdbd. (ISBN 0-674-77235-0). Harvard U Pr., MA.

Brown, John M. Letters from Greenroom Ghosts. (Essay Index Reprint Ser). 1967. (1934) $9.25 Hdbd. (ISBN 0-8369-0258-0). Books for Libraries, NY.

Campbell, Mrs. Patrick. My Life & Some Letters. 1922. $12.50 Hdbd. Banjamin Blom, NY.

Carlisle, Carol J. Shakespeare from the Greenroom: Actors' Criticisms of Four Major Tragedies. 1969. $12.50 Hdbd. (ISBN 0-8078-1115-7). U of NC Pr., NC.

Chaplin, Charles. My Autobiography. $0.95 pa. Pocket Books, Inc., NY.

Chaplin, Charles. My Autobiography. 1964. $6.95 Hdbd. Simon & Schuster, NY.

Charters, Ann. Nobody: The Story of Bert Williams. 1970. $6.95 Hdbd. Macmillan, NY.

Cibber, Colley. Apology for the Life of Colley Cibber Written by Himself, 2 Vols. rev. ed. Lowe, R. W., ed. 1889. $14.50 Hdbd. (ISBN 0-404-01544-1). AMS Pr., NY.

Cohan, George M. Twenty Years on Broadway & the Years It Took to Get There. (1925) $12.25 Hdbd. (ISBN 0-8371-5682-3). Greenwood Pr., CT.

Cole, Toby & Chinoy, Helen K., eds. Actors on Acting: Theories, Techniques,

& Practices of the World's Great Actors, Told in Their Own Words. rev. ed. 1970. $8.95 Hdbd. Crown, NY.

Coleman, John & Coleman, Edward. Memoirs of Samuel Phelps. 1886. $12.50 Hdbd. Benjamin Blom, NY.

Cook, Edward D. Hours with the Players. 1883. $12.50 Hdbd. Benjamin Blom, NY.

Crawford, Joan. Joan Crawford: My Way of Life. 1971. $7.50 Hdbd. (ISBN 0-671-20970-1). Simon & Schuster, NY.

Davidge, William. Footlight Flashes. 1866. $12.50 Hdbd. Benjamin Blom, NY.

Didbin, Thomas. Reminiscences of Thomas Didbin, 2 Vols. 1970. (1827) Set. $32.50 Hdbd. (ISBN 0-404-02124-7). AMS Pr., NY.

Diderot, Dennis. The Paradox of Acting. Incl. Masks of Faces: Archer William. (Orig.). 1957. $1.65 pa. (ISBN 0-8090-0504-2). Hill & Wang, NY.

Dodd, Loring H. Celebrities at Our Hearthside. $5.00 Hdbd. Dresser, Chapman & Grimes, Inc., MA.

Donaldson, Frances. The Actor-Managers. 1971. $6.95 Hdbd. Regnery, NY.

Douglas, Jack. Funny Thing Happened to Me on My Way to the Grave. 1962. $3.50 Hdbd. E. P. Dutton, NY.

E. S. P. & the Stars. $5.95 Hdbd. (1871). Grosset & Dunlap, NY.

Fitzgerald, Percy. World Behind the Scenes. 1881. $12.50 Hdbd. Benjamin Blom, NY.

Forbes-Robertson, Johnston. Player Under Three Reigns. 1925. $9.75 Hdbd. Benjamin Blom, NY.

Fowler, Gene. Goodnight Sweet Prince. (Playbill Ser). 1971. (1944) $0.95 pa. (ISBN 0-345-02182-7). Ballantine Books, NY.

Funke, Lewis & Booth, John E., eds. Actors Talk About Acting. 1967. $1.25 pa. Avon Books, NY.

Gargan, William. Why Me: The Autobiography of William Gargan. 1969. $5.95 Hdbd. Doubleday, NY.

Garrick, David. Letters of David Garrick, 3 Vols. Little, David M., et al. eds. 1963. Set. boxed $35.00 Hdbd. (ISBN 0-674-52650-3). Harvard Univ. Pr., MA.

Gielgud, John. Stage Directions. 1964. $8.95 Hdbd. (ISBN 0-394-44683-6). Random House, NY.

Gielgud, John. Stage Directions. 1966. $1.45 pa. (130, Cap). Putnam, NY.

Gilder, Rosamond. Enter the Actress. $1.95 pa. (2). Theatre Arts Books, NY.

Gilder, Rosamond. Enter the Actress. facs. ed. (Essay Index Reprint Ser). 1931. $14.75 Hdbd. (ISBN 0-8369-2158-5). Books for Libraries, NY.

Goodman, Ezra. Fifty-Year Decline & Fall of Hollywood. 1961. $5.95 Hdbd. Simon & Schuster, NY.

Gordon, Ruth. Myself Among Others.

1971. $10.00 Hdbd (ISBN 0-689-10404-9). Atheneum Publ., NY.

Graham, Franklin. Histrionic Mono-real. 1902. $18.75 Hdbd. Benjamin Blom, NY.

Grau, Robert. Stage in the Twentieth Century. 1912. $15.00 Hdbd. Benjamin Blom, NY.

Grau, Robert. Theatre of Science. 1914. $15.00 Hdbd. Benjamin Blom, NY.

Guthrie, Tyrone. My Life in the Theatre. 1959. $6.95 Hdbd. (ISBN 0-07-025292-0). McGraw Hill, NY.

Hallowell, John. Truth Game. 1969. $5.95 Hdbd. Simon & Schuster, NY.

Hallowell, John. Truth Game. (1970) $0.95 pa. Bantam Books, NY.

Hammerton, J. A., ed. Actor's Art. 1897. $10.75 Hdbd. Benjamin Blom, NY.

Hardwicke, Cedric. Let's Pretend. 1932. $10.75 Hdbd. Benjamin Blom, NY.

Harris, Julie & Tarshis, Barry. Julie Harris Talks to Young Actors. $4.95 Hdbd. Lothrop, Lee & Shephard & Co., NY.

Hart, William S. My Life East & West. 1968. $10.75 Hdbd. Benjamin Blom, NY.

Harvey, John Martin. Autobiography of Sir John Martin-Harvey. 1933. $12.50 Hdbd. Benjamin Blom, NY.

Harvey, John Martin. Book of Martin Harvey. 1928. $12.50 Hdbd. Benjamin Blom, NY.

Hayden, Sterling. Wanderer. 1963. $7.95 Hdbd. Knopf, NY.

Hayes, Helen & Dody, Sandford. On Reflection: An Autobiography. 1969. $7.50 (ISBN 0-912120-00-2). Lanewood Pr., MA.

Hazlitt, William. Hazlitt on Theatre. Archer, William & Lowe, Robert, eds. (Orig.). 1957. $1.25 pa. (ISBN 0-8090-0507-7, Drama). Hill & Wang, NY.

Hecht, Ben. Child of the Century. (Playbill Bk). 1970. (1954) $1.25 pa. (ISBN 0-345-02087-1). Ballantine Bks., NY.

Hill, George H. Scenes from the Life of an Actor. 1853. $12.50 Hdbd. Benjamin Blom, NY.

Izay. For Actors While Waiting in the Unemployment Line. $2.50 pa. Heritage Printers, NC.

Jefferson, Joseph. Autobiography of Joseph Jefferson. Downer, Alan S., ed. (John Harvard Library Ser). 1964. $9.50 Hdbd. (ISBN 0-674-05350-8). Harvard Univ. Pr., MA.

Joseph, Bertram. Tragic Actor. 1959. $9.95 Hdbd. Theatre Arts Books, NY.

Keese, William L. Group of Comedians. 1901. $7.00 Hdbd. Benjamin Blom, NY.

Keese, William L. Group of Comedians. (Drama Ser). 1970 (1901) $14.50 Hdbd. (ISBN 0-8337-1903-3). Burt Franklin, NY.

Kitchin, Laurence. Mid-Century

Drama. 2nd rev. ed. 1962. $6.50 Hdbd. Humanities Pr., NY.

Leman, Walter M. Memories of an Old Actor. 1970. (1886) $12.50 Hdbd. (ISBN 0-403-00199-4). Scholarly Pr., MI.

Leslie, Amy. Some Players. 1899. $12.50 Hdbd. Benjamin Blom, NY.

Lewes, George H. On Actors & the Art of Acting. 1968. (1957) $10.75 Hdbd. Greenwood Pr., CT.

McCallum, John. Scooper. 1961. $4.95 Hdbd. (ISBN 0-8323-0191-4). Binfords & Mort Publ., OR.

MacCarthy, Desmond. Drama. 1940. $9.75 Hdbd. Benjamin Blom, NY.

McHugh, Roger, ed. Ah, Sweet Dancer: W. B. Yeats & Margot Ruddock, a Correspondence. 1971. $4.95 Hdbd. Macmillan, NY.

MacLaine, Shirley. Don't Fall off the Mountain. 1970. $6.50 Hdbd. (ISBN 0-393-07338-6). Norton, NY.

MacLaine, Shirley. Don't Fall off the Mountain. 1971. $1.50 pa. Bantam Books, NY.

MacLiammoir, Michael. All for Hecuba. $6.95 Hdbd. (ISBN 0-8283-1137-4). Branden Pr., MA.

Macready, William C. Diaries of William Charles Macready, 2 Vols. Macready, William C., ed. Toynbee, William C., tr. 1912. $28.50 Hdbd. Benjamin Blom, NY.

Macready, William. Journal of William Charles Macready, 1832–1851. Trewin,

John C., ed. 1970. (1967) $2.85 pa. (ISBN 0-8093-0423-6, AB). Southern Illinois Univ Pr., IL.

Macready, William C. Macready's Reminiscences. Pollock, Frederick, ed. 1875. $12.50 Hdbd. Benjamin Blom, NY.

Maeder, Clara F. Autobiography of Clara Fisher Maeder. Douglas, Taylor, ed. (Drama Ser). 1970. (1897) $14.50 Hdbd. (ISBN 0-8337-3477-6). Burt Franklin, NY.

Maeder, Clara F. Autobiography of Clara Fisher Maeder. 1897. $9.75 Hdbd. Benjamin Blom, NY.

Martin, Pete. Pete Martin Calls On. 1962. $5.95 Hdbd. Simon & Schuster, NY.

Martin-Harvey, John. Autobiography of Sir John Martin-Harvey. 1971. (1933) $19.00 Hdbd. (ISBN 0-403-01015-2). Scholarly Pr., MI.

Matthews, Brander, ed. Papers on Acting. (Orig.). $3.75 Hdbd. (ISBN 0-8090-7510-5, Drama); $1.65 pa. (ISBN 0-8090-0511-5). Hill & Wang, NJ.

Melville, Lewis, pseud. More Stage Favorites of the Eighteenth Century. facs. ed. (Essay Index Reprint Ser). 1929. $9.00 Hdbd. (ISBN 0-8369-0194-0). Books for Libraries, NY.

Merrill, Mary. Survey of Rural Taste for Movie Stars. 1968. $10.00 Hdbd. (ISBN 0-911948-00-7). $5.00 pa. (ISBN 0-911948-29-5). Bormerl Oaks Pr., IN.

Mills, Earl. Dorothy Dandridge: A

Portrait in Black. $1.50 pa. (ISBN 0-87067-411-0). Holloway House Publ., CA.

Montgredien, Georges. Grandes Comediens Du Dix-Septieme Siecle. 1968. (1927) $16.50 Hdbd. (ISBN 0-8337-2444-4). Burt Franklin, NY.

Murdock, James E. Stage. 1880. $12.50 Hdbd. Benjamin Blom, NY.

Nemirovitch-Dantchenko, Vladimir. My Life in the Russian Theatre. 1968. $9.50 Hdbd. $3.45 pa. Theatre Arts Books, NY.

O'Brady, Frederic. All Told. 1964. $4.95 Hdbd. Simon & Schuster, NY.

Oppenheimer, George, ed. Passionate Playgoer. $1.95 pa. (ISBN 0-670-00119-8). Viking Pr., NY.

Ormsbee, Helen. Backstage with Actors. 1938. $10.75 Hdbd. Benjamin Blom, NY.

Ormsbee, Helen. Backstage with Actors. (Essay Index Reprint Ser). $11.75 Hdbd. (ISBN 0-8369-1934-3). Books for Libraries, NY.

Pate, Michael. Film Actor. 1969. $9.50 Hdbd. (ISBN 0-498-06941-9). A. S. Barnes & Co., NJ.

Pickett, L. Across My Path. (Essay Index Reprint Ser). $7.75 Hdbd. (ISBN 0-8369-1841-X). Books for Libraries, NY.

Picon, Molly. So Laugh a Little. 1962. $3.00 Hdbd. Simon & Schuster, NY.

Picon, Molly & Rosenberg, Ethel. So Laugh a Little. $0.60 pa. Paperback Library, NY.

Playboy Editors, ed. Playboy Interviews Peter Fonda & Elliot Gould. (Orig.). 1971. $1.75 pa. Playboy Pr., Ill.

Redfield, William. Letters from an Actor. 1969. (1967) $1.75 pa. (ISBN 0-670-00264-X). Viking Pr., NY.

Redfield, William H. Letters from an Actor. 1967. $5.75 Hdbd. (ISBN 0-670-42582-6). Viking Pr., NY.

Redgrave, Michael. Mask or Face. $4.15 Hdbd. Theatre Arts Books, NY.

Reed, Dena. Success Tips from Young Celebrities. (Self-Help Ser). 1968. $0.75 pa. (ISBN 0-448-04893-0). Grosset & Dunlap, NY.

Reed, Dena. Success Tips from Young Celebrities. (Jr. Hi.). $2.95 Hdbd. (ISBN 0-448-01545-5). Grosset & Dunlap, NY.

Robson, William. Old Playgoer. $18.00 Hdbd. (ISBN 0-87556-304-X). Albert Saifer, PA.

Ross, Lillian & Ross, Helen. Player: A Profile of an Art. 1968. $2.95 pa. Simon & Schuster, NY.

Ryley, S. W. Itinerant, 2 Vols. in 1. 1808. $27.50 Hdbd. Benjamin Blom, NY.

Salvini, Tommaso. Leaves from the Autobiography of Tommaso Salvini. 1893. $12.50 Hdbd. Benjamin Blom, NY.

Scott, George G. Personal & Professional Recollections. 1971. price "n.g." Humanities Pr., NY.

Stanislavski, Constantin. My Life in Art. $4.95 pa. World Publ. Co., OH.

Stanislavski, Constantin. My Life in Art. $6.75 Hdbd. Theatre Arts Books, NY.

Stoker, Bram. Personal Reminiscences of Henry Irving, 2 Vols. 1906. Set. $28.00 Hdbd. (ISBN 0-8371-2845-5). Greenwood Pr., CT.

Stoker, Bram. Personal Reminiscences of Henry Irving, 2 Vols. enl. ed. 1906. $18.75 Hdbd. Benjamin Blom, NY.

Strang, Lewis C. Players & Plays of the Last Quarter Century, 2 Vols. 1903. $10.75 ea. Hdbd. Benjamin Blom, NY.

Terry, Ellen. Ellen Terry's Memoirs. St. John, Christopher & Craig, Edith, eds. $12.50 Hdbd. Benjamin Blom, NY.

Terry, Ellen. Ellen Terry's Memoirs. Craig, Edith & St. John, Christopher, eds. 1932. $14.00 Hdbd. (ISBN 0-8371-4039-0). Greenwood Pr., CT.

Towse, John R. Sixty Years of the Theatre. 1916. $12.50 Hdbd. Benjamin Blom, NY.

Wagenknecht, Edward C. Merely Players. 1966. $5.95 Hdbd. (ISBN 0-8061-0717-0). U of Okla Pr., OK.

Wagenknecht, Edward C. Seven Daughters of the Theater. 1964. $5.95 Hdbd. (ISBN 0-8061-0618-2). U of Okla Pr., OK.

Wallack, Lester. Memories of Fifty Years. 1889. $9.75 Hdbd. Benjamin Blom, NY.

Wemyss, Francis C. Wemyss Chronology of the American Stage, from 1752–1852. 1968. $12.50 Hdbd. Benjamin Blom, NY.

West, Mae. Goodness Had Nothing to Do with It. rev. ed. (1970) $0.95 pa. Macfadden Bartell, NY.

Wilkinson, Tate. Memoirs of His Own Life, 4 Vols. in 2. (1968). $37.50 Hdbd. Benjamin Blom, NY.

Willard, George O. History of the Providence Stage 1762–1891. N.Y. 1891. $12.50 Hdbd. Benjamin Blom, NY.

Winter, William. Other Days. (Essay Index Reprint Ser). $12.50 Hdbd. (ISBN 0-8369-1816-9). Books for Libraries, NY.

Wood, William B. Personal Recollections of the Stage. 1855. $12.75 Hdbd. Benjamin Blom, NY.

Zavattini, C. Zavattini: Sequences from a Cinematic Life. 1969. $10.50 Hdbd. Prentice-Hall, NY.

American

Arliss, George. Up the Years from Bloomsbury: An Autobiography. (1930) $15.75 Hdbd. (ISBN 0-8371-5431-6). Greenwood Pr., CT.

Brown, Thomas A. History of the American Stage. (1968) $18.75 Hdbd. Benjamin Blom, NY.

Clapp, J. B. & Edgett, E. Players of the Present, 3 Vols. (Drama Ser). 1970. (1901) $14.50 ea. Hdbd. (ISBN 0-8337-0577-6). Burt Franklin, NY.

Clapp, John B. & Edgett, Edwin F. Players of the Present, 3 Vols. in 1. 1899–1901. $12.50 Hdbd. Benjamin Blom, NY.

Coad, Oral S. & Mims, Edwin, Jr. American Stage. (Yale Pageant of America Ser., Vol. 14). $10.75 Hdbd. US Publ. Assn., NY.

Cohan, George M. Twenty Years on Broadway & the Years It Took to Get There. (1925) $12.25 Hdbd. (ISBN 0-8371-5682-3). Greenwood Pr., CT.

Eustis, Morton. Players at Work. 1937. $8.75 Hdbd. Benjamin Blom, NY.

Eustis, Morton. Players at Work: Acting According to the Actors. facs. ed. (Essay Index Reprint Ser). 1937. $7.00 Hdbd. (ISBN 0-8369-0432-X). Books for Libraries, NY.

Frohman, Daniel. Encore. (Essay Index Reprint Ser). 1937. $12.50 Hdbd. (ISBN 0-8369-1466-X). Books for Libraries, NY.

Frohman, Daniel. Memories of a Manager. 1911. $9.75 Hdbd. Benjamin Blom, NY.

Gladding, W. J. Group of Theatrical Caricatures. (Drama Ser). 1970. (1897) $14.50 Hdbd. (ISBN 0-8337-1362-0). Burt Franklin, NY.

Goodale, Katherine. Behind the Scenes with Edwin Booth. 1931. $10.75 Hdbd. Benjamin Blom, NY.

Hammond, Percy. This Atom in the Audience. 1940. $10.50 Hdbd. Benjamin Blom, NY.

Harding, Alfred. Revolt of the Actors. 1929. $12.50 Hdbd. Benjamin Blom, NY.

Hayman, Ronald. John Gielgud. 1971. $10.00 Hdbd. Random House, NY.

Hill, Norman, ed. Lonely Beauties. (Orig.). 1971. $0.95 pa. Popular Library, NY.

McKay, Frederic E. & Wingate, Charles E. Famous American Actors of Today. (American Biography Ser). 1896. $19.50 Hdbd. (ISBN 0-512-00507-9). Garrett Pr., NY.

McKay, Frederick E. & Wingate, Charles E. L., eds. Famous American Actors of Today. (1896) $20.00 Hdbd. (ISBN 0-8337-5307-X). Burt Franklin, NY.

Matthews, Brander & Hutton, Laurence, eds. Actors & Actresses of Great Britain & the United States: Vol. 1, Garrick & His Contemporaries. 1900. $12.50 Hdbd. Benjamin Blom, NY.

Matthews, Brander & Hutton. Actors & Actresses of Great Britain & the United States: Vol. 2, The Kembles & Their Contemporaries. 1886. $12.50 Hdbd. Benjamin Blom, NY.

Matthews, Brander & Hutton. Actors & Actresses of Great Britain & the United States: Vol. 3, Kean & Booth, & Their Contemporaries. 1886. $12.50 Hdbd. Benjamin Blom, NY.

Matthews, Brander & Hutton. Actors & Actresses of Great Britain & the United States: Vol. 4, Macready & Forrest & Their Contemporaries. 1886. $12.50 Hdbd. Benjamin Blom, NY.

Matthews, Brander & Hutton. Actors & Actresses of Great Britain & the United States: Vol. 5, The Life & Art of Edwin Booth & His Contemporaries. 1886. $12.50 Hdbd. Benjamin Blom, NY.

Moses, Montrose J. Famous Actor Families in America. (Miscellany of the Theatre Ser). 1969. (1906) $12.00 Hdbd. Johnson Reprint, NY.

Moses, Montrose J. Famous Actor-Families in America. 1968. (1906) $16.50 Hdbd. (ISBN 0-8371-0177-8). Greenwood Pr., CT.

Moses, Montrose J. Famous Actor-Families in America. 1968. (1906) $10.75 Hdbd. Benjamin Blom, NY.

Murray, William. Starlet. 1971. $7.95 Hdbd. Dutton, NY.

Rigdon, Walter, ed. Biographical Encyclopaedia & Who's Who of the American Theatre. 1966. $82.50 Hdbd. James H. Heineman, NY.

Robinson, Edward G. & Robinson, Jane. Edward G. Robinson's World of Art. 1971. $15.00 Hdbd. (ISBN 0-06-013579-4, Harp T). Harper & Row, NY.

Ross, Murray. Stars & Strikes, Unionization in Hollywood. 1941. $9.50 Hdbd. (ISBN 0-404-05408-0). AMS Pr, NY.

Strang, Lewis C. Famous Actors of the Day in America, 2 Sers. 1900–1902. $9.75 ea. Hdbd. Benjamin Blom, NY.

Strang, Lewis C. Famous Actresses of the Day in America, 2 Sers. 1899–1902. $9.75 ea. Hdbd. Benjamin Blom, NY.

Strang, Lewis C. Famous Stars of Light Opera. 1907. $10.75 Hdbd. Benjamin Blom, NY.

Wilson, Garff B. History of American Acting. 1966. $7.95 Hdbd. (ISBN 0-253-13770-5). Indiana Univ Pr., IN.

Winter, William. Brief Chronicles, 3 Vols. in One. 1890. $12.50 Hdbd. Benjamin Blom, NY.

Winter, William. Brief Chronicles, 3 Vols. (Drama Ser). 1971. Repr. of 1899 ed. $14.50 ea. Hdbd. (ISBN 0-8337-3826-7). Burt Franklin, NY.

Winter, William. Other Days. (Essay Index Reprint Ser). $12.50 Hdbd. (ISBN 0-8369-1816-9). Books for Libraries, NY.

Winter, William. Wallet of Time. (Essay Index Reprint Ser). 1913. $42.50 Hdbd. (ISBN 0-8369-1113-X). Books for Libraries, NY.

Winter, William. Wallet of Time, 2 Vols. 1913. $28.75 Hdbd. Benjamin Blom, NY.

Zierold, Norman. Garbo. 1971. $0.60 pa. (445-02582-060). Popular Library, NY.

English

Actors & Actresses of Great Britain & the United States: Vol. 2, the Kembles & Their Contemporaries. 1886. $12.50 Hdbd. Benjamin Blom, NY.

Agate, James. These Were Actors: Extracts from a Newspaper Cutting Book, 1811–1833. 1943. $10.75 Hdbd. Benjamin Blom, NY.

Agate, James. Those Were the Nights. 1947. $10.75 Hdbd. Benjamin Blom, NY.

Armstrong, Cecil F. Century of Great Actors 1750–1850. 1912. $12.50 Hdbd. Benjamin Blom, NY.

Arthur, George. From Phelps to Gielgud. 1936. $12.50 Hdbd. Benjamin Blom, NY.

Arthur, George C. From Phelps to Gielgud: Reminiscences of the Stage Through Sixty-Five Years. (Essay Index Reprint Ser). 1967. (1936) $9.50 Hdbd. (ISBN 0-8369-0160-6). Books for Libraries, NY.

Baker, Barton. History of the London Stage & Its Famous Players 1576–1903. 1904. $12.50 Hdbd. Benjamin Blom, NY.

Baldwin, Thomas W. Organization & Personnel of the Shakespearean Company. 1961. (1927) $15.00 Hdbd. Russell & Russell, NY.

Bentley, G. E. The Jacobean & Caroline Stage. Incl. Vol. 1–2. Dramatic Companies & Players. 1941. $24.00 Hdbd. (ISBN 0-19-811503-2); Vol. 3–5. Plays & Playwrights. 1956. $38.50 Hdbd. (ISBN 0-19-811504-0); Vol. 6–7. Theatres, Appendixes to Vol. 6 & General Index. 1968. $22.50 Hdbd. (ISBN 0-19-811626-8). Oxford Univ Pr., NY.

Bentley, Gerald E. Seventeenth-Century Stage: A Collection of Critical Essays. (Patterns of Literary Criticism Ser., No. 6). 1968. $9.75 Hdbd. (ISBN 0-8020-1561-1). $2.95 pa. (ISBN 0-8020-1560-3). Univ. of Toronto Pr., Toronto, Canada.

Burton, Hal, ed. Great Acting. 1968. $8.95 Hdbd. (ISBN 0-8090-5110-9). Hill & Wang, NY.

Chambers, Edmund K. Elizabethan Stage, 4 Vols. 1923. Set—$38.50 Hdbd. (ISBN 0-19-811511-3). Oxford Univ Pr., NY.

Cibber, Colley. Apology for the Life of Colley Cibber Written by Himself, 2 Vols. rev. ed. Lowe, R. W., ed. 1889. $14.50 Hdbd. (ISBN 0-404-01544-1). AMS Pr., NY.

Coleman, John. Players & Playwrights I Have Known, 2 Vols. in 1. 1890. $18.75 Hdbd. Benjamin Blom, NY.

Collier, J. Payne. Memoirs of the Principal Actors in the Plays of Shakespeare. 1846. $15.00 Hdbd. (ISBN 0-404-01599-9). AMS Pr., NY.

Darbyshire, Alfred. Art of the Victorian Stage. 1907. $10.75 Hdbd. Benjamin Blom, NY.

David, Richard. Shakespeare & the Players. 1961. $3.50 Hdbd. Folcroft Pr., PA.

Disher, Maurice W. Music Hall Parade. 1938. $12.50 Hdbd. Benjamin Blom, NY.

Doran, John. Their Majesties Servants: Annals of the English Stage from Thomas Bettertan to Edmund Kean, 2 Vols. 1970. (1865) Set—$40.00 Hdbd. (ISBN 9-403-00234-6). Scholarly Pr., MI.

Doran, John. Their Majesties' Servants: Or Annals of the English Stage, 3 Vols. Lowe, R. W., ed. 1888. Set—$36.00

Hdbd. (ISBN 0-404-02170-0). AMS Pr., NY.

Filon, Augustin. English Stage. Whyte, Frederic, tr. 1970. (1897) $10.00 Hdbd. (ISBN 0-8046-0753-2).

Filon, Pierre M. English Stage. 1897. $10.75 Hdbd. Benjamin Blom, NY.

Frohman, Daniel. Encore. (Essay Index Reprint Ser). 1937. $12.50 Hdbd. (ISBN 0-8369-1466-X). Books for Libraries, NY.

Fyvie, John. Comedy Queens of the Georgian Era. 1906. $12.50 Hdbd. Benjamin Blom, NY.

Fyvie, John. Tragedy Queens of the Georgian Era. 1909. $12.50 Hdbd. Benjamin Blom, NY.

Gilder, Rosamond. John Gielgud's Hamlet: a Record of Performance. (Select Bibliographies Reprint Ser). (1937) $11.00 Hdbd. (ISBN 0-8369-5675-3). Books for Libraries, NY.

Goddard, Arthur. Players of the Period, 2 Vols. in 1. 1891. $12.50 Hdbd. Benjamin Blom, NY.

Highfill, Philip H., Jr., et al. Biographical Dictionary of Actors, Actresses, Musicians, Dancers, Managers & Other Stage Personnel in London, 1660-1800. 2 Vols. 1971. $17.50 ea. Hdbd. (ISBN 0-8093-0517-8) (ISBN 0-8093-0518-6). Southern Illinois Univ. Pr., IL.

Hill, John. Actor. 1750. $18.50 Hdbd. Benjamin Blom, NY.

Hill, John. Actor. 1755. $17.50 Hdbd. Benjamin Blom, NY.

Hotson, J. Leslie. Commonwealth & Restoration Stage. 1962. (1928) $12.50 Hdbd. Russell & Russell, NY.

Lanier, Henry W. First English Actresses. 1930. $12.50 Hdbd. Benjamin Blom, NY.

Lichtenberg, G. C. Lichtenberg's Visits to England. Mare, Margaret L. & Quarrell, ·W. H., eds. 1938. $12.50 Hdbd. Benjamin Blom, NY.

Marston, Westland. Our Recent Actors, 2 Vols. 1888. $12.75 Hdbd. Benjamin Blom, NY.

Matthews, Brander & Hutton, Laurence, eds. Actors & Actresses of Great Britain & the United States: Vol. 4, Macready & Forrest & Their Contemporaries. 1886. $12.50 Hdbd. Benjamin Blom, NY.

Matthews, Brander & Hutton, Laurence, eds. Actors & Actresses of Great Britain & the United States: Vol. 3, Kean & Booth, & Their Contemporaries. 1886. $12.50 Hdbd. Benjamin Blom, NY.

Matthews, Brander & Hutton, Laurence, eds. Actors & Actresses of Great Britain & the United States: Vol. 5, the Life & Art of Edwin Booth & His Contemporaries. 1886. $12.50 Hdbd. Benjamin Blom, NY.

Matthews, Brander & Hutton, Laurence, eds. Actors & Actresses of Great Britain & the United States: Vol. 1, Garrick & His Contemporaries. 1900. $12.50 Hdbd. Benjamin Blom, NY.

Melville, Lewis. More Stage Favorites of the Eighteenth Century. 1929. $12.50 Hdbd. Benjamin Blom, NY.

Melville, Lewis. Stage Favorites of the Eighteenth Century. 1928. $12.50 Hdbd. Benjamin Blom, NY.

Merrill, Mary. Richard Basehart: An Analysis of His Work, Vols. 1 & 2. 1968. Vols. 1 & 2 In One Vol. $10.00 Hdbd. (ISBN 0-911948-05-8); Vols. 1 & 2 In One Vol. $5.00 pa. (ISBN 0-911948-26-0). Bormerl Oaks Pr., IN.

Merrill, Mary. Richard Basehart: An Analysis of His Work, Vols. 3 & 4. 1969. $10.00 ea. Hdbd. (ISBN 0-911948-06-6) (ISBN 0-911948-34-1). $5.00 ea. pa. (ISBN 0-911948-27-9) (ISBN 0-911948-40-6). Bormerl Oaks Pr., IN.

Nungezer, E. Dictionary of Actors of Plays in England Before 1642. 1929. $17.50 Hdbd. (ISBN 0-404-04806-4). AMS Pr., NY.

Nungezer, Edwin. Dictionary of Actors & of Other Persons Associated with the Public Representation of Plays in England Before 1642. 1971. (1929). $19.00 Hdbd. (ISBN 0-403-01132-9). Scholarly Pr., MI.

Nungezer, Edwin. Dictionary of Actors & of Other Persons Associated with the Public Representation of Plays in England Before 1642. 1969. (1929) $15.75 Hdbd. (ISBN 0-8371-0593-5). Greenwood Pr., CT.

Pascoe, Charles E. Our Actors & Actresses. 2nd rev. ed. 1880. $12.50 Hdbd. Benjamin Blom, NY.

Pearson, Hesketh. Last Actor-Managers. (Biography Index Reprint Ser.,

Vol. 2). 1950. $12.50 Hdbd. (ISBN 0-8369-8072-7). Books for Libraries, NY.

Russell, William C. Representative Actors. 1894. $12.50 Hdbd. Benjamin Blom, NY.

Scott, Clement W. Some Notable Hamlets of the Present Time. 1900. $9.75 Hdbd. Benjamin Blom, NY.

Simpson, Harold & Braun, Charles. Century of Famous Actresses 1750-1850. 1913. $12.50 Hdbd. Benjamin Blom, NY.

Skinner, Otis. Mad Folk of the Theatre. (Essay Index Reprint Ser). $11.50 Hdbd. (ISBN 0-8369-1851-7). Books for Libraries, NY.

Sprague, Arthur C. Shakespearian Players & Performances. 1953. $12.75 Hdbd. (ISBN 0-8371-0664-8). Greenwood Pr., CT.

Thaler, Alwin. Shakespeare to Sheridan. (Illus.). 1922. $12.50 Hdbd. Benjamin Blom, NY.

Thespian Dictionary: Or, Dramatic Biography of the 18th Century. 2nd ed. 1805. $25.00 Hdbd. Benjamin Blom, NY.

Watson, Ernest B. Sheridan to Robertson: A Study of the Nineteenth-Century London Stage. 1926. $12.50 Hdbd. Benjamin Blom, NY.

Wilkinson, Tate. Wandering Patentee, Or, History of the Yorkshire Theatres from 1770 to the Present Time, 4 Vols. in 2. 1968. $37.50 Hdbd. Benjamin Blom, NY.

Wilson, A. E. Christmas Pantomine: The Story of an English Institution. 1934. $12.50 Hdbd. Benjamin Blom, NY.

French

Fransen, J. Comediens Francais En Hollande Au Dix-Septieme & Au Dix-Huitiene Siecles. (Fr). 1925. $22.50 Hdbd. (ISBN 0-8337-4117-9). Burt Franklin, NY.

Gribble, Francis H. Romances of the French Theatre. 1912. $12.75 Hdbd. Benjamin Blom, NY.

Lyonnet, Henry. Dictionnaire Des Comediens Francais, 2 Vols. 1968. (1911) $35.00 Hdbd. (ISBN 0-8337-2158-5). Burt Franklin, NY.

Lyonnet, Henry. Dictionnaire Des Comediens Francais, 2 Vols. 1902-1908. $67.50 Hdbd. Benjamin Blom, NY.

Williams, Hugh N. Later Queens of the French Stage. 1906. $12.50 Hdbd. Benjamin Blom, NY.

Williams, Hugh N. Queens of the French Stage. 1905. $12.50 Hdbd. Benjamin Blom, NY.

Greek

Loehrer, Robert. Mienenspiel und Maske in der Griechischen Tragoedie. 1927. $8.00 pa. Johnson Reprint Corp., NY.

O'Connor, John B. Chapters in the History of Actors & Acting in Ancient Greece. (Drama Ser., No. 39). 1969. (1908) $9.95 Hdbd. (ISBN 0-8383-0602-0). Haskell House Publ., NY.

Italian

McLeod, Addison. Plays & Players in Modern Italy. 1970. (1912) $13.00 Hdbd. (ISBN 0-8046-0758-3). Kennikat Pr., NY.

Rasi, Luigi. I Comici Italiani: Biografia, Bibliografia, Iconografia, 2 Vols. in 3. 1897-1910. $75.00 Hdbd. Benjamin Blom, NY.

Salvini, Tommaso. Leaves from the Autobiography of Tommaso Salvini. 1893. $12.50 Hdbd. Benjamin Blom, NY.

Smith, Winifred. Italian Actors of the Renaissance. 1968. $12.50 Hdbd. Benjamin Blom.

Spanish

Rennert, Hugo A. Spanish Actors & Actresses 1560-1680. 1909. $12.50 Hdbd. Benjamin Blom, NY.

AMATEUR THEATRICALS

Alexander, Martha. Behind the Footlights: From Amateur to Repertory. 1955. $3.00 Hdbd. Transatlantic Arts, NY.

Bourne, John. Teach Yourself Amateur Acting. $2.50 Hdbd. (ISBN 0-486-21426-5). Dover Publ., NY.

Bradbury, Arthur J., et al. Production & Staging of Plays. 1963. lib. $3.50 Hdbd.

(ISBN 0-668-01051-7); $0.95 pa. (ISBN 0-668-01052-5). Arco Publ., NY.

Buerki, Frederick A. Stagecraft for Nonprofessionals. 2nd ed. 1955. $2.50 pa. (ISBN 0-299-01294-8). Univ. of Wisconsin Pr., Madison, WI.

Burger, Isabel B. Creative Play Acting: Learning Through Drama. 2nd ed. 1966. $6.00 text ed. Ronald Pr., NY.

Burton, Peter & Lane, John. New Directions: Ways of Advance for the Amateur Theatre. 1971. $10.50 Hdbd. Hillary House, NY.

Cartmell, Van H. Amateur Theater: A Guide for Actor & Director. 1961. $4.95 Hdbd. Van Nostrand-Reinhold, NY

Chilver, P. Improvised Drama. 1967. $4.00 Hdbd. Lawrence Verry, Mystic, CT.

Chilver, Peter. Staging a School Play. 1968. $4.95 Hdbd. (ISBN 0-06-000793-1). Harper & Row, NY.

Chilver, Peter & Jones, Eric. Designing a School Play. 1970. $6.95 Hdbd. (ISBN 0-8008-2171-8). Taplinger Publ., NY.

Citron, Samuel J. Dramatics the Year Round. 1956. $7.50 Hdbd. (ISBN 0-8381-0211-5). United Synagogue Book Service, NY.

Dolman, John, Jr. Art of Play Production. rev. ed. 1946. $9.50 text ed. (ISBN 0-06-041680-7). Harper & Row, NY.

Dwyer, Terence. Opera in Your School. 1964. $3.40 Hdbd. (ISBN 0-19-317407-3). Oxford Univ. Pr., NY.

Fuchs, Theodore. Home-Built Lighting Equipment. 1939. $3.50 Hdbd. French, Samuel, Inc., NY.

Geen, Michael. Theatrical Costume & the Amateur Stage. 1968. $4.95 Hdbd. (ISBN 0-8238-0095-4). Plays. Boston, MA.

Gross, Edwin & Gross, Nathalie. Teen Theatre: A Guide to Play Production & Six Comedies. 1953. $3.50 Hdbd. (ISBN 0-07-024975-X). McGraw-Hill, NY.

Hedde, Wilhelmina, G. & Brigance, William N. New American Speech. 1963. $6.40 text ed. teacher's key, $0.20. Lippincott, Philadelphia, PA.

Hedde, Wilhelmina G., et al. New American Speech. 1957. $6.40 text ed. Lippincott, Philadelphia, PA.

Hedde, Wilhelmina G., et al. New American Speech. 3rd ed. 1968. $6.40 Hdbd., $4.80 s.p.; teacher's guide, free. Lippincott, Philadelphia, PA.

Heffner, Hubert C., et al. Modern Theatre Practice: Handbook of Play Production. 4th ed. 1959. $7.95 text ed. (ISBN 0-390-43101-X). Appleton-Century-Croft, NY.

Huff, Betty T. Teen-Age Comedies for the Amateur Stage. 1968. $7.95 Hdbd. (ISBN 0-8238-0029-6). Plays. Boston, MA.

Johnson, Albert & Johnson, Bertha. Drama for Junior High, with Selected Scenes. 1971. $6.95 Hdbd. (ISBN 0-498-07587-7). A S Barnes, Cranbury, NJ.

McGee, Cecil. Drama for Fun. 1969. $3.95 Hdbd. (ISBN 0-8054-7505-2). Broadman Pr., Nashville, TN.

MacKenzie, Frances. Amateur Actor. $3.00 Hdbd. Theatre Arts, NY.

Martens, Anne C. Popular Plays for Teen-Agers. 1968. $7.95 Hdbd. (ISBN 0-8238-0063-6). Plays. Boston, MA.

Nolan, Paul T. Drama Workshop Plays for Young People. rev. ed. 1970. $6.95 Hdbd. (Jr Hi–Hi-Sch.). Plays. Boston, MA.

Nolan, Paul T. Round-The-World Plays for Young People. rev. ed. (Elem–Jr Hi). 1970. $6.95 Hdbd. (ISBN 0-8238-0055-5). Plays. Boston, MA.

Nuttall, Kenneth. Play Production for Young People. 1963. $4.95 Hdbd. (ISBN 0-8238-0085-7). Plays. Boston, MA.

Olfson, Lewy. Dramatized Classics for Radio-Style Reading, 2 Vols. 1964. $6.95 ea. Hdbd. (ISBN 0-8238-0056-3) (ISBN 0-8238-0057-1). Plays. Boston, MA, Jr Hi–Hi-Sch.

Ommanney, Katharine A. Stage & the School. 3rd ed. 1960. $7.96 text ed. (ISBN 0-07-047669-1). McGraw Hill, NY.

Shepherd, Jack. Black City Stage. 1968.

$0.70 pa. Pendle Hill Pamphlets, Wallingford, PA.

Smith, Milton M. Play Production. 1948. $7.00 text ed. (ISBN 0-390-82499 2). Appleton-Century-Croft, NY.

Spolin, Viola. Improvisation for the Theater: A Handbook of Teaching & Directing Techniques. 1963. $8.50 Hdbd. (ISBN 0-8101-0249-8); $6.95 text ed. (ISBN 0-8101-0018-5). Northwestern Univ Pr., Evanston, IL.

Wallace, Karl R., ed. History of Speech Education in America. 1960. $9.50 text ed. (ISBN 0-390-91429-0). Appleton-Century-Croft, NY.

Ward, Winifred. Theatre for Children. rev. ed. 1958. $4.00 Hdbd. Anchorage Pr., Anchorage, KY.

White, Edwin C. & Battye, Marguerite. Acting & Stage Movement. 1963. $0.95 pa. (ISBN 0-668-01054-1). Arco Publ., NY.

BIBLIOGRAPHY

Amateur Theatricals

Mersand, Joseph, ed. Guide to Play Selection. 1959. $3.50 text ed. (ISBN 0-390-63171-X). Appleton-Century-Croft, NY.

American Drama

Bergquist, G. William, ed. Three Centuries of English & American Plays: A Check List—England 1500–1800 &

United States 1714–1830. 1963. $25.00 Hdbd. Hafner Publ. Co., NY.

Dunlap, William. History of the American Theatre. (Research & Source Ser., No. 36). 1968. (1797) $23.50 Hdbd. (ISBN 0-8337-0964-X). Burt Franklin, NY.

Gaer, Joseph, ed. Theatre of the Gold Rush Decade in San Francisco. (Bibliography & Reference Ser., No. 391). 1971. (1935) $10.00 Hdbd. (ISBN 0-8337-1261-6). Burt Franklin, NY.

Hill, Frank P. American Plays. (Bibliography & Reference Ser., No. 387). 1971. (1934) $15.00 Hdbd. (ISBN 0-8337-1705-7). Burt Franklin, NY.

Hill, Frank P. American Plays Printed 1740–1830. 1968. $12.50 Hdbd. Benjamin Blom, NY.

Long, E. Hudson, ed. American Drama from Its Beginnings to the Present. (Goldentree Bibliographies in Language & Literature Ser). (Orig.). 1970. $1.95 text ed. (ISBN 0-390-57130-X). Appleton-Century-Crofts, NY.

Pence, James H. Magazine & the Drama: An Index. (Drama Ser). 1970. (1896) $14.50 Hdbd. (ISBN 0-8337-2707-9). Burt Franklin, NY.

Roden, Robert F. Later American Plays, 1831–1900. 1964. $14.50 Hdbd. (ISBN 0-8337-3042-8). Burt Franklin, NY.

U.S. Copyright Office. Dramatic Compositions Copyrighted in the United States, 1870–1916, 2 Vols. 1918. Set—

$95.00 Hdbd. Johnson Reprint Corp., NY.

Wegelin, Oscar. Early American Plays. (Drama Ser). 1970. (1900) $14.50 Hdbd. (ISBN 0-8337-3721-X). Burt Franklin, NY.

Wegelin, Oscar. Early American Plays, 1714–1830. rev. 2nd ed. 1968. $6.00 Hdbd. Johnson Reprint Corp., NY.

Wegelin, Oscar. Early American Plays, 1714–1830. (Drama Ser., No. 39). 1969. (1900) $5.95 Hdbd. (ISBN 0-8383-0256-4). Haskell House, NY.

Weingarten, Joseph A. Modern American Playwrights, 1918–1945. 1967. (1947) $10.00 Hdbd. (ISBN 0-8337-3723-6). Burt Franklin, NY.

Costume

Baker, Blanch M. Dramatic Bibliography. 1968. $17.50 Hdbd. Benjamin Blom, NY.

Baker, Blanche M. Theatre & Allied Arts. $17.50 Hdbd. Blom.

Colas, Rene. Bibliographie Generale Du Costume, 2 Vols. (1648) $30.00 Hdbd. Hacker Art Books, NY.

Hiler, Hilaire & Hiler, Meyer. Bibliography of Costume. 1967. Repr. $18.50 Hdbd. Benjamin Blom, NY.

Lipperheid'Schen. Costume Catalog, 2 Vols. (Illus., Ger. & Eng.). Set—$80.00 Hdbd. (ISBN 0-87556-203-5). Albert Saifer, PA.

Lipperheide, Frank T. Von. Katalog der

Lipperheideschen Kostumbibliothek, 2 Vols. rev. ed. Nienholdt, Eva & Wagner, G., eds. $90.00 Hdbd. Hacker Art Books, NY.

Drama

Baker, Blanch M. Dramatic Bibliography. 1968. $17.50 Hdbd. Benjamin Blom, NY.

Baker, Blanche M. Theatre & Allied Arts. $17.50 Hdbd. Benjamin Blom, NY.

Bates, Alfred, et al, eds. Drama, Its History, Literature & Influence of Civilization, 22 Vols. 1970. (1904) Set— $470.00 Hdbd. (ISBN 0-404-02190-5); $22.50 ea. Hdbd. AMS Pr., NY.

Besterman, Theodore. Music & Drama. (Besterman World Bibliographies Ser). 1971. $15.00 Hdbd. (ISBN 0-87471-046-4). Rowman & Littlefield, NY.

Boston Public Library. Allen A. Brown Collection. 1919. $42.50 Hdbd. Kraus Reprint Co., NY.

Burton, Ernest J. British Theatre: Its Repertory & Practice, 1100–1900 A.D. 1960. $5.00 Hdbd. Dufour Editions, PA.

Chicorel Index Series. Marietta Chicorel, ed. Vol. 1 Chicorel Theater Index to Plays in Anthologies, Periodicals, Discs & Tapes. 1970. $38.25 Hdbd. (ISBN 87729-001-6). Vol. 2 1971. $42.50 Hdbd. (ISBN 87729-002-3). Vol. 3 1972. $42.50 Hdbd. (ISBN 87729-003-7). Vol. 4 Chicorel Library Publishing, NY.

Chicorel Index to Poetry on Discs & Tapes: Poetry-On-Media; Readings by Well Known Actors and Poets. 1972. $42.50 Hdbd. (ISBN 87729-004-9). Chicorel Library Publishing, NY.

Drury, Francis K. Guide to Best Plays. 2nd ed. Salem, James M., ed. 1969. $15.00 Hdbd. (ISBN 0-8108-0254-6). Scarecrow Pr., NJ.

F. W. Faxon Co. Cumulated Dramatic Index, 1909–1949. $540.00 Hdbd. G. K. Hall & Co., MA.

Firkins, Ina T., ed. Index to Plays, 1800–1926. 1927. $10.00 Hdbd. (ISBN 0-404-02386-X). AMS Pr., NY.

Gaer, Joseph, ed. Theatre of the Gold Rush Decade in San Francisco. (Bibliography & Reference Ser., No. 391). 1971. (1935) $10.00 Hdbd. (ISBN 0-8337-1261-6). Burt Franklin, NY.

Hunter, Frederick J., ed. Drama Bibliography: A Short-Title Guide to Extended Reading in Dramatic Art for the English-Speaking Audience & Students in Theatre. 1971. $25.00 Hdbd. G. K. Hall & Co., MA.

Index to Full-Length Plays, 3 vols. Incl. Vol. 1. 1895–1925. Thomson, Ruth G. $8.00 Hdbd. (ISBN 0-87305-085-1); Vol. 2. 1926–1944. Thomson, Ruth G. $8.00 Hdbd. (ISBN 0-87305-071-1); Vol. 3. 1944–1964. Ireland. Norma O. $10.00 Hdbd. (ISBN 0-87305-092-4). 1965. F. W. Faxon Co., MA.

Keller, Dean H. Index to Plays in Periodicals. 1971. $15.00 Hdbd. (ISBN 0-8108-0335-6). Scarecrow Pr., NJ.

Logasa, Hannah & Ver Nooy, Winifred. Index to One-Act Plays, Suppl. 1. 1932. $9.00 Hdbd. (ISBN 0-87305-046-0). F. W. Faxon Co., MA.

McKenzie, Agnes. Playgoer's Guide to the Renaissance Drama. 1927. $15.00 Hdbd. Folcroft Pr., PA.

Mersand, Joseph, ed. Guide to Play Selection. 1959. $3.50 text ed. (ISBN 0-390-63171-X). Appleton-Century-Crofts, NY.

New York Public Library. Catalog of the Theatre & Drama Collections, 2 pts. Pt. 1, No. 1. Drama Collection: Listing by Cultural Origin, 6 vols. Set—$585.00 Hdbd.; Pt. 1, No. 2. Drama Collection: Author Listing, 6 vols. Set—$790.00 Hdbd.; Pt. 2. Theatre Collection: Books on the Theatre, 9 vols. Set—$530.00 Hdbd. 1967. G. K. Hall Co., MA.

Newman, Ralph. Performing Arts Books in Print. 3rd ed. $35.00 Hdbd. Drama Book Shop, NY.

Ottemiller, John H. Index to Plays in Collections. 4th ed. 1964. $9.50 Hdbd. (ISBN 0-8108-0070-5). Scarecrow Pr., NJ.

Pence, James H. Magazine & the Drama: An Index. (Drama Ser). 1970. (1896) $14.50 Hdbd. (ISBN 0-8337-2707-9). Burt Franklin, NY.

Play Index. Incl. 1949–1952 Vol. West, Dorothy H. & Peake, Dorothy M., eds. 1953. $8.00 Hdbd.; 1953–1960 Vol. Fidell, Estelle A. & Peake, Dorothy M., eds. 1963. $11.00 Hdbd. (ISBN 0-8242-0382-8); 1961–1967 Vol. Fidell, Estelle

A., ed. 1968. $16.00 Hdbd. (ISBN 0-8242-0383-6). H. W. Wilson Co., NY.

Salem, James M. Drury's Guide to Best Plays. rev. 2nd ed. 1969. $15.00 Hdbd. (ISBN 0-8108-0254-6). Scarecrow Pr., NJ.

Stratman, Carl J. Bibliography of Medieval Drama, 2 Vols. Set—$35.00 Hdbd. (3272-4). Frederick Ungar, NY.

U.S. Copyright Office. Dramatic Compositions Copyrighted in the United States, 1870–1916, 2 Vols. 1918. Set—$95.00. Johnson Repr. Corp., NY.

Walbridge, Earle. Literary Characters Drawn from Life. 1936. $17.50 Hdbd. Folcroft Pr., PA.

Drama—

History and Criticism

Adelman, Irving & Dworkin, Rita. Modern Drama: A Checklist of Critical Literature on 20th Century Plays. 1967. $9.00 Hdbd. (ISBN 0-8108-0096-9). Scarecrow Pr., NJ.

Baker, Blanch M. Dramatic Bibliography. 1968. $17.50 Hdbd. Benjamin Blom, NY.

Baker, Blanche M. Theatre & Allied Arts. $17.50 Hdbd. Benjamin Blom, NY.

Breed, Paul F. & Sniderman, Florence M. Dramatic Criticism Index: Bibliography of Commentaries on Playwrights from Ibsen to the Avant-Garde.

1971. $20.00 Hdbd. Gale Research Co., MI.

Chicorel Index Series. Marietta Chicorel, ed. Vol. 1 Chicorel Theater Index to Plays in Anthologies, Periodicals, Discs & Tapes. 1970. $38.25 Hdbd. (ISBN 87729-001-6). Vol. 2 1971. $42.50 Hdbd. (ISBN 87729-002-3). Vol. 3 1972. $42.50 Hdbd. (ISBN 87729-003-7). Vol. 4 Chicorel Index to Poetry on Discs & Tapes: Poetry-On-Media; Readings by Well Known Actors and Poets. 1972. $42.50 Hdbd. (ISBN 87729-004-9). Chicorel Library Publishing, NY.

Coleman, Arthur & Tyler, Gary R. Drama Criticism, 2 vols. Incl. Vol. 1. A Checklist of Interpretation Since 1940 of English & American Plays. $9.50 Hdbd.; Vol. 2. A Checklist of Interpretation Since 1940 of Classical & Continental Plays. $12.50 Hdbd. Swallow Pr., IL.

Gohdes, Clarence. Literature & Theater of the States & Regions of the U.S.A.: An Historical Bibliography. 1967. $10.00 Hdbd. (ISBN 0-8223-0071-0). Duke Univ. Pr., NC

Litto, Fredric M. American Dissertations on the Drama & Theatre: A Bibliography. $12.50 Hdbd. (ISBN 0-87338-036-3). Kent St. Univ. Pr., OH.

Palmer, Helen H. & Dyson, Anne J., eds. American Drama Criticism: Interpretations, 1890-1965 Inclusive, of American Drama Since the First Play Produced in America. 1967. $7.50 Hdbd. (ISBN 0-208-00110-7). Shoe String Pr., CT.

Palmer, Helen H. & Dyson, Anne J. European Drama Criticism: Interpretations of European Drama. 1968. $9.00 Hdbd. Shoe String Pr., CT.

Riggs, David. Shakespeare's Heroical Histories: Henry Six & Its Literary Tradition. 1971. $6.50 Hdbd. (ISBN 0-674-80400-7). Harvard Univ. Pr., MA.

English Drama

Arnott, James F. & Robinson, J. W. English Theatrical Literature 1559-1900: A Bibliography. 1971. $45.00 Hdbd. (ISBN 0-8277-0415-1). British Book Center, NY.

Baker, David E., et al. Biographia Dramatica, or Companion to the Playhouse, 3 Vols. 1812. Set—$110.00 Hdbd. ISBN 0-404-00530-6); $39.50 Hdbd. (ISBN 0-404-00531-4) (ISBN 0-404-00532-2) (ISBN 0-404-00533-0). AMS Pr., NY.

Bergquist, G. William, ed. Three Centuries of English & American Plays: A Check List—England 1500-1800 & United States 1714-1830. 1963. $25.00 Hdbd. Hafner Publ. Co., NY.

Capell, E. Notes and Various Readings to Shakespeare. 1970. (1783) Set—$60.00 text ed. (ISBN 0-8337-0465-6). Burt Franklin, NY.

Capell, Edward. Notes & Various Readings to Shakespeare, 3 Vols. 1779-83. Set—$97.50 Hdbd. (ISBN 0-404-01400-3). AMS Pr., NY.

Clarence, Reginald. Stage Cyclopedia: A Bibliography of Plays. 1968. (1909)

$30.00 Hdbd. (ISBN 0-8337-0581-4). Burt Franklin, NY.

Coleman, Edward D. Bible in English Drama: An Annotated Bibliography. rev. ed. 1969. $8.95 Hdbd. (ISBN 0-87068-034-X). Ktav Publ. House, NY.

Coleman, Edward D. Bible in English Drama: An Annotated List of Plays. 1969. $8.95 Hdbd. (ISBN 0-87104-021-2, Co-Pub by Ktav). New York Public Library, NY.

Coleman, Edward D. Jew in English Drama: An Annotated Bibliography. rev. ed. 1969. $8.95 Hdbd. (ISBN 0-87068-011-0). Ktav Publ. House, NY.

Downes, John. Roscius Anglicanus. Summers, Montague, ed. 1968. $12.50 Hdbd. Benjamin Blom, NY.

Farmer, Richard. Bibliotheca Farmeriana. 1798. $27.50 lib. bdg. (ISBN 0-404-52309-9). AMS Pr., NY.

Greg, W. W. Bibliography of the English Printed Drama to the Restoration, 4 Vols. Vols. 1–3, $29.00 ea. Hdbd.; Vol. 4, $21.75 Hdbd. Oxford Univ. Pr., NY.

Greg, Walter W. List of English Plays Written Before 1643 & Printed Before 1700. (Drama Ser., No. 39). 1969. (1900) $6.96 Hdbd. (ISBN 0-8383-0950-X). Haskell House Publ., NY.

Greg, Walter W. List of Masques, Pageants, Etc. Supplementary to a List of English Plays. (Drama Ser., No. 39). 1969. (1902) $9.95 Hdbd. (ISBN 0-8383-0942-9). Haskell House Publ., NY.

Harbage, Alfred. Annals of English Drama: 975–1700. rev. ed. Schoenbaum, S., ed. 1964. $18.00 Hdbd. (ISBN 0-8122-7483-0). Univ. of Pennsylvania Pr., PA.

Hazlitt, William C. Manual for the Collector & Amateur of Old English Plays. 1892. $9.50 Hdbd. Johnson Reprint Corp., NY.

Hazlitt, William C. Manual for the Collector & Amateur of Old English Plays. 1965. (1892) $22.50 Hdbd. (ISBN 0-8337-1629-8). Burt Franklin, NY.

Hughes, S. C. Pre-Victorian Drama in Dublin. (Research & Source Works Ser., No. 708). 1970. (1904) $10.00 Hdbd. (ISBN 0-8337-1760-X). Burt Franklin, NY.

Langbaine, Gerard. Momus Triumphans. 1970. (1688) $15.00 Hdbd. (ISBN 0-404-03873-5). AMS Pr., NY.

Ribner, Irving, ed. Tudor & Stuart Drama. $1.35 pa. (ISBN 0-390-73560-4). Appleton-Century-Crofts, NY.

Stratman, Carl J. Bibliography of English Printed Tragedy, 1565–1900. 1966. $15.00 Hdbd. (ISBN 0-8093-0230-6). Southern Illinois Univ. Pr., IL.

Stratman, Carl J. Dramatic Play Lists: 1591–1963. 1966. $2.50 pa. (ISBN 0-87104-065-4). New York Public Library, NY.

Summers, Montague. Bibliography of the Restoration Drama. 1970. (1934) $8.00 Hdbd. Russell & Russell Publ., NY.

German Drama

Binger, Norman. Bibliography of German Plays on Microcards. 1970. $10.00 Hdbd. (ISBN 0-208-00891-8). Shoe String Pr., CT.

Italian Drama

Bentley, Eric, ed. Genius of the Italian Theater: Follies of Calandro, Deceived, Candle Bearer, Turandot, Emperor, Amyntas, Filumena Marturano. $0.95 pa. New American Library, NY.

Collison-Morley, Lacy. Shakespeare in Italy. 1916. $9.75 Hdbd. Benjamin Blom, Bronx, NY.

Duchartre. P. L. Italian Comedy. $8.00 Hdbd. Peter Smith Publ., Magnolia, MA.

Herrick, Marvin T. Italian Comedy in the Renaissance. 1960. $1.75 pa. (ISBN 0-252-72737-1, 33, IB). Univ. of Illinois Pr., Urbana, IL.

Herrick, Marvin T., ed. Italian Plays: 1500–1700. 1966. $5.75 Hdbd. (ISBN 0-252-72743-6). Univ. of Illinois Pr., Urbana, IL.

Herrick, Marvin T. Italian Tragedy in the Renaissance. 1964. $6.75 Hdbd. (ISBN 0-252-72493-3). Univ. of Illinois Pr., Urbana, IL.

Kennard, Joseph S. Italian Theatre, 2 Vols. 1932. $18.50 Hdbd. Benjamin Blom, Bronx, NY.

MacClintock, Lander. Age of Pirandello. (Indiana University Humanities Ser., No. 25). 1951. $16.00 Hdbd. Kraus Repr., NY.

McLeod, Addison. Plays & Players in Modern Italy. 1970. (1912) $13.00 Hdbd. (ISBN 0-8046-0758-3). Kennikat Pr., Port Washington, NY.

Orr, David. Italian Renaissance Drama in England Before 1625. 1970. $6.00 Hdbd. (ISBN 0-8078-7049-8). Univ. of North Carolina Pr., Chapel Hill, NC.

Radcliff-Umstead, Douglas. Birth of Modern Comedy in Renaissance Italy. 1969. $12.50 Hdbd. Univ. of Chicago Pr., Chicago, IL.

Solerti, Angelo. Musica, Ballo E Drammatica Alla Corte Medicea Dal 1600 Al 1637. (It). 1968. $18.50 Hdbd. Benjamin Blom, Bronx, NY.

Religious Drama

Coleman, Edward D. Bible in English Drama: An Annotated Bibliography. rev. ed. 1969. $8.95 Hdbd. (ISBN 0-87068-034-X). Ktav Publ. House, NY.

Coleman, Edward D. Bible in English Drama: An Annotated List of Plays. 1969. $8.95 Hdbd. (ISBN 0-87104-021-2). New York Public Library, NY.

Spanish Drama

McCready, Warren T. Bibliografia Tematica De Estudios Sobre el Teatro Espanol Antiguo (Span). 1966. $15.00 Hdbd. (ISBN 0-8020-1408-9). Univ. of Toronto Pr., Toronto, Can.

MacCurdy, Raymond R., ed. Spanish Drama of the Golden Age. 1971. $10.00

text ed. (ISBN 0-390-58471-1). Appleton-Century-Croft, NY.

Molinaro, J. A., et al, eds. Bibliography of Comedias Sueltas in the University of Toronto Library. 1959. $6.00 Hdbd. (ISBN 0-8020-1101-2). Univ. of Toronto Pr., Toronto, Can.

Theater

Angotti, Vincent L. Source Materials in the Field of Theatre. 1967. $2.00 pa. (BB00001). Univ. Microfilms, MI.

Baker, Blanche M. Dramatic Bibliography. 1968. $17.50 Hdbd. Benjamin Blom, NY.

Baker, Blanche M. Theatre & Allied Arts. $17.50 Hdbd. Benjamin Blom, NY.

Belknap, S. Yancey. Guide to the Performing Arts, 5 vols. Incl. Vol. 1. 1963. $11.00 Hdbd. (ISBN 0-8108-0164-7); Vol. 2. 1964. $11.00 Hdbd.; Vol. 3. 1965. $12.00 Hdbd. (ISBN 0-8108-0166-3); Vol. 4. 1966. $10.00 Hdbd. (ISBN 0-8108-0167-1); Vol. 5. 1967. $15.00 Hdbd. (ISBN 0-8108-0150-7). Scarecrow Pr., NJ.

Boston Public Library. Allen A. Brown Collection. 1919. $42.50 Hdbd. Kraus Reprint Co., NY.

Gilder, Rosamond & Freedley, George. Theatre Collections in Libraries & Museums, an International Handbook. (Library of Literature, Drama & Criticism). 1970. Repr. of 1936 ed. $10.00 Hdbd. Johnson Reprint Co., NY.

Hunter, Frederick J., ed. Drama Bibliography: A Short-Title Guide to Extended Reading in Dramatic Art for the English-Speaking Audience & Students in Theatre. 1971. $25.00 Hdbd. G. K. Hall & Co., MA.

Kent, Violette. Player's Library, & Bibliography of the Theatre. Repr. of 1930 ed. $25.00 Hdbd. (ISBN 0-8337-4897-1). Burt Franklin, NY.

Litto, Fredric M. American Dissertations on the Drama & Theatre: A Bibliography. $12.50 Hdbd. (ISBN 0-87338-036-3). Kent St. Univ. Pr., OH.

New York Public Library. Catalog of the Theatre & Drama Collections, 2 pts. Incl. Pt. 1, No. 1. Drama Collection: Listing by Cultural Origin, 6 vols. Set—$585.00 Hdbd.; Pt. 1, No. 2. Drama Collection: Author Listing, 6 vols. Set—$790.00 Hdbd.; Pt. 2. Theatre Collection: Books on the Theatre, 9 vols. Set—$530.00 Hdbd. 1967. G. K. Hall & Co., MA.

Palmer, Helen H. & Dyson, Anne J. European Drama Criticism: Interpretations of European Drama. 1968. $9.00 Hdbd. Shoe String Pr., CT.

Palmer, Helen H. & Dyson, Anne J., eds. American Drama Criticism: Interpretations, 1890–1965 Inclusive, of American Drama Since the First Play Produced in America. 1967. $7.50 Hdbd. (ISBN 0-208-00110-7). Shoe String Pr., CT.

Palmer, Helen H. & Dyson, Anne J., eds. American Drama Criticism: Supplement 1 to January, 1969. 1970. $4.50 Hdbd.

(ISBN 0-208-00980-9). Shoe String Pr., CT.

Rowell, George. Victorian Theatre: A Survey. 1967. $6.50 Hdbd. (ISBN 0-19-800653-5). Oxford Univ. Pr., NY.

Stratman, Carl J., et al, eds. Restoration & Eighteenth Century Theatre Research Bibliography, 1961-68. 1969. $10.50 Hdbd. (ISBN 0-87875-000-2). Whitston Pub., NY.

BLACK DRAMA

Abramson, Doris E. Negro Playwrights in the American Theatre. Orig. Title: Study of Plays by Negro Playwrights. 1969. $12.50 Hdbd. (ISBN 0-231-03248-X); $2.95 pa. (ISBN 0-231-08593-1). Columbia Univ. Pr., NY.

Bond, Frederick W. Negro & the Drama. 1969. (1940) $12.00 Hdbd. McGrath Publ. Co., MD.

Brasmer, William & Consolo, Dominick, eds. Black Drama: An Anthology. (gr. 9-12). 1970. $7.95 text ed. (ISBN 0-675-09347-3); $3.95 pa. (ISBN 0-675-09380-5). Charles E. Merrill, OH.

Charters, Ann. Nobody: The Story of Bert Williams. 1970. $6.95 Hdbd. Macmillan, NY.

Couch, William, Jr., ed. New Black Playwrights: An Anthology. 1968. $6.95 Hdbd. (ISBN 0-8071-0409-4). Louisiana State Univ. Pr., LA.

Hatch, James, ed. Black Image on the American Stage: A Bibliography of Plays & Musicals 1770-1970. Orig. Title: Bibliography of American Plays That Present Negro Characters. 1970. $8.00 Hdbd. (ISBN 0-910482-17-9). DBS Publ., NY.

Isaacs, Edith J. Negro in the American Theatre. 1969. (1947) $18.00 Hdbd. McGrath Publ., MD.

Le Roy, Alain. Plays of Negro Life: A Sourcebook of Native American Drama. (1927) $6.50 Hdbd. (ISBN 0-8371-5037-X). Negro Univ. Pr., CT.

Mitchell, Loften. Black Drama: The Story of the American Negro in the Theatre. 1970. $6.95 Hdbd.; $2.45 pa. Hawthorn Bks., NY.

Patterson, Lindsay, ed. Black Theater: A Twentieth-Century Collection of the Works of Its Best Playwrights. 1971. $12.95 Hdbd. (ISBN 0-396-06254-7). Dodd, Mead, NY.

Reardon, William R. & Pawley, Thomas D. Black Teacher & the Dramatic Arts: A Dialogue, Bibliography & Anthology. 1970. $13.50 Hdbd. (ISBN 0-8371-1850-6). Negro Univ. Pr., CT.

Rollins, Charlemae. Famous Negro Entertainers of Stage, Screen & TV. (Jr. Hi). 1967. $3.50 Hdbd. (ISBN 0-396-05503-6). Dodd, Mead & Co., NY.

BLACK MOVING-PICTURE ACTORS AND ACTRESSES

Noble, Peter. Negro in Films. (Literature of Cinema Ser). (1949) $9.00

Hdbd. (ISBN 0-405-01629-8). Arno Pr., NY.

Noble, Peter. Negro in Films. 1969. (1948) $10.00 Hdbd. (ISBN 0-8046-0525-4). Kennikat Pr., NY.

Null, Gary. Black Hollywood: The Negro in Motion Pictures. 1971. $9.95 Hdbd. (ISBN 0-8065-0263-0). Citadel Pr., NY.

Rollins, Charlemae. Famous Negro Entertainers of Stage, Screen & TV. (Jr Hi.). 1967. $3.50 Hdbd. (ISBN 0-396-05503-6). Dodd, Mead & Co., NY.

Sprecher, Daniel, ed. Guide to Films About Negroes, 16mm. 1970. $3.95 pa. Serina Pr., VA.

CHILDREN'S THEATER

Alington, Argentine F. Drama & Education. 1961. $2.50 Hdbd. Dufour Editions, PA.

Armour, Richard. Twisted Tales from Shakespeare. $0.75 pa. New American Library, NY.

Armour, Richard. Twisted Tales from Shakespeare. 1957. $4.95 Hdbd. ISBN 0-07-002252-6). $1.75 pa. (ISBN 0-07-002251-8). McGraw-Hill, NY.

Austin, Ellen L. School Playhouse. (Elem.). 1934. $2.50 Hdbd. (ISBN 0-8283-1156-0). Branden Pr., MA.

Baker, Kitty & Wagner, Jearnine. Place for Ideas: Our Theater. 1965. $8.00 Hdbd. (ISBN 0-911536-01-9). Trinity Univ. Pr., TX.

Bendick, Jeanne & Berk, Barbara. First Book of How to Have a Show. (Elem.). 1957. $3.75 Hdbd. (ISBN 0-531-01691-9). Franklin Watts, NY.

Bennett, Rowena. Creative Plays & Programs for Holidays. (Elem.). 1966. $7.95 Hdbd. (ISBN 0-8238-0005-9). Plays Inc., MA.

Bowers, Gwendolyn. At the Sign of the Globe. 1966. $4.50 Hdbd. (ISBN 0-8098-3049-3). Henry Z. Walck, NY.

Brown, Ivor. Shakespeare & His World. (Illus.). 1964. $5.00 Hdbd. (ISBN 0-8098-3059-0). Henry Z. Walck, NY.

Brown, Ivor. Shakespeare in His Time. 1960. $6.00 Hdbd. (ISBN 0-8407-4023-9). Nelson, NJ.

Brown, Regina. Play at Your House. (Elem.). 1962. $3.50 Hdbd. (ISBN 0-8392-3027-3). Astor-Honor Inc., NY.

Burack, Abraham S., ed. One Hundred Plays for Children. (Elem.). 1970. $8.95 Hdbd. (ISBN 0-8238-0002-4). Plays Inc., MA.

Byers, Ruth. Creating Theatre. (Paul Baker Studies in Theatre, No. 2). 1968. $8.00 Hdbd. (ISBN 0-911536-05-1). Trinity Univ. Pr., TX.

Carlson, Bernice W. Act It Out. (Elem.). 1956. $2.50 Hdbd. (ISBN 0-687-00713-5); $1.60 pa. (ISBN 0-687-00714-3). Abingdon Pr., TN.

Carlson, Bernice W. Play a Part. (Elem.). 1970. $5.95 Hdbd. (ISBN 0-687-31637-5). Abingdon Pr., TN.

Carlson, Bernice W. Right Play for You. (Elem.). 1960. $3.00 Hdbd. (ISBN 0-687-36376-4); $1.60 pa. (ISBN 0-687-36401-9). Abingdon Pr., TN.

Chorpenning, Charlotte B. Twenty-One Years with Children's Theatre. 1954. $3.50 Hdbd. Anchorage Pr., KY.

Chute, Marchette. Introduction to Shakespeare. $3.95 Hdbd. (ISBN 0-525-32587-5). Dutton, NY.

Chute, Marchette. Stories from Shakespeare. 1971. $0.95 pa. New American Library, NY.

Conrad, Edna & Van Dyke, Mary. History on the Stage: Children Make Plays from Historical Novels. 1971. $7.95 Hdbd. Van Nostrand Reinhold, NY.

Davis, Jed H., et al. Children's Theatre. 1960. $9.75 text ed. (ISBN 0-06-041570-3). Harper & Row, NY.

Durland, Frances C. Creative Dramatics for Children: A Practical Manual for Teachers & Leaders. 1952. $2.75 Hdbd. (ISBN 0-87338-063-0); $1.50 pa. (ISBN 0-87338-064-9). Kent State Univ. Pr., OH.

Fenner. Phyllis & Hughes, Avah. Entrances & Exits. (Elem.). 1960. $3.75 Hdbd. (ISBN 0-396-04431-X). Dodd, Mead & Co., NY.

Green, Roger L. Tales from Shakespeare. 1965. $4.95 Hdbd. (ISBN 0-689-20120-6); $4.43 Hdbd. (ISBN 0-689-20117-6). Atheneum Publ., NY.

Hanes, Charles. William Shakespeare & His Plays. (Immortals' Biographies). (Illus.). 1968. $4.50 Hdbd. (ISBN 0-531-00923-8). Watts, NY.

Hodges, C. Walter. Shakespeare & the Players. rev. ed. 1971. $3.00 text ed. Coward, NY.

Hodges, C. Walter. Shakespeare's Theatre. 1964. $6.50 Hdbd. Coward, NY.

Horizon Magazine & Wright, Louis B., eds. Shakespeare's England. (Horizon Caravel Books). 1964. $5.95 Hdbd. (ISBN 0-06-022590-4); $5.49 Hdbd. (ISBN 0-06-022591-2). Harper & Row, NY.

Howard, Vernon. Acts for Comedy Shows: How to Perform & Write Them. (Elem.). $2.99 Hdbd. Sterling Publ. Co., NY.

Howard, Vernon, ed. Complete Book of Children's Theater. 1969. $8.95 Hdbd. Doubleday & Co., NY.

Hughes, Ted, ed. With Fairest Flowers While Summer Lasts: Poems from Shakespeare. (Paperback Ser). 1971. $1.95 pa. Doubleday & Co., NY.

Johnson, Richard. Producing Plays for Children. (Theatre Student Ser). (Hi-Sch.). 1971. $6.96 Hdbd. (ISBN 0-8239-0225-0). Richards Rosen Pr., NY.

Jones, Elizabeth O. How Far Is It to Bethlehem. 1955. $1.50 Hdbd. (ISBN 0-87675-075-7). Horn Bk. Inc., MA.

Kerman, Gertrude L. Plays & Creative Ways with Children. (Elem.). 1961. $6.95 Hdbd. (ISBN 0-8178-3201-7); $6.19 Hdbd. (ISBN 0-8178-3202-5). Harvey House Inc., NY.

Lamb, Charles & Lamb, Mary. Tales from Shakespeare. (Illustrated Juvenile Classics). $3.95 Hdbd. Tudor Publ., NY.

Lamb, Charles & Lamb, Mary. Tales from Shakespeare. $2.45 Hdbd. (ISBN 0-00-422571-6); $4.25 Hdbd. (ISBN 0-00-423571-1). William Collins, NY.

Lamb, Charles & Lamb, Mary. Tales from Shakespeare. (Elem.-Hi-Sch.) 1942. $3.75 Hdbd. (ISBN 0-690-80192-0). Thomas Y Crowell, NY.

Lamb, Charles & Lamb, Mary. Tales from Shakespeare. (New Children's Classics). 1963. $4.95 Hdbd. Macmillan, NY.

Lamb, Charles & Lamb, Mary. Tales from Shakespeare. (Children's Illustrated Classics). $3.95 Hdbd. (ISBN 0-525-40714-6). E. P. Dutton, NY.

Lamb, Charles & Lamb, Mary. Ten Tales from Shakespeare. (Elem.). 1969. $5.95 Hdbd. (ISBN 0-531-01371-5). Franklin Watts, NY.

Lamb, Mary & Lamb, Charles. Tales from Shakespeare. (Children's Illustrated Classics). $2.95 Hdbd. (ISBN 0-460-00008-X). E. P. Dutton, NY.

Montague, C. J. Sixty Years in Waifdom. 1904. $15.00 Hdbd. (ISBN 0-678-08450-5). Augustus M. Keeley, NJ.

Nesbit, Edith. Children's Shakespeare. $2.95 Hdbd. (ISBN 0-394-81014-7); $4.99 Hdbd. (ISBN 0-394-91014-1). Random House, NY.

Noble, Iris. William Shakespeare. (Jr. Hi.). 1961. $3.34 Hdbd. Julian Messner, Inc., NY.

Norman, Charles. Playmaker of Avon: A Biography of Shakespeare. (Hi-Sch.). $1.45 pa. David McKay Co., NY.

Sanders, Sandra. Creating Plays with Children. (Illus., Orig.). 1970. $1.25 pa. (ISBN 0-590-09099-2, Citation). Intl. Schol Bk Serv., OR.

Sesame Street Puppets. (Elem.). 1971. $1.50 Hdbd. (823311). Random House, NY.

Severn, Bill & Severn, Sue. Let's Give a Show. (Elem.). 1956. $4.59 Hdbd. Alfred A. Knopf, NY.

Siks, Geraldine B. Creative Dramatics: An Art for Children. (Jr. Hi.). 1958. $9.00 Hdbd. (ISBN 0-06-046160-8, Harper & Row, NY.

Siks, Geraldine B. & Dunnington, Hazel B., eds. Children's Theatre & Creative Dramatics. YA. (Hi-Sch.). 1961. $6.95 Hdbd.; $3.95 pa. (ISBN 0-295-97875-9, WP29). Univ. of Wash Pr., WA.

Sisson, Rosemary A. Young Shakespeare. (Young Biographies Ser). (Elem. Jr-Hi–Hi-Sch.). 1960. $3.25 Hdbd. Roy Publ., NY.

Smith, Moyne R. Plays & How to Put Them On. (gr. 4–6). 1961. $5.75 Hdbd. (ISBN 0-8098-2352-7). Burgess Publ. Co., MN.

Smith, Moyne R. Plays & How to Put Them On. (Elem.). 1961. $5.75 Hdbd. (ISBN 0-8098-2352-7). Henry Z. Walck, NY.

Summers, Montague. Shakespearean Adaptations. Incl. The Tempest; The Mock Tempest; King Lear. 1969. (1922) $11.95 Hdbd. (ISBN 0-8383-0682-9). Haskell House, NY.

Summers, Montague. Shakespeare's Adaptations, 3 vols. Incl. The Tempest; The Mock Tempest; King Lear. (1922) $11.95 Hdbd. (ISBN 0-8383-0682-9). Haskell House, NY.

Summers, Montague, ed. Shakespeare Adaptations. 1922. $12.50 Hdbd. Benjamin Blom, NY.

Taylor, Loren E. Formal Drama & Children's Theatre. 1966. $1.75 pa. (ISBN 0-8087-2005-8). Burgess Publ. Co., MN.

Walker, Pamela P. Seven Steps to Creative Children's Dramatics. 1957. $3.00 Hdbd. (ISBN 0-8090-8560-7). Hill & Wang, NY.

Ward, Winifred. Theatre for Children. rev. ed. 1958. $4.00 Hdbd. Anchorage, Pr., KY.

White, Anne T. Shakespeare & the Globe Theater. (World Landmark). (Jr Hi.–Hi-Sch.). 1955. $1.95 Hdbd. (ISBN 0-394-80521-6); $3.47 Hdbd. (ISBN 0-394-90521-0). Random House, NY.

Zaidenberg, Arthur. How to Draw Shakespeare's People. (Elem.–Jr Hi–Hi-Sch.). 1967. $3.75 Hdbd. (B39481). Abelard-Schuman Ltd., NY.

COMEDIANS

Blistein, Elmer. Comedy in Action. 1964. $5.00 Hdbd. (ISBN 0-8223-0017-6). Duke Univ Pr., Durham, NC.

Cahn, William. Pictorial History of the Great Comedians. Powers, Thetis, ed. Orig. Title: Laugh Makers. 1970. (1957) $7.95 Hdbd. Grosset & Dunlap, NY.

De Voren Hoffman, Stanton. Comedy & Form in the Fiction of Joseph Conrad. (Studies in English Literature Ser., No. 49). 1970. $7.50 Hdbd. Humanities Pr., NY

Eastman, Max. Enjoyment of Laughter. 1971. (1937) $12.50 Hdbd. Johnson Repr., NY

Enck, John J., et al, eds. Comic in Theory & Practice. 1960. text ed. $3.25 pa. (ISBN 0-390-29055-6). Appleton-Century-Crofts, NY.

Flogel, Karl F. Geschichte Des Grotesk-Komischen, 2 Vols. 1914. $37.50 Hdbd. Benjamin Blom, NY.

Funke, Lewis. Curtain Rises: The Story of Ossie Davis. Duenewald, Doris, ed. 1971. $2.95 Hdbd. (ISBN 0-448-02465-9). Grosset Dunlap, NY.

Greig, John Y. Psychology of Laughter & Comedy. 1969. (1923) $7.50 Hdbd. (ISBN 0-8154-0295-3). Cooper Sq. Pr., NY.

Harmon, Jim. Great Radio Comedians. 1970. $6.95 Hdbd. Doubleday, NY.

Kallen, Horace M. Liberty, Laughter & Tears. 1968. $8.50 Hdbd. (ISBN 0-

87580-006-8). Northern IL. Univ. Pr., Dekalb, IL.

Kaul, A. M. Action of English Comedy: Studies in the Encounter of Abstraction & Experience from Shakespeare to Shaw. 1970. $8.75 Hdbd. (ISBN 0-300-01278-0). Yale Univ Pr., New Haven, CT.

Keese, William L. Group of Comedians. (Drama Ser). 1970. (1901) $14.50 Hdbd. (ISBN 0-8337-1903-3). Burt Franklin, NY.

Kerr, Walter. Tragedy & Comedy. 1967. $5.95 Hdbd. Simon & Schuster, NY.

Lahue, Kalton C. & Gill, Samuel. Clown Princes & Court Jesters. 1970. $8.50 Hdbd. (ISBN 0-498-06949-4). A S Barnes, Cranbury, NJ.

Olson, Elder. Theory of Comedy. 1970. (1968) $1.95 pa. Indiana Univ. Pr., Bloomington, IN.

Olson, Elder. Theory of Comedy. 1969. $5.00 Hdbd. (ISBN 0-253-18790-7, MB). Indiana Univ. Pr., Bloomington, IN.

Piddington, Ralph. Psychology of Laughter: A Study in Social Adaptation. $6.00 Hdbd. $1.95 pa. Gamut Pr., NY.

Strang, Lewis. Celebrated Comedians of Light Opera & Musical Comedy in America. (American Biography Ser). 1970. $14.75 Hdbd. (ISBN 0-512-00696-2). Garrett Pr., NY.

Swabey, Marie C. Comic Laughter: A Philosophical Essay, 1970. (1961) $8.00 Hdbd. (ISBN 0-208-00825-X). Shoe String Pr., Hamden, CT.

Thornbury, Ethel M. Henry Fielding's Theory of the Comic Prose Epic. 1966. (1931) $7.00 Hdbd. Russell & Russell, NY.

COMEDY

Bergson, Henri & Meredith, George. Comedy: Two Classic Studies. Incl. Laughter. Bergson, Henri; Essay on Comedy. Meredith, George. $1.45 pa. Doubleday, NY.

Bergson, Henry. Laughter. Incl. Essays on Comedy by George Meredith. $3.75 Hdbd. Peter Smith Publ. Magnolia, MA.

Blaumanis, Rudolfs. Drama un Komedija. $12.60 Hdbd. (ISBN 0-87908-127-9). Rota Pr., Waverly, IA.

Blistein, Elmer. Comedy in Action. 1964. $5.00 Hdbd. (ISBN 0-8223-0017-6). Duke Univ. Pr., Durham, NC.

Boughner, Daniel C. Braggert in Renaissance Comedy: A Study in Comparative Drama from Aristophanes to Shakespeare. 1954. $14.50 Hdbd. (ISBN 0-8371-3006-9). Greenwood Pr., Westport, CT.

Bronson, Bertrand H., et al. Studies in the Comic. $15.00 Hdbd. Folcroft Pr., Folcroft, PA.

Colby, Elbridge. Early American Comedy. 1919. $3.00 Hdbd. Folcroft Pr., Folcroft, PA.

Cook, Albert. Dark Voyage & the

Golden Mean. 1966. $1.75 pa. (ISBN 0-393-00357-4). W. W. Norton, NY.

Cooper, L. Aristotelian Theory of Comedy. (1922) $12.00 Hdbd. Kraus Reprint, NY.

Corrigan, Robert W., ed. Comedy: A Critical Anthology. 1970. $5.50 pa. Houghton Mifflin, Boston, MA.

Corrigan, Robert W., ed. Comedy: Meaning & Form. 1965. $6.75 pa. (ISBN 0-8102-0070-8). Chandler Publications, San Francisco, CA.

Corrigan, Robert W. & Loney, Glenn M., eds. Comedy: A Critical Anthology. 1971. text ed. price n.g., pa. Houghton Mifflin, Boston, MA.

Corsa, Helen S. Chaucer, Poet of Mirth & Morality. 1964. $3.25 pa. (ISBN 0-268-00363-7). Univ. of Notre Dame Pr., Notre Dame, IN.

Cox, James E. Rise of Sentimental Comedy. 1926. $10.00 Hdbd. Folcroft Pr., Folcroft, PA.

Dalman, Knut O. Aedibus Scaenicis Comoediae Novae. (1929) $6.75 Hdbd. Johnson Reprint, NY.

Feibleman, James K. In Praise of Comedy. 1970. (1962) $2.95 pa. (ISBN 0-8180-1152-1). Horizon Pr., NY.

Feibleman, James K. In Praise of Comedy: A Study in Its Theory & Practice. 1962. (1939) $11.00 Hdbd. Russell & Russell, NY.

Felheim, Marvin, ed. Comedy: Plays, Theory & Criticism. Incl. Birds by Aris-tophanes; Twelfth Night by William Shakespeare; Misanthrope by Moliere; Critic by Richard B. Sheridan; Wedding; or A Joke in One Act by Anton Chekhov; Man of Destiny by George B. Shaw; Importance of Being Earnest by Oscar Wilde; Phoenix Too Frequent by Christopher Fry. text ed. $3.95 pa. (ISBN 0-15-512280-0). Harcourt Brace, NY.

Garvin, W. Development of the Comic Figure. (Studies in Comparative Literature, No. 35). 1970. (1923) $6.95 Hdbd. (ISBN 0-8383-1087-7). Haskell House, NY.

Hadow, W. H. Use of Comic Episodes in Tragedy. 1915. $3.00 Hdbd. Ridgeway Bks., Philadelphia, PA.

Hartman, John G. Development of American Social Comedy from 1787 to 1936. 1971. (1939) $6.50 Hdbd. Lansdowne Pr., Philadelphia, PA.

Herrick, Marvin T. Comic Theory in the Sixteenth Century. 1964. $1.75 pa. (ISBN 0-252-72348-1, 18, IB). Univ. of Illinois Pr., Urbana, IL.

Hogan, Robert & Molin, Sven E. Drama: The Major Genres, an Introductory Critical Anthology. 1962. $5.95 pa. (ISBN 0-396-06108-7). Dodd Mead, NY.

Hoy, Cyrus H. Hyacinth Room: An Investigation into the Nature of Comedy, Tragedy, & Tragicomedy. 1964. $6.95 Hdbd. Knopf, NY.

Kaul, A. M. Action of English Comedy: Studies in the Encounter of Abstraction

& Experience from Shakespeare to Shaw. 1970. $8.75 Hdbd. (ISBN 0-300-01278-0). Yale Univ. Pr., New Haven, CT.

Krutch, Joseph W. Comedy & Conscience After the Restoration, rev. ed. 1924. $2.75 pa. (ISBN 0-231-08516-8, 16). Columbia Univ. Pr., NY.

Lahue, Kalton C. World of Laughter: The Motion Picture Comedy Short 1910–1930. 1971. (1966) $6.95 Hdbd. Univ. of Okla. Pr., Norman, OK.

McCollom, William G. Divine Average: A View of Comedy. 1971. $7.50 Hdbd. (ISBN 0-8295-0202-5). Press of Case Western Press, Cleveland, OH.

Meredith, George. Essay on Comedy & the Uses of the Comic Spirit. Cooper, Lane, ed. 1971. (1918) $10.00 Hdbd. (ISBN 0-8046-1540-3). Kennikat Pr., NY.

Moore, John B. Comic & the Realistic in English Drama. 1965. (1925) $7.50 Hdbd. Russell & Russell, NY.

Morris, Corbyn. Essay Towards Fixing the True Standards of Wit & Humor. 1744. $5.00 Hdbd. (ISBN 0-404-04501-4). AMS Pr., NY.

Olson, Elder. Theory of Comedy. 1969. $5.00 Hdbd. (ISBN 0-253-18790-7). Indiana Univ. Pr., IN.

Olson, Elder. Theory of Comedy. 1970. (1968) $1.95 pa. Indiana Univ. Pr., IN.

Perry, Henry T. Comic Spirit in Restoration Drama. 1962. (1925) $7.00 Hdbd. Russell & Russell, NY.

Perry, Henry T. Masters of Dramatic Comedy & Their Social Themes. 1968. (1939) $13.50 Hdbd. (ISBN 0-8046-0363-4). Kennikat Pr., NY.

Potts, Leonard J. Comedy. 1966. $1.45 pa. Putnam, NY.

Sand, Maurice. History of the Harlequinade, 2 Vols. 1968. $25.00 Hdbd. Benjamin Blom, NY.

Schilling, Bernard N. Comic Spirit: Boccaccio to Thomas Mann. 1967. $7.95 Hdbd. (ISBN 0-8143-1271-3); $2.50 pa. (ISBN 0-8143-1272-1). Wayne St. Univ. Pr., MI.

Servandoni, Jean N. Observations Sur L'Art Du Comedien. ed. 1776. $27.50 Hdbd. Benjamin Blom, NY.

Seyler, Athene & Haggard, Stephen. Craft of Comedy. $2.75 Hdbd. Theatre Arts, NY.

Simon, Neil. Comedy of Neil Simon. $12.95. Random House, NY.

Smith, John H. Gay Couple in Restoration Comedy. 1971. $9.25 Hdbd. (ISBN 0-374-97508-6). Octagon Books, NY.

Smith, Willard. Nature of Comedy. 1930. $15.00 Hdbd. Folcroft Pr., PA.

Sorell, Walter. Facets of Comedy. 1971. $6.95 Hdbd. (ISBN 0-448-00678-2). Grosset & Dunlap, NY.

Vos, Nelvin. Drama of Comedy: Victim & Victor. (Hi-Sch.). 1966. $1.00 pa. John Knox, VA.

Webster, T. B. Birth of Modern Comedy of Manners. 1959. $4.00 Hdbd. Folcroft Pr., PA.

COMMEDIA DELL'ARTE

Duchartre, Pierre L. Italian Comedy: The Improvisation, Scenarios, Lives, Attributes, Portraits & Masks of the Illustrious Characters of the Commedia Dell'arte. 1965. $4.00 pa. (ISBN 0-486-21679-9). Dover Publ., NY.

Kennard, Joseph S. Masks & Marionettes. 1935. $7.50 Hdbd. (ISBN 0-8046-0247-6). Kennikat Pr., NY.

Lea, Kathleen M. Italian Popular Comedy: A Study in the Commedia Dell'arte, 1560-1620, with Special Reference to the English Stage, 2 Vols. 1962. (1934) Set—$17.00 Hdbd. Russell & Russell Publ., NY.

Nicoll, Allardyce. Masks, Mimes & Miracles. 1931. $17.50 Hdbd. (ISBN 0-8154-0163-9). Cooper Sq. Publ., NY.

Nicoll, Allardyce. World of Harlequin. 1963. $22.50 Hdbd. Cambridge U Pr., NY.

Oreglia, Giacomo. Commedia Dell'arte. Edwards, Lovett F., tr. 1968. $5.95 Hdbd. (ISBN 0-8090-3570-7, Drama); $1.95 pa. (ISBN 0-8090-0545-X). Hill & Wang, NY.

Scala, Flaminio. Scenarios of the Commedia Dell'arte: Flaminio Scala's Il Teatro Delle Ravole Rappresentative. Salerno, Henry F., ed. 1967. $10.95 Hdbd. (ISBN 0-8147-0373-9). NYU Pr., NY.

Smith, Winifred. Commedia Dell'arte. rev. ed. $13.75 Hdbd. Benjamin Blom, NY.

COSTUME

Bakst, Leon. Designs of Leon Bakst for the Sleeping Princess. 1969. $27.50 Hdbd. Benjamin Blom, NY.

Barton, Lucy. Appreciating Costume. 1969. $2.95 pa. Walter H. Baker Co., MA.

Barton, Lucy. Historic Costume for the Stage. 1961. $9.95 Hdbd. Walter H. Baker Co., MA.

Barton, Lucy & Edson, Doris. Period Patterns. 1942. $3.25 Hdbd. Walter H. Baker Co., MA.

Boucher. History of Costume in the West. $29.95 Hdbd. (ISBN 0-87245-037-6). Textile Book Serv., NJ.

Bradfield, Nancy. Costume in Detail. 1968. $16.95 Hdbd. (ISBN 0-8238-0091-1). Plays Inc., MA.

Bradley, Carolyn G. Western World Costume: An Outline History. $6.50 text ed. (ISBN 0-390-11674-2). Appleton-Century-Crofts, NY.

Bradshaw, Angela. World Costumes. 1961. $12.95 Hdbd. Macmillan Co., NY.

Broby-Johansen, R. Body & Clothes: An Illustrated History of the Art of Costume. 1968. $12.95 Hdbd. VanN-Rein.

Brooke, Iris. English Costume of the Early Middle Ages: Tenth to Thirteenth Centuries. 1964. $3.00 Hdbd. Barnes & Noble, NY.

Brooke, Iris. Medieval Theatre Costume. 1968. $6.95 Hdbd. Theatre Arts Books, NY.

Buck, Anne M. Victorian Costume & Costume Accessories. (Victorian Collector Ser). 1970. Repr. $8.95 Hdbd. (ISBN 0-87663-125-1). Universe Books, NY.

Casson-Scott, J. Fashion & Costume in Color. 1971. $4.95 Hdbd. Macmillan Co., NY.

Corey, Irene. Mask of Reality: An Approach to Design for Theatre. 1968. $20.00 Hdbd. Anchorage Pr., KY.

Crawford, M. C. One World of Fashion. 3rd ed. Zelin, Beatrice, et al, eds. 1967. $25.00 Hdbd. (ISBN 0-87005-053-2). Fairchild Publ., NY.

Cunnington, C. Willett & Cunninghton, Phillis. Handbook of English Costume in the Nineteenth Century. 1971. $14.95 Hdbd. (ISBN 0-8238-0080-6). Plays Inc., NY.

Cunnington, C. Willett & Cunnington, Phillis. Handbook of English Medieval Costume. 1969. $8.95 Hdbd. (ISBN 0-8238-0092-X). Plays Inc., NY.

Cunnington, Phillis. Costume in Pictures. 1964. $1.95 pa. (ISBN 0-289-79001-8). E. P. Dutton, NY.

Cunnington, Phillis. Costumes of the Nineteenth Century. (Illus). 1971. $3.95 Hdbd. (ISBN 0-8238-0093-8). Plays Inc., MA.

Cunnington, Phillis. Costumes of the Seventeenth & Eighteenth Century.

1971. $3.95 Hdbd. (ISBN 0-8238-0086-5). Plays Inc., MA.

Cunnington, Phillis. Medieval & Tudor Costume. (Jr Hi.). 1968. $3.95 Hdbd. (ISBN 0-8238-0094-6). Plays Inc., MA.

Davenport, Millia. Book of Costume. 1964. $14.95 Hdbd. Crown Publ., NY.

Evans, Mary. Costume Throughout the Ages. 3rd ed. 1950. $8.95 text ed. $4.00 pa. J. B. Lippincott, PA.

Fairservis, Walter A. Costumes of the East: Traditional Eurasian Dress from the American Museum of Natural History Collection. 1971. $15.00 Hdbd. (ISBN 0-85699-028-0). Chatham Pr., CT.

Fernald, Mary. Costume Design & Making. 1967. $4.75 Hdbd. Theatre Arts Books, NY.

Fox, Lilla M. Folk Costumes of Western Europe. 1971. $3.95 Hdbd. (ISBN 0-8238-0087-3). Plays Inc., MA.

Gorsline, Douglas. What People Wore. (Hi-Sch.). 1952. $12.95 Hdbd. (ISBN 0-670-75841-8). Viking Pr., NY.

Green, Michael. Theatrical Costume & the Amateur Stage. (Hi-Sch.). 1968. $4.95 Hdbd. (ISBN 0-8238-0095-4). Plays Inc., MA.

Hansen, Henny H. Costumes & Styles: The Evolution of Fashion from Early Egypt to the Present. 1956. $8.95 Hdbd. (ISBN 0-525-08673-0). E. P. Dutton, NY.

Hartley, Dorothy. Medieval Costume &

Life. (1931) price n.g. Hdbd. Gale Research Co., MI.

Huenefeld, Irene P. International Directory of Historical Clothing. 1967. $5.00 Hdbd. (ISBN 0-8108-0076-4). Scarecrow Pr., NJ.

Jackson, Sheila. Simple Stage Costumes. 1969. $8.50 Hdbd. (ISBN 0-8230-4840-3). Watson-Guptill Publs., NY.

Jones, Inigo. Designs by Inigo Jones for Masques & Plays at Court. Simpson, Percy & Bell, C. F., eds. 1966. Repr. of 1924 ed. $35.00 Hdbd. Russell & Russell, NY.

Kelly, F. M. Shakespearian Costume. 2nd rev. ed. Mansfield, A., ed. 1970. $8.75 Hdbd. (ISBN 0-87830-117-8). Theatre Arts Books, NY.

Kelly, Francis M. & Schwabe, Randolph. Historic Costume: A Chronicle of Fashion in Western Europe 1490–1790. 2nd ed. 1968. $13.75 Hdbd. Benjamin Blom, NY.

Kelly, Francis M. & Schwabe, Randolph. Short History of Costume & Armour, Chiefly in England 1066–1800, 2 Vols. in 1. 1968. Repr. $13.75 Hdbd. Benjamin Blom, NY.

Koehler, Carl & Von Sichart, Emma. History of Costume. Dallas, Alexander K., ed. $3.00 pa. (ISBN 0-486-21030-8). Dover Publ. Inc., NY.

Kohler, Carl. History of Costume. $4.50 Hdbd. (ISBN 0-87245-166-6). Textile Bk. Service, NJ.

Kohler, Carl. History of Costume. $5.50 Hdbd. Peter Smith Publ., MA.

Komisarjevsky, Theodore. Costume of the Theatre. 1968. $12.50 Hdbd. Benjamin Blom, NY.

Komisarjevsky, Theodore & Simonson, Lee. Settings & Costumes of the Modern Stage. 1933. $15.00 Hdbd. Benjamin Blom, NY.

Kybalova, Ludmila, et al. Pictorial Encyclopedia of Fashion, Rosoux, Claudia, tr. 1969. $10.00 Hdbd. Crown Publ., NY.

Laver, James. Concise History of Costume & Fashion. 1969. $7.50 Hdbd. (ISBN 0-8109-2021-2). $3.95 pa. New American Library, NY.

Laver, James. Concise History of Costume & Fashion. 1969. $7.50 Hdbd. (ISBN 0-8109-0056-4). Harry N. Abrams, NY.

Laver, James. Costume. $7.50 Hdbd. Boston Book & Art Shop, MA.

Laver, James. Costume in the Theatre. 1965. $6.50 Hdbd. (ISBN 0-8090-3650-9, Drama). $1.95 pa. (ISBN 0-8090-0543-3). Hill & Wang, NY.

Laver, James, ed. Costume Through the Ages. 1964. $5.95 Hdbd. Simon & Schuster, NY.

Laver, James, ed. Costume Through the Ages. (Jr Hi-Hi-Sch.). 1967. $2.45 pa. Simon & Schuster, NY.

Lester, Katherine M. & Kerr, Rose N. Historic Costume. rev. ed. (Hi-Sch.). 1967. $6.44 text ed. $4.56 s.p. (ISBN 0-87002-257-1). Charles A. Bennett Co., IL.

Lister, Margot. Costume: An Illustrated Survey from Ancient Times to the Twentieth Century. (Hi-Sch.). 1968. $12.95 Hdbd. (ISBN 0-8238-0096-2). Plays Inc., MA.

Lister, Margot. Costumes of Everyday Life. 1971. $10.00 Hdbd. (ISBN 0-8238-0097-0). Plays Inc., MA.

McClellan, E. History of American Costume, Bk. 1, 1607–1870. $15.00 Hdbd. (ISBN 0-87245-212-3). Textile Book Serv., NJ.

Moussinac, Leon. New Movement in the Theatre. 1967. Repr. $35.00 Hdbd. Benjamin Blom, NY.

Parish, Peggy. Costumes to Make. 1970. $3.95 Hdbd. Macmillan Co., NY.

Payne, Blanche. History of Costume. 1965. $15.00 text ed. (ISBN 0-06-045070-3). Harper & Row, NY.

Peters, Joan & Sutcliffe, Anna. Making Costumes for School Plays. (Jr Hi-Hi-Sch.). 1971. $6.95 Hdbd. (ISBN 0-8238-0083-0). Plays Inc., MA.

Prisk, Berneice. Stage Costume Handbook. 1966. $7.50 pa. (ISBN 0-06-045294-3, HarpC). Harper & Row, NY.

Roach, Mary Ellen & Eicher, Joanne B., eds. Dress, Adornment, & the Social Order. 1970. $5.95 pa. (ISBN 0-471-72476-9). John Wiley & Sons, NY.

Rubens, Alfred. History of Jewish Costume. 1967. $10.00 Hdbd. Funk & Wagnalls, NY.

Simonson, Lee, ed. Theatre Art. 1969. (1934) $7.50 Hdbd. (ISBN 0-8154-0289-9). Cooper Sq. Pr., NY.

Snook, Barbara. Costumes for School Plays. $3.95 Hdbd. (ISBN 0-8231-1003-6). Charles T. Branford Co., MA.

Stavridi, Margaret. History of Costume, Vol. 1, Nineteenth Century. (Hi-Sch.). 1966. $15.00 Hdbd. (ISBN 0-8238-0076-8). Plays Inc., MA.

Stavridi, Margaret. History of Costume, Vol. 2, 1600–1800. (Hi-Sch.). 1967. $15.00 Hdbd. (ISBN 0-8238-0077-6). Plays Inc., MA.

Stavridi, Margaret. History of Costume, Vol. 3, 1500–1600. 1969. $15.00 Hdbd. (ISBN 0-8238-0078-4). Plays Inc., MA.

Stavridi, Margaret. History of Costume, Vol. 4, 500 B.C. to 1500 A.D. 1970. $15.00 Hdbd. (ISBN 0-8238-0079-2). Plays Inc., MA.

Tompkins, Julia. Stage Costumes & How to Make Them. 1969. $4.95 Hdbd. (ISBN 0-8238-0064-4). Plays Inc., MA.

Truman, N. Historic Costuming. $1.95 Hdbd. (ISBN 0-87245-367-7). Textile Book Serv., NJ.

Vlack, G. Fantastic Costumes of Trades & Professions. $15.00 Hdbd. (ISBN 0-82330-344-9). Albert Saifer, PA.

Von Boehn, Max. Ornaments, Lace, Fans, Gloves, Walking-Sticks, Parasols,

Jewelry & Trinkets: Modes and Manners. $18.50 Hdbd. Benjamin Blom, NY.

Von Boehm, Max & Fischel, Oskar. Modes & Manners of the Nineteenth Century, 4 Vols. in 2. $47.50 Hdbd. Benjamin Blom, NY.

Walkup, Fairfax P. Dressing the Part: A History of Costume for the Theatre. rev. ed. $8.25 text ed. (ISBN 0-390-91322-7). Appleton-Century-Crofts, NY.

Wilcox, R. Turner. Dictionary of Costume. 1969. $15.00 Hdbd. (ISBN 0-684-10660-4). Charles Scribner's Sons, NY.

Wilcox, R. Turner. Mode in Costume. 1969. Repr. of 1942 ed. $3.95 pa. (ISBN 0-684-41487-2). Charles Scribner's Sons, NY.

Young, Agatha. Recurring Cycles of Fashion, 1760-1937. 1937. $6.95 Hdbd. (ISBN 0-8154-0262-7). Cooper Sq. Pr., NY.

Zirner, Laura. Costuming for the Modern Stage. 1957. $3.95 pa. (ISBN 0-252-72365-1). Univ. of Ill. Pr., IL.

Children's Literature

Barfoot, Audrey I. Discovering Costume. (Elem-Jr. Hi). 1963. $3.25 Hdbd. Dufour Editions, PA.

Berk, Barbara. First Book of Stage Costume & Makeup. (Elem.). 1954. $3.75 Hdbd. (ISBN 0-531-00642-5). Franklin Watts, Inc., NY.

Cooper, Edmund. Let's Look at Costume. (Elem-Jr. H.). 1965. $2.75 Hdbd. $2.06 s.p. (ISBN 0-8075-4470-1). Albert Whitman & Co., IL.

Cummings, Richard. One Hundred One Costumes for All Ages, All Occasions. (Elem.). 1970. $4.95 Hdbd. David McKay Co., NY.

Cunnington, Phillis. Costume. (Junior Reference Bks.). (Elem-Jr. Hi-Hi-Sch.). 1970. $2.95 Hdbd. (ISBN 0-8023-1152-0). Dufour Editions, PA.

Fox, Lilla M. Folk Costumes of Western Europe. (Elem-Jr. Hi-Hi-Sch.). 1971. $3.95 Hdbd. (ISBN 0-8238-0087-3). Plays Inc., MA.

Leeming, Joseph. Costume Book for Parties & Plays. (Jr. Hi-Hi-Sch.). 1938. $4.95 Hdbd. J. B. Lippincott, PA.

Zaidenberg, Arthur. How to Draw Costumes & Clothes. (Elem-Jr. Hi-Hi-Sch.). 1964. $3.75 Hdbd. Abelard-Schuman Ltd., NY.

Design

Doten, Hazel & Boulard, Constance. Fashion Drawing: How to Do It. rev. ed. (Hi-Sch.). 1953. $8.50 Hdbd. (ISBN 0-06-031770-1). Harper & Row, NY.

Fernald, Mary. Costume Design & Making. 1967. $4.75 Hdbd. Theatre Arts Book Co., NY.

Hillhouse, Marion S. Dress Selection & Design. 1963. $8.95 Hdbd. (35453). Macmillan Co., NY.

Ireland, P. J. Fashion Design Drawing. 1970. $6.95 Hdbd. (ISBN 0-471-42835-3). John Wiley & Sons, NY.

Montagna, Pier. Key to Dress Design. $2.00 Hdbd. Wehman Brothers, NJ.

Prisk, Berneice & Byers, Jack. Costuming. (Theatre Student Ser). (Hi-Sch.). 1969. $6.96 Hdbd. (ISBN 0-8239-0147-5). Rosen Richards Assoc., NY.

Roberts, Eva. Art of Designing Clothes. price "n.g." Van Nostrand-Reinhold Books, NY.

Sharaff, Irene. Irene Sharaff Book on Costume Design. price "n.g." Van Nostrand-Reinhold, NY.

Sheldon, Martha. Design Through Draping. 1967. $4.75 pa. (ISBN 0-8087-1906-8). Burgess Publ. Co., MN.

Tompkins, Julia. Stage Costumes & How to Make Them. 1969. $4.95 Hdbd. (ISBN 0-8238-0064-4). Plays Inc., MA.

National

China

Arlington, Lewis C. Chinese Drama. $32.50 Hdbd. Benjamin Blom, NY.

Chambers, William. Designs of Chinese Buildings, Furniture, Dresses, Machines & Utensils. 1968. $32.50 Hdbd. Benjamin Blom, NY.

Chinese Opera Costumes. 1967. $20.00 Hdbd. (ISBN 0-87902-008-3). Orientalia, Inc., NY.

Mahler, Jane G. Westerners Among the Figurines of the T'ang Dynasty of China.

(Roma Oriental Ser. No. 20). 1959. $14.00 Hdbd. Paragon Book, NY.

Scott, A. C. Chinese Costume in Transition. $3.25 pa. Theatre Arts Books, NY.

Zung, Cecilia S. Secrets of the Chinese Drama. 1937. $15.00 Hdbd. Benjamin Blom, NY.

Egypt

Houston, Mary G. Ancient Egyptian, Mesopotamian & Persian Costume & Decoration. 2nd ed. 1954. $8.50 Hdbd. Barnes & Noble, NY.

England

Barnes, R. M. History of the Regiments & Uniforms of the British Army. 1967. $8.50 Hdbd. Fernhill House, NY.

Barnes, R. M. Military Uniforms of Britain & the Empire, 1742 to the Present. 1960. $8.50 Hdbd. Fernhill House, NY.

Brooke, Iris. English Children's Costume Since Seventeen Seventy-Five. 1958. $3.00 Hdbd. Barnes & Noble, NY.

Brooke, Iris. English Costume in the Age of Elizabeth: Sixteenth Century. 2nd ed. 1963. $3.00 Hdbd. Barnes & Noble, NY.

Brooke, Iris. English Costume of the Early Middle Ages: Tenth to Thirteenth Centuries. 1964. $3.00 Hdbd. Barnes & Noble, NY.

Brooke, Iris. English Costume of the Eighteenth Century. Laver, James, ed.

1964. $3.00 Hdbd. Barnes & Noble, NY.

Brooke, Iris. English Costume of the Later Middle Ages: Fourteenth to Fifteenth Centuries. 1963. $3.00 Hdbd. Barnes & Noble, NY.

Brooke, Iris. English Costume of the Nineteenth Century. Laver, James, ed. 1964. $3.00 Hdbd. Barnes & Noble, NY.

Brooke, Iris. English Costume of the Seventeenth Century. 2nd ed. 1964. $3.00 Hdbd. Barnes & Noble, NY.

Brooke, Iris. History of English Costume. 3rd ed. 1969. (1949) $6.00 Hdbd. $3.50 pa. Hillary House Publ., NY.

Calthrop, Dion C. English Costume Ten Sixty-Six to Eighteen Thirty. 1906. $5.00 Hdbd. Barnes & Noble, NY.

Cunington, C. Willett & Cunnington, Phillis. Handbook of English Costume in the Sixteenth Century. rev. ed. enl. ed. 1970. $10.95 Hdbd. (ISBN 0-8238-0081-4). Plays Inc., MA.

Cunnington, C. W., et al. Dictionary of English Costume. 1971. (1960) $7.50 Hdbd. Barnes & Noble, NY.

Cunnington, C. Willett. English Women's Clothing in the Present Century. 1959. $15.00 Hdbd. (ISBN 0-498-07250-9). A. S. Barnes, NY.

Cunnington, C. Willett & Cunnington, Phillis. Handbook of English Costume in the Nineteenth Century. 1971. $14.95 Hdbd. (ISBN 0-8238-0080-6). Plays Inc., MA.

Cunnington, C. Willett & Cunnington, Phillis. Handbook of English Costume in the 18th Century. rev. ed. 1971. $12.95 Hdbd. (ISBN 0-8238-0128-4). Plays Inc., MA.

Cunnington, C. Willett & Cunnington, Phillis. Handbook of English Medieval Costume. 1969. $8.95 Hdbd. (ISBN 0-8238-0092-X). Plays Inc., MA.

Cunnington, Phillis. Costume. (Junior Reference Bks). (Elem. Jr Hi–Hi-Sch.). 1970. $2.95 Hdbd. (ISBN 0-8023-1152-0). Dufour Editions, PA.

Cunnington, Phillis. Costumes of the Nineteenth Century. 1971. $3.95 Hdbd. (ISBN 0-8238-0093-8). Plays Inc., MA.

Cunnington, Phillis. Costumes of the Seventeenth & Eighteenth Century. (Illus.). 1971. $3.95 Hdbd. (ISBN 0-8238-0086-5). Plays Inc., MA.

Cunnington, Phillis. Medieval & Tudor Costume. (Elem.). 1968. $3.95 Hdbd. (ISBN 0-8238-0094-6). Plays Inc., MA.

Cunnington, Phillis & Lucas, Catherine. Occupational Costume in England: From the 11th Century to 1914. 1967. $11.50 Hdbd. Barnes & Noble, NY.

Kelly, F. M. Shakespearian Costume. 2nd rev. ed. Mansfield, A., ed. 1970. $8.75 Hdbd. (ISBN 0-87830-117-8). Theatre Arts Book Co., NY.

La Mar, Virginia A. English Dress in the Age of Shakespeare. (Folger Booklet on Tudor & Stuart Civilization Ser). (Hi-Sch.). 1958. $1.50 pa. (ISBN 0-8139-0088-3). Univ. Pr. of Va., VA.

Linthicum, Marie C. Costume in the Drama of Shakespeare & His Contemporaries. 1963. (1936). $7.50 Hdbd. Russell & Russell, NY.

Yarwood, Doreen. English Costume. 1953. $8.50 Hdbd. Dufour Editions, PA.

Yarwood, Doreen. Outline of English Costume. 1968. $4.95 Hdbd. Plays Inc., MA.

Europe

Anderson, Ruth M. Costumes Painted by Sorolla in His Provinces of Spain. 1957. $4.00 Hdbd. Hispanic Society, NY.

Anderson, Ruth M. Spanish Costume: Extremadura. 1951. $11.00. Hdbd. Hispanic Society, NY.

Anderson, Ruth M. & Spalding, Frances. Costume of Candelario, Salamanca. 1932. $1.50 Hdbd. Hispanic Society, NY.

Bogatyrev, Petr. Functions of Folk Costume in Moravian Slovakia. 1971. $8.50 Hdbd. Humanities Pr., NY.

Brooke, Iris. Western European Costume & Its Relation to the Theatre, Vol. 1: 13th To 17th Centuries. $2.85 pa. Theatre Arts Books, NY.

Brooke, Iris. Western European Costume & Its Relation to the Theatre, Vol. 2: 17th Through 19th Centuries. 1963. $2.85 pa. Theatre Arts Books, NY.

Fairservis, Walter A. Costumes of the East: Traditional Eurasian Dress from the American Museum of Natural History Collection. 1971. $15.00 Hdbd. (ISBN 0-85699-028-0). Chatham Pr., CT.

Fox, Lilla M. Folk Costumes of Southern Europe. (Elem., Jr. Hi-Hi-Sch.). 1971. $3.95 Hdbd. (ISBN 0-8238-0088-1). Plays Inc., MA.

Fox, Lilla M. Folk Costumes of Western Europe. (Elem., Jr. Hi-Hi-Sch.). 1971. $3.95 Hdbd. (ISBN 0-8238-0087-3). Plays Inc., MA.

Fox, Lilla M. Folk Costumes of Western Europe. (Elem., Jr. Hi-Hi-Sch.). 1970. $3.95 Hdbd. (ISBN 0-8238-0087-3). Plays Inc., MA.

Gaborjan, Alice. Hungarian Peasant Costumes. 1971. $4.00 Hdbd. International Publ. Serv., NY.

Houston, Mary G. Medieval Costume in England & France. 1965. $8.50 Hdbd. Barnes & Noble, NY.

Mann, Kathleen. Peasant Costume in Europe. 1950. $7.50 Hdbd. Humanities Pr., NY.

Oaks, Alma & Hamilton-Hill, M. Rural Costume. 1970. $12.95 Hdbd. Van Nostrand-Reinhold Books, NY.

Stibbert, Frederic. Civil & Military Clothing in Europe: From the First to the Eighteenth Century. 1968. $25.00 Hdbd. Benjamin Blom, NY.

Sumberg, Samuel L. Nuremberg Schembert Carnival. 1941. $12.00 Hdbd. (ISBN 0-404-50462-0). AMS Pr., NY.

Greece

Hope, T. Costumes of the Greeks & Romans. $4.95 Hdbd. (ISBN 0-87245-142-9). Textile Bk. Service, NJ.

Hope, Thomas. Costumes of the Greeks & Romans, 2 Vols. in 1. $5.00 Hdbd. Peter Smith Publ., MA.

Hope, Thomas. Costumes of the Greeks & Romans. Orig. Title: Costumes of the Ancients. 1812. $2.50 pa. (ISBN 0-486-20021-3). Dover Publ. Inc., NY.

Houston, Mary G. Ancient Greek, Roman & Byzantine Costume & Decoration. 2nd ed. 1965. $8.50 Hdbd. Barnes & Noble, NY.

Paracas, Necropolis. Headdress & Face Ornaments, Vol. 21. (Museum Workshop Notes). $1.95 Hdbd. (ISBN 0-87245-357-X). Textile Bk. Service, NJ.

India

Ambrose, Kay. Classical Dances & Costumes of India. 1965. $6.50 Hdbd. Hillary House Publ., NY.

Dar, S. N. Costumes of India & Pakistan. $15.00 Hdbd. (ISBN 0-87245-079-1). Textile Book Serv., NJ.

Dar, S. N. Costumes of India & Pakistan: A Historical & Cultural Study. 1971. $22.00 Hdbd. International Publ. Serv., NY.

Flynn, Dorris. Costumes of India. 1971. $9.95 Hdbd. (ISBN 0-87799-017-4). Walter A. Haessner & Assoc., NJ.

Ghurye, Govind S. Bharatanatya & Its

Costume. 1959. $1.50 Hdbd. Humanities Pr., NY.

Ghurye, Govind S. Indian Costume. 2nd ed. 1966. $17.50 Hdbd. Humanities Pr., NY.

Italy

Hope, T. Costumes of the Greeks & Romans. $4.95 Hdbd. (ISBN 0-87245-142-9). Textile Bk. Service, NJ.

Hope, Thomas. Costumes of the Greeks & Romans. Orig. Title: Costumes of the Ancients. (Illus.). 1812. $2.50 pa. (ISBN 0-486-20021-3). Dover Publ. Inc., NY.

Hope, Thomas. Costumes of the Greeks & Romans, 2 Vols. in 1. $5.00 Hdbd. Peter Smith Publ., MA.

Houston, Mary G. Ancient Greek, Roman & Byzantine Costume & Decoration, 2nd ed. 1965. $8.50 Hdbd. Barnes & Noble, NY.

Saunders, Catharine. Costume in Roman Comedy. 1909. $7.50 Hdbd. (ISBN 0-404-05563-X). AMS Pr., NY.

Japan

Minnich, Helen B. Japanese Costume & the Makers of Its Elegant Tradition. 1963. $19.50 Hdbd. (ISBN 0-8048-0287-4). CE Tuttle, VT.

Shaver, Ruth. Kabuki Costume. 1966. $22.50 Hdbd. (ISBN 0-8048-0331-5). CE Tuttle, VT.

Mexico

Mexican Native Costumes. $4.00 Hdbd. Rogers Bk. Service, NY.

Persia

Houston, Mary G. Ancient Egyptian, Mesopotamian & Persian Costume & Decoration. 2nd ed. 1954. $8.50 Hdbd. Barnes & Noble, NY.

U.S.

Earle, Alice M. Two Centuries of Costume in America, 2 vols. (Illus.). Set— $16.00 Hdbd. Peter Smith Publ., MA.

Earle, Alice M. Two Centuries of Costume in America, 2 Vols. 1968. $15.00 Hdbd. Benjamin Blom, NY.

Earle, Alice M. Two Centuries of Costume in America, 2 Vols. 1971. Set— $5.00 pa. (ISBN 0-8048-0969-0). C E Tuttle, VT.

Earle, Alice M. Two Centuries of Costume in America, 2 Vols. 1970. (1903) $3.75 ea. pa. (ISBN 0-486-22551-8) (ISBN 0-486-22552-6). Dover Publ. Inc., NY.

Earle, Alice M. Two Centuries of Costume in America, 1620–1820, 2 Vols. Set —$12.50 Hdbd. Peter Smith Publ., MA.

McClellan, Elisabeth. Historic Dress in America 1607–1870, 2 Vols. in 1. $17.50 Hdbd. Benjamin Blom, NY.

McClellan, Elizabeth. History of American Costume 1607–1870. 1969. Repr. $12.50 Hdbd. (ISBN 0-8148-0135-8). Tudor Publ. Co., NY.

Wilcox, R. Turner. Five Centuries of American Costume. (Illus.). (Jr Hi-Hi-Sch.). 1963. $10.00 Hdbd. (ISBN 0-

684-10661-2). Charles Scribner's Sons, NY.

Wyckoff, Alexander, et al. Early American Dress. rev. ed. $17.50 Hdbd. Benjamin Blom, NY.

DANCE

American Association For Health—Physical Education—And Recreation. Designs for Dance. 1968. $1.25 pa. AAHPER. Washington, D.C.

American Association For Health—Physical Education—And Recreation. Focus on Dance, Vol. 6, 1971. $3.95 pa. AAHPER. Washington, D.C.

American Association For Health—Physical Education—And Recreation. Focus on Dance—Book 4: Dance As a Discipline. 1966. $4.00 pa. AAHPER. Washington, D.C.

American Association For Health—Physical Education—And Recreation. Focus on Dance—Book 5. 1969. $3.00 pa. AAHPER. Washington, D.C.

Arbeau, T. Orchesography. Evans, Mary S., $4.50 Hdbd. Peter Smith. M.A.

Baskerville, Charles R. Elizabethan Jig. 1929 $3.50 pa. (ISBN 0-486-21365-X). Dover Publ. NY.

Baskerville, Charles R. Elizabethan Jig & Related Song Drama. $5.00 Hdbd. Peter Smith. MA.

Blasis, Carlo. Elementary Treatise Upon the Theory & Practice of the Art of Dancing. 3rd. ed. Evans, Mary

S., 1968. (1954). $1.35 pa. (ISBN 0-486-21592-X). Dover Publ. NY.

Boas, Franciska. The Function of Dance in Human Society. $1.95 pa. (ISBN 0-87127-03203). Dance Horizons. NY.

Bruce, Violet R. Dance & Dance Drama in Education. 1965. $3.95 Hdbd. (ISBN 0-08-010882-2); $2.95 pa. (ISBN 0-08-010881-4). Pergamon Pr. NY.

Bruce, Violet R. & Tooke, Joan D. Lord of the Dance: An Approach to Religious Education. 1966. $3.95 Hdbd. (ISBN 0-08-011955-7); $2.95 pa. (ISBN 0-08-011954-9). Pergamon Pr. NY.

Castle, C. Better Dancing. 1967. $4.50 Hdbd. International Publ. Serv. NY.

Cole, Arthur C. Puritan & Fair Terpsichore. $1.95 pa. (ISBN 0-87127-004-8). Dance Horizons. NY.

Cressey, Paul G. Taxi-Dance Hall. 1932. $8.50 Hdbd. (ISBN 0-404-01839-4). AMS Pr. NY.

Cressey, Paul G. Taxi-Dance Hall: A Sociological Study in Commercialized Recreation & City Life. 1969 (1932) $12.00 Hdbd. (ISBN 0-87585-076-6). Patterson Smith. NJ.

Cressey, Paul G. Taxi-Dance Hall: A Sociological Study in Commercialized Recreation & City Life. 1968. (1932). $16.25 Hdbd. (ISBN 0-0371-0366-5). Greenwood. Pr. CT.

Duncan, Isadora. Art of the Dance.

$12.50 Hdbd. Theatre Arts Books, NY.

Eames, Marian. When All the World Was Dancing. 2nd ed. $3.00 pa. (ISBN 0-87104-510-9). NY Public Library, NY.

Frazer, Lilly G. Dancing: A Handbook of the Terpsichorean Arts in Diverse Places & Times, Savage & Civilized. 1969. (1895). $13.50 Hdbd. Singing Tree Pr. MI.

Haberman, Martin. Dance—an Art in Academe. 1970. $7.95 Hdbd. (ISBN 0-8077-1480-1). Teachers College Pr. NY.

Harris, Jane A., et al. Dance a While. 1968. $6.50 Hdbd. (ISBN 0-8087-0811-2). Burgess Publ. Co. MN.

Haskell, Arnold L. Balletomania: Story of an Obsession. 1934. $14.50 Hdbd. (ISBN 0-404-03154-4). AMS Pr. NY.

Hayes, Elizabeth R. Dance Composition & Production for High Schools & Colleges. 1955. $6.00 Hdbd. $5.00 pa. Ronald Pr. Co. NY.

H'Doubler, Margaret N. Dance: A Creative Art Experience. 2nd ed. 1957. $1.45 pa. (ISBN 0-299-01324-6). Univ. of Wisconsin Pr. WI.

Heaton, Alma. Fun Dances & Games: A Fun Dance & Game for Every Purpose. 1969. $3.00 pa. (ISBN

0-8425-0023-5). Brigham Young Univ. Pr. UT.

Heyman, C. A. Dances of the Three-Thousand-League Land. (1963). $4.00 pa. Johnson Reprint Corp. NY.

Horst, Louis. Pre-Classic Dance Forms. 1969. (1937). $2.95 pa. (ISBN 0-87127-021-8). Dance Horizons, Inc. NY.

Horst, Louis & Russell, Carroll. Modern Dance Forms in Relation to the Other Modern Arts. $2.95 pa. (ISBN 0-87127-011-0). Dance Horizons, Inc. NY.

Ishaq, Shahid. Evolution of Classical Dancing in Pakistan. $1.00 Hdbd. International Publ. Service. NY.

Kirstein, Lincoln, et al., eds. Dance Index 1942 Thru 1948, 7 Vols. (Contemporary Art Ser). 1970. (1948) Set. $200.00 (ISBN 0-405-00730-2). Arno Pr. NY.

Lambranzi, Gregorio. New & Curious School of · Theatrical Dancing. De Moroda, Derra, $3.95 pa. (ISBN 0-87127-005-6). Dance Horizons, Inc. NY.

Martin, John. America Dancing: The Background & Personalities of the Modern Dance. 1968. $4.95 pa. (SBN 0-87127-010-2). Dance Horizons, Inc. NY.

Martin, John. Days of Divine Indiscipline. (1961). $4.00 pa. Johnson Reprint Corp. NY.

Martin, John. Introduction to the Dance. $4.95 pa. (ISBN 0-87127-002-1). Dance Horizons, Inc. NY.

Martin, John. John Martin's Book of the Dance. 1963. $8.95 Hdbd. (ISBN 0-8148-0164-1). Tudor Publ. Co. NY.

Meyer-Baer, Kathi. Music of the Spheres & the Dance of Death. 1970. $13.50 Hdbd. (ISBN 0-691-09110-2). Princeton Univ. Pr. NY.

Mikulova, Milada, Coppelia. (Curtain-Raiser Bks). (Elem.) 1971. $4.95 Hdbd. (ISBN 0-531-01926-8). Franklin Watts, Inc. NY.

Moore, Lillian. Artists of the Dance. 1969. (1938). $4.95 pa. (ISBN 0-87127-018-8). Dance Horizons, Inc., NY.

Nadel, Myron H. & Nadel, Constance G. Readings in Dance Appreciation. 1970. $13.95 Hdbd.; text ed. $10.00 Hdbd. Praeger Publ. NY.

Natan, Alex. Prima Donna. 1971. $17.50 Hdbd. (ISBN 0-87597-064-8). Crescendo Publ. MA.

Natan, Alex. Primo Uomo. 1971. $17.50 Hdbd. (ISBN 0-87597-063-X). Crescendo Publ. MA.

Northbrooke, John. Treatise Against Dicing, Dancing, Plays & Interludes. 1971. (1843) $7.50 Hdbd. (ISBN 0-404-04793-9). AMS Pr. NY.

Noverre, Jean G. Letters on Dancing & Ballets. Beaumont, Cyril W., 1803. $3.95 pa. (ISBN 0-87127-006-4). Dance Horizons, NY.

Pecour, Louis, Recueil de Danses & la Nouvelle Galliarde $2.95 pa. Dance Horizons, NY.

Pelmont, R. A. Paul Valery et les Beaux-Arts. 1949. $8.00 pa. Kraus Reprint Corp. NY.

Penrod, James & Plastino, Janice G. Dancer Prepares: Modern Dance for Beginners. (Hi-Sch.) 1970. $3.75 Hdbd.; $1.25 pa. National Pr. CA.

Richardson, J.P. Selection of European Folk Dances, 3 Vols. $1.50 pa. (ISBN 0-08-010833-4). (ISBN 0-08-010842-3) (ISBN 0-08-011926-3) Pergamon Pr. NY.

Rust, Frances. Dance in Society: An Analysis of the Relationship Between the Social Dance & Society, in England, from the Middle Ages to the Present Day. 1970. $8.50 Hdbd. Humanities Pr. NY.

Saint Denis, Ruth. Unfinished Life. $5.95 pa. (ISBN 0-87127-030-7). Dance Horizons, NY.

Scholes, Percy, A. Puritans & Music in England & New England: A Contribution to the Cultural History of Two Nations. 1962. (1934). $10.00 Hdbd. Russell & Russell, NY.

Schramm, John & Anderson, David. Dance in Steps of Change. 1970. $2.95 pa. Thomas Nelson, NJ.

Seldes, Gilbert. Seven Lively Arts. 1962. $2.45 pa. (ISBN 0-498-04076-3) A.S. Barnes. NJ.

Shawn, Ted. Every Little Movement:

The Principles of Francois Delsarte. 1968. $2.95 pa. (ISBN 0-87127-015-3). Dance Horizons, NY.

Sheets, Maxine. Phenomenology of Dance. 1966. $6.50 Hdbd. (ISBN 0-299-03830-0). Univ. of Wisconsin Pr. WI.

Sherbon, Elizabeth. On the Count of One: A Guide to Movement & Progression in Dance. (Hi-Sch.) 1968 $5.00 pa. (ISBN 0-87484-131-3) National Pr. CA.

Sorell, Walter. Dance Through the Ages. 1967. $7.95 Hdbd. (ISBN 0-448-01912-4) Grosset & Dunlap, NY.

Sorell, Walter, ed. Dance Has Many Faces (Hi-Sch.) 1966. $9.00 Hdbd. (ISBN 0-231-02968-3). Columbia Univ. Pr. NY.

Sorrell, Walter. Dancer's Image: Points & Counterpoints. 1971. $15.00 Hdbd. Columbia Univ. Pr. NY.

Swan, G. Old Time Popular Dances. $1.00 Hdbd. Wehman Bros. NJ.

Terry, W. Carrers for the 70's: Dance 1971 $4.95 Hdbd. Macmillan. NY.

Tomlinson, Kellom. The Art of Dancing & Six Dances. $4.95 pa. (ISBN 0-87127-033-1). DAnce Horizons, NY.

Tuner, Mangery J. New Dance: Approaches to Nonliteral Choreography 1971. $7.95 (ISBN 0-8229-3215-6). Univ. of Pittsburgh Pr. PA.

Van Tuyl, Marlan, ed. Anthology of Impulse: Annual of Contemporary Dance 1951-1966. 1969. $2.95 pa. (ISBN 0-87127-017-X). Dance Horizons, NY.

Veale, Tom. Dancing Prices of Denmark. 1961) $4.00 pa. Johnson Reprint. NY.

Walker, Kathryn S. Dance & Its Creators. 1971 $5.95 Hdbd. John Day, NY.

Wigman, Mary. Language of Dance. Sorell, Walter, transl. 1966. $12.50 Hdbd. (ISBN 0-8195-3066-2). Eseleyan Univ. Pr. CT.

Willis, J., ed. Dance World, 5 Vols. 1966-1970. $10.00 Hdbd. Crown Publ., NY.

Wrights, Del. Acrobatic & Adagio Manual. 1962. $5.00 pa. Wehman Bros., NJ.

Zorn, Friedrich A. Grammar of the Art of Dancing Theoretical & Practical. 1970. $37.50 Hdbd. (ISBN 0-8337-3923-9). Burt Franklin, NY.

Children

Bauer, Lois M. & Reed, Barbara A. Dance & Play Activities for the Elementary Grades, 2 Vols. 1951-1967. Vol. 1. $4.50 Hdbd. (ISBN 0-910354-02-2); Vol. 2. $4.98 Hdbd. (ISBN 0-910354-07-3). Chartwell House, NY.

Boorman, Joyce. Creative Dance in the First Three Grades. 1969. $4.50 Hdbd. David McKay, NY.

Carroll, Jean & Lofthouse, Peter. Creative Dance for Boys. 1971. $5.00 Hdbd. International Publ. Serv. NY.

Dimondstein, G. Children Dance in the Classroom. 1971. $7.95 Hdbd. Macmillan. NY.

Haberman, Martin. Dance—an Art in Academe. 1970. $7.95 Hdbd. (ISBN 0-8077-1480-2). Teachers College Pr. NY.

International Council on Health—Physical Education And Recreation. ICHPER Book of Worldwide Games & Dances. 1967. $4.00 pa. AAHPER, Washington, D.C.

Latchaw, Marjorie & Pyatt, Jean. Pocket Guide of Dance Activities. 1956. $4.75 Hdbd. (ISBN 0-13-684837-0). Prentice-Hall, NJ.

Maynards, Olga. Children & Dance & Music. 1968. $6.95 Hdbd. (ISBN 0-684-10382-6). Scribner. NY.

Murray, Ruth L. Dance in Elementary Education. 1963. $9.95 Hdbd. (ISBN 0-06-044680-3). Harper & Row Publ. NY.

Neilson, Neils P., et al. Physical Education for Elementary Schools. 1966. $7.50 Hdbd. Ronald Pr. NY.

Russell, Joan. Creative Dance in the Primary School. 1968. $6.00 Hdbd. Praeger Publ., NY.

Sato, Satoru. Coppelia. Brannen, Ann, transl. (Elem.) 1970. $2.50 Hdbd. Japan Publ., CA.

Wiener, Jack & Lidstone, John. Creative Movement for Children: A Dance Program for the Classroom. 1969. $7.50 Hdbd. Van Nostrand Reinhold, NY.

Dancers

Atkinson, Margaret F. & Hillman, May. Dancers of the Ballet. (Jr. Hi-Sch.) 1955. $5.59 Hdbd. Knopf, NY.

Haskell, Arnold L. Balletomania: Story of an Obsession. 1934. $14.50 Hdbd. (ISBN 0-404-03154-4). AMS Pr. NY.

Le Clercg, Tanaquil. Ballet Cook Book. 1967. $12.50 Hdbd. (ISBN 0-8128-1019-8). Stein & Day, NY.

Martin, John. John Martin's Book of the Dance. 1963 $8.95 Hdbd. (ISBN 0-8148-0164-1). Tudor Publ., NY.

Maynard, Olga. American Modern Dancers: The Pioneers. (Hi-Sch.) 1965. $4.50 Hdbd. (ISBN 0-316-55191-0) Little, Brown, MA.

Moore, Lillian, Artists of the Dance. 1969. (1938). $4.95 pa. (ISBN 0-87127-018-8). Dance Horizons, NY.

Parker, Henry T. Eighth Notes: Voices & Figures of Music & the Dance. 1922. $9.00 Hdbd. (ISBN 0-8369-0768-X). Books for Libraries, NY.

Seroff, Victor. Real Isadora. 1971. $10.00 Hdbd. Dial Pr. NY.

Wagenknecht, Edward C. Seven

Daughters of the Theater. 1964. $5.95 Hdbd. (ISBN 0-8061-0618-2). Univ. of Oklahoma Pr. OK.

Zaidenberg, Arthur. How to Draw Ballet & Other Dancers. (Jr. Hi-Sch.) 1968. $3.75 Hdbd. Abelard-Schuman, NY.

Biography

De Mille, Agnes. Dance to the Piper (Hi-Sch.) 1952. $7.50 Hdbd. (ISBN 0-316-18034-3) Little, Brown, MA.

De Mille, Agnes. Promenade Home. 1958. $6.50 Hdbd. (ISBN 0-316-18033-5) Little, Brown, MA.

Duncan, Irma. Duncan Dancer: An Autobiography. 1966. $6.95 Hdbd. (ISBN 0-8195-3061-1). Weslyan Univ. Pr. CT.

Duncan, Isadora. Isadora. 1968. $.95 pa. Universal Publ. & Dist. NY.

Duncan, Isadora. Mi Vida. $1.75 pa. French & European Publ.; NY.

Dunham, Katherine. Katherine Dunham's Journey to Accompong. (1946) $9.50 Hdbd. (ISBN 0-8371-5187-2). Negro Univ. Pr. CT.

Markova, Alicia. Giselle & I. 1961. $5.95 Hdbd. (ISBN 0-8149-0154-9). Vanguard Pr. NY.

Massine, Leonide. My Life in Ballet. Hartnoll, Phyllis & Rubens, Robert, eds. 1969. $8.95 Hdbd. St. Martin's Pr. NY.

Nijinsky, Vaslav. Diary of Vaslav

Nijinsky. Nijinsky, Romola, ed. 1968. $2.25 pa. (ISBN 0-520-00945-2). Univ. of California Pr. CA.

Nureyev, Rudolph. Nureyev: An Autobiography with Pictures. 1963. $5.95 Hdbd. (ISBN 0-525-16986-5). E.P. Dutton, NY.

Percival, John. Experimental Dance. 1971. $7.95 Hdbd. (ISBN 0-87663-148-0). Universe Books, NY.

Historical

Brinson, Peter. Background to European Ballet: A Notebook from Its Archives. 1966. $.50 pa. Humanities Pr. NY.

Dance Perspectives, 1959-1964. Repr. Set. $80.00 Johnson Reprint, NY.

Dean, Beth. Many Worlds of Dance. 1966. $6.60 Hdbd. Tri-Ocean, CA.

Knight. Dancing, a History of the Dance. 1.00 pa. Borden Publ., CA.

Kraus, Richard. History of the Dance: In Art & Education. 1969. $9.50 Hdbd. (ISBN 0-13039005401). Prentice-Hall, NJ.

Meerloo, Joost A. Dance Craze & Sacred Dance. 1962. $6.50 Hdbd. Humanities Pr. NY.

Ridgeway, William. Dramas & Dramatic Dances of Non-European Races. 1810. $17.50 Hdbd.Benjamin Blom, NY.

Sachs, Curt, Commonwealth of Art. 1946. $10.00 Hdbd. (ISBN 0-393-04158-1) W.W. Norton, NY.

Sachs, Curt. World History of the Dance. 1963. $2.95 pa. (ISBN 0-393-00209-8) W.W. Norton, NY.

Stearns, Marshall & Stearns, Jean. Jazz Dance. 1968. $9.95 Hdbd. Macmillan, NY.

Vuillier, Gaston. History of Dancing. 1971. (1898) $45.00 Hdbd. (ISBN 0-87821-087-3). Milford House, ME.

Illustrated

Armitage, Merle. Dance Memoranda. Corle, Edwin, ed. 1947. $22.50 Hdbd. (ISBN 0-8369-0001-4). Books for Libraries, NY.

Kirstein, Lincoln, et al, eds. Dance Index 1942 Thru 1948, 7 Vols. 1970 (1948) Set. $200.00 Hdbd. (ISBN 0-405-00730-2). Arno Pr. NY.

Meerloo, Joost A. Dance Craze & Sacred Dance. 1962. $6.50 Hdbd. Humanities Pr. NY.

Moore, Lillian. Images of the Dance: Historical Treasures of the Dance Collection, 1581-1861. 1965 $6.75 Hdbd. (ISBN 0-87104-093-X). NY Public Library, NY.

Instruction

American Association for Health—Physical Education—and Recreation. Dance Directory. 1969 $2.00 pa. AAHPER. Washington, D.C.

Carroll, Jean & Lofthouse, Peter. Creative Dance for Boys. 1970 $4.95

Hdbd. (ISBN 0-7121-0318-X). Dufour Eds., PA.

Duggan, Anne S., et al. Teaching of Folk Dance 1948. $6.00 Hdbd. Ronald Pr., NY.

Hayes, Elizabeth R. Introduction to the Teaching of Dance. 1964. $6.50 Hdbd. $5.50 text ed. Ronald Pr., NY.

Joulouze, Michel. L'Art et Instruction de Bien Danser. $2.95 pa. (ISBN 0-87127-036-6). Dance Horizons, NY.

LaSalle, Dorothy. Rhythms & Dances for Elementary Schools. 1951 $6.00 text ed. Ronald, Pr., NY.

Murray, Ruth L. Dance in Elementary Education 1963. $9.95 text ed. Harper & Row, NY.

Pemberton, E. An Essay for the Further Improvement of Dancing. $2.95 pa. (ISBN 0-87127-035-8). Dance Horizons, NY.

Preston-Dunlop, Valerie. Handbook for Modern Educational Dance. 1970 $5.50 Hdbd. (ISBN 0-7121-0801-7), Dufour, Eds., PA.

Rudman, Jack. Teachers License Examination Passbook: Dance Jr. H.S. $8.00 Hdbd. $5.00 pa. National Learning, NY.

Sheehy, Emma D. Children Discover Music & Dance. 1968. $3.95 pa. (ISBN 0-8077-2150-6). Teachers College Pr., NY.

Sherbon, Elizabeth. On the Count of One: A Guide to Movement & Progression in Dance. (Hi-Sch.) 1968.

$5.00 pa (ISBN 0-87474-131-3). National Pr., CA.

Shurr, Gertrude & Yocom, R. D. Modern Dance: Techniques & Teaching. 1949. $6.00 Hdbd. Ronald Pr., NY.

Musical

Gilbert, Pia & Lockhart, Aileene. Music for the Modern Dance. 1961. $9.25 Hdbd. $7.95 text ed. (ISBN 0-697-07427-7). Wm. C. Brown, IA.

Lambranzi, Gregorio. New & Curious School of Theatrical Dancing. De Moroda, Derra, transl. $3.95 pa. (ISBN 0-87127-00506). Dance Horizons, NY.

Nettl, Paul. Story of Dance Music. 1947. $13.50 Hdbd. (ISBN 0-8371-2114-0). Greenwood, Pr., CT.

Newman, Joel, ed. Sixteenth Century Italian Dances. 1966. $3.00 Hdbd. (ISBN 0-271-73102-8). Pennsylvania State Univ. Pr., PA.

National

Africa

Gaskin, L. J., ed. Select Bibliography of Music in Africa. 1965. $11.25 Hdbd. International Publ. Service, NY.

Gorer, Geoffrey. Africa Dances. 1962 $2.25 pa. (ISBN 0-393-00173-3). W.W. Norton, NY.

Argentina

Garcia Jiminez, Francisco. Asi

Nacieton los Tangos. $1.75 pa. French & European Publ., NY.

Asia

Mathur, Jagdish C. Drama in Rural India. (Illus.). 1964. $7.50 Hdbd. (ISBN 0-210-22572-6). Asia, Publ. House, NY.

Ceylon

De Zoete, Berly. Dance & Magic Drama in Ceylon. $4.50 Hdbd. Theatre Arts Books, NY.

Great Britain

Fletcher, Ifan K., et al. Famed for Dance: Essays on the Theory & Practice of Theatrical Dancing in England 1660-1740. 1960. $1.50 pa. (ISBN 0-87104-072-7). New York Public Library, NY.

Greece

Lawler, B.L. Terpsichore, the Story of the Dance in Ancient Greece. (1962) $4.00 pa. Johnson Reprint, NY.

Lawler, Lillian B. Dance in Ancient Greece (1967) $2.95 pa. (ISBN 0-295-97873-2). Univ. of Washington Pr., WA.

Lawler, Lillian B. Dance in Ancient Greece. 1964. $5.75 Hdbd. (ISBN 0-8195-3050-6). Wesleyan Univ. Pr., CT.

Lawler, Lillian B. Dance of Ancient Greek Theatre. 1964 $3.75 text ed. (ISBN 0-87745-014-5); $2.75 pa.

(ISBN 0-87745-015-3). Univ. of Iowa Pr., IA.

Webster, Thomas B. Greek Chorus. 1970. $8.00 Hdbd. Barnes & Noble, NY.

Wright, Frederick A. Arts in Greece. 1969. (1923) $6.00 Hdbd. (ISBN 0-8046-0719-2). Kennikat Pr., NY.

India

Ambrose, Kay. Classical Dances & Costumes of India. 1965 $6.50 Hdbd. Hillary House Publ., NY.

Bowers, Faubion. Dance in India. 1953. $10.00 Hdbd. (ISBN 0-4-4-00963-8). AMS Pr., NY.

Coomaraswamy, Ananda, transl. Mirror of Gesture—Being the Abhinaya Darpana of Nandikesvara. 1970. (1917). $7.50 Hdbd. Lawrence Verry, CT.

Devi, Ragini. Dances of India with an Appendix on Indian Music. 1962. $3.50 Hdbd. Lawrence Verry, CT.

Gesture Language of the Hindu Dance. $17.50 Hdbd. Benjamin Blom, NY.

Jones, Clifford & Jones, Betty T. Kathakali: An Introduction to the Dance-Drama of Kerala. 1970. $3.95 pa. (ISBN 0-87830-530-0). Theatre Arts Books, NY.

Massey, Reginald & Singha, Rina. Indian Dances: Their History & Growth. 1967. $12.50 Hdbd. (ISBN

0-8076-0427-5). George Braziller, NY.

Vatsyayan, Kapela. Classical Indian Dance in Literature & the Arts. 1968. $20.00 Hdbd. Lawrence Verry, CT.

Latin America

Borrows, Frank. Latin American Dancing. $4.95 Hdbd. Wehman Brothers, NJ.

De Hoyos, Benjamin F. Latin American Rhythms, 2 Vols. 1967. Vol. 1 $2.00 text ed. (ISBN 0-8425-0231-9); Vol. 2 $2.20 text ed. (ISBN 0-8425-0022-7). Brigham Young Univ. Pr., UT.

Lehman, L. Latin American Dances. $1.00 Hdbd. Wehman Brothers, NJ.

Mexico

Stone, Martha. At the Sign of Midnight: The Concheros Dance Cult of Mexico. Price "n.g." (ISBN 0-8165-0337-0). Univ. of Arizona Pr., AZ.

Nepal

Jerstad, Luther G. Mani-Rimdu, Sherpa Dance Drama. 1969. $6.95 Hdbd. Univ. of Washington Pr., WA.

Russia

Bakst, Leon. Designs of Leon Bakst for the Sleeping Princess. 1969. $27.50 Hdbd. Benjamin Blom, NY.

Barrie, J.M. Truth About the Russian Dancers. 1962 $4.00 pa. Johnson Reprint, NY.

Haskell, Arnold L. Balletomania: Story of an Obsession. 1934. $14.50 Hdbd. (ISBN 0-404-03154-4). AMS Pr., NY.

Haskell, Arnold L. Russian Genius in Ballet. 1963. $2.25 (ISBN 0-08-009791-X). Pergamon Pr., NY.

Slonimsky, Juri. Soviet Ballet. 1970. (1947) $15.00 Hdbd. (ISBN 0-306-71897-9) Da Capo Pr., NY.

Swift, Mary G. Art of the Dance in the U.S.S.R. 1968. $15.00 Hdbd. (ISBN 0-268-00305-X). Univ. of Notre Dame Pr., IN.

Scotland

Emmerson, George S. Rantin Pipe & Tremblin String: A History of Scottish Dance Music. 1971. $13.00 text ed. (ISBN 0-7735-0116-9). McGill-Queens Univ. Pr., CAN.

Emmerson, George S. Social History of Scottish Dance: Ane Celestial Recreatioun. 1971. $25.00 text ed. (ISBN 0-7735-0087-1). McGill-Queens Univ. Pr., CAN.

Spain

Bonald, Caballero. Andalusian Dances. 1959. $4.50 Hdbd. International Publ. Serv., NY.

Ivanova, Anna. Dance in Spain: A History. 1970. $10.00 Hdbd. Praeger Publ., NY.

U.S.

Berger, M. Curious & Wonderful Gymnastic. (1961) $4.00 pa. Johnson Reprint, NY.

Mason, Bernard S. Dances & Stories of the American Indian. 1944 $7.00 text ed. Ronald Pr., NY.

Maynard, Olga. American Modern Dancers: The Pioneers. (Elem.) 1965. $4.50 Hdbd. (ISBN 0-316-55191-0). Little, Brown, MA.

Schlundt, Christena L., ed. Professional Appearances of Ted Shawn & His Men Dancers: A Chronology & an Index of Dances 1933-1940. 1967. $3.75 pa. (ISBN 0-87104-148-0). New York Public Library, NY.

Sherman, John K. Music & Theater in Minnesota History. 1958. $1.00 pa. (ISBN 0-8166-0174-7). Univ. of Minnesota Pr., MN.

Sociology & History of Popular American Music & Dance, 1920-1968. $3.00 pa. Ann Arbor Publ., MI.

Terry, Walter. Dance in America. 1956. $8.95 Hdbd. (ISBN 0-06-006750-0,) Harper & Row, NY.

Terry, Walter. Dance in America. rev. ed. 1971. $8.95 Hdbd. (ISBN 0-06-014244-8). Harper & Row, NY.

Terry, Walter. Legacy of Isadora Duncan & Ruth St. Denis. (1959) $4.00 pa. Johnson Reprint, NY.

Notation

Benesh, Joan & Benesh, Rudolf. Introduction to Benesh Movement-Notation: Dance. $1.95 pa. (ISBN 0-87127-016-1). Dance Horizons, NY.

Hutchinson, Ann. Labanotation: The System for Recording Movement. $4.95 pa. Theatre Arts Books, NY.

Laban, Rudolf. Principles of Dance & Movement Notation. $1.95 pa. (ISBN 0-87127-020-X). Dance Horizons, NY.

Stepanov, V.I. Alphabet of Movements of the Human Body. Lister, 1969. (1958) $1.95 pa. (ISBN 0-87127-012-9). Dance Horizons, NY.

Orchestration

Fernett, Gene. Swing Out. 1970. $10.00 Hdbd. (ISBN 0-87812-009-2). Pendell Publ. MI.

Fernett, Gene. Thousand Golden Horns. (Illus.). 1966 $7.50 (ISBN 0-87812-004-1). Pendell Publ., MI.

McCarthy, Albert. Dance Band Era: The Dancing Decades, 1910-1050. 1971. $10.00 Hdbd. (ISBN 0-8019-5681-1). Chilton Book Co., PA.

Simon, George T. Big Bands. 1967 $9.95 Hdbd. Macmillan, NY.

Production

Ellfeldt, Lois & Carnes, Edwin.

Dance Production Handbook, or Later Is Too Late. 1971. $8.95 text ed. (ISBN 0-87484-182-8); $5.95 pa. (ISBN 0-87484-181-X). National Pr., CA.

Reference

American Association for Health–Physical Education–and Recreation. Dance Research. 1964 $2.00 pa. AAHPER. Washington, D.C.

American Association for Health–Physical Education–and Recreation. Research in Dance, Vol. 1. From 1964 To Present. 1968. $2.00 pa. AAHPER. Washington, D.C.

Beaumont, Cyril W. Bibliography of Dancing. $12.50 Hdbd. Benjamin Blom, NY.

Belknap, S. Yancey, ed. Guide to Dance Periodicals: An Analytical Index of Articles. Incl. Vol. 1. 1931-35. 1959; Vol. 5. 1951-52. 1955: Vol. 6. 1953-54. 1956; Vol. 7. 1955-56. 1958. $7.50 Hdbd. Univ. of Fl. Pr., FL.

Chujoy, Anatole & Manchester, P.W. Dance Encyclopedia. 1967. $20.00 Hdbd. Simon & Schuster, NY.

Eames, Marian. Dancing in Prints, 1634-1870. 1964. $10.00 Hdbd. (ISBN 0-87104-060-3). NY Public Library, NY.

Eames, Marian. When All the World Was Dancing: Rare & Curious Books from the Cia Fornaroli Collection. 1971. (1958) $3.00 pa. (ISBN 0-405-01750-2); $3.00 pa. (ISBN 0-405-01750-2). Arno Pl., NY.

Johnston, Jill. Marmalade Me. $8.95 Hdbd. $2.45 pa. E.P. Dutton, NY.

Longstreet, Stephen. Dance in Art. $4.47 Hdbd. $1.75 pa. Borden Publ., CA.

Magriel, Paul, ed. Bibliography of Dancing. 1936. $17.50 Hdbd. Banjamin Blom, NY.

Raffe, Walter G. Dictionary of the Dance. $20.00 Hdbd. (ISBN 0-498-06074-8). A.S. Barnes, NJ.

Vatsyayan, Kapela. Classical Indian Dance in Literature & the Arts. 1968. $20.00 Hdbd. Lawrence Verry, CT.

Zorn, Friedrich A. Grammar of the Art of Dancing Theoretical & Practical. 1970. $37.50 Hdbd. (ISBN 0-8337-3923-9). Burt Franklin, NY.

Religious

Iyer, K.B. Kathakali: The Sacred Dance-Drama of Malabar. 1955. $12.50 Hdbd. Lawrence Verry, CT.

Kinkeldey, Otto. Jewish Dancing Master of the Renaissance: Guglielmo Ebreo. 1966. $1.95 pa. (ISBN 0-87127-008-0). Dance Horizons, NY.

Theatrical

Lambranzi, Gregorio. New & Curious School of Theatrical Dancing. De Moroda, Derra, transl. $3.95 pa. (ISBN 0-87127-005-6). Dance Horizons, NY.

Oesterley, W.O. Sacred Dance. 1968. $3.95 pa. (ISBN 0-87127-013-7). Dance Horizons, NY.

Stone, Martha. At the Sign of Midnight: The Concheros Dance Cult of Mexico. Price "n.g." (ISBN 0-8165-1337-0). Univ. of Arizona Pr., AZ.

Therapautic

Barlin, Anne & Barlin, Paul. Art of Learning Through Movement. 1971. $7.50 Hdbd. (ISBN 0-378-09181-6). Ward Ritchie Pr., CA.

Canner, Norma. And a Time to Dance. 1968. $5.95 Hdbd. (ISBN 0-8070-2394-9). Beacon Pr., MA.

Vocations

Denis, Paul. Opportunities in Dancing. rev. ed. (Hi-Sch.) text ed. $3.75 Hdbd. $1.95 pa. Universal Publ. & Dist., NY.

Feuillet, Raoul A. For the Further Improvement of Dancing. Essex, John, tr. $2.95 pa. (ISBN 0-87127-025-0). Dance Horizons, NY.

Woody, Regina J. Young Dancer's Career Book. (Jr. Hi-Sch.) $4.50 Hdbd. (ISBN 0-525-43606-5). E.P. Dutton, NY.

Young Adult

Haskell, Arnold. Wonderful World of Dance. (Jr. Hi-Sch.) 1970 $3.95 Hdbd. Doubleday, NY.

Plotz, Helen, ed. Untune the Sky; Poems of Music & the Dance. 1957. $4.50 Hdbd. (ISBN 0-690-85020-4). Thomas Y. Crowell, NY.

DISCOGRAPHY

Phonorecord Libraries

Association For Recorded Sound Collections. Preliminary Directory of Sound Recordings Collections in the United States & Canada. 1968. $3.00 pa. (ISBN 0-87104-144-8). NY Pub Library, NY.

Breaking Loose, Records. (Crossroads Ser). (Jr Hi.). 1969. $1.48 pa. Noble & Noble, NY.

Currall, H. F. Phonograph Record Libraries. enl. ed. 1970. $9.50 Hdbd. (ISBN 0-208-00381-9). Shoe String Pr., CT.

Gelatt, Roland. Fabulous Phonograph. 1966. $6.95 Hdbd. (ISBN 0-696-59534-6). Hawthorn Books, NY.

High Fidelity Magazine. Records in Review. 1971.. $10.00 Hdbd. Charles Scribner's Sons, NY.

Hurst, Walter E. & Hale, William S. Record Industry Book. (Entertainment Industry Ser., Vol. 1). 1961. $25.00 Hdbd. (ISBN 0-911370-01-3). Seven Arts Pr., CA.

Murray, Don M. World of Sound Recording. (Jr Hi.). 1965. $3.95 Hdbd. J. B. Lippincott, NY.

Pearson, Mary D. Recordings in the Public Library. 1963. $4.00 Hdbd. (ISBN 0-8389-0051-8). American Library Assn., IL.

Ruscha, Edward. Records. 1971. pa. price "n.g." (ISBN 0-8150-0484-2). George Wittenborn, NY.

Taubman, Hyman H. How to Build a Record Library. (1953) $6.00 Hdbd. (ISBN 0-8371-4438-8). Greenwood Pr., CT.

DRAMA

Dictionaries & Indexes

Adams, William D. Dictionary of the Drama Vol. 1, A–G. 1965. (1904) $28.50 Hdbd. Burt Franklin, NY.

Babault, et al. Annales Dramatiques, Ou Dictionnaire General Des Theatres, 9 Vols. $25.00 ea. Hdbd. Burt Franklin, NY.

Barnet, Sylvan, et al. Aspects of the Drama: A Handbook. $3.50 pa. (ISBN 0-316-08178-7). Little, Brown & Co., MA.

Bowman, Walter P. & Ball, Robert H. Theatre Language, a Dictionary. $7.95 Hdbd. Theatre Arts Books, NY.

Chicorel Index Series. Marietta Chicorel, ed. Vol. 1 Chicorel Theater Index to Plays in Anthologies, Periodicals, Discs & Tapes. 1970. $38.25 Hdbd. (ISBN 87729-001-6). Vol. 2 1971. $42.50. Hdbd. (ISBN 87729-002-3). Vol. 3 1972. $42.50 Hdbd. (ISBN 87729-003-

7). Vol. 4 Chicorel Index to Poetry on Discs & Tapes: Poetry-On-Media: Readings by Well Known Actors and Poets. 1972. $42.50 Hdbd. (ISBN 87729-004-9). Chicorel Library Publishing, NY.

Drury, Francis K. Guide to Best Plays. 2nd ed. Salem, James M., ed. 1969. $15.00 Hdbd. (ISBN 0-8108-0254-6). Scarecrow Pr., NJ.

Gassner, John & Quinn, Edward, eds. Reader's Encyclopedia of World Drama. 1969. $15.00 Hdbd. (ISBN 0-690-67483-X). Thomas Y. Crowell, NY.

Granville, Wilfred. Theater Dictionary: British & American Terms in the Drama, Opera, and Ballet. 1952. $10.00 Hdbd. (ISBN 0-8371-4428-0). Greenwood Pr., CT.

Halliday, Frank E. Shakespeare Companion: 1564–1964. rev. ed. 1964. $12.00 Hdbd. (ISBN 0-8052-3237-0). Schocken Books, Inc., NY.

Halliday, Frank E. Shakespeare Companion: 1564–1964. (Hi-Sch.). 1964. $2.65 pa. (ISBN 0-14-053011-8). Penguin Books, Inc., MD.

Mersand, Joseph. Index to Plays with Suggestions for Teaching. 1966. $3.50 Hdbd. (ISBN 0-8108-0069-1). Scarecrow Pr., NJ.

Play Index. Incl. 1949–1952 Vol. West, Dorothy H. & Peake, Dorothy M., eds. 1953. $8.00 Hdbd.: 1953–1960 Vol. Fidell, Estelle A. & Peake, Dorothy M., eds. 1963. $11.00 Hdbd. (ISBN 0-8242-

0382-8); 1961-1967 Vol. Fidell, Estelle A., ed. 1968. $16.00 Hdbd. (ISBN 0-8242-0383-6). H. W. Wilson, NY.

Silk, Agnes K. & Fanning, Clara E. Index to Dramatic Readings. 1971. (1925) $17.00 Hdbd. Scholarly Pr., MI.

Symons, Arthur. Dramatis Personae. (Essay Index Reprint Ser). 1923. $12.50 Hdbd. (ISBN 0-8369-2177-1). Books for Libraries, NY.

English Drama

Dietrich, R. F., et al, eds. Art of Modern Drama. 1969. text ed. $4.15 pa. (ISBN 0-03-074660-4); instructor's manual $1.05. Holt-Rinehart & Winston, NY.

Frankenstein, Louise. Dialect Play-Readings. 1937. $2.00 Hdbd. Samuel French, NY.

Frankenstein, Louise. Playreadings. 1933. $2.00 Hdbd. Samuel French, NY.

Franklin, Miriam A. Rehearsal: The Principles & Practice of Acting for the Stage. 4th ed. 1963. $8.75 pa. (ISBN 0-13-771568-4). Prentice-Hall, NY.

Hodapp, William, ed. Face Your Audience. (Communication Arts Books Ser). 1956. $2.95 Hdbd. (ISBN 0-8038-2230-8). Hastings House Publ., NY.

Kester, Katharine. Problem—Projects in Acting. 1937. $2.00 Hdbd. Samuel French, NY.

Medieval

Block, K. S., ed. Ludus Coventriae, Or, the Place Called Corpus Christi. 1922.

$9.75 Hdbd. (ISBN 0-19-722560-8). Oxford Univ. Pr., NY.

Cawley, A. C., ed. Everyman & Medieval Miracle Plays. $2.95 Hdbd. E. P. Dutton, NY.

Cawley, Arthur C., ed. Everyman & Medieval Miracle Plays. $1.45 pa. (ISBN 0-525-47036-0). E. P. Dutton, NY.

Twentieth Century

Marowitz, Charles, et al, eds. Encore Reader: A Chronicle of the New Drama. 1970. $3.25 pa. (ISBN 0-416-18130-9. Oxford Univ. Pr., NY.

Millett, Fred B. & Bentley, Gerald E. Play's the Thing. $6.95 text ed. (ISBN 0-390-64107-3). Appleton-Century-Crofts, NY.

Price, Pamela V. Drama Review. $2.00 Hdbd. Simon & Schuster, NY.

Ridgeway, William. Dramas & Dramatic Dances of Non-European Races. 1971. (1915) $19.00 Hdbd. Scholarly Pr., MI.

Ritter, Charles C. Lively Art of Theatre. 1970. $6.50 text ed. Allyn, Inc., NJ.

Roby, R. C. & Ulanov, B. Introduction to Drama. 1962. $8.95 text ed. (ISBN 0-07-053335-0). McGraw-Hill, NY.

Roennfeldt, M. J. Drama in Action. 2 Vols. 1969. Vol. 1. $2.00 Hdbd. Vol. 2. $2.50 Hdbd. Tri-Ocean, Inc., CA.

Seng, Peter J. & Cooper, Burton L. Plays: Wadsworth Handbook & Anthology. 1969. $4.95 pa. Wadsworth Publ. Co., CA.

Weiss, Samuel. Drama in the Western World. Incl. Fifteen Plays with Essays. 1964. $5.95 pa. Nine Plays with Essays. 1968. $4.95 pa. D. C. Heath & Co., MA.

Essays

Bevis, Richard W., ed. Eighteenth Century Drama: Afterpieces. 1970. $2.75 pa. (ISBN 0-19-281086-3). Oxford Univ. Pr., NY.

Bonazza, Blaze O. & Roy, Emil. Studies in Drama. 2nd ed. $5.95 pa. (ISBN 0-06-040831-6). Harper-Row, NY.

Boynton, Robert W. & Mack, Maynard. Introduction to the Play. (Hi-Sch.). 1969. $5.45 text ed. $3.95 pa. Hayden Book Co., NY.

Calderwood, James & Toliver, Harold E. Forms of Drama. 1969. $7.50 text ed. (ISBN 0-13-329573-7). Prentice-Hall, NY.

Chandler, Frank W. Aspects of Modern Drama. 1971. (1922) $22.00 Hdbd. Scholarly Pr., MI.

Cohn, Ruby, et al. Classics for Contemporaries: Old Dramas for New Theaters. 1968. $4.75 pa. Random House, NY.

Congdon, S. P., ed. Drama Reader. $3.00 text ed. $2.00 Hdbd. Odyssey Pr., Inc., NY.

Corrigan, Robert W. & Loney, Glenn M., eds. Tragedy: A Critical Anthology.

1971. text ed. $5.50 pa. TN7-8050 Houghton-Mifflin, NY.

Dietrich, R. F., et al, eds. Art of Drama. text ed. $5.25 pa. (ISBN 0-03-074665-5). Holt, Rinehart & Winston, NY.

Goldstone, Richard A. Contexts of the Drama. 1968. $5.05 text ed. (ISBN 0-07-023662-3). McGraw-Hill, NY.

Goodman, R. From Script to Stage: Eight Modern Plays. (Rinehart Editions). 1971. $11.95 text ed. (ISBN 0-03-025870-7). Holt, Rinehart & Winston, NY.

Hogan, Robert & Molin, Sven E. Drama: The Major Genres, an Introductory Critical Anthology. 1962. $5.95 pa. (ISBN 0-396-06108-7). Dodd, Mead & Co., NY.

Hunter, G. K. & Hunter, S. K. John Webster. (Penguin Critical Anthologies). $4.25 Hdbd. Peter Smith Publ., MA.

Kahan, Stanley. Actor's Workbook. $6.50 pa. (ISBN 0-15-500500-6). Harcourt, Brace & World, NY.

Kernan, Alvin B., ed. Character & Conflict: An Introduction to Drama. 1969. $5.50 pa. (ISBN 0-15-506271-9); $5.50 pa. earlier ed. (ISBN 0-15-506270-0). Harcourt, Brace & World, NY.

Kirsch, Arthur C. Dryden's Heroic Drama. 1971. (1965) $7.50 text ed. (ISBN 0-87752-136-0). Gordian Pr., NY.

Lacroix, Paul, pseud. Bibliotheque Dramatique de Monsieur de Soleinne, 9 vols. in 8. Incl. Bibliotheque Dramatique de Pont de Vesle, Augmentee et Complete par les Soins du Bibliophile Jacob (Paul Lacroix; Essai d'une Bibliographie General du Theatre, Ou Catalogue Raisonne de la Bibliotheque d'un Amateur; Table des Pieces de Theatre Descrites dans le Catalogue de la Bibliotheque de M. de Soleinne, par Charles Brunet. Repr. $30.00 Hdbd.; Set— $200.00 Hdbd. Burt Franklin, NY.

Leeson, R. Voyage a Paris. (Fr.). (Jr Hi–Hi-Sch.). 1969. $2.00 pa. St. Martin's Pr., NY.

Levin, Richard. Tragedy: Plays, Theory & Criticism. Incl. Oedipus Rex. Sophocles; Othello. Shakespeare, William; Ghosts. Ibsen, Henrik; Hairy Ape. O'Neill, Eugene. $3.95 pa. (ISBN 0-15-592346-3). Harcourt, Brace & World, NY.

Levin, Richard. Tragedy: Plays, Theory & Criticism. alt. ed. Incl. Antigone. Sophocles; Coriolanus. Shakespeare, William; Wild Duck. Ibsen, Henrik; Murder in the Cathedral. Eliot, T. S. $3.95 pa. (ISBN 0-15-592347-1). Harcourt, Brace & World, NY.

Lid, Richard W., ed. Essays: Classic & Contemporary. 1967. $3.75 pa. J. B. Lippincott, PA.

Lid, Richard W. & Bernd, Daniel, eds. Plays: Classic & Contemporary. 1967. $3.95 pa. J. B. Lippincott, PA.

MacDonald, J. W. & Saxton, J. C., eds.

Four Stages: The Development of World Drama. (Hi-Sch.). 1968. $3.00 text ed. St. Martin's Pr., NY.

Mandel, Oscar, ed. Theatre of Don Juan: A Collection of Plays & Views, 1630-1963. 1963. $10.00 Hdbd. (ISBN 0-8032-0109-5). Univ. of Nebraska Pr., NB.

Nettleton, George H. & Case, Arthur E., eds. British Dramatists from Dryden to Sheridan. 2nd ed. 1969. $12.50 Hdbd. Houghton-Mifflin, NY.

Steinberg, M. W. Aspects of Modern Drama. 1960. $6.25 pa. (ISBN 0-03-010095-X). Holt-Rinehart & Winston, NY.

Tiedje, Egon. Tradition Ben Jonsons in der Restaurations Komoedie. (Britannica et Americana, No. 11). (Ger). 1963. $4.60 pa. (ISBN 3-11-000045-8). De Gruyter, Germany.

Wiley, Autrey N., ed. Rare Prologues & Epilogues 1642-1700. 1970. (1940) $12.50 Hdbd. (ISBN 0-8046-0988-8). Kennikat Pr., NY.

Folk Drama

Brody, Alan. English Mummers & Their Plays: Traces of Ancient Mystery. (Folklore & Folklife Ser). 1971. $9.50 Hdbd. (ISBN 0-8122-7611-6). Univ. of Pa. Pr., Philadelphia, PA.

Chambers, Edmund K. English Folk Play. (Drama Ser., No. 39). 1969. $6.50 Hdbd. (ISBN 0-8383-0521-0). Haskell House, NY.

Chambers, Edmund K. English Folk-Play. 1933. $6.50 Hdbd. (ISBN 0-19-811670-5). Oxford Univ. Pr., NY.

Chambers, Edmund K. English Folk-Play. (Illus.). 1964. (1933) $7.00 Hdbd. Russell & Russell, NY.

Selden, Samuel, ed. International Folk Plays. 1949. $5.00 Hdbd. (ISBN 0-8078-0554-8). Univ. of North Carolina Pr., Chapel Hill, NC.

Tiddy, Reginald J. Mummers' Play. 1923. $17.50 Hdbd. Folcroft Pr., Folcroft, PA.

History and Criticism

Mathur, Jagdish C. Drama in Rural India. 1964. $7.50 Hdbd. (ISBN 0-210-22572-6). Asia Society, NY.

Armistead, Samuel G. & Silverman, Joseph H. Folk-Literature of the Sephardic Jews, Vol. 1. The Judeo-Spanish Ballad Chapbooks Of Yacob Abraham Yona. 1970. $12.00 text ed. (ISBN 0-520-01648-3). Univ. of California Pr., Berkeley, CA.

French Drama

Benay, Jacques G. & Kuhn, Reinhard, eds. Panorama du Theatre Nouveau: Theatre de la Cruaute, Vol. 2. Incl. Balcon. Genet, Jean. (Orig., Fr.). text ed. $2.45 pa. (ISBN 0-390-08011-X). Appleton-Century-Crofts, NY.

Bermel, Albert, ed. Genius of the French Theater: Imaginery Invalid, Andormache, Barber of Seville, Hernani, Pots of Money, Romantics, Songs of Songs,

Lark. 1961. $0.95 pa. New American Library, NY.

Borgerhoff, Joseph L., ed. Nineteenth Century French Plays. (Fr). 1931. $7.75 text ed. (ISBN 0-390-10881-2). Appleton-Century-Crofts, NY.

Bree, G. & Kroff, A. Y. Twentieth Century French Drama. 1969. $11.95 text ed. (31382). Macmillan Co., NY.

Brenner, Clarence D. & Goodyear, Nolan A., eds. Eighteenth-Century French Plays. (Fr). 1927. $8.50 text ed. (ISBN 0-390-12249-1). Appleton-Century-Crofts, NY.

Chiari, Joseph. Contemporary French Theatre: The Flight from Naturalism. 1970. $8.00 text ed. (ISBN 0-87752-126-3). Gordian Pr., NY.

Evans, I. A. Choisissez Vos Roles. (Fr. & Eng.). Elem Jr Hi-Hi-Sch. 1967. $1.60 pa. St. Martin's Pr., NY.

Four Contemporary French Plays. $2.95 Hdbd. (90). Modern Lib.

Fournier, Edouard. Theatre Francais Avant La Renaissance, 1430-1550. 1965. (1872) $25.00 Hdbd. (ISBN 0-8337-1225-X). Burt Franklin, NY.

Grant, Elliott. Chief French Plays of the Nineteenth Century. 1934. $9.95 text ed. (ISBN 0-06-042450-8). Harper & Row Publ., NY.

Grant, Elliott M., ed. Four French Plays of the Twentieth Century. 1949. $12.00 Hdbd. (ISBN 0-8371-2212-0). Greenwood Pr., CT.

Lyons, John C. & Scarles, C. Eight French Classic Plays. 1932. $9.00 Hdbd. (ISBN 0-03-015900-8). Holt, Rinehart & Winston, NY.

Mason, Hamilton. French Theatre in New York. 1940. $12.50 Hdbd. (ISBN 0-404-04224-4). AMS Pr., NY.

Pronko, Leonard, ed. Three Modern French Plays of the Imagination. (Fr). $0.75 pa. Dell Publ., NY.

Scronde, Joseph & Peyre, Henri, eds. Nine Classic French Plays. 1936. $7.95 text ed. D.C. Heath, MA.

Stanton, Stephen, ed. Camille & Other Plays. 1960. $3.50 Hdbd. Peter Smith Publ., MA.

Stone, Donald, ed. Four Renaissance Tragedies. Incl. Jephte ou le Vocu. Buchanan, George; Abraham Sacrifiant. De Beze, Theodore; Didon: Se Sacrifiant. Jodelle, Etienne; Saul le Furicux. De La Taille, Jean. 1966. $2.50 pa. text ed. (ISBN 0-674-31550-2). Harvard Univ. Pr., MA.

Thompson, Lawrence S. Bibliography of French Plays on Microcards. 1967. $18.00 Hdbd. (ISBN 0-208-00301-0). Shoe String Pr., CT.

Turgeon, Frederick. Quatre Pieces Modernes En un Acte. 1951. $4.40 Hdbd. (ISBN 0-03-016475-3). Holt, Rinehart & Winston, NY.

Turgeon, Frederick K. Cinq Comedies: Du Moyen Age a Nos Jours. 1964. $3.95 pa. (ISBN 0-03-067560-X); tapes dual track 7.5 ips $90.00 Hdbd. (ISBN 0-03-045385-2). Holt, Rinehart & Winston, NY.

Wicks, C. Beaumont, ed. Parisian Stage, 4 Vols. Vol. 1. $4.00 pa. (ISBN 0-8173-9502-4); Vol. 2. $2.50 pa. (ISBN 0-8173-9503-2); Vol. 3 $4.00 pa. (ISBN 0-8173-9504-0); Vol. 4 $6.95 pa. (ISBN 0-8173-9505-9). Univ. of Alabama Pr., AL.

Farces

Bower, Barbara C. Caracteristiques Essentielles De la Farce Francaise et Leur Survivance. 1964. $7.50 Hdbd. (ISBN 0-252-00046-3); $6.50 pa. (ISBN 0-252-72333-3). Univ of Illinois Pr., IL.

Cohen, Gustave, ed. Recueil De Farces Francaises Inedites Du Quinzieme Siecle. 1949. $15.00 Hdbd. (ISBN 0-910956-21-9). Mediaeval Academy of America, MA.

Fournier, Edouard. Theatre Francais Avant La Renaissance, 1430–1550. 1965. (1872) $25.00 Hdbd. (ISBN 0-8337-1225-X). Burt Franklin, NY.

Greshman, Herbert S. & Whitworth, Kernan B., Jr., eds. Anthology of Critical Prefaces to the Nineteenth-Century French Novel. 1962. $4.95 Hdbd. (ISBN 0-8262-0546-1). Univ. of Missouri Pr., MO.

Maxwell, Ian. French Farce & John Heywood. 1946. $20.00 Hdbd. Lansdowne Pr., PA.

Maxwell, Ivan. French Farce & John Heywood. $3.00 Hdbd. (ISBN 0-522-83654-2). Library Assn. London, Eng.

General Studies

Abel, Lionel. Metatheatre: A New View of Dramatic Form. $3.95 Hdbd. (ISBN 0-8090-6915-6); $1.45 pa. (ISBN 0-8090-0533-6). Hill & Wang, NY.

Adler, Renata. Year in the Dark. 1971. $1.50 pa. (ISBN 0-425-01977-2). Berkley Publ. Corp., NY.

Altman, Richard & Kaufman, Norman. Making of a Musical: Fiddler on the Roof. 1971. $4.95 Hdbd. Crown Publ., NY.

Anderson, Maxwell. Essence of Tragedy & Other Footnotes & Papers. 1970. (1939) text ed. $6.50. Russell & Russell Publ., NY.

Archer, William. Old Drama & the New. $8.00 Hdbd. Benjamin Blom, NY.

Barnet, Sylvan, et al. Aspects of the Drama: A Handbook. $3.50 pa. (ISBN 0-316-08178-7). Little, Brown & Co., MA.

Barranger, M. S. & Dodson, Daniel B. Generations: An Introduction to Drama. 1971. $3.95 pa. (ISBN 0-15-529534-9). Harcourt-Brace & World, NY.

Beckerman, Bernard. Dynamics of Drama: Theories & Methods of Analysis. 1970. $3.50 pa. Alfred A. Knopf, NY.

Bennetton, Norman A. Social Significance of the Duel in Seventeenth Century Drama. (1938) $13.50 Hdbd. Greenwood Pr., CT.

Bentley, Eric, ed. Theory of the Modern Stage: An Introduction to Modern Theatre & Drama. (Hi-Sch.) 1968. $2.45 pa. (ISBN 0-14-020947-6). Penguin Books, MD.

Blaumanis, Rudolfs. Drama un Komedija. $12.60 Hdbd. (ISBN 0-87908-127-9). Rota Pr., IA.

Blistein, Elmer M., ed. Drama of the Renaissance: Essays for Leicester Bradner. 1970. $7.00 Hdbd. (ISBN 0-87057-117-6). Brown Univ. Pr., RI.

Brook, Peter. Empty Space. 1969. (1967) $1.65 pa. Avon Books, NY.

Brook, Peter. Empty Space: A Book About the Theatre: Deadly, Holy, Rough, Immediate. 1968. $5.00 Hdbd. (ISBN 0-689-10049-3). Atheneum Publ., NY.

Bryden, Ronald. Unfinished Hero & Other Essays. 1970. $5.50 Hdbd. Fernhill House, NY.

Calderwood, James L. & Toliver, Harold E., eds. Perspectives on Drama. 1968. $2.95 pa. (ISBN 0-19-500839-1). Oxford Univ. Pr., NY.

Cameron, Kenneth M. & Hoffman, Theodore J. Theatrical Response. 1969. text ed. $8.50. Macmillan Co., NY.

Carroll, Sidney W. Some Dramatic Opinions. 1968. (1923) $9.50 Hdbd. (ISBN 0-8046-0059-4). Kennikat Pr., NY.

Centano Y Rilova, Augusto & Sutherland, Donald. Blue Clown: Dialogues.

1971. $5.00 Hdbd. (ISBN 0-8032-0791-3). Univ. of Nebraska Pr., NB.

Chiari, Joseph. Landmarks of Contemporary Drama. 1971. (1965) text ed. $8.50. (ISBN 0-87752-144-1). Gordian Pr., NY.

Chilver, Peter. Improvised Drama. 1967. $4.50 Hdbd. Dufour Editions, PA.

Corrigan, Robert W. Forms of Drama. 1969. price "n.g." Hdbd. Houghton-Mifflin, NY.

Dawson, S. W. Drama & the Dramatic. (Critical Idiom Ser., Vol. 11). 1970. $3.00 Hdbd. (ISBN 0-416-17270-9); $1.25 pa. (ISBN 0-416-17280-6). Barnes & Noble, NY.

Dekker, Thomas. Shoemaker's Holiday. Lawlis, Merritt, ed. (Jr. Hi). 1970. $0.95 pa. Barron's Educational Serv., NY.

Dobree, Bonamy. Byron's Dramas. 1962. $3.50 Hdbd. Folcroft, Pr., PA.

Dow, Marguerite R. Magic Mask: A Basic Textbook of Theatre Arts. (Hi Sch.). 1968. text ed. $5.00. St. Martin's Pr., NY.

Driver, Tom F. Romantic Quest & Modern Query: History of the Modern Theatre. 1971. price "n.g." pa. Dell Publ., NY.

Dryden, John. Essay of Dramatic Poesy & Other Critical Writings. Mahoney, John L., ed. 1965. $1.25 pa. Bobbs, Merrill Co., IN.

Dukes, Ashley. Modern Dramatists. $6.50 Hdbd. Folcroft Pr., PA.

Dukore, B. F. Documents for Drama & Revolution. 1971. $1.95 pa. (ISBN 0-03-083651-4). Holt, Rinehart & Winston, NY.

Ellis-Fermor, Una. Shakespeare the Dramatist. 1948. $3.00 Hdbd. Folcroft Pr., PA.

English Institute. Ideas in the Drama. Gassner, John, ed. 1964. $5.50 Hdbd. (ISBN 0-231-02733-8). Columbia Univ. Pr., NY.

Evreinoff, Nicolas. Theatre in Life. 1927. $10.75 Hdbd. Benjamin Blom, NY.

Ferlita, Ernest. Theatre of Pilgrimage. 1971. $6.00 Hdbd. (ISBN 0-8362-1065-4); $2.95 pa. (ISBN 0-8362-0489-1). Sheed & Ward, NY.

Gassner, John. Dramatic Soundings: Evaluations & Retractions Culled from Thirty Years of Dramatic Criticism. 1968. $7.50 Hdbd. Crown Publ., NY.

Gassner, John & Allen, Ralph. Theatre & Drama in the Making, 2 Vols. $5.95 pa. Houghton-Mifflin, NY.

Geddes, Virgil. Beyond Tragedy, Footnotes on the Drama. 1930. $4.00 Hdbd. Folcroft Pr., PA.

Goodman, R. Drama on Stage. (Rinehart Editions). 1961. $8.50 pa. (ISBN 0-03-010455-6). Holt-Rinehart & Winston, NY.

Granville-Barker, Harley. On Dramatic Method. 1956. $1.50 pa. (ISBN 0-8090-0502-6). Hill & Wang, NY.

Granville-Barker, Harley. Study of Drama. 1934. $8.50 Hdbd. Lansdowne Pr., PA.

Granville-Barker, Harley G. Use of the Drama. 1971. (1945) $7.50 Hdbd. Russell & Russell Publ., NY.

Grene, David. Reality & the Heroic Pattern: Last Plays of Ibsen, Shakespeare, & Sophocles. 1967. $6.00 Hdbd. (ISBN 0-226-30788-3). Univ. of Chicago Pr., IL.

Hatlen, Theodore W. Orientation to the Theater. $3.95 pa. (ISBN 0-390-42301-7). Appleton-Century-Crofts, NY.

Hill, P. G. Living Art: An Introduction to Theater & Drama. (Rinehart Editions). 1971. text ed. $10.95. (ISBN 0-03-083049-4). Holt-Rinehart & Winston, NY.

Ionesco, Eugene. Notes & Counternotes. Watson, Donald, trans. 1964. $2.45 pa. Grove Pr., NY.

Ionesco, Eugene. Notes et Contre-Notes. 1966. $1.85 pa. French & European Publ., NY.

Kienzle, Siegfried. Modern World Theatre: A Guide to Productions Since 1945. 1970. $12.50 Hdbd. (ISBN 0-8044-3129-9). Frederick Ungar, NY.

Lamm, Martin. Modern Drama. 1952. $20.00 Hdbd. Folcroft Pr., PA.

Leech, Clifford. Dramatist's Experience: With Other Essays on Literary Theory. 1970. $7.50 Hdbd. (ISBN 0-389-03993-4). Barnes & Noble, NY.

LeMaaitre, Jules. Theatrical Impressions. 1970. (1924) $11.75 Hdbd. (ISBN 0-8046-0757-5). Kennikat Pr., NY.

Lewisohn, Ludwig. Drama & the Stage. 1971. $8.00 Hdbd. (ISBN 0-403-00654-6). Scholarly Pr., MI.

McCrindle, Joseph F., ed. Behind the Scenes: Theater & Film Interviews from the Transatlantic Review. 1971. $7.95 Hdbd. (ISBN 0-03-085091-6); $3.45 pa. Holt-Rinehart & Winston, NY.

MacKaye, Percy. Playhouse & the Play, & Other Addresses Concerning the Theatre & Democracy in America. 1969. (1909) $10.50 Hdbd. (ISBN 0-8371-0550-1). Greenwood Pr., CT.

Marowitz, Charles, et al, eds. Encore Reader: A Chronicle of the New Drama. 1970. $3.25 pa. Barnes & Noble, NY.

Marx, Milton. Enjoyment of Drama. 2nd ed. $2.25 pa. (ISBN 0-390-60198-5). Appleton-Century-Crofts, NY.

Munsterberg, Hugo. Film: A Psychological Study. $4.00 Hdbd. Peter Smith, Publ., MA.

Nathan, George. Magic Mirror. 1960. $5.95 Hdbd. Knopf, NY.

Nathan, George Jean. Mister George Jean Nathan Presents. $10.00 Hdbd.

(ISBN 0-8386-7967-6). Fairleigh Dickinson Univ. Pr., NJ.

Nicoll, Allardyce. Theory of Drama. 1967. $10.75 Hdbd. Benjamin Blom, NY.

Norman, C. H. Revolutionary Spirit in Modern Literature & Drama & the Class War in Europe. 1937. $5.00 Hdbd. Folcroft Pr., PA.

O'Hara, Frank H. Invitation to the Theater. (1951) $9.50 Hdbd. (ISBN 0-8371-3842-6). Greenwood Pr., CT.

Oppenheimer, George, ed. Passionate Playgoer, a Personal Scrapbook. (1958) $16.50 Hdbd. (ISBN 0-678-03182-7). Augustus M. Kelley, NY.

Otway, Thomas. Venice Preserved. Griffith, Benjamin W. Jr., ed. (Theatre Classics Ser). 1971. $0.95 pa. Barrons Educational Series, NY.

Reed, Rex. Conversations in the Raw. 1970. (1969) $1.25 pa. New American Library, NY.

Rosenheim, Edward W., Jr. What Happens in Literature. A Student's Guide to Poetry, Drama, & Fiction. 1960. $4.50 Hdbd. (ISBN 0-226-72792-0). Univ of Chicago Pr., IL.

Rosenheim, Edward W., Jr. What Happens in Literature: A Student's Guide to Poetry, Drama & Fiction. 1960. $1.50 pa. (ISBN 0-226-72793-9, P77). Univ of Chicago Pr., IL.

Saint-Denis, Michel. Theatre: The Rediscovery of Style. 1969. (1960) $2.85 pa. Theatre Arts Books, NY.

Schechner, Richard. Public Domain. Essays on the Theatre. $6.95 Hdbd. Bobbs-Merrill Co., IN.

Schechner, Richard. Public Domain: Essays on the Theatre. 1970. (1969) $1.65 pa. Avon Books, NY.

Schevill, James. Breakout: In Search of New Theatrical Environments. 1971. $8.50 Hdbd; $3.50 pa. Swallow Pr., IL.

Scholes, Robert & Klaus, Carl H. Elements of Drama. 1971. $0.95 pa. (ISBN 0-19-501272-0). Oxford Univ Pr., NY.

Selden, Samuel. Man in His Theatre. 1957. $4.00 Hdbd. (ISBN 0-8078-0716-8). Univ of North Carolina Pr., NC.

Seltzer, Daniel. Modern Theatre: Readings & Documents. 1967. $5.95 pa. (ISBN 0-316-78108-8). Little, Brown & Co., MA.

Seng, Peter J. & Cooper, Burton L. Plays: Wadsworth Handbook & Anthology. 1969. $4.95 pa. Wadsworth Publ. Co., CA.

Sharp, William. Language in Drama. $2.50 pa. (ISBN 0-8102-0014-7). Chandler Publ. Co., CA.

Shaw, George B. Shaw on Theatre. West, E. J., ed. 1959. $4.50 Hdbd. (ISBN 0-8090-8650-6, Drama); $1.75 pa. (ISBN 0-8090-0518-2). Hill & Wang, NY.

Simon, John. Private Screenings. 1971. $1.25 pa. (ISBN 0-425-01951-9). Berkley Publ., NY.

Synge, John M. Letters to Molly: John Millington Synge to Marie O'Neill. Saddlemyer, Ann, ed. 1971. $10.00 Hdbd. (ISBN 0-674-52834-4). Harvard Univ. Pr., MA.

Tennyson, G. B. Introduction to Drama. (Rinehart English Pamphlets). 1967. $1.85 pa. (ISBN 0-03-060820-1). Holt, Rinehart & Winston, NY.

Thompson, Alan R. Anatomy of Drama. 2nd ed. (Essay Index Reprint Ser). 1946. $12.75 Hdbd. (ISBN 0-8369-0932-1). Books for Libraries, NY.

Tulane Drama Review. Theatre in the Twentieth Century. Corrigan, Robert W., ed. (Essay Index Reprint Ser). 1963. $12.50 Hdbd. (ISBN 0-8369-1631-X). Books for Libraries, NY.

Ubright, H. Wayang Purwa: Shadows of the Past. 1970. $9.50 Hdbd. Oxford Univ. Pr., NY.

Walkley, Arthur B. Drama & Life. (Essay Index Reprint Ser). 1967. (1908) $10.00 Hdbd. (ISBN 0-8369-0967-4). Books for Libraries, NY.

Weiss, Theodore. Breath of Clowns & Kings: A Book on Shakespeare. 1971. $10.00 Hdbd. (ISBN 0-689-10329-8). Atheneum Publ., NY.

Wellarth, George E. Theatre of Protest & Paradox: Developments in Avante-Garde Drama. 2nd ed. 1970. $10.00 text ed. (ISBN 0-8147-9150-6); $3.95 pa. (ISBN 0-8147-9151-4). New York Univ. Pr., NY.

Wichelns, Herbert A., et al, eds. Studies in Speech & Drama in Honor of Alexander M. Drummond. 1968. (1944) $13.50 Hdbd. Russell & Russell Publ., NY.

Wilson, John H. Preface to Restoration Drama. $3.95 pa. Houghton-Mifflin, NY.

Wright, Edward A. & Downs, Lenthiel H. Primer for Playgoers. 2nd ed. (Speech & Drama Ser). 1969. $8.95 text ed. $6.95 Hdbd. (ISBN 0-13-700443-5). Prentice-Hall, NY.

History and Criticism

NOTE: Arranged by Country, Country and Period, and Chronological Period.

Adams, Henry H. & Hathaway, Baxter, eds. Dramatic Essays of the Neoclassic Age. $12.50 Hdbd. Benjamin Blom, NY.

Adams, William, et al, eds. Afro-American Literature: Drama. (Afro-American Literature Ser). (Hi-Sch.). $2.40 pa. Houghton-Mifflin, NY.

Agate, James. Red Letter Nights. 1944. $12.50 Hdbd. Benjamin Blom, NY.

Altshuler, Thelma & Janaro, Richard P. Responses to Drama: An Introduction to Plays & Movies. 1967. $4.25 pa. (3-00962). Houghton-Mifflin, NY.

Barbeau, Anne T. Intellectual Design of John Dryden's Heroic Plays. 1970. $8.50 Hdbd. (ISBN 0-300-01111-3). Yale Univ. Pr., CT.

Barroll, J. Leeds, ed. Shakespeare Studies: An Annual Gathering of Research, Criticism, & Reviews, 4 Vols. 1965-1969. $14.75 Hdbd. (ISBN 0-697-03850-5, 03851-3, 03852-1, 03853-X). William C. Brown, IA.

Barry, Jackson G. Dramatic Structure: The Shaping of Experience. 1970. $9.75 Hdbd. (ISBN 0-520-01624-6). Univ. of California Pr., CA.

Bates, Alfred, et al, eds. Drama, Its History, Literature & Influence of Civilization, 22 Vols. 1970. (1904) Set—$470.00 Hdbd. (ISBN 0-404-02190-5); $22.50 Hdbd. AMS Pr., NY.

Bentley, Eric. Dramatic Event. 1956. $1.25 pa. (ISBN 0-8070-6479-3, BP23). Beacon Pr., NY.

Bentley, Eric. Life of the Drama. 1964. $2.95 pa. (ISBN 0-689-70011-3, 112). Atheneum Publ., NY.

Bodkin, Maud. Quest for Salvation in an Ancient & a Modern Play. 1941. $12.50. Ridgeway Books, PA.

Boughner, Daniel C. Braggert in Renaissance Comedy: A Study in Comparative Drama from Aristophanes to Shakespeare. 1954. $14.50 Hdbd. (ISBN 0-8371-3006-9). Greenwood Pr., CT.

Boulton, Marjorie. Anatomy of Drama. 1960-1968. $4.50; $1.75 pa. Hillary House Publ., NY.

Bowen, James K. & Van Der Beets, Richard, eds. Drama: A Critical Introduction. 1971. $5.95 pa. (ISBN 0-06-040889-8). Harper-Row, NY.

Brockett, Oscar G. History of the Theatre. 1968. $12.50 text ed. (491974). Allyn, Inc., NJ.

Brockett, Oscar G. Theatre: An Introduction. 2nd ed. (Rinehart Editions). 1969. $12.95 Hdbd. (ISBN 0-03-082874-0). $10.95 text ed. (ISBN 0-03-080270-9). Holt, Rinehart & Winston, NY.

Campbell, G. A. Strindberg. (Studies in Drama, No. 39). 1971. lib. bdg. $9.95 Hdbd. (ISBN 0-8383-1320-5). Haskell House Publ., NY.

Cheney, Sheldon. Theatre. 1971. $12.95 Hdbd. David McKay, NY.

Cheney, Sheldon. Theatre. rev. & enl. ed. 1971. $12.95 Hdbd. David McKay, NY.

Clark, Barrett H. European Theories of the Drama. rev. ed. Popkin, Henry, ed. Hi-Sch. 1965. $7.50 Hdbd. Crown Publ., NY.

Clarke, R. F. Growth & Nature of Drama. 1965. $1.75 Hdbd. Cambridge Univ. Pr., NY.

Claudel, Paul. Claudel on the Theatre. Petit, Jacques & Kempf, Jean-Pierre, eds. Trollope, Christine, tr. 1971. $10.00 Hdbd. (ISBN 0-87024-158-3). Univ. of Miami Pr., FL.

Clay, James H. & Krempel, D. Theatrical Image. 1967. text ed. $7.95. (ISBN 0-07-011286-X). McGraw-Hill, NY.

Cole, Douglas. Suffering & Evil in the Plays of Christopher Marlowe. 1971. (1962) $9.00 Hdbd. (ISBN 0-87752-134-4). Gordian Pr., NY.

Coleman, Arthur & Tyler, Gary R. Drama Criticism, 2 vols. Incl. Vol. 1. A Checklist of Interpretation Since 1940 of English & American Plays. $9.50; Vol. 2. A Checklist of Interpretation Since 1940 of Classical & Continental Plays. $12.50 Hdbd. Swallow Pr., IL.

Cooke, Richard. Pier Francesco Mola: A Critical Study & Catalogue Raisonne. 1971. $19.25 Hdbd. Oxford Univ. Pr., NY.

Courtney, William L. Idea of Tragedy in Ancient & Modern Drama. 1967. (1900) $6.00 Hdbd. Russell & Russell Publ., NY.

Deane, Cecil V. Dramatic Victory & the Rhymed Heroic Play. 1967. (1931) $7.50 Hdbd. Barnes & Noble, NY.

Deane, Cecil V. Dramatic Theory & the Rhymed Heroic Play. (1931) $6.50 Hdbd. Folcroft Pr., PA.

Downer, Alan S. Art of the Play. 1955. $9.95 text ed. (ISBN 0-03-005310-2). Holt, Rinehart & Winston, NY.

Drew, Elizabeth. Discovering Drama. 1968. (1937) $8.00 Hdbd. (ISBN 0-8046-0116-X). Kennikat Pr., NY.

Dryden, John. Of Dramatick Poesie: An Essay. Boulton, James T., ed. 1964. $1.85 Hdbd. (ISBN 0-19-831380-2). Oxford Univ. Pr., NY.

DuBois, Arthur E. Beginnings of Tragic Comedy in the Drama of the Nineteenth Century. 1934. $4.00 Hdbd. Folcroft Pr., PA.

Dukes, Ashley. Modern Dramatists.

(Essay Index Reprint Ser). 1912. $7.75 Hdbd. (ISBN 0-8369-0396-X). Books for Libraries, NY.

Dunne, E. Catherine, et al, eds. Medieval Drama & It's Claudelian Revival. $10.00 pa. McGrath Publ. Co., MD.

Ellis-Fermor, Una. Frontiers of Drama. 2nd ed. 1964. $2.00 pa. (ISBN 0-416-68420-3, 92). Barnes & Noble, NY.

Faguet, Emile. Drame Ancien, Drame Moderne. (Fr). 1898. $18.50 Hdbd. (ISBN 0-8337-4093-8). Burt Franklin, NY.

Fergusson, Francis. Idea of a Theater: A Study of Ten Plays, the Art of Drama in Changing Perspective. 1968. (1949) $7.50 Hdbd. (ISBN 0-691-06143-2); $1.95 pa. (ISBN 0-691-01288-1, 126). Princeton Univ. Pr., NJ.

Frenz, Horst, ed. American Playwrights on Drama. 1965. $3.95 Hdbd. (ISBN 0-8090-2550-7); $1.65 pa. (ISBN 0-8090-0540-9). Hill & Wang, NY.

Freytag, Gustav. Technique of the Drama. McEwan, E. J., tr. 1968. (1895) $12.00 Hdbd. Johnson Reprint Corp., NY.

Frye, Prosser H. Romance & Tragedy: A Study of Classic & Romantic Elements in the Great Tragedies of European Literature. $1.95 pa. (ISBN 0-8032-5066-5, 118). Univ. of Nebraska Pr., NB.

Fuller, Edmund. Pageant of the Theatre. (Jr. Hi.). 1965. $5.95 Hdbd. (ISBN 0-690-60809-8). Thomas Y. Crowell, NY.

Gassner, John. Directions in Modern Theatre & Drama. rev. ed. 1965. $9.95 text ed. (ISBN 0-03-051370-7). Holt, Rinehart & Winston, NY.

Gassner, John. Masters of the Drama. 3rd ed. 1953. $8.50 Hdbd. (ISBN 0-486-20100-7). Dover Publ., NY.

Goldberg, Isaac. Theatre of George Jean Nathan. 1926. $12.50 Hdbd. (ISBN 0-404-02859-4). AMS Pr., NY.

Goodman, R. From Script to Stage: Eight Modern Plays. (Rinehart Editions). 1971. $11.95 text ed. (ISBN 0-03-025870-7, Holt C). Holt, Rinehart & Winston, NY.

Granville-Barker, Harley G. Use of the Drama. 1971. (1945) $7.50 Hdbd. Russell & Russell Publ., NY.

Gray, Charles H. Theatrical Criticism in London to Seventeen Ninety-Five. 1931. $12.50 Hdbd. Benjamin Blom, NY.

Greenberger, Howard. Off-Broadway Experience. 1971. $6.95 Hdbd. (ISBN 0-13-630616-0). Prentice-Hall, NY.

Greene, J. J. One Act Play: A Laboratory for Drama. (Aspects of English: Literature Ser.). (Hi-Sch.). 1969. $1.52 pa., $1.14 s.p. (ISBN 0-03-071120-7). Holt, Rinehart & Winston, NY.

Grein, Jacob T. Dramatic Criticism, 5 Vols. 1899–1905. $12.50 ea. Hdbd. Benjamin Blom, NY.

Hardison, O. B., Jr. Christian Rite & Christian Drama in the Middle Ages: Essays in the Origin & Early History of Modern Drama. (1965) $10.00 Hdbd.

(ISBN 0-8018-0254-7); $2.45 pa. (ISBN 0-8018-1044-2). Johns Hopkins Pr., MD.

Hathorn, Richmond Y. Tragedy, Myth & Mystery. $4.75 Hdbd. Peter Smith Publ., MA.

Hathorn, Richmond Y. Tragedy, Myth & Mystery. 1962. $2.65 pa. (ISBN 0-253-20092-X). Indiana Univ. Pr., IN.

Havemeyer, Loomis. Drama of Savage Peoples As Revealed in Their Rites. (Drama Ser. No. 39). 1969. (1916) $12.95 Hdbd. (ISBN 0-8383-0663-2). Haskell House Publ., NY.

Heinsius, Daniel. On Plot in Tragedy. 1971. $7.00 Hdbd. $5.00 pa. San Fernando Valley St. College, CA.

Hewitt, Barnard W. Theatre U.S.A., 1668 to 1957. 1959. $9.50 text ed. (ISBN 0-07-028585-3). McGraw-Hill, NY.

Hoy, Cyrus H. Hyacinth Room: An Investigation into the Nature of Comedy, Tragedy, & Tragicomedy. 1964. $6.95 Hdbd. Alfred A. Knopf, NY.

Hughes, Leo. Drama's Patrons: A Study of the Eighteenth-Century London Audience. 1971. $7.50 Hdbd. (ISBN 0-292-70091-1). Univ. of Texas Pr., TX.

Huncker, James G. Iconoclasts, a Book of Dramatists: Ibsen, Strindberg, Becque, Hauptmann, Sudermann, Hervieu, Gorky, Duse & D'Annunzio, Maeterlinck & Bernard Shaw. 1969. (1905) $14.50 Hdbd. (ISBN 0-8371-0930-2). Greenwood Pr., CT.

Hunt, Irene. No Promises in the Wind. (Fiction Ser). (Elem.). 1970. (ISBN 0-695-80065-5); $4.98 Hdbd. (ISBN 0-695-40065-7). Follett Publ. Co., IL.

Hurtik, Emil & Yarber, Robert E., eds. Introduction to Drama & Criticism. 1971. $5.50 pa. (ISBN 0-536-00277-0). Xerox College Publ., MA.

James, Henry. Scenic Art: Notes on Acting & the Drama, 1872–1901. Wade, Allan, ed. 1957. $1.35 pa. (ISBN 0-8090-0505-0, Drama). Hill & Wang, NY.

Kernan, Alvin B. Modern Shakespearean Criticism: Essays on Style Dramaturgy & the Major Plays. $3.95 pa. (ISBN 0-15-563375-9). Harcourt, Brace & World, NY.

Kernan, Alvin B., ed. Character & Conflict: An Introduction to Drama. 1969. $5.50 pa. (ISBN 0-15-506271-9); $5.50 pa. earlier ed. (ISBN 0-15-506270-0). Harcourt, Brace & World, NY.

Kernodle, George R. Invitation to the Theatre. 1967. $9.95 text ed. (ISBN 0-15-546921-5). Harcourt, Brace & World, NY.

Kerr, Walter. God on the Gymnasium Floor. $7.95 Hdbd. 1971. Simon & Schuster, Inc., NY.

Kerr, Walter. How Not to Write a Play. 1955. $5.95 text ed. (ISBN 0-87116-035-8). Writer, Inc., MA.

Kirby, Michael. Futurist Performance. 1971. $8.95 Hdbd.; $3.95 pa. E. P. Dutton, NY.

Kraft, Hy. On My Way to the Theater. Friede, Eleanor, ed. 1971. $7.95 Hdbd. Macmillan Co., NY.

Landa, M. J. Jew in Drama. 1968. (1926) $11.00 Hdbd. (ISBN 0-8046-0257-3). Kennikat Pr., NY.

Landa, Myer J. Jew in Drama. rev. ed. 1969. $8.95 Hdbd. (ISBN 0-87068-074-9). Ktav Publ. House, NY.

Langner, Lawrence. Play's the Thing. (Hi-Sch.). 1960. $6.95 text ed. (ISBN 0-87116-036-6). Writer, Inc., MA.

Lawson, John H. Theory & Technique of Playwriting. 1960. $1.95 pa. (ISBN 0-8090-0525-5). Hill & Wang, NY.

Leathes, Edmund. Actor Abroad: Or, Gossip Dramatic, Narrative, & Descriptive. 1880. $12.75 Hdbd. Benjamin Blom, NY.

Lemaitre, Jules. Theatrical Impressions. Whyte, Frederic, ed. $12.00 Hdbd. Benjamin Blom, NY.

Lewisohn, Ludwig. Drama & the Stage. (Essay Index Reprint Ser). 1922. $8.00 Hdbd. (ISBN 0-8369-1089-3). Books for Libraries, NY.

MacCarthy, Desmond. Drama. 1940. $9.75 Hdbd. Benjamin Blom, NY.

McCarthy, Mary. Theatre Chronicles, Nineteen Thirty Seven to Nineteen Sixty Two. 1963. $4.50 Hdbd. Farrar, Straus & Giroux, NY.

McCarthy, Mary. Theatre Chronicles, Nineteen Thirty Seven to Nineteen Sixty Two. $1.95 pa. Farrar, Straus & Giroux, NY.

MacGowan, Kenneth & Melnitz, W. Golden Ages of the Theater. 1959. $1.95 pa. (ISBN 0-13-357830-5, S8). Prentice-Hall, NY.

Mahr, August C. Dramatische Situationsbilder und-Bildtypen: Eine Studie Zur Kunstgeschichte Des Dramas. 1928. $9.00 Hdbd. (ISBN 0-404-51806-0). AMS Pr., NY.

Marx, Milton. Enjoyment of Drama. 2nd ed. $2.25 pa. (ISBN 0-390-60198-5). Appleton-Century-Crofts, NY.

Matthews, Brander. Playwrights on Playmaking & Other Studies on the Stage. (Essay Index Reprint Ser). 1923. $9.75 Hdbd. (ISBN 0-8369-0698-5). Books for Libraries, NY.

Matthews, Brander. Principles of Playmaking. (Essay Index Reprint Ser). $10.75 Hdbd. (ISBN 0-8369-1989-0). Books for Libraries, NY.

Matthews, Brander. Rip Van Winkle Goes to the Play. (1967) $8.00 Hdbd. (ISBN 0-8046-0303-0). Kennikat Pr., NY.

Matthews, Brander, ed. Papers on Playmaking. (Essay Index Reprint Ser). $10.75 Hdbd. (ISBN 0-8369-1890-8). Books for Libraries, NY.

Matthews, Brander, ed. Papers on Playmaking. 1957. $1.35 pa. (ISBN 0-8090-0510-7). Hill & Wang, NY.

Merchant, W. Moelwyn. Creed & Drama. 1966. $1.95 Hdbd. (ISBN 0-8006-0178-5, 1-178). Fortress Pr., PA.

Mersand, Joseph. Play's the Thing. 1968. (1940) $6.00 Hdbd. (ISBN 0-8046-0311-1). Kennikat Pr., NY.

Millett, Fred B. & Bentley, Gerald E. Art of the Drama. $4.50 text ed. (ISBN 0-390-64088-3). Appleton-Century-Crofts, NY.

Nathan, George J. Critic & the Drama. $6.75 Hdbd. (ISBN 0-8386-7964-1). Fairleigh Dickinson Univ. Pr., NJ.

Nelson, Robert J. Play Within a Play. (Theatre Ser). (1958) price "n.g." (ISBN 0-306-71580-5). Plenum Publ. Corp., NY.

Nicoll, Allardyce. Development of the Theatre. 5th ed. 1967. $15.00 Hdbd. (ISBN 0-15-125327-7). Harcourt, Brace & World, NY.

Nicoll, Allardyce. English Theatre: A Short History. 1936. $11.50 Hdbd. (ISBN 0-8371-3133-2). Greenwood Pr., CT.

Nicoll, Allardyce. World Drama. 1949. $9.75 Hdbd. (ISBN 0-15-198603-7). Harcourt, Brace & World, NY.

O'Hara, Frank H. Invitation to the Theater. (1951) $9.50 Hdbd. (ISBN 0-8371-3842-6). Greenwood Pr., CT.

Olson, Elder. Tragedy & the Theory of Drama. 1961. $2.95 pa. (ISBN 0-8143-1149-0). Wayne St. Univ. Pr., MI.

Ommanney, Katharine A. Stage & the School. 3rd ed. 1960. $7.96 text ed. (ISBN 0-07-047669-1). McGraw-Hill, NY.

Oppenheimer, George, ed. Passionate Playgoer. $1.95 pa. (ISBN 0-670-00119-8). Viking Pr., NY.

Palmer, Helen H. & Dyson, Anne J. European Drama Criticism: Supplement 1, to January, 1970. 1970. $5.50 Hdbd. (ISBN 0-208-01044-0). Shoe String Pr., CT.

Parone, Ed, ed. New Theatre for Now. 1971. $2.25 pa. (440-06384-225). Dell Publ., NY.

Pomeroy, Marcus M. Nonsense, or Hits & Criticisms on the Follies of the Day. (American Humorists, Vol. 20). 1969. (1868) $10.50 Hdbd. (ISBN 0-8398-1572-7). Gregg Pr., N.J.

Quinn, Arthur H. A History of the American Drama, from the Beginning to the Civil War. 2nd ed. (1951) $21.00 Hdbd. (ISBN 0-8371-6183-5). Greenwood Pr., CT.

Reaske, Christopher R. Monarch Literature Notes on How to Analyze Drama. $1.50 pa. Monarch Pr., NY.

Ridgeway, William. Dramas & Dramatic Dances of Non-European Races. 1810. $17.50 Hdbd. Benjamin Blom, NY.

Rothman, John. Origin & Development of Dramatic Criticism in the New York Times 1851-1880. $8.00 Hdbd. (ISBN 0-405-02560-2). Arno Pr., NY.

Rowe, Kenneth T. Theater in Your Head. 1967. $6.95 Hdbd. Funk & Wagnalls, NY.

Rowe, Kenneth T. Write That Play.

1969. $6.95 Hdbd. Funk & Wagnalls, NY.

Salerno, Henry F. & Nelson, Conny E., eds. Drama & Tradition: The Major Genres. 1968. $5.95 pa. Van Nostrand-Reinhold Books, NY.

Samachson, Dorothy & Samachson, Joseph. Dramatic Story of the Theatre. (Jr Hi.). 1955. $4.95 Hdbd. Abelard-Schuman Ltd., NY.

Sedgewick, Garnett G. Of Irony: Especially in Drama—with Special Reference to Shakespeare, Ibsen, & the Greek Tragedians. (Canadian University Paperbooks). 1948. $5.00 Hdbd. (ISBN 0-8020-5003-4); $2.25 pa. (ISBN 0-8020-6064-1). Univ. of Toronto Pr., Canada.

Shaw, George B. Dramatic Criticism, 1895-1898: A Selection by John F. Matthews. (1959) $12.75 Hdbd. (ISBN 0-8371-5234-8). Greenwood Pr., CT.

Shaw, George B. Plays & Players: Essays on the Theatre. 1954. $3.00 Hdbd. (ISBN 0-19-250535-1). Oxford Univ. Pr., NY.

Shaw, George B. Shaw's Dramatic Criticism from the Saturday Review 1895-1898. Matthews, John F., ed. $3.50 Hdbd. Peter Smith Publ., MA.

Sievers, David. Freud on Broadway. 1971. (1955) $12.50 Hdbd. (ISBN 0-8154-0366-6). Cooper Sq. Pr., NY.

Singh, S. Theory of Drama in the Restoration Period. 1968. $6.00 Hdbd. Lawrence Verry, Inc., CT.

Slonim, Marc. Russian Theatre: From

the Empire to the Soviets. 1962. $1.50 pa. Macmillan Co., NY.

Smith, Hallett D., ed. Twentieth Century Interpretations of the Tempest. 1969. $1.25 pa. (ISBN 0-13-903302-5). Prentice-Hall, NY.

Steinberg, M. W. Aspects of Modern Drama. 1960. $6.25 Hdbd. (ISBN 0-03-010095-X). Holt, Rinehart & Winston, NY.

Steiner, George. Death of Tragedy. 1961. $5.95 Hdbd. Alfred A. Knopf, NY.

Stoll, Elmer E. Shakespeare & Other Masters. 1962. (1940) $9.50 Hdbd. Russell & Russell Publ., NY.

Stuart, Donald C. Development of Dramatic Art. $6.00 Hdbd. Peter Smith Publ., MA.

Stuart, Donald C. Development of Dramatic Art. 1928. $4.00 pa. (ISBN 0-486-20693-9). Dover Publ., NY.

Styan, J. L. Elements of Drama. 1960. $6.50 Hdbd.; $2.25 pa. (ISBN 0-521-09201-9, 201). Cambridge Univ. Pr., NY.

Symons, James M. Meyerhold's Theatre of the Grotesque: The Post-Revolutionary Productions, 1920–1932. (Theatre Bks. No. 8). 1971. $10.00 Hdbd. (ISBN 0-87024-192-3). Univ. of Miami Pr., Coral Gables, FL.

Temkine, Raymonde. Grotowski. 1971. $7.50 Hdbd. (ISBN 0-8180-0502-5). Horizon Pr., NY.

Tunison, R. S. Dramatic Traditions of the Middle Ages. 1907. $16.50 Hdbd. (ISBN 0-8337-3578-0). Burt Franklin, NY.

Valency, Maurice J. Tragedies of Herod & Mariamne. 1940. $10.00 Hdbd. (ISBN 0-404-06750-6). AMS Pr., NY.

Waith, Eugene M. Ideas of Greatness: Heroic Drama in England. 1971. $9.50 Hdbd. Barnes & Noble, NY.

Wellarth, George E. Theatre of Protest & Paradox: Developments in Avante-Garde Drama. 2nd ed. 1970. $10.00 text ed. (ISBN 0-8147-9150-6); $3.95 pa. (ISBN 0-8147-9151-4). New York Univ. Pr., NY.

Whitfield, George J. Introduction to Drama. 1938. $2.75 Hdbd. (ISBN 0-19-831226-1). Oxford Univ. Pr., NY.

Whitman, Robert F. Play-Reader's Handbook. 1966. $1.95 pa. Bobbs-Merrill Co., IN.

Whitmore, Charles E. The Supernatural in Tragedy. (1915) $10.00 Hdbd. (ISBN 0-911858-24-5). Phaeton Pr., NY.

Yates, Frances A. Theatre of the World. 1971. $3.45 pa. (ISBN 0-226-95005-0, P348, Phoen). Univ. of Chicago Pr., IL.

General Studies

Lukacs, George. Historical Novel. 1962. $6.50 Hdbd. Humanities Pr., NY.

McCalmon, George & Moe, Christian. Creating Historical Drama: A Guide for the Community & The Interested Individual. 1965. $12.50 Hdbd. (ISBN 0-

8093-0189-X). Southern Ill. Univ. Pr., Carbondale, IL.

Ribner, Irving. English History Play in the Age of Shakespeare. 1965. $5.75 Hdbd. Barnes & Noble, NY.

Roberts, Spencer E. Soviet Historical Drama. 1965. $9.00 pa. Humanities Pr., NY.

Schelling, Felix E. English Chronicle Play. (Burt Franklin Research & Source Works, No. 180). 1968. (1902) $13.50 Hdbd. (ISBN 0-8337-3140-8). Burt Franklin, NY.

Schelling, Felix E. English Chronicle Play. (Drama Ser., No. 39). 1969. (1902) $11.95 Hdbd. (ISBN 0-8383-0618-7). Haskell House, NY.

Schelling, Felix E. English Chronicle Play. 1902. $12.50 Hdbd. (ISBN 0-404-05578-8). AMS Pr., NY.

Smith, Robert M. Froissart & the English Chronicle Play. 1915. $10.00 Hdbd. Benjamin Blom, NY.

Walsh, Henry H. Six Plays in American History. $5.95 Hdbd. (ISBN 0-8289-0087-6). Stephen Greene Pr., Brattleboro, VT.

Medieval

Bevington, David M. From Mankind to Marlowe: Growth of Structure in the Popular Drama of Tudor England. 1962. $8.50 Hdbd. (ISBN 0-674-32500-1). Harvard Univ. Pr., Cambridge, MA.

Cargill, Oscar. Drama & Liturgy. 1969.

(1930) $7.50 Hdbd. Octagon Books, NY.

Chambers, Edmund K. Medieval Stage, 2 Vols. 1903. Set—$16.00 Hdbd. (ISBN 0-19-811512-1). Oxford Univ. Pr., NY.

Creizenach, Wilhelm. Geschichte Des Neueren Dramas, 3 Vols. Set—$65.00 Hdbd.; $27.50 Hdbd. Benjamin Blom, NY.

Fournier, Edouard. Theatre Francais Avant La Renaissance, 1430-1550. 1965. (1872) $25.00 Hdbd. (ISBN 0-8337-1225-X). Burt Franklin, NY.

Gayley, Charles M. Plays of Our Forefathers & Some of the Traditions Upon Which They Were Founded. 1968. (1907) $12.50 Hdbd. (ISBN 0-8196-0209-4). Biblo & Tannen, NY.

Hunningher, Benjamin. Origin of the Theater. 1961. $1.35 pa. (ISBN 0-8090-0528-X). Hill & Wang, NY.

Kretzmann, Paul E. Liturgical Element in the Earliest Forms of Medieval Drama. (Drama Ser., No. 39). 1969. (1916) $9.95 Hdbd. (ISBN 0-8383-0578-4). Haskell House Publ., NY.

MacKenzie, W. Roy. English Moralities from the Point of View of Allegory. (Drama Ser., No. 39). 1969. (1914) $9.95 Hdbd. (ISBN 0-8383-0592-X). Haskell House Publ., NY.

MacKenzie, William R. English Moralities from the Point of View of Allegory. 1966. (1914) $7.50 Hdbd. (ISBN 0-87752-066-6). Gordian Pr., Staten Island, NY.

MacKenzie, William R. English Moralities from the Point of View of Allegory. (Harvard Studies in English Ser). 1969. (1914) $12.50 Hdbd. Johnson Repr., NY.

Maidment, J. & Logan, W. H., eds. Dramatics of the Restoration. (1872) Set—$335.00 Hdbd. Adler's Foreign Books, NY.

Mill, Anna J. Medieval Plays in Scotland. 1969. (1927) $12.50 Hdbd. Benjamin Blom, NY.

Moore, E. Hamilton. English Miracle Plays & Moralities. 1970. (1907) $7.50 Hdbd. (ISBN 0-404-00598-5). AMS Pr., NY.

Ridley, Hugh. Renaissance Drama: Essays Principally on Drama in Its Intellectual Context, New Ser. 3. 1971. $12.50 Hdbd. (ISBN 0-8101-0338-9). Northwestern Univ. Pr., IL.

Tunison, Joseph S. Dramatic Traditions of the Dark Ages. 1907. $25.00 Hdbd. Folcroft Pr., PA.

Tunison, R. S. Dramatic Traditions of the Middle Ages. 1907. $16.50 Hdbd. (ISBN 0-8337-3578-0). Burt Franklin, NY.

Young, Karl. Drama of the Medieval Church, 2 Vols. 1933. $32.00 Hdbd. (ISBN 0-19-811586-5). Oxford Univ. Pr., NY.

National (China)

Chang Pe-Chin & Yutang, Lin. Chinese Opera & Painted Face. $30.00 Hdbd.

(ISBN 0-910482-25-X). DBS Publications, NY.

Hung, Josephine H. Ming Drama. 1966. $2.95 pa. Paragon Book Reprint, NY.

Scott, A. C. Introduction to the Chinese Theatre. 1959. $2.95 pa. Theatre Arts, NY.

Wells, Henry W. Classical Drama of the Orient. $8.50 Hdbd. (ISBN 0-210-22620-X). Asia Soc., NY.

Zung, Cecilia S. Secrets of the Chinese Drama. 1937. $15.00 Hdbd. Benjamin Blom, NY.

National (England)

Agate, James. James Agate: An Anthology. Thal, Herbert Van, ed. 1961. $6.00 Hdbd. (ISBN 0-8090-2380-6). Hill & Wang, NY.

Armstrong, Cecil F. Shakespeare to Shaw: Studies in the Life's Work of Six Dramatists of the English Stage. (Essay Index Reprint Ser). 1913. $11.75 Hdbd. (ISBN 0-8369-0157-6). Books for Libraries, NY.

Barish, Jonas A. Ben Jonson & the Language of Prose Comedy. 1970. (1967) $2.45 pa. (ISBN 0-393-00554-2). W. W. Norton, NY.

Birdsall, Virginia O. Wild Civility: The English Comic Spirit on the Restoration Stage. 1971. $10.50 Hdbd. (ISBN 0-253-19037-1). Indiana Univ. Pr., IN.

Bradbrook, Muriel C. English Dramatic

Form. 1965. $4.50 Hdbd. Barnes & Noble, NY.

Brawley, Benjamin. Short History of the English Drama. (Select Bibliographies Reprint Ser). 1921. $12.50 Hdbd. (ISBN 0-8369-5112-3). Books for Libraries, NY.

Burton, Ernest J. Student's Guide to British Theatre & Drama. 1964. $5.25 Hdbd. International Publ. Serv., NY.

Cibber, Colley. Apology for the Life of Colley Cibber. Fone, B. R., ed. 1968. $9.75 Hdbd. (ISBN 0-472-08210-8). Univ. of Michigan Pr., MI.

Cibber, Colley. Apology for the Life of Colley Cibber Written by Himself, 2 Vols. rev. ed. Lowe, R. W., ed. 1889. $14.50 Hdbd. (ISBN 0-404-01544-1). AMS Pr., NY.

Coleman, Edward D. Jew in English Drama: An Annotated Bibliography. rev. ed. 1966. $8.95 Hdbd. (ISBN 0-87104-101-4). New York Public Library, NY.

Craig, Hardin, ed. Essays in Dramatic Literature: The Parrott Presentation Volume, by Pupils of Prof. Thomas M. Parrott. 1967. (1935) $12.50 Hdbd. Russell & Russell Publ., NY.

Donaldson, Ian. World Upside-Down: Comedy from Jonson to Fielding. 1970. $7.25 Hdbd. (ISBN 0-19-811694-2). Oxford Univ. Pr., NY.

Downer, Alan S. British Drama: A Handbook & Brief Chronicle. 1950.

$5.25 text ed. (ISBN 0-390-27364-3). Appleton-Century-Crofts, NY.

Ellehauge, Martin. English Restoration Drama. 1933. $15.00 Hdbd. Folcroft Pr., PA.

Elwin, Malcolm. Playgoer's Handbook to Restoration Drama. 1928. $12.50 Hdbd. Folcroft Pr., PA.

Evans, Ifor. Short History of English Drama. 1965. $6.50 Hdbd. Humanities Pr., NY.

Gaw, Allison. Studies in English Drama. (1917) $15.00 Hdbd. (ISBN 0-8337-4868-8). Burt Franklin, NY.

Gayley, Charles M. Plays of Our Forefathers & Some of the Traditions Upon Which They Were Founded. 1968. (1907) $12.50 Hdbd. (ISBN 0-8196-0209-4). Biblo & Tannen, NY.

Gentleman, Francis. Dramatic Censor (Or, Critical Companion, 2 Vols. 1770. $20.00 lib. bdg. (ISBN 0-404-02697-4). AMS Pr., NY.

Gentleman, Francis. Dramatic Censor: Or, Critical Companion, 2 Vols. 1770. $37.50 Hdbd. Benjamin Blom, NY.

Granville-Barker, Harley. On Dramatic Method. 1960. $3.75 Hdbd. Peter Smith Publ., MA.

Granville-Barker, Harley. On Dramatic Method. 1956. $1.50 pa. (ISBN 0-8090-0502-6). Hill & Wang, NY.

Greacen, Robert. Art of Noel Coward. 1953. $6.50 Hdbd. Folcroft Pr., PA.

Hazlitt, William. Hazlitt on Theatre.

Archer, William & Lowe, Robert, eds. 1957. $1.25 pa. (ISBN 0-8090-0507-7). Hill & Wang, NY.

Jones, Henry A. Foundations of a National Drama. facs. ed. (Essay Index Reprint Ser). 1967. (1913) $11.50 Hdbd. (ISBN 0-8369-0579-2). Books for Libraries, NY.

Knight, G. Wilson. Golden Labyrinth. 1962. $6.00 Hdbd. (ISBN 0-393-04253-7). W. W. Norton, NY.

Kronenberger, Louis. Thread of Laughter. (Dramabooks). 1970. (1952) $2.45 pa. (ISBN 0-8090-0548-4). Hill & Wang, NY.

Krutch, Joseph W. Comedy & Conscience After the Restoration. (1924, 1949, (1967). $8.50 Hdbd. Russell & Russell Publ., NY.

Landa, M. J. Jew in Drama. 1968. (1926) $11.00 Hdbd. (ISBN 0-8046-0257-3). Kennikat Pr., NY.

Landa, Myer J. Jew in Drama. rev. ed. 1969. $8.95 Hdbd. (ISBN 0-87068-074-9). Ktav Publ. House, NY.

Leathers, Victor. British Entertainers in France, 1600–1900. 1959. $7.50 Hdbd. (ISBN 0-8020-5077-8). Univ. of Toronto Pr., Canada.

Mackenzie, Agnes M. Playgoer's Handbook to the English Renaissance Drama. 1971. (1927) $6.00 Hdbd. (ISBN 0-8154-0373-9). Cooper Sq. Pr., NY.

Manly, J. M. Specimens of Preshakespearean Drama. (Studies in Shakespeare Ser., No. 24). 1971. $28.95

Hdbd. (ISBN 0-8383-1278-0). Haskell House Publ., NY.

Margeson, J. M. Origins of English Tragedy. 1967. $8.00 Hdbd. (ISBN 0-19-811650-0). Oxford Univ. Pr., NY.

Moore, E. Hamilton. English Miracle Plays & Moralities. 1970. (1907) $7.50 Hdbd. (ISBN 0-404-00598-5). AMS Pr., NY.

Moore, John B. Comic & the Realistic in English Drama. 1965. (1925) $7.50 Hdbd. Russell & Russell Publ., NY.

Morgan, Arthur E. English Domestic Drama. $5.50 Hdbd. Folcroft Pr., PA.

Motter, Thomas H. School Drama in England. (1968) $11.00 Hdbd. (ISBN 0-8046-0325-1). Kennikat Pr., NY.

Newton, H. Chance. Crime & the Drama. 1970. (1927) $11.00 Hdbd. (ISBN 0-8046-0761-3). Kennikat Pr., NY.

Nicoll, Allardyce. British Drama: An Historical Survey from the Beginnings to the Present Time. 5th rev. ed. 1963. $6.00 Hdbd. Barnes & Noble, NY.

Nicoll, Allardyce. English Drama: A Modern Viewpoint. 1968. $3.50 Hdbd. Barnes & Noble, NY.

Nicoll, Allardyce. History of English Drama, 1660–1900, 6 vols. Incl. Vol. 1. The Restoration Drama; Vol. 2. Early Eighteenth Century Drama; Vol. 3. Late Eighteenth Century Drama; Vol. 4. Early Nineteenth Century Drama, 1800–1850; Vol. 5. Late Nineteenth Century Drama; Vol. 6. Alphabetical Catalogue of the

Plays. 1959. $14.50 ea. Hdbd. Cambridge Univ. Pr., NY.

Noyes, Robert G. Neglected Muse: Restoration & Eighteenth-Century Tragedy in the Novel 1740–1780. 1958. $4.00 Hdbd. (ISBN 0-87057-052-8). Brown Univ. Pr., RI.

Paine, Clarence S. Comedy of Manners. 1941. $6.50 Hdbd. Folcroft Pr., PA.

Penniman, Josiah. War of the Theatres. 1897. $15.00 Hdbd. Folcroft Pr., PA.

Penniman, Josiah H. War of the Theatres. 1970. (1897) $8.50 Hdbd. (ISBN 0-404-04992-3). AMS Pr., NY.

Prior, Moody E. Language of Tragedy. 1966. $2.95 pa. (ISBN 0-253-20086-5). Indiana Univ. Pr., IN.

Prior, Moorly E. The Language of Tragedy. $6.00 Hdbd. Peter Smith Publ., MA.

Pritchett, Victor S. George Meredith & English Comedy. 1970. $5.00 Hdbd. (ISBN 0-394-42621-5). Random House, NY.

Reynolds, George F. Some Principles of Elizabethan Staging. 1905. $4.00 Hdbd. Folcroft Pr., PA.

Ristine, Frank H. English Tragicomedy. Its Origin & History. 1963. (1910) $7.50 Hdbd. Russell & Russell Publ., NY.

Schelling, Felix B. English Drama. 1963. $4.00 Hdbd. Lawrence Verry, Inc., CT.

Schelling, Felix E. English Chronicle Play. 1902. $12.50 Hdbd. (ISBN 0-404-05578-8). AMS Pr., NY.

Schelling, Felix E. English Chronicle Play. (Burt Franklin: Research & Source Works, No. 180). 1968. (1902) $13.50 Hdbd. (ISBN 0-8337-3140-8). Burt Franklin, NY.

Sherbo, Arthur. English Sentimental Drama. 1957. $5.75 Hdbd. (ISBN 0-87013-026-9). Michigan St. Univ. Pr., MI.

Smith, Winifred. Commedia Dell'arte. rev. ed. $13.75 Hdbd. Benjamin Blom, NY.

Thaler, Alwin. Shakespeare to Sheridan. 1922. $12.50 Hdbd. Benjamin Blom, NY.

Thorndike, Ashley H. English Comedy. 1929. $10.00 Hdbd. (ISBN 0-8154-0238-4). Cooper Sq. Pr., NY.

Thorndike, Ashley H. English Tragedy. 1908. $7.50 Hdbd. (ISBN 0-8154-0237-6). Cooper Sq. Pr., NY.

Wallace, Charles W. Evolution of the English Drama up to Shakespeare. 1912. $7.50 Hdbd. Folcroft Pr., PA.

Ward, Adolphus W. History of English Dramatic Literature to the Death of Queen Anne, 3 Vols. 1966. $50.00 Hdbd. Octagon Books, Inc., NY.

Ward, Adolphus W. History of English Dramatic Literature to the Death of Queen Anne, 3 Vols. 1970. (1899) Set— $55.00 Hdbd. (ISBN 0-8044-2962-6). Frederick Ungar, NY.

Ward, Alfred C. Specimens of English Dramatic Criticism, Seventeenth–Twentieth Centuries. (1945) $15.50 Hdbd. (ISBN 0-8371-5545-2). Greenwood Pr., CT.

Watson, Harold F. Sailor in English Fiction & Drama: 1550-1800. 1931. $8.00 Hdbd. (ISBN 0-404-06873-1). AMS Pr., NY.

Watt, Laughlan M. Attic & Elizabethan Tragedy. (1968) $12.00 Hdbd. (ISBN 0-8046-0490-8). Kennikat Pr., NY.

Welsford, Enid. Court Masque: A Study in the Relationship Between Poetry & the Revels. 1962. (1927) $11.50 Hdbd. Russell & Russell Publ., NY.

Wheatley, Katherine E. Racine & English Classicism. 1956. $12.00 Hdbd. (ISBN 0-8371-3161-8). Greenwood Pr., CT.

Wimsatt, William K., ed. Idea of Comedy: Essays in Prose & Verse: Ben Johnson to George Meredith. 1969. ref. ed. $8.50 Hdbd. (ISBN 0-13-449546-2); $4.95 pa. (ISBN 0-13-449538-1). Prentice-Hall, NY.

National (England)—Periods: Medieval

Bates, Katherine L. English Religious Drama. 1893. $8.50 Hdbd. (ISBN 0-8046-0020-1). Kennikat Pr., NY.

Boas, Frederick S. Shakespeare & His Predecessors. 1969. $18.50 Hdbd. (ISBN 0-8371-0316-9). Greenwood Pr., CT.

Boas, Frederick S. Shakespeare & His Predecessors. (Studies in Shakespeare Ser., No. 24). 1969. (1896) $9.95 Hdbd. (ISBN 0-8383-0914-3). Haskell House Publ., NY.

Boas, Frederick S. Shakespeare & His Predecessors. 1968. (1902) $8.50 Hdbd. (ISBN 0-87752-011-9). Gordian Pr., NY.

Clarke, Sidney M. Miracle Play in England. 1897. $4.00 Hdbd. Folcroft Pr., PA.

Craig, Hardin. English Religious Drama of the Middle Ages. 1955. $13.00 Hdbd. (ISBN 0-19-811520-2). Oxford Univ. Pr., NY.

Davidson, Charles. Studies in the English Mystery Plays. (Drama Ser., No. 39). 1969. (1892) $9.95 Hdbd. (ISBN 0-8383-0536-9). Haskell House Publ., NY.

Davis, Norman, ed. Non-Cycle Plays & Fragments. 1970. $8.50 Hdbd. (ISBN 0-19-722401-6). Oxford Univ. Pr., NY.

Gardiner, Harold C. Mysteries' End: An Investigation of the Last Days of the Medieval Religious Stage. (Yale Studies in English 103). 1967. (1946) $4.50 Hdbd. Shoe String Pr., CT.

Hone, William. Ancient Mysteries Described. 1969. (1823) $9.50 Hdbd. Singing Tree Pr., MI.

Hudson, Henry N. Shakespeare: His Life, Art, & Character, 2 Vols. 1872. Set—$35.00 Hdbd. AMS Pr., NY.

Levin, Richard. Multiple Plot in English Renaissance Drama. 1971. $9.50

Hdbd. (ISBN 0-226-47526-3). Univ. of Chicago Pr., IL.

Prosser, Eleanor. Drama & Religion in the English Mystery Plays: A Re-Evaluation. (Stanford Studies in Language & Literature). 1961. $7.00 Hdbd. (ISBN 0-8047-0060-5). Stanford Univ. Pr., CA.

Rossiter, Arthur P. English Drama from Early Times to the Elizabethans: Its Background, Origins & Developments. 1959. $5.00 Hdbd.; $1.95 pa. (ISBN 0-389-03341-3, 429). Barnes & Noble, NY.

Salter, Frederick M. Medieval Drama in Chester. 1968. (1955) $7.50 Hdbd. Russell & Russell Publ., NY.

Symonds, John A. Shakespeare's Predecessors in the English Drama. (1967) $9.95 Hdbd. (ISBN 0-8154-0301-1). Cooper Sq. Pr., NY.

Wallace, Charles W. Evolution of the English Drama up to Shakespeare: With a History of the First Blackfriars Theatre. 1968. (1912) $8.50 Hdbd. (ISBN 0-8046-0668-4). Kennikat Pr., NY.

Whiting, B. J. Proverbs in the Earlier English Drama. 1969. (1938) $15.00 Hdbd. Octagon Books, Inc., NY.

Williams, Arnold. Drama of Medieval England. 1961. $6.00 Hdbd. (ISBN 0-87013-057-9). Michigan St. Univ. Pr., MI.

Wilson, Frank P. English Drama, Fourteen Eighty Five–Fifteen Eighty Five. 1969. $7.00 Hdbd. (ISBN 0-19-500203-2). Oxford Univ. Pr., NY.

National (England)—Periods: 16th Century—Early Modern & Elizabethan

Acheson, Arthur. Shakespeare, Chapman & Sir Thomas More. 1970. (1931) $11.00 Hdbd. (ISBN 0-404-00278-1). AMS Pr., NY.

Adams, Henry H. English Domestic or Homiletic Tragedy. $12.50 Hdbd. Benjamin Blom, NY.

Albright, Evelyn M. Dramatic Publications in England: 1580–1640. 1970. $10.00 text ed. (ISBN 0-87752-127-1). Gordian Pr., NY.

Alleyn, Edward. Alleyn Papers: Illustrative of the Early English Stage. 1970. (1843) $6.00 Hdbd. (ISBN 0-404-00329-X). AMS Pr., NY.

Baker, Howard. Induction to Tragedy. 1965. (1939) $7.50 Hdbd. Russell & Russell Publ., NY.

Baldwin, Thomas W. On the Literary Genetics of Shakespeare's Plays, 1592–1594. 1959. $10.50 Hdbd. (ISBN 0-252-72587-5). Univ. of Illinois Pr., IL.

Barber, C. L. Idea of Honour in the English Drama 1591–1700. 1957. $27.50 Hdbd. Lansdowne Pr., PA.

Barish, Jonas A. Ben Jonson & the Language of Prose Comedy. 1960. $8.50 Hdbd. (ISBN 0-674-06600-6). Harvard Univ. Pr., MA.

Baskervill, Charles R. Elizabethan Jig. 1929. $3.50 pa. (ISBN 0-486-21365-X). Dover Publ., NY.

Baskervill, Charles R. Elizabethan Jig & Related Song Drama. $5.00 Hdbd. Peter Smith Publ., MA.

Baskervill, Charles R. English Elements in Johnson's Early Comedy. (1911) $5.00 pa. Johnson Reprint Corp., NY.

Bastiaenen, J. A. Moral Tone of Jacobean & Caroline Drama. (Drama Ser. No. 39). 1969. (1930) $9.95 Hdbd. (ISBN 0-8383-0507-5). Haskell House Publ., NY.

Bentley, Gerald E. The Jacobean & Caroline Stage. Incl. Vol. 1-2. Dramatic Companies & Players. 1941. $24.00 Hdbd. (ISBN 0-19-811503-2); Vol. 3-5. Plays & Playwrights. 1956. $38.50 Hdbd. (ISBN 0-19-811504-0); Vol. 6-7. Theatres, Appendixes to Vol. 6 & General Index. 1968. $22.50 Hdbd. (ISBN 0-19-811626-8). Oxford Univ. Pr., NY.

Bernard, Jules E., Jr. Prosody of the Tudor Interlude. (Yale Studies in English No. 90). 1969. (1939) $6.50 Hdbd. (ISBN 0-208-00782-2). Shoe String Pr., CT.

Bevington, David M. From Mankind to Marlowe: Growth of Structure in the Popular Drama of Tudor England. 1962. $8.50 Hdbd. (ISBN 0-674-32500-1). Harvard Univ. Pr., MA.

Bevington, David M. Tudor Drama & Politics: A Critical Approach to Topical Meaning. 1968. $10.00 Hdbd. (ISBN 0-674-91230-6). Harvard Univ. Pr., MA.

Blackburn, Ruth H. Biblical Drama Under the Tudors. 1970. price "n.g." Humanities Pr., NY.

Bluestone, Max & Rabkin, Norman. Shakespeare's Contemporaries: Modern Studies in English Renaissance Drama. 2nd ed. 1970. (ISBN 0-13-807677-4). $4.95 pa. (ISBN 0-13-807651-0). Prentice-Hall, NY.

Boas, Frederick S. Introduction to Stuart Drama. 1946. $6.75 Hdbd. (ISBN 0-19-811507-5). Oxford Univ. Pr., NY.

Boas, Frederick S. Introduction to Tudor Drama. 1933. $3.40 Hdbd. (ISBN 0-19-811508-3). Oxford Univ. Pr., NY.

Boas, Frederick S. Queen Elizabeth in Drama & Related Studies. (Select Bibliographies Reprint Ser). 1950. $9.50 Hdbd. (ISBN 0-8369-5397-5). Books for Libraries, NY.

Boas, Frederick S. Shakespeare & His Predecessors. 1969. $18.50 Hdbd. (ISBN 0-8371-0316-9). Greenwood Pr., CT.

Boas, Frederick S. Shakespeare & His Predecessors. 1968. (1902) $8.50 Hdbd. (ISBN 0-87752-011-9), Gordian Pr., NY.

Boas, Frederick S. Shakespeare & His Predecessors. (Studies in Shakespeare Ser., No. 24). 1969. (1896) $9.95 Hdbd. (ISBN 0-8383-0914-3). Haskell House Publ., NY.

Boas, Frederick S. Shakespeare & the Universities. 1923. $12.50 Hdbd. Benjamin Blom, NY.

Boas, Frederick S. University Drama in the Tudor Age. 1914. $12.50 Hdbd. Benjamin Blom, NY.

Boas, Frederick S., ed. Five Pre-Shakespearean Comedies. 1970. $1.75 pa. (ISBN 0-19-281085-5). Oxford Univ. Pr., NY.

Bowers, Fredson, ed. Dramatic Works in the Beaumont & Fletcher Canon, Vol. 2. 1970. $22.50 Hdbd. (ISBN 0-52i-07253-0). Cambridge Univ. Pr., NY.

Bowers, Fredson. Elizabethan Revenge Strategy. 1958. $4.75 Hdbd. Peter Smith Publ., MA.

Bowers, Fredson. Elizabethan Revenge Tragedy, Fifteen Eighty-Seven–Sixteen Forty-Two. 1940. $2.95 pa. (ISBN 0-691-01259-8, 30). Princeton Univ. Pr., NJ.

Bowers, Fredson. On Editing Shakespeare. 1966. $4.50 Hdbd. (ISBN 0-8139-0030-1); $2.45 pa. (ISBN 0-8139-0031-X). Univ. Pr. of Virginia, VA.

Bowers, Fredson. Textual & Literary Criticism. 1959. $5.00 Hdbd.; $1.65 pa. (ISBN 0-521-09407-0, 407). Cambridge Univ. Pr., NY.

Boyer, Clarence V. Villain As Hero in Elizabethan Tragedy. 1964. (1914) $10.00 Hdbd. Russell & Russell Publ., NY.

Bradbrook, Muriel C. Growth & Structure of Elizabethan Comedy. 1955. $5.50 Hdbd. Hillary House Publ., NY.

Bradbrook, Muriel C. Themes & Conventions of Elizabethan Tragedy. 1952–1960. $7.00 Hdbd.; $1.95 pa. (ISBN 0-521-09108-X, 108). Cambridge Univ. Pr., NY.

Bradford, Gamaliel. Elizabethan Women. facs ed. White, Harold O., ed. (Select Bibliographies Reprint Ser). 1936. $10.00 Hdbd. (ISBN 0-8369-5001-1). Books for Libraries, NY.

Brodwin, Lenora L. Elizabethan Love Tragedy: 1587–1625. 1971. $12.50 Hdbd.; $12.50 text ed. (ISBN 0-8147-0955-9). New York Univ. Pr., NY.

Brooke, C. F. Tudor Drama: A History of English National Drama to the Retirement of Shakespeare. 1970. $10.50 Hdbd. (ISBN 0-208-00578-1). Shoe String Pr., CT.

Brooke, Charles F. & Paradise, Nathaniel B. English Drama, 1580–1642. 1933. text ed. $11.95 Hdbd. D. C. Heath & Co., MA.

Brooke, Rupert. John Webster & the Elizabethan Drama. 1967. (1916) $8.00 Hdbd. Russell & Russell Publ., NY.

Brown, John R. & Harris, Bernard. Jacobean Theatre. 1967. $1.65 pa. G. P. Putnam's Sons, NY.

Brown, John R. & Harris, Bernard, eds. Elizabethan Theatre. (Stratford-Upon-Avon Studies, Vol. 9). 1967. $6.95 Hdbd. St. Martin's Pr., NY.

Brown, John R. & Harris, Bernard, eds. Jacobean Theatre. (Stratford-Upon-Avon Studies, Vol. 1). 1960. $8.95. St. Martin's Pr., NY.

Bulana, M. Presentation of Time in the Elizabethan Drama. (Drama Ser., No. 39). 1969. (1912) $13.95 Hdbd. (ISBN 0-8383-0517-2). Haskell House Publ., NY.

Busby, Olive M. Studies in the Development of the Fool in Elizabethan Drama. 1923. $5.00 Hdbd. (ISBN 0-404-07849-4). AMS Pr., NY.

Busby, Olive M. Studies in the Development of the Fool in the Elizabethan Drama. 1923. $10.00 Hdbd. Folcroft Pr., PA.

Campbell, Eva M. Satire in the Early English Drama. 1914. $10.00 Hdbd. Folcroft Pr., PA.

Cardozo, J. L. Contemporary Jew in Elizabethan Drama. rev. ed. 1970. $10.00 Hdbd. (ISBN 0-87068-032-3). Ktav Publ. House, NY.

Cardozo, Jacob L. Contemporary Jew in the Elizabethan Drama. (Burt Franklin: Research & Source Works, No. 175). (1925) $18.50 Hdbd. (ISBN 0-8337-0466-4). Burt Franklin, NY.

Carpenter, Frederic I. Metaphor & Simile in Minor Elizabethan Drama. 1967. (1901) $5.75 Hdbd. (ISBN 0-87753-007-6). Phaeton Pr., NY.

Carpenter, Frederic I. Metaphor & Simile in the Minor Elizabethan Drama. 1895. $5.50 Hdbd. Folcroft Pr., PA.

Carpenter, Frederic I. Metaphor & Simile in the Minor Elizabethan Drama. 1895. $6.00 Hdbd. (ISBN 0-404-50264-4). AMS Pr., NY.

Cawley, Robert R. Voyagers & Elizabethan Drama. 1938. $17.00 pa. Kraus Reprint Co., NY.

Chambers, Edmund K. Elizabethan Stage, 4 Vols. 1923. Set—$38.50 Hdbd. (ISBN 0-19-811511-3). Oxford Univ. Pr., NY.

Clark, Eleanor G. Ralegh & Marlowe, a Study in Elizabethan Fustian. 1965. (1941) $11.50 Hdbd. Russell & Russell Publ., NY.

Clarkson, Paul S. & Warren, Clyde T. Law of Property in Shakespeare & the Elizabethan Drama. 1968. $10.00 Hdbd. (ISBN 0-87752-022-4). Gordian Pr., NY.

Clemen, Wolfgang H. English Tragedy Before Shakespeare: The Development of Dramatic Speech. Dorsch, T. S., tr. 1967. $3.50 pa. (ISBN 0-416-69750-X, 205). Barnes & Noble, NY.

Cole, Howard C. Quest of Inquiry: Some Contexts of Tudor Literature. (Backgrounds in English Literature Ser). 1971. $6.95 Hdbd.; $2.25 pa. Pegasus, NY.

Collier, John P. History of English Dramatic Poetry to the Time of Shakespeare & the Annals of the Stage to the Restoration, 3 vols. 1970. (1831) Set—$42.50 Hdbd. (ISBN 0-404-01730-4). AMS Pr., NY.

Craik, T. W. Tudor Interlude. 1958. $4.50 Hdbd. Humanities Pr., NY.

Crane, Milton. Shakespeare's Prose.

1951. $5.50 Hdbd. (ISBN 0-226-11859-2). Univ. of Chicago Pr., IL.

Creizenach, Wilhelm. English Drama in the Age of Shakespeare. 1916. $12.50 Hdbd. Folcroft Pr., PA.

Creizenach, Wilhelm. English Drama in the Age of Shakespeare. (Drama Ser., No. 39). 1969. (1916) $12.50 Hdbd. (ISBN 0-8383-0533-4). Haskell House Publ., NY.

Creizenach, Wilhelm. English Drama in the Age of Shakespeare. rev. ed. Schuster, Alfred, ed. Hugon, Cecile, tr. 1967. (1916) $15.00 Hdbd. Russell & Russell Publ., NY.

Cunliffe, John W. Influence of Seneca on Elizabethan Tragedy. 1965. (1893) $5.00 Hdbd. (ISBN 0-208-00038-0). Shoe String Pr., CT.

Cushman, L. W. Devil & the Vice in the English Dramatic Literature Before Shakespeare. (1971) $7.00 Hdbd. Humanities Pr., NY.

Doran, Madeleine. Endeavors of Art: A Study of Form in Elizabethan Drama. 1954. $2.95 pa. (ISBN 0-99-01084-8). Univ. of Wisconsin PR., WI.

Eliot, T. S. Elizabethan Essays. (Studies in Eliot Ser., No. 11). 1969. (1934) $9.95 Hdbd. (ISBN 0-8383-0542-3). Haskell House Publ., NY.

Eliot, T. S. Essays on Elizabethan Drama. pap. $1.65 Hdbd. (ISBN 0-15-629051-0). Harcourt, Brace & World, NY.

Ellison, Lee M. Early Romantic Drama at the English Court. 1917. $12.50 Hdbd. Folcroft Pr., PA.

Elze, Karl. Notes on Elizabethan Dramatists with Conjectural Emendations of the Text. 1880. $5.75 Hdbd. (ISBN 0-404-02327-4). AMS Pr., NY.

Fansler, Harriott E. Evolution of Technic in Elizabethan Tragedy. 1968. (1914) $7.50 Hdbd. (ISBN 0-87753-014-9). Phaeton Pr., NY.

Farmer, John S., ed. Lost Tudor Plays, with Some Others. 1966. (1907) $7.50 Hdbd. Barnes & Noble, NY.

Farnham, Willard. Medieval Heritage of Elizabethan Tragedy. 1936. $9.50 Hdbd. Barnes & Noble, NY.

Feldman, Sylvia D. Morality-Patterned Comedy of the Renaissance. (Proprietatibus Litterarum Ser., Practica 12). 1971. $5.50 pa. Humanities Pr., NY.

Fleay, Frederick G. Biographical Chronicle of the English Drama, 1559–1642, 2 Vols. 1962. (1891) $28.50 Hdbd. (ISBN 0-8337-1151-2). Burt Franklin, NY.

Fleay, Frederick G. Chronicle History of London Stage, 1559–1642. 1964. (1890) $18.50 Hdbd. (ISBN 0-8337-1152-0). Burt Franklin, NY.

Fleay, Frederick G. Shakespeare Manual. 1970. (1876) $14.00 Hdbd. (ISBN 0-404-02408-4). AMS Pr., NY.

Fluchere, Henri. Shakespeare. $2.75 pa. Fernhill House, NY.

Forsythe, Robert S. Relations of Shirley's Plays to the Elizabethan Drama. 1914. $12.50 Hdbd. Benjamin Blom, NY.

Fraser, Russell. War Against Poetry. 1971. $7.50 Hdbd. (ISBN 0-691-06190-4). Princeton Univ. Pr., NJ.

Freeburg, Victor O. Disguise Plots in Elizabethan Drama. 1965. $12.50 Hdbd. Benjamin Blom, NY.

Frost, D. L. School of Shakespeare: The Influence of Shakespeare on English Drama, 1600–42. 1968. $9.50 Hdbd. (8). Cambridge Univ. Pr., NY.

Gibbons, Brian. Jacobean City Comedy: A Study of Satiric Plays by Jonson, Marston & Middleton. 1968. $6.00 Hdbd. (ISBN 0-674-47000-1). Harvard Univ. Pr., MA.

Graves, Thornton S. Act Time in Elizabethan Theatres. (Studies in Drama Ser., No. 39). (1970) $2.95 pa. (ISBN 0-8383-0043-X). Haskell House Publ., NY.

Green, A. Wigfall. Inns of Court & Early English Drama. 1931. $12.50 Hdbd. Benjamin Blom, NY.

Greenfield, Thelma N. Induction in Elizabethan Drama. 1970. $6.00 Hdbd. Univ of Oregon Books, OR.

Greg, Walter W. Dramatic Documents from Elizabethan Playhouses: Stage Plots: Actors' Parts: Prompt Books, 2 Vols. 1931. $38.40 Hdbd. (ISBN 0-19-811672-1). Oxford Univ. Pr., NY.

Greg, Walter W. Pastoral Poetry & Pastoral Drama. 1959. (1906) $11.50 Hdbd. Russell & Russell Publ., NY.

Griffin, Alice V. Pageantry on the Shakespearean Stage. 1962. $2.95 pa. College & Univ. Pr., CT.

Harbage, Alfred. Cavalier Drama. 1964. (1936) $10.00 Hdbd. Russell & Russell Publ., NY.

Harbage, Alfred. Shakespeare & the Rival Traditions. 1968. (1952) $10.00 Hdbd. Barnes & Noble, NY.

Harrison, G. B. Elizabethan Plays & Players. 1956. $4.95 Hdbd. (ISBN 0-472-09002-X). Univ. of Michigan Pr., MI.

Harrison, George B. Elizabethan Plays & Players. 1956. $2.25 pa. (ISBN 0-472-06002-3, 2). Univ. of Michigan, MI.

Harrison, George B. Introducing Shakespeare. rev. ed. (Hi-Sch.). 1966. $1.75 pa. (ISBN 0-14-020043-6). Penguin Books, MD.

Harrison, George B. Shakespeare at Work, 1592–1603. 1958. $1.95 pa. (ISBN 0-472-06016-3, 16, AA). Univ. of Michigan Pr., MI.

Harrison, George B. Shakespeare's Fellows. 1923. $10.00 Hdbd. Folcroft Pr., PA.

Harrison, George B. Story of Elizabethan Drama. 1924. $10.00 Hdbd. Folcroft Pr., PA.

Herndl, George C. High Design: English Renaissance Tragedy & the Natural

Law. 1970. $8.00 Hdbd. (ISBN 0-8131-1217-6). Univ. Pr. of Kentucky, KY.

Hogrefe, Pearl. Sir Thomas More Circle: A Program of Ideas & Their Impact on Secular Drama. 1959. $6.95 Hdbd. (ISBN 0-252-72653-7). Univ. of Illinois Pr., IL.

Holmes, Elizabeth. Aspects of Elizabethan Imagery. 1966. (1929) $7.50 Hdbd. Russell & Russell Publ., NY.

Hosley, Richard, ed. Essays on Shakespeare & Elizabethan Drama in Honor of Hardin Craig. 1962. $9.50 Hdbd. (ISBN 0-8262-0014-1). Univ. of Missouri Pr., MO.

Jewkes, Wilfred T. Act Division in Elizabethan & Jacobean Plays, 1583–1616. 1958. $10.00 Hdbd. AMS Pr., NY.

Jones, Eldred. Othello's Countrymen: The African in English Renaissance Drama. 1965. $6.50 Hdbd. Oxford Univ. Pr., NY.

Joseph, Bertram L. Elizabethan Acting. 2nd ed. 1964. $5.75 Hdbd. (ISBN 0-19-811606-3). Oxford Univ. Pr., NY.

Kaufmann, Ralph J., ed. Elizabethan Drama: Modern Essays in Criticism. (Orig.). 1961. $2.95 pa. (ISBN 0-19-500696-8, GB). Oxford Univ. Pr., NY.

Kerr, Mina. Influence of Ben Jonson on English Comedy, 1598–1642. 1967. (1912) $6.00 Hdbd. (ISBN 0-87753-024-6). Phaeton Pr., NY.

Klein, David. Elizabethan Dramatists As Critics. (Illus.). 1968. (1963) $15.25

Hdbd. (ISBN 0-8371-0131-X). Greenwood Pr., CT.

Knights, Lionel C. Drama & Society in the Age of Jonson: A Study of the Economic & Social Background of the Early 17th Century & Bearing on the Works of Contemporary Dramatists. 1968. $5.00 Hdbd. Barnes & Noble, NY.

Knights, Lionel C. Drama & Society in the Age of Jonson. 1968. $2.25 pa. (ISBN 0-393-00451-1). W. W. Norton, NY.

Lawrence, W. J. Those Nut-Cracking Elizabethans. (Drama Ser., No. 39). 1970. (1935) $8.95 Hdbd. (ISBN 0-8383-0988-7). Haskell House Publ., NY.

Lawrence, William J. Pre-Restoration Stage Studies. (1967) $12.50 Hdbd. Benjamin Blom, NY.

Lawrence, William J. Speeding up Shakespeare. 1968. $12.50 Hdbd. Benjamin Blom, NY.

Lea, Kathleen M. Italian Popular Comedy: A Study in the Commedia Dell'arte, 1560–1620, with Special Reference to the English Stage, 2 Vols. 1962. (1934) Set—$17.00 Hdbd. Russell & Russell Publ., NY.

Leech, Clifford. Shakespeare's Tragedies & Other Studies in Seventeenth Century Drama. 1950. $4.25 Hdbd. Oxford Univ. Pr., NY.

Lindabury, Richard V. Study of Patriotism in the Elizabethan Drama. (Drama Ser., No. 39). 1969. (1931) $9.95 Hdbd.

(ISBN 0-8383-0584-9). Haskell House Publ., NY.

Linthicum, Marie C. Costume in the Drama of Shakespeare & His Contemporaries. 1963. (1936) $7.50 Hdbd. Russell & Russell Publ., NY.

Long, John H., ed. Music in English Renaissance Drama. $7.50 Hdbd. (ISBN 0-8131-1157-9). Univ. Pr. of Kentucky, KY.

Lucas, F. L. Seneca & Elizabethan Tragedy. (Studies in Comparative Literature Ser., No. 35). 1969. (1922) $5.95 Hdbd. (ISBN 0-8383-0668-3). Haskell House Publ., NY.

Lucas, Frank L. Seneca & the Elizabethan Tragedy. 1923. $6.50 Hdbd. Folcroft Pr., PA.

McDonald, Charles O. Rhetoric of Tragedy: Form in Stuart Drama. 1966. $7.50 Hdbd. (ISBN 0-87023-012-3). Univ. of Massachusetts Pr., MA.

Mellwraith, Archibald K., ed. Five Elizabethan Tragedies. (1971) $2.75 pa. (ISBN 0-19-281118-5). Oxford Univ. Pr., NY.

Mehl, Dieter A. Elizabethan Dumb Show: The History of a Dramatic Convention. 1965. $5.75 Hdbd. (ISBN 0-674-24700-0). Harvard Univ. Pr., MA.

Meyer, Edward S. Machiavelli & the Elizabethan Drama. 1897. $11.00 Hdbd. (ISBN 0-8337-2380-4). Burt Franklin, NY.

Miller, Edwin H. Professional Writer in Elizabethan England: A Study of Non-dramatic Literature. 1959. $8.00 Hdbd. (ISBN 0-674-71300-1). Harvard Univ. Pr., MA.

Myers, Aaron M. Representation & Misrepresentation of the Puritan in Elizabethan Drama. 1931. $12.50 Hdbd. Folcroft Pr., PA.

Nethercot, A. H. Elizabethan Plays. rev. ed. 1971. $7.50 pa. (ISBN 0-03-083030-3). Holt, Rinehart & Winston, NY.

Oras, Ants. Pause Patterns in Elizabethan & Jacobean Drama. (Humanities Monographs Ser. No. 3). 1960. $3.00 pa. (ISBN 0-8130-0170-6). Univ. of Florida Pr., FL.

Ornstein, Robert. Moral Vision of Jacobean Tragedy. 1960. $3.25 pa. (ISBN 0-299-02184-X). Univ. of Wisconsin Pr., WI.

Orsini, Gian N. T. S. Eliot & the Doctrine of Dramatic Conventions. 1954. $3.50 Hdbd. Folcroft Pr., PA.

Parr, Johnstone. Tamburlaine's Malady, & Other Essays on Astrology in Elizabethan Drama. 1971. (1953) $9.00 Hdbd. (ISBN 0-8371-5759-5). Greenwood Pr., CT.

Parrott, T. M. & Ball, R. H. Short View of Elizabethan Drama. $4.75 Hdbd. Peter Smith Publ., MA.

Parrott, Thomas M. & Ball, Robert H. Short View of Elizabethan Drama. $2.65 pa. (ISBN 0-684-71860-X, 11). Charles Scribner's Sons, NY.

Partridge, A. C. Orthography in Shakespeare & Elizabethan Drama: A Study of Colloquial Contractions, Elision, Prosody & Punctuation. 1964. $4.75 Hdbd. (ISBN 0-8032-0143-5). Univ. of Nebraska Pr., NB.

Peers, Edgar A. Elizabethan Drama & Its Mad Folk. 1914. $12.50 Hdbd. Folcroft Pr., PA.

Rabkin, Norman, ed. Reinterpretations of Elizabethan Drama. (Selected Papers from the English Institute). 1969. $5.50 Hdbd. (ISBN 0-231-03328-1). Columbia Univ. Pr., NY.

Reed, A. W. Early Tudor Drama. 1969. (1926) $9.00 Hdbd. Octagon Books, Inc., NY.

Reed, Robert R., Jr. Occult on the Tudor & Stuart Stage. 1965. $6.50 Hdbd. (ISBN 0-8158-0170-X). Christopher Publ. House, MA.

Reyher, Paul. Masques Anglais. 1909. $17.50 Hdbd. Benjamin Blom, NY.

Ribner, Irving. English History Play in the Age of Shakespeare. 1965. $5.75 Hdbd. Barnes & Noble, NY.

Righter, Anne. Shakespeare & the Idea of the Play. 1963. $5.00 Hdbd. Barnes & Noble, NY.

Righter, Anne. Shakespeare & the Idea of the Play. (1967) $1.65 pa. (ISBN 0-14-053001-0, SL1). Penguin Books, MD.

Robertson, John M. Introduction to the Study of the Shakespeare Canon. facsimile ed. (Select Bibliographies Reprint Ser). 1924. $16.50 Hdbd. (ISBN 0-8369-5268-5). Books for Libraries, NY.

Robertson, John M. Introduction to the Study of the Shakespeare Canon, Proceeding on Problem of Titus Andronicus. 1924. $17.00 Hdbd. (ISBN 0-8371-3744-6). Greenwood Pr., CT.

Rollins, Hyder E. Contribution to the History of English Commonwealth Drama. (Studies in Drama, No. 39). (1970) $3.95 pa. (ISBN 0-8383-0065-0). Haskell House Publ., NY.

Schelling, Felix E. Elizabethan Drama, 1558–1642: A History of the Drama in England, 2 Vols. 1959. (1908) Set— $25.00 Hdbd. Russell & Russell Publ., NY.

Schelling, Felix E. Elizabethan Playwrights. 1925. $12.50 Hdbd. Benjamin Blom, NY.

Schelling, Felix E. Foreign Influences in Elizabethan Plays. 1969. (1923) $12.00 Hdbd. (ISBN 0-06-107699-6). Harper-Row, NY.

Schelling, Felix E. Foreign Influences in Elizabethan Plays. 1970. (1923) $10.00 Hdbd. (ISBN 0-404-05579-6). AMS Pr., NY.

Schelling, Felix E. Foreign Influences in Elizabethan Plays. 1923. $15.00 Hdbd. Folcroft Pr., PA.

Schelling, Felix E. & Black, Matthew W., eds. Typical Elizabethan Plays. (Play Anthology Reprint Ser). 1949. $29.50 Hdbd. (ISBN 0-8369-8219-3). Books for Libraries, NY.

Schoenbaum, Samuel. Internal Evidence & Elizabethan Dramatic Authorship:

An Essay in Literary History & Method. 1966. $7.50 Hdbd. (ISBN 0-8101-0218-8). Northwestern Univ. Pr., IL.

Schucking, Levin L. Baroque Character of the Elizabethan Tragic Hero. 1938. $3.00 Hdbd. Folcroft Pr., PA.

Sharpe, Robert B. Real War of the Theatres: Shakespeare's Fellows in Rivalry with the Admiral's Men. 1935. $10.00 pa. Kraus Reprint Co., NY.

Silvette, Herbert. Doctor on the Stage: Medicine & Medical Men in Seventeenth-Century England. Butler, Francelia, ed. 1967. $7.50 Hdbd. (ISBN 0-87049-074-5). Univ. of Tennessee Pr., TN.

Simpson, Percy. Studies in Elizabethan Drama. 1955. $15.00 Hdbd. Folcroft Pr., PA.

Simpson, Percy. Theme of Revenge in Elizabethan Tragedy. 1935. $3.50 Hdbd. Folcroft Pr., PA.

Sisson, C. J. Lost Plays of Shakespeare's Age. (English Literature Ser). 1971. (1936) $9.00 Hdbd. (ISBN 0-391-00151-5). Humanities Pr., NY.

Sisson, Charles J. Elizabethan Dramatists. 1928. $8.50 Hdbd. Folcroft Pr., PA.

Slater, Gilbert. Seven Shakespeare. 1931. $15.00 Hdbd. Folcroft Pr., PA.

Small, Roscoe A. Stage-Quarrel Between Ben Jonson & the So-Called Poetasters. 1889. $9.00 Hdbd. (ISBN 0-404-06099-4). AMS Pr., NY.

Spens, Janet. Elizabethan Drama. 1970. (1922) $9.50 Hdbd. Russell & Russell Publ., NY.

Steele, Mary S. Plays & Masques at Court During the Reigns of Elizabeth, James & Charles, 1558–1642. 1968. (1926) $9.00 Hdbd. Russell & Russell Publ., NY.

Stoll, Elmer E. Poets & Playwrights: Shakespeare, Jonson, Spenser, Milton. 1930. $2.95 pa. (ISBN 0-8166-0440-1, Mp1). Univ. of Minnesota Pr., MN.

Stroup, Thomas B. Microcosmos: The Shape of the Elizabethan Play. 1965. $6.00 Hdbd. (ISBN 0-8131-1110-2). Univ. Pr. of Kentucky, KY.

Swinburne, Algernon C. Age of Shakespeare. 1908. $22.50 Hdbd. (ISBN 0-404-06314-4). AMS Pr., NY.

Sykes, H. Dugdale. Sidelights on Elizabethan Drama. 1919. $6.50 Hdbd. Folcroft Pr., PA.

Symonds, John A. Shakespeare's Predecessors in the English Drama. (1967) $9.95 Hdbd. (ISBN 0-8154-0301-1). Cooper Sq. Pr., NY.

Symonds, John A. Shakespeare's Predecessors in the English Drama. 1900. $18.75 Hdbd. (ISBN 0-8371-1154-4). Greenwood Pr., CT.

Symonds, John A. Shakespeare's Predecessors in the English Drama. 1884. $12.50 Hdbd. AMS Pr., NY.

Symons, Arthur. Studies in the Elizabethan Drama. 1920. $7.50 Hdbd. (ISBN 0-404-06331-4). AMS Pr., NY.

Thorp, Willard. Triumph of Realism in Elizabethan Drama. 1970. $6.50 text ed. (ISBN 0-87752-110-7). Gordian Pr., NY.

Thorp, William. Triumph of Realism in the Elizabethan Drama. (Drama Ser., No. 39). 1969. (1928) $5.95 Hdbd. (ISBN 0-8383-0636-5). Haskell House Publ., NY.

Tomlinson, T. B. Study of Elizabethan & Jacobean Tragedy. 1964. $6.00 Hdbd. (ISBN 0-522-83814-6). Library Assn. London, England.

Tomlinson, T. B. Study of Elizabethan & Jacobean Tragedy. $9.00 Hdbd. Cambridge Univ. Pr., NY.

Waith, Eugene, M. Herculean Hero in Marlowe, Chapman, Shakespeare & Dryden. 1962. $7.00 Hdbd. (ISBN 0-231-02506-8). Columbia Univ. Pr., NY.

Waith, Eugene M. Ideas of Greatness: Heroic Drama in England. 1971. $9.50 Hdbd. (ISBN 0-389-04181-5). Barnes & Noble, NY.

Wallace, Charles W. Evolution of the English Drama up to Shakespeare: With a History of the First Blackfriars Theatre. 1968. (1912) $8.50 Hdbd. (ISBN 0-8046-0668-4). Kennikat Pr., NY.

Wallis, Lawrence B. Fletcher, Beaumont & Company. 1968. (1947) $9.00 Hdbd. Octagon Books, Inc., NY.

West, Robert H. Invisible World: A Study of Pneumatology in Elizabethan Drama. 1969. $9.00 Hdbd. Octagon Books, Inc., NY.

White, Richard G. Memoirs of the Life of William Shakespeare. 1865. $22.50 Hdbd. (ISBN 0-404-06933-9). AMS Pr., NY.

Wickham, Glynne. Shakespeare's Dramatic Heritage: Collected Studies in Mediaeval Tudor & Shakespearean Drama. 1969. $7.50 Hdbd. Barnes & Noble, NY.

Wilson, Frank P. Elizabethan Theatre. 1955. $5.00 Hdbd. Folcroft Pr., PA.

Wilson, Frank P. English Drama, Fourteen Fighty Five–Fifteen Eighty Five. 1969. $7.00 Hdbd. (ISBN 0-19-500203-2). Oxford Univ. Pr., NY.

Winslow, Ola E. Low Comedy As a Structural Element in English Drama from the Beginnings to 1642. 1926. $12.50 Hdbd. Folcroft Pr., PA.

Witherspoon, Alexander M. Influence of Robert Garnier on Elizabethan Drama. (Yale Studies in English Ser, No. 65). 1968. $6.00 Hdbd. Shoe String Pr., CT.

Wynne, Arnold. Growth of English Drama. (Essay Index Reprint Ser). 1914. $9.75 Hdbd. (ISBN 0-8369-1014-1). Books for Libraries, NY.

Yearsley, Macleod. Doctors in Elizabethan Drama. 1933. $10.00 Hdbd. Folcroft Pr., PA.

National (England)—Periods: 17th Century–Restoration

Allen, Ned B. Sources of John Dryden's Comedies. 1967. (1935) $7.50 Hdbd. (ISBN 0-87752-002-X). Gordian Pr., NY.

Barber, C. L. Idea of Honour in the English Drama 1591–1700. 1957. $27.50 Hdbd. Lansdowne Pr., PA.

Bentley, Gerald E. Seventeenth-Century Stage: A Collection of Critical Essays. (Patterns of Literary Criticism Ser., No. 6). 1968. $9.75 Hdbd. (ISBN 0-8020-1561-1); $2.95 pa. (ISBN 0-8020-1560-3). Univ. of Toronto Pr., CAN.

Birdsall, Virginia O. Wild Civility: The English Comic Spirit on the Restoration Stage. 1971. $10.50 Hdbd. (ISBN 0-253-19037-1). Indiana Univ. Pr., IN.

Boswell, Eleanor. Restoration Court Stage, 1660–1702. 1932. $12.50 Hdbd. Benjamin Blom, NY.

Boswell, Eleanore. Restoration Court Stage Sixteen Sixty to Seventeen Two. 1966. $8.50 Hdbd. Barnes & Noble, NY.

Brown, John R. & Harris, Bernard. Restoration Theatre. 1967. $1.65 pa. G. P. Putnam's Sons, NY.

Brown, John R. & Harris, Bernard, eds. Restoration Theatre. (Stratford-Upon-Avon Studies, Vol. 6). 1965. $5.75 Hdbd. St. Martin's Pr., NY.

Chase, Lewis N. English Heroic Play: A Critical Description of the Rhymed Tragedy of the Restoration. 1965. (1903) $8.50 Hdbd. Russell & Russell Publ., NY.

Davis, Joe L. Sons of Ben: Jonsonian Comedy in Caroline England. 1967. $8.95 Hdbd. (ISBN 0-8143-1302-7). Wayne St. Univ. Pr., MI.

Deane, Cecil V. Dramatic Theory & the Rhymed Heroic Play. 1931. $6.50 Hdbd. Folcroft Pr., PA.

Deane, Cecil V. Dramatic Theory & the Rhymed Heroic Play. 1967. $7.50 Hdbd. Barnes & Noble, NY.

Dobree, Bonamy. Restoration Comedy, 1660–1720. 1924. $4.00 Hdbd. (ISBN 0-19-811527-X). Oxford Univ. Pr., NY.

Dobree, Bonamy. Restoration Tragedy, 1660–1720. 1929. $4.00 Hdbd. (ISBN 0-19-811528-8). Oxford Univ. Pr., NY.

Falle, G. G., ed. Three Restoration Comedies. $1.50 pa. Odyssey Pr., NY.

Fujimura, Thomas H. Restoration Comedy of Wit. 1968. (1952) $6.00 Hdbd. Barnes & Noble, NY.

Gagen, Jean E. New Woman. $3.50 Hdbd. Twayne Publ., NY.

Harbage, Alfred. Cavalier Drama. 1964. (1936) $10.00 Hdbd. Russell & Russell Publ., NY.

Krutch, Joseph W. Comedy & Conscience After the Restoration. rev. ed. 1924. $2.75 pa. (ISBN 0-231-08516-8, 16). Columbia Univ. Pr., NY.

Krutch, Joseph W. Comedy & Conscience After the Restoration. (1924, 1949, 1967). $8.50 Hdbd. Russell & Russell Publ., NY.

Lever, J. W. Tragedy of State. 1971. $6.50 Hdbd. (ISBN 0-416-08140-1). Barnes & Noble, NY.

Loftis, John. Comedy & Society from Congreve to Fielding. (Stanford Studies in Language & Literature). 1959. $5.75 Hdbd. (ISBN 0-8047-0591-7). Stanford Univ. Pr., CA.

Loftis, John. Politics of Drama in Augustan England. 1963. $4.80 Hdbd. (ISBN 0-19-811611-X). Oxford Univ. Pr., NY.

Loftis, John. Restoration Drama: Modern Essays in Criticism. (Hi-Sch.). 1966. $2.95 pa. (ISBN 0-19-500728-X). Oxford Univ. Pr., NY.

Lynch, Kathleen M. Social Mode of Restoration Comedy. 1965. $7.00 Hdbd. Octagon Books, Inc., NY.

McCall, John. Monarch Literature Notes on Eighteenth Century Restoration Plays. $1.95 pa. Monarch Pr., NY.

Miles, Dudley H. Influence of Moliere on Restoration Comedy. (1971) $10.00 Hdbd. (ISBN 0-374-95652-9). Octagon Books, Inc., NY.

Miner, Earl, ed. Restoration Dramatists: A Collection of Critical Essays. (Twentieth Century Views Ser). $1.95 pa. (ISBN 0-13-774901-5). Prentice-Hall, NY.

Miner, Earl, ed. Restoration Dramatists: A Collection of Critical Essays. $5.95 Hdbd. (ISBN 0-13-774901-5). Prentice-Hall, NY.

Muir, Kenneth. Comedy of Manners. 1970. $4.50 Hdbd.; $2.00 pa. Hutchinson Univ. Library, NY.

Nethercot, A. H. Stuart Plays. rev. & enl. ed. 1971. $8.95 text ed. (ISBN 0-03-083029-X). Holt, Rinehart & Winston, NY.

Nettleton, George H. English Drama of the Restoration & Eighteenth Century, 1642–1780. 1932. $7.95 Hdbd. (ISBN 0-8154-0162-0). Cooper Sq. Pr., NY.

Nicoll, Allardyce. Restoration Drama. (History of English Drama—Vol. 1). $14.50 Hdbd. Cambridge Univ. Pr., NY.

Noyes, Robert G. Neglected Muse: Restoration & Eighteenth-Century Tragedy in the Novel 1740–1780. 1958. $4.00 Hdbd. (ISBN 0-87057-052-8). Brown Univ. Pr., RI.

Palmer, John L. Comedy of Manners. 1962. (1913) $8.50 Hdbd. Russell & Russell Publ., NY.

Pendlebury, Bevis J. Dryden's Heroic Plays, A Study of the Origins. 1967. (1923) $6.50 Hdbd. Russell & Russell Publ., NY.

Perry, Henry T. Comic Spirit in Restoration Drama. 1962. (1925) $7.00 Hdbd. Russell & Russell Publ., NY.

Rosenfield, Sybil. Strolling Players & Drama in the Provinces 1660–1765. 1939. $12.50 Hdbd. Benjamin Blom, NY.

Schneider, Ben R., Jr. Ethos of Restoration Comedy. 1971. $8.50 Hdbd. (ISBN 0-252-00151-6). Univ. of Illinois Pr., IL.

Sharma, R. C. Themes & Conventions in the Comedy of Manners. 1965. $17.50 Hdbd. Folcroft Pr., PA.

Sherwood, Margaret P. Dryden's Dramatic Theory & Practice. 1966. (1898) $7.00 Hdbd. Russell & Russell Publ., NY.

Singh, Sarup. Theory of Drama in the Restoration Period. 1963. $17.50 Hdbd. Folcroft Pr., PA.

Sprague, Arthur C. Beaumont & Fletcher on the Reformation Stage. 1926. $12.50 Hdbd. Benjamin Blom, NY.

Summers, Montague. Playhouse of Pepys. 1964. $13.50 Hdbd. Humanities Pr., NY.

Summers, Montague. Restoration Theater. $13.50 Hdbd. Humanities Pr., NY.

Underwood, Dale. Etherege & the Seventeenth-Century Comedy of Manners. (Yale Studies in English No. 135). 1969. (1957) $5.50 Hdbd. (ISBN 0-208-00764-4). Shoe String Pr., CT.

Waith, Eugene M. Ideas of Greatness: Heroic Drama in England. 1971. $9.50 Hdbd. (ISBN 0-389-04181-5). Barnes & Noble, NY.

Wilcox, John. Relation of Moliere to the Restoration Comedy. 1938. $12.50 Hdbd. Benjamin Blom, NY.

Wilson, John H. Influence of Beaumont & Fletcher on Restoration Drama. Drama. Ser., No. 39). 1969. lib. bdg. $7.95 Hdbd. (ISBN 0-8383-0645-4). Haskell House Publ., NY.

Wilson, John H. Influence of Beaumont & Fletcher on the Restoration Stage.

(1967) $8.50 Hdbd. Benjamin Blom, NY.

Wilson, John H. Preface to Restoration Drama. 1968. (1965) $6.00 Hdbd. (ISBN 0-674-69950-5). Harvard Univ. Pr., MA.

Wilson, John H. Preface to Restoration Drama. $3.95 pa. Houghton-Mifflin, NY.

National (England)—Periods: 18th Century

Bateson, Frederick W. English Comic Drama, 1700–1750. 1963. (1929) $8.00 Hdbd. Russell & Russell Publ., NY.

Bernbaum, Ernest. The Drama of Sensibility: A Sketch of the History of English Comedy and Domestic Tragedy. $5.00 Hdbd. Peter Smith Publ., MA.

Boas, Frederick S. Introduction to Eighteenth Century Drama: 1700–1780. 1953. $6.75 Hdbd. (ISBN 0-19-811505-9). Oxford Univ. Pr., NY.

Clarke, T. Blake. Oriental England. 1969. $7.50 Hdbd. Octagon Books, Inc.

Gagen, Jean E. New Woman. $3.50 Hdbd. Twayne Publ., NY.

Gagey, Edmond M. Ballad Opera. 1937. $12.50 Hdbd. Benjamin Blom, NY.

Goldstein, Malcom. Pope & the Augustan Stage. 1958. $10.00 Hdbd. (ISBN 0-404-51827-3). AMS Pr., NY.

Green, Clarence C. Neo-Classic Theory of Tragedy in England During the 18th

Century. 1934. $12.50 Hdbd. Benjamin Blom, NY.

Kinne, Willard A. Revivals & Importations of French Comedies in England, 1749–1800. 1939. $10.00 Hdbd. (ISBN 0-404-03705-4). AMS Pr., NY.

Loftis, John. Comedy & Society from Congreve to Fielding. (Stanford Studies in Language & Literature). 1959. $5.75 Hdbd. (ISBN 0-8047-0591-7). Stanford Univ. Pr., CA.

Loftis, John. Politics of Drama in Augustan England. 1963. $4.80 Hdbd. (ISBN 0-19-811611-X). Oxford Univ. Pr., NY.

Nettleton, George H. English Drama of the Restoration & Eighteenth Century. 1642–1780. 1932. $7.95 Hdbd. (ISBN 0-8154-0162-0). Cooper Sq. Pr., NY.

Nolte, Fred O. Early Middle Class Drama. 1935. $12.50 Hdbd. Folcroft Pr., PA.

Noyes, Robert G. Neglected Muse: Restoration & Eighteenth-Century Tragedy in the Novel 1740–1780. 1958. $4.00 Hdbd. (ISBN 0-87057-052-8). Brown Univ. Pr., RI.

Rosenfeld, Sybil. Strolling Players & Drama in the Provinces, 1660–1765. (1970) $11.00 Hdbd. Octagon Books, Inc., NY.

Rosenfield, Sybil. Strolling Players & Drama in the Provinces 1660–1765. 1939. $12.50 Hdbd. Benjamin Blom, NY.

Sawyer, Newell W. Comedy of Manners from Sheridan to Maugham. 1961. $1.95 pa. (ISBN 0-498-04057-7). A. S. Barnes, NY.

Trussler, Simon. Burlesque Plays of the Eighteenth Century. 1969. $3.25 pa. (ISBN 0-19-281055-3). Oxford Univ. Pr., NY.

Wurzbach, Natascha, ed. British Theatre: Eighteenth-Century English Drama, 20 Vols. 1969. Set—$470.00 Hdbd. Johnson Reprint Corp., NY.

National (England)—Periods: 19th Century

Agate, James. These Were Actors: Extracts from a Newspaper Cutting Book, 1811–1833. 1943. $10.75 Hdbd. Benjamin Blom, NY.

Booth, Michael. English Melodrama. 1965. $6.00 Hdbd. Fernhill House, NY.

Chew, Samuel C. Dramas of Lord Byron. 1964. (1915) $8.00 Hdbd. Russell & Russell Publ., NY.

Chew, Samuel C. Dramas of Lord Byron: A Critical Study. 1970. (1915) $8.00 Hdbd. (ISBN 0-403-00552-3). Scholarly Pr., MI.

Clark, Barrett H. British & American Drama of To-Day. 1921. $10.00 Hdbd. (ISBN 0-404-01547-6). AMS Pr., NY.

Cordell, Richard A. Henry Arthur Jones & the Modern Drama. 1968. (1932) $9.00 Hdbd. (ISBN 0-8046-0089-9). Kennikat Pr., NY.

Cunliffe, John W. Modern English Playwrights. (Essay and General Literature Index Reprint Ser). 1969. (1927) $9.25 Hdbd. (ISBN 0-8046-0553-X). Kennikat Pr., NY.

Filon, Augustin. English Stage. Whyte, Frederic, tr. 1970. (1897) $10.00 Hdbd. (ISBN 0-8046-0753-2). Kennikat Pr., NY.

Filon, Pierre M. English Stage. 1897. $10.75 Hdbd. Benjamin Blom, NY.

Fletcher, Richard. English Romantic Drama, 1795-1843. 1967. $6.50 Hdbd. (ISBN 0-682-44127-9). Exposition Pr., NY.

Howe, Percival P., ed. Dramatic Portraits. 1969. (1913) $10.00 Hdbd. (ISBN 0-8046-0615-3). Kennikat Pr., NY.

Morgan, Arthur E. Tendencies of Modern English Drama. (Essay Index Reprint Ser). 1923. $9.50 Hdbd. (ISBN 0-8369-1061-3). Books for Libraries, NY.

Reynolds, Ernest. Early Victorian Drama. 1936. $7.50 Hdbd. Benjamin Blom, NY.

Rowell, George. Victorian Theatre: A Survey. 1967. $6.50 Hdbd. (ISBN 0-19-811653-5). Oxford Univ. Pr., NY.

Sawyer, Newell W. Comedy of Manners from Sheridan to Maugham. 1961. $1.95 pa. (ISBN 0-498-04057-7). A. S. Barnes, NY.

Taylor, John R. Rise & Fall of the Well Made Play. 1969. (1967) $5.75 Hdbd. (ISBN 0-8090-8230-6); $1.95 pa. (ISBN 0-8090-0546-8). Hill & Wang, NY.

Tolles, Winton. Tom Taylor & the Victorian Drama. 1940. $17.00 Hdbd. (ISBN 0-404-06474-4). AMS Pr., NY.

Van Der Vat, Daniel G. Fabulous Opera. (Studies in Comparative Literature Ser., No. 35). 1969. (1936) $10.95 Hdbd. (ISBN 0-8383-0724-8). Haskell House Publ., NY.

Watson, Ernest B. Sheridan to Robertson: A Study of the Nineteenth-Century London Stage. 1926. $12.50 Hdbd. Benjamin Blom, NY.

National (England)—Periods: 20th Century

Agate, James. Amazing Theatre. 1939. $12.50 Hdbd. Benjamin Blom, NY.

Agate, James. At Half-Past Eight: Essays on the Theatre 1921-1922. 1923. $10.75 Hdbd. Benjamin Blom, NY.

Agate, James. Contemporary Theatre, Nineteen Twenty-Five. 1926. $10.75 Hdbd. Benjamin Blom, NY.

Agate, James. Contemporary Theatre, Nineteen Twenty-Four. 1925. $10.75 Hdbd. Benjamin Blom, NY.

Agate, James. Contemporary Theatre, Nineteen Twenty-Six. 1927. $12.50 Hdbd. Benjamin Blom, NY.

Agate, James. Contemporary Theatre, Nineteen Twenty-Three. 1924. $10.75 Hdbd. Benjamin Blom, NY.

Agate, James. First Nights. 1934. $12.50 Hdbd. Benjamin Blom, NY.

Agate, James. My Theatre Talks. 1933. $10.75 Hdbd. Benjamin Blom, NY.

Agate, James E. Alarums & Excursions. (Essay Index Reprint Ser). 1922. $9.75 Hdbd. (ISBN 0-8369-0138-X). Books for Libraries, NY.

Agate, James E. Short View of the English Stage, 1900–1926. (Select Bibliographies Reprint Ser). 1926. $8.00 Hdbd. (ISBN 0-8369-5037-2). Books for Libraries, NY.

Bickley, Francis. J. M. Synge & the Irish Dramatic Movement. 1968. (1912) $6.50 Hdbd. Russell & Russell Publ., NY.

Bickley, Francis. J. M. Synge & the Irish Dramatic Movement. 1912. $5.00 Hdbd. Folcroft Pr., PA.

Brown, J. Modern British Dramatists: Collection of Critical Essays. $5.95 Hdbd. (ISBN 0-13-588053-X). Prentice-Hall, NY.

Brown, John R., ed. Modern British Dramatists: A Collection of Critical Essays. (Twentieth Century Views). (Orig.). 1968. $1.95 pa. (ISBN 0-13-588046-7). Prentice-Hall, NY.

Brown, John R. & Harris, Bernard, eds. Contemporary Theater. (Stratford-Upon-Avon Studies, Vol. 4). 1963. $5.75 Hdbd. St. Martin's Pr., NY.

Clark, Barrett H. British & American

Drama of To-Day. 1921. $10.00 Hdbd. (ISBN 0-404-01547-6). AMS Pr., NY.

Cordell, Richard A. Henry Arthur Jones & the Modern Drama. 1968. (1932) $9.00 Hdbd. (ISBN 0-8046-0089-9). Kennikat Pr., NY.

Cunliffe, John W. Modern English Playwrights. (Essay and General Literature Index Reprint Ser). 1969. (1927) $9.25 Hdbd. (ISBN 0-8046-0553-X). Kennikat Pr., NY.

Darlington, William A. Literature in the Theatre, & Other Essays. (Essay Index Reprint Ser). 1925. $9.00 Hdbd. (ISBN 0-8369-0362-5). Books for Libraries, NY.

Darlington, William A. Through the Fourth Wall. (Essay Index Reprint Ser). 1922. $9.00 Hdbd. (ISBN 0-8369-0363-3). Books for Libraries, NY.

Donoghue, Denis. Third Voice: Modern British & American Verse Drama. $7.50 Hdbd. (ISBN 0-691-06130-0); $1.95 pa. (ISBN 0-691-01285-7, 64). Princeton Univ. Pr., NJ.

Dooley, Roger B. Monarch Literature Notes on Modern British & Irish Drama. $1.00 pa. Monarch Pr., NY.

Ellehauge, Martin. Striking Figures Among Modern English Dramatists. 1931. $15.00 Hdbd. Folcroft Pr., PA.

Ellis-Fermor, Una. Irish Dramatic Movement. 2nd ed. 1967. $2.75 pa. (ISBN 0-416-69740-2, 204). Barnes & Noble, NY.

Howe, Percival P., ed. Dramatic Portraits. 1969. (1913) $10.00 Hdbd. (ISBN 0-8046-0615-3). Kennikat Pr., NY.

Mansfield, Katherine. Novels & Novelists. Murry, John M., ed. 1959. $1.65 pa. (ISBN 0-8070-6457-2). Beacon Pr., NY.

Marowitz, Charles & Trussler, Simon, eds. Theatre at Work: Playwrights & Productions in the Modern British Theatre. 1968. $5.00 Hdbd. (ISBN 0-8090-9270-0). Hill & Wang, NY.

Mills, John A. Language & Laughter: Comic Diction in the Plays of Bernard Shaw. 1969. $6.50 Hdbd. (ISBN 0-8165-0182-3). Univ. of Arizona Pr., AZ.

Morgan, Arthur E. Tendencies of Modern English Drama. (Essay Index Reprint Ser). 1923. $9.50 Hdbd. (ISBN 0-8369-1061-3). Books for Libraries, NY.

Popkin, Henry. Modern British Drama. 1969. text ed. $3.95 Hdbd. Grove Pr., NY.

Sawyer, Newell W. Comedy of Manners from Sheridan to Maugham. 1961. $1.95 pa. (ISBN 0-498-04057-7). A. S. Barnes, NY.

Sutton, Graham. Some Contemporary Dramatists. 1925. $7.50 Hdbd. (ISBN 0-8046-0452-5). Kennikat Pr., NY.

Taylor, John R. Angry Theatre: New British Drama. rev & enl. ed. 1969. $7.50 Hdbd. (ISBN 0-8090-2663-5). Hill & Wang, NY.

Taylor, John R. Rise & Fall of the Well Made Play. 1969. (1967) $5.75 Hdbd. (ISBN 0-8090-8230-6). $1.95 pa. (ISBN 0-8090-0546-8). Hill & Wang, NY.

Thouless, Priscilla. Modern Poetic Drama. (Essay Index Reprint Ser). 1968. (1934) $8.50 Hdbd. (ISBN 0-8369-0942-9). Books for Libraries, NY.

Weales, Gerald. Religion in Modern English Drama. 1961. $9.00 Hdbd. (ISBN 0-8122-7267-6). Univ. of Pennsylvania Pr., PA.

Wickham, Glynne. Drama in a World of Science. 1962. $5.00 Hdbd. (ISBN 0-8020-1198-5). Univ. of Toronto Pr., CAN.

National (France)

Affron, Charles. Stage for Poets: Studies in the Theatre of Hugo & Musset. 1971. $9.50 text ed. (ISBN 0-691-06201-3). Princeton Univ. Pr., NJ.

Allard, Louis. Comedie De Moeurs En France Au Dixneuvieme Siecle, Vol. 1. 1923. $20.00 pa. Kraus Reprint Co., NY.

Arvin, Neil C. Eugene Scribe & the French Theatre, 1815–1860. 1924. $12.50 Hdbd. Benjamin Blom, NY.

Bermel, Albert, ed. Genius of the French Theater: Imaginary Invalid, Andromache, Barber of Seville, Hernani, Pots of Money, Romantics, Songs of Songs, Lark. 1961. $0.95 pa. New American Library, NY.

Bishop, Thomas. Pirandello & the French Theater. 1970. $6.95 Hdbd. (ISBN 0-8147-0047-0); $2.25 pa. (ISBN 0-8147-0048-9). New York University Pr., NY.

Carnahan, David H. Prologue in the Old French & Provencal Mystery. (French Literature Ser., No. 45). 1969. (1905) $9.95 Hdbd. (ISBN 0-8383-0519-9). Haskell House Publ., NY.

Chasles, Emile. Comedie En France Au Seizieme Siecle. 1968. (1862) $15.00 Hdbd. (ISBN 0-8337-0546-6). Burt Franklin, NY.

Chiari, Joseph. Contemporary French Theatre: The Flight from Naturalism. 1970. $8.00 text ed. (ISBN 0-87752-126-3). Gordian Pr., NY.

Daniel, May. French Drama of the Unspoken. 1953. $15.00 Hdbd. Folcroft Pr., PA.

Davis, James H., Jr. Tragic Theory & the Eighteenth-Century French Critics. (Romance Languages & Literatures Studies Ser). 1967. $5.00 pa. (ISBN 0-8078-9068-5). Univ. of North Carolina Pr., NC.

Fowlie, Wallace. Dionysus in Paris: A Guide to Contemporary French Theatre. $5.00 Hdbd. Peter Smith Publ., MA.

Frank, Grace. Medieval French Drama. 1954. $8.00 Hdbd. (ISBN 0-19-815317-1). Oxford Univ. Pr., NY.

Frederick, Edna C. Plot & Its Construction in Eighteenth Century Criticism of French Comedy. (1934) $15.00 Hdbd. (ISBN 0-8337-4118-7). Burt Franklin, NY.

Green, Frederick C. Literary Ideas in Eighteenth Century France & England. 1965. $9.50 Hdbd. (ISBN 0-8044-2299-0). Frederick Ungar, NY.

Griffiths, Richard. Dramatic Technique of Antoine De Montchrestien: Rhetoric & Style in French Renaissance Tragedy. 1970. $9.75 Hdbd. (ISBN 0-19-815395-3). Oxford Univ. Pr., NY.

Grossvogel, David I. Twentieth Century French Drama. Orig. Title: Self-Conscious Stage in Modern French Drama. 1958. $2.25 pa. (ISBN 0-231-08522-2, 22). Columbia Univ. Pr., NY.

Grossvogel, David I. Twentieth Century French Drama. 1966. (1961) $7.50 Hdbd. (ISBN 0-87752-048-8). Gordian Pr., NY.

Guicharnaud, Jacques. Modern French Theatre: From Giraudoux to Genet. rev. ed. 1967. $10.00 Hdbd. (ISBN 0-300-00524-5); $2.75 pa. (ISBN 0-300-00106-1, Y51) Yale Univ. Pr., CT.

Harvey, H. G. Theatre of the Basoche: The Contribution of the Law Societies to French Medieval Comedy. 1941. $12.00 pa. Kraus Reprint Co., NY.

Hawkins, Frederick W. Annals of the French Stage from Its Origin to the Death of Racine, 2 Vols. (Drama Ser. No. 39). 1969. (1884) $23.95 Hdbd.

(ISBN 0-8383-0161-4). Haskell House Publ., NY.

Hawkins, Frederick W. Annals of the French Stage from Its Origin to the Death of Racine. 1968. (1884) $23.95 Hdbd. Scholarly Pr., MI.

Hawkins, Frederick W. Annals of the French Stage from Its Origin to the Death of Racine, 2 Vols. 1969. (1884) $26.75 Hdbd. Greenwood Pr., CT.

Hawkins, Frederick W. French Stage in the Eighteenth Century, 2 Vols. (Studies in Drama Ser., No. 39). 1969. (1888) Set lib bdg.—$24.95 Hdbd. (ISBN 0-8383-0162-2). Haskell House Publ., NY.

Hawkins, Frederick W. French Stage in the Eighteenth Century, 2 Vols. rev. ed. 1968. (1888) Set—$24.95 Hdbd. (ISBN 0-403-00085-8). Scholarly Pr., MI.

Hawkins, Frederick W. French Stage in the Eighteenth Century, 2 Vols. 1969. (1888) $29.00 Hdbd. (ISBN 0-8371-2746-7). Greenwood Pr., CT.

Hobson, Harold. French Theatre Today. 1953. $8.75 Hdbd. Benjamin Blom, NY.

Jeffery, Brian. French Renaissance Comedy, Fifteen Fifty-Two to Sixteen Thirty. 1969. $7.25 Hdbd. (ISBN 0-19-815391-0). Oxford Univ. Pr., NY.

Jones, Robert E. Alienated Hero in Modern French Drama. 1962. $4.00 pa. (ISBN 0-8203-0014-4). Univ. of Georgia Pr., GA.

Jourdain, Eleanor F. Dramatic Theory & Practice in France 1690–1808. 1968. $12.50 Hdbd. Benjamin Blom, NY.

Knowles, Dorothy. French Drama of the Inter-War Years, 1918–39. 1968. $6.00 Hdbd. Barnes & Noble, NY.

Kurz, Harry. European Characters in French Drama of the Eighteenth Century. 1916. $10.00 Hdbd. (ISBN 0-404-50617-8). AMS Pr., NY.

Lancaster, Henry C. French Tragi-Comedy. 1966. (1907) $6.00 Hdbd. (ISBN 0-87752-059-3). Gordian Pr., NY.

Lancaster, Henry C. History of French Dramatic Literature in the Seventeenth Century, 9 vols. Incl. Pt. 1, Vol. 1. The Classical Period. 1610–1634. $12.50 Hdbd.; Pt. 1, Vol. 2. The Pre-Classical Period. 1610–1634. $12.50 Hdbd.; Pt. 2, Vol. 1. The Period of Corneille. 1635–1651. $12.50 Hdbd.; Pt. 2, Vol. 2. The Period of Corneille. 1635–1651. $14.00 Hdbd.; Pt. 3, Vol. 1. The Period of Moliere. 1652–1672. $12.50 Hdbd.; Pt. 3, Vol. 2. The Period of Moliere. 1652–1672. $14.00 Hdbd.; Pt. 4, Vol. 1. The Period of Racine. 1673–1700. $14.00 Hdbd.; Pt. 4, Vol. 2. The Period of Racine. 1673–1700. $14.00 Hdbd.; Pt. 5. Recapitulation. 1610–1700. $10.00 Hdbd. 1966. (1929) Set—$100.00 Hdbd. (ISBN 0-87752-060-7). Gordian Pr., NY.

Lanson, Gustave. Esquisse D'une Histoire De la Tragedie Francaise. 1920. $11.50 Hdbd. (ISBN 0-404-50627-5). AMS Pr., NY.

Lemaitre, Jules. Theatrical Impressions. Whyte, Frederic, ed. $12.00 Hdbd. Benjamin Blom, NY.

Lockert, Lacy. Studies in French: Classical Tragedy. 1958. $7.50 Hdbd. (ISBN 0-8265-1049-3). Vanderbilt Univ. Pr., TN.

Lough, John. Paris Theatre Audiences in the Seventeenth & Eighteenth Centuries. 1957. $9.00 Hdbd. (ISBN 0-19-713112-3). Oxford Univ. Pr., NY.

McKean, Sr. M. Faith. Interplay of Realistic & Flamboyant Art Elements in the French Mysteries. (Catholic University of America Studies in Romance Languages & Literatures Ser). 1969. (1959) $12.50 Hdbd. (ISBN 0-404-50360-8). AMS Pr., NY.

Marsan, Jules. Pastorale Dramatique En France a la Fin Du 16ieme & Au Commencement Du 17ieme Siecle. (Research & Source Works Ser., No. 745). 1971. (1905) $25.00 Hdbd. (ISBN 0-8337-4254-X). Burt Franklin, NY.

Matthews, Brander. French Dramatists of the Nineteenth Century. 1968. $12.50 Hdbd. Benjamin Blom, NY.

Moore, Will G. Classical Drama of France. 1971. $4.00 Hdbd.; $1.95 pa. Oxford Univ. Pr., NY.

Nolte, Fred O. Early Middle Class Drama. 1935. $12.50 Hdbd. Folcroft Pr., PA.

Norman, Hilda. Swindlers & Rogues in French Drama. 1968. Repr. $9.00 Hdbd. (ISBN 0-8046-0337-5). Kennikat Pr., NY.

Pafaict, F. & Pafaict, C. Histoire Du Theatre Francois Depuis Son Origine Jusqu'a Present, 15 Vols. 1966. (1749) $190.00 Hdbd. (ISBN 0-8337-2660-9). Burt Franklin, NY.

Petersen, Christine E. Doctor in French Drama: 1700–1775. 1938. $9.50 Hdbd. (ISBN 0-404-04996-6). AMS Pr., NY.

Pronko, Leonard C. Avant-Garde: The Experimental Theater in France. 1962. $6.50 Hdbd. (ISBN 0-520-01038-8); $1.50 pa. (ISBN 0-520-01039-6, 96). Univ. of California Pr., CA.

Reiss, T. J. Toward Dramatic Illusion: Theatrical Technique & Meaning from Hardy to Horace. (Yale Romanic Studies, 2nd Ser., No. 22). 1971. $7.50 Hdbd. (ISBN 0-300-01328-0). Yale Univ. Pr., CT.

Rhodes, Solomon A. Contemporary French Theater. (Fr). 1942. $6.95 text ed. (ISBN 0-390-73446-2). Appleton-Century-Crofts, NY.

Roaten, Darnell. Structural Forms in the French Theater. 1960. $7.00 Hdbd. (ISBN 0-8122-7230-7). Univ. of Pennsylvania Pr., PA.

Sherrell, Richard E. Human Image: Avant-Garde & Christian. 1969. $4.95 Hdbd. (ISBN 0-8042-1965-6). John Knox Pr., VA.

Smith, Hugh A. Main Currents of Modern French Drama. (Essay Index Reprint Ser). 1925. $11.75 Hdbd.

(ISBN 0-8369-0883-X). Books for Libraries, NY.

Wade, Ira O. Philosophie in the French Drama of the Eighteenth Century. 1926. $6.50 pa. Kraus Reprint Co., NY.

Waxman, Samuel M. Antoine & the Theatre Libre. $10.75 Hdbd. Benjamin Blom, NY.

Whiting, B. J. Proverbs in the Earlier English Drama. 1969. (1938) $15.00 Hdbd. Octagon Books, NY.

Translations

Benedikt, Michael & Wellwarth, George E., eds. Modern French Theatre: The Avant-Garde, Dada & Surrealism. 1964. $2.95 pa. (ISBN 0-525-47176-6). E. P. Dutton, NY.

National (Germany)

Bauland, Peter. Hooded Eagle: Modern German Drama on the New York Stage. 1968. $9.00 Hdbd. (ISBN 0-8156-2119-1). Syracuse Univ. Pr., NY.

Diebold, Bernhard. Anarchie Im Drama. 1971. (1928) $22.50 Hdbd. Johnson Reprint Corp., NY.

Dohn, Walter. Jahr 1848 Im Deutschen Drama und Epos. (1912) $15.00 pa. Johnson Reprint Corp., NY.

Garten, H. F. Modern German Drama. 1962. $2.45 pa. Grove Pr., NY.

Garvin, W. Development of the Comic Figure. (Studies in Comparative Literature, No. 35). 1970. (1923) $6.95 Hdbd.

(ISBN 0-8383-1087-7). Haskell House Publ., NY.

Glatzel, Max. Julius Leopold Klein Als Dramatiker. (1914) $7.50 pa. Johnson Reprint Corp., NY.

Gryphius, Andreas. Herr Peter Squentz. Powell, H., ed. 1957. $3.25 Hdbd. Humanities Pr., NY.

Heins, O. Johann Rist und das Niederdeutsche Drama das Siebzehn Jahrhunderts. 1930. $10.00 pa. Johnson Reprint Corp., NY.

Heitner, Robert R. German Tragedy in the Age of Enlightenment: A Study in the Development of Original Tragedies, 1724–1768. 1963. $10.00 Hdbd. (ISBN 0-520-00545-7). Univ. of California Pr., CA.

Hellonius, Ludwig. Jomnium Vitae Humanae: Drama. Wiercinski, Dorothea Glodny, ed. (Komedia, No. 16). (Ger. & Lat.). 1970. $3.00 pa. (ISBN 3-11-006350-6). De Gruyter, GER.

Helmrich, Elsie W. History of the Chorus in the German Drama. 1912. $7.50 Hdbd. (ISBN 0-404-50415-9). AMS Pr., NY.

Hes, Else. Charlotte Birch-Pfeiffer Als Dramatikerin. (1914) $10.00 pa. Johnson Reprint Corp., NY.

Hill, Claude & Ley, Ralph. Drama of German Expressionism: A German-English Bibliography 1960. $10.00 Hdbd. (ISBN 0-404-50928-2). AMS Pr., NY.

Hille, Curt. Deutsche Komadie Unter

der Einwirkung Des Aristophanes. (Ger). (1907) $7.50 pa. Johnson Reprint Corp., NY.

Hortenbach, Jenny C. Freiheitsstreben & Destruktivitat: Frauen in Den Dramen August Strindbergs & Gerhardt Hauptmanns. 1965. $5.30 Hdbd. Universitetsforlaget, MA.

Kaufmann, Friedrich W. German Dramatists of the Nineteenth Century. (Essay Index Reprint Ser). 1940. $8.75 Hdbd. (ISBN 0-8369-1578-X). Books for Libraries, NY.

Kistler, Mark O. Drama of the Storm & Stress. (World Authors Series No. 83). $5.50 Hdbd. Twayne Publ., NY.

Liebenow, Peter K., ed. Kunzelsauer Fronleichnamspiel. (Ger). 1969. $23.50 Hdbd. (ISBN 3-11-000355-4). De Gruyter, GER.

Lowack, Alfred. Mundarten Im Hoch Deutschen Drama Bis Gegen das Ende Des 18 Jahrhunderts. (Ger.). (1905) $7.50 pa. Johnson Reprint Corp., NY.

Moschner, Alfred. Holtei Als Dramatiker. (1911) $7.50 pa. Johnson Reprint Corp., NY.

Nolte, Fred O. Early Middle Class Drama. 1935. $12.50 Hdbd. Folcroft Pr., PA.

Osborne, John. Naturalist Drama in Germany. 1971. $8.75 Hdbd. (ISBN 0-87471-027-8). Rowman & Littlefield, NY.

Roessler, Erwin W. Soliloquy in German Drama. 1915. $10.00 Hdbd. (ISBN 0-404-50419-1). AMS Pr., NY.

Shaw, Leroy R. Playwright & Historical Change: Dramatic Strategies in Brecht, Hauptmann, Kaiser, & Wedekind. 1970. $6.50 Hdbd. (ISBN 0-299-05500-0). Univ. of Wisconsin Pr., WI.

Spalter, Max. Brecht's Tradition. 1967. $9.00 Hdbd. (ISBN 0-8018-0607-0). Johns Hopkins Pr., MD.

Stachel, Paul. Seneca und das Deutsche Renaissancedrama. 1907. $19.00 Hdbd.; $17.00 pa. Johnson Reprint Corp., NY.

Van Abbe, Derek. Drama in Renaissance Germany & Switzerland. 1962. $6.00 Hdbd. (ISBN 0-522-83766-2). Library Assn. London, Eng.

Von Klenze, Camillo. From Goethe to Hauptmann: Studies in a Changing Culture. 1926. $7.50 Hdbd. (ISBN 0-8196-0178-0). Biblo & Tannen Booksellers, NY.

Wiese, Benno. Deutsche Tragoedie Von Lessing Bis Hebbel. $10.50 Hdbd. Adler's Foreign Books, NY.

Witkowski, Georg. German Drama of the Nineteenth Century. 1968. $12.50 Hdbd. Benjamin Blom, NY.

National (Greece)

Aylen, Leo. Greek Tragedy & the Modern World. 1964. $7.25 Hdbd. Methuen, Barnes & Noble, NY.

Baldry, H. C. Greek Tragic Theater.

1971. $6.00 Hdbd. (ISBN 0-393-04337-1). W. W. Norton, NY.

Barnett, Lionel. Greek Drama. 1900. $7.50 Hdbd. Folcroft Pr., PA.

Bieber, M. History of the Greek & Roman Theater. rev. ed. 1961. $25.00 Hdbd. (ISBN 0-691-03521-0). Princeton Univ. Pr., NJ.

Chapman, John J. Greek Genius, & Other Essays. (Essay Index Reprint Ser). 1915. $9.00 Hdbd. (ISBN 0-8369-0289-0). Books for Libraries, NY.

Dale, Amy M. Collected Papers of Amy M. Dale. Turner, E. G. & Webster, T. B., eds. $13.00 Hdbd. Cambridge Univ. Pr., NY.

Dale, Amy M. Lyric Metres of Greek Drama. 2nd ed. 1968. $9.50 Hdbd. Cambridge Univ Pr., NY.

De Romilly, Jacqueline. Time in Greek Tragedy. 1968. $6.50 Hdbd. (ISBN 0-8014-0361-8). Cornell Univ. Pr., NY.

Driver, Tom F. Sense of History in Greek & Shakespearean Drama. 1960. $2.25 pa. (ISBN 0-231-08576-1, 76). Columbia Univ Pr., NY.

Else, Gerald F. Origin & Early Form of Greek Tragedy. (Martin Classical Lectures Ser). 1965. $3.75 Hdbd. (ISBN 0-674-64401-8). Harvard Univ. Pr., MA.

Flickinger, Roy C. Greek Theater & Its Drama. 4th ed. 1936. $8.50 Hdbd. (ISBN 0-226-25369-4). Univ. of Chicago Pr., IL.

Flint, William W. Use of Myth to Create

Suspense. (Studies in Comparative Literature, No. 35). 1970. (1921) $4.95 pa. (ISBN 0-8383-0030-8). Haskell House Publ., NY.

Glen, R. S. Two Muses: An Introduction to Fifth-Century Athens by Way of the Drama. 1968. $4.00 text ed. St. Martin's Pr., NY.

Goodell, Thomas D. Athenian Tragedy. 1969. (1920) $10.00 Hdbd. (ISBN 0-8046-0612-9). Kennikat Pr., NY.

Greek Poetry & Life: Essays Presented Gilbert Murray on His Seventieth Birthday, January 2, 1936. (Essay Index Reprint Ser). 1936. $14.75 Hdbd. (ISBN 0-8369-0496-6). Books for Libraries, NY.

Haigh, A. E. Attic Theatre. 3rd enl. ed. (1907) $13.00 Hdbd. Kraus Reprint Co., NY.

Haigh, A. E. Tragic Drama of the Greeks. 1969. (1896) $3.50 pa. (ISBN 0-486-22018-4). Dover Publ., NY.

Haigh, Arthur E. Attic Theatre: A Description of the Stage & Theatre of the Athenians. (Drama Ser., No. 39). 1969. (1898) $12.95 Hdbd. (ISBN 0-8383-0951-8). Haskell House Publ., NY.

Harry, Joseph E. Greek Tragic Poets. (Studies in Poetry Ser., No. 38). 1969. (1914) $10.95 Hdbd. (ISBN 0-8383-0567-9). Haskell House Publ., NY.

Harsh, Philip W. Handbook of Classical Drama. 1944. $10.00x Hdbd. (ISBN

0-8047-0380-9); $3.85 pa. (ISBN 0-8047-0381-7, SP20). Stanford Univ Pr., CA.

Jones, John. On Aristotle & Greek Tragedy. 1962. $6.50 Hdbd. Oxford Univ. Pr., NY.

Jones, John. On Aristotle & Greek Tragedy. 1968. (1962) $2.25 pa. (ISBN 0-19-500443-4). Oxford Univ. Pr., NY.

Kamerbeek, J. C. The Plays of Sophocles: Commentaries. Incl. Pt. 1. Ajax. 1963. $14.75 Hdbd.; Pt. 2. Trachinae. 1970. $14.00 Hdbd.; Pt. 3. Antigone. price "n.g."; Pt. 4. Oepidus Tyrannus. $14.75 Hdbd. 1967. Humanities Pr., NY.

Kitto, Humphrey D. Form & Meaning in Drama. 1956. $3.25 pa. (ISBN 0-416-67520-4, 2) Barnes & Noble, NY.

Kitto, Humphrey D. Form & Meaning in Drama. 1956. $5.75 Hdbd. Barnes & Noble, NY.

Kitto, Humphrey D. Greek Tragedy: A Literary Study. 3rd rev. ed. 1961. $6.75 Hdbd. Barnes & Noble, NY.

Kitto, Humphrey D. Greek Tragedy: A Literary Study. 3rd rev. ed. 1969. $3.50 pa. (ISBN 0-416-68900-0, 140). Barnes & Noble, NY.

Lattimore, Richmond. Poetry of Greek Tragedy. 1958. $5.00 Hdbd. (ISBN 0-8018-0364-0). Johns Hopkins Pr., MD.

Lattimore, Richmond. Story Patterns in Greek Tragedy. 1964. $4.00 Hdbd. (ISBN 0-472-55494-8). Univ. of Michigan Pr., MI.

Lattimore, Richmond. Story Patterns in Greek Tragedy. 1969. (1964) $1.95 pa. (ISBN 0-472-06146-1, 146). Univ. of Michigan Pr., MI.

Lawler, Lillian B. Dance of the Ancient Greek Theatre. 1964. $3.75 text ed. (ISBN 0-87745-014-5); $2.75 pa. (ISBN 0-87745-015-3). Univ. of Iowa Pr., IA.

Legrand, Philippe E. New Greek Comedy. Loeb, James, tr. 1917. $19.00 Hdbd. (ISBN 0-8371-3122-7). Greenwood Pr., CT.

Lesky, Albin. Greek Tragedy. 2nd ed. rev. ed. Frankfort, H. A., tr. 1967. $7.50 Hdbd. (389); $2.95 pa. (ISBN 0-389-02802-9, 449). Barnes & Noble, NY.

Little, Alan M. Myth & Society in Attic Drama. 1967. $6.50 Hdbd. Octagon Books, NY.

Loehrer, Robert. Mienenspiel und Maske in der Griechischen Tragoedie. 1927. $8.00 pa. Johnson Reprint Corp., NY.

Lucas, Donald W. Greek Tragic Poets. 1964. $1.75 pa. (ISBN 0-393-00253-5). W. W. Norton, NY.

Miller, Walter. Daedalus & Thespis: The Contributions of the Ancient Dramatic Poets to Our Knowledge of the Arts & Crafts of Greece. 1931–1932. $10.00 Hdbd. (ISBN 0-8262-0590-9); Vol. 3 Pt. 1. $1.25 pa. Univ. of Missouri Pr., MO.

Nietzsche, Friedrich. The Birth of Tragedy. Kaufman, Walter, tr. Incl. The

Case of Wagner. $1.65 pa. Random House, NY.

Nietzsche, Friedrich. The Birth of Tragedy. Golffing, Francis, trans. Incl. The Genealogy of Morals. 1956. $1.45 pa. (Anchor Bks.) Doubleday & Co., NY.

Norwood, Gilbert. Greek Comedy. 1963. $1.95 pa. (ISBN 0-8090-0536-0). Hill & Wang, NY.

Norwood, Gilbert. Greek Comedy. $4.25 Hdbd. Peter Smith Publ., MA.

Norwood, Gilbert. Greek Comedy. $6.95 Hdbd. Crescendo Publ., MA.

Norwood, Gilbert. Greek Tragedy. 1960. $1.95 pa. (ISBN 0-8090-0521-2). Hill & Wang, NY.

Pickard-Cambridge, Arthur. Dramatic Festivals of Athens. 2nd ed. Lewis, D. M. & Gould, J. P., eds. 1968. $19.25 Hdbd. (ISBN 0-19-814258-7). Oxford Univ. Pr., NY.

Pickard-Cambridge, Arthur W. Dithyramb, Tragedy & Comedy. 2nd ed. Webster, T. B., ed. 1962. $8.00 Hdbd. (ISBN 0-19-814227-7). Oxford Univ. Pr., NY.

Prentice, William K. Those Ancient Dramas Called Tragedies. 1969. (1942) $9.50 Hdbd. Russell & Russell Publ., NY.

Reinhold, Meyer. Barron's Simplified Approach to Ten Greek Tragedies. (Hi-Sch.). 1965. $0.95 pa. Barron's Educational Series, NY.

Renault, Mary. Mask of Apollo. $0.95 pa. New American Library, NY.

Ridgeway, William. Dramas & Dramatic Dances of Non-European Races. 1810. $17.50 Hdbd. Benjamin Blom, NY.

Ridgeway, William. Origin of Tragedy. 1910. $12.50 Hdbd. Benjamin Blom, NY.

Robinson, Cyril E., tr. Genius of the Greek Drama. (Play Anthology Reprint Ser). 1921. $7.00 Hdbd. (ISBN 0-8369-8217-7). Books for Libraries, NY.

Rosenmeyer, Thomas G. Masks of Tragedy, Essays on Six Greek Dramas. 1971. (1963) $8.50 text ed. (ISBN 0-87752-140-9). Gordian Pr., NY.

Schlesinger, Alfred C. Boundaries of Dionysus: Athenian Foundations for the Theory of Tragedy. (Martin Classical Lecture Ser. No. 17). 1963. $4.50 Hdbd. (ISBN 0-674-08000-9). Harvard Univ. Pr., MA.

Snell, Bruno. Scenes from Greek Drama. 1965. $7.00 Hdbd. (ISBN 0-520-01191-0). Univ. of California Pr., CA.

Thomson, George. Aeschylus & Athens. (Drama Ser., No. 39). 1969. (1940) $15.95 Hdbd. (ISBN 0-8383-0723-X). Haskell House Publ., NY.

Thomson, George. Aeschylus & Athens. 3rd ed. 1969. $3.45 pa. (ISBN 0-448-01103-4). Grosset & Dunlap, NY.

Watt, Laughlan M. Attic & Elizabethan

Tragedy. 1968. $12.00 Hdbd. (ISBN 0-8046-0490-8). Kennikat Pr., NY.

Webster, T. Birth of Modern Comedy of Manners. 1959. $0.50 pa. (ISBN 0-424-05690-9). Library Assn., London, Eng.

Webster, T. B. Birth of Modern Comedy of Manners. 1959. $4.00 Hdbd. Folcroft Pr., PA.

Webster, Thomas B. Greek Chorus. 1970. $8.00 Hdbd. (ISBN 0-406-16350-5). Barnes & Noble, NY.

Webster, Thomas B. Studies in Later Greek Comedy. 2nd ed. 1970. $9.50 Hdbd. (ISBN 0-389-03989-6). Barnes & Noble, NY.

White, John W. Verse of Greek Comedy. 1968. (1912) $21.00 Hdbd. Adler's Foreign Books, NY.

National (Japan)

Japanese National Commission for UNESCO, ed. Theatre in Japan. $7.25 Hdbd. Japan Publ., San Francisco, CA.

Lombard, Frank A. Outline History of Japanese Drama. (Drama Ser., No. 39). 1969. (1928) $12.95 Hdbd. (ISBN 0-8383-0585-7). Haskell House, NY.

Scott, Adolphe C. Kabuki Theatre of Japan. 1966. $2.95 pa. Macmillan Co., NY.

Wells, Henry W. Classical Drama of the Orient. $8.50 Hdbd. (ISBN 0-210-22620-X). Asia Society, NY.

National (Russia)

Chekhov, Anton. Letters on the Short Story, the Drama & Other Literary Topics. Friedland, Louis S., ed. $4.00 Hdbd. Peter Smith Publ., MA.

Chekhov, Anton. Letters on the Short Story, the Drama & Other Literary Topics. Friedland, Louis S., ed. 1966. $2.50 pa. (ISBN 0-486-21635-7). Dover Publ., NY.

Chekhov, Anton P. Chekhov's Letters on the Short Story, the Drama, & Other Literary Topics. Friedland, Louis S., ed. $8.50 Hdbd. Benjamin Blom, NY.

Coleman, Arthur P. Humor in the Russian Comedy from Catherine to Gogol. (1925) $6.50 Hdbd. (ISBN 0-404-01589-1). AMS Pr., NY.

Roberts, Spencer E. Soviet Historical Drama. 1965. $9.00 pa. Humanities Pr., NY.

Welsh, David I. Russian Comedy, 1765-1823. 1966. $7.00 Hdbd. Humanities Pr., NY.

Wiener, Leo. Contemporary Drama of Russia. 1924. $10.00 Hdbd. (ISBN 0-404-06943-6). AMS Pr., NY.

Wiener, Leo. Contemporary Drama of Russia. 1971. (1924) $10.00 Hdbd. (ISBN 0-404-06943-6). AMS Pr., NY.

National (Spain)

Crawford, J. P. Spanish Drama Before Lope De Vega. rev. ed. $9.00 Hdbd.

(ISBN 0-8122-7562-4). Univ. of Pa. Pr., Philadelphia, PA.

Crawford, J. Wickersham, Spanish Pastoral Drama. 1915. $10.00 Hdbd. Folcroft Pr., PA.

Gregersen, H. Ibsen & Spain: A Study in Comparative Drama. 1936. $10.00 pa. Kraus Reprint Co., NY.

Kyd, Thomas. Spanish Tragedy. Mulryne, J. R., ed. 1971. $4.50 Hdbd. (ISBN 0-8090-8788-X, Drama); $1.75 pa. (ISBN 0-8090-1118-2). Hill & Wang, NY.

McClelland, I. L. Spanish Drama of Pathos, 1750–1808, 2 Vols. 1970. Set—$30.00 Hdbd. (ISBN 0-8020-1694-4). Univ. of Toronto Pr., Toronto, CAN.

MacCurdy, Raymond R., Jr. Francisco De Rojas Zorrilla & the Tragedy. (Language & Literature Ser., No. 13). 1958. $2.50 pa. (ISBN 0-8263-0119-3). Univ. of New Mexico Pr., Albuquerque, NM.

Ruiz Ramin, Francisco. Historia Del Teatro Espanol. $2.50 pa. French & European Publications, NY.

Wilson, M. Spanish Drama of the Golden Age. $6.50 Hdbd. (ISBN 0-08-013955-8); $4.50 pa. (ISBN 0-08-013954-X). Pergamon Publ. Co., Elmsford, NY.

National (United States)

Brown, John M. & Moses, Montrose J., eds. American Theatre As Seen by Its Critics, 1752–1934. 1934. $10.00 Hdbd. (ISBN 0-8154-0033-0). Cooper Sq. Publ., NY.

Cohn, Ruby. Dialogue in American Drama. 1971. $9.50 pa. (ISBN 0-253-11620-1). Ind. Univ. Pr., IN.

Cohn, Ruby. Dialogue in American Drama. 1971. $9.50 Hdbd. (ISBN 0-253-11620-1). Ind. Univ. Pr., IN.

Dickinson, Thomas H. Playwrights of the New American Theater. facs. ed. (Essay Index Reprint Ser). 1925. $10.00 Hdbd. (ISBN 0-8369-0373-0). Books for Libraries, NY.

Dunlap Society Publications: A Series of Publications Relating to the Drama, Stage & Theatre in Early America, 30 Vols. 1968. (1904) Set. prepub. $360.00 Hdbd.; $14.50 Hdbd. (ISBN 0-8337-0958-5); prepub. $14.50 Hdbd.; $390.00 pa. Burt Franklin, NY.

Erkard, Thomas A. Lynn Riggs: Southwest Playwright. Lee, James W., ed. (Southwest Writers Ser). 1970. $1.00 pa. (ISBN 0-8114-3889-9). Steck-Vaughn Co., TX.

Ford, Paul L. Some Notes Towards an Essay on the Beginnings of American Dramatic Literature, 1606–1789. 1969. (1893) $7.50 Hdbd. (ISBN 0-8337-1197-0). Burt Franklin, NY.

Freedman, Morris. American Drama in Social Context. 1971. $5.95 Hdbd. (ISBN 0-8093-0526-7), Southern Ill. Univ. Pr., IL.

Freedman, Morris. American Drama in Social Context. Moore, Harry T., ed. (Crosscurrents—Modern Critiques Ser).

1971. $5.95 Hdbd. (ISBN 0-8093-0526-7). Southern Ill. Univ. Pr., IL.

Gallagher, Kent G. Foreigner in Early American Drama. 1966. $9.00 Hdbd. Humanities Pr., NY.

Hartman, John G. Development of American Social Comedy from 1787 to 1936. (1971) $7.50 Hdbd. Octagon Books, NY.

Herron, Ima H. Small Town in American Drama. 1969. $12.50 Hdbd. S. Meth. Univ. Pr., TX.

Hodge, Francis. Yankee Theatre: The Image of America on the Stage, 1825–1850. 1964. $6.00 Hdbd. (ISBN 0-292-73436-0). Univ. of Tex. Pr., TX.

Lass, Abraham & Levin, Milton, eds. Student's Guide to Fifty American Plays. 1969. $0.75 pa. (ISBN 0-671-46873-1). Washington Sq. Pr., NY.

Long, E. Hudson, ed. American Drama from Its Beginnings to the Present. (Goldentree Bibliographies in Language & Literature Ser). 1970. $1.95 text ed. (ISBN 0-390-57130-X). Appleton-Century-Crofts, NY.

Mayorga, Margret G. Short History of the American Drama: Commentaries of Plays Prior to 1920. (1932) $25.00 Hdbd. (ISBN 0-8337-5312-6). Burt Franklin, NY.

Meserve, Walter J. Outline History of American Drama. Date n.g. $7.95 lib. bdg. Rowman & Littlefield, NY.

Meserve, Walter J. Outline History of American Drama. 1965. $7.95 Hdbd.; $2.25 pa. Littlefield, Adams & Co., NJ.

Miller, Jordan Y. American Dramatic Literature: Ten Modern Plays in Historical Perspective. 1961. $11.75 Hdbd. (ISBN 0-07-042050-5). McGraw-Hill, NY.

Moody, Richard. America Takes the Stage. 1955. $15.00 Hdbd. Kraus Reprint Co., NY.

Moses, Montrose J. American Dramatist. rev. ed. $12.50 Hdbd. Benjamin Blom, NY.

Nannes, Caspar H. Politics in the American Drama. $18.00 Hdbd. McGrath Publ., MD.

Simonson, H. P. Closed Frontier: Studies in American Literary Tragedy. 1970. $8.25 text ed. (ISBN 0-03-079405-6). Holt, Rinehart & Winston, NY.

Spearman, Walter. Carolina Playmakers: The First Fifty Years. 1970. $7.50 Hdbd. (ISBN 0-8078-1137-8). Univ. of N.C. Pr., NC.

Sper, Felix. From Native Roots. $4.00 Hdbd. Brown Book Co., NY.

Yatron, Michael. Americas Literary Drama. (Essay Index Reprint Ser). 1959. $9.00 Hdbd. (ISBN 0-8369-1437-6). Books for Libraries, NY.

National (US)—Indians

Heath, Virginia S. Dramatic Elements in American Indian Ceremonials. (Americana Ser., No. 37). 1970. $2.95 pa.

(ISBN 0-8383-0093-6). Haskell House Publ., NY.

Radin, Paul. Road of Life & Death. (Bollingen Series, Vol. 5). 1945. $6.50 Hdbd. (ISBN 0-691-09819-0). Princeton Univ. Pr., Princeton, NJ.

National (US)—20th Century

Abramson, Doris E. Negro Playwrights in the American Theatre. Orig. Title: Study of Plays by Negro Playwrights. 1969. $12.50 Hdbd. (ISBN 0-231-03248-X); $2.95 pa. (ISBN 0-231-08593-1). Columbia Univ. Pr., NY.

Bigsby, C. W. Confrontation & Commitment: A Study of Contemporary American Drama, 1959–1966. 1969. $4.95 Hdbd.; $2.50 pa. (ISBN 0-8262-0064-8). Univ. of Mo. Pr., MO.

Broussard, Louis. American Drama, Contemporary Allegory from Eugene O'Neill to Tennessee Williams. 1966. (1962) $4.95 Hdbd. (ISBN 0-8061-0536-4). Univ. of Okla. Pr., OK.

Brown, John R. & Harris, Bernard, eds. American Theatre. (Stratford-Upon-Avon Studies Vol. 10). 1967. $5.75 Hdbd. St. Martin's Pr., NY.

Clark, Barrett H. British & American Drama of To-Day. 1921. $10.00 Hdbd. (ISBN 0-404-01547-6). AMS Pr., NY.

Donoghue, Denis. Third Voice: Modern British & American Verse Drama. $7.50 Hdbd. (ISBN 0-691-06130-0); $1.95 pa. (ISBN 0-691-01285-7, 64). Princeton Univ. Pr., NJ.

Downer, Alan S. Fifty Years of American Drama, 1900–1950. 1966. $1.25 pa. Henry Regnery, IL.

Downer, Alan S., ed. American Drama & Its Critics: A Collection of Critical Essays. 1965. $6.50 Hdbd. (ISBN 0-226-16061-2); $2.45 pa. (ISBN 0-226-16061-0, 4). Univ. of Chicago Pr., IL.

Downer, Alan S. American Theater Today. (Hi-Sch.). 1967. $5.95 Hdbd. (ISBN 0-465-00224-2). Basic Books, NY.

Dusenbury, Winifred L. Theme of Loneliness in Modern American Drama. 1960. $6.50 Hdbd. (ISBN 0-8130-0068-8). Univ. of Fla. Pr., FL.

Flanagan, Hallie. Arena: The History of the Federal Theatre. $12.50 Hdbd. Benjamin Blom, NY.

Flexner, Eleanor. American Playwrights: 1918–1938. (Essay Index Reprint Ser). 1938. $14.50 Hdbd. (ISBN 0-8369-1412-0). Books for Libraries, NY.

Golden, Joseph. Death of Tinker Bell: The American Theatre in the 20th Century. 1967. $5.00 Hdbd. (ISBN 0-8156-0054-2). Syracuse Univ. Pr., NY.

Gould, Jean. Modern American Playwrights. 1966. $6.50 Hdbd. (ISBN 0-396-05357-2). Dodd, Mead & Co., NY.

Gould, Jean. Modern American Playwrights. (Hi-Sch.). $1.95 pa. Apollo Editions, NY.

Kerr, Walter. Pieces at Eight. 1957. $3.95 Hdbd. Simon & Schuster, NY.

Kerr, Walter. Pieces at Eight. $1.55 pa. (ISBN 0-525-47216-9). E. P. Dutton, NY.

Kinne, Wisner P. George Pierce Baker & the American Theatre. 1968. (1954) $15.75 Hdbd. (ISBN 0-8371-0129-8). Greenwood Pr., CT.

Krutch, Joseph W. American Drama Since 1918. 1957. $6.00 Hdbd. (ISBN 0-8076-0042-3). George Braziller, NY.

Lewis, Allan. American Plays & Playwrights of the Contemporary Theatre. 1970. $5.95 Hdbd. Crown Publ., NY.

Lewis, E. Stages: The Fifty-Year Childhood of the American Theater. $8.50 Hdbd. (ISBN 0-13-840306-6). Prentice-Hall, NY.

Mersand, Joseph. American Drama Since Nineteen Thirty: Essays on Playwrights & Plays. 1968. (1949) $7.50 Hdbd. (ISBN 0-8046-0310-3). Kennikat Pr., NY.

Meserve, Walter J., ed. Discussions of Modern American Drama. (Discussions of Literature). (Hi-Sch.). 1965. $2.25 text ed. D. C. Heath, MA.

Nathan, George J. Encyclopedia of the Theatre. 1970. $10.00 Hdbd. (ISBN 0-8386-7721-5). Fairleigh Dickinson Univ. Pr., NJ.

O'Hara, Frank H. Today in American Drama. 1969. (1939) $12.25 Hdbd. Greenwood Pr., CT.

Philips, Elizabeth & Rogers, David. Monarch Literature Notes on Modern American Drama. $1.95 pa. Monarch Pr., NY.

Porter, Thomas E. Myth & Modern American Drama. 1969. $7.95 Hdbd. (ISBN 0-8143-1360-4). Wayne State Univ. Pr., MI.

Taylor, William E. Modern American Drama: Essays in Criticism. 1968. $10.00 Hdbd. Everett Edwards Pr., FL.

Weales, Gerald. American Drama Since World War Two. $6.50 Hdbd. (ISBN 0-15-105575-0). Harcourt Brace Jovanovich, NY.

Weales, Gerald. Jumping-off Place: American Drama of the 1960's. 1969. $6.95 Hdbd. Macmillan Co., NY.

Weinberg, Helen A. New Novel in America: The Kafkan Mode in Contemporary Fiction. 1970. $6.95 Hdbd. (ISBN 0-8014-0537-8). Cornell Univ. Pr., NY.

19th Century

Alexander, Nigel. Shaw: Arms & the Man—Pygmalion. (Macmillan Critical Commentaries). 1968. $1.00 pa. Fernhill House, NY.

Bentley, Eric. Playwright As Thinker. YA. Hi-Sch. $2.85 pa. (ISBN 0-15-672040-X). Harcourt Brace Jovanovich, NY.

Block, Haskell M. Mallarme & the Symbolist Drama. 1963. $5.00 pa. (ISBN 0-8143-1221-7). Wayne St. Univ. Pr., MI.

Bogard, Travis & Oliver, William I., eds.

Modern Drama: Essays in Criticism. (Hi-Sch.). 1965. $2.50 pa. (ISBN 0-19-500717-4). Oxford Univ. Pr., NY.

Dahlstrom, Carl E. Strindberg's Dramatic Expressionism. $12.50 Hdbd. Benjamin Blom, NY.

Dickinson, Thomas H. Outline of Contemporary Drama. 1969. (1927) $8.50 Hdbd. (ISBN 0-8196-0249-3). Biblo & Tannen, NY.

Driver, Tom F. Romantic Quest & Morgan Query. 1970. $7.50 Hdbd. Delacorte Pr., NY.

Dukes, Ashley. Youngest Drama. 1924. $12.50 Hdbd. Folcroft Pr., PA.

Ellehauge, Martin. Position of Bernard Shaw in European Drama & Philosophy. (Drama Ser., No. 39). 1969. (1931) $14.95 Hdbd. (ISBN 0-8383-0659-4). Haskell House Publ., NY.

Foulkes, Peter & Lehner, Edgar. Nineteenth Century Drama. price "n.g." Houghton-Mifflin, NY.

Hale, Edward E. Dramatists of To-Day. (Essay Index Reprint Ser). 1911. $9.75 Hdbd. (ISBN 0-8369-1261-6). Books for Libraries, NY.

Huneker, James G. Iconoclasts. (Essay Index Reprint Ser). 1905. $12.50 Hdbd. (ISBN 0-8369-1472-4). Books for Libraries, NY.

James, Henry. Scenic Art: Notes on Acting & the Drama, 1872-1901. Wade, Allan, ed. 1957. $1.35 pa. (ISBN 0-8090-0505-0). Hill & Wang, NY.

Krutch, Joseph W. Modernism in Modern Drama. 1962. (1953) $6.00 Hdbd. Russell & Russell Publ., NY.

Krutch, Joseph W. Modernism in Modern Drama: A Definition & an Estimate. (Hi-Sch.). 1953. $1.45 pa. (ISBN 0-8014-9030-8). Cornell Univ. Pr., NY.

Miller, Anne I. Independent Theatre in Europe, Eighteen Eighty-Seven. 1931. $12.50 Hdbd. Benjamin Blom, NY.

Peacock, Ronald. Poet in the Theatre. $1.45 pa. (ISBN 0-8090-0523-9, Drama). Hill & Wang, NY.

Shaw, George B. Shaw's Dramatic Criticism: 1895-98. Matthews, John F., ed. $1.45 pa. (ISBN 0-8090-0517-4, Drama). Hill & Wang, NY.

Valency, Maurice. Fiower & the Castle: An Introduction to Modern Drama. $2.95 pa. (ISBN 0-448-00202-7, UL). Grosset & Dunlap, NY.

Van Szeliski, John. Tragedy & Fear: Why Modern Tragic Drama Fails. 1971. $9.95 Hdbd. (ISBN 0-8078-1177-7). Univ. of N.C. Pr., NC.

Williams, Raymond. Drama from Ibsen to Brecht. 1969. $6.50 Hdbd. (ISBN 0-19-519077-7). Oxford Univ. Pr., NY.

20th Century

Alexander, Nigel. Shaw: Arms & the Man—Pygmalion. (Macmillan Critical Commentaries). 1968. $1.00 pa. Fernhill House, NY.

Anderson, Michael, et al. Crowell's

Handbook of Contemporary Drama. 1971. $10.00 Hdbd. (ISBN 0-690-22643-8). Thomas Y Crowell, NY.

Baxter, Kay M. Contemporary Theatre & the Christian Faith. 1965. $2.75 Hdbd. (ISBN 0-687-09528-X). Abingdon Pr., TN.

Belli, Angela. Ancient Greek Myths & Modern Drama: A Study in Continuity. (Studies in Comparative Literature). 1969. $8.50 text ed. (ISBN 0-8147-0034-9); $2.50 pa. (ISBN 0-8147-0959-1). New York Univ. Pr., NY.

Bentley, Eric. Playwright As Thinker. (Hi-Sch.). $2.85 pa. (ISBN 0-15-672040-X). Harcourt Brace Jovanovich, NY.

Bentley, Eric. Theatre of Commitment. 1967. $5.00 Hdbd. (ISBN 0-689-10034-5). Atheneum Publ., NY.

Blau, H. Impossible Theatre. 1964. $10.00 Hdbd. Macmillan Co., NY.

Blau, Herbert. Impossible Theater. 1966. $1.95 pa. Macmillan Co., NY.

Bogard, Travis & Oliver, William I., eds. Modern Drama: Essays in Criticism. (Hi-Sch.). 1965. $2.50 pa. (ISBN 0-19-500717-4). Oxford Univ. Pr., NY.

Brown, John M. Broadway in Review. (Essay Index Reprint Ser). 1940. $9.00 Hdbd. (ISBN 0-8369-0007-3). Books for Libraries, NY.

Brown, John M. Dramatis Personae: A Retrospective Show. 1963. $2.25 pa. (ISBN 0-670-00171-6). Viking Pr., NY.

Brown, John M. Two on the Aisle.

(Essay & General Literature Index Reprint Ser). (1938) $10.00 Hdbd. (ISBN 0-8046-0546-7). Kennikat Pr., NY.

Brustein, Robert. Theatre of Revolt: An Approach to the Modern Drama. 1964. $8.50 Hdbd. (ISBN 0-316-11288-7; $2.45 pa. (ISBN 0-316-11287-9). Little, Brown & Co., MA.

Cheney, Sheldon. New Movement in the Theatre. $12.50 Hdbd. Benjamin Blom, NY.

Chiari, Joseph. Landmarks of Contemporary Drama. 1965. $5.00 Hdbd. Fernhill House, NY.

Clark, Barrett H. British & American Drama of Today. 1971. (1921) $10.00 Hdbd. (ISBN 0-404-01547-6). AMS Pr., NY.

Clark, Barrett H. & Freedley, George. History of Modern Drama. 1947. $9.50 text ed. (ISBN 0-390-19413-1). Appleton-Century-Crofts, NY.

Clurman, Harold. Naked Image. 1966. $6.50 Hdbd. Macmillan Co., NY.

Coe, R., et al. Aspects of Drama & the Theatre. 1965. $1.00 pa. (ISBN 0-424-05050-1). Library Assn., London, ENG.

Cohn, Ruby. Currents in Contemporary Drama. (Midland Quality Paperback Ser., No. 141). 1971. $2.95 pa. (ISBN 0-253-20141-1). Indiana Univ. Pr., IN.

Cohn, Ruby. Currents in Contemporary Drama. 1969. $5.95 Hdbd. (ISBN 0-253-11525-6). Indiana Univ. Pr., IN.

Corrigan, Robert W. Modern Theatre.

1964. $11.95 Hdbd. Macmillan Co., NY.

Dickinson, Hugh. Myth on the Modern Stage. 1969. $8.50 Hdbd. (ISBN 0-252-78400-6). Univ. of Illinois Pr., IL.

Dickinson, Thomas H. Outline of Contemporary Drama. 1969. (1927) $8.50 Hdbd. (ISBN 0-8196-0249-3). Biblo & Tannen, NY.

Driver, Tom F. Romantic Quest & Morgan Query. 1970. $7.50 Hdbd. Delacorte Pr., NY.

Dukes, Ashley. Youngest Drama. 1924. $12.50 Hdbd. Folcroft Pr., PA.

Esslin, Martin. Reflections: Essays on Modern Theatre. 1969. $5.95 Hdbd. Doubleday & Co., NY.

Esslin, Martin. Theatre of the Absurd. 1969. $2.50 pa. Doubleday & Co., NY.

Esslin, Martin. Theatre of the Absurd. $4.00 Hdbd. Peter Smith Publ., MA.

Freedman, Morris. Essays in the Modern Drama. 1964. $4.95 pa. D. C. Heath, MA.

Freedman, Morris. Moral Impulse: Modern Drama from Ibsen to the Present. 1967. $4.95 Hdbd. (ISBN 0-8093-0235-7, Crosscurrents). Southern Ill. Univ. Pr., IL.

Gascoigne, Bamber. Twentieth Century Drama. 1963. $4.00 Hdbd. Hutchinson Univ. Library, NY.

Gascoigne, Bamber. Twentieth Century Drama. 1966. $1.75 pa. (ISBN 0-389-02217-9, 423). Barnes & Noble, NY.

Gassner, John. Theatre at the Crossroads: Plays & Playwrights on the Mid-Century American Stage. 1960. $5.95 Hdbd. (ISBN 0-03-030290-0). Holt, Rinehart & Winston, NY.

Gassner, John. Theatre in Our Times. 1954. $7.50 Hdbd.; $2.95 pa. Crown Publ., NY.

Hale, Edward E. Dramatists of To-Day. (Essay Index Reprint Ser). 1911. $9.75 Hdbd. (ISBN 0-8369-1261-6). Books for Libraries, NY.

Hamilton, Clayton. Conversations: A Contemporary Drama. 1970. (1925) $9.50 Hdbd. (ISBN 0-403-00619-8). Scholarly Pr., MI.

Hamilton, Clayton M. Conversations on Contemporary Drama. (Essay Index Reprint Ser). 1924. $9.50 Hdbd. (ISBN 0-8369-1354-X). Books for Libraries, NY.

Huneker, James G. Iconoclasts. (Essay Index Reprint Ser). 1905. $12.50 Hdbd. (ISBN 0-8369-1472-4). Books for Libraries, NY.

Kernan, Alvin, ed. Modern American Theater: A Collection of Critical Essays. 1967. $5.95 Hdbd. (ISBN 0-13-586271-X). Prentice-Hall, NY.

Kernan, Alvin B., ed. Modern American Theatre: A Collection of Critical Essays. (Orig., Twentieth Century Views). (Hi-Sch.). 1967. $1.95 pa. Prentice-Hall, NY.

Kerr, Walter. Theater in Spite of Itself.

1963. $5.00 Hdbd. Simon & Schuster, NY.

Kitchin, Laurence. Drama in the Sixties: Form & Interpretation. 1966. $7.50 Hdbd. Humanities Pr., NY.

Krutch, Joseph W. Modernism in Modern Drama. 1962. (1953) $6.00 Hdbd. Russell & Russell Publ., NY.

Krutch, Joseph W. Modernism in Modern Drama: A Definition & an Estimate. (Hi-Sch.). 1953. $1.45 pa. (ISBN 0-8014-9030-8). Cornell Univ. Pr., NY.

Lewis, Allan. Contemporary Theatre. rev. ed. 1971. $5.95 Hdbd. Crown Publ., NY.

Lumley, Frederick. New Trends in Twentieth Century Drama: A Survey Since Ibsen & Shaw. 3rd ed. 1967. $8.50 Hdbd. Oxford Univ. Pr., NY.

McCrindle, Joseph F., ed. Behind the Scenes: Theater & Film Interviews from the Transatlantic Review. 1971. $7.95 Hdbd. (ISBN 0-03-085091-6); $3.45 pa. Holt, Rinehart & Winston, NY.

McMillan, James. Sensual Sixties. 1971. $5.95 Hdbd. (ISBN 0-87695-030-6). Aurora Publ., TN.

Melchinger, Siegfried. Concise Encyclopedia of Modern Drama. Popkin, Henry, ed. Wellworth, George, tr. $15.00 Hdbd. (ISBN 0-8180-0500-9). Horizon Pr., NY.

Miller, Anne I. Independent Theatre in Europe, Eighteen Eighty-Seven. 1931. $12.50 Hdbd. Benjamin Blom, NY.

Miller, J. William. Modern Playwrights at Work, Vol. i. 1968. $10.00 Hdbd. Samuel French, NY.

Millett, Fred B. Reading Drama. (Play Anthology Reprint Ser). 1950. $11.00 Hdbd. (ISBN 0-8369-8203-7). Books for Libraries, NY.

Nathan, George J. Passing Judgments. (Essay Index Reprint Ser). 1935. $8.50 Hdbd. (ISBN 0-8369-1150-4). Books for Libraries, NY.

Nathan, George J. Passing Judgments. 1969. (1935) $9.00 Hdbd. Johnson Reprint Corp., NY.

Nathan, George J. Passing Judgments. 1970. $8.00 Hdbd. (ISBN 0-8386-7722-3). Fairleigh Dickinson Univ. Pr., NJ.

Nathan, George J. Passing Judgments. 1935. $10.50 Hdbd. (ISBN 0-8371-2302-X). Greenwood Pr., CT.

Nathan, George J. Since Ibsen. $8.00 Hdbd. (ISBN 0-8386-7780-0). Fairleigh Dickinson Univ. Pr., NJ.

The New York Times Theatre Reviews 1920–1970. Set. 8 vols. & 2 vol. index $1050.00 Hdbd. Arno Pr., NY.

Palmer, John L. Studies in the Contemporary Theatre. (Essay Index Reprint Ser). 1927. $8.50 Hdbd. (ISBN 0-8369-1369-8). Books for Libraries, NY.

Peacock, Ronald. Poet in the Theatre. $1.45 pa. (ISBN 0-8090-0523-9). Hill & Wang, NY.

Phelps, William L. Essays on Modern Dramatists. (Essay Index Reprint Ser).

1921. $9.50 Hdbd. (ISBN 0-8369-1476-7). Books for Libraries, NY.

Schechner, Richard, ed. Drama Review: Summer 1969. 1969. $2.00 Hdbd. Simon & Schuster, NY.

Scott, Nathan A., Jr., ed. Man in the Modern Theatre. (Chime Paperback Ser). 1965. $1.00 pa. John Knox Pr., VA.

Sheed, Wilfrid. Morning After. 1971. $7.95 Hdbd. Farrar, Straus & Giroux, NY.

Styan, J. L. Dark Comedy: The Development of Modern Comic Tragedy. 2nd ed. $9.50 Hdbd. (ISBN 0-521-06572-0); $2.95 pa. (ISBN 0-521-09529-8, 529). Cambridge Univ. Pr., NY.

Swales, M. W. Arthur Schnitzler: Professor Bernhardi. price "n.g." Hdbd. Pergamon Publ. Co., NY.

Van Szeliski, John. Tragedy & Fear: Why Modern Tragic Drama Fails. 1971. $9.95 Hdbd. (ISBN 0-8078-1177-7). Univ. of N.C. Pr., NC.

Williams, Raymond. Drama from Ibsen to Brecht. 1969. $6.50 Hdbd. (ISBN 0-19-519077-7). Oxford Univ. Pr., NY.

Irish Drama

Barnet, Sylvan, et al, eds. Genius of the Irish Theater: John Bull's Other Island, Canavans, Deidre of the Sorrows, Words Upon the Window-Pane, la la Noo, in The Train, Purple Dust. $0.75 pa. New American Library, NY.

Bickley, Francis, J. M. Synge & the Irish Dramatic Movement. 1968. (1912) $6.50 Hdbd. Russell & Russell, NY.

Bickley, Francis J. J. M. Synge & the Irish Dramatic Movement. 1912. $5.00 Hdbd. Folcroft Pr., PA.

Robinson, L. Irish Theatre. (Drama Ser., No. 39). 1969. (1939) $8.95 Hdbd. (ISBN 0-8383-1201-2). Haskell House Publ., NY.

History and Criticism

Dooley, Roger B. Monarch Literature Notes on Modern British & Irish Drama. $1.00 pa. Monarch Pr., NY.

Duggan, George C. Stage Irishman. 1937. $12.50 Hdbd. Benjamin Blom, NY.

Ellis-Fermor, Una. Irish Dramatic Movement. 2nd ed. 1967. $2.75 pa. (ISBN 0-416-69740-2, 204). Barnes & Noble, NY.

Hogan, Robert. After the Irish Renaissance: A Critical History of the Irish Drama Since the Plough & the Stars. 1967. $6.95 Hdbd. (ISBN 0-8166-0457-6). Univ. of Minn. Pr., MN.

Hughes, S. C. Pre-Victorian Drama in Dublin. (Research & Source Works Ser., No. 708). 1970. (1904) $10.00 Hdbd. (ISBN 0-8337-1760-X). Burt Franklin, NY.

Malone, Andrew E. Irish Drama. 1929. $10.75 Hdbd. Benjamin Blom, NY.

Robinson, L. Irish Theatre. (Drama Ser., No. 39). 1969. (1939) $8.95 Hdbd.

(ISBN 0-8383-1201-2). Haskell House Publ., NY.

Weygandt, Cornelius. Irish Plays & Playwrights. 1913. $10.00 Hdbd. (ISBN 0-8046-0498-3). Kennikat Pr., NY.

Masques

Brotanek, Rudolf. Die Englishen Maskenspiele. 1902. $13.50 pa. Johnson Reprint Corp., NY.

Evans, Herbert A. English Masques. 1897. $20.00 Hdbd. Folcroft Pr., PA.

Greg, Walter W. List of Masques, Pageants, Etc. Supplementary to a List of English Plays. (Drama Ser., No. 39). 1969. (1902) $9.95 Hdbd. (ISBN 0-8383-0942-9). Haskell House Publ., NY.

Jones, Inigo. Designs by Inigo Jones for Masques & Plays at Court. Simpson, Percy & Bell, C. F., eds. 1966. (1924) $35.00 Hdbd. Russell & Russell, NY.

Jonson, et al. Book of Masques. 1967. $13.50 Hdbd. Cambridge Univ. Pr., NY.

Jonson, Ben. Score for Lovers Made Men, a Masque by Ben Jonson. Sabol, Andrew J., ed. 1963. $4.00 pa. (ISBN 0-87057-073-0). Brown Univ. Pr., Providence, RI.

Nicoll, Allardyce. Stuart Masques & the Renaissance Stage. 1938. $17.50 Hdbd. Benjamin Blom, NY.

Orgel, Stephen. Jonsonian Masque. 1965. $6.00 Hdbd. (ISBN 0-674-48250-6). Harvard Univ. Pr., Cambridge, MA.

Reyher, Paul. Masques Anglais. 1909. $17.50 Hdbd. Benjamin Blom, NY.

Steele, Mary S. Plays & Masques at Court During the Reigns of Elizabeth, James & Charles, 1558-1642. 1968. (1926) $9.00 Hdbd. Russell & Russell, NY.

Welsford, Enid. Court Masque: A Study in the Relationship Between Poetry & the Revels. 1962. (1927) $11.50 Hdbd. Russell & Russell, NY.

Melodrama

Booth, Michael. English Melodrama. 1965. $6.00 Hdbd. Fernhill House, NY.

Grimsted, David. Melodrama Unveiled: American Theater & Culture, 1800–1850. 1968. $8.95 Hdbd. (ISBN 0-226-30901-0). Univ. of Chicago Pr., Chicago, IL.

Heilman, Robert B. Tragedy & Melodrama: Versions of Experience. 1968. $8.95 Hdbd. Univ. of Wash. Pr., Seattle, WA.

Rahill, Frank. World of Melodrama. 1967. $9.50 Hdbd. (ISBN 0-271-73113-3). Penn. St. Univ. Pr., University Park, PA.

Periodicals

Schoenbaum, Samuel. Renaissance Drama, New Ser. 2, Essays Principally on Dramatic Theory & Form. 1969. $7.50 Hdbd. (ISBN 0-8101-0000-2). Northwestern Univ. Pr., IL.

Schoenbaum, Samuel, ed. Essays Principally on Masques & Entertainments. (Renaissance Drama, New Series 1). 1968. $10.50 Hdbd. (ISBN 0-8101-0222-6). Northwestern Univ. Pr., IL.

Schoenbaum, Samuel, ed. Renaissance Drama, Vol. 7. 1964. $4.75 Hdbd. (ISBN 0-8101-0219-6). Northwestern Univ. Pr., IL.

Schoenbaum, Samuel, ed. Renaissance Drama, Vol. 8. 1965. $7.50 Hdbd. (ISBN 0-8101-0220-X). Northwestern Univ. Pr., IL.

Schoenbaum, Samuel, ed. Renaissance Drama, Vol. 9. 1966. $9.75 Hdbd. (ISBN 0-8101-0221-8). Northwestern Univ. Pr., IL.

Shakespeare Society Of New York. Publications, 33 Vols. 1885-1926. Set— $400.00 Hdbd. (ISBN 0-404-54200-X). AMS Pr., NY.

Smith, Michael. Theatre Journal: Winter, 1967. (Literary Frontiers Series, No. 3). 1968. $1.50 pa. Univ. of Missouri Pr., MO.

Stratman, Carl J. Britain's Theatrical Periodicals, 1720-1966: A Bibliography. 2nd ed. 1970. price "n.g." Hdbd. (ISBN 0-87104-034-4). New York Public Library, NY.

Tallish Dramatic Magazine. (Tallish's Shakespeare Gallery of Engravings). 1850-1853. $25.00 Hdbd. Benjamin Blom, NY.

Plots and Characters

Cartmell, Van H., ed. Plot Outlines of One Hundred Famous Plays. $3.50 Hdbd. Peter Smith Publ., MA.

Dipple, Elizabeth. Plot. (Critical Idiom Ser., Vol. 12). 1970. $3.00 Hdbd. (ISBN 0-416-19770-1); $1.25 pa. (ISBN 0-416-19780-9). Barnes & Noble, NY.

Drury, Francis K. Guide to Best Plays. 2nd ed. Salem, James M., ed. 1969. $15.00 Hdbd. (ISBN 0-8108-0254-6). Scarecrow Pr., NJ.

Fenton, Doris. Extra Dramatic Moment in Elizabethan Plays. 1930. $15.00 Hdbd. Folcroft Pr., PA.

Freeburg, Victor O. Disguise Plots in Elizabethan Drama. 1965. $12.50 Hdbd. Benjamin Blom, Bronx, NY.

Halford, Aubrey S. & Halford, Giovanna M. Kabuki Handbook: A Guide to Understanding & Appreciation. 1955. $3.50 Hdbd. (ISBN 0-8048-0332-3). Charles E. Tuttle, VT.

Hamburger, Kate. From Sophocles to Sartre: Figures from Greek Tragedy, Classical & Modern. Sebba, Helen, tr. 1969. $6.50 Hdbd. (ISBN 0-8044-2340-7). Frederick Ungar Publ., NY.

Kienzle, Siegfried. Modern World Theatre: A Guide to Productions Since 1945. 1970. $12.50 Hdbd. (ISBN 0-8044-3129-9). Frederick Ungar, NY.

Laffont-Bompiani, ed. Dictionnaire Des Personnages Litteraires Et Dramatiques De Tous Les Temps Et De Tous Les

Pays. (Illus.). $40.00 Hdbd. French & European Publications, NY.

Lovell, John, Jr., ed. Great American Plays in Digest Form. $2.25 pa. Apollo Editions, NY.

Polti, Georges. Thirty-Six Dramatic Situations. 1921. $4.00 Hdbd. (ISBN 0-87116-043-9). Writer. Boston, MA.

Rogers, David. Monarch Literature Notes on Modern European Drama. $1.00 pa. Monarch Pr., NY.

Salem, James M. Drury's Guide to Best Plays. rev. 2nd ed. 1969. $15.00 Hdbd. (ISBN 0-8108-0254-6). Scarecrow Pr., NJ.

Shackford, Martha H. Shakespeare, Sophocles: Dramatic Themes & Modes. 1960. $1.45 pa. College & Univ. Pr., CT.

Shank, Theodore J., ed. Digest of Five Hundred Plays: Plot Outlines & Production Notes. 1966. $1.95 pa. Macmillan Co., NY.

Sprinchorn, Evert, ed. Twentieth-Century Plays in Synopsis. 1966. $6.95 Hdbd. (ISBN 0-690-84061-6). Thomas Y. Crowell, NY.

Young, James N. One Hundred One Plots Used & Abused. $3.95 Hdbd. (ISBN 0-87116-059-5). Writer. Boston, MA.

Religious

Cohen, Gustave. Histoire De la Mise En Scene Dans le Theatre Religieux Français Au Moyen Age. rev. ed. (Fr). 1926. $20.00 Hdbd. (ISBN 0-8337-4048-2). Burt Franklin, NY.

Craig, Hardin. English Religious Drama of the Middle Ages. 1955. $13.00 Hdbd. (ISBN 0-19-811520-2). Oxford Univ. Pr., NY.

Gaster, Theodor H. Thespis: Ritual, Myth & Drama in the Ancient Near East. rev. ed. $2.95 pa. (ISBN 0-06-131281-9). Harper-Row, NY.

Merchant, W. Moelwyn. Creed & Drama. 1966. $1.95 Hdbd. (ISBN 0-8006-0178-5, 1-178). Fortress Pr., PA.

Moseley, J. Edward. Using Drama in the Church. $1.00 pa. (ISBN 0-8272-3800-2). Bethany Pr., MO.

Roston, Murray. Biblical Drama in England. 1968. $10.00 Hdbd. (ISBN 0-8101-0211-0). Northwestern Univ. Pr., IL.

Wardropper, Bruce W., ed. Teatro Espanol Del Siglo De Oro. 1970. $11.95 text ed. (ISBN 0-684-41474-0). Charles Scribner's Sons, NY.

Weales, Gerald. Religion in Modern English Drama. 1961. $9.00 Hdbd. (ISBN 0-8122-7267-6). Univ. of Pennsylvania Pr., PA.

Skits, Stunts, Etc.

Carlson, Bernice W. Do It Yourself: Tricks, Stunts & Skits. (Elem.). 1952. $2.50 Hdbd. (ISBN 0-687-11007-6);

$1.60 pa. (ISBN 0-687-11008-4). Abingdon. Nashville, TN.

Depew, Arthur M. Cokesbury Stunt Book. Rev. ed. (Elem.). 1953. $4.50 Hdbd. (ISBN 0-687-08838-0). Abingdon. Nashville, TN.

Eisenberg, Helen & Eisenberg, Larry. Fun with Skits, Stunts & Stories. 1955. $3.50 Hdbd. (ISBN 0-8096-1266-6). Assn. Pr., NY.

Eisenberg, Helen & Eisenberg, Larry. Handbook of Skits & Stunts. 1953. $3.95 Hdbd. (ISBN 0-8096-1086-8). Assn. Pr., NY.

Fontaine, Robert. Humorous Skits for Young People. Rev. ed. (Elem.). 1970. $5.95 Hdbd. (ISBN 0-8238-0023-7). Plays. Boston, MA.

Howard, Vernon. Pantomimes, Charades & Skits. (Elem.). 1959. $2.95 Hdbd. Sterling, NY.

Ireland, Norma O. Index to Skits & Stunts. 1958. $10.00 Hdbd. (ISBN 0-87305-088-6). Faxon. Westwood, MA.

Mulac, Margaret E. Games & Stunts for Schools, Camps & Playgrounds. 1964. $5.95 Hdbd. (ISBN 0-06-004500-0). Har-Row., NY.

Rodgers, Martin A. Handbook of Stunts. Repr. 1928 price n.g. Hdbd. Gale. Detroit, MI.

Vaughn, Ruth. Skits That Win. 1968. $1.00 pa. Zondervan. Grand Rapids, MI.

Whitman, Virginia. Plays & Playlets. 1959. $1.00 pa. Moody. Chicago, IL.

Technique

Archer, William. Plant Materials of Decorative Gardening: Identification of Trees & Shrubs. 1959. $2.50 pa. (ISBN 0-486-20651-3). Dover Publs., NY.

Archer, William. Play-Making, a Manual of Craftsmanship. $4.50 Hdbd. Peter Smith Publ., MA.

Art of Playwriting: Lectures Delivered at the University of Pennsylvania on the Mask & Wig Foundation. (Essay Index Reprint Ser). 1967. $7.75 Hdbd. (ISBN 0-8369-0159-2). Books for Libraries, NY.

Baker, George P. Dramatic Technique. (Theatre Ser). (1919). price "n.g." Hdbd. (ISBN 0-306-71344-6). Plenum Publ. Corp., NY.

Baker, George P. Dramatic Technique. 1919. $16.75 Hdbd. (ISBN 0-8371-3005-0). Greenwood Pr., CT.

Baldwin, Thomas W. Shakespeare's Five-Act Structure. 1947. $10.00 Hdbd. (ISBN 0-252-72647-2). Univ. of Ill. Pr., IL.

Boulton, Marjorie. Anatomy of Drama. 1960–1968. $4.50 Hdbd.; $1.75 pa. Hillary House Publ., NY.

Buland, M. Presentation of Time in the Elizabethan Drama. (Drama Ser., No. 39). 1969. (1912) $13.95 Hdbd. (ISBN 0-8383-0517-2). Haskell House Publ., NY.

Busfield, Roger M. The Playwright's Art: Stage, Radio, Television, Motion Pictures. (1958) $11.50 Hdbd. (ISBN 0-8371-5741-2). Greenwood Pr., CT.

Dobree, Bonamy. Histriophone: A Dialogue on Dramatic Diction. 1925. $4.00 Hdbd. Folcroft Pr., PA.

Drew, Elizabeth. Discovering Drama. 1968. (1937) $8.00 Hdbd. (ISBN 0-8046-0116-X). Kennikat Pr., NY.

Fansler, Harriott E. Evolution of Technic in Elizabethan Tragedy. 1968. (1914) $7.50 Hdbd. (ISBN 0-87753-014-9). Phaeton Pr., NY.

Fleming, William H. Shakespeare's Plots. 1971. (1902) $22.50 Hdbd. (ISBN 0-404-02437-8). AMS Pr., NY.

Freytag, Gustav. Technique of Drama. 1895. $12.00 Hdbd. (ISBN 0-403-00019-X). Scholarly Pr., MI.

Freytag, Gustav. Technique of the Drama. McEwan, Elias J., tr. 1968. (1895) $12.00 Hdbd. Johnson Reprint Corp., NY.

Freytag, Gustav. Technique of the Drama. MacEwan, Elias J., tr. 1968. (1904) $10.75 Hdbd. Benjamin Blom, NY.

Graves, Thornton S. Act Time in Elizabethan Theatres. (Studies in Drama Ser., No. 39). (1970) $2.95 pa. (ISBN 0-8383-0043-X). Haskell House Publ., NY.

Jewkes, Wilfred T. Act Division in Elizabethan & Jacobean Plays, 1583–1616. 1958. $10.00 Hdbd. (ISBN 0-404-03568-X). AMS Pr., NY.

Jourdain, Eleanor F. Dramatic Theory & Practice in France 1690-1808. 1968 $12.50 Hdbd. Benjamin Blom, NY.

King, Nancy. Theatre Movement: The Actor & His Space. $7.50 Hdbd. (ISBN 0-910482-28-4). DBS Publ., NY.

Langner, Lawrence. Play's the Thing. (Hi-Sch.). 1960. $6.95 text ed. (ISBN 0-87116-036-6). Writer, Inc., MA.

Lessing, Gotthold Ephraim. Hamburg Dramaturgy. Zimmern, tr. $2.75 pa. (ISBN 0-486-20032-9). Dover Publ., NY.

Lessing, Gotthold Ephraim. Hamburg Dramaturgy. $4.75 Hdbd. Peter Smith Publ., MA.

Lewis, B. Roland. Technique of the One Act Play. $2.00 Hdbd. Humphries Pr., NY.

Mahr, August C. Dramatische Situationsbilder und Bildtypen: Eine Studie Zur Kunstgeschichte des Dramas. 1928. $9.00 Hdbd. (ISBN 0-404-51806-0). AMS Pr., NY.

Matthews, Brander. Principles of Playmaking. (Essay Index Reprint Ser). $10.75 Hdbd. (ISBN 0-8369-1989-0). Books for Libraries, NY.

Matthews, Brander, ed. Papers on Acting. $3.75 Hdbd. (ISBN 0-8090-7510-5, Drama); $1.65 pa. (ISBN 0-8090-0511-5). Hill & Wang, NY.

Matthews, Brander, ed. Papers on Playmaking. 1957. $1.35 pa. (ISBN 0-8090-0510-7, Drama). Hill & Wang, NY.

Matthews, Brander, ed. Papers on Playmaking. (Essay Index Reprint Ser). $10.75 Hdbd. (ISBN 0-8369-1890-8). Books for Libraries, NY.

Miller, J. William. Modern Playwrights at Work, Vol. 1. 1968. $10.00 Hdbd. Samuel French, NY.

Millett, Fred B. Reading Drama. (Play Anthology Reprint Ser). 1950. $11.00 Hdbd. (ISBN 0-8369-8203-7). Books for Libraries, NY.

Millett, Fred B. & Bentley, Gerald E. Art of the Drama. $4.50 text ed. (ISBN 0-390-64088-3). Appleton-Century-Crofts, NY.

Minot, Stephen. Three Genres: The Writing of Poetry, Fiction & Drama 2-E. 2nd ed. 1971. $6.95 text ed. (ISBN 0-13-920348-6). Prentice-Hall, NY.

Moulton, R. G. Shakespeare As a Dramatic Artist. $5.00 Hdbd. Peter Smith Publ., MA.

Moulton, Richard G. Shakespeare As a Dramatic Artist: A Popular Illustration of the Principles of Scientific Criticism. rev. & enl. ed. 1966. $3.00 pa. (ISBN 0-486-21546-6). Dover Publ., NY.

Niggli, Josefina. New Pointers on Playwriting. rev. & enl. ed. (Hi-Sch.). 1967. $5.00 text ed. (ISBN 0-87116-041-2). Writer Inc., MA.

O'Hara, Frank H. Invitation to the Theater. (1951) $9.50 Hdbd. (ISBN 0-8371-3842-6). Greenwood Pr., CT.

Polti, Georges. Thirty-Six Dramatic Situations. 1921. $4.00 Hdbd. (ISBN 0-87116-043-9). Writer Inc., MA.

Ratermanis, J. B. & Irwin, William R. Comic Style of Beaumarchais. 1961. $8.00 Hdbd. (ISBN 0-8371-2298-8). Greenwood Pr., CT.

Robertson, John G. Lessing's Dramatic Theory. 1939. $15.00 Hdbd. Benjamin Blom, NY.

Roessler, Erwin W. Soliloquy in German Drama. 1915. $10.00 Hdbd. (ISBN 0-404-50419-1). AMS Pr., NY.

Rowe, Kenneth T. Write That Play. 1969. $6.95 Hdbd. Funk & Wagnalls, NY.

Van Druten, John. Playwright at Work. 1953. $9.50 Hdbd. (ISBN 0-8371-3847-7). Greenwood Pr., CT.

Van Laan, Thomas F. Idiom of Drama. 1969. $11.75 Hdbd. (ISBN 0-8014-0543-2). Cornell Univ. Pr., NY.

Weston, Harold. Form in Literature. 1932. $15.00 Hdbd. Folcroft Pr., PA.

Tragicomedy

Guthke, Karl S. Modern Tragicomedy. $4.00 Hdbd. Peter Smith Publ., MA.

Guthke, Karl S. Modern Tragicomedy: An Investigation into the Nature of the Genre. 1966. $2.95 text ed. Random House, NY.

Herrick, Marvin T. Tragicomedy: Its Origin & Development in Italy, France & England. 1962. $1.95 pa. (ISBN 0-252-72685-5, 4, IB). Univ. of Ill. Pr., IL.

Hogan, Robert & Molin, Sven E. Drama: The Major Genres, an Introductory Critical Anthology. 1962. $5.95 pa. (ISBN 0-396-06108-7). Dodd, Mead & Co., NY.

Hoy, Cyrus H. Hyacinth Room: An Investigation into the Nature of Comedy, Tragedy, & Tragicomedy. 1964. $6.95 Hdbd. Alfred A. Knopf, NY.

Lancaster, Henry C. French Tragi-Comedy. 1966. (1907) $6.00 Hdbd. (ISBN 0-87752-059-3). Gordian Pr., NY.

Ristine, Frank H. English Tragicomedy, Its Origin & History. 1963. (1910) $7.50 Hdbd. Russell & Russell Publ., NY.

Styan, J. L. Dark Comedy: The Development of Modern Comic Tragedy. 2nd ed. $9.50 Hdbd. (ISBN 0-521-06572-0); $2.95 pa. (ISBN 0-521-09529-8, 529). Cambridge Univ. Pr., NY.

Verse Drama

Spanos, William V. Christian Tradition in Modern British Verse Drama: Poetics of Sacramental Time. 1967. $12.50 Hdbd. (ISBN 0-8135-0554-2). Rutgers Univ. Pr., NJ.

DRAMATIC CRITICISM

Breed, Paul F. & Sniderman, Florence M. Dramatic Criticism Index: Bibliography of Commentaries on Playwrights from Ibsen to the Avant-Garde. 1971. $20.00 Hdbd. Gale Research Co., MI.

Clapp, Henry A. Reminiscences of a Dramatic Critic, with an Essay on the Art of Henry Irving. (1902) $14.50 Hdbd. (ISBN 0-8337-5273-1). Burt Franklin, NY.

Colman, Arthur & Tyler, Gary. Drama Criticism, Vol. 2, A Checklist Of Interpretation Since 1940 Of Classical & Continental Plays. 1971. $12.50 Hdbd. (ISBN 0-8040-0500-1). Swallow Pr., IL.

Dubose, Estelle & Dubose, Larocque. Cyrano De Bergerac Notes. 1971. $1.00 pa. (ISBN 0-8220-0346-5). Cliff's Notes, NB.

Klein, David. Elizabethan Dramatists As Critics. 1968. (1963) $15.25 Hdbd. (ISBN 0-8371-0131-X). Greenwood Pr., CT.

Montague, C. E. Dramatic Values. 1971. (1925) $12.75 Hdbd. (ISBN 0-403-01112-4). Scholarly Pr., MI.

Smith, Samuel S. Craft of the Critic. (Essay Index Reprint Ser). 1931. $11.00 Hdbd. (ISBN 0-8369-1180-6). Books for Libraries, NY.

Walkley, A. B. Dramatic Criticism. 1970. (1903) $6.00 Hdbd. (ISBN 0-8046-0765-6). Kennikat Pr., NY.

DRAMATISTS

Antoine, Andre. Memories of the Theatre-Libre. Carlson, Marvin, ed. (Books of the Theatre, No. 5). 1964. $6.50 Hdbd. (ISBN 0-87024-034-X). Univ. of Miami Pr., Coral Gables, FL.

Bentley, Eric, ed. Great Playwrights, 2 Vols. 1970. Set—$22.50 Hdbd. Doubleday & Co., NY.

Bentley, G. E. Profession of Dramatist in Shakespeare's Time, 1590-1642. $10.00 Hdbd. Princeton Univ. Pr., NJ.

Chandler, Frank W. Modern Continental Playwrights. 1969. (1931) $20.00 Hdbd. (ISBN 0-06-101060-X). Harper-Row, NY.

Cohan, George M. Twenty Years on Broadway & the Years It Took to Get There. (1925) $12.25 Hdbd. (ISBN 0-8371-5682-3). Greenwood Pr., CT.

Coleman, John. Players & Playwrights I Have Known, 2 Vols. in 1. 1890. $18.75 Hdbd. Benjamin Blom, NY.

De Selincourt, Aubrey. Six Great Playwrights. $12.50 Hdbd. Folcroft Pr., PA.

Flexner, Eleanor. American Playwrights: 1918-1938. (Essay Index Reprint Ser). 1938. $14.50 Hdbd. (ISBN 0-8369-1412-0). Books for Libraries, NY.

Frisch, Max. Biografie: Ein Spiel. (Ger). 1971. $1.25 pa. Harcourt, Brace & World, NY.

Gassner, John. Masters of the Drama. 3rd ed. 1953. $8.50 Hdbd. (ISBN 0-486-20100-7). Dover Publ., NY.

Gilder, Rosamond. Enter the Actress. $1.95 pa. Theatre Arts Books, NY.

Griffin, Gerald. Life & Works of Gerald Griffin, 8 Vols. (1843) Set—$135.00 Hdbd. (ISBN 0-404-08860-0); $17.00 Hdbd. (ISBN 0-404-08861-9) (ISBN 0-404-08862-7) (ISBN 0-404-08863-5) (ISBN 0-404-08864-3) (ISBN 0-404-08865-1). AMS Pr., NY.

Henderson, Archibald. European Dramatists. (Essay Index Reprint Ser). 1926. $15.75 Hdbd. (ISBN 0-8369-2163-1). Books for Libraries, NY.

Huneker, James G. Iconoclasts. (Essay Index Reprint Ser). 1905. $12.50 Hdbd. (ISBN 0-8369-1472-4). Books for Libraries, NY.

Huneker, James G. Iconoclasts, a Book of Dramatists: Ibsen, Strindberg, Becque, Hauptmann, Sudermann, Hervieu, Gorky, Duse & D'annunzio, Maeterlinck & Bernard Shaw. 1969. (1905) $14.50 Hdbd. (ISBN 0-8371-0930-2). Greenwood Pr., CT.

Kaufmann, Friedrich W. German Dramatists of the Nineteenth Century. (Essay Index Reprint Ser). 1940. $8.75 Hdbd. (ISBN 0-8369-1578-X). Books for Libraries, NY.

Kennard, Joseph S. Italian Theatre, 2 Vols. 1932. $18.50 Hdbd. Benjamin Blom, NY.

Little, Stuart & Cantor, Arthur. Playmakers. 1971. $2.95 Hdbd. (ISBN 0-525-47278-9). E. P. Dutton, NY.

March, Harold. Frederic Soulie: Novelist & Dramatist of the Romantic Period. (1931) $15.00 Hdbd. (ISBN 0-404-53203-9). AMS Pr., NY.

Melchinger, Siegfried. Concise Encyclopedia of Modern Drama. Popkin,

Henry, ed. Wellworth, George, tr. $15.00 Hdbd. (ISBN 0-8180-0500-9). Horizon Pr., NY.

Mersand, Joseph. American Drama Since Nineteen Thirty: Essays on Playwrights & Plays. 1968. (1949) $7.50 Hdbd. (ISBN 0-8046-0310-3). Kennikat Pr., NY.

Monahan, Michael. Nova Hibernia, Irish Poets & Dramatists of Today & Yesterday. (Essay Index Reprint Ser). 1914. $9.00 Hdbd. (ISBN 0-8369-0713-2). Books for Libraries, NY.

Moon, Harold K. Alejandro Casona: Playwright. (Merrill Monograph Ser). 1970. $1.50 pa. (ISBN 0-8425-0216-5). Brigham Young Univ. Pr. UT.

Moses, Montrose J. American Dramatist. rev. ed. $12.50 Hdbd. Benjamin Blom, NY.

Robinson, L. Irish Theatre. (Drama Ser., No. 39). 1969. (1939) $8.95 Hdbd. (ISBN 0-8383-1201-2). Haskell House Publ., NY.

Weygandt, Cornelius. Irish Plays & Playwrights. 1913. $10.00 Hdbd. (ISBN 0-8046-0498-3). Kennikat Pr., NY.

Zuckmayer, Carl. Part of Myself. 1970. $7.95 Hdbd. (ISBN 0-15-170970-X). Harcourt, Brace & World, NY.

Zweig, Stefan. World of Yesterday: An Autobiography. $4.00 Hdbd. Peter Smith Publ., MA.

EDUCATION

Alington, Argentine F. Drama & Education. 1961. $2.50 Hdbd. Dufour Editions, PA.

Altenbernd, Lynn & Lewis, Leslie L. Handbook for the Study of Drama. rev. ed. 1966. $1.50 pa. Macmillan Co., NY.

Barnfield, Gabriel. Creative Drama in Schools. 1969. $10.00 Hdbd.; $2.95 pa. (ISBN 0-8055-1057-5). Hart Publ. Corp., NY.

Bazagonov, M. S. Shakespeare in the Red. 1964. $3.50 Hdbd. (ISBN 0-668-01321-4); $0.95 pa. (ISBN 0-668-01322-2). Arc Bks., NY.

Boas, Frederick S. University Drama in the Tudor Age. 1914. $12.50 Hdbd. Benjamin Blom, NY.

Bordan, Sylvia D. Plays As Teaching Tools in the Elementary School. 1970. $7.95 Hdbd. (ISBN 0-13-684498-7). Parker Publ. Co., NY.

Bordon, S. Plays As Teaching Tools in the Elementary School. $8.95 Hdbd. (ISBN 0-13-684498-7). Prentice-Hall, NY.

Boy Scouts of America. Skits & Puppets. 1967. $0.50 pa. Boy Scouts of America, NJ.

Boynton, Robert W. & Mack, Maynard. Introduction to the Play. (Hi-Sch.). 1969. $5.45 text ed.; $3.95 pa. Hayden Book Co., NY.

Bruford, Rose. Teaching Mime. 1958. $4.00 Hdbd. Barnes & Noble, NY.

Buckman, Irene. Twenty Tales from Shakespeare. (Elem–Jr Hi). 1965. $5.39 Hdbd. Random House, NY.

Burger, Isabel B. Creative Play Acting: Learning Through Drama. 2nd ed. 1966. $6.00 text ed. Ronald Pr. Co., NY.

Chambers, Dewey W. Literature for Children: Storytelling & Creative Drama. Lamb, Pose, ed. 1970. $1.95 pa. (ISBN 0-697-06201-5). William C. Brown, IA.

Chilver, Peter. Staging a School Play. 1968. $4.95 Hdbd. (ISBN 0-06-000793-1). Harper & Row, NY.

Citron, Samuel J. Dramatics for Creative Teaching. 1961. $7.50 Hdbd. (ISBN 0-8381-0212-3). United Synagogue Book Serv., NY.

Courtney, Richard. Play, Drama & Thought: The Intellectual Background to Dramatic Education. 1968. $10.50 Hdbd. International Publ. Serv., NY.

Courtney, Richard. School Play. 1966. $4.00 Hdbd. Intl. Publications Service, NY.

Creegan, George. Sir Georges' Book of Hand Puppetry. 1966. $1.98 Hdbd. (ISBN 0-695-48003-0). Follett Publ., IL.

Crosscup, Richard. Children & Dramatics. 1966. $5.95 Hdbd. (ISBN 0-684-10091-6). Charles Scribner's Sons, NY.

Cullum, Albert, ed. Greek Tears & Roman Laughter. Ten Tragedies & Five Comedies for Schools. 1970. $4.50 pa. (ISBN 0-590-09100-X). Scholastic Book Service, NY.

Cummings, Richard. One Hundred & One Hand Puppets. 1962. $3.95 Hdbd. McKay, David, NY.

Currell, David. Puppetry for School Children. (Elem.). 1970. $4.25 Hdbd. (ISBN 0-8231-3028-2). Charles T. Branford, MA.

Dow, Marguerite R. Magic Mask: A Basic Textbook of Theatre Arts. (Hi-Sch.). 1968. $5.00 text ed. St. Martin's Pr., NY.

Durland, Frances C. Creative Dramatics for Children: A Practical Manual for Teachers & Leaders. 1952. $2.75 Hdbd. (ISBN 0-87338-063-0); $1.50 pa. (ISBN 0-87338-064-9). Kent St. Univ. Pr., OH.

Dwyer, Terence. Opera in Your School. 1964. $3.40 Hdbd. (ISBN 0-19-317407-3). Oxford Univ. Pr., NY.

Fitzgerald, Burdett S. World Tales for Creative Dramatics & Storytelling. 1962. $8.70 Hdbd. (ISBN 0-13-969022-0). Prentice-Hall, NY.

Foster, John. Shakespeare Word-Book, Being a Glossary of Archaic Forms & Varied Usages of Words Employed by Shakespeare. 1969. (1908) $17.50 Hdbd. Russell & Russell Publ., NY.

Gofflot, L. V. Theatre Au College Du Moyen Age a Nos Jours, Avec Bibliographie Et Appendices. 1907. $17.50

Hdbd. (ISBN 0-8337-1365-5). Burt Franklin, NY.

Goodridge, Janet. Creative Drama & Improvised Movement for Children. Orig. Title: Drama in the Primary School. 1971. $5.95 Hdbd. (ISBN 0-8238-0120-9). Plays, Inc., MA.

Green, M. C. & Targett, B. R. Space Age Puppets & Masks. (Elem–Hi-Sch.). 1969. $5.95 Hdbd. (ISBN 0-8238-0070-9). Plays, Inc., MA.

Haggerty, Joan. Please Can I Play God. 1967. $4.00 Hdbd. Bobbs-Merrill Co., IN.

Hatcher, Orie L. Book for Shakespeare Plays & Pageants. 1916. $16.50 Hdbd. (ISBN 0-8371-3105-7). Greenwood Pr., CT.

Hatcher, Orie L. Book for Shakespeare Plays & Pageants. (Select Bibliographies Reprint Ser). 1916. $16.50 Hdbd. (ISBN 0-8369-5258-8). Books for Libraries, NY.

Inverarity, Bruce. Manual of Puppetry. (Jr–Hi). 1938. $3.50 Hdbd. (ISBN 0-8323-0168-X). Binfords & Mort, OR.

Jagendorf, Moritz. Puppets for Beginners. (Elem). 1952. $3.95 Hdbd. (ISBN 0-8238-0072-5). Plays Inc., MA.

Johnson, Albert. Shakespeare Vignettes: Adaptations for Acting. 1970. $6.75 Hdbd. (ISBN 0-498-06768-8). A. S. Barnes, NJ.

Johnson, Albert & Johnson, Bertha. Drama for Classroom & Stage. 1969.

$9.50 Hdbd. (ISBN 0-498-06711-4). A. S. Barnes, NJ.

Kerman, Gertrude L. Plays & Creative Ways with Children. (Elem). 1961. $6.95 Hdbd. (ISBN 0-8178-3201-7); $6.19 Hdbd. (ISBN 0-8178-3202-5). Harvey House, NY.

Kinne, Wisner P. George Pierce Baker & the American Theatre. 1968. (1954). $15.75 Hdbd. (ISBN 0-8371-0129-8). Greenwood Pr., CT.

Lewis. Roger. Puppets & Marionettes. (Elem). 1952. $3.59 Hdbd. Alfred A. Knopf, NY.

Lewis, Shari. Making Easy Puppets. (Elem–Hi-Sch.). 1967. $4.50 Hdbd. (ISBN 0-525-34484-5). E. P. Dutton, NY.

Lowndes, Betty. Movement & Creative Drama for Children. Orig. Title: Movement & Drama in the Primary School. 1970. $5.95 Hdbd. (ISBN 0-8238-0121-7). Plays, Inc., MA.

McCaslin, Nellie. Creative Dramatics in the Classroom. 1968. $3.75 text ed.; $2.95 pa. David McKay, NY.

McIntyre, Barbara. Informal Dramatics: A Language Arts Activity for the Special Pupil. 1963. $2.25 pa. (ISBN 0-87076-803-4). Stanwix House, PA.

Malcolm, John, ed. Music Drama in Schools. (Resources of Music Ser). 1971. $12.50 Hdbd. (ISBN 0-521-08003-7). Cambridge Univ Pr., NY.

Mersand, Joseph. Teaching the Drama

in Secondary Schools. 1969. $7.50 Hdbd. (ISBN 0-8108-0260-0). Scarecrow Pr., NJ.

Moffett, James. Teaching the Universe of Discourse. 1968. text ed. $3.60 s.p.; $3.75 pa. Houghton-Mifflin, NY.

Motter, Charlotte K. Theatre in High School: Planning, Teaching, Directing. (Drama Ser). 1970. $6.95 Hdbd. (ISBN 0-13-913012-8). Prentice-Hall, NY.

Motter, Thomas H. School Drama in England. 1968. $11.00 Hdbd. (ISBN 0-8046-0325-1). Kennikat Pr., NY.

Orr, Andrew A. Invitation to Drama. (Hi-Sch.). 1969. $2.80 text ed. St. Martin's Pr., NY.

Pels, Gertrude. Easy Puppets. (Elem.). 1951. $3.95 Hdbd. (ISBN 0-690-25377-X). Thomas Y. Crowell, NY.

Pemberton-Billing, Robin. Teaching Drama. 1965. $2.45 pa. Dufour Editions, PA.

Pierini, M. Francis. Creative Dramatics: A Guide for Educators. 1971. $3.95 Hdbd. Herder & Herder, NY.

Ranger, Paul. Experiments in Drama. 1971. $6.25 Hdbd. International Publ. Serv., NY.

Reardon, William R. & Pawley, Thomas D. Black. Teacher & the Dramatic Arts: A Dialogue, Bibliography & Anthology. 1970. $13.50 Hdbd. (ISBN 0-8371-1850-6). Negro Univ. Pr., CT.

Renfro, Nancy. Puppets for Play Pro-

duction. (Elem.). 1969. $6.95 Hdbd. Funk & Wagnalls, NY.

Ross, Laura. Puppet Shows Using Poems & Stories. (Elem.). 1970. $4.95 Hdbd. Lothrop, Lee & Shephard., NY.

Schattner, Regina. Creative Dramatics for Handicapped Children. (Special Education Bks). 1966. $6.00 Hdbd. John Day Co., NY.

Shakespeare, William. Hamlet. (E-Z Learner Study Test Ser). (Hi-Sch.). 1971. $1.25 pa. (ISBN 0-524-99112-X). Coshad Inc. Apollo Books, CT.

Sievers, David W. Directing for the Theater. 2nd ed. 1965. $6.50 Hdbd. (ISBN 0-697-04250-2). William C. Brown, IA.

Siks, Geraldine B. Creative Dramatics: An Art for Children. (Elem.). 1958. $9.00 text ed. (ISBN 0-06-046160-8). Harper & Row, NY.

Siks, Geraldine B. & Dunnington, Hazel B., eds. Children's Theatre & Creative Dramatics. (Hi-Sch.). 1961. $6.95 Hdbd.; $3.95 pa. (ISBN 0-295-97875-9). Univ. of Washington Pr., WA.

Slade, P. Introduction to Child Drama. 1958. $2.50 Hdbd. Lawrence Verry, Inc., CT.

Slade, Peter. Child Drama. 1954. $7.50 Hdbd. Lawrence Verry, Inc., CT.

Smilansky, Sara. Effects of Sociodramatic Play of Disadvantaged Pre-School Children. 1968. $8.00 Hdbd. (ISBN 0-471-79950-5). John Wiley & Sons, NY.

Stahl, E. L. Iphigenie Auf Tauris by Goethe. Foster, L. W. & Rowley, B. A., eds. (Studies in German Literature Ser). (Orig., Critical Analysis Only). Hi-Sch. 1961. $2.50 Hdbd.; $1.00 pa. Barron's Educ. Series, NY.

Storch, C. Fun Time Puppets. (Elem.). $2.75 Hdbd. Childrens Pr., IL.

Styan, J. L. Dramatic Experience. 1965. $6.95 Hdbd. Cambridge Univ. Pr., NY.

Taylor, Loren E. Pageants & Festivals. 1965. $1.75 pa. (ISBN 0-8087-2007-4). Burgess Publ. Co., MN.

Tichenor, Tom. Tom Tichenor's Puppets. 1971. $5.95 Hdbd. (ISBN 0-687-42363-5). Abingdon Pr., TN.

Usherwood, Stephen. Shakespeare Play by Play. (Hi-Sch.). 1968. $5.95 Hdbd. (ISBN 0-8090-8620-4). Hill & Wang, NY.

Walker, Pamela P. Seven Steps to Creative Children's Dramatics. 1957. $3.00 Hdbd. (ISBN 0-8090-8560-7). Hill & Wang, NY.

Ward, Winifred. Playmaking with Children from Kindergarten Through Junior High School. 2nd ed. 1957. text ed. $5.75. (ISBN 0-390-92325-7). Appleton-Century-Crofts, NY.

Ward, Winifred. Stories to Dramatize. 1952. $6.00 Hdbd. Anchorage Pr., KY.

Wargo, Dan & Wargo, Dorothy. Dramatics in the Christian School. 1966. $5.25 pa. Concordia Publ. House, MO.

Way, Brian. Development Through Drama. 1966. $2.75 pa. Humanities Pr., NY.

Television

Adams, John C., et al. College Teaching by Television. 1958. $5.00 Hdbd. (ISBN 0-8268-1242-2). Ace Books, Inc., NY.

Anglo-Norwegian Symposium – Oslo – 1968. Use of Television in Adult Education: Report. 1969. $2.00 pa. Universitetsforlaget, MA.

Association For Educational Communications And Technology. Survey of Instructional Closed-Circuit Television, 1967. 1967. $3.00 pa. (071-02890). National Educ. Assn., NY.

Ball, Samuel & Bogatz, Gerry A. First Year of Sesame Street: An Evaluation. 1970. text ed. $7.50 pa. (ISBN 0-8077-1043-1). Teachers Coll. Pr., NY.

Benton, Charles et al. Television in Urban Education. 1969. $15.00. Frederick A. Praeger, NY.

Bessant, Wailand, et al. Adoption & Utilization of Instructional Television. 1968. $2.00 pa. (ISBN 0-292-73451-4). Univ. of Texas Pr., TX.

Burke, Richard C., ed. Instructional Television Bold New Venture. (Bold New Venture Ser). 1971. $5.95 Hdbd. (ISBN 0-253-33018-1). Ind. Univ. Pr., IN.

Connochie, T. D. TV for Education & Industry. 1969. $7.00 Hdbd. William S. Heinman, NY.

Costello, Lawrence F. & Gordon, George N. Teach with Television. 2nd ed. (Communication Arts Books Ser). 1961. $5.95 Hdbd. (ISBN 0-8038-7019-1); $3.45, PA. (ISBN 0-8038-7018-3). Hastings House, NY.

Davis, Harold S., ed. Instructional Media Center Bold New Venture. (Bold New Venture Ser). 1971. $7.50 Hdbd. (ISBN 0-253-33010-6). Ind. Univ. Pr., IN.

Diamond, Robert M., ed. Guide to Instructional Television. 1964. $8.95 Hdbd. (ISBN 0-07-016725-7). McGraw-Hill, NY.

Division of Educational Technology. Guide to the N E a for Education Industries. 1969. pa. price "n.g." National Educ. Assn., NY.

Division Of Educational Technology. Professional Rights & Responsibilities of Television Teachers: An N E a Policy Statement. 1969. pa. price "n.g." National Educ. Assn.,NY.

Division Of Educational Technology. Schools & Cable Television. 1971. $2.25 pa. National Educ. Assn., NY.

Division Of Educational Technology. Television for World Understanding. 1970. $1.50 pa. National Educ. Assn., NY.

Evans, Richard I. & Leppmann, Peter K. Resistance to Innovation in Higher Education. 1967. $7.50 Hdbd. (ISBN 0-87589-010-5). Jossey-Bass Inc., CA.

Feinstein, Phyllis. All About Sesame Street. 1971. $0.75 pa. (T075-19). Tower Publ., NY.

Gordon, George N. Classroom Television: New Frontiers in ITV. 1970. $8.95 Hdbd. (ISBN 0-8038-1144-6); text ed. $5.80 pa. (ISBN 0-8038-1149-7). Hastings House, NY.

Kinross, Felicity. Television for the Teacher. 1968. $6.95 Hdbd. (ISBN 0-241-91293-8). Dufour Editions, PA.

Koenig, Allen E. & Hill, Ruane B., eds. Farther Vision; Educational Television Today. 1969. $3.95 pa. (ISBN 0-299-04584-6). Univ. of Wis. Pr., WI.

Levenson, William B. & Stasheff, Edward. Teaching Through Radio & Television. rev. ed. 1952. $18.00 Hdbd. (ISBN 0-8371-2414-X). Greenwood Pr., CT.

Lewis, William C. Through Cable to Classroom: A Guide to ITV Distribution Systems. Ingle, Henry T., ed. 1967. $2.00 pa. National Educ. Assn., NY.

Midwest Program On Airborne Television Instruction. Using Television in the Classroom. 1961. text ed. $3.95. (ISBN 0-07-041911-6). McGraw-Hill, NY.

Modern Language Association. Research & Studies About the Use of Television & Film in Foreign Language Instruction: A Bibliography with Abstracts. Svobodny, Dolly D., ed. (ERIC). 1969. $2.50 pa. (ISBN 0-87352-054-8). Modern Language Assn., NY.

Moir, Guthrie. Teaching & Television: ETV Explained. 1967. $6.00 Hdbd. (ISBN 0-08-012355-4); $4.00 pa. (ISBN 0-08-012354-6). Pergamon Publishing Co., NY.

National Association Of Educational Broadcasters Conference – 1964. Improvement of Teaching by Television. MacLennan, Donald W. & Griffith, Barton L., eds. 1964. $4.00 Hdbd. (ISBN 0-8262-0034-6); $2.50 pa. Univ. of Missouri Pr., MO.

National Education Association – Division Of Educational Technology. Creating Visuals for TV: A Guide for Educators. 1962. $1.25 pa. National Educ. Assn., NY.

National Education Association – Division Of Educational Technology. Instructional Television Fixed Service: What It Is... How to Plan. 1967. $1.00 pa. National Educ. Assn., NY.

National Education Association – Elementary School Principals Department. Beyond Sesame Street. 1971. $2.00 pa. National Educ. Assn., NY.

Postman, Neil. Television & the Teaching of English. $1.65 pa. (ISBN 0-390-71420-8). Appleton-Century-Crofts, NY.

Schramm, Wilbur L., et al. People Look at Educational Television a Report of Nine Representative E. T. V. Stations. 1963. $6.50 Hdbd. (ISBN 0-8047-0172-5). Stanford Univ. Pr., CA.

Taylor, Calvin W. & Williams, Frank E.

Instructional Media & Creativity. $9.95 text ed. $5.95 pa. John Wiley & Sons, NY.

Treneman, Joseph M. Communication & Comprehension. 1968. $6.50 Hdbd. Humanities Pr., NY.

Unesco. New Educational Media in Action, 3 Vols. 1969. Set—$13.50 Hdbd. (UNESCO). Unipub Inc., NY.

FINANCE

Angels' Bible: Theatre & Film Finance. 1971. $95.00 Hdbd. (ISBN 0-8277-0725-8). British Book Center, NY.

Archer, William & Barker, H. Granville, eds. National Theatre: Scheme & Estimates. 1970. (1907) $9.50 Hdbd. (ISBN 0-8046-0749-4). Kennikat Pr., NY.

Bernheim, Alfred L. Business of the Theatre. 1932. $17.50 Hdbd. Benjamin Blom, NY.

Cullman, Marguerite. Occupation: Angel. 1963. $3.95 Hdbd. (ISBN 0-393-07440-4). W. W. Norton, NY.

Davis, Christopher. The Producer. 1972. $8.95 Hdbd. (ISBN 06-010994-7). Harper & Row, NY.

Donohue, Joseph W., Jr., ed. Theatrical Manager in England & America: Players of a Perilous Game. 1971. $8.50 Hdbd. (ISBN 0-691-06188-2). Princeton Univ. Pr., NJ.

Farber, Donald C. From Option to

Opening: A Guide for the off Broadway Producer. rev. 2nd ed. 1970. $7.50 Hdbd. (ISBN 0-910482-24-1). DBS Publ., NY.

Farber, Donald C. Producing on Broadway: A Comprehensive Guide. 1969. $15.00 Hdbd. DBS Publ., NY.

Moore, Thomas G. Economics of the American Theater. 1968. $8.25 Hdbd. (ISBN 0-8223-0118-0). Duke Univ. Pr., NC.

Poggi, Jack. Theater in America: The Impact of Economic Forces, 1870–1967. 1968. $10.00 Hdbd. (ISBN 0-8014-0340-5). Cornell Univ. Pr., NY.

Ripenhausen, Bernhard. Das Arbeitsrecht der Buehne: Systematische Darstellung der Gesamten Rechtsprechung des Buehneoberschiedsgerichts. (Labor Law as applied to theater in Germany; 2nd enl. ed. Incl. Ergaenzungsband. 1965. $13.20 Hdbd. (ISBN 3-11-001029-1). (Ger.). 1956. $9.85 Hdbd. (ISBN 3-11-001028-3). De Gruyter, Germany.

MOTION PICTURE

Actors and Actresses

Anderson, Robert G. Faces, Forms, Films. The Artistry Of Lon Chaney. $8.50 Hdbd. (ISBN 0-498-07726-8). A.S. Barnes, NJ.

Cameron, Ian & Cameron, Elizabeth. Dames. 1969. $4.95 Hdbd. $2.50 pa. Frederick Praeger, NY.

Cameron, Ian & Cameron, Elizabeth.

Heavies. 1969. $4.95 Hdbd. $2.50 pa. Frederick Praeger, NY.

Cameron, Ian, ed. Second Wave. 1970. $4.95 Hdbd. $2.50 pa. Frederick Praeger, NY.

Corneau, Ernest N. Hall of Fame of Western Films Stars. 1969. $9.75 Hdbd. (ISBN 0-8158-0124-6). Christopher Publ. House, MA.

Croce, Arlene. Fred Astaire — Ginger Rogers Movie Book. 1971. $10.00 Hdbd. (ISBN 0-87690-027-9). Outerbridge and Diens & Frey, NY.

Deschner, Donald. Films of Cary Grant. 1971. $9.95 Hdbd. (ISBN 0-8065-0229-0). Citadel Pr., NY.

Eyles, Allen & Billings, Pat. Hollywood Today. 1971. $2.95 pa. (ISBN 0-498-07858-2). A.S. Barnes, NJ.

Gelman, Barbara, Photoplay Treasury. 1971. $9.95 Hdbd. Crown Publ, NY.

Gifford, Dennis. British Cinema. $2.95 pa. (ISBN 0-498-06930-3). A.S. Barnes, NJ.

Gomes, P.E. Salles. Jean Vigo. Francovich, Allan, transl. $8.95 Hdbd. (ISBN 0-520-01676-9). Univ. of California. Pr. CA.

Graham, Peter. Dictionary of the Cinema. 1968. $4.95 Hdbd. (ISBN 0-498-06839-0); $2.95 pa. (ISBN 0-498-06838-2). A.S. Barnes, NJ.

Graham, Sheilah. Garden of Allah. 1970. $5.95 Hdbd. Crown Publ., NY.

Griffith, Richard. Movie Stars. 1970.

$25.00 Hdbd. Doubleday & Co., NY.

Hughes, Elinor. Famous Stars of Fildom: Men. 1932. $12.50 Hdbd. (ISBN 0-8369-1518-6). Books for Libraries, NY.

Lacalamita, M. & Di Gammatteo, F., eds. Filmlexicon Degli Autori E Delle Opere, 7 Vols. 1968. $200.00 Hdbd. Benjamin Blom, NY.

Lahue, Kalton C. Ladies in Distress. 1971. $10.00 Hdbd. (ISBN 0-498-07634-2). A.S. Barnes, NJ.

Lahue, Kalton C. Winners of the West: The Sagebrush Heroes of the Silent Screen. 1970. $10.00 Hdbd. (ISBN 0-498-07396-3). A.S. Barnes, NJ.

Lake, Veronica & Bain, Donald. Veronica: The Autobiography of Veronica Lake. 1971. $6.95 Hdbd. (ISBN 0-8065-0226-6). Citadel Pr., NY.

McDonald, Gerald D., Films of Charlie Chaplin. 1971. $3.95 pa. (ISBN 0-8065-0236-3). Citadel Pr., NY.

Maltin, Leonard. Movie Comedy Teams. 1970. $1.50 pa. New American Library, NY.

Michael, Paul. American Movies Reference Book: The Sound Era. 1968. $29.95 Hdbd. (ISBN 0-13-028134-4). Prentice-Hall, NY.

Miller, Edwin. Seventeen Interviews: Film Stars & Super-Stars of the Sixties. 1970. $6.95 Hdbd. Macmillan Publ., NY.

Morella, Joe & Epstein, Edward Z.

Lana Turner. 1971. $6.95 Hdbd. (ISBN 0-8065-0226-6). Citadel Pr., NY.

Morella, Joseph & Epstein, Edward Z. Rebel in Films. 1971. $9.95 Hdbd. Citadel Pr., NY.

Quirk, Lawrence J. Films of Fredric March. 1971. $9.95 Hdbd. (ISBN 0-8065-0259-2). Citadel Pr., NY.

Quirk, Lawrence J. Films of Paul Newman. (Illus.). 1971. $9.95 Hdbd. Citadel Pr., NY.

Sarris, Andrew. American Cinema: Directors & Directions: Nineteen Twenty-Nine–Nineteen Sixty-Eight. 1969. $2.95 pa. (ISBN 0-525-47227-4). E.P. Dutton, NY.

Taylor, John R. Cinema Eye, Cinema Ear: Some Key Film-Makers of the Sixties. $5.95 Hdbd. (ISBN 0-8090-3460-3); $2.25 pa. (ISBN 0-8090-1328-2). Hill & Wang, NY.

Twomey, Alfred E. & McClure, Arthur F. Versatiles. 1969. $10.00 Hdbd. (ISBN 0-498-06792-0). A.S. Barnes, NJ.

Wagenknecht, Edward. Movies in the Age of Innocence. 1962. $7.95 Hdbd. (ISBN 0-8061-0539-9). Univ. of Oklahoma Pr.

Walker, Alexander. Stardom. 1970. $10.00 Hdbd. (ISBN 0-8128-1309-X). Stein & Day, NY.

Zierold, Norman. Moguls. 1969. $6.95 Hdbd. Coward McCann, NY.

Audiences

Seldes, Gilbert V. Great Audience. 1950. $11.00 Hdbd. (ISBN 0-8371-2802-1). Greenwood Pr., CT.

Shuttleworth, Frank K. & May, Mark A. Social Conduct & Attitudes of Movie Fans. $8.00 Hdbd. (ISBN 0-405-01630-1). Arno Pr., NY.

Cameras

Lahue, Kalton C. & Bailey, Joseph C. Collecting Vintage Cameras, Vol. 1, The American 35mm. 1971. $4.50 Hdbd. (ISBN 0-8174-0176-8). American Photographic Book Publ., NY.

Pittaro, Ernest. T.V. & Film Production Data Book. 1959. $2.95 Hdbd. (ISBN 0-87100-067-9). Morgan & Morgan, NY.

Souto, H. Mario. Technique of the Motion Picture Camera. 1967. $16.00 Hdbd. (ISBN 0-8038-7088-4). Hastings House Publ., NY.

Surgenor. Bolex H16-H8 Guide. $2.50 pa. American Photographic Book Publ., NY.

Tydings, Kenneth. Bolex 8-16 Mm Movie Guide $2.50 pa. American Photographic Book Publ., NY.

Cartoons

Anderson, Yvonne. Make Your Own Animated Movies. (Elem.) 1970. $5.95 Hdbd. (ISBN 0-316-03940-3). Little, Brown & Co., MA.

Andersen, Yvonne. Teaching Film Animation. 1970. $8.95 Hdbd. VanNostrand-Reinhold Books, NY.

Halas, John. Film & TV Graphics. Herdeg, Walter, ed. 1967. $17.95 Hdbd. (ISBN 0-8038-2237-5). Hastings House Publ., NY.

Halas, John & Manwell, Roger. Technique of Film Animation. 1968. $10.95 Hdbd. (ISBN 0-8038-7024-8). Hastings House Publ., NY.

Halas, John & Manwell, Roger. Art in Movement: New Frontiers in Animation. 1970 $17.50 Hdbd. (ISBN 0-8038-0344-3). Hastings House Publ., NY.

Hepworth, Cecil M. Animated Photography: The ABC of the Cinematograph. $5.00 Hdbd. (ISBN 0-405-01615-8). Arno Pr., NY.

Kinsey, Anthony. How to Make Animated Movies. 1970. $6.95 Hdbd. (ISBN 0-670-38391-0). Viking Pr., NY.

Stephenson, Ralph. Animation in the Cinema. $2.95 pa. (ISBN 0-498-06640-1). A.S. Barnes, NJ.

Criticism

Adler, Renata. Year in the Dark. 1970. $7.95 Hdbd. (ISBN 0-394-45293-3). Random House, NY.

Altshuler, Thelma & Janaro, Richard P. Responses to Drama: An Introduction to Plays & Movies. 1967. $4.25 pa. Houghton Mifflin, MA.

Balazs, Bela. Theory of the Film. 1971. $12.95 Hdbd. (ISBN 0-8277-0616-2). British Book Center, NY.

De Bartolo, Dick. Return of Mad Look at Old Movies. $.60 pa. New American Library, NY.

Huss, Roy, ed. Focus on Blow-Up. 1971. $5.95 Hdbd. (ISBN 0-13-077784-6); $2.45 pa. (ISBN 0-13-077776-5). Prentice-Hall, NY.

Jones, G. William. Sunday Night at the Movies. 1967. $1.95 pa. (ISBN 0-8042-1977-X). John Knox Pr., VA.

Kael, Pauline. Going Steady. 1971. $1.95 pa. Bantam Books, NY.

Kael, Pauline. I Lost It at the Movies. 1965. $7.50 Hdbd. (ISBN 0-316-48164-5). Little Brown & Co., MA.

Kael, Pauline. Kiss Kiss Bang Bang. 1968 $8.95 Hdbd. (ISBN 0-316-48162-9). Little Brown & Co., MA.

Kael, Pauline. Kiss Kiss Bang Bang. 1971. $1.95 pa. Bantam Books, N.Y.

Kauffmann, Stanley. Figures of Light: Film Criticism & Comment. 1971. $8.95 Hdbd. (ISBN 0-06-012274-9). Harper & Row, NY.

MacDonald, Dwight. Dwight MacDonald on Movies. 1971. $1.50 pa. (ISBN 0-425-01938-1). Berkley Publ. Co., NY.

Rosenbaum, Jonathan, ed. Film Masters: An Anthology of Criticism on

Thirty-Two Film Directors. 1971. $12.95 Hdbd. Grosset & Dunlap, NY.

Sarris, Andrew. Film. 1968. $1.00 pa. Bobbs-Merrill, IN.

Wolfenstein, Martha & Leites, Nathan, Movies: A Psychological Study. $13.95 Hdbd. Hafner Publ. Co., NY.

Film Collections

Chittock, J. World Dictionary of Stockshot & Film Production Library. $12.50 Hdbd. Pergamon Publ., NY.

Gifford. Movie Monsters. $1.95 Hdbd. (ISBN 0-289-79038-7). E.P. Dutton, NY.

Holland, Benjamin F. Status & Prospects of Film Distribution in Texas. (Fred Carlton Ayer Memorial, Vol. 2). 1958. $1.25 pa. (ISBN 0-292-73388-7). Univ. of Texas Pr. TX.

Kula, S. Bibliography of Film Librianship. $3.00 Hdbd. (ISBN 0-85365-140-X). International Scholary Book Serv., OR.

Lahue, Kalton. Collecting Classic Films. 1970. $6.95 Hdbd. (ISBN 0-8038-1141-1). American Photographic Book Publ., NY.

Maltin, Leonard. Classical Movie Shorts. 1971. $9.95 Hdbd. Crown Publ., NY.

Munden, Kenneth, ed. American Film Institute Catalog, Feature Films 1911-1920. price "n.g." (ISBN 0-8352-0437-5). R.R. Bowker, NY.

Screen Monographs One. $5.00 Hdbd.

(ISBN 0-405-01626-3). Arno Pr., NY.

Screen Monographs Two. (1970) $7.00 Hdbd. (ISBN 0-405-01627-1). Arno Pr., NY.

Industry

Anderson, Joseph L. & Ritchie, Donald. Japanese Film: Art & Industry. 1960. $3.95 pa. Grove Pr., NY.

Cameron, Ian. Movie Reader. 1971. $12.50 Hdbd. $4.50 pa. Frederick Praeger, NY.

French, Philip. Movie Moguls: An Informal History of the Hollywood Tycoons. 1971. $5.95 Hdbd. Henry Regnery Co., IL.

Guback, Thomas H. International Film Industry: Western Europe & America Since 1945. 1969. $10.00 Hdbd. (ISBN 0-253-33050-5). Indiana Univ. Pr., IN.

Jobes, Gertrude. Motion Picture Empire. 1966. $10.00 Hdbd. (ISBN 0-208-00169-7). Shoe String Pr., CT.

Kelly, Terence. Competitive Cinema. 1966. $7.50 Hdbd. International Public Serv., NY.

Lahue, Kalton C. Dreams for Sale: The Rise & Fall of the Triangle Film Corporation. 1971. $8.50 Hdbd. (ISBN 0-498-07684-9). A.S. Barnes, NJ.

Minus, Johnny & Hale, William S. Movie Industry Book. (Entertainment Industry Ser., Vol. 5). Orig. Title: Movie Producers First Business & Law

Book. 1970. $35.00 Hdbd. (ISBN 0-911370-05-6). Seven Arts Pr., CA.

Moving Picture World, 1907-1911, 10 vols. Set. $750.00 Hdbd. Arno Pr., NY.

Pechter, William S. Twenty-Four Times a Second: Films & Film-Makers. 1971. $7.95 Hdbd. (ISBN 0-06-013321-X). Harper & Row, NY.

Rosenberg, Bernard & Silverstein, Harry. Real Tinsel: The Story of Hollywood Told by the Men and Women Who Lived It. 1970. $9.95 Hdbd. Macmillan & Co., NY.

Sinclair, Upton. Upton Sinclair Presents William Fox. $12.50 Hdbd. (ISBN 0-405-01637-9). Arno Pr., NY.

Music

Bachrach & David. Bachrach-David Songbook. 1970. $7.50 Hdbd. Simon & Schuster, NY.

Croce, Arlene. Fred Astaire-Ginger Rogers Movie Book. 1971. $10.00 Hdbd. (ISBN 0-87690-027-0). Outerbridge & Dienstfrey, NY.

Foort, Reginald. The Cinema Organ. $6.00 Hdbd. (ISBN 0-911572-05-8). Vestal Pr., NY.

Gershwin, George & Gershwin, Ira. George & Ira Gershwin Songbook. 1960. $10.00 Hdbd. Simon & Schuster, NY.

Hofmann, Charles. Sounds for Silents. 1969. $10.00 Hdbd. DBS Publs., NY.

Lang, Edith & West, George. Musical Accompaniment of Moving Pictures. (1920) $4.00 Hdbd. (ISBN 0-405-01620-4). Arno Pr., NY.

London, Kurt. Film Music. (1936) $9.50 Hdbd. (ISBN 0-405-01622-0). Arno Pr., NY.

Manwell, Roger & Huntley, John. Technique of Film Music. 1957. $11.50 Hdbd. (ISBN 0-8038-7028-0). Hastings House Publ., NY.

Okun, Milton, ed. Great Songs of the Sixties. 1970. $17.50 Hdbd. (ISBN 0-8129-0153-3). Quadrangle Books, IL.

Porter, Cole. Cole Porter Song Book. 1959. $12.50 Hdbd. Simon & Schuster, NY.

Rapee, Erno. Encyclopedia of Music for Pictures. $15.50 Hdbd. (ISBN 0-405-01634-4). Arno Pr., NY.

Rapee, Erno. Motion Picture Moods for Pianists & Organists, a Rapid Reference Collection of Selected Pieces. $30.00 Hdbd. (ISBN 0-405-01635-2). Arno Pr., NY.

Skinner, Frank. Underscore. $6.00 Hdbd. Wehman Brothers, NJ.

Plays

Amberg, G., intro. by. Film Society Programmes, 1925-1939. 1971. $25.00 Hdbd. (ISGN 0-405-00741-8). Arno Pr., NY.

Antonioni. Antonioni: Four Screenplays. 1971. $3.95 pa. (ISBN 0-670-12944-5). Grossman Publ., NY.

Beylie, Claude, ed. Jean Renoir Films, 1924-1939. Lane, Helen R., transl. 1971. $50.00 Hdbd. Grove Pre., NY.

Blacker, Irwin R. Film Script. 1971. $5.95 Hdbd. (ISBN 0-8402-1208-9). $2.95 pa. (ISBN 0-8402-8208-7). Nash Publ. Corp., CA.

Bunuel, Luis. Bunuel: Three Screenplays. Bozzetti, Piergiuseppi, transl. 1970. $6.95 Hdbd. (ISBN 0-670-19466-2); $3.50 pa. (ISBN 0-670-19467-0). Grossman Publ., NY.

Clair, Rene. Clair: Four Screenplays. Bozzetti, Piergiuseppi, transl. 1970 $10.00 Hdbd. (ISBN 0-670-22488-X); $4.95 pa. (ISBN 0-670-22489-8). Grossman Publ., NY.

Clair, Rene. Clair: Four Screenplays. Bozzetti, Piergiuseppi, trans. 1970. $10.00 Hdbd. (ISBN 0-670-22488-X); $4.95 pa. (ISBN 0-670-22489-8). Grossman Publ., NY.

Clair, Rene. Nous La Liberte Entr'Acte. 1970. $1.95 pa. (ISBN 0-671-20617-6). Simon & Schuster, NY.

Dreyer, Carl T. Four Screenplays. Stallybrass, Oliver, transl. 1971. $3.95 pa. (ISBN 0-253-28140-7). Indiana Univ. Pr., IN.

Eastman, Charles. Little Fauss & Big Halsy. 1970. $4.95 Hdbd. $2.25 pa. (ISBN 0-374-18904-8). Farrar, Straus & Giroux, NY.

Eisler, Hanns. Composing for the

Films. (1947) $9.75 Hdbd. (ISBN 0-8369-5674-5). Books for Libraries, NY.

Fellini, Federico. Fellini: Early Screenplays. Green, Judith, transl. 1971. $6.95 Hdbd. (ISBN 0-670-31150-2). Grossman Publ., NY.

Herman, Lewis. Practical Manual of Screen Playwriting for Theater & Television Films. $3.95 pa. World Publ. Co., OH.

Kurosawa, Akira. Seven Samurai. 1970. $2.95 Hdbd. (ISBN 0-671-20619-2). Simon & Schuster, NY.

Lahue, Kalton C. Bound & Gagged. 1968. $7.50 Hdbd. (ISBN 0-498-06762-9). A.S. Barnes, NJ.

Lelouche, Claude. Man & a Woman. 1970. $1.95 pa. (ISBN 0-671-20963-9). Simon & Schuster, NY.

McCarty, Clifford. Published Screenplays: A Checklist. 1971. $6.50 Hdbd. (ISBN 0-87338-112-2). Kent St. Univ. Pr., OH.

Martin, Marcel, eds. Complete Works of S.M. Eisenstein. 1971. $50.00 Hdbd. Grove Pr., NY.

Mayer, David. Eisenstein's Potemkin. 1971. $8.95 Hdbd. (ISBN 0-670-29079-3); $4.95 pa. Grossman Publ., NY.

Pabst, G.W. Pandora's Box. 1970. $1.95 pa. (ISBN 0-671-20615-X). Simon & Schuster, NY.

Parker, Norton S. Audiovisual Script Writing. 1968. $12.50 Hdbd. (ISBN 0-8135-0576-3). Rutgers Univ. Pr., NJ.

Pasolini, Pier P. Oedipus Rex. 1970. $1.95 pa. (ISBN 0-671-20964-7). Simon & Schuster, NY.

Phillips, Henry A. Photodrama. (1914). $7.00 Hdbd. (ISBN 0-405-01632-8). Arno Pr., NY.

Prevert, Jacques & Carne, Marcel. Jour Se Leve. 1970. $1.95 pa. (SIBN 0-671-20616-8). Simon & Schuster, NY.

Pudovkin, V. Film Technique & Acting. $3.95 Hdbd. Wehman Brothers, NY.

Robinson, William R., ed. Man & the Movies. 1969. (1967) $2.25 pa. (ISBN 0-14-021061-X). Penguin Books, MD.

Visconti, Luchino. Visconti, Five Screenplays: Vol. 1 Terra Trema & Senso, Vol. 2 White Nights, Rocco & His Brothers, Job. Green, Judith, transl. 1969. Vol. 1. $6.95 Hdbd. (ISBN 0-67074705-X); $3.50 pa. (ISBN 0-670-74708-4) (ISBN 0-670-74706-8). Grossman Publ., NY.

Visconti, Luchino. Visconti, Three Screenplays: White Nights, Rocco & His Brothers, The Job. Green, Judith, transl. 1970. $7.95 Hdbd. (ISBN 0-670-74705-X); $3.50 pa. (ISBN 0-670-74706-8). Grossman Publ., NY.

Visconti, Luchino. Visconti: Two Screenplays la Terra Trema Senso. Green, Judith, transl. $6.95 Hdbd.

(ISBN 0-670-74707-6); $2.50 pa. (ISBN 0-670-74708-4). Grossman Publ., NY.

Von Stroheim, Erich. Greed. 1970. $4.95 Hdbd. (ISBN 0-671-20614-1). Simon & Schuster, NY.

Warhol, Andy. Blue Movie. 1970. $1.75 pa. Grove Pr., NY.

Weine, Robert. Cabinet of Dr. Caligari. 1970 $1.95 pa. Simon & Schuster, NY.

Welles, Orson. Trial. 1970. $1.95 pa. (ISBN 0-671-20620-6). Simon & Schuster, NY.

History and Criticism

Battcock, Gregroy, ed. New American Cinema: A Critical Anthology. 1967. $1.95 pa. (ISBN 0-525-47200-2). E.P. Dutton, NY.

Blacker, Irwin R. Best Film Plays, 1970-1971. 1971. $8.50 Hdbd. (ISBN 0-8402-1243-7). Nash Publ. Co, CA.

Boyum, Joy G. & Scott, Adrienne. Film As Film: Critical Responses to Film Art. 1971. $4.95 pa. Allyn Inc., NJ.

Eich, Gunter. Journeys. Hamburger, Michael, transl. 1970. $3.50 Hdbd. (ISBN 0-670-40956-1); $1.50 pa. (ISBN 0-670-40957-X). Grossman Publ., NY.

Gessner, Robert. Moving Image. 1970. (1968). $3.95 pa. (ISBN 0-525-47275-4). E.P. Dutton, NY.

Gessner, Robert. Moving Image: A Guide to Cinematic Literacy. 1968.

$8.95 Hdbd. (ISBN 0-525-16068-X). E.P. Dutton, NY.

Gottesman, R. & Geduld, H. Guide to Film Study. $3.95 pa. (ISBN 0-03-085292-7). Holt, Rinehart & Winston, NY.

Huss, Roy & Silverstein, Norman. Film Experience. $1.95 pa. Dell Publ. Co., NY.

Kauffmann, Stanley. World on Film. 1966. $7.95 Hdbd. (ISBN 0-06-012273-0). Harper & Row, NY.

Kracauer, Siegfried. From Caligari to Hitler: A Psychological History of the German Film. $9.00 Hdbd. (ISBN 0-691-08708-3); $2.95 pa. (ISBN 0-691-02505-3). Princeton Univ. Pr., NJ.

Robinson, William R., ed. Man & the Movies: Essays on the Art of Our Time. 1967. $7.95 Hdbd. (ISBN 0-8071-0718-2). Louisiana State Univ. Pr., LA.

Projection

Rudman, Jack. Civil Service Examination Passbook: Motion Picture Operator. $8.00 Hdbd. $5.00 pa. National Learning Corp., NY.

Wheeler, Leslie J. Principles of Cinematography. 1969. $15.95 Hdbd. (ISBN 0-87100-009-1). Morgan & Morgan, NY.

Serials

Barbour, Alan G. Days of Thrills &

Adventure. 1970. $6.95 Hdbd. Macmillan, NY.

Theaters

Aloi, Roberto. Architecture for the Theatre. 1958. $30.00 Hdbd. William Heinman, NY.

Grau, Robert. Stage in the Twentieth Century. 1912. $15.00 Hdbd. Benjamin Blom, NY.

Hulfish, David. Motion-Picture Work. (1915). $25.00 Hdbd. (ISBN) 0-405-01617-4). Arno Pr., NY.

Sharp, Dennis. Picture Palace & Other Buildings for the Movies. 1969. $12.50 Hdbd. Frederick Praeger, NY.

MOTION PICTURES

Amberg, G. Film Society Programmes, 1925. 1939. 1971. 1925. $25.00 Hdbd. (ISBN 0-405-00741-8). Arno Pr., NY.

Angels' Bible: Theatre & Film Finance. 1971. $95.00 Hdbd. (ISBN 0-8277-0725-8). British Book Center, NY.

Arnheim, Rudolf. Film As Art. 1957. $1.95 pa. (ISBN 0-520-00035-8). Univ. of California Pr., CA.

Balazs, Bela. Theory of Film: Character & Growth of a New Art. 1971. $2.75 pa. (ISBN 0-486-22685-9). Dover Publ., NY.

Barbour, Alan. Days of Thrills & Adventure. 1970. $3.95 pa. Macmillan, NY.

Barbour, Alan. Thousand & One Delights. 1971. $7.95 Hdbd. Macmillan, NY.

Barbour, Alan. Thrill of It All. 1971. $7.95 Hdbd. $3.95 pa. Macmillan, NY.

Battcock, Gregory, ed. New American Cinema: A Critical Anthology. 1967. $1.95 pa. (ISBN 0-525-47200-2). E.P. Dutton, NY.

Baxter, John. Gangster Film. 1970. $3.50 pa. (ISBN 0-498-07714-4). A.S. Barnes, NJ.

Baxter, John. Science Fiction in the Cinema. $2.95 pa. (ISBN 0-498-07416-1). A.S. Barnes, NJ.

Bazin, Andre. What Is Cinema. Gray, Hugh, transl. 1967. $5.75 Hdbd. (ISBN 0-520-00091-9); $2.25 pa. (ISBN 0-520-00092-7). Univ. of California Pr., CA.

Bazin, Andre. What Is Cinema, Vol. 2. Gray, Hugh, transl. $7.95 Hdbd. (ISBN 0-520-02034-0). Univ. of California Pr., NY.

Bellone, Julius. Renaissance of the Film. 1970. $2.95 pa. Macmillan, NY.

Benoit-Levy, Jean. Art of the Motion Picture. (1946). $9.00 Hdbd. (ISBN 0-405-01603-4). Arno Pr., NY.

Bluestone, George. Novels into Film. 1957. $2.45 pa. (ISBN 0-520-00130-3). Univ. of California Pr., NY.

Blumer, Herbert. Movies, Delinquency,

& Crime. $8.00 Hdbd. (ISBN 0-87585-152-5). Patterson Smith, NJ.

Bobker, Lee. Elements of Film. 1969. $4.75 pa. (ISBN 0-15-522094-2). Harcourt Brace Jovanovich, NY.

Buckle, Gerald F. Mind & the Film, a Treatise on the Psychological Factors in the Film. (1926). $4.50 Hdbd. (ISBN 0-405-01604-2). Arno Pr., NY.

Butler, Ivan. Horror in the Cinema. 1970. $2.95 pa. (ISBN 0-498-07651-2). A.S. Barnes, NJ.

Carson, L. Kit & McBride, Jim. David Holzman's Diary. 1970. $4.95 Hdbd. $2.25 pa. (ISBN 0-374-50872-0). Farrar, Straus & Giroux, NY.

Casty, Alan. Dramatic Art of the Film. 1971. $3.50 pa. (ISBN 0-06-041214-3). Harper & Row, NY.

Cocteau, Jean. On Film. 1971. $2.00 pa. (ISBN 0-486-22777-4). Dover Publ., NY.

Commercial Television Yearbook 1971-72. 1970. $15.00 Hdbd. International Publ. Serv., NY.

Cooper, John C. & Skrade, Carl, eds. Celluloid & Symbols. 1970. $2.95 pa. (ISBN 0-8006-0138-6). Fortress Pr., PA.

Cowie, Peter, ed. International Film Guide, Vols. 3-5, 1966-68. 1966-69. Vol. 1968 $5.95 Hdbd. (ISBN 0-498-06872-2); $3.95 pa. (ISBN 0-498-06686-X). A.S. Barnes, NJ.

Cowie, Peter, ed. International Film Guide, Vol. 6, 1969. $3.95 pa. (ISBN 0-498-06979-6). A.S. Barnes, NJ.

Cowie, Peter, ed. International Film Guide, Vol. 7, 1970. 1969. $5.95 Hdbd. (ISBN 0-498-07513-3); $3.95 pa. (ISBN 0-498-07513-3). A.S. Barnes, NJ.

Cowie, Peter, ed. International Film Guide 1972. $3.95 pa. (ISBN 0-498-07995-3). A.S. Barnes, NJ.

Crist, Judith. Private Eye, the Cowboy & the Very Naked Girl: Movies from Cleo to Clyde. 1968. $6.95 Hdbd. (ISBN 0-03-072495-3). Holt, Rinehart & Winston, NY.

Curtis, David. Experimental Cinema. 1971. $6.95 Hdbd. (ISBN 0-87663-131-6). Universe Books, NY.

Dale, Edgar. Content of Motion Pictures. 1935. $7.50 Hdbd. (ISBN 0-405-01644-1). Arno Pr., NY.

Dale, Edgar. Content of Motion Pictures. (1935). $7.50 Hdbd. (ISBN 0-405-01644-1). Arno Pr., NY.

Dale, Edgar. How to Appreciate Motion Pictures. (1937). $8.50 Hdbd. (ISBN 0-405-01645-X). Arno Pr., NY.

Davy, Charles. Footnotes to the Film. (1938). $12.00 Hdbd. (ISBN 0-405-01610-7). Arno Pr., NY.

De Nitto, D. Media for Our Time: An Anthology. 1971. $6.95 pa. (ISBN 0-03-084700-1). Holt, Reinhart & Winston, NY.

Durgnat, Raymond. Films & Feelings.

1971. $1.95 pa. (ISBN 0-262-54016-9). M.I.P. Pr., MA.

Eisenstein, Sergei. Film Essays & a Lecture. Leyda, Jay, transl. 1970. $6.95 Hdbd. $2.95 pa. Frederick Praeger, NY.

Eisenstein, Sergei. Film Form. 1969. (1949). $2.45 pa. (ISBN 0-15-630920-3). Harcourt Brace Jovanovich, NY.

Eisenstein, Sergei. Film Sense. 1969. (1947). $2.45 pa. (ISBN 0-15-630935-1). Harcourt Brace Jovanovich, NY.

Eisenstein, Sergei. Notes of a Film Director. Danko, X., transl. 1970. (1959). $3.00 pa. (ISBN 0-486-22392-2). Dover Publ., NY.

Eyles, Allen. Western: An Illustrated Index. $2.95 pa. (ISBN 0-498-06688-6). A.S. Barnes, NJ.

Farber, Manny. Negative Space: Manny Farber on the Movies. 1971. $7.95 Hdbd. Frederick Praeger, NY.

Fischer, Edward. Screen Arts: A Guide to Film & Television Appreciation. 1969 (1960). $1.95 pa. (ISBN 0-8362-0060-8). Sheed & Ward, NY.

Freeburg, Victor O. Art of Photoplay Making. (1918). $9.00 Hdbd. (ISBN 0-405-01612-3). Arno Pr., NY.

Freeburg, Victor O. Pictorial Beauty on the Screen. (1923). $7.00 Hdbd. (ISBN 0-405-01613-1). Arno Pr., NY.

Furhammar, Leif & Isaksson, Folke. Politics & Film. 1971. $12.50 Hdbd.

Frederick Praeger, NY.

Gifford, Denis. Science Fiction Film. 1971. $2.25 pa. E.P. Dutton, NY.

Goodman, Ezra. Fifty-Year Decline & Fall of Hollywood. 1961. $5.95 Hdbd. Simon & Schuster, NY.

Gow, Gordon. Suspense in the Cinema. $2.95 Pa. (ISBN 0-498-06841-2). A.S. Barnes, NJ.

Grau, Robert. Theatre of Science. 1914. $15.00 Hdbd. Benjamin Blom, NY.

Griffith, Mrs. D.W. When the Movies Were Young. 1968. (1925). $9.75 Hdbd. Benjamin Blom, NY.

Griffith, Richard, ed. Photoplay: An Anthology. 1971 $3.50 pa. (ISBN 0-486-22762-6). Dover Publ., NY.

Halliwell, Leslie. Film Goer's Companion. 1971. (1965). $3.95 pa. Avon Books, NY.

Hamblett, Charles. Hollywood Cage. 1970. $7.95 Hdbd. (ISBN 0-8055-1062-1); $2.95 pa. (ISBN 0-8055-0095-2). Hart Publ., NY.

Harman, Bob. Hollywood Panorama. 1971. $3.95 pa. (ISBN 0-525-45323-8) E.P. Dutton, NY.

Henderson, Ron, ed. Image Maker. 1971. Price "n.g." John Knox Pr., VA.

Holaday, Perry W. & Stoddard, George D. Getting Ideas from the Movies. (1933). $4.00 Hdbd. (ISBN 0-405-01647-6). Arno Pr., NY.

Hoppe, I. Bernard. Basic Motion Picture Technology. 1970. $10.00 Hdbd. (ISBN 0-8038-0729-5). Hastings House Publ., NY.

Hopwood, Henry V. Living Pictures: Their History, Photo-Production & Practical Working. (1899). $10.00 Hdbd. (ISBN 0-405-01616-6). Arno Pr., NY.

Houston, Penelope. Contemporary Cinema. (Hi-Sch.) 1963. $1.45 pa. (ISBN 0-14-020636-1). Penguin Books, MD.

Hughes, Robert, ed. Film, Bk. 2. Films Of Peace & War. 1962. $2.45 pa. Grove Pr., NY.

Hulfish, David. Motion-Picture Work. (1915). $25.00 Hdbd. (ISBN 0-405-01617-4). Arno Pr., NY.

Jacobs, Lewis. Introduction to the Art of the Movies. 1970. $9.00 Hdbd. Octagon Books, NY.

Jacobs, Lewis. Introduction to the Art of the Movies. 1960. $2.25 pa. Farrar, Straus & Giroux, NY.

Jacobs, Lewis, ed. Movies As Medium. 1970. $8.50 Hdbd. $3.65 pa. Farrar, Straus & Giroux, NY.

Jarvie, I.C. Movies & Society. 1970. $10.00 Hdbd. (ISBN 0-465-04737-8). Basic Books, NY.

Kael, Pauline. I Lost It at the Movies. 1965. $7.50 Hdbd. (ISBN 0-316-48164-5). Little, Brown, MA.

Katz, John S. Perspectives on the Study of Film. 1971. Price "n.g." Little, Brown, MA.

Kennedy, Donald. So You Think You Know Movies. 1970. $0.60 pa. Ace Publ., NY.

Kirschner, Allen & Kirschner, Linda. Film Readings in the Mass Media. $4.35 pa. Odyssey Pr., IN.

Kirschner, Allen & Kirschner, Linda, eds. Film: Readings in the Mass Media. 1971. $4.35 pa. Bobbs-Merrill, IN.

Kirstein, Lincoln, eds. Films No. One—Four. 1968 (1940). $25.00 Hdbd. (ISBN 0-405-00717-5). Arno Pr., NY.

Kitses, Jim. Horizons West. 1970. $5.95 Hdbd. (ISBN 0-253-13870-1); $2.25 pa. Indiana Univ. Pr., IN.

Koenigil, Mark. Movies in Society. 1962. $5.95 Hdbd. (ISBN 0-8315-0000-X). Robert Speller & Sons, NY.

Kracauer, Siegfried. Theory of Film: The Redemption of Physical Reality. 1960. $12.50 Hdbd. (ISBN 0-19-500605-4). Oxford Univ. Pr., NY.

Kracauer, Siefgried. Theory of Film: The Redemption of Physical Reality. 1965. $2.75 pa. (ISBN 0-19-500721-2). Oxford Univ. Pr., NY.

Kuhns, William. Mobile Image: Movies. 1970. $1.25 pa. Herder & Herder, NY.

Lawson, John H. Film: The Creative Process. 1967. $7.95 Hdbd. (ISBN 0-8090-4460-9). $2.95 pa. (ISBN 0-8090-1337-1). Hill & Wang, NY.

Lee, Raymond & Van Hecke, B.C. Gangsters & Hoodlums: The Underworld in the Cinema. 1970. $8.95 Hdbd. (ISBN 0-498-06994-X). A.S. Barnes, NJ.

Linden, George W. Reflections on the Screen. 1970. $10.60 Hdbd. $7.95 text ed. Wadsworth Publ., CA.

Lindgren, Ernest. Art of the Film. 1963. $7.50 Hdbd. $2.95 pa. Macmillan, NY.

Lindsay, Vachel. Art of the Moving Picture. 1970. (1922) $7.95 Hdbd. (ISBN 0-87140-508-3); $2.95 pa. (ISBN 0-87140-004-9). Liveright, NY.

MacCann, Richard D. Film & Society. 1964. $2.95 pa. (ISBN 0-684-41342-6). Charles Scribner's Sons, NY.

MacCann, Richard D., ed. Film: A Montage of Theories. $2.45 pa. (ISBN 0-525-47181-2). E.P. Dutton, NY.

McClure, Arthur F. Movies: An American Idiom. $15.00 Hdbd. Fairleigh Dickinson Univ. Pr., NJ.

McCrindle, Joseph F., ed. Behind the Scenes: Theater & Film Interviews from the Transatlantic Review. 1971. $7.95 Hdbd. (ISBN 0-03-085091-6); $3.45 pa. Holt, Rinehart & Winston, NY.

MacDonald, Dwight. Dwight MacDonald on Movies. 1969. $9.95 Hdbd. (ISBN 0-13-221150-5). Prentice-Hall, NJ.

McKowen, Clark & Sparke, William.

It's Only a Movie. 1971. $8.95 Hdbd. (ISBN 0-13-509208-6); $3.95 pa. (ISBN 0-13-509190-X). Prentice-Hall, NJ.

MacPherson, Kenneth & Bryher, Winifred, eds. Close-Up: A Magazine Devoted to the Art of Films, Vols. 1-10. (1927). Set. $245.00 Hdbd. (ISBN 0-405-00732-9). Arno Pr., NY.

Manchel, F. Terrors of the Screen. 1970. $4.25 Hdbd. (ISBN 0-13-906792-2). Prentice-Hall, NJ.

Manvell, Roger, ed. Experiment in the Film. (1949). $10.00 Hdbd. (ISBN 0-405-01623-9). Arno Pr., NY.

Mayer, Michael F. Foreign Films on American Screens. 1965. $4.50 Hdbd. (ISBN 0-668-01248-X); $2.00 pa. (ISBN 0-668-01249-8). Arco Publ., NY.

Mayersberg, Paul. Hollywood-the Haunted House. 1969 (1967). $0.95 pa. Ballantine Books, NY.

Michael, Paul. American Movies Reference Book: The Sound Era. 1968. $29.95 Hdbd. (ISBN 0-13-028134-4). Prentice-Hall, NJ.

Montagu, Ivor. Film World. (Hi-Sch.) 1964. $1.75 pa. (ISBN 0-14-020686-8). Penguin Books, MD.

Munsterberg, Hugo. Film: A Psychological Study. Orig. Title: Photoplay: A Psychological Study. 1969 (1916). $2.00 pa. (ISBN 0-486-22476-7). Dover Publ., NY.

Munsterberg, Hugo. Photoplay: A

Psychological Study. (1916). $7.50 Hdbd. (ISBN 0-405-01628-X). Arno Pr., NY.

Nilsen, Vladimir. Cinema As a Graphic Art. 1959. $6.95 Hdbd. (ISBN 0-8090-3450-6). Hill & Wang, NY.

Parish, James R., ed. Great Movie Series. $15.00 Hdbd. (ISBN 0-498-07847-7). A.S. Barnes, NJ.

Pechter, William S. Twenty-Four Times a Second: Films & Film-Makers. 1971. $7.95 Hdbd. (ISBN 0-06-013321-X). Harper & Row, NY.

Peil, Paul. How to Make a Dirty Movie. 1970. $1.25 pa. (ISBN 0-87067-310-6). Holloway House Publ., CA.

Perry, George S. Films of Alfred Hitchcock. $1.95 pa. (ISBN 0-289-79014-X). E.P. Dutton, NY.

Pudovkin, V. Film Technique & Acting. $3.95 Hdbd. Wehman Brothers, NJ.

Pudovkin, V. Film Techniques & Film Acting. 1959. $3.75 Hdbd. Crown Publ., NY.

Reile, Louis. Films in Focus. 1970 $1.25 pa. Abbey Pr., IN.

Renan, Sheldon. Introduction to the American Underground Film. (Hi-Sch.) 1967. $2.25 pa. (ISBN 0-525-47207-X). E.P. Dutton, NY.

Rhode, Eric. Tower of Babel: Speculations on the Cinema. 1967. $5.95 Hdbd. (ISBN 0-8019-5206-9). Chilton Book Co., PA.

Richardson, Robert. Literature & Film. 1969. $4.95 Hdbd. (ISBN 0-253-14845-6). Indiana Univ. Pr., IN.

Ross, Murray. Stars & Strikes: Unionization in Hollywood. 1941. $9.50 Hdbd. (ISBN 0-404-05408-0). AMS Pr., NY.

Samuels, Charles T. Casebook on Film. 1970. $3.50 pa. Van Nostrand Reinhold, NY.

Sarris, Andrew. Confessions of a Cultist. 1970. $8.95 Hdbd. $3.95 pa. Simon & Schuster, NY.

Seldes, Gilbert. Public Arts. 1957. $1.95 pa. Simon & Schuster, NY.

Seldes, Gilbert. Seven Lively Arts. 1962. $2.45 pa. (ISBN 0-498-04076-3). A.S. Barnes, NJ.

Sennett, Ted. Warner Brothers, Presents. 1971. $11.95 Hdbd. (ISBN 0-87000-136-1). Arlington House Publ., NY.

Sheridan, Marion C. Motion Picture & the Teaching of English. 1965. $1.95 pa. (ISBN 0-390-80420-7). Appleton-Century-Crofts, NY.

Simon, John. Private Screenings. 1967. $6.95 Hdbd. Macmillan, NY.

Simon, John & Schickel, Richard, eds. Film, 67-68. 1968. $6.95 Hdbd. $1.95 pa. Simon & Schuster, NY.

Sontag, Susan. Duet for Cannibals. 1970. $4.95 Hdbd. $2.25 pa. (ISBN 0-374-14424-9). Farrar, Straus & Giroux, NY.

Speed, Maurice, ed. Film Review 1969-70. 1970. $6.95 Hdbd. (ISBN 0-498-07579-6). A.S. Barnes, NJ.

Speed, Maurice, ed. Film Review 1968-69. 1968. $2.95 Hdbd. (ISBN 0-498-06978-8). A.S. Barnes, NJ.

Speed, Maurice, ed. Film Review 1966-68. 1967. $2.95 Hdbd. (ISBN 0-498-06750-5). A.S. Barnes, NJ.

Spottiswoode, Raymond. Grammar of the Film: An Analysis of Film Technique. 1950. $1.75 pa. (ISBN 0-520-01200-3). Univ. of California Pr., CA.

Starr, Cecile. Discovering the Movies. Price "n.g." Van Nostrand Reinhold, NY.

Stauffacher, Frank, ed. Art in Cinema: A Symposium of Avant-Garde Film. 1968 (1947). $7.50 Hdbd. (ISBN 0-405-00724-8). Arno Pr., NY.

Stern, Seymour & Jacobs, Lewis, eds. Experimental Cinema. Nos. 1-5. 1971 (1934). Set. $20.00 Hdbd. (ISBN 0-405-00739-6). Arno Pr., NY.

Svitak, Ivan. Film in a Manipulated World. 1971. $6.95 Hdbd. Atheneum Publ., NY.

Sweeting, Charles. Film Course Manual. 1971. $2.25 pa. (ISBN 0-8211-1821-8). McCutchan Publ., CA.

Talbot, Daniel, ed. Film: An Anthology. (Hi-Sch.) 1966. $2.45 pa. (ISBN 0-520-01251-8). Univ. of California Pr., CA.

Taylor, John R. Cinema Eye. Cinema Ear: Some Key Film-Makers of the Sixties. $5.95 Hdbd. (ISBN 0-8090-3460-3); $2.25 pa. (ISBN 0-8090-1328-2). Hill & Wang, NY.

Thomson, David. Movie Man. 1969. $2.95 pa. (ISBN 0-8128-1235-2). Stein & Day, NY.

Thorp, Margaret. America at the Movies. (1939). $11.00 Hdbd. (ISBN 0-405-01639-5). Arno Pr., NY.

Tyler, Parker. Hollywood Hallucination. 1970. $5.95 Hdbd. $1.95 pa. Simon & Schuster, NY.

Tyler, Parker. Magic & Myth of the Movies. 1970. $5.95 Hdbd. $1.95 pa. Simon & Schuster, NY.

Tyler, Parker. Sex, Psyche, Etcetera in the Film. 1969. $7.50 Hdbd. (ISBN 0-8180-0700-1). Horizon Pr., NY.

Tyler, Parker. Underground Film: A Critical History. 1970. $7.50 Hdbd. Grove Pr., NY.

Vance, Malcolm F. Movie Quiz Book. 1970. $1.25 pa. Paperback Library, NY.

Weinberg, Herman G. Saint Cinema: Selected Writings, 1929-1970. 1970. $8.95 Hdbd. (ISBN 0-910482-16-0). DBS Publ., NY.

White, David M. & Averson, Richard, eds. Sight & Sound, & Society. 1968. $7.50 Hdbd. (ISBN 0-8070-6186-7). Beacon Pr., MA.

Wolfenstein, Martha & Leites, Nathan. Movies: A Psychological Study. 1970 (1950). $3.45 pa. (ISBN

0-689-70252-3). Atheneum Publ., NY.

Wollen, Peter. Signs & Meaning in the Cinema. 1969. $5.95 Hdbd. (ISBN 0-253-18140-2); $1.95 pa. (ISBN 0-253-18142-9). Indiana Univ. Pr., IN.

Wright, Edward A. & Downs, Lenthiel H. Primer for Playgoers. 1969. $8.95 Hdbd. $6.95 text ed. (ISBN 0-13-700443-5). Prentice-Hall, NJ.

Wysotsky, Michael Z. Wide-Screen Cinema & Stereophonic Sound. 1970. $15.00 Hdbd. (ISBN 0-8038-8044-8). Hastings House Publ., NY.

Young, Vernon. Cinema Borealis. 1970. Price ''n.g.'' (ISBN 0-912012-09-9). David Lewis, NY.

Youngblood, Gene. Expanded Cinema. 1970. $9.95. Hdbd. (ISBN 0-525-10152-7). E.P. Dutton, NY.

As Art

Carey, Gary. Lost Films. 1970. $4.95 pa. (ISBN 0-87070-429-X). Museum of Modern Art, NY.

Griffith, Richard & Mayer, Arthur. Movies. 1957. $15.00 Hdbd. Simon & Schuster, NY.

Knight, Arthur. Liveliest Art. 1971. $1.25 pa. New American Library, NY.

O'Leary, Liam. Silent Cinema. 1965. $1.95 pa. (ISBN 0-289-79012-3). E.P. Dutton, NY.

Parish, James R. Fox Girls. 1971 $11.95 Hdbd. (ISBN 0-87000-127-2). Arlington House Publ., NY.

Shipman, David. Great Movie Stars: The Golden Years. 1970. $10.00 Hdbd. Crown Publ., NY.

Bibliography

Eyles, Allen. Western: An Illustrated Index. $2.95 pa. (ISBN 0-498-06688-6). A.S. Barnes, NJ.

Film Index: A Bibliography, Vol. 1: The Film As Art. (1941) $22.50 Hdbd. (ISBN 0-405-01512-7). Arno Pr., NY.

Gottesman, R. & Gould, H. Guidebook to Film an Eleven in One Reference. $7.95 Hdbd. (ISBN 0-03-086707-X). Holt, Rinehart & Winston, NY.

Library Of Congress. National Union Catalog, a Cumulative Author List, Consolidated Edition of the Fourth & Fifth Supplements to the National Union Catalog: Re-1956 Imprints, 1956-67, 120 Vols. 1970. Set. $2100.00 Hdbd. Rowman and Littlefield, NJ.

Library Of Congress. National Union Catalog, a Cumulative Author List, 1953-57, 23 Vols. Set. $310.00 Hdbd.; Vol. 27 Music & Phonorecords. $25.00 Hdbd.; Vol. 28 Motion Pictures & Film Strips. $25.00 Hdbd.; Rowman & Littlefield, NJ.

Niver, Kemp R. Motion Pictures from the Library of Congress Paper Print Collection, 1894-1912. 1967. $35.00 Hdbd. (ISBN 0-520-00947-9). Univ. of California Pr., CA.

Pickard, R.A. Dictionary of One-Thousand Best Films. 1971.

$12.00 Hdbd. (ISBN 0-8096-1805-2). Association Pr., NY.

Rotha, Paul. Documentary Film. 1964. $10.00 Hdbd. (ISBN 0-8038-1529-8). Hastings House Publ., NY.

Vincent, Carl, et al, eds. General Bibliography of Motion Pictures. 1971. (1953). $15.00 Hdbd. (ISBN 0-405-00769-8). Arno Pr., NY.

Weiss, Ken & Goodgold, Ed. To Be Continued. 1971. $9.95 Hdbd. Crown Publ., NY.

Catalogs

American Association Of Industrial Management. Film Guide for Industrial Training. 1969. $10.00 pa. Research Serv., NY.

American Film Institute, ed. American Films, 1893-1910. 1971. Price "n.g." (ISBN 0-8352-0436-7). R.R. Bowker, NY.

Cowie, Peter, ed. International Film Guide 1971. 1970. $5.95 Hdbd. (ISBN 0-498-07710-1); $3.95 pa. (ISBN 0-498-07704-7). A.S. Barnes, NJ.

Dimmit, Richard B. Actors Guide to the Talkies, 1949-1964, 2 Vols. 1967. $35.00 Hdbd. (ISBN 0-8108-0000-4). Scarecrow Pr., NJ.

Dimmitt, Richard B. Title Guide to the Talkies, 2 Vols. 1967. $47.50 Hdbd. (ISBN 0-8108-0171-X). Scarecrow Pr., NJ.

Films: 1969 Catalogue of the Film Collection in the New York Public Library. 1969. $1.50 pa. (ISBN 0-87104-073-5). New York Public Library, NY.

Gluski, J. Proverbs. Price "n.g." (ISBN 0-444-40904-1). American Elsevier, NY.

International Film Guide Series, 5 Vols. $6.25 pa. Paperback Library, NY.

Munden, Kenneth W., ed. American Film Institute Catalog, Feature Films 1911-1920. price "n.g." (ISBN 0-8352-0437-5). R.R. Bowker, NY.

Munden, Kenneth W., ed. Feature Films 1921-1930, 2 Vols. 1971. Set. $55.00 (ISBN 0-8352-0440-5). Bowker, NY.

National Information Center For Educational Media. Nicem Media Indexes, 3 Vols. 1969. Vol. 1. Index To 16mm Educ. Films. $39.50 (ISBN 0-8352-0275-5); Vol. 2. Index To 8mm Educ. Motion Cartridges. $16.00 Hdbd. (ISBN 0-8352-027603); Vol. 3. Index To Overhead Transparancies. $22.50 Hdbd. (ISBN 0-8352-0277-1); Vol. 4. Index To 35mm Educ. Films. $34.00 Hdbd. (ISBN 0-9352-0278-X). R.R. Bowker, NY.

Solomon, Martin B., Jr. & Lovan, Nora G. Annotated Bibliography of Films in Automation, Data Processing & Computer Science. 1967. $3.00 pa. (ISBN 0-8131-1145-5). Univ. Pr. of Kentucky, KY.

Williams, Tess M., ed. Directory of

Non-Royalty Films for Television. 1954. $1.00 pa. (ISBN 0-8138-1160-0). Iowa St. Univ. Pr., IA.

Censorship

Carmen, Ira H. Movies, Censorship & the Law. 1966. $7.95 Hdbd. (ISBN 0-472-19880-7). Univ. of Michigan Pr., MI.

Hunnings, Neville M. Film Censors & the Law. 1967. $12.50 Hdbd. Hillary House, NY.

Randall, Richard S. Censorship of the Movies: The Social & Political Control of a Mass Medium. 1970. $10.00 Hdbd. (ISBN 0-299-04731-8); $2.95 pa. (ISBN 0-299-4734-2). Univ. of Wisconsin Pr., WI

Vizzard, John A. See No Evil. 1970. $6.95 Hdbd. Simon & Schuster, NY.

Children's Literature

Buchanan, Andrew. Going to the Cinema. (Hi-Sch.) 1970. $3.75 Hdbd. International Publ. Serv., NY.

Charters, W.W. Motion Pictures & Youth: A Summary. (1933) $4.00 Hdbd. (ISBN 0-4-5-01642-5). Arno Pr., NY.

Dale, Edgar. Children's Attendance of Motion Pictures. $7.00 Hdbd. Arno Pr., NY.

Dysinger, Wendell S. & Buckmick, Christian A. Emotional Responses of Children to the Motion Picture Situation. $7.00 Hdbd. (ISBN 0-405-01643-3). Arno Pr., NY.

Field, Mary & Miller, M. Boys' & Girls' Book of Films & Television (Jr. Hi-Sch.) $3.95 Hdbd. Roy Publ., NY.

Forman, Henry J. Our Movie Made Children. (1935) $9.00 Hdbd. (ISBN 0-4-5-01646-8). Arno Pr., NY.

Jennings, Gary. Movie Book. 1963. $3.95 Hdbd. Dial Pr., NY.

Manchel, Frank. Cameras West. 1971. $4.25 Hdbd. (ISBN 0-13-112730-6); Prentice-Hall, NY.

Manchel, Frank. When Movies Began to Speak. 1969. $4.25 Hdbd. (ISBN 0-13-955328-2). Prentice-Hall, NY.

Manchel, Frank. When Pictures Began to Move. (Jr. Hi-Sch.) 1969. $4.25 (ISBN 0-13-955328-2). Prentice-Hall, NY.

Manchel, Frank. Movies & How They Are Made. (Elem.) 1968. $4.50 Hdbd. (ISBN 0-13-604702-5). Prentice-Hall, NY.

Renshaw, Samuel. Chilcren's Sleep: A Series of Studies on the Influence of Motion Pictures. (1933) $10.00 Hdbd. (ISBN 0-405-01631-X). Arno Pr., NY.

Directing and Producing

Bare, Richard L. Film Director: A Practical Guide to Motion Pictures & Television Techniques. 1971. $8.95 Hdbd. Macmillan, NY.

Bayer, William. Breaking Through, Selling Out, Dropping Dead. 1971. $6.95 Hdbd. Macmillan, NY.

Butler, Ivan. Making of Feature Films: A Guide. 1971. $1.75 pa. (ISBN 0-14-021232-9). Penguin Books, MD.

Cameron, Ian. Directors for the Seventies. 1971. $6.95 Hdbd. $1.95 pa. Frederick Praeger, NY.

Carter, Rich & Carroll, David C. Action Camera. (Jr. Hi.) 1971. $5.95 Hdbd. (ISBN 0-684-12490-4). Charles Scribner's Sons, NY.

Cocteau, Jean. Beauty & the Beast: Diary of a Film. 1971. $2.00 pa. (ISBN 0-486-22776-6). Dover Publ., NY.

Farber, Donald & Baumgarten, Paul. Financing & Producing the Film. Price "n.g." (ISBN 0-910482-31-4). DBS Publ., NY.

French, Philip. Movie Moguls: An Informal History of the Hollywood Tycoons. 1971. $5.95 Hdbd. Henry Regnery, IL.

Garrett, George P., et al, eds. Film Scripts One. 1971. $4.95 pa. (ISBN 0-390-34945-3). Appleton-Century-Crofts, NY.

Garrett, George P., et al, eds. Film Scripts Two. 1971. Price "n.g." pa. (ISBN 0-390-34946-1). Appleton-Century-Crofts, NY.

Geduld, Harry M., ed. Film Makers on Film Making. 1967. $7.50 Hdbd. (ISBN 0-253-12600-2). Indiana Univ. Pr., IN.

Geduld, Harry M., ed. Film-Makers on Film-Making. 1969. $2.35 pa. (ISBN 0-253-20104-7). Indiana Univ. Pr., IN.

Gelmis, Joseph. Film Director As Superstar. 1970 $3.50 pa. Doubleday, NY.

Gomes, P.E. Salles. Jean Vigo. Francovich, Allan, transl. $8.95 Hdbd. (ISBN 0-520-01676-9). Univ. of California Pr., CA.

Goodwin, N. & Manilla, J. Make Your Own Professional Movies. 1971. $5.95 Hdbd. $1.50 pa. Macmillan, NY.

Grey, Elizabeth B. Behind the Scenes in a Film Studio. (Jr. Hi.) 1968. $3.50 Roy Publ., NY.

Gussow, Mel. Dont Say Yes Until I Finish Talking: A Biography of Darryl F. Zanuck. 1971. $7.95 Hdbd. Doubleday, NY.

Harwood, Ronald. Making of One Day in the Life of Ivan Denisovich. Aitken, Gillon, transl. 1971. $1.25 pa. (ISBN 0-345-02295-5). Ballantine Books, NY.

Henderson, Ron, ed. Image Maker. 1971. Price "n.g." pa. John Knox Pr., VA.

Higham, Charles. Films of Orson Welles. 1971. $5.95 pa. (ISBN 0-520-02048-0). Univ. of California Pr., CA.

Higham, Charles & Greenberg, Joel. Celluloid Muse: Hollywood Directors Spead. 1971. $7.95 Hdbd. Henry Regnery, IL.

Huss, Roy & Silverstein, Norman. Film Experience. 1969. $1.95 pa. Dell Publ., NY.

Huss, Roy & Silverstein, Norman. Film Experience. 1968. $6.95 Hdbd. (ISBN 0-06-032967-X). Harper & Row, NY.

Kantor, Bernard. Directors at Work: Interviews with American Film Makers. 1970. $10.00 Hdbd. Funk & Wagnalls, NY.

Livingston, Don. Film & the Director: A Handbook & Guide to Film Direction. 1969. (1958) $1.95 pa. G.P. Putnam's Sons, NY.

Marner, Terence, ed. Directing Motion Pictures. $2.95 pa. (ISBN 0-498-07993-7). A.S. Barnes, NJ.

Mascelli, Joseph. Five C's of Cinematography. 1970. (1965) $15.00 Hdbd. (ISBN 0-9600240-0-X). CineGraphic Publ., CA.

Mascelli, Joseph. Five C's of Cinematography. $15.00 Hdbd. Borden Publ., CA.

Milne, Tom. Mamoulian. 1970. $5.95 Hdbd. (ISBN 0-253-15015-9); $2.95 pa. (ISBN 0-253-15016-7). Indiana Univ. Pr., IN.

Monoogian, Haig P. Film-Maker's Art. 1966. $7.50 Hdbd. (ISBN 0-465-02398-3). Basic Books. NY.

Nizhny, Vladimir. Lessons with Eisenstein. 1969 (1962) $5.75 Hdbd. (ISBN 0-8090-6515-0); $1.95 pa. (ISBN 0-8090-1350-9). Hill & Wang, NY.

Parsons, Christopher. Making Wildlife Movies: A Beginners Guide. 1971. $7.95 Hdbd. (ISBN 0-8117-0966-3).

Stackpole Books, PA.

Pratley, Gerald. Cinema of Otto Preminger. 1971. $2.95 pa. (ISBN 0-498-07860-4). A.S. Barnes, N.J.

Pudovkin, V. Film Technique & Film Acting. Montagu, Ivor, ed. 1970. $1.95 pa. Grove Pr., NY.

Quick, J. & Lebeau, T. Handbook of Film Production. 1971. $12.95 Hdbd. Macmillan, NY.

Reynertson, A.J. Work of the Film Director. 1970. $13.50 Hdbd. (ISBN 0-8038-8042-1); $7.60 pa. (ISBN 0-8038-8045-6). Hastings House Publ., NY.

Rilla, Wolf. A-Z of Movie-Making. 1970. $6.95 Hdbd. (ISBN 0-670-13978-5). Viking Pr., NY.

Roberts, Kenneth H. & Sharples, Winston S., Jr. Primer for Film-Making: A Complete Guide to 16 & 35mm Film Production. 1971. $15.00 Hdbd. $6.75 pa. Bobbs-Merrill, IN.

Robinson, William R., ed. Man & the Movies. 1969 (1967) $2.25 pa. (ISBN 0-14-021061-X). Penguin Books, MD.

Robinson, William R., ed. Man & the Movies: Essays on the Art of Our Time. 1967. $7.95 Hdbd. (ISBN 0-8071-0718-2). Louisiana State Univ. Pr., LA.

Rosenthal, Alan. Documentary in Action: A Casebook in Film-Making. 1971. $8.00 Hdbd. (ISBN 0-520-01888-5). Univ. of California Pr., CA.

Sarris, Andrew. Interviews with Film Directors. 1969. (1968) $1.65 pa. Avon Books, NY.

Shavelson, Melville. How to Make a Jewish Movie. 1971. $6.95 Hdbd. (ISBN 0-13-418483-1). Prentice-Hall, NJ.

Sherman, Eric & Rubin, Martin. Director's Event: Interviews with Five American Film-Makers. 1970. $6.95 Hdbd. (ISBN 0-689-10249-6). Atheneum Publ., NY.

Smith, John M. Jean Vigo. 1971. $6.95 Hdbd. $2.95 pa. Praeger Publ., NY.

Stephenson, Ralph & Debrix, J.R. Cinema As Art. (Hi-Sch.) 1965. $1.65 pa. (ISBN 0-14-020677-9). Penguin Books, MD.

Talbot, Frederick A. Moving Pictures: How They Are Made & Worked. (1912) $14.00 Hdbd. (ISBN 0-4-5-01638-7). Arno Pr., NY.

Taylor, Theodore. People Who Make Movies. (Hi-Sch.) 1967. $3.95 Hdbd. Doubleday, NY.

Walker, Alexander. Stanley Kubrick Directs. 1971. Price "n.g." Harcourt Brace Jovanovich, NY.

Directories

Dougall, Lucy. The War-Peace Film Guide. 1970. $.75 pa. (ISBN 0-912018-09-7). World Without War Council Publ., CA.

Kemp's Film & Television Yearbook 1971. 1971. $20.00. International Publ. Serv., NY.

Limbacher, James L. Feature Films on 8mm & 16mm: A Directory of Feature Films Available for Rental, Sale, & Lease in the United States. 1971. Price "n.g." pa. (ISBN 0-8352-0492-8). R.R. Bowker, NY.

Slide, Anthony. Early American Cinema. (International Film Guide Ser). 1970 $1.95 pa. (ISBN 0-498-07717-9). A.S. Barnes, NJ.

Weaver, John T. Twenty Years of Silents, 1908-1928. 1971. $15.00 Hdbd. (ISBN 0-8108-0401-8). Scarecrow Pr., NJ.

Documentary

Baddeley, W. Hugh. Technique of Documentary Film Production 1963. $10.00 Hdbd. (ISBN 0-8038-7021-3). Hastings House Publ., NY.

Bellocchio, Marco. Bellicho's China Is Near. Green, Judith, transl. from It. 1970. $1.9 pa. (ISBN 0-670-15609-4). Grossman Publ., NY.

Hardy, Forsyth. Grierson on Documentary. 1971. $10.95 Hdbd. $5.50 pa. Frederick Praeger, NY.

Knight, Derrick & Porter, Vincent. Long Look at Short Films: An A.C.T.T. Report on the Short Entertainment & Factual Film. $2.45 pa. (ISBN 0-08-012259-0). Pergamon Pr., NY.

Leyda, Jay. Films Beget Films: A Study of the Compilation Film. 1971.

(1964) $4.95 Hdbd. (ISBN 0-8090-4500-1). $1.95 pa. (ISBN 0-8090-1355-X). Hill & Wang, NY.

Rotha, Paul. Documentary Film. 1964 $10.00 Hdbd. (ISBN 0-8038-1529-8). Hastings House Publ., NY.

Snyder, Robert L. Pare Lorentz & the Documentary Film. 1968. $6.95 Hdbd. (ISBN 0-8061-0784-7). Univ. of Oklahoma Pr., OK.

Spottiswoode, Raymond. Film & Its Techniques. 1951. $9.50 Hdbd. (ISBN 0-520-01201-1). Univ. of California Pr., CA.

Williams, Tess M., ed. Directory of Non-Royalty Films for Television. 1954. $1.00 pa. (ISBN 0-8138-1160-0). Iowa State Univ. Pr., IA.

Editing

Burder, John. Technique of Editing 16mm Films. 1968. $9.50 Hdbd. (ISBN 0-8038-7022-1). Hastings House Publ., NY.

Leyda, Jay. Films Beget Films: A Study of the Compilation Film. 1971. (1964) $4.95 Hdbd. (ISBN 0-8090-4500-1); $1.95 pa. (ISBN 0-8090-1355-X). Hill & Wang, NY.

Reisz, Karel & Millar, Gavin. Technique of Film Editing. 1967. $13.50 Hdbd. (ISBN 0-8038-7026-4); $7.20 pa. (ISBN 0-8038-7025-6). Hastings House Publ., NY.

Rudman, Jack. Civil Service Examination Passbook: Film Editor. $8.00 Hdbd. $5.00 pa. National Learning, NY.

Walter, Ernst. Technique of the Film Cutting Room. 1969. $11.50 Hdbd. (ISBN 0-8038-7091-4). Hastings House Publ., NY.

Education

Cushing, Jane. One Hundred One Films for Character Growth. 1969. $1.50 pa. (ISBN 0-8190-0500-2). Fides Publ., IN.

Dale, Edgar. Motion Pictures in Education: A Summary of the Literature. $15.00 Hdbd. (ISBN 0-405-01609-3). Arno Pr., NY.

Forsdale, Louis. Eight MM Sound Film & Education. 1962. $2.95 pa. (ISBN 0-8077-1374-0). Teachers college Pr., NV.

Groves, Peter D., ed. Film in Higher Education & Research. 1966. $7.00 Hdbd. (ISBN 0-08-011358-3); $4.95 pa. (ISBN 0-08-011357-5). Pergamon Pr., NY.

Herman, Lewis. Educational Films: Writing, Directing, Producing for Classroom, Television & Industry. (Hi-Sch.) 1965. $5.95 Hdbd. Crown Publ., NY.

Hoban, Charles F. & Van Orner, Edward B. Instructional Film Research, Nineteen Eighteen to Nineteen Fifty. (1950) $8.00 Hdbd. (ISBN 0-405-01621-2). Arno Pr., NY.

Index to Eight MM Motion Cartridges. (NICEM Media Indexes, Vol. 3). 1969. $19.50 Hdbd. (ISBN 0-8352-0276-3). R.R. Bowker, NY.

Index to Thirty-Five Millimeter Filmstrips. 1970. $34.00 Hdbd. (ISBN 0-8352-0278-X). R.R. Bowker, NY.

National Council for the Social Studies. How to Use a Motion Picture. 1965. $.25 pa. National Council for Social Studies, DC.

National Information Center for Educational Media. Nicem Media Indexes, 3 Vols. 1969. Vol. 1. Index To 16mm Educ. Films. $39.50 Hdbd. (ISBN 0-8352-0275-5); Vol. 2. Index To 8mm Educ. Motion Cartridges. $16.00 Hdbd. (ISBN 0-8352-0276-3); Vol. 3. Index To Overhead Transparancies. $22.50 Hdbd. (ISBN 0-8352-0277-1); Vol. 4. Index To 35mm Educ. Films. $34.00 Hdbd. (ISBN 0-8352-0278-X). R.R. Bowker, NY.

Ross, Theodore J. Film & the Liberal Arts. 1970. $5.25 pa. (ISBN 0-03-081104-X). Holt, Rinehart & Winston, NY.

Rulon, P.J. Sound Motion Picture in Science Teaching. 1933. $10.00 pa. Johnson Reprint, NY.

Schillaci, Anthony & Culkin, John M., eds. Films Deliver: Teaching Creatively with Film. 1970. $5.25 pa. (ISBN 0-590-09155-7). Scholastic Book Serv., NY.

Stewart, David C., ed. Film Study in Higher Education. 1966. $3.50 Hdbd. (ISBN 0-8268-1288-0). American Council on Educ., DC.

Evaluation

Boyum, Joy G. & Scott, Adrienne. Film As Film: Critical Responses to Film Art. 1971. $4.95 pa. Allyn & Bacon, NJ.

Kauffman, Stanley. World on Film. 1966. $7.95 Hdbd. (ISBN 0-06-012273-0). Harper & Row, NY.

Thompson, Howard, ed. New York Times Guide to Movies on TV. 1971. $1.95 pa. (ISBN 0-8129-6126-9). Quadrangle Books, OH.

Tyler, Parker. Three Faces of the Film. 1967. $2.95 Hdbd. (ISBN 0-498-06591-X). A.S. Barnes, NJ.

History

Agee, James. Five Film Scripts: Noa Noa, African Queen, Night of the Hunter, Bride Comes to Yellow Sky, Blue Hotel. 1964. $2.75 pa. (ISBN 0-8070-6455-6). Beacon Pr., MA.

Alloway, Lawrence. Violent America: The Movies, 1946-1964. 1971. $7.95 Hdbd. (ISBN 0-87070-623-3). New York Graphic Society, CT.

Anderson, John & Fulop-Miller, Rene. American Theater & the Motion Picture in America. 1970. (1938) $22.50 Hdbd. Johnson Reprint, NY.

Ball, Robert H. Shakespeare on Silent Film. 1968. $12.50 Hdbd. Theatre Arts Books, NY.

Balshofer, Fred J. & Miller, Arthur C. One Reel a Week. 1968. $6.95 Hdbd. (ISBN 0-520-00073-0). Univ. of California Pr., CA.

Barbour, A. Movie Going Fun in the Forties. 1971. $7.95 Hdbd. Macmillan, NY.

Bardeche, Maurice & Brasillach, Robert. History of Motion Pictures. (1938) $14.00 Hdbd. (ISBN 0-405-01602-6). Arno Pr., NY.

Baxter, John. Hollywood in the Thirties. $2.95 pa. (ISBN 0-498-06927-3). A.S. Barnes, NJ.

Baxter, John. Hollywood in the Thirties. (International Film Guide Ser). 1970. (1968) $1.25 pa. Paperback Library, NY.

Blum, Daniel. Pictorial History of the Silent Screen. $7.95 Hdbd. (ISBN 0-448-01477-7). Grosset & Dunlap, NY.

Blum, Daniel & Kobal, John. New Pictorial History of the Talkies. Powers, Thetis, ed. 1970. (1968) $9.95 Hdbd. Grosset & Dunlap, NY.

Brownlow, Kevin. Parade's Gone By. 1968. $15.00 Hdbd. Alfred A. Knopf, NY. $3.95 pa. Ballantine Books, NY.

Carter, Huntly. New Spirit in the Cinema (1930) $14.00 Hdbd. (ISBN 0-405-01605-0). Arno Pr., NY.

Ceram, C.W. Archaeology of the Cinema. Winston. Richard, transl. 1965. $6.50 Hdbd. (ISBN 0-15-107871-8). Harcourt Brace

Jovanovich, NY.

Clair, Rene. Cinema Yesterday & Today. Appelbaum, Stanley, transl. 1971. $3.00 pa. (ISBN 0-486-22775-8). Dover Publ., NY.

Cocteau, Jean. Beauty & the Beast; Diary of a Film. (Dover Film Ser). 1971. $2.00 pa. (ISBN 0-486-22776-6). Dover Publ., NY.

Cowie, Peter. Seventy Years of Cinema. 1968. $15.00 Hdbd. (ISBN 0-498-06635-5). A.S. Barnes, NJ.

Cowie, Peter, ed. Concise History of the Cinema. 2 Vols. (International Film Guide Ser). 1970. $3.50 pa. (ISBN 0-498-07715-2) (ISBN 0-498-07716-0). A.S. Barnes, NJ.

Crowther, Bosley. Great Films: Fifty Golden Years of Motion Pictures. 1967. $10.00 Hdbd. Putnam, NY.

Deming, Barbara. Running Away from Myself: A Dream Portrait of America Drawn from the Films of the Forties. 1969. $6.95 Hdbd. (ISBN 0-670-61089-5). Grossman Publ., NY.

Everson, William K. Pictorial History of the Western Film. 1971. (1969) $3.95 Hdbd. (ISBN 0-8065-0257-6). Citadel Pr., NY.

Eyles, Allen. American Comedy Since Sound. (International Film Guide Ser). 1969. $3.50 pa. (ISBN 0-498-07510-9). A.S. Barnes, NJ.

Fescourt, Henri. Cinema Des Origines a Nos Jours. $12.50 Hdbd. Boston Book & Art Shop, MA.

Fulton, Albert R. Motion Pictures: The Development of an Art from Silent Films to the Age of Television. 1970. (1960) $6.95 Hdbd. (ISBN 0-8061-0467-8). Univ. of Oklahoma Pr., OK.

Furhammar, Leif & Isaksson, Folke. Politics & Film. 1971. $12.50 Hdbd. Praeger Publ., NY.

Gow, Gordon. Hollywood in the Fifties. 1971. $2.95 pa. (ISBN 0-498-07859-0). A.S. Barnes, NJ.

Gow, Gordon. Suspense in the Cinema. (International Film Guide Ser). 1971. (1968) $1.25 pa. Paperback Library, NY.

Griffith, D.W. When the Movies Were Young. 1970. (1925) $2.50 pa. (ISBN 0-486-22300-0). Dover Publ., NY.

Griffith, D.W. When the Movies Were Young. $5.00. Peter Smith, MA.

Griffith, Richard & Mayer, Arthur. Movies. 1970. $19.95 Hdbd. Simon & Schuster, NY.

Griffith, Richard & Mayer, Arthur. Movies. 1957. $15.00 Hdbd. Simon & Schuster, NY.

Hampton, Benjamin B. History of the American Film Industry from Its Beginning to 1931. $7.50 Hdbd. Peter Smith, MA.

Hampton, Benjamin B. History of the American Film Industry from the Beginnings to 1931. Griffith, Richard, ed. 1970. $4.00 pa. (ISBN 0-486-22403-1). Dover Publ., NY.

Hampton, Banjamin B. History of the Movies. (1931) $20.00 (ISBN 0-405-01614-X). Arno Pr., NY.

Harmon, Jim & Glut, Donald F. Movie Serials: Their Sound & Fury. 1971. $4.95 Hdbd. Doubleday, NY.

Hendricks, Gordon. Beginnings of the Biograph. 1964. $6.00 Hdbd. Beginnings of the American Film, NY.

Hendricks, Gordon. Edison Motion Picture Myth. 1961. Price "n.g." (ISBN 0-306-70297-5). Plenum Publ., NY.

Higham, Charles. Hollywood in the Forties. $2.95 pa. (ISBN 0-498-06928-1). A.S. Barnes, NJ.

Higham, Charles & Greenberg, Joel. Hollywood in the Forties. (International Film Guide Ser). 1970. (1968) $1.25 pa. Paperback Library, NY.

Huaco, George A. Sociology of Film Art. 1965. $5.50 Hdbd. (ISBN 0-465-08034-0). Basic Books, NY.

Jacobs, Lewis. Emergence of Film Art. 1970. $10.00 Hdbd. (ISBN 0-87460-245-9); $4.95 pa. (ISBN 0-87460-246-7). Lion Pr., NY.

Jacobs, Lewis. Introduction to the Art of the Movies. 1960. $2.25 pa. Farrar, Straus & Giroux, NY.

Jacobs, Lewis. Rise of the American Film. 1968. $12.50 Hdbd. (ISBN 0-8077-1556-5); $5.25 pa. (ISBN 0-8077-155-7). Teacher's College Pr., NY.

Kardish, Lawrence. Reel Plastic Magic:

A History of Films & Filmmaking in America. (Jr. Hi-Sch.) 1971. $6.95 Hdbd. Little, Brown, MA.

Kelman, Ken. History of Reflections on Film. 1972. Price "n.g." Red Dust, NY.

Knight, Arthur. Liveliest Art. 1971. $1.25 pa. New American Library, NY.

Lahue, Kalton C. Continued Next Week: A History of the Moving Picture Serial. 1969. (1964) $6.95 Hdbd. (ISBN 0-8061-0633-6). Univ. of Oklahoma Pr., OK.

Lahue, Kalton C. Winners of the West: The Sagebrush Heroes of the Silent Screen. 1970. $10.00 Hdbd. (ISBN 0-498-07396-3). A.S. Barnes, NJ.

Lahue, Kalton C. World of Laughter: The Motion Picture Comedy Short 1910-1930. 1971. (1966) $6.95 Hdbd. Univ. of Oklahoma Pr., OK.

McCallum, John. Scooper. 1961. $4.95 Hdbd. (ISBN 0-8323-0191-4). Binfords & Mort, Publ., OR.

MacGowan, Kenneth. Behind the Screen. 1967. $2.95 pa. Dell Publ., NY.

MacGowan, Kenneth. Behind the Screen. 1965. $12.50 Hdbd. Delacorte Pr., NY.

Manchel, Frank. When Movies Began to Speak. (Jr. Hi-Sch.) 1969. $4.25 Hdbd. (ISBN 0-13-955328-2). Prentice-Hall, NY.

Manvell, Roger. New Cinema in the U.S.A. 1966. $1.95 pa. (ISBN 0-289-79025-5). E.P. Dutton, NY.

Martin, Marcel. France. (International Film Guide Ser). 1971. $3.50 Hdbd. (ISBN 0-498-07518-4). A.S. Barnes, NJ.

Mast, Gerald. Short History of the Movies. 1971. $4.95 Hdbd. Pegasus, NY.

McVay, Douglas. Musical Film. $2.95 pa. (ISBN 0-498-06687-8). A.S. Barnes, NJ.

O'Leary, Liam. Silent Cinema. 1965. $1.95 pa. (ISBN 0-289-79012-3). E.P. Dutton, NY.

Quigley, Martin & Gertner, Richard. Films in America. 1970. $12.95 Hdbd. Western Publ., NY.

Quigley, Martin. Magic Shadows: The Story of the Origin of Motion Pictures. 1969. $10.00 Hdbd. (SBN 0-8196-0254-X). Biblo & Tannen, NY.

Ramsaye, Terry. Million & One Nights. 1964. $10.00 Hdbd. $3.95 Hdbd. Simon & Schuster, NY.

Robinson, David. Hollywood in the Twenties. $2.95 pa. (ISBN 0-498-06926-5). A.S. Barnes, NJ.

Robinson, David. Hollywood in the Twenties. (International Film Guide Set). 1970. (1968). $1.25 pa. Paperback Library, NY.

Rotha, Paul & Griffith, Richard. Film till Now. $15.00 Hdbd. Twayne Publ., NY.

Schickel, Richard. Movies: The History of an Art & an Institution. 1964. $5.95

Hdbd. (ISBN 0-465-04736-X). Basic Books, NY.

Slide, Anthony. Early American Cinema. (International Film Guide Ser). 1970. $2.95 pa. (ISBN 0-498-07717-9). A.S. Barnes, NJ.

Spears, Jack. Hollywood: The Golden Era. 1970. $12.00 Hdbd. (ISBN 0-498-07552-4). A.S. Barnes, NJ.

Stern, Seymour & Jacobs, Lewis, eds. Experimental Cinema, 1971. (1934). Set. $20.00 (ISBN 0-405-00739-6). Arno Pr., NY.

Vardac, A. Nicholas. Stage to Screen: Theatrical Method from Garrick to Griffith. 1968. $12.50 Hdbd. Benjamin Blom, NY.

Wagenknecht, Edward. Movies in the Age of Innocence. 1962. $7.95 Hdbd. (ISBN 0-8061-0539-9). Univ. of Oklahoma Pr., OK.

Wilk, Max. Wit & Wisdom of Hollywood: From the Squaw Man to the Hatchet Man. 1971. $8.95 Hdbd. (ISBN 0-689-10370-0). Atheneum Publ., NY.

Wilson, Earl. Show Business Nobody Knows. 1971. $6.95 Hdbd. Cowles Book, IL.

Wiseman, Thomas. Cinema. 1965. $12.00 Hdbd. (ISBN 0-498-06344-5). A.S. Barnes, NJ.

Media Technology

Fensch, Thomas. Films on the Campus. 1970. $15.00 Hdbd. (ISBN 0-498-07428-5). A.S. Barnes, NJ.

Lowndes, Douglas. Film Making in Schools. (Hi-Sch.) 1969. $8.95 text ed. Watson-Guptill, NY.

Moral and Religious

Blumer, Herbert. Movies & Conduct. (1933). $9.00 Hdbd. (ISBN 0-405-01640-9). Arno Pr., NY.

Blumer, Herbert & Hauser, Philip M. Movies Delinquency & Crime. (1933). $7.50 Hdbd. (ISBN 0-405-01641-7). Arno Pr., NY.

Cinema Commission Of Inquiry. Cinema: Its Present Position & Future Possibilities. (1917). $15.00 Hdbd. (ISBN 0-405-01608-5). Arno Pr., NY.

Cooper, John C. & Skrade, Carl, eds. Celluloid & Symbols. 1970. $2.95 pa. (ISBN 0-8006-0138-6). Fortress Pr., PA.

Dale, Edgar. Content of Motion Pictures. (1935). $7.50 Hdbd. (ISBN 0-405-01644-1). Arno Pr., NY.

Durgnat, Raymond. Eros in the Cinema. 1966. $4.50 Hdbd. Fernhill House, NY.

Harris, Larry. Stag Movies. $4.75 Hdbd. Academy Pr. Books, CA.

Hurley, Neil P. Theology Through Film. 1970. $5.95 Hdbd. (ISBN 0-06-064082-0). Harper & Row Publ., NY.

Jackson, B.F., Jr., ed. Television-Radio-Film for Churchmen. 1969.

$6.50 Hdbd. (ISBN 0-687-4294-4). Abdingdon Pr., TN.

Jones, G. William. Sunday Night at the Movies. 1967. $1.95 pa. (ISBN 0-8042-1977-X). John Knox Pr., VA.

Koenigil, Mark. Movies in Society. 1962. $5.95 Hdbd. (ISBN 0-8315-0000-X). Robert Speller & Sons, NY.

Martin, Olga J. Hollywood's Movie Commandments, a Handbook for Motion Picture Writer & Reviewers. (1937). $9.00 Hdbd. (ISBN 0-405-01624-7). Arno Pr., NY.

Peters, Charles C. Motion Pictures & Standards of Morality. (1933). $9.00 Hdbd. (ISBN 0-405-01648-4). Arno Pr., NY.

Peterson, Ruth C. & Thurstone, L.L. Motion Pictures & the Social Attitudes of Children. $8.00 Hdbd. (ISBN 0-405-01630-1). Arno Pr., NY.

Tyler, P. Homosexuality in the Movies. 1971. $8.50 Hdbd. (ISBN 0-03-086583-2). Holt, Rinehart & Winston, NY.

National

Europe

Hibbin, Nina. Eastern Europe: A Screen Guide. 1969. $3.50 Hdbd. (ISBN 0-498-07412-9). A.S. Barnes, NJ.

Manvell, Roger. New Cinema in Europe. $1.95 pa. (ISBN 0-289-79018-2). E.P. Dutton, NY.

Quinn, James. Film & Television As an Aspect of European Culture. 1969. $4.50 pa. Humanities Pr., NY.

Whyte, Alistair. New Cinema in Eastern Europe. 1971. pa. Price "n.g." Dutton, NY.

France

Armes, Roy. French Cinema. 1970. $2.25 pa. (ISBN 0-289-79045-X). Dutton, NY.

Armes, Roy. French Cinema Since Nineteen Forty Six, 2 Vols. (International Film guide Ser). 1970. $2.45 pa. (ISBN 0-498-07652-0) (ISBN 0-498-07655-5). A.S. Barnes, NJ.

Graham, Peter, ed. New Wave: Critical Landmarks. 1968. $1.29 pa. Doubleday. NY.

Martin, Marcel. France. (International Film Guide Ser). 1971. $3.50 Hdbd. (ISBN 0-498-07518-4). A.S. Barnes, NJ.

Germany

Bucher, Felix. Germany. 1970. $3.50 pa. (ISBN 0-498-07517-6). A.S. Barnes, NJ.

Bucher, Felix. Screen Guide: Germany. (International Film Guide Ser). 1969. $3.50 pa. (ISBN 0-498-07517-6). A S. Barnes, NJ.

Eisner, Lotte. Haunted Screen: Expressionism in the German Cinema & the Influence of Max Reinhardt. 1969. $10.95 Hdbd. (ISBN

0-520-01519-3). Univ. of California Pr., CA.

Hull, David S. Film in the Third Reich: A Study of the German Cinema, 1933-1945. 1969. $8.95 Hdbd. (ISBN 0-520-01489-8). Univ. of California Pr. CA.

Manvell, Roger & Fraenkel, Heinrich. German Cinema. 1971. $10.00 Hdbd. Praeger Publ., NY.

Semprun, J. La Guerre Est Finie. Seaver, Richard, transl. $4.50 Hdbd. Peter Smith, MA.

Great Britain

Durgnat, Raymond. Mirror for England: British Films from Austerity to Affluence. 1971. $11.95 Hdbd. Praeger Publ. NY.

Knight, Derrick & Porter, Vincent. Long Look at Short Films: An A.C.T.T. Report on the Short Entertainment & Factual Film. $2.45 pa. (ISBN 0-08-012259-0). Pergamon Pr., NY.

Low, Rachael. History of the British Film, Vol. 2. 1906-1914. 1949. $6.50 Hdbd. Vol. 3. 1914-1918. $6.50 Hdbd. Fernhill House, NY.

Manvell, Roger. New Cinema in Britain. 1969. $1.95 pa. (ISBN 0-289-79034-4). E.P. Dutton, NY.

India

Barnouw, Erik & Krishnaswamy, S. Indian Film. 1963. $10.00 Hdbd. (ISBN 0-231-02538-6). Columbia

Univ. Pr., NY.

Shah, Panna. Indian Film. 1950. $12.00 Hdbd. (ISBN 0-8371-3144-8). Greenwood Pr., CT.

Wood, Robin. Apu Trilogy. 1971. $5.50 Hdbd. $1.95 pa. Praeger Publ., NY.

Italy

Salachas, Gilbert. Federico Fellini. Siegel, Rosalie, transl. 1969. $2.95 pa. Crown Publ. NY.

Wlaschin, Ken. Italian Cinema Since the War. 1970. $2.95 Hdbd. (ISBN 0-498-07650-4). A.S. Barnes, NJ.

Japan

Anderson, Joseph L. & Ritchie, Donald. Japanese Film: Art & Industry. 1960. $3.95 pa. Grove Pr. NY.

Near East

Landau, Jacob M. Studies in the Arab Theatre & Cinema. 1958. $10.00 Hdbd. (ISBN 0-8122-7188-2). Univ. of Pennsylvania Pr., PA.

Russia

Carter, Huntly. New Theatre and Cinema of Soviet Russia. $10.00 Hdbd. (ISBN 0-405-01607-7). Arno Pr., NY.

Leyda, Jay. Kino: A History of the Russian & Soviet Film. 1960. $10.00 Hdbd. Hillary House, NY.

Moussinac, Leon. Sergei Eisenstein. Petrey, D. Sandy, transl. (Editions

Seghers' Cinema D'Aujourd'hui). 1970. $2.95 pa. Crown Publ., NY.

Sweden

Cowie, Peter. Sweden, 2 Vols. $2.95 pa. (ISBN 0-498-07419-6) (ISBN 0-498-07447-1). A.S. Barnes, NJ.

Plots, etc.

Baxter, John. Science Fiction in the Cinema $2.95 pa. (ISBN 0-498-07416-1). A.S. Barnes, NJ.

Butler, Ivan. Horror Film. $2.95 pa. (ISBN 0-498-06689-4). A.S. Barnes, NJ.

Butler, Ivan. Religion in the Cinema. $1.95 pa. (SIBN 0-498-07417-X). A.S. Barnes, NJ.

Clarens, Carlos. Illustrated History of the Horror Film. 1968. $2.75 pa. Putnam's Sons, NY.

Crowther, Bosley. Great Films: Fifty Golden Years of Motion Pictures. 1967. $10.00 Hdbd. G.P. Putnam's Sons, NY.

Douglas, Drake. Horror. 1969. (1966). $6.95 Hdbd. $1.50 pa. Macmillan, NY.

McClelland, C. Kirk & Cannon, Doran W. On Making a Movie: Brewster McLoud. 1971. $1.50 pa. New American Library, NY.

Tyler, Parker. Sex, Psyche Etcetera in the Film. 1971. $1.65 pa. (ISBN 0-14-021302-3). Penguin Books, MD.

Wood, Robin. Hitchcock's Films $2.95 pa. (ISBN 0-498-07418-8). A.S. Barnes, NJ.

Zinman, David. Fifty Classic Motion Pictures. 1970. $9.95 Hdbd. Crown Publ., NY.

Reviews

Crist, Judith. Private Eye, The Cowboy & The Very Naked Girl: Movies from Cleo to Clyde. 1968. $6.95 Hdbd. (ISBN 0-03-072495-3). Holt, Rinehart & Winston, NY. $.95 pa. Paperback Library, NY.

Farber, Manny. Negative Space: Manny Farber on the Movies. 1971. $7.95 Hdbd. Praeger Publ., NY.

Kael, Pauline. Citizen Kane Book. 1971. $15.00 Hdbd. (ISBN 0-316-48171-8). Little, Brown, MA.

New York Times Film Reviews, Nineteen Thirteen to Nineteen Sixty-Eight, 6 Vols. $395.00 Hdbd. (ISBN 0-405-02191-7). Arno Pr., NY.

Reed, Rex. Big Screen, Little Screen. 1971. $7.95 Hdbd. Macmillan, NY.

Salem, James M. Guide to Critical Reviews: The Screenplay from the Jazz Singer to Dr. Strangelove. 1971. $30.00 Hdbd. (ISBN 0-8108-0367-4). Scarecrow Pr., NJ.

Sarris, Andrew. Confessions of a Cultist. 1970 $8.95 Hdbd. $3.95 pa. Simon & Schuster, NY.

Simon, John. Movies into Films: Film Criticism 1967-1970. 1971. $9.95 Hdbd. Dial Pr., NY.

Simon, John & Schickel, Richard, eds. Film, Sixty Seven to Sixty Eight. 1968. $6.95 Hdbd. $1.95 pa. Simon & Schuster, NY.

Speed, Maurice. Film Review Nineteen Seventy-Seventy One. 1970. $6.95 Hdbd. (ISBN 0-498-07723-3). A.S. Barnes, NJ.

Vocations

Colman, Hila. Making Movies: Student Films to Features. (Hi-Sch.) 1971. $4.95 Hdbd. World Publ. NY.

Gordon, George N. & Falk, Irving A. Your Career in Film Making. (Hi-Sch.) 1969. $3.95 Hdbd. (ISBN 0-671-32195-1). Julian Messner, NY.

Jones, Charles R. Your Career in Motion Pictures, Radio & Television. $5.00 Hdbd. Sheridan House, NY.

Photoplay Research Society. Opportunities in the Motion Picture Industry & How to Qualify for Positions in Its Many Branches. (1922). $5.00 Hdbd. (ISBN 0-405-01633-6). Arno Pr., NY.

Yearbooks

Blum, Daniel. Screen World, 10 Vols. 1949, 1951-1959. 1969. Set. 1 $35.00; $15.00 ea. (ISBN 0-8196-0255-8). Set. $135.00. Biblo & Tannen Booksellers & Publ., NY.

Film Daily Yearbook of Motion Pictures & Television. 1970. $25.00 Hdbd. (ISBN 0-405-02550-5). Arno Pr., NY.

Film Daily Yearbook of Motion Pictures 1918-1969. 51 Vols. $2100.00 Hdbd. (ISBN 0-405-02557-2); $45.00 per vol. Arno Pr., NY.

Morgenstern, Joseph & Kanfer, Stefan. Film, 1969-1970. 1971. $7.95 Hdbd. $2.95 pa. Simon & Schuster, NY.

Morgenstern, Joseph & Kanfer, Stefan, eds. Film, 1969-1970. 1970. $6.95 Hdbd. $2.50 pa. Simon & Schuster, NY.

OPERA

Appia, Adolphe. Music & the Art of the Theatre. Hewitt, Barnard, ed. (Books of the Theatre, No. 3). 1963. $6.50 Hdbd. (ISBN 0-87024-018-8). Univ. of Miami Pr., FL.

Kerman, Joseph. Opera as Drama. 1956 (ISBN 0-394-75088-8). $1.95 pa. (ISBN 0-394-70088-0). Random House, NY.

Mitchell, Ronald. Opera-Dead or Alive: Production, Performance, & Enjoyment of Musical Theatre. 1970. $12.50 Hdbd. (ISBN 0-299-05811-5). Univ. of Wisconsin PR., WI.

Bibliography

Langbaine, Gerard. Account of the English Dramatic Poets. 2nd ed. 1965. (1691) $37.50 Hdbd. (ISBN 0-8337-2003-1). Burt Franklin, NY.

Monterde, Francisco, ed. Bibliografia Del Teatro En Mexico. (Bibliografia Del Teatro En Mexico. (Bibliography & Reference Ser., No. 369). (Span). 1970. (1934) $25.00 Hdbd. (ISBN 0-8337-2240-1). Burt Franklin, NY.

Children's Literature

Hurd, Michael. Young Person's Guide to Opera. (Jr Hi). 1966. $3.25 Hdbd. Roy Publ., NY.

Samachson, Dorothy & Samachson, Joseph. Fabulous World of Opera. (Jr Hi–Hi-Sch.). $4.95 Hdbd. Rand, McNally & Co., IL.

Streatfeild, Noel. First Book of the Opera. (Elem.). 1967. $3.75 Hdbd. (ISBN 0-531-00602-6). Franklin Watts, Inc., NY.

Dictionaries

Brockway, Wallace & Weinstock, Herbert. World of Opera. 1962. $12.50 Hdbd. Pantheon, NY.

Clement, Felix & Larousse, Pierre. Dictionnaire Des Operas, 2 Vols. (Music Reprint Ser). 1969. (1905). $47.50 Hbdb. (ISBN 0-306-71197-4). Plenum Publ. Co., NY

Granville, Wilfred. Theater Dictionary: British & American Terms in the Drama, Opera, and Ballet. 1952. $10.00 Hbdb. (ISBN 0-8371-4428-0). Greenwood Press, Inc., CT.

Maretzek, Max. Crochets & Quavers (Or, Revelations of an Opera Manager in America. 2nd ed. (Music Ser). 1966. $6.95 Hdbd. (ISBN 0-306-70915-5). Plenum Publ. Co., NY.

Mates, Julian. American Musical Stage Before 1800. 1962. $10.00 Hbdb. (ISBN 0-8135-0393-0). Rutgers Univ. Pr., NJ.

Matthews, Thomas. Splendid Art: A History of the Opera. (Jr Hi–Hi–Sch.). 1970. $5.95 Hdbd. Macmillan Co., NY.

Pauly, Reinhard G. Music & the Theater: An Introduction to Opera. 1970. $13.95 Hdbd. (ISBN 0-13-607010-8); $9.95 text ed. (ISBN 0-13-607002-7). Prentice-Hall, NY.

Scouten, Arthur H., ed. London Stage, 1600–1800, Pt. 3 1729-1747 A Critical Introduction. 1968. $2.25 pa. (ISBN 0-8093-0338-8, AB). Southern Illinois Univ. Pr., IL.

Scouten, Arthur H., ed. London Stage, 1600–1800, Pt. 3 1729-1747. 2 Vols. 1961. $25.00 Hdbd. (ISBN 0-8093-0053-2). Southern Illinois Univ. Pr., IL.

Sheppard, F. H., et al, eds. Theatre Royal, Drury Lane & the Royal Opera House, Vol. 35. 1970. $19.25 Hdbd. Oxford Univ. Pr., NY.

Slonim, Marc. Russian Theatre: From the Empire to the Soviets. 1962. $1.50 pa. Macmillan Co., NY.

Solerti, Angelo. Musica, Ballo E Drammatica Alla Corte Medicea Dal 1600 Al 1637. 1968. $18.50 Hdbd. Benjamin Blom, NY.

Sonneck, Oscar G. Early Opera in America. 1915. $15.00 Hdbd. Benjamin Blom. NY.

Stone, George W., Jr., ed. London Stage, 1600–1800, Pt. 4 1747–1776 A Critical Introduction. 1968. $2.25 pa. (ISBN 0-8093-0339-6). Southern Illinois Univ. Pr., IL.

Stone, George W., Jr., ed. London Stage, 1600–1800, Pt. 4 1747–1776, 3 Vols. 1963. $25.00 Hdbd. (ISBN 0-8093-0094-X). Southern Illinois Univ. Pr., IL.

History and Criticism

Jell, George C. Master Builders of Opera. (Essay Index Reprint Ser). $9.50 Hdbd. (ISBN 0-8369-1964-5). Books for Libraries, NY.

Opera and Plots

Glennon, James. Making Friends with Gilbert & Sullivan. (Making Friends Ser). 1970. $1.50 pa. (ISBN 0-87597-

051-6). Crescendo Publ., MA.

Newman, Ernest. Stories of the Great Operas. 1930. Price "n.g." Hdbd. Alfred A. Knopf., NY.

Producing and Directing

Boarder, Sylvia. They Made an Opera: A Primary School's Adventure in Music Making. 1966. $4.00 Hdbd. Lawrence Verry, Inc., CT.

Dwyer, Terence. Opera in Your School. 1964. $3.40 Hdbd. (ISBN 0-19-317407-3). Oxford Univ. Pr., NY.

Eaton, Quaintance. Opera Production: A Handbook. 1961. $6.50 Hdbd. (ISBN 0-8166-0249-2). Univ. of Minnesota Pr., MN.

Gollancz, Victor. Ring at Bayreuth. 1966. $3.50 Hdbd. E.P. Dutton, NY.

Maretzek, Max. Revelations of an Opera Manager in Nineteenth Century America. $4.75 Hdbd. Peter Smith Publ., MA.

Robinson, Douglas. Act Two Beginners Please. Incl. Melody $2.25 pa. (ISBN 0-521-07417-7); Piano. $2.50 Hdbd. (ISBN 0-521-07416-9). 1970. Cambridge Univ. Pr., NY.

Skelton, Geoffrey. Wieland Wagner: The Positive Sceptic. 1971. $6.95 Hdbd. St. Martin's Pr., NY.

Volbach, Walther R. Problems of Opera Production. 2nd ed. 1967. $10.00 Hdbd. (ISBN 0-208-00166-2); $6.00 pa. (ISBN 0-208-00166-2). Shoe String Pr., CT.

PANTOMIME

Alberts, David. Pantomime: Elements & Exercises. 1971. $5.50 Hdbd. (ISBN 0-7006-0075-2). Univ. Pr. of Kansas, Lawrence, KS.

Aubert, Charles. Art of Pantomime. 1969. (1927) $10.75 Hdbd. Benjamin Blom, NY.

Broadbent, R. J. History of Pantomime. 1901. $5.75 Hdbd. Benjamin Blom, NY.

Enters, Angna. On Mime. 1965. $5.00 Hdbd. (ISBN 0-8195-3058-1). Wesleyan Univ. Pr., CT.

Mayer, David, 3rd. Harlequin in His Element: The English Pantomime, 1806–1836. 1969. $15.00 text ed. (ISBN 0-674-37275-1). Harvard Univ. Pr., MA.

Mehl, Dieter A. Elizabethan Dumb Show: The History of a Dramatic Convention. 1965. $5.75 Hdbd. (ISBN 0-674-24700-0). Harvard Univ. Pr., MA.

Sand, Maurice, pseud. History of the Harlequinade, 2 Vols. 1968. $25.00 Hdbd. Benjamin Blom, NY.

Wilson, A. E. Christmas Pantomine: The Story of an English Institution. 1934. $12.50 Hdbd. Benjamin Blom, NY.

PANTOMIMES

Disher, Maurice W. Clowns & Pantomimes. 1968. $17.50 Hdbd. Benjamin Blom, NY.

Howard, Vernon. Pantomimes, Charades & Skits. (Elem.). 1959. $2.95 Hdbd. Sterling Publ., NY.

Hunt, Kari & Hunt, Douglas. Panto-mime: The Silent Theater. (Elem–Hi-Sch.). 1964. $3.95 Hdbd. (ISBN 0-689-20191-5); Atheneum Publ., NY.

Schell, Stanley. Recitations: Panto-mimes. $1.50 Hdbd. Wheman Bros., NJ.

PERIODICALS

Dancing

Association Of College And University Concert Managers Bulletin. 1958. 7-8xyr. Free. College Printing and Typing Co., 453 W. Gilman St., Madison, WI. 53703.

Arabesque. 1962. 5xyr. 50 fr. ($1). Mr. & Mrs. Lartelier, 67 av. Dailly, Brussels 3, Belgium.

Ballet Today. 1946 6xyr. 20s. ($3.50). I.E. Herf, 33 Shepherd St., London W.1, England.

Balletopics. (Formerly: National Ballet News). 1953 4xyr. Can. $1. Ed. Lynda Woodcock. National Ballet of Canada, 157 King St. E., Toronto 1, Ont., Canada.

Ballet-Who. 1953. 4xyr. Vancouver Ballet Society, 3694 W. 16th Ave., Vancouver 8, B.C., Canada.

Courrier Musical De France. 1963. 40 F. Association pour la Diffusion de la Pensee Francaise, 23 rue la Perouse, 75 Paris (16e), France.

Dance and Dancers. 1950. mo. 60s. ($8.50). Hansom Books, Artillery Man-sions, 75 Victoria St., London SW 1, England.

Dance Films Newsletter. 1967. Dance Films Association, 250 W. 57th St., Rm. 2202, New York, NY. 10019.

Dance Magazine. 1926. mo. $9. Dance Magazine, Inc., 268 W. 47th St., New York, NY. 10036.

Dance News. 1942. mo. $3. P.W. Manchester, 119 W. 57th St., New York NY. 10019.

Dance Perspectives. 1959. 4xyr. $7. 29 E. 9th St., New York, NY. 10003.

Dance Scope. 1965. 2xyr. $2. American Dance Guild Inc., 124-16 84th Rd., Kew Gardens, NY. 11415.

Dancing Times. 1910. 52s. 18 Hand Court, High Holborn, London WC 1, England.

Danses. 1966. 4xyr. $1. Institut Bonnecompaignie, 51 rue Saint-Bernard, Brussels 6, Belgium.

English Dance and Song. 1936. 4xyr. 12s. ($1.44). English Folk Dance and Song Society, Cecil Sharp House, 2 Regents Park Rd., London NW 1, England.

Modern Dance and Dancer. 1934. mo. 29s.6d. Lawrence, Pritchard & Pickett Ltd., 2 Norfolk House, Brixton Oval, London SW 2, England.

Northern Junket. 1950. 6xyr. $3. for 12 nos. 117 Washington St., Keene, NH. 03431.

Seven Arts. 1958. mo. 300s ($43.)

Hansom Books, Artillery Mansions, 75 Victoria, London SW1, England.

Motion Pictures

ABC Film Review. 1951. mo. 18s. Associated British Cinemas Ltd., 30/31 Golden Sq., London W.1, England.

Action (U.S.) 1966. 6xyr. $4. Directors Guild of America, Inc., 7950 Sunset Blvd., Hollywood, CA. 90046.

Amatersky Film. (Supersedes: Filmovym Objektivem) 1969. mo. 48 Kcs. Orbis, Vinohradska 46, Prague 2, Czechoslovakia.

Amis Du Film & De La Television. 1955. mo. $3. Centre Catholique d'Action Cinematographique, 10 rue de l'Orme, Brussels 4, Belgium.

Arcadie. 1954. mo. 50 F. ($12.) 19 rue Beranger, Paris (3e), France.

Artes. 1965. mo. $7.70. Rua Nestor Pestana 30.21 Conj. 216, Sao Paulo 3 S.P., Brazil.

Association of College and University Concert Managers Bulletin. 1958. 7-8xyr. Free. College Printing and Typing Co., 453 W. Gilman St., Madison, WI. 53703.

Audiovisivi. 1961. mo. L.3000. Via dei Faggella 4, Rome, Italy.

Audiovisual Instruction. 1956. mo. $8. National Education Assoc., Dept. of Audiovisual Instruction, 1201 16th St., N.W., Washington, D.C. 20036.

Avant-Scene Du Cinema. (Paris) Ceased.

Beaux-Arts. 1934. 4xmo. 60 fr. ($13.) Palais des Beaux-Arts, 10 rue Royal, Brussels 1, Belgium.

Bianco E Nero. 1965. L.6800. Edizioni di Bianco e Nero, via Antonio Musa 15, Rome, Italy.

Bild Und Ton. 1948. mo. M.1.50. VEB Fotokinoverlag Leipzig, Karl-Heine-Str. 16,7031 Leipzig E. Germany.

Billboard. 1894. 4xmo. $20. Billboard Publishing Co., 165 W. 46 St., New York, NY.

Boxoffice. 1967. 4xmo. $5. Associated Publications, Inc., 825 Van Brunt Blvd., Kansas City, MO. 64124.

British Kinematography, Sound & Television. (Formerly: British Kinematography) 1936. mo. 72s. ($15). British Kinematograph Sound and Television Society, 110-112 Victoria House, Vernon Place, London, WC 1, England.

Bulletin Fipresci. 1963. 3-4xyr. Free. Federation Internationale de la Presse Cinematographique, General Secretary, Via Somaini 6, Lugano, Switzerland.

Cahiers D'Etudes De Presse. 1965. 12 F. Institut Francais de Presse, Universite de Paris, 27 rue Saint Guillaume, Paris (7e), France.

Cahiers Du Cinema. 1951. mo. 66 F. 8 rue Marbeuf, Paris (8e), France.

Camera (E. Germany). 4xyr. M.O. 20. Staatliches Filmarchiv der DDR, Kronensta. 10,108 Berlin, E. Germany.

Cameral. 1966. mo. 15 F. Association Cineastes de Marseille-Provence, 55 bd. Rodocanachi, Marseille (8e), France.

Canadian Film & TV Bi-Weekly. (Formerly: Canadian Film Weekly) 1942. 2xmo. Can. $7.50. ($8.50). Film Publications of Canada Lts., 175 Bloor St. E., Toronto 4, Canada.

Celuloide. 1957. mo. $8. Rua David Manuel da Fonseca 88, Rio Maior, Portugal.

Centre National De La Cinematographie. Bulletin D'Information. 1947. 6xyr. 15.F. ($3). Centre National de la Cinematographie, 12 rue de Lubeck, Paris (16e), France.

Challenge for Change Newsletter. 1968. 3-4xyr. Free. National Film Board of Canada, Box 6100. Montreal, Que., Canada.

Changes. 1969. 2xmo. $11. 80 Fifth Ave., New York, NY. 10011.

Christian Communications. 1962. Can. $2. Saint Paul University, Institute of Social Communications. 223 Main St., Ottawa 1, Canada.

Cine Cubano. 1961. mo. $2.75. 1153 Calle 23, Vedado, Havana, Cuba.

Cine Photo Amateur. (Formerly: Cine Amateur) 1930. mo. 40F. Federation Francaise des Clubs de Cinema d'Amateur, 54 rue Rene Boullan, Paris (9e), France.

Cine Technicians' Association of South India. Journal. 1947. mo. Rs. 12. ($3). Cine Technicians' Assoc. of South India, 34 Usman Rd., Madras 17, India.

Cine Universal. 1956. 4xmo. Mex. $90. ($9). Editore Mexico, S.R.L. de C.V., Arteaga No. 33, Mexico 3, D.F., Mexico.

Cine World. 1964 6xyr. $2. K. Godzinski, Box 86, Toronto 9, Canada.

Cineaste. 1967. 4xyr, $2. Cineaste Magazine, 27 W. 11th St., New York, NY. 10011.

Cinecronache. N.S. 1967. mo. Price "n.g." Circolo del Cinema de Rovigo, Via All'ara 8, Rovigo, Italy.

Cinema (S. Africa). 1959. 2xyr. $.15. Johannesburg Film Society, Box 10849, Johannesburg, S. Africa.

Cinema (U.S.) 1963. 6xyr. $1. Box 5271, Plaza Station, Kansas City, Mo. 64112.

Cinema Canada. (Formerly: Canadian Cinematography) 1961. 6xyr. Can. $3. Canadian Society of Cinematographers.

Cinema De Amadores. 1945 4xyr. Esc. 50. ($2). Pathe Baby Portugal, R.S. Nicolau 22, Lisbon 2, Portugal.

Cinema E Scienza-Televisione. 1956. mo. L.4500. ($7). Istituto per la Cinematografia Scientifica, Universita di Roma, Via A. Papa 11, Rome, Italy.

Cinema International. 1964 6xyr. 16 fr. Ed. Bd. Imprimene Robert S.A., 2740 Moutier, Switzerland.

Cinema Nuovo. 6xyr. L. 6000. Capo Santa Chiara 6, 16146 Genoa, Italy.

Cinema Pratique. 1955. 9xyr. 40 F. Editions Techniques Europeennes, 45 rue St. Roch, 75 Paris (1er), France.

Cinema Studies. 1960. 4xyr. 25s. ($4). Society for Film History Research, College of Preceptors, 2 Bloomsbury Sq., London WC 1, England.

Cinemasud. 1958. mo. L.5000 ($7). Via Cavour 8, Avellino, Italy.

Cinematografia Ita. 1933 mo. L.5000 ($20.) Gino Caserta, Via Baiamonti, 10, Rome, Italy.

Classic Film Collector. (Formerly: Eight MM Collector) 1962. 4xyr. $3. Samuel K. Rubin, 734 Philadelphia St., Indiana, Pa. 15701.

Coloquio. 1967. 4xyr. Esc. 100. Fundacao Calouste Gulbenkian, Avenida de Berna 45a, Lisbon 1, Portugal.

Communication Arts International. 4xyr. Leeward Publications, Box 2801, Washington, D.C. 20013.

Continental Film Review. 1952. mo. 30s. ($6). Eurap Publishing Co. Ltd., 71 Oldhill St., London N16, England.

Count Dracula Society Quarterly. 1967. 4xyr. $2. Gordon R. Guy,

Gothick Gateway, 22 Canterbury Street, East Hartford, CT. 06118.

CTVD: Cinema—TV—Digest. Winter 1961/62 4xyr. $3. Hampton Books, Drawer H, Hampton Bays, NY. 11946.

Cultural Events in Africa. 1965. mo. Institutions & libraries 100s. Transcription Centre, 84c Warwick Ave., London. W. 9, England.

Czechoslovak Film. 1965. 7xyr. Price "n.g." Vaolavske num. 28, Prague 1, Czechoslovakia.

Czechoslovak Film Press News. 1965. 20xyr. Vaclavske nam. 28, Prague 1, Czechoslovakia.

Dance Films Newsletter. 1967. Dance Films Association, 250 W. 57th St., Rm. 2202, New York, NY. 10019.

Deutsche Kameramann. 1950. mo. DM. 16.50. DDK. Verlag I. Weber, Rotbuchenstr. 21, 8 Munich 90, W. Germany.

Dzuboks Magazin. 1966. mo. 1.50 din. Novinsko Izdavacko Preduzece "Duga," Vlajkoviceva 8, Belgrade, Yugoslavia.

Educational Media (Canada). (Formerly: Canadian Audio Visual Review) 1965. 6xyr. Can. $6.(6). Seccombe House Canada Ltd., 443 Mt. Pleasant Rd., Toronto 7, Canada.

EFLA Bulletin. 1943. mo. $5. Educational Film Library Assoc., 250 W. 57th St., New York, NY. 10019.

Ekran. 1957. 4xmo. $9.50. RSW Prasa, Bagatela 1-3, Warsaw, Poland.

Educational Screen & Audio Visual Guide. 1922. mo. $4. Trade Periodicals Inc., 434 S. Wabash, Chicago, IL. 60605.

Eight MM. Magazine. 1962. mo. 30s.($6). Haymarket Press Ltd., 9 Harrow Rd., London W2, England.

Especta'culos. 1967. mo. Free. Uniao de Gremios dos Espectaculos, Av. Duque de Loule, 86-20 DT, Lisbon 1, Portugal.

Esquire. 1933. mo. $6.50. Esquire, Inc., 488 Madison Ave., New York, NY. 10022.

Etudes Cinematographiques. 1960. 3-4xyr. 37 F. for 10 nos. Lettres Modernes, 73 rue du Cardinal-Lemoine, Paris (5e), France.

Eumig-Lupe. 1956. 6xyr. Price "n.g." Elektrizitaets-und-Metallwaren-Industrie, Buchengasse 11-15, A-1101 Vienna, Austria.

Evangelischer Film-Beobachter. 1948. 4xmo. DM.26.40. Evang. Presserverband fuer Bayern, Birkerstr. 22, 8 Munich 2, W. Germany.

Fackel (Austria). 1966. 4xyr. S.30. ($1.50). Box 70, A-1094 Vienna, Austria.

Fantasy Film Review—67. 1969. 25s. ($4). 10 Dartmouth Ave., Oldfield Pari, Bath BA2 IAT, Somerset, England.

Fernseh-Und Kino-Technik. (Formerly: Kino-Technik) 1951. mo. DM.56.60 Verlad fuer Radio-Foto-Kinotechnik GmbH, 1 Berlin.52, W. Germany.

Fiche Filmographique. 1967. ?. Price "n.g." Institud des Hautes Etudes Cinematographiques, 92 Champs-Elysees, Paris (8e), France.

Film (Eng). 1952 4xyr. 12s ($1.50). British Federation of Film Societies, 81 Dean St., London W1, England.

Film (Poland). 1946. 4xmo. 156 zl.($7.50). Wydawnictwa Artystyczne Filmowe, Pulawska 61, Warsaw, Poland.

Film (W. Germany). 1963. mo. DM.44. Erhard Friedrichverlag, 3001 Velber&Hannover, W. Germany.

Film A. Doba. 1954. mo. 54 Kcs. Vaclavske Nam 43, Prague 1, Czechoslovakia.

Film & Bio. 1967. 9xyr. Kr. 30. Filmbranschens Forlagsaktiebolog, Stureplan 13, Stockholm C, Sweden.

Film & Televisie. mo. 100fr ($3). Centre CAtholique d'Action Cinematographique, 10 Olmstraat, Brussels 4, Belgium.

Film & Television Daily. (Formerly: Film Daily) 1918. 20xmo. $20. Wid's Films and Film Folk, Inc., 1600 Broadway, New York, NY. 10019.

Film & Television Technician. 1935. mo. 1s.6d. Assoc. of Cinematograph,

Television and Allied Technicians, 2 Soho Sq. London W.1. England.

Film & Ton-Magazin. (Formed by the Merger Of: Film-Kreis & Ton-Magazin) 1966. mo. DM.36. Heering-Verlag GmbH., Ortlerstr. 8, Munich 25, W. Germany.

Film Artiste. 1964. 4xyr. 7s6d. Film Artistes' Assoc., 61 Marloes Rd., Kensington, London W8, England.

Film Blaetter. (Formerly: Film-Echo/Filmwoche) 1947. 2xmo. DM.90. Kommanditgesellschaft Verlag Horst Axtmann GmbH & Co., Wilhelmstr. 42, 62 Wiesbaden, W. Germany.

Film Bulletin (U.S.) 1935. 2xmo. $3. Wax Publications, Inc., 1239 Vine St., Philadelphia, PA. 19107.

Film Comment. 1963. 4xyr. $6. Film Comment Publishing Corp., 100 Walnut Pl., Brookline, MA. 02146.

Film Culture. 1962 4xyr. $4. Box 1499, G.P.O., New York, NY. 10001.

Film Critics' Guild. Bulletin. 1950. 4xmo. ($10.) Film Critics' Guild, 9 Compayne Gardens, London NW 6, England.

Film Fan Monthly. 1961. mo. $3.75. 77 Grayson Pl., Teaneck, NJ. 07666.

Film Fernsehen Filmerziehung. 1963. 2xyr. MDN.6 Volkseigener Verlag, Lindenstr. 54a, 108 Berlin, E. Germany.

Film Forum Society. Bulletin. 1952.

mo. Free. Film & Forum Society, Somerset West, S. Africa.

Film Francais—Cinematographie Francaise. 1918. 4xmo. 100 F. Dir. Maurice Bessy. 40 rue du Cherche Midi, Paris (6e), France.

Film Heritage. 1965. 4xyr. $2. University of Dayton, Box 652, Dayton, OH. 45409.

Film Italiano. 1950. Free. Unitalia Film, Via Veneto 108, Rome, Italy.

Film Journal Advertiser. mo. 391 Hoboken Ave., Jersey City, NJ. 07306.

Film-Lyd-Bilde. 4xyr. Fabritius & Sonners Forlag. Ovre Slottsgt 25, Oslo 1, Norway.

Film News. 1939. 6xyr. $6. Rohama Lee, 250 W. 57th St., New York, NY. 10019.

Film OG Kino. (Formerly: Norsk Filmblad) 1930. 10xyr. Kr.30. ($.90). Kommunale Kinematografers Landsforbund, Stortingsgaten 16, Oslo 1, Norway.

Film Polski. 6xyr. $1.20. Mazowiecka 6-8, Warsaw, Poland.

Film Quarterly. 1945. 4xyr. $4. University of California Press, Berkeley, CA. 94720.

Film Society Review. 1965. mo. $5. American Federation of Film Societies, 144 Bleecker St., New York, NY. 10012.

Film, Szinhaz, Muzsika/Picture,

Theatre, Music. 1959. 4xmo. $8. Kultura, Box 149, Budapest 62, Hungary.

Film Technikum; 1948. mo. DM.33.60. Kommanditgesellschaft Verlag Horst, Axtmann GmbH. Wilhelmstr. 42, 52 Wiesbaden, W. Germany.

Film User. 1946. mo. 30s. ($4.50). Current Affairs Ltd., Box 109, Croydon, Surrey, England.

Film Weekly. 1926. 4xmo. 60s. Derwent Enterprises Pty. Ltd., 340 Pitt St., Sydney 2000, Australia.

Film World. 1964 4xyr. Rs. 15. ($5). T.M. Ramachandran, A-15, Anand Nagar, Juhu Tara Rd., Juhu, Santa Cruz (W), Bombay 54, India.

Filmblaetter. 1948. 4xmo. DM.50.40. Verlag fuer Kultur and Wirtschaft GmbH, Tauentzienstr. 16, 1 Berlin 30, W. Germany.

Filmclub Action-Mitteilungen. 1966. 6xyr. Free. Filmclub Action, A-1152 Vienna, Austria.

Filmcritica. 1950. mo. L.4000. Via Carlo Fea 6, Rome, Italy.

Filmdienst Und Fernsehvorschau, 8xmo. Evangelische Filmgilde in Oesterreich, Schellinggasse 12-3, 1010 Vienna 1, Austria.

Filme Cultura. 1966. 6xyr. Cr. $12. ($5.) Instituto Nacional do Cinemana, Rua 20 de Abril, 28, -2 Andar, Sala 201, Centro, Rio de Janeiro, Brazil.

Filmfacts. 1958. 2xmo. $25. Grosset & Dunlap, Inc., 51 Madison Ave, New York, N.Y. 10010.

Filmfare. 1952 2xmo. Rs. 23. Bennett, Coleman & Co. Ltd., D. Naoroji Rd., Bombay 1, India.

Filmjournalen. 1940. mo. Kr. 32. ($8.) Kaare Messel Birkelund, Skippergaten 9v, Oslo, Norway.

Filmkritik. 1967. mo. DM. 24. Verlag Filmkritik GmbH, Rueckerstr. 38, Frankfurt a.M., W. Germany.

Filmkunst. 1949. 4xyr. S.75 ($3.50). Schwarzenbergstr. 5, Vienna 1, Austria.

Filmlist. mo. Price "n.g." Educational Film Library, 250 W. 57th St., New York, N.Y. 10019.

Filmmakers' Newsletter. 1967. mo. $3. Filmmakers' Newsletter Co., 80 Wooster St., New York, N.Y. 10012.

Filmore Informace. 1965 4xmo. 52 Kcs. Narodni fr. 28, Prague 1, Czechoslovakia.

Filmovy Prehled. 1965 4xmo. 52 Kcs. Cesky Filmovy Ustav, Narodni 28, Prague, Czechoslovakia.

Filmowy Osrodek Doswiadczalno-Uslugowy. Przeglad Dokumentacyjny. 1960 mo. 220 zl. ($7). Branzowy Osrodek Informacji Technicznej i Ekonomicznej, ul Dominikanska 9, Warsaw, Poland.

Films and Filming. 1954. mo.60s. ($8.50). Hansom Books, Artillery Mansions, 75 Victoria St., London, England.

Films in Review. 1950. mo. $7. National Board of Review of Motion Pictures, Inc., 31 Union Square, New York, N.Y. 10003.

Filmschau. 1951. 4xmo. S.100. Katholische Filmkommission fuer Oesterreich, Goldschmiedgasse 6, Vienna 1, Austria.

Filmska Kultura. 1966 6xyr. 12 din. Praska 8/2, Zagreb, Yugoslavia.

Filmski Svet. 1966. 4xmo. 39 din. Novinsko Izdacko Preduzece "Duga", Vlajkoviceva 8, Belgrade, Yugoslavia.

Filmspiegel (Austria). 1956 2xmo. Free. Oesterreichischer Gewerkschaftsbund, Hohenstaufengasse 10-12, Vienna 1, Austria.

Filmspiegel (E. Germany). 1954. 2xmo. M. 10.40. Henschelverlag Kunst und Gesellschaft, Oranienburger Str. 67-68, 104 Berlin, E. Germany.

Filmtheater-Praxis. 1954. mo. DM. 13.80. Kommanditgesellschaft Verlag Horst Axtmann GmbH & Co., Wilhelmstr. 42,62 Wiesbaden, W. Germany.

Filmwissenschaftliche Bibliothek. 1967. 4xyr. MDN.6. Institut fuer Filmwissenschaft, Kronenstr. 10, 108 Berlin, E. Germany.

Filmwissenschaftliche Mitteilungen. 1967. 4xyr. MDN.6 Institut fuer Filmwissenschaft, Kronenstr. 10, 108 Berlin, E. Germany.

F M & Fine Arts. 1960 mo. $5.00. FM & Fine Arts Guide Inc., 291 S. La Cienega Blvd, Beverley Hills, CA. 90211.

F M Music Program Guide. 1963 mo. $7. Raymond Gombach, 200 Hudson St., New York, N.Y. 10013.

Foto-Kino Revija. 1948. mo. 72 din. ($7). "Technicka Knjiga", Bulevar Revolucije 44, 7 Jula 26, Belgrade, Yugoslavia.

Fotocine. 1968. mo. L.3000. ($6.) Briano Editore Genova, Via Caffaro 19, 16124 Genoa, Italy.

Fox-Report. 1967. mo. Centfox-Film GmbH, Kirchnerstr. 2, 600 Frankfurt 1, E. Germany.

Greater Amusements and International Projectionist. (Formed by the Merger Of: Greater Amusements & International Projectionist) 1965. mo. $3. Gallo Publishing Corp., 1600 Broadway, 514-D, New York, NY. 10019.

Griffith. 1965. mo. 220 ptas. ($6). Ediciones Griffith, Calle de Emilio Vargas 19, Madrid 17, Spain.

Hamburger Jugendbrief. 1948 mo. DM.3. Jugendbehoerde der Frein und Hansestadt Hamburg, Hachmannplatz 1, Bieberhaus, 2 Hamburg 1, W. Germany.

Harbinger (U.S.). 1967 2xyr. $4.50 for 4 nos. Cassandra Publications, Box 7817, Austin,

Ifida Bulletin. 1959. 2xyr. Free.

International Film Importers & Distributors of America, Inc., 477 Madison Ave., New York, NY. 10022.

Ikon (Italy). 1969 4xyr. L.3000. Instituto "Agostino Gemelli", Corso Monforte 33, Milan, Italy.

Image et Son. 10xyr. 30 F. Ligue Francaise de l'Enseignement, 3 rue Recamier, Paris (E), France.

Indian Movie News. 1952. mo. S. $8.50. Chinese Pictorial Review Ltd, 112/120 Robinson Road, Singapore.

Independent Film Journal. 2xmo. 1937. $2. Morton Sunshine, ITOA Independent, Inc., 165 W. 46th St., New York, NY. 10036.

International Press Bulletin. 1964. 4xyr. $4. N. A. Kovach, 4801-09 Second Ave., Los Angeles, CA. 90043.

Iskusstvo Kino. 1931. mo. 12 rub. Soyuz Rabotnikov Kinematografii SSSR, ul. Usiyevicha 9, Moscow A-319, USSR.

Jugend Film Fernsehen. 1955. 6xyr. DM.14. Arbeitszentrum Jugend Film Fernsehen e.V., Wissenschaftl. Inst. f. Jugend-u. Bildungsfragen in Film u. Fernsehen, Waltherstr. 23, D-8000 Munich 15, W. Germany.

Kaleidoscope (U.S.) 1965. 3xyr. $2. 95 Dearborn St., East Longmeadow, MA. 01028.

Kinderzeitung. 1930. 6xyr. $2. Workmen's Circle Educational Dept.,

175 E. Broadway, New York, NY. 10002.

Kinematograph Weekly (Kine). 1907. 4xmo. 140s. Longacre Press Ltd., 161 Fleet St., London EC4, England.

Kino. 1966. mo. $8.60. Wydawnictwa Artystyczne i Filmowe, Krakowskie Przedmiescie 21/23, Warsaw, Poland.

Kinomekhanik. 1937. mo. 3.60 rub. Mezhdunarodnaya Kniga, Smolenskaya Sennayo.

Kosmorama. 1954. 6xyr. Kr.30. Danske Filmmuseum, Store Sondervoldstraede, 1419 Copenhagen K, Denmark.

Landers Film Reviews. 1956. 10xyr. $35. Landers Associates, Box 69760, Los Angeles, CA.

Lara Lamont. 1967. mo. R.2. Golden Film Productions (Edms) Bpk, Dunwell-Gebou 112, Jorrissenstraat, Braamfontein, Johannesburg, South Africa.

Listener and BBC Television Review. 1929. 4xmo. $75s.($11.) British Broadcasting Corp. Broadcasting House, London W1, England.

Making Films in New York. 1967. 6xyr. $3. 120 E. 56th St., New York, NY. 10022.

Marshall McLuhan Dew-Line. 1968. 6xyr. $25. Human Development Corp., 200 Madison Ave., New York, NY. 10016.

Medion. 1969. 6xyr. Free. Museum of

Media, 1 Union Square W., New York, NY. 10003.

Medium (U.S.) 1967 4xyr. $2.75. Filmage Inc., 180 Centre St., New York, NY. 10013.

Modern Screen. 1930. mo. $5. Dell Publishing Co. Inc., 750 Third Ave., New York, NY. 10017.

Moj Pas. 1966. mo. 14 din. Kinoloskog Saveza SR Hrvatske, Ilica 61, Zagreb, Yugoslavia.

Mon Film. 1924. mo. 2F. Publications Ventillard, 2-12 rue de Bellevue, 75-Paris (19e), France.

Monthly Film Bulletin, 1934. mo. 30s($4.50). British Film Institute, 81 Dean St., London W1, England.

Motion Picture Daily. 1931. 20xmo. $15. Quigley Publishing Co., Inc., 1270 Sixth Ave., Rockefeller Center, New York, NY. 10020.

Motion Picture Exhibitor. (Incorporating: Showmen's Trade Review) 1918. 4xmo. $2. Shain Enterprises, Inc., 317 N. Broad St., Philadelphia, PA. 19107.

Motion Picture Herald. 1907. 4xmo. $5. Quigley Publishing Co., 1270 Sixth Ave., New York, NY. 10020.

Motion Picture Magazine. 1911. mo. $3. Macfadden-Bartell Corp., 205 E. 42nd St., New York, NY. 10017.

Movie. 1962. 4xyr. 20s($4). Movie Magazine Ltd., 3 Cork St., London W1, England.

Movie Life. 1937. mo. $4.20. Ideal Publishing Corp., 295 Madison Ave., New York, NY. 10017

Movie Maker. (Incorporating: Amateur Cine World and Eight MM Movie Maker) 1934. mo. 50s($8). Fountain Press Ltd., 46-47 Chancery Lane, London WC2. England.

Movie Mirror. 1957. mo. $3. Sterling Group, Inc., 315 Park Ave., S., New York, NY. 10010.

Movie News. 1948. mo. S$8.50. Chinese Pictorial Review Ltd., 112/120 Robinson Rd., 1 Singapore.

Movie Stars. 1940. mo.$4.50. Ideal Publishing Corp., 295 Madison Ave., New York, NY. 10017.

Movie World. 1952. 6xyr. $4.50. Magazine Management Co., 625 Madison Ave., New York, NY. 10022.

Movies. 1968. mo.$2. Vanity Fair, 5614 Greene St., Philadelphia PA. 19144.

New Republic. 1914. 4xmo. $9. 1244 19th St., N.W., Washington, DC.

New York Critics Guide to Films and Plays. (Formerly Critics Guide to Movies and Plays) 1967. mo.$5. 485 Fifth Ave., New York, NY. 10017.

Nouveau Cinema Canadien/New Canadian Film. (Supersedes: Objectif Sixty-Fiver) 1968. 5-6xyr. La Cinematheque Canadienne, 3834 rue Saint Deinis, Montreal 13, Quebec, Canada.

Nouveau Cinemonde. (Formerly: Cinemonde) 1966. 2xmo. 90 F. Societe Francaise d'Editions et de Publications Illustrees, 2a 12 rue de Bellevue, 75 Paris (19e), France.

Nuestro Cine. 1969. mo. 260ptas. Santiago de la Heras, Macarena, 23-Madrid-16, Spain.

Oesterreichische Gesellschaft Fuer Filmwissenschaft. Mitteilungen. 1952. 6xyr. S.30. Oesterreichische Gesellschaft fuer Filmwissenschaft, Ranhensteingasse 5, 1010 Vienna, Austria.

Olympic Training Film Digest. 1968. 6xyr. $3. Olympic Film Service, 161 W. 22nd St., New York, NY. 10011.

Ontario Film Association. Bulletin. 1957. 3xyr. Ontario Film Assoc., Inc., Box 728, Adelaide St. P.O., Toronto 1, Ont., Canada.

Photo Screen. 1965. mo. $4. Morris S. Latzen, 315 Park Ave. S., New York, NY. 10010.

Photoplay. 1911. mo $5. Macfadden-Bartell Corp., 205 E. 42nd St., New York, NY. 10017.

Presence du Cinema. 1959. mo. 60F. ($12). 25 Passage des Princes, Paris (2e), France.

Preview (U.S.) 1969. 4xyr. Free. Indiana University, Audio-Visual Center, Field Services, Bloomington, IN.

Producers Guild of America. Journal. (Formerly: Screen Producers Guild. Journal) 1953. 4xyr. 141 el Camino

Dr., Beverly Hills, CA. 90212.

Programme News. 1945. mo. ($2). Johannesburg Film Society, Box 10849, Johannesburg, S. Africa.

Reel Four. 1968. 4xyr. Screen ACtors Guild, New York Branch, 551 Fifth Ave., New York, NY. 10017.

Repertuar Khudozhestvennoi Samodeiatel'nosti. 1966. 7 kop. IZD "Iskusstvo," Tsvetnoi Buc'var, Moscow 1-51, USSR.

Research Film. 1952. 2xyr. Institut fuer den Wissenschaftlichen Film, 72 Nonnenstieg, Goettingen, W. Germany.

Revue Internationale du Cinema. 1949. mo. 15F($3.) Office Catholique International du Cinema, Secretariat Information, 129 Fg. St. Honore, Paris (8e), France.

Rivista del Cinematografo. 1928. mo. L.4000. Edicine s.r.l., Via della Conciliazione 2C, 00193 Rome, Italy.

Rivista Tecnica di Cinematografia. 1950. 4xyr. L.1000. Viale Campania 23, Milan, Italy.

RPM Weekly. 4xmo. Can.$5. ($15.) RPM Music Publications, 1560 Bayview Ave., Toronto 17, Ont. Canada.

San Francisco's Openings. 1969. 2xmo. $2.50. Jay Bail, P.O. Box 14143, San Francisco, CA. 94114.

Schmalfilm. 1948. mo. DM.18. Fachverlag Schiele & Schon,

Markgrafenstr. 11, 1 Berlin 61, Germany.

SCJ&Sydney Cinema Journal. 4xyr. Aus.$3.50. Ken Quinell & Michael Thornhill, Box 4430, Sydney, N.S.W., Australia.

Screen. 1959. 6xyr. 6s($1.) Society for Education in Film and Television, 81 Dean Street, London, W1, England.

Screen Facts. 1963. 6xyr. $7. Alan G. Barbour, 123-40 83rd Ave., Kew Gardens, NY. 11415.

Screenland. 1920. mo.$3.75. Macfadden-Bartell Corp., 205 E. 42nd St., New York, NY. 10017.

Seven Arts. 1958. mo.300s($43.) Hansom Books, Artillery Mansions, 75 Victoria, London SW1, England.

SMPTE Journal. 1916. mo.($16). Society of Motion Picture and Television Engineers, 9 E. 41 St., New York, NY. 10017.

Stage and Cinema. 1915. 4xmo. R.S. Stag and Cinema Newspapers, Ltd., Box 1574 Johannesburg, South Africa.

Tanzarchiv. 1953. DM.30. Stadion-Aacherstr., 5 Cologne-Muengerdsorf, W. Germany.

TV Picture Life. 1957. mo.$4. Publication House, Inc., 260 Park Ave. S., New York, NY. 10010.

Variety. 1905. 4xmo. $20. Variety, Inc., 154 W. 46th St., New York, NY. 10036.

Opera

Central Opera Service Bulletin. 1954. 6xyr. $5. Central Opera Service, Metropolitan Opera, Lincoln Center, New York, NY. 10023.

Corriere Internazionale del Teatro. 1960. 6xyr. L.2500. Via Goldoni 32, Milan, Italy.

Gilbert and Sullivan Journal. 1925. 3xyr. 6s($1). J. Antony Gowers, 23 Burnside, Sawbridgeworth, Herts, England.

Opera/Canada. 1960. 4xyr. $3. Canadian Opera Assoc., 129 Adelaide St. W. Ste. 517, Toronto 110, Ont., Canada.

Opera (Eng). 1950. mo. 65s($12.) Seymour Press Ltd., 334 Brixton Road, London SW9, England.

Opera (France). 1961. mo. 30f. 19 rue du Depart, Paris (14e). France.

Opera (Italy). 1965. 4xyr. L.15,000($24.) Editoriale Fenarete, Via Beruto 7, Milan, Italy.

Opera Journal. (Formerly: National Opera Assoc. Newsletter). 1968. 4xyr. $5. University of Mississippi, University Extension, University, MS. 38677.

Opera (Netherlands). 1960. 6xyr. f.3. Nederlandse Opera Stichting, Stadsschouwburg, Amsterdam, Netherlands.

Opera News. 1936. 4xmo. 2smo. (Spring and Fall). Metropolitan Opera

Guild, Inc., 1865 Broadway, New York, NY. 10023.

Oper Und Konzert. 1963. mo. DM.18. Arnold Hanuschik, Leopoldstr. 173, Munich 23, Germany.

Opern Journal. 1961. mo. pf.80. Hauszeitschrift der Deutschen Oper Berlin-W., Richard-Wagner-Str. 10, 1 Berlin 10, W. Germany.

Sound Recording and Broadcasting

Atlantic Monthly. 1857. mo.$9. Atlantic Monthly Co., 8 Arlington St., Boston, MA. 02116.

Audio (U.S.) 1917. mo.$5. North American Publishing Co., 134 N. 13th St., Philadelphia, PA. 19107.

Audio Engineering Society. Journal. 1953. 6xyr. ($22.50). Audio Engineering Society, 60 E. 42nd St., Rm. 428, New York, NY. 10017.

Audio Record Review. (Incorporating: Gramophone Record and Record Review) 1933. mo.40s.($6). Heathcock Press Ltd., Pembroke House, Wellesly Rd., West Croydon, CR9 2BX, England.

Audio Times. 1959. 2xmo. $3. Audio Times Inc., 145 E. 42nd St., New York, NY. 10022.

Audio Visual Communication Review. 1953. 4xyr. $8. Dept. of Audio Visual Instruction, 1201 16th St., N.W., Washington, D.C. 20036.

Audio-Visual Media/Moyens Audio-Visuels. (Formerly: ICEF Review). 1967. 4xyr. 80s. Pergamon Press, Inc., Journals Dept., Maxwell House, Fairview Park, Elmsford, NY. 10523 and Headington Hill Hall, Oxford OX3 OBW, England.

Bandopname. 1962. mo.f.1.75. Nederlandse Vereniging voor Geluid-en Beeldregistratie, Box 3520, Amsterdam, Netherlands.

Billboard. (Formerly: Billboard Music Week) 1894. 4xmo. $2. Billboard Publishing Co., 165 W. 46 St., New York, NY. 10036.

Broadcasting. 1931. 4xmo. $10. Broadcasting Publications, Inc., 1735 De Sales St. N.W., Washington, D.C. 20036.

Broadcasting & Communications. 1965. 6xyr. Tomar Publications Ltd., 146 Bates Rd., Montreal 26, Canada.

Budavox Telecommunication Review. (Formerly BHG Telecommunication Review) 2xyr. $4. Editorial Board. Budavox Telecommunication Foreign Trading Co. Ltd., Box 267, Budapest 62, Hungary.

Christian Communications. 1962. 6xyr. Can.$2. Saint Paul University, Institute of Social Communications, 223 Main St., Ottawa 1, Canada.

Communications News. 1964. mo. $3.50. Brookhill Publishing Co., 402 W. Liberty Drive, Wheaton, IL. 60187.

Cultural Events in Africa. 1965. mo. 100x. Transcription Centre, 84c

Warwick Ave., London W.9, England.

DB, The Sound Engineering Magazine. 1967. mo. $6. Sagamore Publishing Co. Inc., 980 Old Country Rd, Plainview, NY. 11803.

Educational Development. 1946. 3xyr. 20s. Educational Development Assoc., 192 Stonelow Road, Dronfield, Nr. Sheffield S18 6EQ, England.

Educational/Instructional Broadcasting. 1968. $15. Acolyte Publications, Inc., 647 N. Sepulveda Blvd, Bel Air, Los Angeles, CA 90049.

Educational Television International. (Formerly: CETO News) 1967. 4xyr. 100s.($12.50). Pergamon Press, Inc., Journals Dept., Maxwell House, Fairview Park, Elmsford, NY. 10523 and Headington Hill Hall, Oxford OX3 OBW, England.

Elektron. 1948. mo. S.14. Technisher Verlag, Graben 9, A4020 Linz-Donau, Austria.

Elementary Electronics. 1963. 6xyr. $4. Science & Mechanics Publishing Co., A Subsidiary of David Publications, Inc., 229 Park Ave., S., New York, NY. 10003.

FM & Fine Arts. 1960. mo. $5.00 FM & Fine Arts Guide, Inc., 291 S. La Cienega Blvd., Beverly Hills, CA. 90211.

FM Music Program Guide. 1963. mo. $7. Raymond Gombach, 200 Hudson St., New York, NY. 10013.

Fono Forum. 1957. mo.DM.30($7.50). Bielefelder Verlagsanstalt KG, Schillerplatz 20, 48 Bielefeld, W. Germany.

Fonografiek. 2xmo. f.35 Fonorama N.V., Kon. Wilhelminalaan 12, Postbus 26, Amersfoort, Netherlands.

Format (W. Germany). 6xyr. D.m.68($17.). Verlag Nadolski, Am Vogelherd 14, Postfach 187,7000 Stuttgart-Weilimdorf, W. Germany.

Funk-Technik. 2xmo. DM.63. Verlag fuer Radio Foto-Kinotechnik GmbH, Eichborndamm 141-167, 1 Berlin 52, W. Germany.

Hi-Fi Buyers' Guide. 1965. 2xyr. $1.25. Davis Publishing Co., 229 Park Ave. S., New York, NY. 10003.

Hi-Fi News. 1956. mo.47s.($5.60). Link House Publications Ltd., Link House, Dingwall Ave., Croydon, Surrey Cr9 2TA, England.

Hi-Fi Sound. (Supersedes: Amateur Tape Recording, Video and Hi-Fi) 1967. mo.42s. Gillow House, 5 Winsley St., London W 1, England.

HiFi-Stereo Phonie. 1962. mo.DM (3 mos.) Verlag G. Braun GmbH, Karl-Friedrichstr. 14-18, Postfach 1709, 75 Karlsruhe, W. Germany.

Intermedia Newsletter. 1968. 4xyr. Intermedia Society, 575 Beatty St., Vancouver 3 B.C., Canada.

High Fidelity. 1951. mo. $9. Billboard Publishing Co., 165 W. 46th St., New York, NY. 10036.

High Fidelity/Musical America. 1965. mo. $17. Billboard Publishing Co., 165 W. 46th St., New York, NY. 10036.

Journal of Broadcasting. 1956/57. 4xyr. $8. Assoc. for Professional Broadcasting Education, Temple University, Philadelphia, PA. 19122.

Luister. 1952. mo.f.10. Postbus 43, Amersfoort, Netherlands.

Lyd & Tone. 1955. Kr.26($4.50). Otto Monstedsgade 1, Copenhagen V, 1571 Denmark.

Magnetophone-Haute Fidelite Stereophonie. 1959. 6xyr. 25 F. Publications Nouvelles, 12 rue Richer, 75 Paris (9e), France.

Musical Merchandise Review. 1880. mo. $5. Joseph D. Feldmann, 373 Fifth Ave., New York, NY. 10016.

National Association of Educational Broadcasters Newsletter. 1936. mo. $5. National Assoc. of Educational Broadcasters, 1346 Connecticut Ave., Washington, D.C. 20036.

New Republic. 1914. 4xyr. $9. Robert J. Myers, 1244 19th St., N.W., Washington, D.C. 20036.

Phono. 1954. 6xyr. S.69.($3.) Symphonia T.A. GmbH., Konzerthaus, Lothringerstr. 20, Vienna 3, Austria.

Phonotheque Nationale Bulletin. 1961. 2xyr. Free Phonotheque Nationale, 19 rue des Berhardins, Paris (5e), France.

Playback. (Formerly: Geluidsjournaal). 1968. 4xyr. Minnesota (Nederland) N.V., Roosevelstraat 55, Leiden, Netherlands.

Populaer Radio OG TV Teknik. 1927. mo. Kr. 42.($5.). Berlingske Tidende, Ny Oestergade 12, 1147 Copenhagen, Denmark.

Quarterly Journal of Speech. 1915. 4xyr. $12.50. Speech Assoc. of America, Statler Hilton Hotel, New York, NY. 10001.

Radio and Electronic Engineer. 1926. mo. 130s.($20.). Institution of Electronic and Radio Engineers, 9 Bedford Sq., London WC1, England.

Record Buyer. (Supersedes: Pop Weekly) 1969. mo. 42s. 41 Derby Rd., Heanor, Derbyshire, England.

Record Collector. 1948. 6xyr. 30s.($4.50). James F.E. Dennis, 61 Fore St., Ipswich, Suffolk, England.

Record World. 4xmo. $20. Record World Pub. Co. Inc., 200 W. 57th St., New York, NY. 10019.

Recorded Sound. 1961 4xyr. 40s.($6.). British Institute of Recorded Sound, 29 Exhibition Rd., London SW7, England.

Recorder and Music Magazine. 1963. 4xyr. 13s.($3.). 48 Great Marlborough St., London W1, England.

Recorder Reporter. 1967. mo. ($2.) American Recorder Society, Chicago

Chapter, 1120 Randolph St., Oak Park, IL. 60302.

Records and Recording. 1957. mo. 42.($6.). Hansom Books, Artillery Mansions, 75 Victoria St., London SW1, England.

Revue Du Son. 1953. mo.40 F. Editions Chiron, 40 rue de Seine, Paris (6e), France.

RPM Weekly. 4xmo. Can.$5.($15.) RPM Music Publications, 1560 Bayview Ave., Toronto 17, Ontario, Canada.

Ruch Muzyczny. 1957. 2xmo. 135 zl.($6.50). Wydawnictwo Artystyczne i Filmowe (Artist and Film Publishers), Teatr Wielki, Plac Zwyciestwa 9, Warsaw, Poland.

Seven Arts. 1958. mo. 300s.($43.) Hansom Books, Artillery Mansions, 75 Victoria, London SW1, England.

Stereo Review. (Formerly HiFi Stereo Review) 1958. mo. $7. Ziff-Davis Publishing Co., One Park Ave., New York, NY. 10016.

Tape Recorder. 1959. mo. 30s.($4.50). Link House Publications Ltd., Dingwall Ave., Croydon, Surrey, England.

Systems Technology. (Formerly: Plessey Communications Journal) 1966. 3xyr. Free. Plessey Co. Ltd., Ilford, Essex, England.

Tape Recording Magazine. 1957. mo. 25s.($3.75). Prestige House, 14-18 Holborn, London EC4, England.

Telecommunications. 1967. mo. Free to qualified personnel, others $20· Horizon House, 610 Washington St., Dedham, MA 02026.

Telecommunications and Radio Engineering. 1964. mo. $75. Institute of Electrical and Electronics Engineers, Inc., Special Subscr. Dept., 275 Madison Ave., New York, NY. 10016.

Today's Speech. 1953. 4xyr. $4.50. Indiana Univ., Bloomington, IN. 47401.

Variety. 1905. 4xmo. $20. Variety, Inc., 154 W. 46th St., New York, NY. 10036.

Voicespondent. 1953. 4xyr. Voicespondence Club, Doswell, VA. 23047.

Television

Arab Film & T.V. Center Informations-News. Arab Film & T.V. Center, P.O. Box 3434, Beirut, Lebanon.

Billboard. 1894. 4xmo. $2. Billboard Publishing Co., 165 W. 46 St., New York, NY.

Broadcasting. 1931. 4xmo. $10. Broadcasting Publications, Inc., 1735 De Sales St., N.W., Washington, D.C. 20036.

Budavox Telecommunication Review. (Formerly: BHG Telecommunication Review) 1965. 2xyr. $4. Editorial Board. Budavox Telecommunication

Foreign Trading Co., Ltd., Box 267, Budapest 62, Hungary.

Cablecasting-Cable TV Engineering. 1966. mo. $8. C.S. Tepfer Publishing Co., Inc., 140 Main St., Ridgefield, CT. 06877.

CATV Weekly. (Formerly: Cable Television Review) 1964. 4xmo. $33. Communications Publishing Corp. 207 N.E. 38th, Oklahoma City, OK. 73106.

CBC Times. 1969. 4xmo. $3. Canadian Broadcasting Corp., Box 500, Terminal "A", Toronto 1, Canada.

Daily Variety. 1933. 20xmo. $20. Daily Variety Ltd., 6404 Sunset Blvd. Hollywood, CA. 90028.

Education Television. 1968. mo. $8. C.S. Tepfer Publishing Co., Inc., 140 Main St., Ridgefield, CT. 06877.

ETV Newsletter. 1967. 2xmo. $40. ETV Newsletter Co., 140 Main St., Ridgefield, CT. 06877.

Format (W. Germany). 1969. 6xyr. D.m.68.($17.). Verlag Nadolski, Am Vogelherd 14, Postfach 187, 7000 Stuttgart-Weilimdorf, W. Germany.

Listener and BBC Television Review. 1929. 4xmo. $75s.($11.) British Broadcasting Corp., Broadcasting House, London. W1 England.

National Academy of Television Arts & Sciences Presidential Newsletter. (Formerly: National Academy of Television Arts & Sciences Newsletters) 6xyr. National Academy of Television Arts and Sciences, 54 West 40th St., New York, NY. 10018.

Populaer Radio OG TV Teknik. 1927. mo.Kr. 42.($5.) Berlingske Tidende, Ny Oestergade 12, 1147 Copenhagen, Denmark.

Ross Reports: Television. 1949. mo.$10. Television Index, Inc., 150 Fifth Ave., New York, NY. 10011.

Rundfunk Und Fernschen. 1953. 4xyr. DM.20. Verlag Hans Bredow Institut, Heimhuderstr. 21, 2 Hamburg 13, W. Germany.

Sound and Vision Broadcasting. 1960. 3xyr. 22s.6d.($3.50). Ed. J. Deveson. The Marconi Co., Ltd., Chelmsford, Essex, England.

Stage and Television Today. 1880. w. 68s.($8.25). Carson and Comerford, Ltd., 19/21 Tavistock St., London WC2, England.

Systems Technology. (Formerly: Plessey Communications Journal) 1966. Free. Plessey Co. Ltd., Ilford, Essex, England.

Television. 1939. 10xyr. 25F.($6.20). Societe des Editions Radio, 42 rue Jacob, Paris (6e), France.

Television Age. 1953. 2xmo. $7. Television Editorial Corp., 1270 Ave. of the Americas, New York, NY. 10020.

Telecommunications. 1967. mo. Free to qualified personnel, others $20.

Horizon House, 610 Washington St., Dedham, MA. 02026.

Telecommunications and Radio Engineering. 1964. mo. $75. Institute of Electrical and Electronics Engineers, Inc., Special Subscr. Dept., 275 Madison Ave., New York, NY. 10016.

Television Quarterly. 1962. 4xyr. ($7.50). National Academy of Television Arts and Sciences, 54 W. 40th St., New York, NY. 10018.

TV & Communications. 1964. mo. $10. Communications Publishing Corp., 207 N.E. 38th, Oklahoma City, OK, 73105.

TV Picture Life. 1957. mo. $4. Publication House, Inc., 260 Park Ave. S., New York, NY. 10010.

Theater

Abel ($12.00/yr.) Abel News Agencies, 300 West 17th Street, New York, NY. 10011.

African Arts/Arts D'Afrique. 4xyr. $10. African Studies Center, University of California, Los Angeles, CA. 90024.

Afro-Asian Theatre Bulletin. (American Educational Theatre Assoc.) 1965. 2xyr. Free. University of Kansas, International Theatre Studies Center, Lawrence, Kan. 66044.

Agentzia. 1967. 6xyr. 30 F.($10.) Editions Agentzia, 25 rue Vandamme, 75 Paris (14e), France.

Amateur Stage. Stacey Publications, 1 Hawthorndene Rd., Hayes, Bromley, Kent, England.

American Place Theatre News. American Place Theatre, 423 W. 46th St., New York, NY. 10036.

ANTA Newsletter. American National Theatre and Academy, 245 W. 52nd St., New York, NY. 10019.

Antaeu's ($8.00/yr.) Box 3121, New York, NY. 10001.

Approaches (France) Compagnie du Cothurne, Theatre du Huiteme, 8 av. Jean-Mermoz, Lyon (8e), France.

Arab Film & TV Center Information-News. Arab Film & TV Center, P.O. Box 3434, Beirut, Lebanon.

Arcoscenico. mo. Lire2000($3.20). Giuseppe Luongo, Via Ormisda 10, Rome, Italy.

Arcadie. 1954. mo. 50F.($12.) 19 rue Beranger, Paris (3e), France.

Artes. 1965. $7.70. Rua Nestor Pestana 30.21 Conj. 216, Sao Paulo 3 S.P., Brazil.

Artistes et Varietes. (Formerly: Revue de l'Accordeoniste et des Instrumentistes de Rythme) 1945. mo. 3.50 F. 48 rue de Berri, Paris (8e), France.

Arts Council of Australia. 1964. 4xyr. Free. North Sydney Printing Pty. Ltd., 207 Miller St., North Sydney, Australia.

Arts Management. 1962. 5xyr. $10. Radius Group Inc., 408 W. 57th St., New York, NY. 10019.

Association of College and University Concert Managers Bulletin. 1958. 7-8xyr. Free. College Printing and Typing Co., 453 W. Gilman St., Madison, WI. 53703.

Atlantic Mirror. 1967. 4xyr. Atlantic Literary Alliance, 4 Hector St., Glace Bay, Nova Scotia, Canada.

Avant Garde. 2xmo. 110 W. 40 St., New York, NY. 10018.

Back Stage. 1960 weekly $15. Back Stage Publications, Inc., 165 W. 46th St., New York, NY. 10036.

Beaux-Arts. 1934. 4xmo. 560 fr.($13.) Palais des Beaux-Arts, 10 rue Royal, Brussels 1, Belgium.

Billboard. (Formerly Billboard Music Week) 1894. 4xmo. $2. Billboard Publishing Co., 165 W. 46 St., New York, NY. 10036.

Black Theatre; a periodical of the black theatre movement. (Formerly: Black Theatre News) 1968. 3xyr. $2.50(for 6 nos.) New Lafayette Publications, Room 103, 200 West 135th St., New York, NY. 10030.

Blaetter Der Freien Volksbuehne Berlin. 2xmo. Freie Volksbuehne Berlin ev, Ruhrstr. 6, 1000 Berlin 31, W. Germany.

Bonner Kultur-Blaetter. 1950. mo. DM.6. Theatergemeinde Bonn, Kronprinzenstr, 10, 53 Bonn, W. Germany.

Bravo. 1960. 4-6xyr. $2.25. 3 E. 54th St., New York, NY. 10022.

Buehne. 1958. mo. S.192. ($8.) Zeitschriftenverlag Austria International, Gesellschaft MbH, Wallnerstr. 8, Vienna 1, Austria.

Buehnengenossenschaft. 1971. mo. DM.12. Buehnenschriften-Vertriebs-Gesellschaft MbH, Feldbrunnenstr. 74, Hamburg 13, W. Germany.

Buehnentechnische Rundschau. 1907. 6xyr. DM 26. ($7.50). Klasing & Co., GmbH., Schoeneberger Ufer 59, Berlin W 30, W. Germany.

Buenos Aires Musical. 1968. 17xyr. Arg.$1000($8.) Alsine 912, Buenos Aires, Argentina.

Bulletin des Livres Nouveaux et Pieces de Theatre. 1969. PolacKultury i Nauki, Warsaw, Poland.

Bulletin of the Comediantes. 1968. $2.50. Romance Languages, University of Arizona, Tucson, AZ. 85721.

Bulletin Signaletique. Part 523: Historire et Science de la Litterature-Arts du Spetacle. (Centre National de la Recherche Scientifique) 4xyr. 65 F. Centre de Documentation du C.N.R.S., 15 Quai Anatole-Fance, Paris (7e), France.

Cahiers Renaud Barrault. 1955. 4xyr. 17 F.($5.) Editions Gallimard, 5 rue

Sebastien Bottin, Paris (7e), France.

California Shavian. 1958. 6xyr. Shaw Society of California, 1933 S. Broadway, Los Angeles CA. 90007.

Call Board. 1931. 2xmo. Catholic Actors Guild of America, Hotel Piccadilly, 227 W. 45th St., New York, NY. 10036.

Call Boy. 1963. 2xmo. 21s.($3). British Music Hall Society, The Studio. 63 Great Cumberland Place, London, W1, England.

Catholic Theatre. 6xyr. C.S.J. National Catholic Theatre Conference, 1701 Pennsylvania Ave., N.W., Washington, D.C. 20006.

Central Ontario Drama League (Publication). 6xyr. Central Ontario Drama League, Apt. 304, F St., Stevens Court, Islington, Ontario, Canada.

Changes. 1969. 2xmo. $11. 80 Fifth Ave., New York, NY. 10011.

Children's Theatre News. 1970. 3xyr. Children's Theatre Conference, Region 14, c-o Ann Battle, 65 Roosevelt Blvd., Edison, NJ. 08817.

Children's Theatre Review. 1970. 4xyr. Membership Ed. Mrs. Donald F. Phillips, 6104 Jocelyn Hollow Rd., Nashville, TN. 37205.

Choragos. 1965. 2xmo. $2.50. Verb Publicatons, 1323 E. 14th Ave., Denver, CO. 80218.

Chronicle mo. Citadel Theatre, 10030-102nd St., Edmonton, Alta, Canada.

Chrysalis. 1948. $4.00. Lily & Baird Hastings, 112 Vernon St., Hartford, CT. 06106.

Coloquio. 1967. 5xyr. Esc. 100. Fundacao Calouste Gulbenkian, Avenida de Berna 45a, Lisbon 1, Portugal.

Communication Arts International. 4xyr. Leeward Publications, Box 2801, Washington, D.C. 20013.

Concerned Theatre Japan. 1969. 4xyr. Yen 2500($10.) Concerned Theatre Japan. Nishi-Azabu3-1-14, Minato-Ku, Tokyo 106, Japan.

Conjunto. 1964. 4xyr. $60 per no. Ed.Bd. Casa de las Americas, Gx 3ra., Vedado, Havana, Cuba.

Creative Drama. 1949. 2xyr. 6s.($4.) Stacey Publications, 1 Hawthorndene Rd., Hayes, Bromley, Kent, England.

Cue of Theta Alpha Phi. 1928. $2.50. Indiana State Univ., Speech Dept, Terre Haute, IN. 47809.

Cultural Events in Africa. 1965. Institutions & libraries 100s. Transcription Centre, 84c Warwick Ave., London W. 9, England.

Daily Variety. 1933. 20xmo. $20. Daily Variety Ltd., 6404 Sunset Blvd., Hollywood, CA. 90028.

Dialog (Poland). 1956 mo. 120zl. Pulawska 61, Warsaw, Poland.

Divadelni Noviny. 1969. 26 Kes.

Valdstejnske nam. 3, Prague 1, Czechoslovakia.

Divadlo/Theatre. 10xyr. 50 Kcs. Svaz Ceskoslovenskych Divadelnich Umelcu, Valentinska 7, Prague 1, Czechoslovakia.

D.O.E./Speel. 1951. 2xmo. f.12.50. Stichting "Ons Leekenspel", Gudelalaan 2, Bussum, Netherlands.

Drama. 1919. 4xyr. British Drama League, 9 Fitzroy Square, London W.1, England.

Drama and Theatre. 1961-1962. 4xyr. $.50. SUNY, Fredonia, Dept. of English, Fredonia, N.Y. 14063.

Drama Review. 1956 4xyr. $6. 32 Washington Pl., New York, N.Y. 10003.

Dramatics. 1929. 8xyr. $5. International Thespian Society, College Hill Sta., Box E, Cincinnati, Oh. 45224.

Dramatika. 1968. 2xyr. $4.50. Lincoln University, Lincoln University, PA. 19352.

Dramatists Guild Quarterly. 1964. 4xyr. Dramatists Guild, Inc., 234 W. 44th St., New York, N.Y. 10036.

Echo (Denmark). 1939. mo. $16. 30 Vesterbrogade, DK1610 Copenhagen V, Denmark.

Educational Theatre Journal. 1949. 4xyr. $12.50 American Educational Theatre Assoc. 1317 FSt. N.W., Washington, D.C. 20004.

Educational Theatre News. 1970-1971. 6xyr. $2. American Educational Theatre Assoc., Southern California District, Cerritos College, 11110 E. Alondra Blvd., Norwalk CA. 90650.

Enact. 1967. mo. Rs.12. ($5) 4 Chamelian Rd., Delhi 6, India.

En Garde. 1967. 3xyr. $1.50 19159 Helen, Detroit, MI.

Equity. 1915. mo. Actors' Equity Assoc. 165 W. 46th St., New York, NY. 10036.

Esquire. 1933. mo. $6.50. Esquire, Inc., 488 Madison Ave., New York, NY. 10022.

Evergreen Review. mo. 80 University Place, N.Y., NY. 10003

Fackel (Austria). 1966. 4xyr. S.30 ($1.50). Box 70, A-1094 Vienna, Austria.

Flourish. 1970. 4xyr. Royal Shakespeare Co., Stratford-upon-Avon, England.

France – Theatre. 1957. mo. 25 F. Syndicat National des Agences, De Theatres de France, 16 Av. l'Opera, Paris, France.

From New York. 1954. 4xmo. Creighton Peet, Room 1138, 22 E. 17th St., New York, NY. 10003.

Gala. 1964. 6xyr. L.3000. Via Zanella 41, 20133 Milan, Italy.

Gambit. 1963. 4xyr. ($6.75). Gambit

Theatre, 40 Old Church Lane, London NW 9, England.

Giornale Dello Spettacolo. 4xmo. L.5000. ($8.) Via di Villa Patrizi 10, Rome 00161, Italy.

Greater London Arts. 1968. 4xyr. 10s. Greater London Arts Assoc., 21 Theobalds Rd., London WC 1, England.

Hamburger Jugendbrief. 1948. mo. DM.3. Jugendbehoerde der Freien und Hansestadt Hamburg, Hachmannplatz 1, Bieberhaus, 2 Hamburg 1, W. Germany.

Humpty Dumpty's Magazine. 1952. $5. Parents Magazine Enterprises, Inc., 52 Vanderbilt Ave., New York, NY.

Dramma. 1925. mo. L.10,000. Corso Bramante 20, Turin, Italy. Il.

Independent Shavian. 1962. 3xyr. (libraries $3). New York Shavians, Inc., 14 Washington Place, New York, NY. 10003.

Innsbrucker Theater-Und Konzertspiegel. 1957. mo. Free. Tiroler Landestheater, Rennweg 2, Konzerte der Stadt Innsbruck, Museumstr. 17 a, Innsbruck, Austria.

Institute of Outdoor Drama Newsletter. 1964. mo. $2. Institute of Outdoor Drama, 202 Graham Memorial, Chapel Hill, NC. 27514.

International Theatre. 1949. 4xyr. 20 fr. ($4.) Institut Internationale du Theatre, 1 rue Miollis, Paris (15e), France.

Junge Theater. 1951. mo. DM. 90 Mundsburger Damm 60, 2 Hamburg 22, W. Germany.

Kammerspiele Munchen. 1912. Price ''n.g.'' EMHA-Verlag, Sendlinger-tor-Platz 8, Munich 2, W. Germany.

Kinderzeitung. 1930. 6xyr $2. Workmen's Circle Educational Dept., 175 E. Broadway, New York, NY. 10002.

Kultur/Art Et Culture. 1968. ($12.) Pointengasse 22, 1170 Vienna, Austria.

Latin American Theatre Review. 1967. 2xyr. $3. University of Kansas, Center of Latin American Studies, Lawrence, KA. 66044.

Letture Drammatiche. 1964. mo. L.1500. Centro Spettacolo, Via M. Ausiliatrice 32, Turin, Italy.

Linzer Theaterzeitung. 1955. mo. S.30.Landestheater Linz, Promenade 39, Linz, Austria.

Literary Cavalcade. 1948. mo. 5xyr. $1.50 Scholastic Magazines, Inc., 50 W. 44th St., New York, NY. 10036.

Mademoiselle. 1935. mo. $5. Conde Nast Publications, Inc., 420 Lexington Ave., New York, NY. 10017.

Madia. 1969. 6xyr. L.2000. Fuuri Porta Bazzano 3, L'aquila, Italy.

Marquee. 1969. 4xyr. $6. Theatre Historical Society, Box 4445, Washington, D.C. 20017.

Maske Und Kothurn. 1955. 4xyr. DM.32 ($8.) Hermann Beohlaus Nachf, Schmalzhofgasse 4, A-1061 Vienna, Austria.

Masque (Australia). 1967. 2xmo. Aus. $3.80. Masque Publications, 22 Steam Mill St., Sydney, N.S.W., 2000, Australia.

Microcritica, 1965. 6xyr. M.n.800 ($5.) Gral. Hornos 1110-2b, Buenos Aires, Argentina.

M i m o s. 1 9 6 5. 4 x y r. Theatersammlung, Bern, Switzerland.

Mirador. 1966. 6xyr. Price "n.g." Inter-American Foundation for the Arts, 55 West 44th St., New York, NY.10036.

Modern International Drama. 1967. 2xyr. $4.50. University of New York, Department of Theatre, Binghamton, NY. 13901.

M o z a i e k. 1 9 6 6. m o. Kultuurcentrum-Beursschouwburg, August Ortsstraat 22, Brussels 1, Belgium.

Musical Show. 1962. 6xyr. Free. Tams-Witmark Music Library, Inc., 757 Third Ave., New York, NY. 10017.

Mystetztvo. 1954. mo. Kultury Ukrayins'koyi RSR, Spilka Kompozytoriv, Spilka kinematohra fistiv Ukrayiny., Spilkakhudozhnikov U k r a y i n y, V u l. Y n r i y a Kotsyubinskogo 5, Kiev, USSR.

Natya. 1969. 4xyr. Rs.12. ($3.50).

Bharatiya Natya Sangh, 34 New Central Market, New Delhi, India.

Neue Blaetter Des Theaters in Der Josefstadt. 1953. 2xmo. Direktion des Theaters in der Josefstadt, Josefstaedterstr. 26, A-1082 Vienna, Austria.

New Jersey Theatre League. Bulletin. 1965 10xyr. $1.50 54 Nestro Rd., W. Orange, N.J. 07052.

New Republic. 1914 4xmo. $9. Robert J. Myers, 1244 19th St., N.W., Washington, D.C. 20036.

New Theatre Magazine. 1959 3xyr. 15s. ($3). Univ. of Bristol, Drama Dept., 29 Park Row, Bristol BS8-5LT, England.

New York State Community Theatre. Journal. 1961. 4xyr. $1. State Univ. of New York, 1223 Western Ave., Albany, NY. 12203.

New York Theatre Critics' Reviews. 1940. 22-30xyr. $40. Proscenium Publications, 150 E. 35th St., New York, N.Y. 10016.

New York Times Magazine. 4 xmo. 229 W. 43 St., N.Y., NY. 10036.

Noda Bulletin. 1935. 3xyr. 75 np. National Operatic and Dramatic Assn., 1 Crestfield St., London WC1 8 AV, England.

Nos Spectacles. 1948. 6xyr. 28 F. Federation Catholique du Theatre d'Amateurs Francais, 31 rue de Fleurus, Paris (6e), France.

Ohio State University Theatre Collection Bulletin. 1968. Price "n.g." Ohio State Univ., Dept. of Theatre, 154 North Oval Drive, Columbus, OH. 43210.

Ontario Puppetry Association Letter. (The Opal). 1962. 6xyr. Kenneth McKay, 10 Skyview Cres., Willowdale, Ont., Canada.

Pamietnik Teatralny. 1952. 4xyr. 72 zl. ($4.) Wydawnictwa Artystycze i Filmowe, Pulawska 61, Warsaw, Poland.

Pantuflas Del Obispo. 1966. S/20. ($1.) Semannario Sabado, Vargas 219, Quito, Ecuador.

Paris Theatre. 1947. mo. 44f. 13 Rue du Sentier, Paris (2e), France.

Performance. 4xyr. ($7.00/yr) New York Public Theater, 425 Lafayette St., New York, NY. 10003.

Performing Arts. 1967. mo. $10. K&K Publishing Inc., 147 South Robertson Blvd., Beverly Hills, CA 90211.

Performing Arts In Canada. 1961. 4xyr. Can. $3. Canadian Stage and Arts Publications, Ltd., 49 Wellington E., Toronto 1, Ont., Canada.

Performing Arts Review. 1969 4xyr. $10. Law-Arts Publishers Inc., 453 Greenwich St., New York, NY. 10013.

Playbill. 1884. mo. $4. Playbill Inc., Joan Rubin, 579 Fifth Ave., New York, NY. 10017.

Players Magazine. (National Collegiate Players) 1924. 6xyr. $5. Northern Illinois Univ., University Theatre, Dekalb, Il. 60115.

Plays. 1941. mo. $8.00 Plays, Inc., 8 Arlington St., Boston, MA.

Plays and Players. (Incorporating: Theatre World & Encore) 1953. mo. 60s. ($10.00). Hansom Books, Artiliery Mansions, 75 Victoria St., London S.W. 1, England.

Primer Acto. 1965. mo. 260 ptas. Sanchez Barcaiztegui 35, 60 Madrid, Spain.

Prologue (U.S.) 1945. 3-4xyr. Free Tufts University Theater, Medford, MA. 02155.

Prompt. 1962. 3xyr. 11s. ($2.) University College London Dramatic Society, Gower St., London WC 1, England.

Puppenspiel Und Puppenspieler. 1960. 2xyr. 8 fr. Schweizerische Vereinigung fuer Puppenspiel und Puppenspieler, Willy Wellstein, Jaegerstr. 14, Ch-4058, Basel, Switzerland.

Puppet Master. N.S. 1962. 2xyr. British Puppet and Model Theatre Guild, 90 the Minories, London EC 3, England.

Puppet Post. 1950 2xyr. Educational Puppetry Assoc., 23a Southampton Place, London. WC1, England.

Puppetry Journal. 1949 6xyr. ($10.) 2015 Novem Dr., Fenton, MO. 63103

Ramparts. 1962. mo. $8.50. Ramparts

Magazine, Inc., 495 Beach St., San Francisco, CA. 94133.

Religious Theatre. 1964. $3.50. Religious Theatre, Box 14, Wichita State University, Wichita, KA. 67208.

Repertorio. (Formerly: Nuevo Teatro Centroamericano) 1964. 4xyr. $3.00 Consejo Superior Universitario Centroamericano (C S U C A), Apdo. 37, Ciudad Universitaria "Rodrigofacio", San Jose, Costa Rica.

Restoration & Eighteenth Century Theatre Research. 1962. 2xyr. $3. Loyola Univ., 820.

Revista De Estudios De Teatro. 1964. Price "n.g." Instituto Nacional de Estudios de Teatro, Cordoba 1199, Buenos Aires, Argentina.

Revista De Teatro. 1942. 6xyr. $4. Sociedade Brasileira de Autores Teatrais, Av. Almirante Barroso 97, 3p Andar-ZC P, Rio de Janeiro, Brazil.

Revue D'Histoire Du Theatre. 1948. 4xyr. $7. Societe d'Histore du Theatre, 98 bd. Kellerman, Paris (13e). France.

Ridotto. 1951. mo. L.2500 Ente Nazionale Assistenza Lavoratori, Casella Postale 374, 30124 Venice, Italy.

R P M Weekly. 4xmo. Can. $5. ($15.) RPM Music Publications, 1560 Bayview Ave., Toronto 17, Ont., Canada.

Samenspel. mo. f.7. Zandpad 28, Maanssen, Netherlands.

San Francisco's Openings. 1969. 2xmo. $2.50. Jay Bail, P.O. Box 14143, San Francisco, CA. 94114.

Scen Och Salong. 1915. mo. Kr. 15. ($3.) Svedenborgsgatan 1, Stockholm So., Sweden.

Scena (E. Germany). 1962. 4xyr. Institut fuer Technologic kultureller Einrichtungen, Unter den Linden 41, 108 Berlin, E. Germany.

Scena (Yugoslavia). 1964. 5xyr. 24 din($2.) "Sterijino Pozorje," Novi Sad, Yugoslavia.

Scenografie. 1963. 4xyr. 20 Kcs. Ed. Vera Ptackova. Theatre Institute of Prague, Valdstenjnske nam. 3, Prague 1, Czechoslovakia.

Scripts. New York Public Theater 10xyr. ($7.50) 425 Lafayette St., New York, N.Y. 10003.

Seven Arts. 1958. mo. 300s ($43.) Hansom Books, Artillery Mansions, 75 Victoria, London SW 1, England.

Shakespeare Newsletter. 1951. 6xyr. $2.50. University of Illinois at Chicago Circle, Dept. of English, Chicago, IL. 60680.

Shakespeare Quarterly. 1950. 4xyr. Shakespeare Assoc. of America, Inc., Box 2653, Grand Central Sta., New York, NY. 10017.

Shavian NS. 1953 3xyr. Shaw Society, 45 Manor Rd., Ashford, Kent, England.

Shaw Review. 1951. 3xyr. $5. Pennsylvania State University Press,

University Park, PA. 16802.

Show Business. 1941. 4xmo. $15. Leo Shull, 136 W. 44th St., New York, NY. 10036.

Show Business (France). 4xmo. 80F. 22rue Huyghens, Paris (16e). France.

Sixty-Minute Hour. 1967. 4xmo. Free. John Gates, 124 E. 38th St., New York, NY. 10016.

Sovetski Ekran. 1957. 6xyr. $4.80. M e z h d u n a r o d n a y a K n i g a, Smolenskaya Sennayo 32/34. Moscow G-200, USSR.

Speech and Drama. 1951. 3xyr. 30s ($3.75). Society of Teachers of Speech and Drama, St. Bride Institute, Bride Lane, London EC 4, England.

Spettacolo. 1951. 4xyr. L.3000($7.) Viale Della, Letteratura 30 (E.U.R.), Rome, Italy.

Spiel in Der Schule. 1960. 4xyr. DM.11.80. Manz Verlag, Anzingerstr. 1, Munich 180, W. Germany.

Spiel und Theater. (Formerly: Laienspieler) 1949. 4xyr. DM.3. Deutscher Theaterverlag GmbH, Koenigsberger Str. 18-22. Postfach 187, D-6940 Weinheim, W. Germany.

Spielplan. 1967. mo. DM.24 Baerenreiter-Verlag Karl Voetterle KG, Heinrich-Schuetz-Allee 29-37, 35 Kassel-Wilhelmshoehe, W. Germany.

Spotlight. 1943. 8xyr. Educational Puppetry Assoc. 23a Southampton Place, London WC1A 2BP, England.

Stage and Cinema. 1915. 4xmo. R.5. Stage and Cinema Newspapers, Ltd., Box 1574, Johannesburg, South Africa.

Stage and Television Today. 1880. w. 68s($8.25). Carson and Comerford Ltd., 19/21 Tavistock St., London WC 2, England.

Stage Centre. 1962 7xyr. Manitoba Theatre Centre, 174 Market Ave., Winnipeg 2, Man., Canada.

Stage in Canada/Scene au Canada. 10xyr. mo. Can. $5.15. Canadian Theatre Centre (Centre Canadien du Theatre), 49 Wellington St. E., Toronto 1, Ont., Canada.

Studii si Cercetari de Istoria Artel. Seria Teatru-Musica-Cinematografie. 1954. 2xyr. $8. Academia Republici Socialiste Romania, Str. Gutemberg 3 bis, Bucharest, Romania Cartimex, Box 134, Bucharest, Romania.

Studi Teatrali. 1966. 4xyr. L.2,800. Marsilio Editore, Via S. Eufemia 5, Padova, Italy.

Szene. 1966. mo. M.1.50 VEB Friedrich Hofmeister Musikverlag, Karlstr. 10, 701 Leipzig, E. Germany.

Szindhdz. 1968. 4xyr. 144ft($8.) Nagymezo utca 22-24, Budapest 6, Hungary.

TDR: The Drama Review (Formerly: Tulane Drama Review) 4xyr. School of the Arts, New York Univ., New York, NY. 10003.

Teater SA. 1968. 4xyr. 4.1.75.$3.)

Reijger Publishers, P.O. Box 2153, Cape Town, South Africa.

Teatern. 1934. 4xyr. KR.1.25 Riksteatern, Jungfrugatan 23, Stockholm O, Sweden.

Teatralnaya Zhizn. 1958. 6xyr. $9. A. Zubkov. ul. Zhdanova 12, Moscow 1-45, USSR.

Teatr (Poland) 2xmo. $6.50 Wydawnictwa Artystyczne (Filmowe Warszawa, Pulawska 61, Warsaw, Poland.

Teatr (USSR). 1937. mo. 12 rub. Kuznetzk Most 9-10, Moscow, USSR.

Teatro. 1964. mo. Arg.$500($6). Concepcion Arenal 3932, Buenos Aires, Argentina.

Teatro E. Cinema. 1968. 4xyr. L.3000($6.50). 1 Salita Salvatore Viale, 28-16128 Genoa, Italy.

Teatrul. 1956. mo. 84 lei. Comitetul de Stat pentru Cultura si Arta si de Uniunea Scriitorilor dir R.P.R., Str. Constantin Mille Nr.4-7-9, Bucharest, Rumania.

Theater der Seit. 1946. 6xyr. M.36. Henschelverlag Kunst und Gesellschaft, Oranienburger Str. 67/68, 104 Berlin, E. Germany.

Theater-Echo. 1962. 4xyr. Ehrhard Reinicke. Harlessem-Str. 27, 32 Hidescheim, Germany.

Theater Mosaik. 1963. DM.26.40. Jurgen Stier, Savigny-Platz 7/8, 1 Berlin 12, Germany.

Theaternachrichten. 1952. 4xmo. S.40 Grazer Theatergemeinschaft, Burggasse 16, A-8010 Graz, Austria.

Theater-Rundschau. 1955 mo. DM.10.80($3.30). Theater-Rundscaue-Verlag, Bonner Talweg 10, Bonn, W. Germany.

Theatre Crafts. 1967. 6xyr. $5. Rodale Press, Emmaus, PΛ. 18049.

Theatre dans le Monde/World Theatre. 1951. 6xyr. 36 F.($7.50). Institut International du Theatre, 6 rue Franklin, Paris (16e), France.

Theatre Design and Technology. 1965. 4xyr. U.S. Institute for Theatre Technology, 245 W. 52nd St., New York, NY.10019.

Theatre Documentation. 1968. 2xyr. International Theatre Studies Centre, Univ. of Kansas, Lawrence, KA. 66044.

Theatre en Pologne/Theatre in Poland. 1958. mo. Free. Polish Centre of the International Theatre Institute, ul. Moliera 1, Warsaw, Poland.

Theatre Heute. 1960. mo. DM.66. Erhard Friedrich Verlag, 3001 Velber Bei Hannover, Germany.

Theatre Inforamtion Bulletin. 1944. 4xmo. $50. Proscenium Publications, 4 Park Ave., New York, NY. 10016.

Theatre Notebook. 1946. 4xyr. 30s. 77 Kinnerton St., London, SW1, England.

Theatre Research (ENG.)/Recherches Theatrales. 1958. 2xyr. International Federation for Theatre Research, 14 Woronzow Rd., London, NW 8, England.

Theatre Research (Scotland)/Recherches Theatrales. 1955. 2xyr. 50s. Drama Dept., Glasgow Univ., Scotland.

Theatre Survey. 1960. 2xyr. $4. Univ. of Pittsburgh, 1117 CL., Pittsburgh, PA. 15213 and Univ. of Victoria, Victoria, BC, Canada.

Theatre Today. 1968. 4xyr. Advanced Institute for Development of American Repertory Theatre, 245 W. 52nd St., New York, NY. 10019.

Theatre Vivant. 1966. 4xyr. Can.$7.($8.) Holt Reinhart et Winston Ltee, 9400 Parkway Anjou, Montreal 437, Canada.

Theatrical Variety Guide. 1966. $5. Ed. Edward H. Hilton. Theatrical Variety Publications, Inc. 7046 Hollywood Blvd., Suite 617, Hollywood, CA. 90028.

Theatron. 1961. 2xmo. L.5000($7). Elda A. Vernara, Via Fabiola 1, 00152 Rome, Italy.

Thespis. (Athens) ceased.

Toneel/Teatraal. 4xyr. f.20. Nieuwe Uitleg 15, The Hague, Netherlands.

Unterhaltungkunst. 1969. mo. M.12. Henschelverlag Kunst und Gesellschaft, Oranienburger Str. 67/68, 104 Berlin, E. Germany.

Variety. 1905. 4xmo. $20. Variety, Inc., 154 W. 46th St., New York, NY. 10036.

Vlaanderen; 1951. 6xyr. 250fr($5.) Christelijk Vlaams Kunstenaarsverbond, Pontonstraat 12, Oestende, Belgium.

Wat Kan Ons Opvoer?/What Can We Stage? 1967. 2xyr. Free. Dramatic Artistic & Literary Rights Organisation Pty. Ltd., 1201 Cavendish Chambers, Jeppe St., Johannesburg, South Africa.

Western Speech. 1968. 4xyr. $5. Western Speech Association, Calif. State at Los Angeles, CA. 00000.

World Theatre. 1950 4xyr. $7.50. Editions Michel Brient, 64 rue de Saintonge, Paris (3e), France.

Yale/Theatre. 1968. 3xyr. $4.50. Box 2046, Yale Sta., New Haven, CT. 06520.

Zpravy Divadelniho Ustavu. 10xyr. Theatre Institute, Valdstejnske Nam. 3, Prague 1, Czechoslovakia.

PLAYWRIGHTS

Aeschylus

Ahrens, Robert H., Jr. Monarch Literature Notes on the Plays of Aeschylus. $1.00 pa. Monarch Pr., NY.

Campbell, Lewis. Tragic Drama in Aeschylus, Sophocles & Shakespeare. 1965. (1904). $8.50 Hdbd. Russell & Russell, NY.

Dawe, R. D. Collation & Investigation of Manuscripts of Aeschylus. 1964. $16.50 Hdbd. Cambridge Univ. Pr., NY.

Dawe, Roger D. Repertory of Conjectures on Aeschylus. 1965. $13.00 Hdbd. Humanities Pr., NY.

Earp, Frank R. Style of Aeschylus. 1970. (1948). $9.00 Hdbd. Russell & Russell, NY.

Finley, John H., Jr. Pindar & Aeschylus. (Martin Classical Lecture Ser. No. 14). 1955. $8.00 Hdbd. (ISBN 0-674-66800-6). Harvard Univ. Pr., MA.

Garvie, A. F. Aeschylus' Supplices: Play & Trilogy. 1969. $12.50 Hdbd. (ISBN 0-521-07182-8). Cambridge Univ. Pr., NY.

Golden, Leon. In Praise of Prometheus: Humanism & Rationalism in Aeschylean Thought. 1966. $6.00 Hdbd. (ISBN 0-8078-0996-9). Univ. of North Carolina Pr., NC.

Greifenhagen, Adolf. Ein Satyrspiel Des Aischylos. (Winckelmannsprogramm der Archaeologischen Gesellschaft Zu Berlin, No. 118). (Ger). 1963. $7.65 pa. (ISBN 3-11-001223-5). De Gruyter, Germany.

Herington, C. J. Author of the Prometheus Bound. (New Delphin Ser. Vol. 1). 1970. $4.75 Hdbd. (ISBN 0-292-70044-X). Univ. of Texas Pr., TX.

Italie, Gabriel. Index Aeschyleus. (Lat). 1964. $19.00 Hdbd. Humanities Pr., NY.

Kuhns, Richard. House, the City & the Judge: The Growth of Moral Awareness in the Oresteia. 1962. $5.00 Hdbd. Bobbs-Merrill, IN.

Mette, Hans J., ed. Supplementum Aeschyleum. (Kleine Texte, No. 1969). (Lat). 1939. $1.65 pa. De Gruyter, Germany.

Milch, Robert. Aeschylus' Oresteia Notes. $1.00 pa. (ISBN 0-8220-0128-4). Cliff's Notes, NB.

Murray, Gilbert. Aeschylus: The Creator of Tragedy. 1940. $8.00 Hdbd. (ISBN 0-19-814319-2). Oxford Univ. Pr., NY.

Murray, R. D. Motif of Io in Aeschylus' Suppliants. 1958. $2.00 Hdbd. Princeton Univ. Pr., NJ.

Podelicki, Anthony J. Political Background of Aeschylean Tragedy. 1966. $7.50 Hdbd. (ISBN 0-472-04732-9). Univ. of Mich. Pr., MI.

Sheppard, J. T. Aeschylus & Sophocles (Their Work & Influence). (Our Debt to Greece & Rome Ser). 1930. $3.50 Hdbd. (ISBN 0-8154-0205-8). Cooper Square Pr., NY.

Smyth, Herbert W. Aeschylean Tragedy. 1969. (1924). $6.50 Hdbd. (ISBN 0-8196-0235-3). Biblo & Tannen, NY.

Smyth, Herbert W. Aeschylean Tragedy. 1924. $7.50 Hdbd. (ISBN 0-404-06137-0). AMS Pr., NY.

Solmsen, Friedrich. Hesiod & Aeschylus. 1949. $15.00 Hdbd. Johnson Reprint, NY.

Thomson, George. Aeschylus & Athens. (Drama Ser., No. 39). 1969. (1940). $15.95 Hdbd. (ISBN 0-8383-0723-X). Haskell House, NY.

Thomson, George. Aeschylus & Athens. 3rd ed. 1969. $3.45 pa. (ISBN 0-448-01103-4). Grosset & Dunlap, NY.

Trevelyan, R. C., tr. Aeschylus. 1922. $5.00 Hdbd. (SBN 0-87556-003-2). Albert Saifer, PA.

Walter, William. Monarch Literature Notes on the Plays of Euripides, Aeschylus & Aristophanes. $1.00 pa. Monarch Pr., NY.

Albee, Edward

Albee, Edward. Edward Albee at Home & Abroad. a Bibliography 1958-June, 1968. Amacher, Richart E. & Rule, Margaret, eds. 1970. $12.50 Hdbd. (ISBN 0-404-07945-8). AMS Pr., NY.

Amacher, Richard E. Edward Albee. (U. S. Authors Ser., No. 141). 1968. $4.95 Hdbd. Twayne Publ., NY.

Cohn, Ruby. Edward Albee. (Pamphlets on American Writers Ser. No. 77). 1969. $0.95 pa. (ISBN 0-8166-0527-0). Univ. of Minn. Pr., MN.

Debusscher, G. Edward Albee: Tradition & Renewal. 1970. $2.95 pa. (Pub. by Center Am Studies). Intl. Schol. Book Serv., OR.

Rutenberg, Michael. Edward Albee: Playwright in Protest. 1969. $6.95 Hdbd. DBS Publ., NY.

Rutenberg, Michael. Edward Albee: Playwright in Protest. 1970. (1969). $1.65 pa. Avon Books, NY.

Anouilh, Jean

Archer, Marguerite. Jean Anouilh. (Essays on Modern Writers Ser. No. 55). 1971. $1.00 Hdbd. (ISBN 0-231-03346-X). Columbia Univ. Pr., NY.

Fazia, Alba Della. Jean Anouilh. (World Authors Series No. 76). $5.50 Hdbd. Twayne Publ., NY.

Harvey, John. Anouilh: A Study in Theatrics. 1964. $6.50 Hdbd. (ISBN 0-300-00540-7). Yale Univ. Pr., CT.

Marsh, Edward O. Jean Anouilh, Poet of Pierrot & Pantaloon. 1968. (1953). $9.50 Hdbd. Russell & Russell, NY.

Pronko, Leonard C. World of Jean

Anouilh. (New Cal Paperbacks No 157).
1968. $5.75 Hdbd. (ISBN 0-520-01035-
3); $2.25 pa. (ISBN 0-520-01036-1).
Univ. of Cal. Pr., CA.

Aristophanes

Aristophanes. Froesche Des Aristophanes. Suess, Wilhelm, ed. (Ger). 1960.
$1.60 pa. (ISBN 3-11-001332-0). De
Gruyter, Germany.

Dunbar, Henry. Complete Concordance
to the Comedies & Fragments of Aristophanes. 1968. (1883). $30.00 Hdbd.
Adler's Foreign Books, NY.

Ehrenberg, Victor. People of Aristophanes: A Sociology of Old Attic Comedy.
3rd ed. 1962. $2.95 pa. (ISBN 0-8052-
0027-4). Schocken Books, NY.

Gum, Coburn. Aristophanic Comedies
of Ben Jonson. 1970. $9.50 Hdbd.
Humanities Pr., NY.

Littlefield, D., ed. Twentieth Century
Interpretations of the Frogs. $4.95
Hdbd. (ISBN 0-13-331843-5). Prentice-
Hall, N.Y.

Littlefield, David J., ed. Twentieth Century Interpretations of the Frogs. 1968.
$1.25 pa. (ISBN 0-13-331835-4). Pren-
tice-Hall, NY.

Lord, Louis E. Aristophanes: His Plays
& His Influence. (Our Debt to Greece &
Rome Ser). 1930. $3.50 Hdbd. (ISBN
0-8154-0140-X). Cooper Sq. Pr., NY.

MacDowell, Douglas M., ed. Aristophanes: Wasps. 1971. $8.00 text ed. (ISBN
0-19-814182-3). Oxford Univ. Pr., NY.

Murray, Gilbert. Aristophanes. 1964.
(1933). $8.00 Hdbd. Russell & Russell,
NY.

Murray, Gilbert. Aristophanes: A Study.
1933. $8.00 Hdbd. (ISBN 0-19-814340-
0). Oxford Univ. Pr., NY.

Neuville, H. Richmond. Monarch Literature Notes on Aristophanes' Plays.
$1.00 pa. Monarch Pr., NY.

Strauss, Leo. Socrates & Aristophanes.
1966. $8.50 Hdbd. (ISBN 0-465-0874-
X). Basic Books, NY.

Todd, O. J. Index Aristophaneus. 1962.
(1932). $13.30 Hdbd. Adler's Foreign
Books, NY.

Walter, William. Monarch Literature
Notes on the Plays of Euripides, Aeschy-
lus & Aristophanes. $1.00 pa. Monarch
Pr., NY.

Whitman, Cedric H. Aristophanes & the
Comic Hero. (Martin Classical Lecture
Ser. No. 19). 1964. $9.00 Hdbd. (ISBN
0-674-04500-9). Harvard Univ. Pr., MA.

Barrie, Sir James Matthew, Bart

Asquith, Cynthia M. Portrait of Barrie.
(1954). $10.25 Hdbd. (ISBN 0-8371-
6115-0). Greenwood Pr., CT.

Block, Andrew. Sir J. M. Barrie: His
First Editions, Points & Values. 1933.
$10.00 Hdbd. Folcroft Pr., PA.

Braybrooke, Patrick. J. M. Barrie: 1924.
$12.50 Hdbd. Folcroft Pr., PA.

Cutler, Bradley D. Sir James M. Barrie:
A Bibliography with Full Collations of
the American Unauthorized Editions.

1967. (1931). $18.50 Hdbd. (ISBN 0-8337-0748-5). Burt Franklin, NY.

Darton, Frederick. J. M. Barrie. 1929. $6.00 Hdbd. Folcroft Pr., PA.

Darton, Frederick. J. J. M. Barrie. (1929). $8.00 Hdbd. (ISBN 0-8371-5369-7). Greenwood Pr., CT.

Darton, Frederick. J. M. Barrie. 1970. (1929). $7.50 Hdbd. (ISBN 0-403-00569-8). Scholarly Pr., MI

Dunbar, Janet. J. M. Barrie: The Man Behind the Image. 1970. $8.95 Hdbd. (ISBN 0-395-10939-6). Houghton-Mifflin, NY.

Elder, Michael. Young James Barrie. (Young Biographies Ser). (Jr Hi.). 1968. $3.50 Hdbd. Roy Publ., NY.

Geduld, Harry M. James Barrie. (Twayne's English Authors Series No. 105). $4.95 Hdbd. Twayne Publ., NY.

Green, Roger L. J. M. Barrie. (Hi-Sch.). 1961. $2.75 Hdbd. (ISBN 0-8098-3903-2). Henry Z. Walck, NY.

Walbrook, H. M. J. M. Barrie & the Theatre. 1969. (1922). $7.25 Hdbd. (ISBN 0-8046-0482-7). Kennikat Pr., NY.

Beckett, Samuel Barclay

Barnard, G. C. Samuel Beckett: A New Approach. 1971. $1.75 pa. Apollo Editions, NY.

Barnard, G. C. Samuel Beckett: A New Approach. 1970. $4.50 Hdbd. (ISBN 0-396-06182-6). Dodd, Mead, NY.

Beckett, Samuel. Samuel Beckett: A Collection of Critical Essays. Esslin, Martin, ed. $1.95 pa. (ISBN 0-13-072983-3). Prentice-Hall, NY.

Beckett, Samuel. Samuel Beckett: A Collection of Critical Essays. Esslin, Martin, ed. 1965. $5.95 Hdbd. (ISBN 0-13-072991-4). Prentice-Hall, NY.

Calder, John. Beckett at Sixty. 1967. $5.95 Hdbd. Dufour Editions, PA.

Chevigny, Bell G., ed. Twentieth Century Interpretations of Endgame. 1969. $1.25 pa. (ISBN 0-13-277285-X, Spec). Prentice-Hall, NY.

Coe, Richard N. Samuel Beckett. 1970. $1.50 pa. Grove Pr., NY.

Cohn, R. Casebook on Waiting for Godot. $4.00 Hdbd. Peter Smith Publ., MA.

Cohn, Ruby. Samuel Beckett: The Comic Gamut. 1962. $7.50 Hdbd. (ISBN 0-8135-0402-3). Rutgers Univ. Pr., NJ.

Cohn, Ruby, ed. Casebook on Waiting for Godot. YA. (Hi-Sch.). 1967. $1.95 text ed. Grove Pr., NY.

Federman, Raymond. Journey to Chaos: Samuel Beckett's Early Fiction. 1965. $7.50 Hdbd. (ISBN 0-520-00398-5). Univ. of Cal. Pr., CA.

Federman, Raymond & Fletcher, John. Samuel Beckett: His Works & His Critics: An Essay in Bibliography, 1929–1966. 1970. $15.00 text ed. (ISBN 0-520-01475-8). Univ. of Cal. Pr., CA.

Fletcher, John. Novels of Samuel Beckett. 2nd ed. 1970. $5.50 Hdbd. (ISBN 0-389-02154-7). Barnes & Noble, NY.

Fletcher, John. Samuel Beckett's Art. 1967. $4.00 Hdbd. Barnes & Noble, NY.

Friedman, Melvin J., ed. Samuel Beckett Now: Critical Approaches to His Novels, Poetry, & Plays. 1970. $7.95 Hdbd. (ISBN 0-226-26346-0). Univ. of Chicago Pr., IL.

Grossvogel, David I. Blasphemers: The Theatre of Brecht, Ionesco, Beckett, Genet. $1.95 pa. (ISBN 0-8014-9006-5). Cornell Univ. Pr., NY.

Grossvogel, David L. Four Playwrights & a Postscript: Brecht, Ionesco, Beckett, Genet. 1962. $6.00 Hdbd. (ISBN 0-8014-0161-5). Cornell Univ. Pr., NY.

Harrison, Robert. Samuel Beckett's Murphy: A Critical Excursion. (Monographs, No. 6). 1968. $4.00 pa. (ISBN 0-8203-0157-4). Univ. of Georgia Pr., GA.

Hart, Clive. Samuel Beckett. $4.50 Hdbd. (ISBN 0-8387-7885-2); $1.95 pa. (ISBN 0-8387-7987-5). Bucknell Univ. Pr., PA.

Harvey, Lawrence E. Samuel Beckett: Poet & Critic. 1970. $12.50 Hdbd. (ISBN 0-691-06176-9). Princeton Univ. Pr., NJ.

Hassan, Ihab. Literature of Silence: Henry Miller & Samuel Beckett. 1967. $4.50 text ed.; $2.25 pa. Random House, NY.

Hassan, Ihab. Literature of Silence: Henry Miller & Samuel Beckett. $4.95 Hdbd. Alfred A. Knopf, NY.

Hassan, Ihab. Literature of Silence: Henry Miller & Samuel Beckett. $4.25 Hdbd. Peter Smith Publ., MA.

Hesla, David H. Shape of Chaos: An Interpretation of the Art of Samuel Beckett. 1971. $9.75 Hdbd. (ISBN 0-8166-0625-0). Univ. of Minn. Pr., MN.

Hoffman, Frederick J. Samuel Beckett: The Language of Self. $1.65 pa. (ISBN 0-525-47143-X). E. P. Dutton, NY.

Hoffman, Frederick J. Samuel Beckett: The Language of Self. 1962. $4.50 Hdbd. (ISBN 0-8093-0056-7). Southern Ill. Univ. Pr., IL.

Kennedy, Sighle. Murphy's Bed: A Study of Real Sources & Sur-Real Associations in Samuel Beckett's First Novel. $12.00 Hdbd. (ISBN 0-8387-7739-2). Bucknell Univ. Pr., PA.

Kenner, Hugh. Samuel Beckett: A Critical Study (New Cal Paperbacks No. 159). 1968. $2.25 pa. (ISBN 0-520-00641-0). Univ. of Cal. Pr., CA.

Kern, Edith. Existential Thought & Fictional Technique: Kierkegaard, Sartre, Beckett. 1970. $6.75 Hdbd. (ISBN 0-300-01203-9). Yale Univ. Pr., CT.

Monarch Literature Notes on Beckett's Waiting for Godot & Other Works. $1.00 pa. Monarch Pr., NY.

O'Hara, J. D., ed. Twentieth Century Interpretations of Molloy, Malone Dies, the Unnamable. (Twentieth Century Interpretations Ser). 1970. $1.45 pa. Prentice-Hall, NY.

Reid, Alec. All I Can Manage, More Than I Could: An Approach to the Plays of Samuel Beckett. 1970. $1.95 Hdbd. Grove Pr., NY.

Reid, Alec. All I Can Manage, More Than I Could: An Approach to the Plays of Samuel Beckett. 1968. $4.50 Hdbd. (ISBN 0-8023-1169-5); $2.95 pa. Dufour Editions, PA.

Robinson, Michael. Long Sonata of the Dead: A Study of Samuel Beckett. 1970. $2.45 pa. Grove Pr., NY.

Scott, Nathan A. Samuel Beckett. 1965. (1963) $3.00 Hdbd. Hillary House, NY.

Tanner, J. F. & Vann, J. Don. Samuel Beckett: A Checklist. 1969. $4.50 Hdbd. (ISBN 0-87338-051-7). Kent State Univ. Pr., OH.

Tindall, William Y. Samuel Beckett. 1964. $1.00 pa. (ISBN 0-231-02659-5). Columbia Univ. Pr., NY.

Via, Dan O. Commentary on Samuel Beckett's Waiting for Godot. Belford, Lee, ed. (Religious Dimensions in Literature Ser). $0.85 pa.; $0.75 pa. 10 or more. Seabury Pr., NY.

Webb, Eugene. Samuel Beckett: A Study of His Novels. 1970. $6.95 Hdbd. (ISBN 0-295-95059-5). Univ. of Wash. Pr., WA.

Behan, Brendan

Behan, Dominic. My Brother Brendan. 1966. $4.50 Hdbd. Simon & Schuster, NY.

Boyle, Ted E. Brendan Behan. (English Authors Ser. No. 91). $4.95 Hdbd. Twayne Publ., NY.

Collis, John S. Brendan Behan. $4.50 Hdbd. (ISBN 0-8387-7868-2); $1.95 pa. (ISBN 0-8387-7971-9). Bucknell Univ. Pr., PA.

McCann, Sean, ed. World of Brendan Behan. 1966. $4.00 Hdbd. Twayne Publ., NY.

O'Connor, Ulick. Brendan. 1971. $6.95 Hdbd. (ISBN 0-13-081851-8). Prentice-Hall, NY.

Benavente Y Martinez Jacinto

Penuelas, Marcelino C. Jacinto Benavente. (World Authors Ser., No. 57). 1969. $5.50 Hdbd. Twayne Publ., NY.

Benet, Stephen Vincent

Fenton, Charles A. Stephen Vincent Benet. 1958. $10.00 Hdbd. (ISBN 0-300-00452-4). Yale Univ. Pr., CT.

Stroud, Parry E. Stephen Vincent Benet. (United States Authors Ser., No. 27). 1962. $4.95 Hdbd. Twayne Publ., NY.

Calderon de la Barca, Pedro

Bauer, Helga. Index Pictorius Calderons: Untersuchangen Zu Seiner Malermetaphorik. (Ger). 1969. $10.40 pa. (ISBN 3-11-002674-0). De Gruyter, Germany.

Engelbert, Manfred. Pedro Calderon De la Barca: El Pleito Matrimonial Del Cuerpo y el Alma (Kritische Ausgabe und Kommentar. (Hamburger Romanistische Studien B 31, Calderoniana 2). (Ger.). 1969. $14.20 pa. (ISBN 3-11-000063-6). De Gruyter, Germany.

Hesse, Everett W. Calderon De La Barca. (World Authors Ser., No. 30). 1968. $5.50 Hdbd. Twayne Publ., NY.

McGarry, Sr. M. Frances. Allegorical & Metaphorical Language in the Autos Sacramentales of Calderon. (Catholic University of America Studies in Romance Languages & Literatures Ser). 1969. (1937) $12.50 Hdbd. (ISBN 0-404-50316-0). AMS Pr., NY.

Paetz, Bernhard. Kirke und Odysseus: Ueberlieferung und Deutung Von Homer Bis Calderon. (Ger.). 1970. $8.75 pa. (ISBN 3-11-002806-9). De Gruyter, Germany.

Parker, Jack H. & Fox, Arthur M., eds. Calderon De la Barca Studies, 1951–69: A Critical Survey & Annotated Bibliography. $12.50 Hdbd. (ISBN 0-8020-1762-2). Univ. of Toronto Pr., Canada.

Schwarz, Egon. Hofmannsthal & Calderon. (German Studies Ser. No. 3). 1962. $4.25 Hdbd. (ISBN 0-674-40500-5). Harvard Univ. Pr., MA.

Trench, R. C. Calderon. (Spanish Literature Ser, No. 36). 1970. (1886) $9.95 Hdbd. (ISBN 0-8383-1151-2). Haskell House, NY.

Wardropper, Bruce W., ed. Critical Essays on the Theater of Calderon. (Gotham Library). 1965. $7.95 Hdbd. (ISBN 0-8147-0425-5); $2.25 pa. (ISBN 0-8147-0426-3). New York Univ. Pr., NY.

Carroll, Lewis   *(See Dodgson)*

Cervantes Saavedra, Miguel De

Allen, John J. Don Quixote: Hero or Fool. (University of Florida Monographs Ser., No. 29). 1969. $2.00 pa. (ISBN 0-8130-0268-0). Univ. of Fla. Pr., FL.

Arbo, Sebastian J. Cervantes: The Man & His Time. $4.00 Hdbd. (ISBN 0-8149-0454-8). Vanguard Pr., NY.

Azorin, pseud. Ruta De Don Quijote. $1.75 pa. French & European Publ., NY.

Barbera, Raymond E. Cervantes, a Critical Trajectory. 1971. $8.00 Hdbd. (ISBN 0-87821-150-0); $3.95 pa. Milford House, NY.

Bardon, Maurice. Don Quichotte En France Au Dix-Septieme & Au Dix-Huitieme Siecles, 1605–1815, Vol. 1 & 2. (Fr). 1931. $35.00 Hdbd. (ISBN 0-8337-3966-2). Burt Franklin, NY.

Bates, Margaret J. Discrecion in the Works of Cervantes. 1945. $5.00 Hdbd. (ISBN 0-404-50331-4). AMS Pr., NY.

Benardete, Mercedes J. & Flores, Angel, eds. Anatomy of Don Quixote: A Symposium. 1968. (1932) $6.50 Hdbd. (ISBN 0-8046-0025-2). Kennikat Pr., NY.

Bergin, T. C. Cervantes. 1970. $4.95 Hdbd. (ISBN 0-07-004854-1). McGraw-Hill, NY.

Busoni, Rafaello. Man Who Was Don Quixote: The Story of Miguel Cervantes. (Jr Hi.). 1958. $4.95 Hdbd. (ISBN 0-13-548362-X). Prentice Hall, NY.

Cherwinski, Joseph. Don Quixote with a Rake. $2.75 Hdbd. Bruce Humphries, MA.

Church, M. Don Quixote: Man of La Mancha. 1971. $7.95 text ed. (ISBN 0-8147-1352-1); $2.45 pa. (ISBN 0-8147-1354-8). New York Univ. Pr., NY.

Crabb, Daniel M. Critical Study Guide to Cervantes' Don Quixote. abr. ed. $1.00 pa. Littlefield, Adams & Co., NJ.

Croft-Cooke, Rupert. Through Spain with Don Quixote. 1960. $5.95 Hdbd. with Don Quixote. (Hi-Sch.). 1960. $5.95 Hdbd. Alfred A. Knopf, NY.

De Madariaga, Salvadore. Don Quixote: An Introductory Essay in Psychology. $1.50 pa. Oxford Univ. Pr., NY.

Diaz-Plaja. Fernando. Cervantes: The Life of a Genius. (Hi-Sch.). 1970. $3.95 Hdbd. (ISBN 0-684-20799-0). Charles Scribner's Sons, NY.

Entwistle, William J. Cervantes. 1940. $5.75 Hdbd. (ISBN 0-19-815367-8). Oxford Univ. Pr., NY.

Fitzmaurice-Kelly, James. Cervantes in England. (Studies in Comparative Literature, No. 35). 1970. (1905) $1.95 pa. (ISBN 0-8383-0029-4). Haskell House, NY.

Flores, Angel & Benardete, M. J. Cervantes Across the Centuries a Quadricentennial Volume. 1969. (1947) $9.00 text ed. (ISBN 0-87752-036-4). Gordian Pr., NY.

Forcione, Alban K. Cervantes, Aristotle, & the Persiles. 1970. $11.50 Hdbd. (ISBN 0-691-06175-0). Princeton Univ. Pr., NY.

Grierson, Herbert. Don Quixote. 1921. $2.50 Hdbd. Folcroft Pr., PA.

Hainsworth, George. Novelas Exemplares De Cervantes En France Au Dix-Septieme Siecle Contribution a L'etude De La Nouvelle En France. 1967. (1933) $15.00 Hdbd. (ISBN 0-8337-1530-5). Burt Franklin, NY.

Klibbe, Lawrence H. Barron's Simplified Approach to Cervantes' Don Quixote. 1970. $0.95 pa. Barron's Educational Series, NY.

Klibbe, Lawrence H. Don Quixote-Cervantes. 1969. $1.00 pa. (ISBN 0-389-00860-5). Barnes & Noble, NY.

Lewis, Dominic W. Shadow of Cervantes. 1962. $4.50 Hdbd. (ISBN 0-8362-0210-4). Sheed & Ward, NY.

Linsalata, Carmine R. Smollett's Hoax: Don Quixote in English. 1956. $9.00 Hdbd. (ISBN 0-404-51824-9). AMS Pr., NY.

Mann, Thomas. Cervantes, Goethe, Freud. $1.25 pa. French & European Publ., NY.

Nelson, Lowry, Jr., ed. Cervantes: A Collection of Critical Essays. (Twentieth Century Views Ser). 1969. $5.95 Hdbd. (ISBN 0-13-123299-1). Prentice-Hall, NY.

Nelson, Lowry, Jr., ed. Cervantes: A Collection of Critical Essays. 1969. $1.95 pa. (ISBN 0-13-123281-9). Prentice-Hall, NY.

Peers, Edgar A. Saint Teresa of Jesus & Other Essays & Addresses. 1953. $6.50 Hdbd. (ISBN 0-8401-1838-4). Alec R. Allenson, IL.

Predmore, R. I. Index to Don Quijote. 1938. $6.00 Hdbd. Kraus Reprint Co., NY.

Predmore, Richard L. World of Don Quixote. 1967. $4.95 Hdbd. (ISBN 0-674-96090-4). Harvard Univ. Pr., MA.

Riley, Edward C. Cervantes's Theory of the Novel. 1962. $8.00 Hdbd. (ISBN 0-19-815338-4). Oxford Univ. Pr., NY.

Rius, D. Leopoldo. Bibliografia Critica De las Obras De Miguel De Cervantes Saavedra, 3 Vols. (Bibliography & Reference Ser., No. 349). (Sp). 1970. (1895) $49.50 Hdbd. (ISBN 0-8337-3005-3). Burt Franklin, NY.

Roy, Gregor. Monarch Literature Notes on Cervantes' Don Quixote. $1.00 pa. Monarch Pr., NY.

Schevill, Rudllph. Cervantes. 1966. $6.50 Hdbd. (ISBN 0-8044-2779-8). Frederick Ungar, NY.

Serrano-Plaja, Arturo. Magic—Realism in Cervantes Don Quixote: As Seen Through Tom Sawyer and the Idiot. Rudder, Robert S., tr. 1970. $6.95 Hdbd. (ISBN 0-520-01591-6). Univ. of Cal. Pr., CA.

Sturman, Marianne. Don Quixote Notes. $1.00 pa. (ISBN 0-8220-0415-1). Cliff's Notes, NB.

Watts, Henry E. Life of Miguel De Cervantes. $11.00 Hdbd. Gale Research, MI.

Watts, Henry E. Life of Miguel De Cervanies. 1971. (1891) $11.00 Hdbd. Plutarch Books, MI.

Woodberry, George E. Great Writers. (Essay Index Reprint Ser). 1907. $8.00 Hdbd. (ISBN 0-8369-1008-7). Books for Libraries, NY.

Woodberry, George E. Literary Essays. 1920. $9.50 Hdbd. (ISBN 0-8046-0510-6). Kennikat Pr., NY.

Cervantes Saavedra, Miguel De—Bibliography

Grismer, R. L. Cervantes: A Bibliography. (1946) $12.00 Hdbd. Kraus Reprint Co., NY.

Rius, D. Leopoldo. Bibliografia Critica De las Obras De Miguel De Cervantes Saavedra, 3 Vols. (Bibliography & Reference Ser., No. 349). (Sp). 1970. (1895) $49.50 Hdbd. (ISBN 0-8337-3005-3). Burt Franklin, NY.

Chekhov, Anton Pavlovich

Avilova, Liddia A. Chekhov in My Life. Magarshack, David, tr. (1950) $8.50

Hdbd. (ISBN 0-8371-5551-7). Greenwood Pr., CT.

Bruford, Walter H. Anton Chekhov. 1957. $1.75 pa. Hillary House, NY.

Bruford, Walter H. Chekhov & His Russia: A Sociological Study. 1971. (1947). $7.25 Hdbd. (ISBN 0-208-01164-1). Shoe String Pr., CT.

Chekhov, Anton. Anton Tchekov: Literary & Theatrical Reminiscences. Koteliansky, S. S., ed. 1927. $12.75 Hdbd. Benjamin Blom, NY.

Gilles, Daniel. Chekhov: Observer Without Illusion. Markmann, Charles L., tr. 1968. $10.00 Hdbd. Funk & Wagnalls, NY.

Goldstone. Chekhov's the Cherry Orchard. $2.95 Hdbd. Allyn Inc., NJ.

Gorky, Maxim. Reminiscences of Tolstoy, Chekhov & Andreyev. $1.25 pa. (ISBN 0-670-00055-8). Viking Pr., NY.

Gorky, Maxim. Reminiscences of Tolstoy, Chekhov & Andreev. 1968. $3.00 Hdbd. Hillary House, NY.

Hingley, Ronald. Chekhov: A Biographical & Critical Study. rev. ed. 1966. $4.00 Hdbd. Barnes & Noble, NY.

Jackson, Robert L. Chekhov: A Collection of Critical Essays. 1967. $5.95 Hdbd. (ISBN 0-13-128249-2). Prentice-Hall, NY.

Jackson, Robert L., ed. Chekhov: A Collection of Critical Essays. 1967. $1.95 pa. (ISBN 0-13-128231-X, STC71). Prentice-Hall, NY.

Kramer, Karl D. Chameleon & the Dream: The Image of Reality in Cexov's Stories. (Slavistic Printings & Reprintings Ser., No. 78). 1971. $11.50 text ed. Humanities Pr., NY.

Magarshack. David. Chekhov, a Life. 1953. $10.50 Hdbd. Greenwood Pr., CT.

Magarshack. David. Chekhov: The Dramatist. 1960. $3.75 Hdbd. Peter Smith Publ., MA.

Melchinger, Siegfried. Anton Chekov. (World Dramatist Ser). $6.50 Hdbd. Frederick Ungar, NY.

Priestley, J. B. Anton Chekhov. (International Profiles Ser). 1970. $1.95 Hdbd. (ISBN 0-498-07407-2). A S Barnes, NJ.

Saunders, Beatrice. Chekhov the Man. 1961. $8.95 Hdbd. Dufour Editions, PA.

Saunders, Beatrice. Tchehov the Man. 1968. $5.00 Hdbd. (ISBN 0-8283-1136-6). Branden Pr., MA.

Saunders, Beatrice. Tchehov the Man. $5.00 Hdbd. (ISBN 0-87556-310-4). Albert Saifer, PA.

Shestov, Leon. Penultimate Words, & Other Essays. (Essay Index Reprint Ser). 1916. $7.25 Hdbd. (ISBN 0-8369-0876-7). Books for Libraries, NY.

Shestov, Leon Chekhov, & Other Essays. 1966. $4.40 Hdbd. (ISBN 0-472-09113-1). Univ. of Mich. Pr., MI.

Shestov, Leon. Chekhov & Other Essays. 1966. $1.95 pa. (ISBN 0-472-06113-5). Univ. of Mich. Pr., MI.

Simmons, Ernest J. Chekhov: A Biography. 1970. $3.95 pa. (ISBN 0-226-75805-2, 372). Univ. of Chicago Pr., IL.

Speirs, Logan. Tolstoy & Chekhov. 1971. $8.00 Hdbd. (ISBN 0-521-07950-0). Cambridge Univ. Pr., NY.

Styan, J. L. Chekhov in Performance: A Commentary of the Major Plays. 1971. $14.50 Hdbd. (ISBN 0-521-07975-6). Cambridge Univ. Pr., NY.

Talento, Louis V. Three Sisters, the Cherry Orchard: Chekhov. 1970. $1.00 pa. (ISBN 0-389-00876-1, 871). Barnes & Noble, NY.

Tansley, Katharine. Vision in Vertebrates. 1965. $3.50 Hdbd. Barnes & Noble, NY.

Toumanova, Nina A. Anton Chekhov. 1937. $6.00 Hdbd. (ISBN 0-231-00935-6); $1.50 pa. (ISBN 0-231-08504-4). Columbia Univ. Pr., NY.

Valency, Maurice. Breaking String: The Plays of Anton Chekhov. 1969. (1966) $1.95 pa. (ISBN 0-19-500792-1). Oxford Univ. Pr., NY.

Valency, Maurice J. Breaking String: The Plays of Anton Chekhov. 1966. $7.50 Hdbd. (ISBN 0-19-500637-2). Oxford Univ. Pr., NY.

Wexford, Jane. Monarch Literature Notes on Chekhov's Plays & Stories. $1.00 pa. Monarch Pr., NY.

Winner, Thomas G. Chekhov & His Prose. 1966. $5.00 Hdbd. (ISBN 0-03-053600-6). Holt, Rinehart & Winston, NY.

Coward, Noel Pierce

Gleacen, Robert. Art and Noel Coward. 1953. $12.50 Hdbd. Folcroft Pr., PA.

Levin, Milton. Noel Coward. (English Authors Series, No. 73). 1969. $4.95 Hdbd. Twayne Publ., NY.

Morley, Sheridan. Talent to Amuse. 1969. $8.95 Hdbd. Doubleday & Co., NY.

Snider, Rose. Satire in the Comedies of Congreve, Sheridan, Wilde & Coward. 1937. $7.50 Hdbd. Folcroft Pr., PA.

Dodgson, Charles Lutwidge (Lewis Carroll)

Collingwood, Stuart D. Life & Letters of Lewis Carroll. 1968. (1898) $7.80 Hdbd. Gale Research, NY.

De La Mare, Walter. Lewis Carroll. 1932. $8.50 Hdbd. Folcroft Pr., PA.

Gernsheim, Helmut. Lewis Carroll: Photographer. rev. ed. 1970. (1949) $2.50 pa. (ISBN 0-486-22327-2). Dover Publ., NY.

Gernsheim, Helmut. Lewis Carroll, Photographer. rev. ed. $5.00 Hdbd. Peter Smith Publ., MA.

Greenacre, Phyllis. Swift & Carroll: A Psychoanalytic Study of Two Lives. 1955. $7.50 Hdbd. (ISBN 0-8236-6280-2). International Universities Pr., NY.

Hudson, Derek. Lewis Carroll. (Writers & Their Work Ser. No. 96). $2.25

Hdbd.; $1.00 pa. British Book Center, NY.

Kirk, Daniel F. Charles Dodgson, Semeiotician. (Humanities Monographs Ser., No. 11). 1963. $2.00 pa. (ISBN 0-8130-0130-7). Univ. of Fla. Pr., FL.

Phillips, Robert, ed. Aspects of Alice: Critical Essays. 1865-1971, on Lewis Carroll's Masterwork. $10.00 Hdbd. (ISBN 0-8149-0700-8). Vanguard Pr., NY.

Rackin, Donald, ed. Alice's Adventures in Wonderland: A Critical Handbook. (Guides to Literary Study Ser). 1969. $3.95 pa. Wadsworth Publ., CA.

Richardson, Joanna. Young Lewis Carroll. (Young Biographies Ser). (Jr Hi). 1965. $3.25 Hdbd. Roy Publ., NY.

Sutherland, Robert D. Language & Lewis Carroll. (Juana Linguarum Ser). 1971. $16.00 Hdbd. Humanities Pr., NY.

Weaver, Warren. Alice in Many Tongues: The Translations of Alice in Wonderland. 1964. $4.74 Hdbd. (ISBN 0-299-03130-6). Univ. of Wisc. Pr., WI.

Wood, James P. Snark Was a Boojum: A Life of Lewis Carroll. (Pantheon Portrait Ser). (Jr. Hi-Hi-Sch.). 1966. $5.17 Hdbd. Pantheon Books, NY.

Dodgson, Charles Lutwidge (Lewis Carroll)—Bibliography

Williams, Sidney H. Bibliography of the Writings of Lewis Carroll 1924. $17.50 Hdbd. Folcroft Pr., PA

Williams, Sidney H. & Madan, Falconer. Lewis Carroll Handbook. rev. ed. Green, Roger L., ed. 1970. $17.50 Hdbd. (ISBN 0-389-01560-1). Barnes & Noble, NY.

Dostoevski, Fedor Mikhailovich

Arco Editorial Board. Arco Notes: Feodor Dostoyevsky's Crime & Punishment. (Jr. Hi.). 1969. $0.95 pa. (ISBN 0-668-01973-5). Arco Publ., NY.

Belknap, Robert L. Structure of the Brothers Karamazov. 1967. $7.00 Hdbd. Humanities Pr., NY.

Berdyaev, Nicholas. Dostoyevsky. Orig. Title: World Outlook of Dostoyevsky. $2.95 pa. World Publ., OH.

Bitsilli, P. M., et al. O Dostoevskom: Stat'i. (Rus). 1966. $4.00 pa. (ISBN 0-87057-098-6). Brown Univ. Pr., RI.

Blackmur, Richard P. Eleven Essays in the European Novel. 1964. $5.75 Hdbd. (ISBN 0-15-128206-4). Harcourt Brace Jovanovich, NY.

Blackmur, Richard P. Eleven Essays in the European Novel. $2.95 pa. (ISBN 0-15-628210-0, HO36). Harcourt Brace Jovanovich, NY.

Carey, Gary. Idiot Notes. 1968. $1.00 pa. (ISBN 0-8220-0627-8). Cliff's Notes, NB.

Cipolla, Thomas M. Brothers Karamazov—Dostoevsky. 1968. $1.00 pa. (ISBN 0-389-00865-6, 860, BN). Barnes & Noble, NY.

Cox, Roger L. Between Earth & Heaven: Shakespeare, Dostoevsky, & the Meaning of Christian Tragedy. 1969. $5.95 Hdbd. (ISBN 0-03-081842-7). Holt, Rinehart & Winston, NY.

Curle, Richard. Characters of Dostoevsky, Studies from Four Novels. 1966. (1950) $10.00 Hdbd. Russell & Russell, NY.

Dostoesky, Fyodor. Notebooks for the Brothers Karamazov. Wasiolek, Edward, tr. 1971. $9.50 Hdbd. Univ. of Chicago Pr., IL.

Dostoeuskaia, Liubov F. Fyodor Dostoyevsky, a Study. (1922) $12.50 Hdbd. Gale Research, NY.

Fanger, Donald. Dostoevsky & Romantic Realism: A Study of Dostoevsky in Relation to Balzac, Dickens, Gogol. 1965. $2.45 pa. (ISBN 0-226-23747-8). Univ. of Chicago Pr., IL.

Fanger, Donald L. Dostoevsky & Romantic Realism: A Study of Dostoevsky in Relation to Balzac, Dickens, & Gogol. (Studies in Comparative Literature Ser. No. 27). 1965. $8.50 Hdbd. (ISBN 0-674-21500-1). Harvard Univ. Pr., MA.

Friedman, Maurice. Problematic Rebel: Melville, Dostoyevsky, Kafka, Camus. 1970. $3.95 pa. (ISBN 0-226-26396-7). Univ. of Chicago Pr., IL.

Garey, Carey & Roberts, James L. Brothers Karamazov Notes. 1967. $1.00 pa. (ISBN 0-8220-0265-5). Cliff's Notes, NB.

Gide, Andre. Dostoevsky. 1961. $1.75 pa. New Directions, NY.

Gooding, David. Monarch Literature Notes on Dostoyevsky's The Idiot. $1.00 pa. Monarch Pr., NY.

Habel, Herbert P. Barron's Simplified Approach to Dostoyevsky's Crime & Punishment. 1968. $0.95 pa. Barron's Educational Series, NY.

Harper, Ralph. Seventh Solitude: Metaphysical Homelessness in Kierkegaard, Dostoevsky, & Nietzsche. $5.50 Hdbd. (ISBN 0-8018-0256-3); $1.95 pa. (ISBN 0-8018-0257-1). Johns Hopkins Univ. Pr., MD.

Hubben, William. Dostoevsky, Kierkegaard, Nietzsche & Kafka. Orig. Title: Four Prophets of Our Destiny. 1966. $0.95 pa. Macmillan Co., NY.

Ivanov, Vyacheslav. Study in Dostoevsky. 1963. $1.45 pa. Farrar, Straus & Giroux, NY.

Jackson, Robert L. Dostoevsky's Quest for Form: A Study of His Philosophy of Art. 1966. $6.00 Hdbd. (ISBN 0-300-00594-6). Yale Univ. Pr., CT.

Juhasz, Leslie. Monarch Literature Notes on Dostoyevsky's Notes from the Underground. $1.00 pa. Monarch Pr., NY.

Kent, Leonard J. Subconscious in Gogol & Dostoevskii & Its Antecedents. (Slavistic Printings & Reprintings, No. 75). 1970. $9.25 Hdbd. Humanities Pr., NY.

Lord, Robert. Dostoevsky: Essays & Perspectives. 1970. $5.95 Hdbd. (ISBN 0-520-01639-4). Univ. of Cal. Pr., CA.

Masaryk, Thomas G. The Spirit of Russia: Studies in History, Literature & Philosophy. rev. ed. Paul, Eden & Paul, Cedar, trs. Incl. Vol. 1. 1961; Vol. 2, 1961. Vols. 1 & 2. 2 vol. set—$16.50 Hdbd.; Vol. 3. Gibian, George, ed. Bass, Robert, tr. 1967. $8.00 Hdbd. Barnes & Noble, NY.

Merezhkovski, Dmitri. Tolstoi As Man & Artist with an Essay on Dostoievski. 1970. (1902) $13.00 Hdbd. (ISBN 0-403-00350-4). Scholarly Pr., MI.

Merezhkovski, Dmitri S. Tolstoi As Man & Artist. 1902. $11.00 Hdbd. (ISBN 0-8371-4098-6). Greenwood Pr., CT.

Miller, Harold A. Crime & Punishment —Dostoevsky. 1966. $1.00 pa. (ISBN 0-389-00800-1). Barnes & Noble, NY.

Mochulsky, Konstantin. Dostoevsky: His Life & Work. Minihan, Michael A., tr. 1971. $3.95 pa. (ISBN 0-691-01299-7). Princeton Univ. Pr., NJ.

Mochulsky, Konstantin. Dostoevsky: His Life & Work. Minihan, M., tr. 1967. $15.00 Hdbd. (ISBN 0-691-06027-4); $3.95 pa. Princeton Univ. Pr., NJ.

Muchnic, Helen. Dostoyevsky's English Reputation: Eighteen Eighty One to Nineteen Thirty-Six. 1969. (1939) $8.00 Hdbd. Octagon Books, NY.

Murry, John M. Fyodor Dostoevsky, a

Critical Study. 2nd ed. 1966. (1924) $8.50 Hdbd. Russell & Russell, NY.

Neuville, H. Richmond, Jr. Monarch Literature Notes on Dostoyevsky's The Brothers Karamazov. $1.00 pa. Monarch Pr., NY.

Passage, Charles E. Dostoevski the Adapter. (Comparative Literature Studies). 1954. $6.50 pa. (ISBN 0-8078-7010-2). Univ. of N.C. Pr., NC.

Payne, Robert. Dostoyevsky: A Human Portrait. (Hi-Sch.). 1961. $7.95 pa. Alfred A. Knopf, NY.

Peace, Richard A. Dostoyevsky. 1971. $11.50 Hdbd. (ISBN 0-521-07911-X); price "n.g." pa. Cambridge Univ. Pr., NY.

Proctor, Thelwall T. Dostoevsky & the Belinsky School of Literary Criticism. (Slavistic Printings: Reprintings Ser., No. 64). 1970. $10.00 Hdbd. Humanities Pr., NY.

Roberts, James L. Crime & Punishment Notes. $1.00 pa. (ISBN 0-8220-0328-7). Cliff's Notes, NB.

Roe, Ivan. Breath of Corruption. 1971. (1946) $7.00 Hdbd. (ISBN 0-8046-1646-9). Kennikat Pr., NY.

Sajkovic, Miriam. F. M. Dostoevsky: His Image of Man. 1962. $8.00 Hdbd. (ISBN 0-8122-7368-0). Univ. of Penna. Pr., PA.

Schutte, William. Six Novelists: Stendahl, Dostoyevsky, Tolstoy, Hardy, Dreiser, Proust. 1959. $12.50 Hdbd. Ridgeway Books, PA.

Seduro, Vladimir I. Dostoyevski in Russian Literary Criticism. 1846–1956. 1959. $12.00 Hdbd. Octagon Books, NY.

Serrano-Plaja, Arturo. Magic—Realism in Cervantes Don Quixote: As Seen Through Tom Sawyer and the Idiot. Rudder. Robert S., tr. 1970. $6.95 Hdbd. (ISBN 0-520-01591-6). Univ. of Cal. Pr., CA.

Shestov, Leo. Penultimate Words, & Other Essays. (Essay Index Reprint Ser). 1916. $7.25 Hdbd. (ISBN 0-8369-0876-7). Books for Libraries, NY.

Shestov, Leon. Chekhov & Other Essays. 1966. $1.95 pa. (ISBN 0-472-06113-5). Univ. of Mich. Pr., MI.

Shestov, Leon. Chekhov, & Other Essays. 1966. $4.40 Hdbd. (ISBN 0-472-09113-1). Univ. of Mich. Pr., MI.

Shestov, Lev. Dostoevsky, Tolstoy & Nietzsche. 1969. $10.00 Hdbd. (ISBN 0-8214-0053-3). Ohio Univ. Pr., OH.

Simmons, Ernest J. Dostoevsky: The Making of a Novelist. $4.00 Hdbd. Peter Smith Publ., MA.

Simmons, Ernest J. Feodor Dostoevsky. (Columbia Essays in Modern Writers No. 40). 1969. $1.00 pa. (ISBN 0-231-03205-6). Columbia Univ. Pr., NY.

Steinberg, A. Dostoievsky. 1966. $2.50 Hdbd. Hillary House, NY.

Steiner, George. Tolstoy or Dostoevsky. 1959. $7.95 pa. Alfred A. Knopf, NY.

Steiner, George. Tolstoy or Dosto-yevsky: An Essay in the Old Criticism. $1.45 pa. (ISBN 0-394-70186-0). Random House, NY.

Terras, Victor. Young Dostoevsky, 1846–1849: A Critical Study. (Slavistic Printings & Reprints, No. 69). 1970. $16.00 Hdbd. Humanities Pr., NY.

Thurneysen, Eduard. Dostoevsky. Crim, Keith R., tr. 1964. $0.50 pa. (ISBN 0-8042-1932-X). John Knox Pr., VA.

Tuten, Frederic. Monarch Literature Notes on Dostoyevsky's Crime & Punishment. $1.00 pa. Monarch Pr., NY.

Van Der Eng, J. Dostoevskij Romancier. (Fr). 1957. $4.00 Hdbd. Humanities Pr., NY.

Van Der Eng, Jan & Meijer, Jan M. Brothers Karamozov by Feodor Dostoevski: Essays. 1971. $9.00 Hdbd. Humanities Pr., NY.

Wasiolek, Edward. Brothers Karamazov & the Critics. (Guides to Literary Study Ser). 1967. $2.95 pa. Wadsworth Publ., CA.

Wasiolek, Edward. Crime & Punishment & the Critics. (Guides to Literary Study Ser). 1961. $2.95 pa. Wadsworth Publ., CA.

Wasiolek, Edward. Dostoevsky: The Major Fiction. $1.95 pa. (ISBN 0-262-73026-X). MIT Pr., MA.

Wasiolek, Edward. Dostoevsky: The Major Fiction. 1971. $1.95 pa. (ISBN 0-262-73026-X). MIT Pr., MA.

Wellek, Rene, ed. Dostoevsky: A Collection of Critical Essays. 1962. $5.95 Hdbd. (ISBN 0-13-218792-2). Prentice-Hall, NY.

Wellek, Rene, ed. Dostoevsky: A Collection of Critical Essays. 1962. $1.95 pa. (ISBN 0-413-218784-1). Prentice-Hall, NY.

Yarmolinsky, Avrahm. Dostoevsky: His Works & Days. 1971. $12.50 Hdbd. Funk & Wagnalls, NY.

Dryden, John

Aden, John M., ed. Critical Opinions of John Dryden: A Dictionary. 1967. $10.00 Hdbd. (ISBN 0-8265-1062-0). Vanderbilt Univ. Pr., TN.

Allen, Ned B. Sources of John Dryden's Comedies. 1967. (1935) $7.50 Hdbd. (ISBN 0-87752-002-X). Gordian Pr., NY.

Amarasinghe, Upali. Dryden & Pope in the Early 19th Century. 1962. $8.00 Hdbd. Cambridge Univ. Pr., NY.

Arundell, D. D. Dryden & Howard. 1929. $20.00 Hdbd. Ridgeway Books, PA.

Baumgartner, Milton D. On Dryden's Relation to Germany in the 18th Century. 1970. (1914) $4.95 pa. (ISBN 0-8383-0084-7). Haskell House, NY.

Bredvold, Louis I. Intellectual Milieu of John Dryden. 1956. $4.40 Hdbd. (ISBN 0-472-09003-1). Univ. of Mich. Pr., MI.

Bredvold, Louis I. Intellectual Milieu of John Dryden. 1956. $1.75 pa. (ISBN 0-472-06003-1). Univ. of Mich. Pr., MI.

Budick, Sanford. Dryden & the Abysse of Light: A Reading of Religio Laici & the Hind & the Panther. 1970. $8.75 Hdbd. (ISBN 0-300-01338-8). Yale Univ. Pr., CT.

Dobree, Bonamy. Dryden. (Writers & Their Work Ser No. 70). $2.25 Hdbd. $1.00 pa. British Book Center, NY.

Eliot, T. S. Homage to Dryden. $2.50 Hdbd. Gordon Publ., NY.

Eliot, T. S. John Dryden. $6.50 Hdbd. Gordon Publ., NY.

Eliot, T. S. John Dryden. (Studies in John Dryden Ser., No. 10). 1969. (1932) $6.95 Hdbd. (ISBN 0-8383-0692-6). Haskell House, NY.

Eliot, T. S. John Dryden. 1971. $7.50 Hdbd. Porter Bern, ME.

Elliot, T. S. Homage to John Dryden. 1971. $4.00 Hdbd. Lansdowne Pr., PA.

Emerson, Oliver F. John Dryden & a British Academy. 1921. $3.00 Hdbd. Folcroft Pr., PA.

Ferry, Anne D. Milton & the Miltonic Dryden. 1968. $7.00 Hdbd. (ISBN 0-674-57576-8). Harvard Univ. Pr., MA.

Frost, William. Dryden & the Art of Translation. (Yale Studies in English No. 128). 1969. (1955) $4.00 Hdbd. (ISBN 0-208-00778-4). Shoe String Pr., CT.

Hamilton, K. G. John Dryden & the Poetry of Statement. $6.20 Hdbd. International Scholarly Book Service, OR.

Hamilton, K. G. John Dryden & the

Poetry of Statement. 1969. $7.50 Hdbd. (ISBN 0-87013-130-3). Mich. State Univ. Pr., MI.

Harth, Phillip. Contexts of Dryden's Thought. 1968. $8.50 Hdbd. (ISBN 0-226-31831-1). Univ. of Chicago Pr., IL.

Hoffman, Arthur W. John Dryden's Imagery. 1962. $6.00 Hdbd. (ISBN 0-8130-0112-9). Univ. of Fla. Pr., FL.

Hollis, Christopher. Dryden. 1933. $15.00 Hdbd. Folcroft Pr., PA.

Hume, Robert D. Dryden's Criticism. 1970. $8.00 Hdbd. (ISBN 0-8014-0585-8). Cornell Univ. Pr., NY.

Huntley, Frank L. On Dryden's Essay of Dramatic Poesy. 1968. (1951) $4.00 Hdbd. Shoe String Pr., CT.

Jensen, H. James. Glossary of John Dryden's Critical Terms. 1969. $5.00 Hdbd. (ISBN 0-8166-0504-1). Univ. of Minn. Pr., MN.

Johnson, Samuel. Six Chief Lives, from Johnson's Lives of the Poets, with Macaulay's Life of Johnson. Arnold, Matthew, ed. 1968. (1881) $10.50 Hdbd. Russell & Russell, NY.

King, Bruce. Dryden's Major Plays. 1966. $6.75 Hdbd. Barnes & Noble, NY.

King, Bruce, ed. Dryden's Mind & Art. (Essays Old & New Ser., Vol. 5). 1971. $7.50 Hdbd. (ISBN 0-389-03985-3). Barnes & Noble, NY.

King, Bruce, ed. Twentieth Century Interpretations of All for Love. 1968. $4.95 Hdbd. (ISBN 0-13-022350-6). Prentice-Hall, NY.

King, Bruce, ed. Twentieth Century Interpretations of All for Love. 1968. $1.25 pa. (ISBN 0-13-022343-3). Prentice-Hall, NY.

Kinsley, James & Kinsley, Helen, eds. Dryden: The Critical Heritage. (Critical Heritage Ser). 1971. $15.00 Hdbd. (ISBN 0-389-04126-2). Barnes & Noble, NY.

Lowell, James R. Among My Books. 1970. (1870) $11.50 Hdbd. (ISBN 0-404-04039-X). AMS Pr., NY.

Lubbock, Allan. Character of John Dryden. 1925. $3.00 Hdbd. Folcroft Pr., PA.

McHenry, Robert & Louges, David, eds. Critics on Dryden. $3.95 Hdbd. (ISBN 0-87024-208-3). Univ. of Miami Pr., FL.

Masson, David. Three Devils: Luther's, Milton's & Goethe's. 1970. (1874) $13.00 Hdbd. (ISBN 0-404-04247-3). AMS Pr., NY.

Masson, David. Three Devils: Luther's, Milton's & Goethe's. 1874. $12.50 Hdbd. Folcroft Pr., PA.

Miner, Earl. Dryden's Poetry. 1967. $12.50 Hdbd. (ISBN 0-253-31835-1). Ind. Univ. Pr., IN.

Monk, Samuel H. John Dryden: A List of Critical Studies Published from 1895–1948. 1950. $6.50 Hdbd. Folcroft Pr., PA.

Montgomery, Guy, et al, eds. Concordance to the Poetical Works of John Dryden. 1967. (1957) $30.00 Hdbd. Russell & Russell, NY.

Moore, Frank H. Nobler Pleasure: Dryden's Comedy in Theory & Practice. 1963. $7.50 Hdbd. (ISBN 0-8078-0868-7). Univ. of N.C. Pr., NC.

Nicoll, Allardyce. Dryden & His Poetry. 1967. (1923) $6.50 Hdbd. Russell & Russell, NY.

Nicoll, Allardyce. Dryden & His Poetry. 1923. $5.50 Hdbd. Folcroft Pr., PA.

Nicoll, Allardyce. Dryden As an Adaptor of Shakespeare. 1922. $5.00 Hdbd. (ISBN 0-404-07848-6). AMS Pr., NY.

Osborn, James M. John Dryden: Some Biographical Facts & Problems. 1965. $8.50 Hdbd. (ISBN 0-8130-0171-4). Univ. of Fla. Pr., FL.

Parkin, Francis. Augustans: Dryden, Pope, Swift. (Hi-Sch.). 1970. $1.52 pa. (ISBN 0-03-080760-3). Holt, Rinehart & Winston, NY.

Pendlebury, Bevis J. Dryden's Heroic Plays, a Study of the Origins. 1967. (1923) $6.50 Hdbd. Russell & Russell, NY.

Proudfoot, L. Dryden's Aeneid & Its Seventeenth Century Predecessors. 1960. $20.00 Hdbd. Ridgeway Books, PA.

Ramsey, Paul. Art of John Dryden. 1969. $6.50 Hdbd. (ISBN 0-8131-1184-6). Univ. Pr. of Ken., KY.

Reaske, Christopher. Monarch Literature Notes on the Poetry of Dryden. $1.00 pa. Monarch Pr., NY.

Roper, Alan. Dryden's Poetric Kingdoms. 1965. $4.50 Hdbd. Barnes & Noble, NY.

Russell, Trusten W. Voltaire, Dryden & Heroic Tragedy. 1946. $9.50 Hdbd. (ISBN 0-404-05467-6). AMS Pr., NY.

Saintsbury, George. Dryden. Morley, John, ed. 1888. $7.80 Hdbd. (ISBN 0-404-51726-9). AMS Pr., NY.

Saintsbury, George E. Dryden. 1968. (1902) $7.80 Hdbd. Gale Research, MI.

Schilling, Bernard N., ed. Dryden: A Collection of Critical Essays. 1963. $1.95 pa. (ISBN 0-13-220863-6). Prentice-Hall, NY.

Schilling, Bernard N., ed. Dryden: A Collection of Critical Essays, 1963. $5.95 Hdbd. (ISBN 0-13-220871-7). Prentice-Hall, NY.

Scott, Walter. Life of Dryden. Kreissman, Bernard, ed. 1963. $5.00 Hdbd. (ISBN 0-8032-0170-2). Univ of Neb. Pr., NB.

Scott, Walter. Life of Dryden. Kreissman, Bernard, ed. 1963. $1.70 pa. (ISBN 0-8032-5177-7). Univ. of Neb. Pr., NB.

Sherwood, Margaret. Dryden's Dramatic Theory & Practice. (Studies in John Dryden, No. 10). 1970. (1898) $5.95 pa. (ISBN 0-8383-0069-3). Haskell House, NY.

Sherwood, Margaret P. Dryden's Dramatic Theory & Practice. 1966. (1898) $7.00 Hdbd. Russell & Russell, NY.

Smith, David N. John Dryden. 1966.

(1950) $4.00 Hdbd. (ISBN 0-208-00118-2). Shoe String Pr., CT.

Swedenberg, H. T., Jr., ed. Essential Articles for the Study of John Dryden. (Essential Articles Ser). 1966. $8.50 Hdbd. (ISBN 0-208-00204-9). Shoe String Pr., CT.

Van Der Welle, Jojakim A. Dryden & Holland. 1962. $17.50 Hdbd. Folcroft Pr., PA.

Van Doren, M. Poetry of John Dryden. (Studies in John Dryden Ser., No. 10). 1969. (1920) $12.95 Hdbd. (ISBN 0-8383-1207-1). Haskell House, NY.

Van Doren, Mark. John Dryden: A Study of His Poetry. 1960. $4.25 Hdbd. Peter Smith Publ., MA.

Van Doren, Mark. John Dryden: A Study of His Poetry. 1960. $1.95 pa. (ISBN 0-253-20022-9). Ind. Univ. Pr., IN.

Waith, Eugene M. Herculean Hero in Marlowe, Chapman. Shakespeare & Dryden. 1962. $7.00 Hdbd. (ISBN 0-231-02506-8). Columbia Univ. Pr., NY.

Ward, Charles E. Life of John Dryden. 1961. $8.50 Hdbd. (ISBN 0-8078-0835-0). Univ. of N.C. Pr., NC.

Wasserman, George. John Dryden. (Eng. Authors Ser., No. 14). 1964. $4.95 Hdbd. Twayne Publ., NY.

Young, Kenneth. John Dryden, a Critical Biography. 1969. (1954) $8.00 Hdbd. Russell & Russell, NY.

Zebouni, Selma A. Dryden: A Study in Heroic Characterization. 1965. $3.00

Hdbd. (ISBN 0-8071-0843-X). La. St. Univ. Pr., LA.

Eliot, Thomas Stearns

Aldington, Richard. Ezra Pound & T. S. Eliot, a Lecture 1970. $0.75 pa. Oriole Editions, NY.

Austin, Allen. T. S. Eliot: The Literary & Social Criticism. 1971. $5.00 pa. (ISBN 0-253-38668-3). Ind. Univ. Pr., IN.

Bantock, G. H. T. S. Eliot & Education. 1969. $1.95 pa. Random House, NY.

Barry, M. Martin. Analysis of the Prosodic Structure of Selected Poems of T. S. Eliot. $9.00 pa. McGrath Publ., MD.

Bergonzi, B. T. S. Eliot. 1971. $5.95 Hdbd. Macmillan Co., NY.

Bergsten, Staffan. Time & Eternity: A Study in Structure & Symbolism of T. S. Eliot's Four Quartets. 1960. $10.00 Hdbd. Hillary House, NY.

Blamires, Harry. Word Unheard: A Guide Through Eliot's Four Quartets. 1969. $5.00 Hdbd. (ISBN 0-389-01307-2). $2.50 pa. (ISBN 0-416-29910-5). Barnes & Noble, NY.

Bodelsen, Carl A. T. S. Eliot's Four Quartets, a Commentary. 1958. $4.50 pa. Hillary House, NY.

Bradbrook, Muriel C. T. S. Eliot. Writers & Their Works Ser No. 8). $2.25 Hdbd.; $1.00 pa. British Book Ctr., NY.

Braybrooke, Neville. T. S. Eliot. Jellema, Roderick, ed. (Contemporary

Writers in Christian Perspective Set) 1967. $0.85 pa. Wm. B. Eerdmans, MI.

Braybrooke, Neville, ed. T. S. Eliot: A Symposium for His Seventieth Birthday. facsimile ed. (Essay Index Reprint Ser). $9.00 Hdbd. (ISBN 0-8369-0100-2). Books for Libraries, NY.

Browne, E. Martin. Making of T. S. Eliot's Plays. 1969. $9.50 Hdbd. Cambridge Univ. Pr., NY.

Buckley, Vincent. Poetry & Morality. 1959. $5.00 Hdbd. Humanities Pr., NY.

Cahill, Audrey F. T. S. Eliot & the Human Predicament. 1967. $6.50 Hdbd. Lawrence Verry, Inc., CT.

Cattaui, Georges. T. S. Eliot. 1969. (1968) $1.95 pa. Funk & Wagnalls, NY.

Cattaui, Georges. T. S. Eliot. $3.95 Hdbd. Funk & Wagnalls, NY.

Clark, D., ed. Twentieth Century Interpretations of Murder in the Cathedral. 1971. $4.95 Hdbd. (ISBN 0-13-60400-0). Prentice-Hall, NY.

Clark, D., ed. Twentieth Century Interpretations of Murder in the Cathedral. 1971. $1.45 pa. (ISBN 0-13-606392-6). Prentice-Hall, NY.

Clark, David R., ed. Twentieth Century Interpretations of Murder in the Cathdral. (Twentieth Century Interpretations Ser). 1971. $4.95 Hdbd. (ISBN 0-13-606400-0); $1.45 pa. (ISBN 0-13-606392-6). Prentice-Hall, NY.

Cornwell, Ethel F. Still Point: Theme & Variations in the Writings of T. S.

Eliot, Coleridge, Yeats, Henry James, Virginia Woolf, & D. H. Lawrence. 1962. $7.50 Hdbd. (ISBN 0-8135-0413-9). Rutgers Univ. Pr., NJ.

Costello, Mary C. Between Fixity & Flux, a Study of the Concept of Poetry in the Criticism of T. S. Eliot. $7.95 pa. McGrath Publ., MD.

Davidson, Arthur. Eliot Enigma. 1959. $6.50 Hdbd. Folcroft Pr., PA.

De Masirevich, Constance. On the Four Quartets of T. S. Eliot. 1965. $3.00 Hdbd. Barnes & Noble, NY.

Drew, Elizabeth. T. S. Eliot: The Design of His Poetry. $3.50 Hdbd. (ISBN 0-684-10131-9). Charles Scribner's Sons, NY.

Drew, Elizabeth. T. S. Eliot: The Design of His Poetry. 1949. $2.45 pa. (ISBN 0-684-71752-2). Charles Scribner's Sons, NY.

Eliot, T. S. Four Quarters. Bergonzi, Bernard, ed. (Casebook Ser). 1970. (1968) $2.50 text ed. (ISBN 0-87695-039-X). Aurora Publ., TN.

Eliot, T. S. Wasteland. Cox, C. B. & Hincheiffe, A. P., eds. (Casebook Ser). 1970. (1968) $2.50 text ed. (ISBN 0-87695-040-3). Aurora Publ., TN.

Freed, Lewis. T. S. Eliot: Aesthetics & History. $5.95 Hdbd.; $2.45 pa. Open Court, IL.

Gallup, Donald. T. S. Eliot: A Bibliography. rev. ed. 1969. $18.50 Hdbd.

(ISBN 0-15-191370-6). Harcourt Brace Jovanovich, NY.

Gannon, Paul & Levensohn, Stephen. Monarch Literature Notes on T. S. Eliot's Murder in the Cathedral & Selected Poems. $1.00 pa. Monarch Pr., NY.

Gardner, Helen. Art of T. S. Eliot. 1959. $1.25 pa. (ISBN 0-525-47043-3). E. P. Dutton, NY.

George, A. G. T. S. Eliot: His Mind & His Art. 1962. $9.00 Hdbd. (ISBN 0-210-33849-0). Asia Soc., NY.

Grudin, Louis. Mr. Eliot Among the Nightingales. 1932. $10.00 Hdbd. Folcroft Pr., PA.

Hamilton, G. Rostrevor. Tell-Tale Article: A Critical Approach to Modern Poetry. 1950. $12.50 Hdbd. Folcroft Pr., PA.

Headings, Philip. T. S. Eliot. (Twayne's United States Authors Ser). 1964. $2.45 pa. Coll. & Univ. Pr., CT.

Headings, Philip R. T. S. Eliot. (U.S. Authors Ser., No. 57). 1964. $4.95 Hdbd. Twayne Publ., NY.

Holder, Alan. Three Voyagers in Search of Europe. 1966. $9.75 Hdbd. (ISBN 0-8122-7486-5). Univ. of Penna. Pr., PA.

Ishak, F. M. Mystical Philosophy of T. S. Eliot. 1970. $6.50 Hdbd.; $2.95 pa. Coll. & Univ. Pr., CT.

Jameson, R. D. Poetry & Plain Sense: Note on the Poetic Method of T. S.

Eliot. 1932. $5.00 Hdbk. Folcroft Pr., PA.

Jones, Genesius. Approach to the Purpose: A Study of the Poetry of T. S. Eliot. 1965. $9.00 Hdbd. Barnes & Noble, NY.

Kaplan, Robert B. T. S. Eliot's Major Poems & Plays Notes. $1.00 pa. (ISBN 0-8220-1246-4). Cliff's Notes, NB.

Kenner, H., ed. T. S. Eliot: A Collection of Critical Essays. 1962. $1.95 pa. (ISBN 0-13-274324-8). Prentice-Hall, NY.

Kenner, H., ed. T. S. Eliot: A Collection of Critical Essays. 1962. $5.95 Hdbd. (ISBN 0-13-274332-9). Prentice-Hall, NY.

Kenner, Hugh. Invisible Poet. 1959. $6.95 Hdbd. (ISBN 0-8392-1053-1). Astor-Honor, NY.

Lane, Robert L. Barron's Simplified Approach to T. S. Eliot. 1968. $0.95 pa. Barron's Educ. Series, NY.

Leavis, Frank R. New Bearings in English Poetry. 1960. $4.40 Hdbd. (ISBN 0-472-09036-4). Univ. of Mich. Pr., MI.

Leavis, Frank R. New Bearings in English Poetry. 1960. $1.85 pa. (ISBN 0-472-06036-8). Univ. of Mich. Pr., MI.

Levy, William T. & Scherle, Victor. Affectionately, T. S. Eliot. 1968. $4.95 Hdbd. J. B. Lippincott, PA.

Lu Fei-Pai. T. S. Eliot: The Dialectical Structure of His Theory of Poetry. 1966.

$5.75. Hdbd. (ISBN 0-226-49628-7). Univ. of Chicago Pr., IL.

Lucy, Sean. T. S. Eliot & the Idea of Tradition. 1960. $6.50 Hdbd. Barnes & Noble, NY.

McGreevey, Thos. T. S. Eliot: A Study. (Studies in T. S. Eliot, No. 11). 1971. $9.95 Hdbd. (ISBN 0-8383-1327-2). Haskell House, NY.

McGeevy, Thomas. Thomas Stearns Eliot. 1931. $5.50 Hdbd. Folcroft Pr., PA.

March, Richard & Tambimuttu, M. J., eds. T. S. Eliot. 1949. $11.50 Hdbd. (ISBN 0-8369-0676-4). Books for Libraries, NY.

Martin, Graham, ed. Eliot in Perspective. 1970. $10.00 Hdbd. (ISBN 0-391-00002-0). Humanities Pr., NY.

Martin, J., ed. Collection of Critical Essays on the Waste Land. 1967. $4.95 Hdbd. (ISBN 0-13-139584-X). Prentice-Hall, NY.

Martin, Jay, ed. Collection of Critical Essays on the Waste Land. (Twentieth-Century Interpretations). 1967. $1.25 pa. (ISBN 0-13-139576-9). Prentice-Hall, NY.

Martin, Mildred. Half a Century of Eliot Criticism. $5.00 Hdbd. (ISBN 0-8387-8808-9). Bucknell Univ. Pr., PA.

Martin, P. W. Experiment in Depth: A Study of Jung, Eliot & Toynbee. 1955. $6.75 Hdbd. Humanities Pr., NY.

Matthiessen, F. O. Achievement of T. S.

Eliot: An Essay on the Nature of Poetry. 3rd ed. 1959. $2.25 pa. (ISBN 0-19-500681-X). Oxford Univ. Pr., NY.

Matthiessen, F. O. Achievement of T. S. Eliot: An Essay on the Nature of Poetry. 3rd ed. 1958. $6.50 Hdbd. (ISBN 0-19-500005-6). Oxford Univ. Pr., NY.

Maxwell, Desmond E. Poetry of T. S. Eliot. 1961. (1952) $6.00 Hdbd.; $6.00 pa. Humanities Pr., NY.

Montgomery, Marion. T. S. Eliot: The American Magus. 1970. $4.50 Hdbd. (ISBN 0-8203-0232-5). Univ. of Ga. Pr., GA.

Mordell, Albert. T. S. Eliot's Deficiencies As a Social Critic. 1951. $8.50 Hdbd. Ridgeway Books, PA.

Morris, David. Poetry of Gerard Manley Hopkins & T. S. Eliot in the Light of the Donne Tradition. 1953. $15.00 Hdbd. Folcroft Pr., PA.

Musgrove, S. T. S. Eliot & Walt Whitman. $6.75 Hdbd. Gordon Publ., NY.

Musgrove, Sydney. T. S. Eliot & Walt Whitman. (English, American & Comparative Literature Ser., No. 150). 1970. Repr. of 1952 ed. $6.95 Hdbd.; $4.95 pa. (ISBN 0-8383-0056-1). Haskell House, NY.

O'Connor, Daniel. T. S. Eliot: Four Quartets, a Commentary. 1969. $3.00 Hdbd. Lawrence Verry, Inc., NY.

Oras, Ants. Critical Ideas of T. S. Elliot. 1932. $10.00 Hdbd. Folcroft Pr., PA.

Orsini, Gian N. T. S. Eliot & the

Doctrine of Dramatic Conventions. 1954. $3.50 Hdbd. Folcroft Pr., PA.

Patterson. Gertrude. T. S. Eliot: Poems in the Making. 1971. $8.00 Hdbd. (ISBN 0-389-04086-X). Barnes & Noble, NY.

Pearce, T. S. T. S. Eliot. 1969. $3.95 Hdbd. (ISBN 0-668-01883-6); $1.95 pa. (ISBN 0-668-01884-4). Arco Publ., NY.

Preston, Raymond. Four Quartets Rehearsed. (Studies in Eliot, No. 11). 1970. $3.95 pa. (ISBN 0-8383-0063-4). Haskell House, NY.

Rajan, B. T. S. Eliot: A Study of His Writings by Several Hands. (Studies in Eliot Ser., No. 11). 1969. (1947) $5.95 Hdbd. (ISBN 0-8383-0545-8). Haskell House, NY.

Rajan, Balachandra, ed. T. S. Eliot: A Study of His Writings by Several Hands. 1966. (1947) $7.50 Hdbd. Russell & Russell, NY.

Sansom, Clive. Poetry of T. S. Eliot. 1947. $5.00 Hdbd. Folcroft Pr., PA.

Sen, Sunil K. Metaphyiscal Tradition & T. S. Eliot. 1965. $15.00 Hdbd. Lansdowne Pr., PA.

Sen, Sunil K. Metaphysical Tradition & T. S. Eliot. 1965. $15.00 Hdbd. Folcroft Pr., PA.

Sharma, H. L. Essential T. S. Eliot. 1971. $7.50 Hdbd. Lawrence Verry, Inc., CT.

Smidt, Kristian. Poetry & Belief in the Work of T. S. Eliot. 2nd rev. ed. $6.75 Hdbd. Humanities Pr., NY.

Smith, Carol H. T. S. Eliot's Dramatic Theory & Practice: From Sweeney Agonistes to the Elder Statesman. $7.50 Hdbd. (ISBN 0-691-06128-9); $2.95 pa. (ISBN 0-691-01286-5, 87). Princeton Univ. Pr., NJ.

Smith, Grover. T. S. Eliot's Poetry & Plays: A Study in Sources & Meaning. 1956. $6.59 Hdbd. (ISBN 0-226-76521-0). Univ. of Chicago Pr., IL.

Smith, Grover, T. S. Eliot's Poetry & Plays: A Study in Sources & Meaning. 1956. $2.45 pa. (ISBN 0-226-76437-0). Univ. of Chicago Pr., IL.

Southam, B. C. Guide to the Selected Poems of T. S. Eliot. 1970. $1.25 pa. (ISBN 0-15-637980-5). Harcourt Brace Jovanovich, NY.

Southam, Brian. Guide to the Selected Poems of T. S. Eliot. 1969. $4.50 Hdbd. (ISBN 0-15-138051-1). Harcourt Brace Jovanovich, NY.

Stead. C. K. New Poetic. 1964. $3.00 Hdbd. Hutchinson Univ. Lib., NY.

Stephenson, Ethel M. T. S. Eliot & the Lay Reader. (Studies in Eliot, No. 11). 1970. $4.95 pa. (1944) (ISBN 0-8383-0101-0). Haskell House, NY.

Tate, Allen, ed. T. S. Eliot: The Man & His Work. $6.50 Hdbd. Delacorte Pr., NY.

Tate, Allen, ed. T. S. Eliot: The Man & His Work. $2.45 pa. Dell Publ., NY.

Thompson, Eric. T. S. Eliot: The Metaphysical Perspective. 1963. $4.95 Hdbd. (ISBN 0-8093-0089-3). Southern Ill. Univ. Pr., IL.

Unger, Leonard. T. S. Eliot. 1961. $0.95 pa. (ISBN 0-8166-0235-2). Univ. of Minn. Pr., MI.

Unger, Leonard. T. S. Eliot. Moments & Patterns. 1967. $5.75 Hdbd. (ISBN 0-8166-0400-2); $1.95 pa. (ISBN 0-8166-0443-6). Univ. of Minn. Pr., MI.

Unger, Leonard, ed. T. S. Eliot: A Selected Critique. 1966. (1948) $12.00 Hdbd. Russell & Russell, NY.

Verma, Rajendra. Royalist in Politics. T. S. Eliot & Political Philosophy. 1968. $5.75 Hdbd. (ISBN 0-210-22733-8). Asia Soc., NY.

Weinberg, Kerry. T. S. Eliot & Charles Baudelaire. (Studies in General & Comparative Literature Ser. No. 5). 1970. $5.00 pa. Humanities Pr., NY.

Whitford, Ruth. Commentary on T. S. Eliot's Waste Land Ash Wednesday, Four Quartets. Belford, Lee, ed. (Religious Dimensions in Literature Ser). 1969. $0.86 pa.; $0.75 pa. 10 or more. Seabury Pr., NY.

Williams, Helen. Waste Land by T. S. Eliot—Critical Analysis Only. 1969. $1.00 pa. Barron's Educ. Serv., NY.

Williamson, George. Reader's Guide to T. S. Eliot. 1953. $6.50 Hdbd. Farrar, Straus & Giroux, NY.

Williamson, George. Reader's Guide to T. S. Eliot with an Epilogue Entitled T. S. Eliot, 1888-1965. rev. ed. 1955. $2.25 pa. Farrar, Straus & Giroux, NY.

Williamson, George C. Talent of T. S. Eliot. 1929. $6.50 Hdbd. Folcroft Pr., PA.

Williamson, H. R. Poetry of T. S. Eliot. (Studies in T. S. Eliot Ser., No. 11). 1971. $12.95 Hdbd. (ISBN 0-8383-1291-8). Haskell House, NY.

Williamson, Hugh R. Poetry of T. S. Eliot. 1932. $10.00 Hdbd. Folcroft Pr., PA.

Euripides

Alinder, Martha W. Hippolytus & Medea-Euripides. $1.00 pa. (ISBN 0-389-00874-5). Barnes & Noble, NY.

Austin, Colinus, ed. Nova Fragmenta Euripidea: In Papyris Reperta. (Lat). 1968. $5.50 pa. (ISBN 3-11-001313-4). De Gruyter, Germany.

Bates, William N. Euripides. (Illus.). 1961. $1.95 pa. (ISBN 0-498-04048-8). A. S. Barnes, NY.

Bates, William N. Euripides, a Student of Human Nature. 1969. (1930) $11.00 Hdbd. Russell & Russell, NY.

Chapman, John J. Greek Genius, & Other Essays. (Essay Index Reprint Ser). 1915. $9.00 Hdbd. (ISBN 0-8369-0289-0). Books for Libraries, NY.

Conacher, D. J. Euripidean Drama: Myth, Theme & Structure, 1967. $10.00 Hdbd. (ISBN 0-8020-5190-1). Univ. of Toronto Pr., CAN.

Daitz, Stephen G. Jerusalem Palimpsest

of Euripides. 1970. $23.50 Hdbd. (ISBN 3-11-001193-X). De Gruyter, Germany.

De Charme, Paul. Euripedes & the Spirit of His Dramas. Loeb, J., tr. 1968. (1906) $12.50 Hdbd. (ISBN 0-8046-0104-6). Kennikat Pr., NY.

Diggle, James. Euripides: Phaethon. (Cambridge Classical Texts & Commentaries No. 12). 1970. $19.50 Hdbd. (ISBN 0-521-07700-1). Cambridge Univ. Pr., NY.

Euripides. Euripides Medea: Mit Scholien. Diehl, Ernst, ed. 1911. $0.75 pa. De Gruyter, Germany.

Euripides. Euripides Medea: Supplementum Euripideum. Von Arnim, H., ed. 1913. $1.05 pa. De Gruyter, Germany.

Harris, Eugenie. Monarch Literature Notes on the Plays of Euripides. $1.00 pa. Monarch Pr., NY.

Lucas, Frank L. Euripides & His Influence. (Our Debt to Greece & Rome Ser). 1930. $3.50 Hdbd. (ISBN 0-8154-0141-8). Cooper Sq. Pr., NY.

Macurdy, G. H. Chronology of the Extant Plays of Euripides. (Drama Ser., No. 39). 1969. (1905) $8.95 Hdbd. (ISBN 0-8383-0590-3). Haskell House, NY.

Milch, Robert. Electra Notes. Incl. Medea Notes. $1.00 pa. (ISBN 0-8220-0355-4). Cliff's Notes, NB.

Murray, Gilbert. Euripides & His Age. 2nd ed. 1965. $1.75 pa. (ISBN 0-19-285013-X). Oxford Univ. Pr., NY.

Norwood, Gilbert. Euripides & Shaw. $6.00 Hdbd. Crescendo Publ., MA.

Ritchie, William. Authenticity of the Rhesus of Euripides. 1964. $10.00 Hdbd. Cambridge Univ. Pr., NY.

Salter, W. H. Essays on Two Moderns: Euripides, Samuel Butler. 1970. (1911) $6.00 Hdbd. (ISBN 0-8046-0976-4). Kennikat Pr., NY.

Segal, Ed., ed. Euripides: A Collection of Critical Essays. 1968. $5.95 Hdbd. (ISBN 0-13-291930-3). Prentice-Hall, NY.

Stevens, P. T., ed. Euripides: Andromache. 1971. $6.50 Hdbd. Oxford Univ. Pr., NY.

Sutherland, Donald. Bacchae of Euripides: A New Translation with a Critical Essay. 1968. $3.95 Hdbd. (ISBN 0-8032-0182-6). Univ. of Nebr. Pr., NB.

Verrall, A. W. Bacchantes of Euripides. 1910. $8.50 text ed. Cambridge Univ. Pr., NY.

Verrall, Arthur W. Euripides the Rationalist. 1967. (1895) $8.00 Hdbd. Russell & Russell, NY.

Walter, William. Monarch Literature Notes on the Plays of Euripides, Aeschylus & Aristophanes. $1.00 pa. Monarch Pr., NY.

Webster, Thomas B. Tragedies of Euripides. 1967. $10.00 Hdbd. Barnes & Noble, NY.

Wilson, John R., ed. Twentieth Century Interpretations of Euripedes' Alcestis. 1968. $4.95 Hdbd. (ISBN 0-13-291880-3). $1.25 text ed. (ISBN 0-13-291872-2). Prentice-Hall, NY.

Zuntz, Guenther. Political Plays of Euripides. 1955. $6.00 Hdbd. Barnes & Noble, NY.

Zuntz, Gunther. Inquiry into the Transmission of the Plays of Euripides. $12.50 Hdbd. Cambridge Univ. Pr., NY.

Euripides—Criticism

Barlow, Shirley A. Imagery of Euripides. 1971. $11.25 Hdbd. (ISBN 0-416-08130-4). Barnes & Noble, NY.

Schwartz, Eduard. Scholia in Euripidem, 2 vols. Incl. Vol. 1. 1959. (1887); Vol. 2. 1967. (1891) Set--$31.75 Hdbd.; $24.75 pa. De Gruyter, Germany.

Frisch, Max

Weisstein, Ulrich, Max Frisch. (World Authors Ser., No. 21). 1968. $5.50 Hdbd. Twayne Publ., NY.

Fry, Christopher

Roy, Emil. Christopher Fry. $4.95 Hdbd. (ISBN 0-8093-0315-9. Southern Ill. Univ. Pr., NY.

Standord, Derek. Christopher Fry. (Writers & Their Work Ser No. 54). $2.25 Hdbd.; $1.00 pa. British Book Ctr., NY.

Wiersma, Stanley. Christopher Fry. Jellema, Roderick, ed. (Contemporary Writers in Christian Perspective Ser). 1970. $0.95 pa. Wm. B. Eerdmans, MI.

Gay, Edwin Francis

Heaton, Herbert. Scholar in Action, Edwin F. Gay. 1968. (1952) $11.75 Hdbd. (ISBN 0-8371-0101-8). Greenwood Pr., CT.

Gay, John

Armens, Sven M. John Gay, Social Critic. 1966. $9.00 Hdbd. Octagon Books, NY.

Dobree, Bonamy. William Congreve: A Conversation Between Swift & Gay. 1929. $5.00 Hdbd. Folcroft Pr., PA.

Hogarth, William & Blake, W. Beggar's Opera: A Portfolio. Lewis, W. S. & Hofer, Philip, eds. 1965. $100.00 Hdbd. (ISBN 0-300-00683-7). Yale Univ. Pr., CT.

Irving, William H. John Gay. Favorite of the Wits. 1962 (1940) $7.50 Hdbd. Russell & Russell, NY.

Irving, William H. John Gay's London, Illustrated from the Poetry of the Time. 1968. (1928) $12.50 Hdbd. Shoe String Pr., CT.

Kidson, Frank. Beggar's Opera: It's Predecessors & Successors. (Music Practice & Theory Ser). 1969. (1922) $7.00 Hdbd. Johnson Reprint Corp., NY.

Kidson, Frank. Beggar's Opera: Its Predecessors & Successor. 1922. $8.00 Hdbd. (ISBN 0-8371-4250-4). Greenwood Pr, CT.

Melville, Lewis S. Life & Letters of

John Gay. 1921. $12.50 Hdbd. Folcroft Pr., PA.

Pearce, Charles E. Polly Peachum: The Story of Lavinia Fenton & the Beggar's Opera. 1968. $12.50 Hdbd. Benjamin Blom, NY.

Plessow, Max. Geschichte der Fabeldichtung in England Bis Zu John Gay. 1906. $29.00 Hdbd.; $27.00 pa. Johnson Reprint Corp., NY.

Schultz, William E. Gay's Beggar's Opera: Its Content, History & Influence. 1967. (1923) $10.00 Hdbd. Russell & Russell, NY.

Spacks, Patricia. John Gay. (Eng. Authors Ser., No. 22). 1965. $4.95 Hdbd. Twayne Publ., NY.

Warner, Oliver. John Gay. (Writers & Their Work Ser No. 171). 1964. $2.25 Hdbd.; $1.00 pa. British Book Ctr., NY.

Genet, Jean

Coe, Richard N. Vision of Jean Genet. 1969. Repr. $2.95 pa. Grove Pr., NY.

Coe, Richard N. Theater of Jean Genet: A Casebook. 1970. $2.95 pa. Grove Pr., NY.

Coe, Richard N. Vision of Jean Genet. 1968. $7.50 Hdbd. Grove Pr., NY.

Driver, Tom F. Jean Genet. 1966. $1.00 pa. (ISBN 0-231-02942-X). Columbia Univ. Pr., NY.

Grossvogel, David I. Blasphemers: The Theatre of Brecht, Ionesco, Beckett, Genet. $1.95 pa. (ISBN 0-8014-9006-5). Cornell Univ. Pr., NY.

Grossvogel, David L. Four Playwrights & a Postscript: Brecht, Ionesco, Beckett, Genet. 1962. $6.00 Hdbd. (ISBN 0-8014-0161-5). Cornell Univ. Pr., NY.

Jacobsen, Josephine & Mueller, William R. Ionesco & Genet: Playwrights of Silence. $5.95 Hdbd. (ISBN 0-8090-5885-5). $1.95 pa. (ISBN 0-8090-0544-1). Hill & Wang, NY.

Knapp, Bettina L. Jean Genet. (World Authors Series, No. 44). 1968. $5.50 Hdbd. Twayne Publ., NY.

McMahon, Joseph H. Imagination of Jean Genet. 1963. $6.50 Hdbd. (ISBN 0-300-00744-2). Yale Univ. Pr., CT.

Sartre, Jean-Paul. Saint Genet. $1.25 pa. $3.95 Hdbd. New American Library, NY.

Sartre, Jean-Paul. Saint Genet: Actor & Martyr. $8.50 Hdbd. (ISBN 0-8076-0243-4). George Braziller, NY.

Sartre, Jean-Paul. Saint Genet, Comedien et Martyr. 1952. $8.50 pa. French & European Publ., NY.

Thody, Philip. Jean Genet: A Critical Appraisal. 1970. $2.45 pa. (ISBN 0-8128-1296-4). Stein & Day, NY.

Gide, Andre Paul Guillaume

Bree, Germaine. Gide. 1963. $6.00 Hdbd. (ISBN 0-8135-0434-1). Rutgers Univ. Pr., NJ.

Brennan, J. G. Three Philosophical

Novelists. 1964. $6.50 Hdbd. Macmillan Co., NY.

Cordle. Thomas. Andre Gide. (World Authors Ser. Nov. 86). $5.50 Hdbd. Twayne Publ., NY.

Delay, Jean. Youth of Andre Gide. Guicharnaud, June, tr. 1963. $7.95 Hdbd. (ISBN 0-226-14207-8). Univ. of Chicago Pr., IL.

Falk, Eugene H. Types of Thematic Structure. 1967. $5.00 Hdbd. (ISBN 0-226-23609-9). Univ. of Chicago Pr., IL

Fowlie, Wallace. Andre Gide: His Life & Art. 1965. $4.95 Hdbd. 1966. $1.95 pa. Macmillan Co., NY.

Freedman, Ralph. Lyrical Novel: Studies in Hermann Hesse, Andre Gide, & Virginia Woolf. 1963. $8.50 Hdbd. (ISBN 0-691-06071-1): $2.95 pa. (ISBN 0-691-01267-9, 62). Princeton Univ. Pr., NJ.

Guerard. Albert J. Andre Gide. rev. ed. 1969. $6.95 Hdbd. (ISBN 0-674-03525-9). Harvard Univ. Pr., MA.

Hytier, Jean. Andre Gide. $5.00 Hdbd. (ISBN 0-8044-2405-5); $1.95 pa. (ISBN 0-8044-6283-6). Frederick Ungar, NY.

Ireland, G. W. Andre Gide: A Study of His Creative Writings. 1970. $16.00 Hdbd. (ISBN 0-19-815397-X). Oxford Univ. Pr., NY.

Laidlaw, G. Norman, Elysian Encounter: Diderot & Gide. 1963. $5.50 Hdbd. (ISBN 0-8156-2054-3). Syracuse Univ. Pr., NY.

Lemaitre, George. Four French Novelists: Marcel Proust, Andre Gide, Jean Giraudoux, Paul Morand. (Essay & General Literature Reprint Ser). 1969. (1938) $13.50 Hdbd. (ISBN 0-8046-0267-0). Kennikat Pr., NY.

Littlejohn, D., ed. Gide: A Collection of Critical Essays. 1970. $5.95 Hdbd. (ISBN 0-13-356212-3). $1.95 pa. (ISBN 0-13-356204-2). Prentice-Hall, NY.

McLaren, James C. Theatre of Andre Gide: Evolution of Moral Philosopher. 1971. $7.00 text ed. Octagon Books, NY.

March, Harold. Gide & the Hound of Heaven. 1961. $2.25 pa. (ISBN 0-498-04044-5). A. S. Barnes, NY.

Naville, Arnold. Bibliographie Des Ecrits De Andre Gide. 1971. (1949) $12.50 Hdbd. (ISBN 0-8337-2503-3). Burt Franklin, NY.

Nersoyan, H. J. Andre Gide: The Theism of an Atheist. 1969. $7.00 Hdbd. (ISBN 0-8156-2135-3). Syracuse Univ. Pr., NY.

O'Neill, K. Andre Gide & the Roman D'adventure. 1969. $3.50 pa. (ISBN 0-424-05990-8). Intl. Schol. Book Serv., OR.

Painter, George D. Andre Gide: A Critical Biography. rev. ed. 1968. $5.00 Hdbd. (ISBN 0-689-10218-6). Atheneum Publ., NY.

Perry, Kenneth I. Religious Symbolism of Andre Gide. (Studies in French Literature Ser 18). 1970. $7.75 pa. Humanities Pr., NY.

Rossi, Vinio. Andre Gide. $1.00 pa. ISBN 0-231-02960-8). Columbia Univ. Pr., NY.

Rossi, Vinio. Andre Gide: The Evolution of an Aesthetic. 1967. $7.50 Hdbd. (ISBN 0-8135-0544-5). Rutgers Univ. Pr., NJ.

Schwerner, Armand. Monarch Literature Notes on Gide's The Immoralist & Strait Is the Gate. $1.00 pa. Monarch Pr., NY.

Stoltzfus, Ben. Gide's Eagles. 1969. $4.95 Hdbd. (ISBN 0-8093-0347-7). Southern Ill. Univ. Pr., IL.

Watson-Williams, Helen. Andre Gide & the Greek Myth: A Critical Study. 1967. $6.10 Hdbd. (ISBN 0-19-815374-0). Oxford Univ. Pr., NY.

Goethe, Johann Wolfgang Von

Andrews, William P. Goethe's Key to Faust. 1913. $5.00 Hdbd. (ISBN 0-8046-0012-0). Kennikat Pr., NY.

Atkins, Stuart. Goethe's Faust: A Literary Analysis. 1958. $8.50 Hdbd. (ISBN 0-674-35600-4). Harvard Univ. Pr., MA.

Baldensperger, Fernand. Bibliographie Critique De Goethe En France. (Fr). 1907. $22.50 Hdbd. (ISBN 0-8337-3961-1). Burt Franklin, NY.

Baldensperger, Fernand. Goethe En

France. 1890. $19.50 Hdbd. (ISBN 0-8337-3962-X). Burt Franklin, NY.

Bapp, Karl. Aus Goethes Griechischer Gedankenwelt. (Ger). (1921) $5.00 pa. Johnson Reprint Corp., NY.

Barnes, H. G. Goeth's Die Wahlverwandstschaften a Literary Interpretation. 1967. $6.75 Hdbd. (ISBN 0-19-815370-8). Oxford Univ. Pr., NY.

Bielschowsky, Albert. Life of Goethe, 3 Vols. (German Literature & Letters Ser., No. 13). 1969. (1905) $39.95 Hdbd. (ISBN 0-8383-1000-1). Haskell House, NY.

Bielschowsky, Albert. Life of Goethe, 3 Vols. Cooper, William A., tr. 1970. (1908) Set—$40.00 Hdbd. (ISBN 0-404-00870-4); $14.00 ea. (ISBN 0-404-00871-2) (ISBN 0-404-00872-0) (ISBN 0-404-00873-9). AMS Pr., NY.

Boehm, Hans. Goethe: Grundzuege Series Lebens und Werkes. 4th ed. (Ger). 1951. $1.50 Hdbd. (ISBN 3-11-003206-6). De Gruyter, Germany.

Boelich, Ernst. Goethes Prophylaen. (1915) $7.50 pa. Johnson Reprint Corp., NY.

Boynton, Henry W. World's Leading Poets. (Essay Index Reprint Ser). 1912. $11.75 Hdbd. (ISBN 0-8369-0238-6). Books for Libraries, NY.

Braun, Frederick A. Margaret Fuller & Goethe. 1910. $15.00 Hdbd. Folcroft Pr., PA.

Brown, P. Hume. Youth of Goethe.

(German Literature, No. 13). 1970. (1913) $10.95 Hdbd. (ISBN 0-8383-1182-2). Haskell House, NY.

Brown, P. Hume. Life of Goethe, 2 Vols. (German Literature & Letters Ser., No. 13). 1971. Set—$29.95 Hdbd. (ISBN 0-8383-1307-8). Haskell House, NY.

Bruford, Walter H. Culture & Society in Classical Weimar, 1775-1806. 1962. $13.50 Hdbd. Cambridge Univ. Pr., NY.

Burckhardt, Sigurd. Drama of Language: Essays on Goethe & Kleist. 1970. $6.95 Hdbd. (ISBN 0-8018-1049-3). Johns Hopkins Univ. Pr., MD.

Butler, Eliza M. Goethe & Byron. 1949. $3.00 Hdbd. Folcroft Pr., PA.

Butler, Eliza M. Byron & Goethe: Analysis of Passion. $6.50 Hdbd. Humanities Pr., NY.

Buxton, Charles R. Prophets of Heaven & Hell. (Studies in Comparative Literature, No. 35). 1970. (1945). $5.95 pa. (ISBN 0-8383-0086-3). Haskell House, NY.

Calvert, George H. Coleridge, Shelley, Goethe. 1880. $17.50 Hdbd. Folcroft Pr., PA.

Cassirer, Ernst. Rousseau, Kant & Goethe. $1.25 pa. (ISBN 0-06-131092-1). Harper & Row, NY.

Cassirer, Ernst. Rousseau, Kant, & Goethe. 1970. $6.00 pa. (ISBN 0-691-01970-3, 195). Princeton Univ. Pr., NJ.

Colby, U. J. Goethe: Egmont. 1970.

$2.95 Hdbd. (ISBN 0-07-011690-3). McGraw Hill, NY.

Croce, Benedetto. Goethe. 1970. (1923) $8.00 Hdbd. (ISBN 0-8046-0816-4). Kennikat Pr., NY.

Danckert, Werner. Goethe: Der Mythische Urgrund Seiner Weltschau. (Ger). 1951. $5.50 Hdbd. (ISBN 3-11-005340-3). De Gruyter, Germany.

Davidson, Thomas. Philosophy of Goethe's Faust. $8.50 Hdbd. Gordon Publ., NY.

Davidson, Thomas. Philosphy of Goethe's Faust. (German Letters & Literature Ser., No. 13). 1969. (1906) $8.95 Hdbd. (ISBN 0-8383-0933-X). Haskell House, NY.

De Quincey, Thomas. Biographies of Shakespeare, Pope Goethe & Schiller & on the Political Parties of Modern England. 1863. $17.50 Hdbd. (ISBN 0-404-02079-8). AMS Pr., NY.

Eissler, Kurt R. Goethe: A Psychoanalytic Study, 1775-1786, 2 Vols. 1963. Set—$35.00 Hdbd. (ISBN 0-8143-1194-6). Wayne State Univ. Pr., MI.

Era of Goethe Essays Presented to James Boyd. (Essay Index Reprint Ser). 1959. $9.75 Hdbd. (ISBN 0-8369-0418-4). Books for Libraries, NY.

Ewen, Frederic. Prestige of Schiller in England, 1788-1885. 1932. $9.00 Hdbd. (ISBN 0-404-02364-9). AMS Pr., NY.

Fahrner, R. Hoelderlins Begebnung

Mit Goethe und Schiller. 1925. $4.50 pa. Johnson Reprint Corp., NY.

Fairley, Barker. Goethe As Revealed in His Poetry. 2nd ed. $5.00 Hdbd. (ISBN 0-8044-2186-2). Frederick Ungar, NY.

Fairley, Barker. Study of Goethe. 1947. $6.50 Hdbd. (ISBN 0-19-815311-2). Oxford Univ. Pr., NY.

Fischer-Lamberg, Hanna, ed. Der Junge Goethe, 5 vols. Incl. Vol. 1. August, 1749 zu Maerz, 1770. 1963. $10.50 Hdbd. (ISBN 3-11-005119-2); Vol. 2. April, 1770 zu September, 1772. 1963. $8.20 Hdbd. (ISBN 3-11-005120-6); Vol. 3. September, 1772 zu Dezember, 1773. 1965. $13.20 Hdbd. (ISBN 3-11-005121-4); Vol. 4. Januar zu Dezember, 1774. 1968. $13.20 Hdbd. (ISBN 3-11-005122-2). (Ger.). De Gruyter, Germany.

Fleissner, Otto S. & Fleissner, E. M. Junge Goethe. (Ger.). 1963. $3.40 pa. Houghton-Mifflin, NY.

Fuchs, Albert. Goethe-Studien. (Kleinere Schriften zur Literaturgeschichte und Geistesgeschicht) . (Ger.). $15.30 Hdbd. (ISBN 3-11-005122-2). De Gruyter, Germany.

Gillies, Alexander. Goethe's Faust: An Interpretation. 1957. $6.00 Hdbd. Fernhill House, NY.

Gray, Ronald D. Goethe: A Critical Introduction. $7.50 Hdbd. (ISBN 0-521-09404-6, 404). Cambridge Univ. Pr., NY.

Grumach, Ernst. Goethe und Die Antike: Eine Sammlung. 2 Vols. (Ger). 1949. $11.00 Hdbd. (ISBN 3-11-003211-2). De Gruyter, NY.

Grumach, Ernst & Grumach, Renate, eds. Goethe: Begegnungen und Gespraeche, 12 vols. Incl. Vol. 1. 1749–1776. 1965. $17.00 Hdbd. (ISBN 3-11-005141-9); Vol. 2 1777–1785. 1966. $21.50 Hdbd. (ISBN 3-11-005142-7). (Ger). De Gruyter, Germany.

Gundolf, Friedrich. Goeth. 1930. $28.50 Hdbd. (ISBN 0-404-02961-2). AMS Pr., NY.

Hammer, Carl, Jr., ed. Goethe After Two Centuries: A Series of Essays. 1969. Repr. $6.00 Hdbd. (ISBN 0-8406-0192-5). Kennikat Pr., NY.

Haskell, Juliana. Bayard Taylor's Translation of Goethe's Faust. 1908. $7.00 Hdbd. (ISBN 0-404-50410-8). AMS Pr., NY.

Hatfield, Henry. Goethe. $1.95 pa. New Directions, NY.

Hatfield, Henry C. Goethe, a Critical Introduction. 1963. $7.00 Hdbd. (ISBN 0-674-35550-4). Harvard Univ. Pr., MA.

Hauhart, William F. Reception of Goethe's Faust in England in the First Half of the Nineteenth Century. 1909. $7.50 Hdbd. (ISBN 0-404-50411-6). AMS Pr., NY.

Heun, Hans G. Satzbau in Der Prosa Des Jungen Goethe. 1930. $9.00 Hdbd. $7.00 pa. Johnson Reprint Corp., NY.

Hopper, Vincent F. Barron's Simplified Approach to Goethe's Faust 1 & 2. (Hi-Sch.). 1964. $0.95 pa. Barron's Educ. Serv., NY.

Howe, Sussanne. Wilhelm Meister & His English Kinsmen. 1930. $11.00 Hdbd. (ISBN 0-404-03367-9). AMS Pr., NY.

Hoyer, Walter. Goethe's Life in Pictures. 1963. $1.75 Hdbd. Adler's Foreign Books, NY.

Hoyer, Walter. Goethe's Life in Pictures. 1969. $2.95 Hdbd. Dufour Editions, PA.

Hungerford, Edward B. Shores of Darkness. $4.00 Hdbd. Peter Smith Publ., MA.

Jantz, Harold. Mothers in Faust: The Myth of Time & Creativity. 1969. $6.95 Hdbd. (ISBN 0-8018-0311-X). Johns Hopkins Univ. Pr., MD.

Jessen, Arnd. Zwoelf Reiche der Seele Nach Goethes Faust-Schema. (Ger). 1951. $1.05 pa. (ISBN 3-11-003213-9). De Gruyter, Germany.

Keenan, Randall. Monarch Literature Notes on Goethe's The Sorrows of Young Werther. $1.00 pa. Monarch Pr., NY..

Knight, G. Wilson. Christian Renaissance. 1962. $1.85 pa. (ISBN 0-393-00197-0). W. W. Norton, NY.

Kuch, Franz. Goethes Gedankenform. (Ger). 1967. $13.20 Hdbd. (ISBN 3-11-005184-2). De Gruyter, Germany.

Kutscher, Arthur. Naturgefuhl in Goethes Lyrik Gis Zur Ausgabe der Schriften. 1789. (1906) $7.50 pa. Johnson Reprint Corp., NY.

Lange, Victor, ed. Goethe: A Collection of Critical Essays. (Twentieth Century Views Series). 1967. $1.95 pa. (ISBN 0-13-357715-5). $5.95 Hdbd. (ISBN 0-13-357723-6). Prentice-Hall, NY.

Leppmann, Wolfgang. German Image of Goethe. 1961. $6.75 Hdbd. (ISBN 0-19-815340-6). Oxford Univ. Pr., NY.

Lewes, George H. Life & Works of Goethe. $3.25 Hdbd. (ISBN 0-460-00269-4). E. P. Dutton, NY.

Lewes, George H. Life of Goethe. 1965. $8.50 Hdbd. (ISBN 0-8044-2521-3). Frederick Ungar, NY.

Lakacs, Georg. Goethe & His Age. 1969. $2.45 pa. (ISBN 0-448-00194-2). Grosset & Dunlap, NY.

Mabie, Hamilton W. Backgrounds of Literature. (Essay Index Reprint Ser). 1904. $12.50 Hdbd. (ISBN 0-8369-1617-4). Books for Libraries, NY.

Macintosh, W. Scott & Goethe. 1970. Repr. $9.00 Hdbd. (ISBN 0-8046-1026-6). Kennikat Pr., NY.

Mann. Thomas. Cervantes, Goethe, Freud. $1.25 pa. French & European Publ., NY.

Mason, Eudo C. Goethe's Faust: Its Genesis & Purport. 1967. $11.05 Hdbd. (ISBN 0-520-00821-9). Univ. of Cal. Pr., CA.

Masson, David. Essays, Biographical & Critical. 1856. $20.00 Hdbd. (ISBN 0-404-04244-9). AMS Pr., NY.

Masson, David. Essays Biographical & Critical: Chiefly on English Poets. 1856. $20.00 Hdbd. Folcroft Pr., PA.

Masson, David. Three Devils: Luther's, Milton's & Goethe's. 1970. (1874) $13.00 Hdbd. (ISBN 0-404-04247-3). AMS Pr., NY.

Masson, David. Three Devils: Luther's, Milton's & Goethe's. 1874. $12.50 Hdbd. Folcroft Pr., PA.

Matthaei, Rupprecht, ed. Goethe's Color Theory. 1971. $27.50 Hdbd. Van Nostrand-Reinhold, NY.

Mendelssohn-Bartholdy, F. Goethe & Mendelssohn. (German Literature & Letters Ser., No. 13). 1970. (1874) $8.95 Hdbd. (ISBN 0-8383-0902-X). Haskell House, NY.

Mendelssohn-Bartholdy, Karl. Goethe & Mendelssohn. 1874. $8.95 Hdbd. (ISBN 0-8383-0902-X). Haskell House, NY.

Menne, Karl. Goethes Werther in der Niederlandischen Literatur (Ger). Repr. of 1905 ed. $7.50 pa. Johnson Reprint, NY.

Milch, Robert J. Faust, Pts. 1 & 2, Notes. $1.00 pa. (ISBN 0-8220-0479-8). Cliff's Notes, NB.

Montgomery, Paul. Monarch Literature Notes on Goethe's Faust. $1.00 pa. Monarch Pr., NY.

Mueller, Curt R. Geschichtlichen Voraussetzungen Des Symbolbegriffs in Goethes Kunstanschauung. 1937. $14.00 Hdbd.; $12.00 pa. Johnson Reprint Corp., NY.

Noolendorfs, Valters. Streit Um Den Urfaust. 1967. $14.00 Hdbd. Humanities Pr., NY.

Orlandi, Enzo, ed. Life & Times of Goethe. (Portraits of Greatness Ser). $1.98 Hdbd. Doubleday & Co., NY.

Orrick, James B. Matthew Arnold & Goethe. 1928. $8.50 Hdbd. Folcroft Pr., PA.

Peacock, Ronald. Goethe's Major Plays. 1959. $5.00 Hdbd. Barnes & Noble, NY.

Pollak, Gustav. International Perspective in Criticism. 1914. $9.50 Hdbd. (ISBN 0-8046-0370-7). Kennikat Pr., NY.

Raphael, Alice. Goethe & the Philosophers' Stone: Symbolical Patterns in the Parable & the Second Part of Faust. $8.50 Hdbd. Garrett Pr., NY.

Reiss, Hans. Geothe's Novels. 1971. $10.00 Hdbd. (ISBN 0-87024-187-7). Univ. of Miami Pr., FL.

Reiss, Hans. Goethe's Novels. $10.00 Hdbd. (ISBN 0-87024-198-2). Univ. of Miami Pr., FL.

Robertson, John G. Goethe & Bryon. 1925. $12.50 Hdbd. Folcroft Pr., PA.

Rolland, Romain. Goethe & Beethoven. 1968. Repr. $12.50 Hdbd. Benjamin Blom., NY.

Rueff, H. Zur Entstehungsgeschichte Von Goethes Torquato Tasso. 1910. $4.50 pa. Johnson Reprint Corp., NY.

Salm, Peter. Poem As Plant: A Biological View of Goethe's Faust. 1971. $5.95 Hdbd. (ISBN 0-8295-0204-1). Pr. of Case Western Reserve, OH.

Sarrayana, George. Three Philosophical Poets. 1971. (1910) $6.00 Hdbd. (ISBN 0-8154-0361-5). Cooper Sq. Pr., NY.

Scott, D. F. Some English Correspondents of Goethe. 1949. $2.00 Hdbd. Barnes & Noble, NY.

Seeley, J. R. Goethe. (Studies in German Literature, No. 13). 1970. (1894) $7.95 Hdbd. (ISBN 0-8383-1136-9). Haskell House, NY.

Sime, James. Life of Johann Wolfgang Goethe. 1971. (1880) $9.50 Hdbd. (ISBN 0-8046-1614-0). Kennikat Pr., NY.

Spalding, John L. Opportunity, & Other Essays & Addresses. (Essay Index Reprint Ser). 1900. $9.00 Hdbd. (ISBN 0-8369-0894-5). Books for Libraries, NY.

Steer, Alfred G., Jr. Goethe's Social Philosophy As Revealed in Campagne in Frankreich & Belagerung Von Mainz. 1955. $10.00 Hdbd. (ISBN 0-404-50915-0). AMS Pr., NY.

Steiner, Rudolf. Goethe the Scientist. 1950. $4.00 Hdbd. (ISBN 0-910142-12-2). Anthroposophic Pr., NY.

Steiner, Rudolf. Theory of Knowledge Based on Goethe's World Conception. 1968. $4.95 Hdbd. (ISBN 0-910142-38-6). Anthroposophic Pr., NY.

Stenger, Gerhard. Goethe Und August Von Kotzebue. (1910) $7.50 pa. Johnson Reprint Corp., NY.

Strich, Fritz. Goethe & World Literature. 1971. (1949) $13.50 Hdbd. (ISBN 0-8046-1648-5). Kennikat Pr., NY.

Strich, Fritz. Goethe & World Literature. (1949) $15.50 Hdbd. (ISBN 0-8371-5645-9). Greenwood Pr., CT.

Vickery, John B. & Sellery, J'Nan, eds. Goethe's Faust Pt. One: Essays in Criticism. (Guides to Literary Study Ser). 1969. $2.95 pa. Wadsworth Publ., CA.

Vietor, Karl. Goethe the Poet. Hadas, Moses, tr. 1970. (1949) $13.00 Hdbd. Russell & Russell, NY.

Von Goethe, Johann W. Boyhood. Wagner & Cartmell, eds. (Ger). $1.10 text ed. Cambridge Univ. Pr., NY.

Von Goethe, Johann W. Italian Journey, 1786–1788. 1968. (1962) $10.00 Hdbd. $3.95 pa. (ISBN 0-8052-0193-9). Schocken Books, NY.

Von Gronicka, Andre. Russian Image of Goethe: Goethe in Russian Literature of the First Half of the Nineteenth Century. (Haney Foundation Ser). 1968. $9.00 Hdbd. (ISBN 0-8122-7573-X). Univ. of Penna. Pr., PA.

Von Klenze, Camillo. From Goethe to Hauptmann: Studies in a Changing Culture. 1926. $7.50 Hdbd. (ISBN 0-8196-0178-0). Biblo & Tannen, NY.

Wackerl, Georg. Goethes Tag-Hefte und Hahres-Hefte. (Quellen und Forschungen Zur Sprachgeschichte und Kulturgeschichte der Germanischen Voelker, No. 35). (Ger). 1970. $9.30 Hdbd. (ISBN 3-11-002683-X). De Gruyter, Germany.

Wahr, Frederick B. Emerson & Goethe. 1915. $12.50 Hdbd. Folcroft Pr., PA.

Wentzlaff-Eggebert, Friedrich W. Schillers Weg Zu Goethe. (Die Kleinen De Gruyter Baende 4). (Ger). 1963. $4.40 (ISBN 3-11-000491-7). De Gruyter, Germany.

Wilkinson, Elizabeth M. & Willoughby, Leonard A. Goethe: Poet & Thinker. 1962. $8.00 Hdbd. Barnes & Noble, NY.

Willoughby, L. A. & Fairley, Barker. Papers About Goethe: Goethe & Wordsworth, Coleridge & His Contemporaries. 1934. $12.50 Hdbd. Folcroft Pr., PA.

Wolfgang Von Goethe, Johann. Goethe's World View: Presented in His Reflections & Maxims. Ungar, Frederick, ed. Norden, Heinz, tr. $5.00 Hdbd. (2264-8). Frederick Ungar, NY.

Wolfgang Von Goethe, Junge Goethe: Goethes Erste Weimarer Gedichtsammlung Mit Varianten. 2nd ed. Leitzmann, Albert, ed. (Kleine Texte, No. 63). (Ger). 1940. $0.30 pa. De Gruyter, Germany.

Wolfgang, Von Goethe. Junge Goethe:

Goethes Roemische Elegien Nach der Aeltesten Reinschrift. Leitzmann, Albert, ed. (Kleine Texte, No. 100). (Ger). 1912. $0.70 pa. De Gruyter, Germany.

Gogol, Nikolai Vasilevich

Annenkov, P. V. Extraordinary Decade: Literary Memoirs. Mendel, Arthur P., ed. 1968. $8.50 Hdbd. (ISBN 0-472-11270-8). Univ. of Mich. Pr., MI.

Debreczeny, Paul. Nikolay Gogol & His Contemporary Critics. 1966. $2.00 pa. Am Philosophical Soc., PA.

Driessen, F. C. Gogol As a Short-Story Writer. Finlay, Ian F., tr. 1965. $13.00 Hdbd. Humanities Pr., NY.

Erlich, Victor. Gogol. (Yale Russian & East European Studies, Ser, No. 8). 1969. $7.50 Hdbd. (ISBN 0-300-01120-2). Yale Univ. Pr., CT.

Fanger, Donald. Dostoevsky & Romantic Realism: A Study of Dostoevsky in Relation to Balzac, Dickens, Gogol. 1965. $2.45 pa. (ISBN 0-226-23747-8). Univ. of Chicago Pr., IL.

Fanger, Donald L. Dostoevsky & Romantic Realism: A Study of Dostoevsky in Relation to Balzac, Dickens, & Gogol. (Studies in Comparative Literature Ser. No. 27). 1965. $8.50 Hdbd. (ISBN 0-674-215000-1). Harvard Univ. Pr., MA.

Gippius, Vasily. Gogol. Fanger, Donald, ed. (Rus). 1963. $4.75 pa. (ISBN 0-87057-069-2). Brown Univ. Pr., RI.

Kent, Leonard J. Subconscious in

Gogol & Dostoevskij & Its Antecedents. (Slavistic Printings & Reprintings, No. 75). 1970. $9.25 Hdbd. Humanities Pr., NY.

Lavrin, Janko. Nikolai Gogol, 1809–1852: A Centenary Survey. 1968. (1951) $6.50 Hdbd. Russell & Russell, NY.

Magarshack, David. Gogol: A Life. 1969. $2.95 pa. Grove Pr., NY.

Nabokov, Vladimir. Nikolai Gogol. $1.95 pa. New Directions, NY.

Proffer, Carl R. Simile & Gogol's Dead Souls. (Slavistic Printings & Reprintings Series No. 62). (1967) 1968. $9.25 Hdbd. Humanities Pr., NY.

Setchkarev, Vsevolod. Gogol: His Life & Works. Kramer, Robert, tr. (Gotham Library). 1965. $7.95 Hdbd. (ISBN 0-8147-0379-8); $2.25 pa. (ISBN 0-8147-0380-1). New York Univ. Pr., NY.

Slonimskii, Alexandr L. Tekhnika Komicheskogo U Gogolia. 1963. $1.50 pa. (ISBN 0-87057-070-6). Brown Univ. Pr., RI.

Goldsmith, Oliver

Balderston, Katherine C. Collected Letters of Oliver Goidsmith. 1971. (1928) $10.00 Hdbd. Lansdowne Pr., PA.

Balderston, Katherine C. The History & Sources of Percy's Memoir of Goldsmith. Incl. Collected Letters. Goldsmith. 1926. $15.00 Hdbd. Kraus Reprint Co., NY.

Black, William. Goldsmith. Morley, John, ed. 1887. $12.50 Hdbd. (ISBN 0-404-51702-1). AMS Pr., NY.

Cliff's Notes Editors. Vicar of Wakefield Notes. $1.00 pa. (ISBN 0-8220-1329-0). Cliff's Notes, NB.

Dobson, Austin. Life of Oliver Goldsmith. 1971. Repr. of 1888 ed. $9.50 Hdbd. (ISBN 0-8046-1570-5). Kennikat Pr., NY.

Emslie, Macdonald. Vicar of Wakefield by Goldsmith. Daiches, David. ed. (Studies in English Literature Ser). (Critical Analysis Only). (Hi-Sch.). 1963. $1.00 pa. Barron's Educ. Serv., NY.

Forster, John. Life of Oliver Goldsmith. 1971. (1903) $23.00 Hdbd. Scholarly Pr., MI.

Forster, John. The Life of Oliver Goldsmith. (Illus.). (1903) $14.50 Hdbd. (ISBN 0-8371-3100-6). Greenwood Pr., NY.

Gooding, David. Monarch Literature Notes on Goldsmith's She Stoops to Conquer & Other Works. $1.00 pa. Monarch Pr., NY.

Hopkins, Robert H. True Genius of Oliver Goldsmith. 1969. $8.00 Hdbd. (ISBN 0-8018-1016-7). Johns Hopkins Univ. Pr., MD.

Hudson, William H. Johnson & Goldsmith & Their Poetry. 1918. $7.50 Hdbd. Folcroft Pr., PA.

Hudson, William H. Johnson & Goldsmith & Their Poetry. 1918. $8.00

Hdbd. (ISBN 0-404-52515-6). AMS Pr., NY.

Jeffares, A. Norman. Oliver Goldsmith. (Writers & Their Work Ser No. 107). $2.25 Hdbd.; $1.00 pa. British Book Ctr., NY.

Kent, Elizabeth. Goldsmith & His Booksellers. 1933. $10.00 Hdbd. Folcroft Pr., PA.

Kent, Elizabeth E. Goldsmith & His Booksellers. 1970. (1933) $7.50 Hdbd. (ISBN 0-678-00725-X). Augustus M. Kelley, NY.

Kirk, Clara M. Oliver Goldsmith. (Eng. Authors Ser., No. 17). 1967. $4.95 Hdbd. Twayne Publ., NY.

Krans, Horatio S. Oliver Goldsmith: A Critical Biography. 1918. $10.00 Hdbd. Folcroft Pr., PA.

Paden, William D. & Hyder, C. K., eds. A Concordance to the Poems of Oliver Goldsmith. 1940. $7.50 Hdbd. Peter Smith Publ., MA.

Piggin, Julia R. Vicar of Wakefield-Goldsmith. 1969. $1.00 pa. (ISBN 0-389-00885-0, 878, BN). Barnes & Noble, NY.

Pitman, James H. Goldsmith's Animated Nature: A Study of Goldsmith. (1924). price "n.g." Hdbd. (ISBN 0-208-01135-8). Shoe String Pr., CT.

Quintana, R. Oliver Goldsmith: A Georgian Study. (Masters of World Lit Series, Vol. 3). 1967. $4.95 Hdbd. Macmillan Co., NY.

Roy, Gregor & Greene, James. Monarch Literature Notes on Goldsmith's Vicar of Wakefield. $1.00 pa. Monarch Pr., NY.

Sherwin, Oscar. Goldy: The Life & Times of Oliver Goldsmith. 1961. $6.00 Hdbd. Twayne Publ., NY.

Smith, H. Goldsmith's Citizen of the World. (Yale Studies in English Ser., No. 71). 1970. (1926) $5.50 Hdbd. (ISBN 0-208-00911-6). Shoe String Pr., CT.

Wardle, Ralph. Oliver Goldsmith. 1969. (1957) $9.00 Hdbd. (ISBN 0-208-00755-5). Shoe String Pr., CT.

Grahame, Kenneth

Chalmers, Patrick R. Kenneth Grahame: Life & Writings. (1936) $10.00 Hdbd. Gale Research, MI.

Chalmers, Patrick R. Kenneth Grahame: Life, Letters & Unpublished Work. 1971. (1933) $12.50 Hdbd. (ISBN 0-8046-1560-8). Kennikat Pr., NY.

Graham, Eleanor. Kenneth Grahame. 1963. $2.75 Hdbd. (ISBN 0-8098-3907-5). Henry Z. Walck, NY.

Green, Paul Eliot

Kenny, Vincent. Paul Green. (United States Authors Ser. No. 186). $4.95 Hdbd. Twayne Publ., NY.

Lazenby, Walter S., Jr. Paul Green (Southern Writers Ser). 1970. $1.00 pa. (ISBN 0-8114-3890-2). Steck-Vaughn, TX.

Grillparzer, Franz

Alker, E. Franz Grillparzer: Ein Kampf Um Leben und Kunst. (Beitraege Zur Deutschen Literaturwissenschaft, No. 36). 1930. $10.00 pa. Johnson Reprint Corp., NY.

Buecher, W. Grillparzers Verhaeltnis Zur Politik Seiner Zeit. 1913. $4.50 pa. Johnson Reprint Corp., NY.

Burkhard, Arthur. Franz Grillparzer in England & America. 1961. $2.00 Hdbd. Arthur Burkhard, MA.

Burkhard, Arthur. Grillparzer in Ausland Munich. (Ger.). 1969. $4.00 Hdbd. Arthur Burkhard, MA.

Coenen, Frederic E. Franz Grillparzer's Portraiture of Men. 1951. $10.00 Hdbd. (ISBN 0-404-50904-5). AMS Pr., NY.

De Walsh, Faust C. Grillparzer As a Poet of Nature. 1910. $5.00 Hdbd. (ISBN 0-404-50412-4). AMS Pr., NY.

Pollak, Gustav. International Perspective in Criticism. 1914. $9.50 Hdbd. (ISBN 0-8046-0370-7). Kennikat Pr., NY.

Wells, G. A. Plays of Grillparzer. $4.75 Hdbd. (ISBN 0-08-012950-1); $3.25 text ed. (ISBN 0-08-012949-8). Pergamon Publ., NY.

Hellman, Lillian

Adler, Jacob H. Lillian Hellman. (Southern Writers Ser). 1969. $1.00 text ed. (ISBN 0-8114-3846-5). Steck-Vaughn, TX.

Triesch, Manfred. Lillian Hellman Collection. 1968. $7.50 Hdbd. (ISBN 0-292-78364-7). Univ. of Texas Pr., TX.

Heywood, Thomas

Clark, Arthur M. Thomas Heywood, Playwright & Miscellanist. 1967. (1931) $9.00 Hdbd. Russell & Russell, NY.

Cromwell, Otelia. Thomas Heywood: A Study in the Elizabethan Drama of Everyday Life. (Yale Studies in English No. 78). 1969. (1928) $7.00 Hdbd. (ISBN 0-208-00767-9, Archon). Shoe String Pr., CT.

Velte, M. Bourgeois Element in the Dramas of Thomas Heywood. (Drama Ser., No. 39). 1969. (1922) $9.95 Hdbd. (ISBN 0-8383-0641-1). Haskell House, NY.

Hughes, Langston

Dickinson, Donald C. Bio-Bibliography of Langston Hughes, 1902-1967. 1967. $10.00 Hdbd. (5,). Shoe String Pr., CT.

Emanuel, James. Langston Hughes. (U.S. Authors Ser., No. 123). 1967. $4.95 Hdbd. Twayne Publ., NY.

Emanuel, James A. Langston Hughes. 1967. $2.45 pa. College & Univ. Pr., CT.

Hughes, Langston. Big Sea. YA. (Hi-Sch.). 1963. $4.95 Hdbd. (ISBN 0-8090-2990-1). $2.45 pa. (ISBN 0-8090-0065-2). Hill & Wang, NY.

Meltzer, Milton. Langston Hughes: A Biography. (Jr Hi-Hi-Sch.). 1968.

$4.50 Hdbd. (ISBN 0-690-48525-5). Thomas Y. Crowell, NY.

Myers, Elisabeth P. Langston Hughes: Poet of His People. (People in the Arts & Sciences Ser). (Illus.). 1970. $2.79 Hdbd. (ISBN 0-8116-4507-X). Garrard Publ., IL.

O'Daniel, Therman, ed. Langston Hughes, Black Genius: A Critical Evaluation. 1971. $5.95 Hdbd. William Morrow, NY.

Rollins, Charlemae. Black Troubador: Langston Hughes. 1970. $4.95 Hdbd. Rand McNally, NY.

Hugo, Victor Marie, Comte

Duclaux, Madame. Victor Hugo. 1971. (1921) $9.50 Hdbd. (ISBN 0-8046-1594-2). Kennikat Pr., NY.

Edwards, Samuel. Victor Hugo: A Tumultuous Life. 1971. $8.95 Hdbd. David McKay, NY.

Gladden, Washington. Witnesses of the Light. (Essay Index Reprint Ser). 1903. $8.75 Hdbd. (ISBN 0-8369-1081-8). Books for Libraries, NY.

Grant, E. M. Career of Victor Hugo. (Harvard Studies in Romance Languages). 1954. $16.00 pa. Kraus Reprint Co., NY.

Grant, Richard B. Perilous Quest: Imagery, Myth & Prophecy in the Narratives of Victor Hugo. 1968. $8.75 Hdbd. (ISBN 0-8223-0076-1). Duke Univ. Pr., NC.

Hooker, Kenneth W. Fortunes of

Victor Hugo in England. 1938. $12.50 Hdbd. (ISBN 0-404-03328-8). AMS Pr., NY.

Hudson, William H. Victor Hugo & His Poetry. 1918. $8.00 Hdbd. (ISBN 0-404-52514-8). AMS Pr., NY.

Jones, Barron's Simplified Approach to Hugo: Les Miserables. 1971. $0.95 pa. Barron's Educ. Serv., NB.

Keating, Clark L. & Moraud, Marcel I. Selections De Moliere, Voltaire, Hugo. text ed. price n.g. Van Nostrand-Reinhold, NY.

Klin, George & Marsland, Amy L. Les Miserables Notes. 1968. $1.00 pa. (ISBN 0-8220-0735-5). Cliff's Notes, NB.

Maurois, Andre. Victor Hugo & His World. Bernard, Oliver, tr. 1966. $6.95 Hdbd. (ISBN 0-670-74587-1). Viking Pr., NY.

Monarch Literature Notes on Hugo's Les Miserables. $1.00 pa. Monarch Pr., NY.

O'Connor, Mary I. Study of the Sources of Han D'Islande & Their Significance in the Literary Development of Victor Hugo. (Catholic University Romance Languages Ser). 1970. (1942) $12.50 Hdbd. (ISBN 0-404-50324-1). AMS Pr., NY.

Olivier, Juste. Paris En Dix-Huit Cent Trente: Journal De Juste Olivier. Delattre, Andre & Denkinger, Marc, eds. 1951. $10.00 Hdbd. (ISBN 0-8078-9019-7, 19). Univ. of N.C. Pr., NC.

Picon, Gaeten. Dessins De Victor Hugo. $15.00 Hdbd. (ISBN 0-8150-0196-7). George Wittenborn, NY.

Saltus, Edgar. Victor Hugo & Golgotha: Two Essays. 1925. $10.00 Hdbd. (ISBN 0-404-05551-6). AMS Pr., NY.

Swinburne, Algernon C. Study of Victor Hugo. 1970. Repr. of 1886 ed. $6.50 Hdbd. (ISBN 0-8046-1000-2). Kennikat Pr., NY.

Hugo, Victor Marie, Comte— Bibliography

Dubois, Pierre. Bio-Bibliographie De Victor Hugo De 1802 a 1825. 1971. (1913) $23.50 Hdbd. (ISBN 0-8337-0929-1). Burt Franklin, NY.

Ibsen, Henrik

Acker, Helen. Four Sons of Norway. (Biography Index Reprint Ser). 1948. $11.00 Hdbd. (ISBN 0-8369-8010-7). Books for Libraries, NY.

Anstensen, Ansten. Proverb in Ibsen: Proverbial Sayings & Citations As Elements in His Style. 1936. $15.00 Hdbd. (ISBN 0-404-50451-5). AMS Pr., NY.

Barranger, Milly S. Barron's Simplified Approach to Ibsen: Ghosts, Wild Duck, & Hedda Gabler. 1969. $0.95 pa. Barron's Educ. Serv., NY.

Barranger, Milly S. Barron's Simplified Approach to Ibsen: Peer Gynt, Doll's House, Enemy of the People. 1969. $0.95 pa. Barron's Educ. Serv., NY.

Bernstein, Alice & Thompson, Rebecca. About Hedda Gabler: On Playing Hedda Gabler & a Short Story of Criticism. 1970. $1.00 Hdbd. Terrain Gallery, NY.

Bolckmans, Alex, et al. Contemporary Approaches to Ibsen. 1966. $5.00 Hdbd. Humanities Pr., NY.

Bradbrook, Muriel C. Ibsen, the Norwegian: A Revaluation. rev ed. 1966. $4.50 Hdbd. (ISBN 0-208-00487-4). Shoe String Pr., CT.

Brandes, Georg. Henrik Ibsen. 1899. $8.75 Hdbd. Benjamin Blom, NY.

Byrnes, Edward. Monarch Literature Notes on Ibsen's Major Plays. $1.00 pa. Monarch Pr., NY.

Downs, Brian W. Ibsen: The Intellectual Background. 1969. (1946) $8.00 Hdbd. Octagon Books, NY.

Eikeland. P. Ibsen Studies. (European Literature Ser., No. 151). 1970. (1934) $7.95 Hdbd. (ISBN 0-8383-1028-1). Haskell House, NY.

Fjelde, Rolf, ed. Ibsen: A Collection of Critical Essays. 1965. $1.95 pa. (ISBN 0-13-448811-3). $5.95 Hdbd. (ISBN 0-13-448829-6). Prentice-Hall, NY.

Franc, Miriam A. Ibsen in England. 1919. $15.00 Hdbd. Folcroft Pr., PA.

Gosse, Edmund. Northern Studies. 1970. (1890) $9.00 Hdbd. (ISBN 0-8046-0862-8). Kennikat Pr., NY.

Gregersen, H. Ibsen & Spain: A Study in Comparative Drama. 1936. $10.00 pa. Kraus Reprint Co., NY.

Grene, David. Reality & the Heroic Pattern: Last Plays of Ibsen, Shakespeare & Sophocles. 1967. $1.95 pa. (ISBN 0-226-30789-1, 349). $6.00 Hdbd. (ISBN 0-226-30788-3). Univ. of Chicago Pr., IL.

Heiberg, Hans. Ibsen: A Portrait of the Artist. Tate, Joan, tr. $10.00 Hdbd. (ISBN 0-87024-156-7). Univ. of Miami Pr., FL.

Holtan, Orley I. Mythic Patterns in Ibsen's Last Plays. 1970. $7.95 Hdbd. (ISBN 0-8166-0582-3). Univ. of Minn. Pr., MN.

James, Henry. Most Unholy Trade, Being Letters on the Drama. 1923. $5.00 Hdbd. Folcroft Pr., PA.

Koht, Halvdan. Life of Ibsen. $17.50 Hdbd. Benjamin Blom, NY.

Kroener, Johanna. Technik des realistischen Dramas bei Ibsen und Galsworthy. 1935. $4.00 pa. Johnson Reprint Corp., NY.

Logeman, Henri. Commentary, Critical, & Explanatory, on the Norwegian Text of Henrik Ibsen's Peer Gynt: Its Language, Literary Association & Folklore. 1917. $15.50 Hdbd. (ISBN 0-8371-3027-1). Greenwood Pr., CT.

Lucas, F. L. Ibsen & Strindberg. 1962. $10.00 Hdbd. Macmillan & Co., NY.

McFarlane, James W., ed. Henrik Ibsen. (Education Ser). 1971. $3.25 pa. (ISBN 0-14-080174-X). Penguin Books, MD.

McFarlane, James W., ed. Discussions of Henrik Ibsen. (Discussions of Literature). (Hi-Sch.). 1962. $2.25 pa. D. C. Heath Co., IN.

Meyer, Hans G. Henrik Ibsen. (World Dramatist Ser). $6.50 Hdbd. Frederick Ungar, NY.

Meyer, Michael. Ibsen: A Biography. 1971. $12.95 Hdbd. Doubleday & Co., NY.

Muir, Kenneth. Last Periods of Shakespeare, Racine, Ibsen. 1961. $5.00 Hdbd. Wayne St. Univ. Pr., MI.

Russell, Edward R. & Standing, Percy C. Ibsen on His Merits. 1971. (1897) $8.50 Hdbd. Kennikat Pr., NY.

Shaw, George B. Quintessence of Ibsenism. $1.75 pa. (ISBN 0-8090-0509-3). Hill & Wang, NY.

Sturman, Marianne. Ibsen's Plays Notes, 2 vols. Incl. Vol. 1, Pt. 1. A Doll's House Notes; Vol. 1, Pt. 2. Hedda Gabler Notes; Vol. 2, Pt. 1. Ghosts Notes; Vol. 2, Pt. 2. The Enemy of the People Notes; Vol. 2, Pt. 3. Wild Ducks. $1.00 pa. Cliff's Notes, NB.

Tedford, Ingrid. Ibsen Bibliography 1928-1957. $6.00 pa. Humanities Pr., NY.

Tedford, Ingrid. Ibsen Bibliography, 1928-1957. 1961. $5.85 pa. Universitets forlaget, MA.

Tennant, P. F. Ibsen's Dramatic Technique. 1965. (1958) $6.00 Hdbd. Humanities Pr., NY.

Thalmann, M. Henrik Ibsen, Ein Erlebnis der Deutschen. 1928. $4.50 pa. Johnson Reprint Corp., NY.

Turnbull, H. G. Shakespeare & Ibsen.

(Studies in Comparative Literature, No. 35). 1970. (1926) $6.95 Hdbd. (ISBN 0-8383-1019-2). Haskell House, NY.

Tysdahl, B. J. Joyce & Ibsen. A Study in Literary Influence. 1968. $7.50 Hdbd. Humanities Pr., NY.

Valency, Maurice. Flower & the Castle: An Introduction to Modern Drama. $2.95 pa. (ISBN 0-448-00202-7). Grosset & Dunlap, NY.

Weigand, Hermann J. Modern Ibsen. $2.25 pa. (ISBN 0-525-47054-9). E. P. Dutton, NY.

Weigand, Hermann J. Modern Ibsen. (Select Bibliographies Reprint Ser). 1953. $14.50 Hdbd. Books for Libraries, NY.

Wicksteed, Philip H. Four Lectures on Henrik Ibsen: Dealing Chiefly with His Metrical Works. 1969. Repr. $5.50 Hdbd. (ISBN 0-8046-0501-7). Kennikat Pr., NY.

Ionesco, Eugene

Bonnefoy, Claude. Conversations with Eugene Ionesco. 1st ed. 1970. $4.95 Hdbd. (ISBN 0-03-081024-8). Holt, Rinehart & Winston, NY.

Coe, Richard N. Eugene Ionesco: A Study of His Work. 1970. $1.50 pa. Grove Pr., NY.

Grossvogel, David I. Blasphemers: The Theatre of Brecht, Ionesco, Beckett, Genet. $1.95 pa. (ISBN 0-8014-9006-5). Cornell Univ. Pr., NY.

Grossvogel, David L. Four Playwrights & a Postscript: Brecht, Ionesco, Beckett, Genet. 1962. $6.00 Hdbd. (ISBN 0-8014-0161-5). Cornell Univ. Pr., NY.

Jacobsen, Josephine & Mueller, William R. Ionesco & Genet: Playwrights of Silence. $5.95 Hdbd. (ISBN 0-8090-5885-5). $1.95 pa. (ISBN 0-8090-0544-1). Hill & Wang, NY.

Pronko, Leonard C. Eugene Ionesco. (Orig.). 1965. $1.00 pa. (ISBN 0-231-02681-1, MW7). Columbia Univ. Pr., NY.

Wulbern, Julian H. Brecht & Ionesco: Commitment in Context. 1971. $8.95 Hdbd. (ISBN 0-252-00129-X). Univ. of Ill. Pr., IL.

Joyce, James

Adams, Robert M. James Joyce: Common Sense & Beyond. $4.00 Hdbd. Peter Smith Publ., MA.

Adams, Robert M. James Joyce: Common Sense & Beyond. 1966. $2.95 pa. Random House, NY.

Adams, Robert M. Surface & Symbol: The Consistency of James Joyce's Ulysses. 1962. $7.95 Hdbd. (ISBN 0-19-500467-1). 1967. $2.50 pa. (ISBN 0-19-500737-9). Oxford Univ. Pr., NY.

Anderson, Chester G. James Joyce & His World. (Photos). 1968. $6.95 Hdbd. (ISBN 0-670-40526-4). Viking Pr., NY.

Andreach, Robert J. Studies in Structure. 1965. $5.00 Hdbd. (ISBN 0-8232-0630-0). Fordham Univ. Pr., NY.

Arnold, Armin. James Joyce. (Modern Literature Monographs Ser). 1969. $5.00 Hdbd. (ISBN 0-8044-2007-6). Frederick Ungar, NY.

Baker, James R. & Staley, Thomas F. James Joyce's Dubliners. (Guides to Literary Study Ser). 1969. $2.95 pa. Wadsworth Publ. Co., CA.

Beck, Warren. Joyce's Dubliners: Substance, Vision & Art. 1969. $8.75 Hdbd. (ISBN 0-8223-0212-8). Duke Univ. Pr., NC.

Benstock, Bernard. Joyce-Again's Wake: An Analysis of Finnegan's Wake. 1966. $7.95 Hdbd; $3.45 pa. (ISBN 0-295-74032-9). Univ. of Wash Pr., WA.

Blamires, Harry. Bloomsday Book: A Guide Through Joyce's Ulysses. 1966. $5.75 Hdbd. $3.00 pa. (ISBN 0-416-69500-0, 180). Barnes & Noble, NY.

Boldereff, Frances M. Hermes to His Son Thoth: Joyce's Use of Giordano Bruno in Finnegans Wake. 1968. $10.50 Hdbd.; $2.95 pa. Classic Nonfiction Library, NJ.

Bonheim, Helmut. Joyce's Benefictions. (Perspectives in Criticism 16). 1964. $5.75 Hdbd. (ISBN 0-520-00147-8). Univ. of Cal. Pr., CA.

Bonheim. Helmut. Lexicon of the German in Finnegans Wake. 1967. $7.00 Hdbd. (ISBN 0-520-00148-6). Univ. of Cal. Pr., CA.

Brandabur, Edward. Scrupulous Meanness: A Study of Joyce's Early Work.

1971. $6.95 Hdbd. (ISBN 0-252-00134-6). Univ. of Ill. Pr., IL.

Brennan, J. G. Three Philosophical Novelists. 1964. $6.50 Hdbd. Macmillan & Co., NY.

Budgen, Frank. James Joyce & the Making of Ulysses. $4.50 Hdbd. Peter Smith Publ., MA.

Budgen, Frank. James Joyce & the Making of Ulysses. 1960. $2.25 pa. (ISBN 0-253-20026-1). Ind. Univ. Pr., IN.

Burgess, Anthony. Re Joyce. 1968. Repr. $2.95 pa. (ISBN 0-393-00445-7). W. W. Norton, NY.

Campbell, Joseph & Robinson, Henry M. Skeleton Key to Finnegans Wake. $1.65 pa. (ISBN 0-670-00074-4). Viking Pr., NY.

Chatterjee, Sisir. James Joyce, a Study in Technique. 1957. $12.50 Hdbd. Folcroft Pr., PA.

Christiani, Dounia B. Scandinavian Elements of Finnegans Wake. 1965. $7.50 Hdbd. (ISBN 0-8101-0063-0). Northwestern Univ. Pr., IL.

Colum, Mary & Colum, Padraic. Our Friend James Joyce. $4.25 Hdbd. Peter Smith Publ., MA.

Connolly, Thomas E. Joyce's Portrait: Criticisms & Critiques. 1962. $3.25 pa. (ISBN 0-390-20610-5). Appleton-Century-Crofts, NY.

Crise, Stelio. Joyce & Trieste. Perez,

Gabriel, tr. $8.00 Hdbd. (ISBN 0-8387-7746-5). Bucknell Univ. Pr., PA.

Curran, Constantine. James Joyce Remembered. 1968. $5.00 Hdbd. (ISBN 0-19-500141-9). Oxford Univ. Pr., NY.

Dalton, Jack P. & Hart, C., eds. Twelve & a Tilly: Essays on the Occasion of the 25th Anniversary of Finnegans Wake. 1966. $5.50 Hdbd. (ISBN 0-8101-0073-8). Northwestern Univ. Pr., IL.

Deming, Robert H., ed. James: The Critical Heritage. 2 Vols. (Critical Heritage Ser). 1970. Set—$18.50 Hdbd. (ISBN 0-389-01023-5). Barnes & Noble, NY.

Doyle, Paul A. Concordance to the Collected Poems of James Joyce. 1966. $5.00 Hdbd. (ISBN 0-8108-0027-6). Scarecrow Pr., NJ.

Duff, Charles. James Joyce & the Plain Reader. 1932. $10.00 Hdbd. Folcroft Pr., PA.

Ellmann, Richard. James Joyce. (1959). $3.95 pa. (ISBN 0-19-500723-9). Oxford Univ. Pr., NY.

Ellmann, Richard. James Joyce. 1959. $15.00 Hdbd. (ISBN 0-19-500541-4). Oxford Univ. Pr., NY.

Enroth, C. A. Joyce & Lawrence. (Hi-Sch.). 1969. $1.52 pa. s.p. 1.14 (ISBN 0-03-082824-4). Holt, Rinehart & Winston, NY.

Freund, Gisele & Carleton, V. B. James Joyce in Paris: His Final Years. 1965. $8.50 Hdbd. (ISBN 0-15-146050-7). Harcourt Brace Jovanovich, NY.

Garrett, Peter K. Scene & Symbol from George Eliot to James Joyce: Studies in Changing Fictional Mode. (Studies in English Ser., No. 172). 1969. $8.75 Hdbd. (ISBN 0-300-01045-1). Yale Univ. Pr., CT.

Garrett, Peter K., ed. Twentieth Century Interpretations of Dubliners. 1968. $4.95 Hdbd. (ISBN 0-13-221036-3). Prentice-Hall, NY.

Garrett, Peter K., ed. Twentieth Century Interpretations of Dubliners. 1968. $1.25 pa. (ISBN 0-13-221028-2). Prentice-Hall, NY.

Gifford, Don & Seidman, Robert. Notes for Joyce: Dubliners & a Portrait of the Artist As a Young Man. 1967. $1.75 pa. E. P. Dutton, NY.

Gilbert, Stuart. James Joyce's Ulysses. 1955. $1.95 pa. (ISBN 0-394-70013-9). Random House, NY.

Givens, Seon, ed. James Joyce: Two Decades of Criticism. (1963). $10.00 Hdbd. (ISBN 0-8149-0107-7). Vanguard Pr., NY.

Glasheen, Adaline. Second Census of Finnegan's Wake: An Index of the Characters & Their Roles. 1963. $7.50 Hdbd. (ISBN 0-8101-0102-5). Northwestern Univ. Pr., IL.

Goldberg, Samuel L. Classical Temper: A Study of James Joyce's Ulysses. 1961. $5.50 Hdbd. Barnes & Noble, NY.

Golding, Louis. James Joyce. 1971. (1933) $8.50 Hdbd. (ISBN 0-8046-1573-X). Kennikat Pr., NY.

Golding, Louis. James Joyce. 1933. $15.00 Hdbd. Folcroft Pr., PA.

Goldman, Arnold. James Joyce. (Profiles in Literature). 1968. $2.75 Hdbd. Humanities Pr., NY.

Goldman, Arnold. Joyce Paradox. 1966. $5.50 Hdbd. (ISBN 0-8101-0104-1). Northwestern Univ. Pr., IL.

Gross, John. James Joyce. Kermode, Frank, ed. (Modern Masters Ser). 1970. $4.95 Hdbd. (ISBN 0-670-40508-6); $1.65 pa. (ISBN 0-670-01914-3, M10). Viking Pr., NY.

Hancock, Leslie. Word Index to James Joyce's Portrait of the Artist. 1967. $6.00 Hdbd. (ISBN 0-8093-0253-5). Southern Ill. Univ. Pr., IL.

Hart, C. James Joyce's Ulysses. 1968. $3.05 Hdbd. Intl. Scholarly Book Serv., OR.

Hart, C. & Senn, F. Wake Digest. 1968. $3.50 pa. (ISBN 0-424-05610-0). Intl. Scholarly Book Serv., OR.

Hart, Clive. Structure & Motif in Finnegans Wake. 1962. $8.00 Hdbd. (ISBN 0-8101-0114-9). Northwestern Univ. Pr., IL.

Hart, Clive, ed. James Joyce's Dubliners: Critical Essays. 1969. $6.50 Hdbd. (ISBN 0-670-40529-9). Viking Pr., NY.

Hayman, David. Ulysses: The Mechanics of Meaning. 1970. $5.95 Hdbd. (ISBN 0-13-935742-4). Prentice-Hall, NY.

James Joyce & the Plain Reader. (Studies in Irish Literature, No. 16). 1971.

$6.95 Hdbd. (ISBN 0-8383-1329-9). Haskell House, NY.

Jones, William P. James Joyce & the Common Reader. rev. ed. 1970. $5.95 Hdbd. (ISBN 0-8061-0324-8); $2.50 pa. (ISBN 0-8061-0930-0). Univ. of Okla. Pr., OK.

Joyce, James. Early Joyce. 1955. $10.00 Hdbd. Ridgeway Bks., PA.

Joyce, James. Passages from Finnegans Wake: A Free Adaptation for the Theater. Manning, Mary, ed. (Poets Theatre Ser. No. 3). 1957. $3.25 Hdbd. (ISBN 0-674-65650-4). Harvard Univ. Pr., MA.

Joyce, Stanislaus. My Brother's Keeper: James Joyce's Early Years by Stanislaus Joyce, Ellman, Richard, ed. 1969. (1958) $1.65 pa. (ISBN 0-670-00263-1, Comp), Viking Pr., NY.

Kain, Richard M. Fabulous Voyager: James Joyce's Ulysses. 1959. $1.65 pa. (ISBN 0-670-00046-9). Viking Pr., NY.

Kronegger, M. E. James Joyce & Associated Image Makers. 1968. $6.00 Hdbd.; $2.25 pa. Coll. & Univ. Pr., CT.

Levin, Harry. James Joyce, a Critical Introduction. 1960. $1.95 pa. New Directions, NY.

Litz, A. Walton. Art of James Joyce: Method & Design in Ulysses & Finnegans Wake. 1964. (1961) $1.25 pa. (ISBN 0-19-500258-X, GB). 1961. $5.50 Hdbd. Oxford Univ. Pr., NY.

Litz, A. Walton. James Joyce. (Eng.

Authors Ser., No. 31). 1966. $4.95 Hdbd. Twayne Publ., NY .

Magalaner, Marvin & Kain, Richard M. Joyce: The Man, The Work, The Reputation. 1956. $8.95 Hdbd. (ISBN 0-8147-0276-7). N. Y. Univ. Pr., NY.

Magalaner, Marvin, ed. James Joyce Miscellany: Second & Third Series. 2nd ser. $5.00 Hdbd. (ISBN 0-8093-0019-2); 3rd ser. $6.50 Hdbd. (ISBN 0-8093-0075-3). Southern Ill. Univ. Pr., IL.

Magalaner, Marvin. Time of Apprenticeship: The Fiction of Young James Joyce. (Select Bibliographies Ser). (1959) $8.50 Hdbd. (ISBN 0-8369-5609-5). Books for Libraries, NY.

Monarch Editors. Monarch Literature Notes on Joyce's Ulysses. $1.00 text ed. Monarch Pr., NY.

Morris, William E. & Nault, Clifford A., Jr., eds. Portraits of an Artist: A Casebook on James Joyce's a Portrait of the Artist As a Young Man. 1962. $2.45 pa. Odyssey Pr., IN.

Morse, Mitchell J. Sympathetic Alien: James Joyce & Catholicism. 1959. $6.95 Hdbd. (ISBN 0-8147-0321-6). N. Y. Univ. Pr., NY.

Moseley, Virginia. Joyce & the Bible. $6.50 Hdbd. (ISBN 0-87580-002-5). Northern Ill. Univ. Pr., IL.

Murillo, Louis A. Cyclical Night: Irony in James Joyce & Jorge Luis Borges. 1968. $8.00 Hdbd. (ISBN 0-674-18040-2). Harvard Univ. Pr., MA.

Noon, William T. Joyce & Aquinas.

(Yale Studies in English Ser., No. 133). 1970. (1957) $5.50 Hdbd. (ISBN 0-208-00928-0). Shoe String Pr., CT.

O'Brien, D. Conscience of James Joyce. 1968. $6.95 Hdbd. (ISBN 0-691-06019-3). Princeton Univ. Pr., NJ.

O'Hehir, Brendan. Gaelic Lexicon for Finnegans Wake & Glossary for Joyce's Other Works. 1968. $10.00 Hdbd. (ISBN 0-520-00952-5). Univ. of Cal. Pr., CA.

Parr, Mary. James Joyce: The Poetry of Conscience. 1962. $5.90 Hdbd. $18.00 ltd. ed. Literary, Mart., WI.

Pearl, Cyril. Dublin in Bloomtime: The City James Joyce Knew. 1969. $5.95 Hdbd. (ISBN 0-670-28570-6, Studio). Viking Pr., NY.

Prescott, Joseph. Exploring James Joyce. 1964. $4.50 Hdbd. (ISBN 0-8093-0123-7). Southern Ill. Univ. Pr., IL.

Quasha, George. Monarch Literature Notes on Joyce's Portrait of the Artist As a Young Man & Other Writings. $1.00 pa. Monarch Pr., NY.

Ross, Martin. Music & James Joyce. 1936. $4.00 Hdbd. Folcroft Pr., PA.

Russell, Francis. Three Studies in Twentieth Century Obscurity: Joyce, Kafka, Gertrude Stein. (Studies in Comparative Literature Ser., No. 35). 1969. (1954). $5.95 Hdbd. (ISBN 0-838-0678-0). Haskell House, NY.

Ryan, John, ed. Bash in the Tunnel. 1971. $12.50. Intl. Publ. Serv., NY.

Ryan, John, ed. Bash in the Tunnel: James Joyce by the Irish. 1970. $5.00 Hdbd. (ISBN 0-901255-15-7). Clifton Books, NY.

Ryf, Robert S. New Approach to Joyce: The Portrait of the Artist As a Guidebook. 1962. $1.95 pa. (ISBN 0-520-01110-4, CAL97). Univ. of Cal. Pr., CA.

Scholes, Robert & Kain, Richard. Scholes, Robert & Kain, Richard. Workshop of Daedalus. 1965. $9.00 Hdbd. (ISBN 0-8101-0223-4). Northwestern Univ. Pr., IL.

Schutte, William M. Joyce & Shakespeare: A Study in the Meaning of Ulysses. (Yale Studies in English Ser., No. 134). 1971. (1957) price "n.g." Hdbd. (ISBN 0-208-01137-4). Shoe String Pr., CT.

Schutte, William M., ed. Twentieth Century Interpretations of A Portrait of the Artist As a Young Man. 1968. $1.25 pa. (ISBN 0-13-686121-0). $4.95 Hdbd. (ISBN 0-13-686147-4). Prentice-Hall, NY.

Senn, Fritz. James Joyce. Carens, James F., ed. (Irish Writers Ser). $4.50 Hdbd. (ISBN 0-8387-7758-9); $1.95 pa. (ISBN 0-8387-7628-0). Bucknell Univ. Pr., PA.

Smidt, Kristian. James Joyce & the Cultic Use of Fiction. 1955. $4.50 Hdbd. Humanities Pr., NY.

Smith, Paul J. Key to the Ulysses of James Joyce. $3.00 Hdbd. Gordon Publ., NY.

Smith, Paul J. Key to the Ulysses of James Joyce. 1927. $4.50 Hdbd. Folcroft. Pr., PA.

Smith, Paul J. Key to the Ulysses of James Joyce. $1.50 pa. City Lights, CA.

Smith, Paul J. Key to Ulysses of James Joyce. (Studies in Fiction Ser., No. 34). 1969. (1934) $3.95 Hdbd. (ISBN 0-8383-0625-X). Haskell House, NY.

Solomon, Margaret C. Eternal Geomater: The Sexual Universe of Finnegans Wake. 1969. $6.95 Hdbd. (ISBN 0-8093-0392-2). Southern Ill. Univ. Pr., IL.

Spoerri, James F. James Joyce: Books & Pamphlets Relating to the Author & His Works. 1955. $4.00 Hdbd. Folcroft Pr., PA.

Staley, Thomas F. Critical Study Guide to Joyce's A Portrait of the Artist As a Young Man. (Pennant Study Guides). 1968. $1.00 pa. Littlefield, Adams & Co., NJ.

Staley, Thomas F., ed. James Joyce Today: Essays on the Major Works. 1970. (1966). $6.50 Hdbd. (ISBN 0-253-14420-5, MB); $1.95 pa. (ISBN 0-253-20126-8). Ind. Univ. Pr., IN.

Staley, Thomas F. & Benstock, Bernard, eds. Approaches to Ulysses: Ten Essays. 1970. $7.95 Hdbd. (ISBN 0-8229-3209-1). Univ. of Pittsburgh Pr., PA.

Stewart, J. I. James Joyce. (Writers & Their Work Ser. No. 91). $2.25 Hdbd.; $1.00 pa. British Book Ctr., NY.

Sullivan, Kevin. Joyce Among the

Jesuits. 1958. $7.00 Hdbd. (ISBN 0-231-02269-7). Columbia Univ. Pr., NY.

Sultan, Stanley. Argument of Ulysses. 1965. $6.95 Hdbd. (ISBN 0-8142-0120-2). Ohio State Univ., Pr.

Svevo, Italo. James Joyce. $1.25 pa. City Lights Pr., CA.

Thompson, Lawrance, Comic Principle in Sterne, Meredith, Joyce. 1954. $10.00 Hdbd. Folcroft Pr., PA.

Thornton, Weldon. Allusions in Ulysses: An Annotated List. 1968. $12.50 Hdbd. (ISBN 0-8078-1056-8). Univ. of N.C. Pr., NC.

Tindall, William Y. James Joyce. 1950. $2.25 pa. (ISBN 0-684-71911-8, 108, SL). Charles Scribner's Sons, NY.

Tindall, William Y. Joyce Country. 1960. $7.50 Hdbd. (ISBN 0-271-73073-0). Pa. State Univ. Pr., PA.

Tindall, William Y. Reader's Guide to Finnegans Wake. 1969. $6.95 Hdbd.; $2.25 pa. Farrar, Straus & Giroux, NY.

Tindall, William Y. Reader's Guide to James Joyce. 1959. $6.95 Hdbd.; $2.25 pa. Farrar, Straus & Giroux, NY.

Tysdahl, B. J. Joyce & Isben: A Study in Literary Influence. (Norwegian Studies in English, Vol. 14). 1968. $7.50 Hdbd. Humanities Pr., NY.

Ussher, Arland. Three Great Irishmen: Shaw, Yeats, Joyce. 1953. $6.75 Hdbd. (ISBN 0-8196-0222-1). Biblo & Tannen, NY.

Waldock, Arthur J. James, Joyce & Others. (Essay Index Reprint Ser). 1937. $7.75 Hdbd. (ISBN 0-8369-0963-1). Books for Libraries, NY.

Joyce, James—Bibliography

Connolly, Thomas E. Personal Library of James Joyce: A Descriptive Bibliography. 1955. $6.50 Hdbd. Ridgeway Books, PA.

Epstein, Edmund L. Ordeal of Stephen Dedalus: The Conflict of Generations in James Joyce's a Portrait of the Artist As a Young Man. 1971. $8.95 Hdbd. (ISBN 0-8093-0485-6). Southern Ill. Univ. Pr., IL.

Scholes, Robert, ed. Cornell Joyce Collection: A Catalogue. 1961. $8.50 Hdbd. (ISBN 0-8014-0370-7). Cornell Univ. Pr., NY.

Slocum, John J. A Bibliography of James Joyce, 1882–1941. (1953) $11.00 Hdbd. (ISBN 0-8371-5639-4). Greenwood Pr., CT.

Spielberg, Peter, ed. James Joyce's Manuscripts & Letters at the University of Buffalo. 1962. $10.00 Hdbd. (ISBN 0-87395-009-7). State Univ. of N.Y. Pr., NY.

Kerouac, Jack

Montgomery. John. Jack Kerouac, a Memoir. $3.95 Hdbd. Giligia Pr., NH.

Kyd, Thomas

Edwards, Philip. Thomas Kyd & Early Elizabethan Tragedy. (Writers & Their Work Ser No. 192). $2.25 Hdbd. $1.00 pa. British Book Center, NY.

Freeman, Arthur. Thomas Kyd; Facts & Problems. 1968. $8.00 Hdbd. (ISBN 0-19-811661-6). Oxford Univ. Pr., NY.

Murray, Peter B. Thomas Kyd. (English Authors Series No. 88). $4.95 Hdbd. Twayne Publ., NY.

Lehar, Franz

Grun, Bernard. Gold & Silver: The Life & Times of Franz Lehar. 1970. $8.95 Hdbd. David McKay, NY.

Lessing, Gotthold Ephraim

Allison, Henry E. Lessing & the Enlightenment. 1966. $7.50 Hdbd. (ISBN 0-472-04112-6). Univ. of Mich. Pr., MI.

Brown, F. Andrew. Gotthold Ephraim Lessing. (Twayne's World Authors Series No. 113). $5.50 Hdbd. Twayne Publ., NY.

Coleridge, Samuel T. Confessions of an Inquiring Spirit. Hart, H. St. J., ed. 1840. (1957) $1.85 pa. (ISBN 0-8047-0331-0). Stanford Univ. Pr., CA.

Fittbogen, Gottfried. Religion Lessings. 1967. (1923) $19.00 Hdbd.; $17.00 pa. Johnson Reprint Corp., NY.

Heller, Peter. Dialectics & Nihilism: Essays on Lessing, Nietzsche, Mann & Kafka. 1969. (1966) $8.00 Hdbd. (ISBN 0-87023-019-0). Univ. of Mass. Pr., MA.

Lachmann, Karl, ed. Lessings Saemtliche Schriften. (Ger). 1968. $328.00 Hdbd. (ISBN 3-11-005161-3). De Gruyter, Germany.

Lowell, James R. English Poets: Lessing,

Rousseau. 1970. (1888) $10.00 Hdbd. (ISBN 0-8046-1047-9). Kennikat Pr., NY.

Mann, Otto. Lessing: Sein und Leistung. (Ger). 1961. $6.05 Hdbd. (ISBN 3-11-000343-0). De Gruyter, Germany.

Metzger, Michael M. Lessing & the Language of Comedy. 1966. $11.50 Hdbd. Humanities Pr., NY.

Robertson, John G. Lessing's Dramatic Theory. 1939. $15.00 Hdbd. Benjamin Blom, NY.

Rolleston, Thomas W. Life of Gotthold Ephraim Lessing. 1971. (1889) $9.50 Hdbd. (ISBN 0-8046-1609-4). Kennikat Pr., NY.

Vail, Curtis C. Lessing's Relation to the English Language & Literature. 1936. $15.00 Hdbd. (ISBN 0-404-50453-1). AMS Pr., NY.

Lorca, Federico Garcia

Barea, Arturo. Lorca, el Poeta y Su Pueblo. $1.25 pa. French & European Pubhs., NY.

Campbell, Roy. Lorca: An Appreciation of His Poetry. (Studies in Poetry Ser., No. 38). 1971. (1952) $6.95 Hdbd. (ISBN 0-8382-e226-8). Haskell House, NY.

Cobb, Carl. Garcia Lorca. (WORLD Authors Ser., No. 23). 1968. $5.50 Hdbd. Twayne Publ., NY.

De Torre, Guillermo. Triptico Del Sacrificio. $1.25 pa. French & European Publ., NY.

Duran, Manuel, ed. Lorca: A Collection of Critical Essays. 1962. $5.95 Hdbd. (ISBN 0-13-540633-1). Prentice-Hall, NY.

Honig, Edwin. Federico Garcia Lorca. rev. ed. 1962. $1.80 pa. New Directions, NY.

Trend, John B. Lorca & the Spanish Poetic Tradition. 1971. (1956) $12.00 Hdbd. Russell & Russell, NY.

Young, Howard T. Victorious Expression: A Study of Four Contemporary Spanish Poets, Unamuno, Machado, Jimenez, & Lorca. 1964. $8.50 Hdbd. (ISBN 0-299-03140-3); $2.95 pa. (ISBN 0-299-03144-6). Univ. of Wisc. Pr., WI.

Lowell, Robert

Cooper, Philip. Autobiographical Myth of Robert Lowell. 1970. $7.50 Hdbd. (ISBN 0-8078-1147-5). Univ. of N.C. Pr., NC.

Fein, R. J. Robert Lowell. (United States Authors Ser. No. 176). $4.95 Hdbd. Twayne Publ., NY.

London, Michael & Boyers, Robert, eds. Robert Lowell: A Portrait of the Artist in His Time. $15.00 Hdbd. David Lewis Publ., NY.

Martin, Jay. Robert Lowell, No. 92. (Pamphlets on American Writers Ser). 1970. $0.95 pa. (ISBN 0-8166-0564-5). Univ. of Minn. Pr., MN.

Mazzaro, Jerome. Poetic Themes of Robert Lowell. 1965. $4.50 Hdbd. (ISBN 0-472-64199-9). Univ. of Mich. Pr., MI.

Parkinson, T., ed. Lowell: A Collection of Critical Essays. $5.95 Hdbd. (ISBN 0-13-541219-6). 1968. $1.95 pa. (ISBN 0-13-541201-3). Prentice-Hall, NY.

Price, Jonathan, ed. Critics on Robert Lowell. $3.95 Hdbd. (ISBN 0-87024-210-5). Univ. of Miami Pr., FL.

Malory, Thomas, Sir

Bennett, Jack A., ed. Essays on Malory. 1963. $5.25 Hdbd. (ISBN 0-19-811604-7). Oxford Univ. Pr., NY.

Bradbrook, Muriel C. Malory. (Writers & Their Work Ser No. 95). $2.25 Hdbd. $1.00 pa. British Book Center, NY.

Gardner, John. Morte D'Arthur Notes. $1.00 pa. (ISBN 0-8220-0726-6). Cliffs Notes, NB.

Hicks, Edward. Sir Thomas Malory: His Turbulent Career. 1970. (1928) $7.00 Hdbd. Octagon Books, NY.

Knight, S. Structure of Sir Thomas Malory's Arthuriad. 1969. $3.50 pa. (ISBN 0-424-05960-6). Intl. School Book Ser., OR.

Lumiansky, M., ed. Malory's Originality. 1964. $9.00 Hdbd. (ISBN 0-8018-0403-5). Johns Hopkins Pr., MD.

Matthews, William. Ill-Framed Knight: A Skeptical Inquiry into the Identity of Sir Thomas Malory. 1966. $7.50 Hdbd. (ISBN 0-520-00830-8). Univ. of Cal. Pr., CA

Moorman, Charles. Book of Kyng Arthur: The Unity of Malory's Morte

D'Arthur . 1965. $5.00 Hdbd. (ISBN 0-8131-1103-X). Univ. Pr. of Ky., KY.

Reiss, Edmund. Sir Thomas Malory. (Eng. Authors Ser., No. 35). 1966. $4.95 Hdbd. Twayne Publ., NY.

Sandved, Arthur O. Studies in the Language of Caxton's Malory & That of the Winchester Manuscript. (Norwegian Studies in English, Vol. 15). 1968. $10.00 Hdbd. Humanities Pr., NY.

Schofield, William H. Chivalry in English Literature. 1912. $10.00 Hdbd. (ISBN 0-404-05621-0). AMS Pr., NY.

Vinaver, Eugene. Malory. 1929. $7.25 Hdbd. (ISBN 0-19-811583-0). Oxford Univ. Pr., NY.

Wilson, Robert H. Characterization in Malory. 1934. $7.50 Hdbd. Folcroft Pr., PA.

Marivaux, Pierre Carlet De Chamblain De

Jamieson, Ruth K. Marivaux: A Study in Sensibility. 1969. (1941) $7.50 Hdbd. Octagon Books, NY.

McKee, Kenneth N. Theater of Marivaux. 1958. $7.95 Hdbd. (ISBN 0-8147-0274-0). N. Y. Univ. Pr., NY.

Tilley, Arthur A. Three French Dramatists: Racine, Marivaux, Musset. 1967. (1933) $8.50 Hdbd. Russell & Russell Publ., NY.

Marlowe, Christopher

Bakeless, John E. Christopher Marlow: The Man in His Time. $0.90 pa. Wash. Sq. Pr., NY.

Bakeless, John E. The Tragical History of Christopher Marlowe, 2 vols. (1942) $30.00 Hdbd. (ISBN 0-8371-3352-1). Greenwood Pr., CT.

Battenhouse, Roy W. Marlowe's Tamburlaine: A Study in Renaissance Moral Philosophy. 1964. $6.50 Hdbd. (ISBN 0-8265-1070-1). Vanderbilt Univ. Pr., TN.

Boas, Frederick S. Christopher Marlowe: A Biographical & Critical Study. 1940. $8.00 Hdbd. (ISBN 0-19-811506-7). Oxford Univ. Pr., NY.

Boas, Frederick S. Marlowe & His Circle: A Biographical Survey. 1968. (1929) $6.00 Hdbd. Russell & Russell Publ., NY.

Brooke, Tucker. Marlowe Canon. (English, American & Comparative Literature Ser., No. 150). 1970. (1922) $2.95 pa. (ISBN 0-8383-0010-3). Haskell House Publ., NY.

Clark, Eleanor G. Ralegh & Marlowe, a Study in Elizabethan Fustian. 1965. (1941) $11.50 Hdbd. Russell & Russell Publ., NY.

Crawford, Charles. Marlowe Concordance, 2 Vols. 1964. $70.00 Hdbd. (ISBN 0-8337-0733-7). Burt Franklin, NY.

Daiches, David, et al, eds. Doctor Faustus by Marlowe: Critical Analysis. (Studies in English Literature Ser). (Hi-Sch.). 1962. $1.00 pa. Barron's Educ. Series, NY.

Eccles, Mark. Christopher Marlowe in

London. (1967) $8.00 Hdbd. Octagon Books, NY.

Ellis-Fermor, Una M. Christopher Marlowe. 1967. (1927) $5.00 Hdbd. (ISBN 0-208-00481-5). Shoe String Pr., CT.

Fanta, Christopher G. Marlowe's Agonists: An Approach of the Ambiguity of His Plays. 1970. $2.50 pa. (ISBN 0-674-55060-9). Harvard Univ. Pr., MA.

Farnham, Willard, ed. Twentieth Century Interpretations of Doctor Faustus. 1969. $1.25 pa. (ISBN 0-13-216291-1). $4.94 Hdbd. (ISBN 0-13-216309-8). Prentice-Hall, NY.

Fieler, Frank B. Tamburlaine, Part One, & Its Audience. (Humanities Monographs, No. 8). 1962. $2.00 pa. (ISBN 0-8130-0077-7). Univ. of Fla. Pr., FL.

Fitzwater, Eva. Doctor Faustus Notes. $1.00 pa. (ISBN 0-8220-0406-2). Cliff's Notes, NB.

Henderson, Philip. Marlowe. (Writers & Their Work Ser No. 81). $2.25 Hdbd.; $1.00 pa. British Book Center, NY.

Hotson, J. Leslie. Death of Christopher Marlowe. 1967. (1925) $7.50 Hdbd. Russell & Russell Publ., NY.

Hotson, J. Leslie. Death of Christopher Marlowe. 1925. $6.95 Hdbd. (ISBN 0-8383-0571-7). Haskell House Publ., NY.

Ingram, John H. Christopher Marlowe & His Associates. 1970. Repr. of 1904 ed. $11.00 lib. bdg. (ISBN 0-8154-0326-7). Copper Sq., NY.

Ingram, John H. Marlowe & His Poetry. 1914. $8.00 Hdbd. (ISBN 0-404-52522-9). AMS Pr., NY.

Ingram, John H. Marlowe & His Poetry. 1914. $8.50 Hdbd. Folcroft Pr., PA.

Knoll, Robert E. Christopher Marlowe, (English Authors Ser., No. 74). 1969. $4.95. Twayne Publ., NY.

Kocher, Paul H. Christopher Marlow: A Study of His Thought, Learning & Character. 1962. (1946) $11.00 Hdbd Russell & Russell Publ., NY.

Leach, Clifford, ed. Marlowe: A Collection of Critical Essays. 1964. $5.95 Hdbd. (ISBN 0-13-558353-5); $1.95 pa. (ISBN 0-13-558346-2). Prentice-Hall, NY.

Levin, Harry. Overreacher: A Study of Christopher Marlowe. 1964. $1.75 pa. (ISBN 0-8070-6497-1). Beacon Pr., NY.

Levin, Harry. Overreacher: A Study of Christopher Marlowe. $4.00 Hdbd. Peter Smith Publ., MA.

Lewis, J. G. Christopher Marlowe. 1891. $5.50 Hdbd. Folcroft Pr., PA.

Marlow, Christopher. Doctor Faustus, 1604–1616. Greg, W. W., ed. (World's Classics). 1950. $13.50 Hdbd. Oxford Univ. Pr., NY.

Marlowe, Christopher. Christopher Marlowe's the Jew of Malta: Text & Major Criticism. Ribner, I., ed. $1.85 pa. Odyssey Pr., NY.

Marlowe, Christopher. Doctor Faustus. Taylor, John, ed. (Casebook Ser). 1970.

$2.50 pa. (ISBN 0-87695-043-8). Aurora Publ., TN.

Marlowe, Christopher. Doctor Faustus: Text & Major Criticism. Ribner, Irving, ed. 1966. $1.45 pa. Odyssey Pr., NY.

Marlowe, Christopher. The Life of Marlowe. Tucker Brooke, C. F., ed. Incl. The Tragedy of Dido Queen of Carthage. (Works & Life of Christopher Marlowe Ser., Vol. 1). 1966. (1930) $10.00 Hdbd. Gordian Pr., NY.

Marlowe, Christopher. Plays of Christopher Marlowe. Gill, Roma, ed. (1971) $4.00 pa. (ISBN 0-19-281062-6). Oxford Univ. Pr., NY.

Marlowe, Christopher. Works & Life of Christopher Marlowe, 6 Vols. Case, R. H., ed. 1966. (1933) Set—$55.00; $10.00 ea. Hdbd. (ISBN 0-87752-067-4). Gordian Pr., NY.

Morris, Brian, ed. Christopher Marlowe. 1969. $4.50 Hdbd. (ISBN 0-8090-6780-3). Hill & Wang, NY.

Mullany, Peter. Monarch Literature Notes on Marlowe's Dr. Faustus & Other Writings. $1.00 pa. Monarch Pr., NY.

Norman, Charles. Christopher Marlowe: The Muse's Darling. $7.50 Hdbd. Bobbs-Merrill Co., IN.

O'Neil, Judith. Critics on Marlowe. (Readings in Literary Criticism No. 4). 1969. $3.95 Hdbd. (ISBN 0-87024-121-4). Univ. of Miami Pr., FL.

Pearce, T. M. Christopher Marlowe,

Figure of the Renaissance. 1934. $10.00 Hdbd. Folcroft Pr., PA.

Poirier, Michel. Christopher Marlowe. 1968. (1950) $4.00 Hdbd. Shoe String Pr., CT.

Rohrman, Hendrik. Marlowe & Shakespeare. 1952. $10.00 Hdbd. Folcroft Pr., PA.

Rohrman, Hendrik. Way of Life, Marlowe & Shakespeare. 1952. $5.00 Hdbd. (ISBN 0-404-05386-6). AMS Pr., NY.

Rowse, Alfred L. Christopher Marlowe. 1965. $8.00 Hdbd. (ISBN 0-06-013690-1). Harper-Row, NY.

Rowse, Alfred L. Christopher Marlowe: His Life & Time. $2.65 pa. (ISBN 0-448-00198-5). Grosset & Dunlap, NY.

Sanders, Wilber. Dramatist & the Received Idea: Studies in the Plays of Marlowe & Shakespeare. 1968. $9.50 Hdbd. Cambridge Univ. Pr., NY.

Sims, James H. Dramatic Uses of Biblical Allusions in Marlowe & Shakespeare. (Humanities Monographs Ser, No. 24). 1966. $2.00 pa. (ISBN 0-8130-0206-0). Univ. of Fla. Pr., FL.

Smith, Marion B. Marlowe's Imagery & the Marlowe Canon. 1940. $15.00 Hdbd. Folcroft Pr., PA.

Steane, J. B. Marlowe: A Critical Study. 1970. $8.95 Hdbd. Cambridge Univ. Pr., NY.

Verity, A. W. Influence of Christopher Marlowe on Shakespeare's Earlier Style. 1886. $6.50 Hdbd. Folcroft Pr., PA.

Waith, Eugene M. Herculean Hero in Marlowe, Chapman, Shakespeare & Dryden. 1962. $7.00 Hdbd. (ISBN 0-231-02506-8). Columbia Univ. Pr., NY.

Wilson, Frank P. Marlowe & the Early Shakespeare. 1953. $4.00 Hdbd. (ISBN 0-19-811585-7). Oxford Univ. Pr., NY.

Wraight, A. D. In Search of Christopher Marlowe. 1965. $12.50 Hdbd. (ISBN 0-8149-0213-8). Vanguard Pr., NY.

Miller, Arthur

Calandra, Denis M. Crucible Notes. 1968. $1.00 pa. (ISBN 0-8220-0337-6). Cliff's Notes, NB.

Corrigan, Robert W., ed. Arthur Miller: A Collection of Critical Essays. (Twentieth Century Views Ser). 1969. $1.95 pa. (ISBN 0-13-582965-8). $5.95 Hdbd. (ISBN 0-13-582973-9). Prentice-Hall, NY.

Evans, Richard I. Psychology & Arthur Miller. 1969. $4.50 Hdbd. (ISBN 0-525-18584-4); $1.75 pa. (ISBN 0-525-47237-1). E. P. Dutton, NY.

Hayman, Ronald. Arthur Miller. (World Dramatist Ser). $6.50 Hdbd. Frederick Ungar, NY.

Hogan, Robert. Arthur Miller. $0.95 pa. (ISBN 0-8166-0332-4). Univ. of Minn. Pr., MN.

Hurrell, John D., ed. Two Modern American Tragedies. (Research Anthology Ser). 1961. $2.95 pa. (ISBN 0-684-41292-6). Charles Scribner's Sons, NY.

Moss, Leonard. Arthur Miller. (U.S. Authors Ser., No. 115). $4.95 Hdbd. Twayne Publ., NY.

Moss, Leonard. Arthur Miller. (Twayne's United States Author Ser). 1968. $2.45 pa. College Univ. Pr., CT.

Murray, Edward. Arthur Miller Dramatist. 1967. $6.50 Hdbd. (ISBN 0-8044-2642-2); $1.95 pa. (ISBN 0-8044-6533-9, 2165). Frederick Ungar, NY.

Nelson, Benjamin. Arthur Miller: Portrait of a Playwright. 1970. $5.95 Hdbd. David McKay, Inc., NY.

Nourse, Joan T. Monarch Literature Notes on Miller's Crucible & View from the Bridge. $1.00 pa. Monarch Pr., NY.

Nourse, Joan T. Monarch Literature Notes on Miller's Death of a Salesman. $1.00 pa. Monarch Pr., NY.

Roberts, James L. Death of a Salesman Notes. $1.00 pa. (ISBN 0-8220-0382-1). Cliffs Notes, NB.

Weales, Gerald, ed. Crucible: Text & Criticism. (Critical Library Ser). 1971. $5.95 Hdbd. (ISBN 0-670-25033-3); $1.95 pa. (ISBN 0-670-01807-4). Viking Pr., NY.

Miller, Arthur—Bibliography

Hayashi, Tetsumaro. Arthur Miller Criticism, 1930–1967. 1969. $5.00 Hdbd. (ISBN 0-8108-0267-8). Scarecrow Pr., NJ.

Milton, John

Adams, Robert M. Ikon: John Milton & the Modern Critics. 1955. $11.25

Hdbd. (ISBN 0-8371-6021-9). Greenwood Pr., CT.

Adams, Robert M. Milton & the Modern Critics. 1966. $1.95 pa. (ISBN 0 8014-9025-1). Cornell Univ. Pr., NY.

Agar, Herbert. Milton & Plato. 1965. $3.50 Hdbd. Peter Smith Publ., MA.

Ames, Percy W. Milton Memorial Lectures 1909. (Studies in Milton Ser., No.22). 1969. (1909) $9.95 Hdbd. (ISBN 0-8383-0501-6). Haskell House Publ., NY.

Anstice, R. H. Satan of Milton. 1910. $5.00 Hdbd. Folcroft Pr., PA.

Arthos, John. Dante, Michelangelo & Milton. 1963. $4.50 Hdbd. Hillary House Publ., NY.

Barker, Arthur E., ed. Milton: Modern Essays in Criticism. (Hi-Sch.). 1965. $2.95 pa. (ISBN 0-19-500720-4). Oxford Univ. Pr., NY.

Barnes, C. L. Parallels in Dante & Milton. 1917. $4.00 Hdbd. Folcroft Pr., PA.

Belloc, Hilaire. Milton. 1935. $12.50 Hdbd. (ISBN 0-404-00744-9). AMS Pr., NY.

Berry, W. Grinton. M. A. John Milton. 1909. $15.00 Hdbd. Folcroft Pr., PA.

Blake, William. Milton. Russell, A. & Maclagan, E., eds. 1907. $6.50 Hdbd. Folcroft Pr., PA.

Bridges, Robert. Milton's Prosody. 1921. $6.50 Hdbd. (ISBN 0-19-811629-2). Oxford Univ. Pr.,NY.

Bridges, Robert. Milton's Prosody with a Chapter on Accentual Verse & Notes. 1921. $4.50 Hdbd. Ridgeway Books, Pa.

Brown, Eleanor G. Milton's Blindness. (Studies in Milton, No. 22). 1970. (1934) $8.95 Hdbd. (ISBN 0-8383-1078-8). Haskell House Publ., NY.

Brown, Eleanor G. Milton's Blindness. 1968. $7.50 Hdbd. Octagon Books, NY.

Bush, Douglas. John Milton. 1964. $3.95 Hdbd. 1967. $1.95 pa. Macmillan Co., NY.

Bush, Douglas. Renaissance & English Humanism. (Congress University Paperbooks). 1939. $1.50 pa. (ISBN 0-8020-6008-0). Univ. of Toronto Pr., CAN.

Byse, Frank. Milton on the Continent. 1903. $10.00 Hdbd. Folcroft Pr., PA.

Candy, Hugh C. Milton the Individualist in Metre. 1930. $4.00 Hdbd. Folcroft Pr., PA.

Carey, John. Milton. (Arco Literary Critiques Ser). 1970. $3.95 Hdbd. (ISBN 0-668-02179-9); $1.95 pa. (ISBN 0-668-02178-0). Arco Publ. Co., NY.

Channing, William E. Character & Writings of John Milton. 1826. $4.00 Hdbd. Folcroft Pr., PA.

Channing, William E. Remarks on the Character and Writings of John Milton, 3rd ed. 1828. $5.00 Hdbd. (ISBN 0-404-01448-8). AMS Pr., NY.

Clark, Donald I. John Milton at St. Paul's School. 1964. Repr. of 1948 ed. $6.00 Hdbd. (ISBN 0-208-00148-4). Shoe String Pr., CT.

Coleridge, Samuel T. Seven Lecture on Shakespeare & Milton by the Late Samuel Taylor Coleridge. Collier, J. Payne, ed. 1856. $12.50 Hdbd. (ISBN 0-404-01617-0). AMS Pr., NY.

Coleridge, Samuel T. Seven Lectures on Shakespeare & Milton. (Research & Source Works Ser., No. 276). 1969. (1856) ed. $16.50 Hdbd. (ISBN 0-8337-0618-7). Burt Franklin, NY.

Cooke, John. John Milton 1608–1674. 1908. $15.00 Hdbd. Folcroft Pr., PA.

Corson, Hiram. Introduction to the Prose & Poetical Works of John Milton. (1899). $8.75 Hdbd. (ISBN 0-911858-11-3). Phaeton Pr., NY.

Critical Essays on Milton. $4.75 Hdbd. Peter Smith Publ., MA.

Curry, Walter C. Milton's Ontology, Cosmogony, & Physics. (Illus.). 1957. $1.95 pa. (ISBN 0-8131-0102-6). Univ. Pr. of Ky., KY.

Daiches, David. Milton. 1966. $1.65 pa. (ISBN 0-393-00347-7). W. W. Norton, NY.

Daiches, David. Milton. 1966. $4.50 Hdbd. Hutchinson Univ. Library, NY.

Daniells, Roy. Milton, Mannerism & Baroque. 1963. $10.00 (ISBN 0-8020-5122-7). Univ. of Toronto Pr., CAN.

Darbishire, Helen. Milton's Paradise Lost. 1951. $4.00 Hdbd. Folcroft Pr., PA.

Darbishire, Helen, ed. Early Lives of Milton. 1971. (1932) $16.00 Hdbd.

(ISBN 0-403-00935-9). Scholarly Pr., MI.

De Selincourt, Ernest. English Poets & the National Ideal. 1915. $8.50 Hdbd. Folcroft Pr., PA.

Douglas, John. Milton Vindicated from the Charge of Plagarism Brought Against Him by Mr. Lauder. 1751. $5.50 Hdbd. (ISBN 0-404-02159-X). AMS Pr., NY.

Dowden. Edward. Milton in the Eighteenth Century 1701–1750. 1908. $3.00 Hdbd. Folcroft Pr., PA.

Downing, John. Testimonies & Criticisms Relating to the Life & Works of John Milton. 1903. $13.50 Hdbd. (ISBN 0-404-02175-1). AMS Pr., NY.

Edmonds, Cyrus R. John Milton: A Biography. 1851. $12.00 Hdbd. (ISBN 0-404-02247-2). AMS Pr., NY.

Edmonds, Cyrus R. John Milton: A Biography. 1851. $17.50 Hdbd. Folcroft Pr., PA.

Edmundson, George. Milton & Vondel. 1885. $10.00 Hdbd. (ISBN 0-404-02249-9). AMS Pr., NY.

Edmundson, George. Milton & Vondel. 1885. $17.50 Hdbd. Folcroft Pr., PA.

Eliot, Thomas Stearns. Note on the Verse of John Milton. 1971. (1936) $4.00 Hdbd. Lansdowne Pr., PA.

Emma, Ronald D. Milton's Grammar. 1964. $15.00 Hdbd. Folcroft Pr., PA.

Emma, Ronald D. & Shawcross, John T., eds. Language & Style in Milton. 1967. $11.50 Hdbd. (ISBN 0-8044-2162-5). Frederick Ungar, NY.

Evans, Robert O. Milton's Elisions. (Humanities Monographs Ser. No. 21). 1966. $2.00 pa. (ISBN 0-8130-0076-9). Univ. of Fla. Pr., FL.

Ferry, Anne D. Milton & the Miltonic Dryden. 1968. $7.00 text ed. (ISBN 0-674-57576-8). Harvard Univ. Pr., MA.

Fiore, Amadeus P. Th'upright Heart & Pure. 1968. $5.95 Hdbd. (J26430). Duquesne Univ. Pr., PA.

Firth, Charles H. Milton As an Historian. 1908. $4.00 Hdbd. Folcroft Pr., PA.

Fletcher, Harris F. Use of the Bible in Milton's Prose. (Studies in Milton Ser., No. 22). 1970. (1929) $6.95 Hdbd. (ISBN 0-8383-0974-7). Haskell House Publ., NY.

Fletcher, Harris F. Intellectual Development of John Milton. Vol. 2. 1956. $10.00 Hdbd. (ISBN 0-252-72492-5). Univ. of Ill. Pr., IL.

Flower, Desmond. Voltaire's Essay on Milton. 1954. $6.50 Hdbd. Folcroft Pr., PA.

French, Joseph M., ed. Life Records of John Milton 1608–1674, 5 Vols. 1966. (1958) Set—$75.00 Hdbd.; $15.00 ea. (ISBN 0-87752-039-9). Gordian Pr., NY.

French, Joseph M. Milton in Chancery. (1939) $26.00 Hdbd. (ISBN 0-8371-5721-8). Greenwood Pr., CT.

Fry, Alfred A. Lecture on Writings, Prose, & Poetic Character, Public & Personal, of John Milton. 1838. $5.00 Hdbd. (ISBN 0-404-02635-4). AMS Pr., NY.

Fry, Alfred A. Milton: Patriot & Poet. 1861. $5.00 Hdbd. (ISBN 0-404-02636-2). AMS Pr., NY.

Garnett, Richard. Life of John Milton. 1970. (1890) $10.00 Hdbd. (ISBN 0-404-02686-9). AMS Pr., NY

Gertsch, Alfred. Der Steigende Ruhm Miltons. 1927. $29.50 pa. Johnson Reprint. Corp., NY.

Gilman, Wilbur, ed. Milton's Rhetoric: Studies in His Defence of Liberty. 1970. $7.50 Hdbd. (ISBN 0-87753-018-1). Phaeton Pr., NY.

Gilman, Wilbur E. Milton's Rhetoric. 1971. (1939) $6.50 Hdbd. Lansdowne Pr., PA.

Gilman, Wilbur E. Milton's Rhetoric: Studies in His Defense of Liberty. 1939. $9.50 Hdbd. (ISBN 0-404-02775-X). AMS Pr., NY.

Good, John W. Studies in the Milton Tradition. 1915. $12.00 Hdbd. (ISBN 0-404-02862-4). AMS Pr., NY.

Good, John W. Studies in the Milton Tradition. 1915. $12.00 Hdbd. Johnson Reprint Corp., NY.

Grace, William J. Ideas in Milton. 1969. (1968). $6.50 Hdbd. (ISBN 0-268-00126-X); $2.95 pa. (ISBN 0-268-00331-9). Univ. of Notre Dame Pr., IN.

Grebanier, Bernard. Barron's Simplified Approach to Milton: Paradise Lost & Other Works. (Hi-Sch.). 1964. $0.95 pa. Barron Ed. Series, NY.

Grierson, Herbert. Criticism & Creation. 1949. $10.00 Hdbd. Folcroft Pr., PA.

Grierson, Herbert J. Milton & Wordsworth. 1960. $4.00 Hdbd. Barnes & Noble, NY.

Grolier Club. Catalogue of an Exhibition Commemorative of the Tercentenary of the Birth of John Milton, 1608–1908. 1908. $6.50 Hdbd. (ISBN 0-404-02937-X). AMS Pr., NY.

Halkett, John. Milton & the Idea of Matrimony: A Study of the Divorce Tracts & Paradise Lost. 1970. $6.50 Hdbd. (ISBN 0-300-01196-2). Yale Univ. Pr., CT.

Hamilton, G. Rostrevor. Hero or Fool. (Studies in Milton, No. 22). 1970. (1924). $2.95 pa. (ISBN 0-8383-0038-3). Haskell House Publ., NY.

Hamilton, G. Rostrevor. Hero or Fool: A Study of Milton's Satan. 1944. $5.00 Hdbd. Folcroft Pr., PA.

Hamilton, John A. Life of John Milton, Englishman. $6.50 Hdbd. Folcroft Pr., PA.

Hamilton, William D. Original Papers Illustrative of the Life & Writings of John Milton. 1859. $10.00 Hdbd. Folcroft Pr., PA.

Hamilton, William D. Original Papers Illustrative of the Life & Writings of John Milton. 1859. $15.00 Hdbd. Johnson Reprint Corp., NY.

Hamilton, William D., ed. Original Papers Illustrative of the Life & Writings of John Milton. 1859. $15.00 Hdbd. (ISBN 0-404-50175-3). AMS Pr., NY.

Hanford, James H. John Milton, Englishman. 1949. $1.45 pa. Crown Publ. Co., NY.

Hanford, James H. John Milton, Poet & Humanist. 1966. $6.00 Hdbd. (ISBN 0-8295-0050-2). Pr. of Case W. R. Univ., OH.

Hanford, James H. Milton Handbook. 4th ed. 1946. $4.00 Hdbd. (ISBN 0-390-40869-7). Appleton-Century-Croft, NY.

Hanford, James H. & Taaffe, James G. Milton Handbook. 5th ed. 1970. $5.75 Hdbd. (ISBN 0-390-40870-0). Appleton-Century-Croft, NY. ·

Hanford, James H., et al. Studies in Shakespeare. Milton & Donne. 1970. $7.50 Hdbd. (ISBN 0-87753-020-3). Phaeton Pr., NY.

Harding, Davis P. Milton & the Renaissance Ovid. 1946. $10.00 Hdbd. Ridgeway Bks., PA.

Harris, W. Melville. John Milton: Puritan, Patriot, Poet. $5.00 Hdbd. Folcroft Pr., PA.

Havens, Raymond D. Influence of Milton on English Poetry. 1961. (1922). $17.50 Hdbd. Russell & Russell Publ., NY.

Hayley, William. Life of Milton. 2nd ed. 1970. $17.50 Hdbd. (ISBN 0-8201-1081-7). Schol. Facsimiles & Reprints, FL.

Herford, Charles H. Dante & Milton. 1924. $5.00 Hdbd. Folcroft Pr., PA.

Herford, Charles H. Post-War Mind of Germany & Other Studies. 1927. $12.50 Hdbd. Folcroft Pr., PA.

Hillis, Newell D. Great Men As Prophets of a New Era. (Essay Index Reprint Ser). 1968. (1922) $8.00 Hdbd. (ISBN 0-8369-0541-5). Bks for Libraries, NY.

Hood, Edwin P. John Milton, the Patriot & Poet. 1852. $11.00 Hdbd. (ISBN 0-404-03319-9). AMS Pr., NY.

Hood, Edwin P. John Milton: The Patriot & the Poet. 1852. $17.50 Hdbd. Folcroft Pr., PA.

Hunter, Joseph. Milton, a Sheaf of Gleanings. 1850. $8.50 Hdbd. Folcroft Pr., PA.

Hunter, William B. Milton on the Nature of Man. 1946. $4.00 Hdbd. Folcroft Pr., PA.

Hunter, William B., et al. Bright Essence: Studies in Milton's Theology. 1970. $6.75 Hdbd. (ISBN 0-87480-061-7). Univ. of Utah Pr., UT.

Ivimey, Joseph. John Milton. 1833. $16.50 Hdbd. (ISBN 0-404-03509-4). AMS Pr., NY.

Ivimey, Joseph. John Milton: His Life & Times, Religious & Political Opinions. 1833. $30.00 Hdbd. Folcroft Pr., PA.

Jenks, Tudor. In the Days of Milton. 1905. $13.75 Hdbd. (ISBN 0-404-03559-0). AMS Pr., NY.

Johnson, Samuel. Six Chief Lives, from

Johnson's Lives of the Poets, with Macaulays' Life of Johnson. Arnold, Matthew, ed. 1968. (1881) $10.50 Hdbd. Russell & Russell, NY.

Kermode, John F., ed. Living Milton: Essays by Various Hands. $4.50 Hdbd. Barnes & Noble, NY.

Knight, G. Wilson. Chariot of Wrath: John Milton. 1942. $15.00 Hdbd. Ridgeway Bks., PA.

Kranidas, Thomas. Fierce Equation. 1965. $8.00 Hdbd. Humanities Pr., NY.

Laguardia, Eric. Nature Redeemed: The Imitation of Order in Three Renaissance Poems. 1966. $8.00 Hdbd. Humanities Pr., NY.

Langdon, Ida. Milton's Theory of Poetry & Fine Art. 1965. (1924) $8.50 Hdbd. Russell & Russell, NY.

Larson, Martin A. Modernity of Milton. 1927. $8.50 Hdbd. Folcroft Pr., NY.

Larson, Martin A. Modernity of Milton: A Theological & Philosophical Interpretation. 1971. $9.00 Hdbd. (ISBN 0-404-03880-8). AMS Pr., NY.

Leach, A. F. Milton As Schoolboy & Schoolmaster. 1908. $3.00 Hdbd. Folcroft Pr., PA.

Le Comte, Edward S. Yet Once More: Verbal & Psychological Pattern in Milton. 1953. $15.00 Hdbd. Ridgeway Bks., PA.

Le Comte, Edward S. Yet One More. 1953. $9.25 Hdbd. (ISBN 0-404-03918-9). AMS Pr., NY.

Lijegren, Sten B. Studies in Milton. (Studies in Milton, No. 22). 1969. (1918) $6.95 Hdbd. (ISBN 0-8383-0718-3). Haskell House Publ., NY.

Lijegren, Sten B. Studies in Milton. 1918. $7.50 Hdbd. Folcroft Pr., PA.

Macaulay, Rose. Milton. 2nd ed. (Great Lives Ser., No. 26). 1968. (1934). $2.95 pa. (L/35-5542). Dufour Editions, PA.

Macaulay, Thomas B. Milton. 1900. $8.75 Hdbd. (ISBN 0-8371-4094-3). Greenwood Pr., CT.

Madsen, William G. From Shadowy Types to Truth: Studies in Milton's Symbolism. 1968. $6.00 Hdbd. (ISBN 0-300-00748-5). Yale Univ. Pr., CT.

Manuel, M. Seventeenth Century Critics & Biographers of Milton. 1962. $12.50 Hdbd. Folcroft Pr., PA.

Marilla, Esmond L. Milton & Modern Man. 1968. $6.00 Hdbd. (ISBN 0-8173-7307-1). Univ. of Ala. Pr., AL.

Marsh, John F. Papers Connected with Affairs of Milton & His Family. 1851. $8.50 Hdbd. Folcroft Pr., PA.

Martyn, W. Carlos. Life & Times of John Milton. 1866. $20.00 Hdbd. Folcroft Pr., PA.

Martz, L., ed. Milton: A Collection of Critical Essays. $5.95 Hdbd. (ISBN 0-13-583146-6). Prentice-Hall, NY.

Martz, L., ed. Milton: A Collection of Critical Essays. 1966. $1.95 pa. (ISBN 0-13-583138-5, Spec). Prentice-Hall, NY.

Masson, David. Life of John Milton: Narrated in Connection with the Political, Literary & Ecclesiastical History of His Time, 7 vols. $73.50 Hdbd. Peter Smith Publ., MA.

Masson, David. Three Devils: Luther's, Milton's & Goethe's. 1970. (1874) $13.00 Hdbd. (ISBN 0-404-04247-3). AMS Pr., NY.

Masterman, John H. Age of Milton. 1897. $12.50 Hdbd. (ISBN 0-404-04248-1). AMS Pr., NY.

Milton, John. Milton on Education: The Tractate of Education with Supplementary Extracts from Other Writings of Milton. Ainsworth, Oliver M., ed. 1971. (1928) $15.00 Hdbd. (ISBN 0-403-01110-8). Scholarly Pr., MI.

Milton, John. Portraits, Prints & Writings of John Milton. 1908. $7.50 Hdbd. Folcroft Pr., PA.

Mohl, Ruth. John Milton & His Commonplace Book. 1969. $11.00 Hdbd. (ISBN 0-8044-2631-7). Frederick Ungar, NY.

Mohl, Ruth. Studies in Spenser, Milton, & the Theory of Monarchy. 1962. $4.50 Hdbd. (ISBN 0-8044-2633-3). Frederick Ungar, NY.

Morris, J. W. John Milton. 1862. $15.00 Hdbd. Folcroft Pr., PA.

Morrison, William. Milton & Liberty. 1909. $5.00 Hdbd. Folcroft Pr., PA.

Murr, Kenneth. John Milton. 2nd ed. 1960. $4.00 Hdbd. Barnes & Noble, NY.

Murray, Patrick. Milton: The Modern Phase: A Survey of Twentieth-Century Criticism. 1967. $5.00 Hdbd. Barnes & Noble, NY.

Mutschmann, H. Milton's Eyesight & the Chronology of His Works. (Studies in Milton, No. 22). 1971. $6.95 Hdbd. (ISBN 0-8383-1325-6). Haskell House Publ., NY.

Mutschmann, H. Milton's Projected Epic on the Rise & Future Greatness of the Britannic Nation. 1936. $10.00 Hdbd. Folcroft Pr., PA.

Mutschmann, H. Secret of John Milton. 1925. $10.00 Hdbd. Folcroft Pr., PA.

Myhr, Ivar L. Evolution & Practice of Milton's Epic Theory. 1942. $6.50 Hdbd. Folcroft Pr., PA.

Nicolson, Marjorie H. John Milton: A Reader's Guide to His Poetry. (Orig.). $2.95 pa. Farrar, Straus, & Giroux, NY.

Nicolson, Marjorie H. John Milton: A Reader's Guide to His Poetry. 1971. $12.00 Hdbd. (ISBN 0-374-96106-9). Octagon Books Inc., NY.

Nicolson, Marjorie H. Milton's Editors & Commentators. (Studies in Milton Ser., No. 22). 1969. (1931) $13.95 Hdbd. (ISBN 0-8383-0604-7). Haskell House Publ., NY.

Nicolson, Marjorie H. Milton's Editors & Commentators from Patrick Hume to Henry John Todd 1695–1801: A Study in Critical Views & Methods. 1931. $14.50 Hdbd. (ISBN 0-19-811690-X). Oxford Univ. Pr., NY.

Nicolson, Marjorie H. Notes on Some Miltonic Usages: Their Background & Later Development. 1938. $8.50 Hdbd. Folcroft Pr., PA.

Orchard, Thomas N. Milton's Astronomy. 1913. $12.50 Hdbd. Folcroft Pr., PA.

Osgood, Charles G. Classical Mythology of Milton's English Poems. 1900. $7.00 Hdbd. (ISBN 0-697-00014-1). William Brown, NY.

Osgood, Charles G. Classical Mythology of Milton's English Poems. 1964. (1900) $5.00 Hdbd. (ISBN 0-87752-080-1). Gordian Pr., NY.

Osgood, Charles G. Classical Mythology of Milton's English Poems. (Studies in Comparative Literature Ser., No. 35). 1969. (1900) $3.95 Hdbd. (ISBN 0-8383-0603-9). Haskell House Publ., NY.

Parker, William R. Milton: A Biography, 2 Vols. 1968. $48.00 Hdbd. (ISBN 0-19-811619-5). Oxford Univ. Pr., NY.

Parker, William R. Milton's Contemporary Reputation. (Studies in Milton, No. 22). 1970. (1940) $9.95 Hdbd. (ISBN 0-8383-1129-6). Haskell House Publ., NY.

Parker, William R. Milton's Contemporary Reputation. 1971. (1940) $10.75 Hdbd. (ISBN 0-374-96255-3). Octagon Books Inc., NY.

Parker, William R. Milton's Contemporary Reputation. 1940. $20.00 Hdbd. Ridgeway Bks., PA.

Patrick, J. Max, ed. Samla Studies in

Milton: 1953. $4.50 pa. (ISBN 0-8130-0183-8). Univ. of Fla. Pr., FL.

Pattison, Mark. Milton. Morley, John, ed. 1887. $12.50 Hdbd. (ISBN 0-404-51725-0). AMS Pr., NY.

Pearsau, R. Spenser & Milton. (gr. 10–12). 1970. $1.52 pa. (ISBN 0-03-080393-4). Holt, Rinehart & Winston, NY.

Pointon, Marcia R. Milton & English Art. $14.50 Hdbd. (ISBN 0-8020-1708-8). Univ. of Toronto Pr., CAN.

Pommer, Henry F. Milton & Melville. 1970. (1950) $6.00 Hdbd. (ISBN 0-8154-0338-0). Cooper Sq. Pr., NY.

Racine, Louis. Life of Milton. 1930. $12.50 Hdbd. Folcroft Pr., PA.

Raleigh, Walter A. Milton. 1967. Repr. $8.75 Hdbd. Blom, NY.

Reaske, Christopher. Monarch Literature Notes on the Poetry of Milton. $1.00 pa. Monarch Pr., NY.

Ricks, Christopher. Milton's Grand Style. 1963. $4.50 Hdbd. (ISBN 0-19-811608-X); $1.50 pa. (ISBN 0-19-881127-6). Oxford Univ. Pr., NY.

Roberts, Margaret K. John Milton. 1904. $5.00 Hdbd. AMS Pr., NY.

Rudrum, Alan, ed. John Milton. (Modern Judgement Ser). 1970. (1968) $2.50 pa. (ISBN 0-87695-100-0). Aurora Publs., TN.

Samuel, Irene. Plato & Milton. 1965. $1.45 pa. (ISBN 0-8014-9092-8). Cornell Univ. Pr., NY.

Saurat, Denis. Blake & Milton. 1965. (1935) $7.50 Hdbd. Russell & Russell, NY.

Saurat, Denis. Milton, Man & Thinker. 1925. $16.00 Hdbd. (ISBN 0-404-05565-6). AMS Pr., NY.

Saurat, Denis. Milton, Man & Thinker. (Studies in Milton, No. 22). 1970. (1925) $13.95 Hdbd. (ISBN 0-8383-1093-1). Haskell House Publ., NY.

Scherpbier, H. Milton in Holland. 1933. $17.50 Hdbd. Folcroft Pr., PA.

Schultz, H. Milton & Forbidden Knowledge. 1955. $11.00 pa. Kraus Reprint Co., NY.

Senior, H. L. John Milton, the Supreme Englishman. $4.50 Hdbd. Folcroft Pr., PA.

Sensabaugh, George F. Milton in Early America. 1964. $9.00 Hdbd. (ISBN 0-691-06077-0). Princeton Univ. Pr., NJ.

Sewell, Arthur. Study in Milton's Christian Doctrine. 1967. $6.50 Hdbd. Shoe String Pr., CT.

Sharma, K. L. Milton Criticism in the Twentieth Century. 1971. $7.50 Hdbd. Lawrence Verry Inc., CT.

Shawcross, John T., ed. Milton: The Critical Heritage. (Critical Heritage Ser). 1970. $8.50 Hdbd. Barnes & Noble, NY.

Simmonds, James D., ed. Milton Studies: Vol. 1. 1969. $8.95 pa. (ISBN 0-8229-3174-5). Univ. of Pittsburgh Pr., PA.

Simmonds, James D. Milton Studies: Vol. 2. (Milton Studies Ser). $9.95 Hdbd. (ISBN 0-8229-3194-X). Vol. 3. 1971. $9.95 Hdbd. (ISBN 0-8229-3218-0). Univ. of Pittsburgh Pr., PA.

Skeat, Walter W. John Milton's Epitaphium Damonis. 1933. $7.50 Hdbd. Folcroft Pr., PA.

Smith, I. P. Milton & His Modern Critics. 1967. (1940) $4.00 Hdbd. Shoe String Pr., CT.

Sobol, Donald J. Milton the Model A. (Elem.). 1971. $3.50 Hdbd. (ISBN 0-8178-4831-2); PLB $3.36 (ISBN 0-8178-4832-0). Harvey House, NY.

Sprott, S. Ernest. Milton's Art of Prosody. 1953. $12.50 Hdbd. Folcroft Pr., PA.

Steadman, John M. Milton & the Renaissance Hero. 1967. $6.50 Hdbd. (ISBN 0-19-811652-7). Oxford Univ. Pr., NY.

Stein, Arnold, et al. Critical Essays on Milton from ELH. ELH Magazine, ed. 1969. $2.45 pa. (ISBN 0-8018-1094-9). Johns Hopkins Pr., MD.

Stevens, David H. Milton Papers. 1927. $10.00 Hdbd. Folcroft Pr., PA.

Stevens, David H. Milton Papers. 1927. $5.00 Hdbd. (ISBN 0-404-06262-8). AMS Pr., NY.

Summers, Joseph H., ed. Lyric & Dramatic Milton. 1965. $5.50 Hdbd. (ISBN 0-231-02863-6). Columbia Univ. Pr., NY.

Symmons, Charles. Life of John Milton. 1970. (1822) $25.50 Hdbd. (ISBN 0-404-06325-X). AMS Pr., NY.

Symmons, Charles. Life of John Milton. 1810. $25.00 Hdbd. Folcroft Pr., PA.

Taylor, George C. Milton's Use of Du Bartas. (1968) $7.00 Hdbd. Octagon Books, NY.

Telleen, John M. Milton Dans la Litterature Francaise. (Fr). 1904. $15.00 Hdbd. (ISBN 0-8337-4446-1). Burt Franklin, NY.

Thompson, Elbert. Essays of Milton. 1910. $7.50 Hdbd. Folcroft Pr., PA.

Thompson, Elbert N. Essays on Milton. 1968. (1914) $7.00 Hdbd. Russell & Russell Publ., NY.

Thorpe, James. Milton Criticism: Selections from Four Centuries. 1966. $11.00 Hdbd. Octagon Books, NY.

Thorpe, James, ed. Milton Criticism: Selections from Four Centuries. 1969. $2.45 pa. Macmillan Co., NY.

Tillyard, Eustace M. Milton. (Writers & Their Work Ser No. 26). $2.25 Hdbd.; $1.00 pa. (26). British Book Center, NY.

Tillyard, Eustace M. Milton. 1967. $2.45 pa. Macmillan Co., NY.

Tillyard, Eustace M. Milton. rev. ed. 1967. $5.00 Hdbd. Barnes & Noble, NY.

Tillyard, Eustace M. Miltonic Setting. 1963. $3.50 Hdbd. Barnes & Noble, NY.

Tillyard, Eustace M. Studies in Milton. 1960. $3.50 Hdbd. Barnes & Noble, NY.

Todd, Henry J. Some Account of the Life & Writings of John Milton. 1826. $30.00 Hdbd. Folcroft Pr., PA.

Todd, Henry J. Some Account of the Life & Writings of John Milton. 1826. $16.50 Hdbd. (ISBN 0-404-06469-8). AMS Pr., NY.

Toland, John. Life of John Milton. 1761. $30.00 Hdbd. Folcroft Pr., PA.

Treip, Mindele. Milton's Punctuation & Changing English Usage 1582-1676. 1970. $8.75 Hdbd. (ISBN 0-416-13650-8). Barnes & Noble, NY.

Trent, William P. John Milton. 1899. $20.00 Hdbd. Folcroft Pr., PA.

Trent, William P. John Milton: A Short Study of His Life & Works. 1899. $13.50 Hdbd. (ISBN 0-404-06523-6). AMS Pr., NY.

Tuckwell, W. Lycidas: A Monograph. 1911. $8.50 Hdbd. Folcroft Pr., PA.

Tuve, Rosemond. Essays by Rosemond Tuve: On Spenser, Herbert, & Milton. Roche, Thomas P., Jr., ed. 1970. $10.00 Hdbd. (ISBN 0-691-06171-8). Princeton Univ. Pr., NJ.

The University of Michigan, English Department Studies in Shakespeare. Milton & Donne. (Studies in Poetry Ser., No. 38). 1969. (1925) $11.95 Hdbd. (ISBN 0-8383-0638-1). Haskell House Publ., NY.

Visiak, E. H. Portent of Milton: Some Aspects of His Genius. 1969. (1958) $6.00 Hdbd. Humanities Pr., NY.

Visiak, E. H. Animus Against Milton. 1945. $3.50 Hdbd. Folcroft Pr., PA.

Wagenknecht, Edward. Personality of Milton. 1970. $5.00 Hdbd. (ISBN 0-8061-0916-5). Univ. of Oklahoma Pr., OK.

Whaler, James. Counterpoint & Symbol: An Inquiry into the Rhythm of Milton's Epic Style. 1956. $15.00 Hdbd. Folcroft Pr., PA.

White, Thomas H. Review of Johnson's Criticism on the Style of Milton's English Prose. 1818. $5.00 Hdbd. (ISBN 0-404-06937-1). AMS Pr., NY.

Williams, Charles. English Poetic Mind. 1963. (1932) $7.50 Hdbd. Russell & Russell Publ., NY.

Williamson, George. Milton & Others. 2nd ed. 1970. $7.50 Hdbd. (ISBN 0-226-89937-3). Univ. of Chicago Pr., IL.

Williamson, George C. Milton. 1905. $15.00 Hdbd. Folcroft Pr., PA.

Williamson, George C. Milton Tercentenary: The Portraits, Prints & Writings on John Milton. 1967. (1908) $19.50 Hdbd. (ISBN 0-8337-3808-9). Burt Franklin, NY.

Wittriech, Joseph A. Romantics on Milton: Formal Essays & Critical Asides. 1970. $15.00 Hdbd. (ISBN 0-8295-0168-1). Pr. of Case-Western Reserve Univ., OH.

Wolfe, Don M. Milton & His England. 1971. $10.00 Hdbd. Princeton Univ. Pr., NJ.

Wolfe, Don M. Milton & His England. 1971. $10.00 Hdbd. (ISBN 0-691-06200-5). Princeton Univ. Pr., NJ.

Wood, Louis A. Form & Origin of Milton's Antitrinitarian Conception. 1911. $15.00 Hdbd. Folcroft Pr., PA.

Woodberry, George E. Great Writers. (Essay Index Reprint Ser). 1907. $8.00 Hdbd. (ISBN 0-8369-1008-7). Books for Libraries, NY.

Wynkoop, William M. Three Children of the Universe: Emerson's View of Shakespeare, Bacon & Milton. 1966. $7.25 Hdbd. Humanities Pr., NY.

Young, Richard B., et al. Three Studies in the Renaissance: Sidney, Johnson, Milton. (Yale Studies in English No. 138). 1969. (1958) $8.00 Hdbd. (ISBN 0-208-00780-6). Shoe String Pr., CT.

Milton John—Areopagitica

Gilman, Wilbur E. Milton's Rhetoric, Studies in His Defense of Liberty. 1939. $6.50 Hdbd. Folcroft Pr., PA.

Jebb, Richard C. Milton's Areopagitica. 1918. $15.00 Hdbd. Folcroft Pr., PA.

Jebb, Richard C. Milton's Areopagitica. 1872. $5.00 Hdbd. (ISBN 0-404-03556-6). AMS Pr., NY.

Milton, John. Areopagitica, 1644. Arber, Edward, ed. $4.00 Hdbd. (ISBN 0-87556-219-1). Albert Saifer, PA.

Ould, Hermon, ed. Freedom of Expression. 1970. (1944) $7.50 Hdbd. (ISBN 0-8046-0968-3). Kennikat Pr., NY.

Milton, John—Bibliography

Brown, Eleanor G. Milton's Blindness. 1971. (1934) $6.50 Hdbd. Lansdowne Pr., PA.

Fletcher, Harris F. Contributions to a Milton Bibliography 1800-1930: (Illinois Studies in Language & Literature). 1969. (1931) $6.00 Hdbd. Johnson Reprint Corp., NY.

Fletcher, Harris F. Contributions to a Milton Bibliography, 1800-1930. 1967. (1931) $8.50 Hdbd. Russell & Russell Publ., NY.

Grolier Club. Catalogue of an Exhibition Commemorative of the Tercentenary of the Birth of John Milton, 1608-1908. 1908. $6.50 Hdbd. (ISBN 0-404-02937-X). AMS Pr., NY.

Haley, William. Life of Milton. 1971. $17.50 Hdbd. Lansdowne Pr., PA.

Hanford, James H., ed. Milton. (Orig.). $1.25 text ed. (ISBN 0-390-40871-9, Gtree). Appleton-Century-Crofts, NY.

Huckabay, Calvin. John Milton: A Bibliographical Supplement. 1960. $32.50 Hdbd. (ISBN 0-404-04346-1). AMS Pr., NY.

Mutschmann, H. Milton's Eyesight & the Chronology of His Works. 1924. $7.50 Hdbd. Folcroft Pr., PA.

Reader's Guide to John Milton. 1971. $10.00 Hdbd. (ISBN 0-8277-0420-8). British Book Center, NY.

Stevens, David H. Reference Guide to Milton from 1800 to the Present Day. 1967. (1930) $10.00 Hdbd. Russell & Russell Publ., NY.

Thompson, Elbert N. John Milton: A Topical Bibliography. 1916. $5.50 Hdbd. (ISBN 0-404-06398-5). AMS Pr., NY.

Thompson, Elbert N. John Milton: Topical Bibliography. 1916. $15.00 Hdbd. Folcroft Pr., PA.

Todd, Henry J. Some Account of the Life & Writings of John Milton. 1826. $16.50 Hdbd. (ISBN 0-404-06469-8). AMS Pr., NY.

Milton, John—Comus

Broadbent, J. B. Comus & Samson Agonistes by John Milton: Critical Analysis. Daiches, David, ed. (Studies in English Literature Ser). (Hi-Sch.). 1961. $1.00 pa. Barron's Educ. Series, NY.

Demaray, John G. Milton & the Masque Tradition: The Early Poems, Arcades & Comus. 1968. $6.00 Hdbd. (ISBN 0-674-57550-4). Harvard Univ. Pr., MA.

Diekhoff, John S., ed. Maske at Ludlow: Essays on Milton's Comus. 1968. $8.95 Hdbd. (ISBN 0-8295-0134-7). Pr. of Case-Western Reserve Univ., OH.

Fletcher, Angus. Transcendental Masque: An Essay on Milton's Comus. 1971. $8.50 Hdbd. (ISBN 0-8014-0620-X). Cornell Univ. Pr., NY.

Rudrum, Alan, ed. Milton: Comus & Shorter Poems. (Macmillan Critical Commentaries). 1967. $1.00 pa. Fernhill House, NY.

Stevens, David H. Milton Papers. 1927. $5.00 Hdbd. (ISBN 0-404-06262-8). AMS Pr., NY.

Milton, John—Dictionaries, Indexes, Etc.

Gilbert, Allan H. Geographical Dictionary of Milton. 1968. (1919) $9.50 Hdbd. Russell & Russell Publ., NY.

Gilbert, Allan H. Geographical Dictionary of Milton. 1971. (1919) $7.50 Hdbd. Lansdowne Pr., PA.

Le Comte, Edward S. Milton Dictionary. 1961. $14.50 Hdbd. (ISBN 0-404-03917-0). AMS Pr., NY.

Lockwood, Laura E. Lexicon to the English Poetical Works of John Milton. 1907. $50.00 Hdbd. Folcroft Pr., PA.

Todd, Henry J. Some Account of the Life & Writings of John Milton. 1826. $16.50 Hdbd. (ISBN 0-404-06469-8). AMS Pr., NY.

Milton, John—History of England

Carpenter, William. Life & Times of John Milton. 1836. $20.00 Hdbd. Folcroft Pr., PA.

Nicholas, Constance. Introduction & Notes for Milton's History of Britain. 1957. $5.00 Hdbd. (ISBN 0-252-00050-1); $4.00 pa. (ISBN 0-252-72488-7). Univ. of Illinois Pr., IL.

Milton, John—Juvenile Literature

Hobbs, Mary. Young John Milton. (Young Biographies Ser). (Elem.-Jr. Hi. Hi-Sch.). 1969. $3.50 Hdbd. Roy Publ., NY.

Strausse, Flora. John Milton. (Jr. Hi. Hi-Sch.). 1960. $4.50 Hdbd. (ISBN 0-8149-0411-4). Vanguard Pr., NY.

Wedgwood, C. V. Milton & His World. (Jr. Hi–Hi-Sch.). 1969. $5.00 Hdbd. (ISBN 0-8098-3082-5). Henry Z. Walck, NY.

Milton, John—Knowledge and Learning

Bailey, M. L. Milton & Jakob Boehme. (Studies in Comparative Literature Ser., No. 35). 1969. (1914) $8.95 Hdbd. (ISBN 0-8383-0505-9). Haskell House Publ., NY.

Banks, Theodore H. Milton's Imagery. 1950. $10.00 Hdbd. (ISBN 0-404-00498-9). AMS Pr., NY.

Cawley, Robert R. Milton & the Literature of Travel. 1970. (1951) $6.50 text ed. (ISBN 0-87752-015-1). Gordian Pr., NY.

Carry, Walter C. Milton's Ontology, Cosmogony, & Physics. 1957. $1.95 pa. (ISBN 0-8131-0102-6). Univ. Pr. of Kentucky, KY.

Fetcher, Harris F. Intellectual Development of John Milton, Vol. 2. 1956. $10.00 Hdbd. (ISBN 0-252-72492-5). Univ. of Illinois Pr., IL.

Fetcher, Harris F. Milton's Rabbinical Readings. 1967. (1930) $10.00 Hdbd. (ISBN 0-208-00335-5). Shoe String Pr., CT.

Fetcher, Harris F. Milton's Rabbinical Readings. 1967. (1930) $7.50 Hdbd. (ISBN 0-87752-034-8). Gordian Pr., NY.

Spaeth, Sigmund. Milton's Knowledge of Music. 1963. $1.75 pa. (ISBN 0-472-06082-1, 82). Univ. of Michigan Pr., MI.

Stein, Arnold. Heroic Knowledge: An Interpretation of Paradise Regained & Samson Agonistes. 1965. (1957) $6.00 Hdbd. (ISBN 0-208-00317-7). Shoe String Pr., CT.

Svendsen, Kester. Milton & Science. 1956. $11.50 Hdbd. (ISBN 0-8371-2410-7). Greenwood Pr., CT.

Warren, William F. Universe As Pictured in Milton's Paradise Lost. 1915. $5.00 Hdbd. Folcroft Pr., PA.

Wittreich, Joseph A., Jr., ed. Calm of Mind: Tercentenary Essays on Paradise Regained & Samson Agonistes. 1971. $15.00 Hdbd. (ISBN 0-8295-0214-9). Pr. of Case WR Univ., OH.

Milton, John—Political and Social Views

Barker, Arthur E. Milton & the Puritan Dilemma, 1641–1660. 1955. $12.50 Hdbd. (ISBN 0-8020-5025-5). Univ. of Toronto Pr., CAN.

Fixler, Michael. Milton & the Kingdoms of God. 1964. $6.50 Hdbd. (ISBN 0-8101-0092-4). Northwestern Univ. Pr., IL.

Ivimey, Joseph. John Milton. 1833. $16.50 Hdbd. (ISBN 0-404-03509-4). AMS Pr., NY.

Ivimey, Joseph. John Milton: His Life & Times, Religious & Political Opinions. 1833. $30.00 Hdbd. Folcroft Pr., PA.

Morand, Paul P. Effects of His Political Life Upon John Milton. 1939. $15.00 Hdbd. Folcroft Pr., PA.

Ross, Malcolm M. Milton's Royalism: A Study of the Conflict of Symbol & Ideas in the Poems. 1970. (1943) $8.50 Hdbd. Russell & Russell, NY.

Sensabaugh, George. That Grand Whig Milton. $10.75 Hdbd. Benjamin Blom, NY.

Wolfe, Don M. Milton in the Puritan Revolution. 1963. $8.50 Hdbd. Humanities Pr., NY.

Milton, John—Religion and Ethics

Acton, Henry. Religious Opinions & Example of Milton, Locke, & Newton. 1833. $5.00 Hdbd. (ISBN 0-404-00283-8). AMS Pr., NY.

Barker, Arthur E. Milton & the Puritan Dilemma, 1641–1660. 1955. $12.50 Hdbd. (ISBN 0-8020-5025-5). Univ. of Toronto Pr., CAN.

Conklin, George N. Biblical Criticism & Heresy in Milton. 1949. $12.50 Hdbd. Ridgeway Bks., PA.

Conklin, George N. Biblical Criticism & Heresy in Milton. 1971. $7.50 Hdbd. (ISBN 0-374-91905-4). Octagon Book Inc., NY.

Eastland, Elizabeth W. Milton's Ethics. 1942. $5.00 Hdbd. Folcroft Press, PA.

Empson, William. Milton's God. 1961. $10.00 Hdbd. New Directions, NY.

Fletcher, Harris F. Use of the Bible in Milton's Prose. $6.00 Hdbd. Gordon Publs., NY.

Hughes, Merritt Y. Ten Perspectives on Milton. 1965. $8.75 Hdbd. Yale Univ. Pr., CT.

Hunter, William B., Jr., et al. Bright Essence: Studies in Milton's Theology. 1971. price "n.g." Hdbd. (ISBN 0-87480-061-7). Univ. of Utah Pr., UT.

Ivimey, Joseph. John Milton. 1833. $16.50 Hdbd. (ISBN 0-404-03509-4). AMS Pr., NY.

Ivimey, Joseph. John Milton: His Life & Times, Religious & Political Opinions. 1833. $30.00 Hdbd. Folcroft Pr., PA.

Kelley, Maurice. This Great Argument. $6.00 Hdbd. Peter Smith Publs., MA.

Kurth, Burton O. Milton & Christian Heroism: Biblical Epic Themes & Forms in Seventeenth-Century England. $5.00 Hdbd. (ISBN 0-208-00099-2). Shoe String Pr., CT.

McDill, Joseph M. Milton & the Pattern of Calvinism. 1942. $25.00 Hdbd. Folcroft Pr., PA.

McLachlan, H. Religious Opinions of Milton, Locke, & Newton. 1941. $20.00 Hdbd. Folcroft Pr., PA.

Morris, Joseph W. John Milton: A Vindication, Specially from the Charge of

Arianism. 1862. $6.50 Hdbd. (ISBN 0-404-04502-2). AMS Pr., NY.

Muldrow, George M. Milton & the Drama of the Soul: A Study of the Theme of the Restoration of Man in Milton's Later Poetry. (Studies in English Literature, Vol. 51). 1970. $11.25 Hdbd. Humanities Pr., NY.

Patrides, C. A. Milton & the Christian Tradition. 1966. $9.00 Hdbd. (ISBN 0-19-811632-2). Oxford Univ. Pr., NY.

Sewell, Arthur. Study in Milton's Christian Doctrine. 1967. Repr. $6.50 Hdbd. (5). Shoe String Pr., CT.

Sewell, Arthur. Study in Milton's Christian Doctrine. 1939. $12.50 Hdbd. Folcroft Pr., PA.

Sims, James H. Bible in Milton's Epics. 1962. $8.00 Hdbd. (ISBN 0-8130-0205-2). Univ. of Fla. Pr., FL.

Stroup, Thomas B. Religious Rite & Ceremony in Milton's Poetry. 1968. $4.50 Hdbd. (ISBN 0-8131-1149-8). Univ. Pr. of Ky., KY.

Whiting, George W. Milton & This Pendant World. 1969. (1958) $8.50 Hdbd. Octagon Books, Inc., NY.

Milton, John—Samson Agonistes

Broadbent, J. B. Comus & Samson Agonistes by John Milton: Critical Analysis. Daiches, David, ed. (Studies in English Literature Ser). (Hi-Sch.). 1961. $1.00 pa. Barron Educational Series, NY.

Crump, Galbraith M., ed. Twentieth Century Interpretations of Samson Agonistes. 1968. $4.95 Hdbd. (ISBN 0-13-790931-4). $1.25 pa. (ISBN 0-13-790923-3). Prentice-Hall, NY.

Kreipe, Christian E. Milton's Samson Agonistes. 1926. $20.00 Hdbd. Folcraft Pr., PA.

Krouse, F. Michael. Milton's Samson & the Christian Tradition. 1949. $7.50 Hdbd. (ISBN 0-404-03783-6). AMS Pr., NY.

Parker, William R. Milton's Debt to Greek Tragedy in Samson Agonistes. 1969. (1937) $6.50 Hdbd. (ISBN 0-389-01169-X). Barnes & Noble, NY.

Rudrum, Alan, ed. Milton: Samson Agonistes. (Macmillan Critical Commentaries). 1969. $1.00 pa. Fernhill House, NY.

Stein, Arnold. Heroic Knowledge: An Interpretation of Paradise Regained & Samson Agonistes. 1965. (1957) $6.00 Hdbd. (ISBN 0-208-00317-7). Shoe String Pr., CT.

Visiak, E. H. Milton's Agonistes. (Studies in Milton, No. 22). 1970. (1922) $4.95 pa. (ISBN 0-8383-0102-9). Haskell House Publ., NY.

Visiak, E. H. Milton's Agonistes: A Metaphysical Criticism. 1922. $6.50 Hdbd. Folcroft Pr., PA.

Wittreich, Joseph A., Jr., ed. Calm of Mind: Tercentenary Essays on Paradise Regained & Samson Agonistes. 1971. $15.00 Hdbd. (ISBN 0-8295-0214-9). Pr. of Case WR Univ., OH

Milton, John—Sources

Fletcher, Harris. Use of the Bible in Milton's Prose. (1929) $8.00 Hdbd. Johnson Reprint Corp., NY.

McColley, Grant. Milton's Technique of Source Adaptation. (Studies in Milton, No. 22). 1970. (1938) $2.95 pa. (ISBN 0-8383-0053-7). Haskell House Publ., NY.

Prince, Frank T. Italian Element in Milton's Verse. 1954. $5.00 Hdbd. (ISBN 0-19-811569-5). Oxford Univ. Pr., NY.

Whiting, George W. Milton's Literary Milieu. 1964. (1939) $9.50 Hdbd. Russell & Russell, NY.

Moliere, Jean Baptiste Poquelin

Bulgakov, Mikhail. Life of Monsieur De Moliere. Ginsburg, Mirra, tr. 1970. $5.95 Hdbd. Funk & Wagnalls, NY.

Calandra, Denis M. Misanthrope Notes. Incl. Bourgeois Gentleman Notes. $1.00 pa. (ISBN 0-8220-0843-2). Cliffs Notes, NB.

Chapman, Percy A. Spirit of Moliere. Bede, Jean-Albert, ed. 1965. (1940) $8.50 Hdbd. Russell & Russell Publ., NY.

Charden, Henri. Nouveaux Documents Sur les Comediens De Campagne et la Vie De Moliere, 2 Vols. (1886–1905 Reprint 1968). $35.00 Hdbd. (ISBN 0-8337-0536-9) Burt Franklin, NY.

Crabb, Daniel M. Critical Study Guide to Moliere's Tartuffe & Other Plays. abr ed. 1966. $1.00 pa. Littlefield, Adams & Co., NJ.

Desfeuilles, Arthur. Lexique De la Langue De Moliere. Vol. 1-2. (Fr). 1900. Set—$38.50 Hdbd. (ISBN 0-8337-4744-4). Burt Franklin, NY.

Desfeuilles, Arthur. Notice Bibliographique De Moliere. (Bibliography & Reference Ser., No. 343). (Fr). 1970. (1893) $25.00 Hdbd. (ISBN 0-8337-0839-2). Burt Franklin, NY.

Faguet, Emile. Rousseau Centre Moliere. (1912) $19.50 Hdbd. (ISBN 0-8337-4951-X). Burt Franklin, NY.

Fernandez, Ramon. Moliere: Man Seen Through the Plays. Follett, Wilson, tr. 1960. $3.75 Hdbd. (ISBN 0-8090-6990-3); $1.45 pa. (ISBN 0-8090-0520-4). Hill & Wang, NY.

Fritsche, H. Moliere-Studien: Ein Namenbuch Zu Moliere's Werken Mit Philologischen & Historischen Erlauterungen. (Ger). 1887. $25.00 Hdbd. (ISBN 0-8337-4750-9). Burt Franklin, NY.

Gossman, Lionel. Men & Masks: A Study of Moliere. 1969. (1963) $9.00 Hdbd. (ISBN 0-8018-0228-8); $2.45 pa. (ISBN 0-8018-1043-4). Johns Hopkins Pr., MD.

Grebanier, Bernard. Barron's Simplified Approach to Moliere: Complete Works. (Hi-Sch.). 1965. $0.95 pa. Barron's Educ. Series, NY.

Guicharnaud, Jacques. Moliere: A Collection of Critical Essays. 1964. $5.95

Hdbd. (ISBN 0-13-599712-7). Prentice-Hall, NY.

Hall, Gaston. Tartuffe by Moliere: Critical Analysis. Moore, W. G., ed. (Studies in French Literature Ser). 1960. $2.50 Hdbd.; $1.00 pa. Barron's Educ. Series, NY.

Hubert, Judd D. Moliere & the Comedy of Intellect. 1971. (1962) $13.50 Hdbd. Russell & Russell Publ., NY.

Keating, Clark L. & Moraud, Marcel I. Selections De Moliere, Voltaire, Hugo. price not set. text ed. Van Nostrand-Reinhold Books, NY.

Klibbe, Lawrence. Monarch Literature Notes on the Plays of Moliere. $1.00 pa. Monarch Pr., NY.

Mander, Gertrud. Moliere. (World Dramatist Ser). $6.50 Hdbd. Frederick Ungar, NY.

Miles, Dudley H. Influence of Moliere on Restoration Comedy. (1971) $10.00 Hdbd. (ISBN 0-374-95652-9). Octagon Books, Inc., NY.

Miles, Dudley H. Influence of Moliere on Restoration Comedy. 1971. (1910) $8.00 Hdbd. (ISBN 0-8154-0374-7). Cooper Sq. Pr., NY.

Moore, Will G. Moliere: A New Criticism. 1949. $3.50 Hdbd. (ISBN 0-19-815321-X); $1.25 pa. (ISBN 0-19-815381-3). Oxford Univ. Pr., NY.

Palmer, John. Moliere. rev. ed. 1968. $12.50 Hdbd. Benjamin Blom., NY.

Roberts, James L. Tartuffe Notes & the

Miser Notes. 1968. $1.00 pa. (ISBN 0-8220-1264-2). Cliffs Notes, NB.

Tilley, Arthur A. Moliere. 1968. (1921) $11.00 Hdbd. Russell & Russell Publ., NY.

Turnell, Martin. The Classical Moment: Studies in Corneille, Moliere & Racine. $11.75 Hdbd. (ISBN 0-8371-5803-6). Greenwood Pr., CT.

Van Zandt, Eleanor R. Misanthrope. the Would-Be Gentlemen-Moliere. (Book Notes Ser., No. 876). 1969. $1.00 pa. (ISBN 0-389-00883-4, 876). Barnes & Noble, NY.

Walker, Hallam. Moliere. (World Authors Ser. No. 176). $5.50 Hdbd. Twayne Publ., NY.

Wilcox, John. Relation of Moliere to the Restoration Comedy. 1938. $12.50 Hdbd. Benjamin Blom., NY.

Montherlant, Henry De

Batchelor, John. Existence & Imagination: The Theatre of Henry De Montherplant. $8.85 Hdbd. International School Book Service, OR.

Batchelor, John. Existence & Imagination: The Theatre of Henry De Montherlant. 1967. $10.00 Hdbd. Humanities Pr., NY.

Becker, Lucille F. Henry De Montherlant: A Critical Biography. 1970. $4.95 Hdbd. (ISBN 0-8093-0411-2, Crosscurrents). Southern Ill. Univ. Pr., IL.

Johnson, Robert B. Henry De Montherlant. (World Authors Series, No. 37). 1968. $5.50 Hdbd. Twayne Publ., NY.

Musset, Alfred De

Clouard, Maurice. Bibliographie Des Oeuvres D'Alfred De Musset, et Des Ouvrages, Gravures et Vignettes Qui S'y Rapportent. $16.50 Hdbd. (ISBN 0-8337-4966-8). Burt Franklin, NY.

Rees, Margaret A. Alfred De Musset. (World Authors Ser. No. 137). $5.50 Hdbd. Twayne Publ., NY.

Tilley, Arthur A. Three French Dramatists: Racine, Marivaux, Musset. 1967. (1933) $8.50 Hdbd. Russell & Russell Publ., NY.

O'Casey, Sean

Armstrong, William A. Sean O'Casey. (Writers & Their Work Ser. No. 198). $2.25 Hdbd.; $1.00 pa. British Book Center, NY.

Ayling, Ronald, ed. Sean O'Casey. (Modern Judgement Ser). 1970. (1968) $2.50 pa. (ISBN 0-87695-097-7). Aurora Publ., TN

Benstock, Bernard. Sean O'Casey. Carens, James F., ed. (Irish Writers Ser). $4.50 Hdbd. (ISBN 0-8387-7748-1); $1.95 pa. (ISBN 0-8387-7618-3). Bucknell Univ. Pr., PA.

Cowasjee, S. Sean O'Casey: Man Behind the Plays. 1963. $7.50 Hdbd. St. Martin's Pr., NY.

Fallon, Gabriel. Sean O'Casey: Man I Knew. 1965. $5.95 Hdbd. (ISBN 0-316-27385-6). Little, Brown & Co., MA.

Krause, David. Sean O'Casey: The Man & His Works. 1960. $6.00 Hdbd. Hillary House Publ., NY.

Krause, David. Self-Portrait of the Artist As a Man. 1968. $2.50 Hdbd. Dufour Editions, Pa.

Malone, Maureen. Plays of Sean O'Casey. 1969. $4.95 Hdbd. (ISBN 0-8093-0386-8). S. Ill. Univ. Pr., IL.

O'Neill, Eugene Gladstone

Alexander, Doris. Tempering of Eugene O'Neill. 1962. $6.50 Hdbd. (ISBN 0-15-188529-X). Harcourt, Brace & World, NY.

Callahan, John. Barron's Simplified Approach to O'Neill's Mourning Becomes Electra. 1969. $0.95 pa. Barron's Educ. Series, NY.

Cargill, Oscar, et al, eds. O'Neill & His Plays. (Gotham Library). 1961. $10.00 Hdbd. (ISBN 0-8147-0075-6); $3.95 pa. (ISBN 0-8147-0076-4). New York Univ. Pr., NY.

Carpenter, Frederic I. Eugene O'Neill. (Twayne's United States Authors Ser). 1964. $2.45 pa. College & Univ. Pr., NY.

Carpenter, Frederic I. Eugene O'Neill. (United States Authors Series, No. 66). 1964. $4.95 Hdbd. Twayne Publ., NY.

Clark, Barrett H. Eugene O'Neill, the Man & His Plays. $1.50 pa. (ISBN 0-486-20379-4). Dover Publ., NY.

Coolidge, Olivia E. Eugene O'Neill. (Jr Hi–Hi-Sch.). 1966. $3.95 Hdbd. (ISBN 0-684-20774-5); $3.63 pa. (ISBN

0-684-82011-0). Charles Scribner's Sons, NY.

Engel, Edwin A. Haunted Heroes of Eugene O'Neill. rev. ed. price "n.g." Hdbd. (ISBN 0-674-38200-5). Harvard Univ. Pr., MA.

Falk, Doris V., Eugene O'Neill & the Tragic Tension. An Interpretive Study of the Plays. 1958. $9.00 Hdbd. Rutgers Univ. Pr., NJ.

Frazer, Winifred D. Love As Death in the Iceman Cometh. (Humanities Monographs Ser, No. 27). 1967. $2.00 pa. (ISBN 0-8130-0081-5). Univ. of Fla. Pr., FL.

Frenz, Horst. Eugene O'Neill. Sebba, Helen, tr. (Modern Literature Monographs). 1971. $5.00 Hdbd. (ISBN 0-8044-2211-7); $1.75 pa. (ISBN 0-8044-6159-7). Frederick Ungar, NY.

Gannon, Paul. Monarch Literature Notes on O'Neill's Long Day's Journey into Night. $1.00 pa. Monarch Pr., NY.

Gannon, Paul, ed. Monarch Literature Notes on O'Neill's Desire Under the Elms. $1.00 pa. Monarch Pr., NY.

Gassner, John. Eugene O'Neill. (Orig.). $0.95 pa. (ISBN 0-8166-0349-9). Univ. of Minn. Pr., MN.

Gassner, John, ed. O'Neill: A Collection of Critical Essays. 1964. $1.95 pa. (ISBN 0-13-634261-2). $5.95 Hdbd. (ISBN 0-13-634279-5). Prentice-Hall, NY.

Geddes, Virgil. Melodramadness of

Eugene O'Neill. 1934. $4.00 Hdbd. Folcroft Pr., PA.

Gelb, Barbara & Gelb, Arthur. O'Neill: A Biography. 1962. $15.00 Hdbd. (ISBN 0-06-011485-1). Harper-Row, NY.

Greene, James. Monarch Literature Notes on O'Neill's Strange Interlude. $1.00 pa. Monarch Pr., NY.

Long, Chester C. Role of Nemesis in the Structure of Selected Plays by Eugene O'Neill. (American Literature Studies Series, Vol. 8). 1968. $9.25 Hdbd. Humanities Pr., NY.

Nugent, Elizabeth. Monarch Literature Notes on O'Neill's Iceman Cometh. $1.00 pa. Monarch Pr., NY.

Nugent, Elizabeth. Monarch Literature Notes on O'Neill's Mourning Becomes Electra. $1.00 pa. Monarch Pr., NY.

Raghavacharyulu, D. V. Eugene O'Neill: A Study. 1965. $4.50 Hdbd. Humanities Pr., NY.

Raleigh, John H. Plays of Eugene O'Neill. 1965. $4.50 Hdbd. (ISBN 0-8093-0154-7). S. Ill. Univ. Pr., IL.

Raleigh, John H., ed. Twentieth Century Interpretations of the Iceman Cometh. 1968. $4.95 Hdbd. (ISBN 0-13-449116-5). $1.25 pa. (ISBN 0-13-449108-4). Prentice-Hall, NY.

Reaver, J. Russell. O'Neill Concordance, 3 Vols. (1969) $87.50 Hdbd. Gale Research Co., MI.

Roberts, James L. Mourning Becomes

Electra Notes. $1.00 pa. (ISBN 0-8220-0911-0). Cliff's Notes, NB.

Rogers, David. Monarch Literature Notes on the Major Plays of O'Neill. $1.00 pa. Monarch Pr., NY.

Sanborn, Ralph & Clark, Barrett H., eds. Bibliography of the Works of Eugene O'Neill with Collected Poems by O'Neill. $12.50 Hdbd. Benjamin Blom., NY.

Scheiber, Rolf. Late Plays of Eugene O'Neill. (Cooper Monographs, Vol. 15). 1971. $9.50 Hdbd. Fernhill House, NY.

Sheaffer, Louis. O'Neill, Son & Playwright. 1968. $10.95 Hdbd. (ISBN 0-316-78335-8). Little, Brown & Co., MA.

Shipley, Joseph T. Art of Eugene O'Neill. 1928. $5.00 Hdbd. Folcroft Pr., PA.

Skinner, Richard D. Eugene O'Neill: A Poet's Quest. 1964. (1935) $8.50 Hdbd. Russell & Russell Publ., NY.

Tiusanen, Timo. O'Neill's Scenic Images. 1968. $12.00 Hdbd. (ISBN 0-691-06145-9). Princeton Univ. Pr., NJ.

Tornqvist, Egil. Drama of Souls: Studies in O'Neill's Super-Naturalistic Technique. 1970. $7.50 Hdbd. (ISBN 0-300-01152-0). Yale Univ. Pr., CT.

Winther, Sophus K. Eugene O'Neill. rev & enl ed. 1961. (1934) $8.50 Hdbd. Russell & Russell Publ., NY.

Pinter, Harold

Burkman, Katherine H. Dramatic World of Harold Pinter: Its Basis in Ritual. 1971. $8.00 Hdbd. (ISBN 0-8142-0146-6). Ohio St. Univ. Pr., OH.

Esslin, Martin. Peopled Wound: The Work of Harold Pinter. 1970. $5.95 Hdbd.; $1.45 pa. Doubleday & Co., NY.

Gordon, Lois G. Stratagems to Uncover Nakedness: The Dramas of Harold Pinter. (Literary Frontiers Ser., No. 6). 1968. $1.50 pa. (ISBN 0-8262-8116-8). Univ. of Mo. Pr., MO.

Hinchcliffe, Arnold P. Harold Pinter. (Eng. Authors Ser., No. 51). $4.95 Hdbd. Twayne Publ., NY.

Hollis, James R. Harold Pinter: The Poetics of Silence. 1970. $4.95 Hdbd. (ISBN 0-8093-0450-3). Southern Ill. Univ. Pr., IL.

Kerr, Walter. Harold Pinter. (Columbia Essays on Modern Writers No. 27). 1968. $1.00 pa. (ISBN 0-231-02964-0). Columbia Univ. Pr., NY.

Schroll, Herman T. Harold Pinter: A Study of His Reputation, 1958–1969. 1971. $5.00 Hdbd. (ISBN 0-8108-0402-6). Scarecrow Pr., NJ.

Sykes, Arlene. Harold Pinter. $3.45 pa. International School Book Service, OR.

Sykes, Arlene. Approach to Harold Pinter. 1971. $5.00 Hdbd.; $2.50 pa. Humanities Pr., NY.

Sykes, Arlene. Harold Pinter. 1970. $6.50 Hdbd.; $3.75 pa. Humanities Pr., NY.

Taylor, John R. Harold Pinter. Beachcroft, T. O., et al, eds. (Writers &

Their Work Ser., No. 212). $2.25 Hdbd., incl. catalog cards; $1.00 pa. British Book Center, NY.

Pirandello, Luigi

Bishop, Thomas. Pirandello & the French Theater. 1970. (1990) $6.95 Hdbd. (ISBN 0-8147-0047-0); $2.25 pa. (ISBN 0-8147-0048-9). New York Univ. Pr., NY.

Monner Sans, Jose M. Pirandello y Su Teatro. $1.25 pa. French & European Publ., NY.

Pirandello, Luigi. Pirandello: A Collection of Critical Essays. Cambon, Glauco, ed. $1.95 pa. (ISBN 0-13-676395-2). 1967. $5.95 Hdbd. (ISBN 0-13-676403-7). Prentice-Hall, NY.

Ragusa, Olga. Luigi Pirandello. 1968. $1.00 pa. (ISBN 0-231-02952-7). Columbia Univ. Pr., NY.

Starkie, Walter. Luigi Pirandello, 1867–1936. 3rd rev. ed. 1965. $5.00 Hdbd. (ISBN 0-520-01206-2); $2.25 pa. (ISBN 0-520-01207-0, CAL 130). Univ. of Cal. Pr., CA.

Vittorini, Domenico. Drama of Luigi Pirandello. 2nd enl. ed. 1969. (1957) $12.50 Hdbd. Russell & Russell Publ., NY.

Racine, Jean Baptiste

Barthes, Roland. On Racine. Howard, Richard, tr. 1964. (ISBN 0-8090-7440-0). $1.75 pa. (ISBN 0-8090-0539-5). Hill & Wang, NY.

Bowra, C. M. Simplicity of Racine. 1956. $4.00 Hdbd. Folcroft Pr., PA.

Canfield, Dorothea F. Corneille & Racine in England. 1904. $12.50 Hdbd. (ISBN 0-404-50605-4). AMS Pr., NY.

Clark, Alexander F. Jean Racine. (1970). $11.00 Hdbd. Octagon Books, Inc., NY.

De Mourgues, Odette. Racine, or the Triumph of Relevance. $6.50 Hdbd.; $2.25 pa. (ISBN 0-521-09428-3, 428). Cambridge Univ. Pr., NY.

Eccles, F. Y. Racine in England. 1922. $3.00 Hdbd. Folcroft Pr., PA.

France, Peter. Racine's Rhetoric. 1965. $8.00 Hdbd. (ISBN 0-19-815361-9). Oxford Univ. Pr., NY.

Freeman, Bryant C., ed. Concordance Du Theatre et Des Poesies De Jean Racine, 2 Vols. (Concordances Series). (Prog. Bk.). 1968. $22.50 Hdbd. (ISBN 0-8014-0142-9). Cornell Univ. Pr., NY.

Giraudoux, Jean. Racine. 1938. $4.00 Hdbd. Folcroft Pr., PA.

Gutwirth, Marcel. Jean Racine: Un Itineraire Poetique. 1970. price not set. Hdbd. International School Book Service, OR.

Harris, Eugenie. Monarch Literature Notes on the Plays of Racine & Corneille. $1.00 pa. Monarch Pr., NY.

Klin, Georgia & Marsland, Amy F. Phaedra Notes & Andromache Notes. 1969. $1.00 pa. (ISBN 0-8220-1012-7). Cliffs Notes, NB.

Knapp, Bettina L. Jean Racine: Mythos & Renewal in Modern Theater. 1971.

$10.00 Hdbd. (ISBN 0-8173-7604-6). Univ. of Ala. Pr., AL.

Knight, R. C., ed. Racine. (Modern Judgement Ser). 1970. (1968) $2.50 pa. (ISBN 0-87695-088-8). Aurora Publ., TN.

Lapp, John C. Aspects of Racinian Tragedy. (Canadian University Paperbooks). 1955. $7.50 Hdbd. (ISBN 0-8020-5040-9). Univ. of Toronto Pr., CAN.

Lockert, Lacy. Studies in French: Classical Tragedy. 1958. $7.50 Hdbd. (ISBN 0-8265-1049-3). Vanderbilt Univ. Pr., TN.

Mesnard, Paul. Notice Bibliographique De Racine. (Bibliography & Reference Ser., No. 375). 1971. (1865) $15.00 Hdbd. (ISBN 0-8337-2374-X). Burt Franklin, NY.

Moore, W. G. Britannicus by Racine: Critical Analysis. (Studies in French Literature Ser). (Hi-Sch.). 1960. $2.50 Hdbd. Barron's Educ. Series, NY.

Muir, Kenneth. Last Periods of Shakespeare, Racine, Ibsen. 1961. $5.00 Hdbd. (ISBN 0-8143-1140-7). Wayne St. Univ. Pr., MI.

Nelson, R., ed. Corneille & Racine: Parallels & Contrasts. 1969. $5.95 text ed. (ISBN 0-13-172742-7). Prentice-Hall, NY.

Robinson, Mary Duclaux Pseud. Of A. M. Life of Racine. 1971. (1925) $9.00 Hdbd. (ISBN 0-8046-1595-0). Kennikat Pr., NY.

Tilley, Arthur A. Three French Dramatists: Racine, Marivaux, Musset. 1967. (1933) $8.50 Hdbd. Russell & Russell Publ., NY.

Tobin, Ronald W. Racine & Seneca. 1971. $5.00 pa. (ISBN 0-8078-9096-0). Univ. of N.C. Pr., NC.

Turnell, Martin. The Classical Moment: Studies in Corneille, Moliere & Racine. $11.75 Hdbd. (ISBN 0-8371-5803-6). Greenwood Pr., CT.

Vossler, Karl. Jean Racine. 1971. $6.50 Hdbd. Frederick Ungar, NY.

Weinberg, Bernard. Art of Jean Racine. 1963. $7.50 Hdbd. (ISBN 0-226-88551-8). 1969. $3.45 pa. (ISBN 0-226-88549-6). Univ. of Chicago Pr., IL.

Wheatley, Katherine E. Racine & English Classicism. 1956. $12.00 Hdbd. (ISBN 0-8371-3161-8). Greenwood Pr., CT.

Raimund, Ferdinand

Michalski, John. Ferdinand Raimund. (World Authors Ser., No. 39). 1968. $5.50 Hdbd. Twayne Publ., NY.

Prohaska, Dorothy. Raimund & Vienna: A Critical Study of Raimund's Plays in Their Viennese Setting. (Anglica Germanica Ser., No. 2). 1971. $13.00 Hdbd. (ISBN 0-521-07789-3). Cambridge Univ. Pr., NY.

Saint Exupery, Antoine De

Breaux, Adele. Saint-Exupery in America, 1942–1943: A Memoir. $8.00 Hdbd.

(ISBN 0-8386-7610-3). Fairleigh Dickinson Univ. Pr., NJ.

Cate, Curtis. Antoine De Saint-Exupery. 1970. $10.00 Hdbd. G. P. Putnam's Sons, NY.

Crane, Helen E. Humanisme Dans L'oeuvre De Saint Exupery. (Fr). 1957. $5.00 Hdbd. (ISBN 0-911536-09-4). Trinity Univ. Pr., TX.

Davis, Harold T. Alexandria, the Golden City, 2 vols. Incl. Vol. 1. City of Ptolemies (ISBN 0-911536-11-6); Vol. 2. Cleopatra's City (ISBN 0-911536-12-4). 1957. $5.40 Hdbd. Trinty Univ. Pr., TX.

Sartre, Jean Paul

Adereth, M. Commitment in Modern French Literature: Politics & Society in Peguy, Aragon, & Sartre. 1970. (1968) $2.95 pa. (ISBN 0-8052-0285-4). Schocken Books Inc., NY.

Aron, Raymond. Marxism & the Existentialists. (World Perspectives Ser). 1969. $5.95 Hdbd. (ISBN 0-06-010132-6). Harper & Row, NY.

Barnes, Hazel E. Existentialist Ethics. 1967. $8.95 Hdbd. Alfred A. Knopf, NY.

Bauer, George H. Sartre & the Artist. 1969. $8.50 Hdbd. (ISBN 0-226-03930-7). Univ. of Chicago Pr., IL.

Belkind, Allen J. Jean-Paul Sartre in English: A Bibliographical Guide. (Serif Ser., No. 10). 1970. $7.50 Hdbd. (ISBN 0-87338-049-5). Kent State Univ. Pr., OH.

Champigny, Robert R. Stages on Sartre's Way, 1938–52. (Indiana University Humanities Ser., No. 42). 1959. $13.00 Hdbd. Kraus Reprint Co., NY.

Desan, Wilfrid. Marxism of Jean-Paul Sartre. $1.45 pa. (A507, Anch). Doubleday & Co., NY.

Desan, Wilfrid. Marxism of Jean-Paul Sartre. $3.50 Hdbd. Peter Smith, Publ., MA.

Desan, Wilfrid. Tragic Finale: An Essay on the Philosophy of Jean-Paul Sartre. $2.45 pa. (ISBN 0-06-131030-1, TB-1030). Harper & Row, NY.

Falk, Eugene H. Types of Thematic Structure. 1967. $5.00 Hdbd. (ISBN 0-226-23609-9). Univ. of Chicago Pr., IL.

Fell, Joseph P., 3rd. Emotion in the Thought of Sartre. 1965. $7.05 Hdbd. (ISBN 0-231-02756-7). Columbia Univ. Pr., NY.

Greene, Norman N. Jean-Paul Sartre: The Existentialist Ethic. 1960. $4.40 Hdbd. (ISBN 0-472-09075-5). $1.75 pa. (ISBN 0-472-06075-9). Univ. of Mich. Pr., MI.

Juhasz, Leslie A. Monarch Literature Notes on Sartre's No Exit, The Flies & Other Writings. $1.00 pa. (00569). Monarch Pr., NY.

Kaelin, Eugene F. Existentialist Aesthetic: The Theories of Sartre & Merleau-Ponty. 1962. $15.00 Hdbd. (ISBN 0-299-02630-2). Univ. of Wis Pr., WI.

Kern, Edith. Existential Thought &

Fictional Technique: Kierkegaard, Sartre, Beckett. 1970. $6.75 Hdbd. (ISBN 0-300-01203-9). Yale Univ. Pr., CT.

Laing, R. D. & Cooper, David. Reason & Violence. 1971. $1.95 pa. (ISBN 0-394-71043-6). Random House, NY.

McCall, Dorothy K. Theatre of Jean-Paul Sartre. 1969. $7.50 Hdbd. Columbia Univ. Pr., NY.

McMahon, Joseph H. Humans Being: The World of Jean-Paul Sartre. 1971. $14.50 Hdbd. (ISBN 0-226-56100-3). Univ. of Chicago Pr., IL.

Molnar, Thomas. Sartre: Idealogue of Our Time. 1968. $5.95 Hdbd. (710800). Funk & Wagnalls, NY.

Murdoch, Iris. Sartre: Romantic Rationalist. 1953. $1.25 pa. (ISBN 0-300-00170-3, Y9). Yale Univ. Pr., CT.

Peyre, Henri. Jean-Paul Sartre. (Essays on Modern Writers, No. 31). (Hi-Sch.). 1968. $1.00 pa. (ISBN 0-231-02987-X, MW31). Columbia Univ. Pr., NY.

Pollmann, Leo. Sartre & Camus: Literature of Existence. $8.50 Hdbd. (2699-6). Frederick Ungar, NY.

Richter, Liselotte. Jean-Paul Sartre. (Modern Literature Monographs). 1970. $5.00 Hdbd. (ISBN 0-8044-2732-1); $1.45 pa. (ISBN 0-8044-6728-5). Frederick Ungar, NY.

Salvan, Jacques L. Scandalous Ghost: Sartre's Existentialism As Related to Vitalism, Humanism, Mysticism, Marxism. 1967. $7.95 Hdbd. (ISBN 0-8143-1303-5). Wayne State Univ. Pr., OH.

Savage, Catharine. Malraux, Sartre, & Aragon As Political Novelists. (Humanities Monographs Ser, No. 17). 1965. $2.00 pa. (ISBN 0-8130-0202-8). Univ. of Fla. Pr., FL.

Sheridan, James F. Sartre: The Radical Conversion. 1969. $7.50 Hdbd. (ISBN 0-8214-0055-X). Ohio Univ. Pr., OH.

Ussher, Arland. Journey Through Dread. 1955. $6.75 Hdbd. (ISBN 0-8196-0221-3). Biblio & Tannen, NY.

Warnock, Mary. Existentialist Ethics. 1967. $1.95 pa. (E 73250). St Martin's Pr., NY.

Warnock, Mary, ed. Sartre: A Collection of Critical Essays. (Orig.). 1971. $2.50 pa. Doubleday & Co., NY.

Schiller, Friedrich von

Berger, Karl. Schiller, Sein Leben und Seine Werke, 2 Vols. rev. ed. 1910-11. Set—$30.00 Hdbd. (ISBN 0-404-00790-2); $15.50 ea. (ISBN 0-404-00791-0) (ISBN 0-404-00792-9). AMS Pr., NY.

Berresheim, Fritz. Schiller Als Herausgeber der Rheinischen Thalia. (1914) $7.50 pa. Johnson Reprint Corp., NY.

Carus, Paul. Friedrich Schiller. $3.00 pa. Open Court Publ. Co., IL.

De Quincey, Thomas Biographies of Shakespeare, Pope, Goethe & Schiller & on the Political Parties of Modern England. 1863. $17.50 Hdbd. (ISBN 0-404-02079-8). AMS Pr., NY.

Ellis, J. M. Schiller's Kalliasbriefe & the Study of His Aesthetic Theory. 1969. $9.50 Hdbd. Humanities Pr., NY.

Ewen, Frederic. Prestige of Schiller in England, 1788–1859. 1932. $9.00 Hdbd. (ISBN 0-404-02364-9). AMS Pr., NY.

Fahrner, R. Hoelderlins Begegnung Mit Goethe und Schiller. 1925. $4.50 pa. Johnson Reprint Corp., NY.

Frey, John R., ed. Schiller, 1759–1959; Commemorative American Studies. 1959. $3.50 pa. (ISBN 0-252-72638-3). Univ. of Ill. Pr., IL.

Garland, H. G. Dramatic Writer: A Study of Style in the Plays. 1969. $11.00 Hdbd. (ISBN 0-19-815387-2). Oxford Univ. Pr., NY.

Hudson, William H. Schiller & His Poetry. 1914. $8.00 Hdbd. (ISBN 0-404-52519-9). AMS Pr., NY.

Keller, Werner. Pathos in Schillers Jugendlyrik. (Quellen und Forschungen Zur Sprachgeschichte und Kulturgeschichte der Germanischen Voelker, No. 15). (Ger). 1964. $7.10 Hdbd. (ISBN 3-11-000206-X). De Gruyter, Germany.

Kerry, Stanley. Schiller's Writings on Aesthetics. 1961. $5.00 Hdbd. Barnes & Noble, NY.

Knippel, Rich. Schillers Verhaltnis Zur Idylle. (Ger). (1909) $3.50 pa. Johnson Reprint Corp., NY.

Kostka, Edmund K. Schiller in Russian Literature. 1965. $9.00 Hdbd. Univ. of Pa. Pr., PA.

London University Institute Of Germanic Studies. Schiller Bicentenary Lectures. rev ed. Norman, F., ed. 1960. $6.00 Hdbd. Dufour Editions, PA.

Longyear, R. M. Schiller & Music. (Germanic Languages & Literature Studies). 1966. $7.50 Hdbd. (ISBN 0-8078-8054-X). Univ. of N.C. Pr., NC.

Miller, R. D. Schiller & the Ideal of Freedom: A Study of Schiller's Philosophical Works with Chapters on Kant. 1970. $5.75 Hdbd. (ISBN 0-19-824349-9). Oxford Univ. Pr., NY.

Petersen, Julius. Schiller und Die Buhne. 1904. $29.00 Hdbd.; $27.00 pa. Johnson Reprint Corp., NY.

Rudolph, Ludwig. Schiller-Lexikon, 2 Vols. (Bibliography & Reference Ser). 1971. (1890) $27.50 Hdbd. (ISBN 0-8337-3092-4). Burt Franklin, NY.

Rudolph, Ludwig. Schiller-Lexikon, 2 Vols. 2nd ed. 1967. (1890) $27.50 Hdbd. (ISBN 0-8337-3092-4). Burt Franklin, NY.

Sandberg, Hans-Joachim. Thomas Manns Schiller-Studien. 1965. $4.65 Hdbd. Universitetsforlaget, MA.

Schiller, Johann C. Schiller Symposium. Willson, A. Leslie, ed. 1961. $4.00 Hdbd. (ISBN 0-292-73367-4). Univ. of Tex. Pr., TX.

Stahl, Ernest L. Friedrich Schiller's Drama. 1954. $5.75 Hdbd. (ISBN 0-19-815326-0). Oxford Univ. Pr., NY.

Witte, William. Schiller & Burns. 1959. $4.50 Hdbd. Fernhill House, NY.

Schnitzler, Arthur

Allen, Richard H. Annotated Arthur Schnitzler Bibliography. 1966. $6.00

Hdbd. (ISBN 0-8078-8056-6). Univ. of N.C. Pr., NC.

Schnitzler, Arthur. Studies in Arthur Schnitzler. Reichert, Herbert W. & Salinger, Herman, eds. 1963. $10.00 Hdbd. (ISBN 0-404-50942-8). AMS Pr., NY.

Swales, M. W. Arthur Schnitzler: Professor Bernhardi. price "n.g." Hdbd. Pergamon Pr., NY.

Schulz, Charles M.

Schulz, Charles M. & Mendelson, Lee. Charlie Brown & Charlie Schulz. 1970. $6.95 Hdbd. World Publ. Co., NY.

Short, Robert L. Gospel According to Peanuts. 1965. $2.95 Hdbd.; $1.75 pa. John Knox Pr., VA.

Short, Robert L. Gospel According to Peanuts. 1970. $0.75 pa. (S3800). Bantam Books, NY.

Seneca

Canter, Howard V. Rhetorical Elements in the Tragedies of Seneca. (1925) $8.00 Hdbd. Johnson Reprint Corp., NY.

Charlton, Henry B. Senecan Tradition in Renaissance Tragedy. 1946. $15.00 Hdbd. Folcroft Pr., PA.

Cunliffe, John W. Influence of Seneca on Elizabethan Tragedy. 1965. (1893) $5.00 Hdbd. (ISBN 0-208-00038-0). Shoe String Pr., CT.

Holland, Francis. Seneca. facs. ed. (Select Bibliographies Reprint Ser). $12.50 Hdbd. (ISBN 0-8369-5131-X). Books for Libraries, NY.

Lausberg, Marion. Untersuchungen Zu Senecas Fragmenten. (Ger). 1971. $17.00 Hdbd. (ISBN 3-11-006351-4). De Gruyter, Germany.

Lenzen, Hubert. Senecas Dialog De Brevitate Vitae. (1937) $5.50 Hdbd. Johnson Reprint Corp., NY.

Lucas, F. L. Seneca & Elizabethan Tragedy. (Studies in Comparative Literature Ser., No. 35). 1969. (1922) $5.95 Hdbd. (ISBN 0-8383-0668-3). Haskell House Publ., NY.

Lucas, F. L. Seneca & Elizabethan Tragedy. $5.00 Hdbd. Gordon Publ., NY.

Lucas, Frank L. Seneca & the Elizabethan Tragedy. 1923. $6.50 Hdbd. Folcroft Pr., PA.

Mendell, Clarence W. Our Seneca. (1968) $8.00 Hdbd. Shoe String Pr., CT.

Reynolds, Leighton D. Medieval Tradition of Seneca's Letters. 1965. $8.00 Hdbd. (ISBN 0-19-814712-0). Oxford Univ. Pr., NY.

Spearing, E. M. Elizabethan Translations of Seneca's Tragedies. 1912. $7.50 Hdbd. Folcroft Pr., PA.

Stachel, Paul. Seneca und das Deutsche Renaissancedrama. 1907. $19.00 Hdbd.; $17.00 pa. Johnson Reprint Corp., NY.

Tobin, Ronald W. Racine & Seneca. 1971. $5.00 pa. (ISBN 0-8078-9096-0). Univ. of N.C. Pr., NC.

Shakespeare, William See Main Heading

Shaw, George Bernard

Adam, Ruth. What Shaw Really Said. (What They Really Said Ser). 1967. $4.00 Hdbd. (ISBN 0-8052-3288-5). Schocken Books, Inc., NY.

Adams, Elsie B. Bernard Shaw & the Aesthetes. 1971. $10.00 Hdbd. (ISBN 0-8142-0155-5). Ohio St. Univ. Pr., OH.

Alexander, Nigel. Shaw: Arms & the Man–Pygmalion. (Macmillan Critical Commentaries). 1968. $1.00 pa. Fernhill House, NY.

Armstrong, Cecil F. Shakespeare to Shaw. 1913. $8.50 Hdbd. (ISBN 0-404-00383-4). AMS Pr., NY.

Barr, Alan P. Victorian Stage Pulpiteer: Bernard Shaw's Crusade. price "n.g." Hdbd. (ISBN 0-8203-0266-X). Univ. of Georgia Pr., GA.

Bentley, Eric. Bernard Shaw. rev. ed. 1947. $1.95 pa. New Directions, NY.

Bevan, E. Dean. Concordance to the Plays & Prefaces of Bernard Shaw. 1971. price "n.g." Hdbd. Gale Research Co., MI.

Boxill, Roger. Shaw & the Doctors. 1969. $5.95 Hdbd. (ISBN 0-465-07772-2). Basic Books, NY.

Braybrooke, Patrick. Genius of Bernard Shaw. 1925. $12.50 Hdbd. Folcroft Pr., PA.

Braybrooke, Patrick. Subtlety of George Bernard Shaw. 1930. $12.50 Hdbd. Folcroft Pr., PA.

Brinser, Ayers. Respectability of Mr. Bernard Shaw. 1931. $6.50 Hdbd. Folcroft Pr., PA.

Broad, Lewis C. & Broad, V. M. Dictionary to Plays & Novels of Shaw. $9.00 Hdbd. Gordon Publ., NY.

Broad, Lewis C. & Broad, A. Dictionary to Plays & Novels of Shaw. (Studies in Irish Literature Ser., No. 16). 1969. (1929) $8.95 Hdbd. (ISBN 0-8383-0961-5). Haskell House Publ., NY.

Broad, Lewis C. & Broad, Violet M. Dictionary to the Plays & Novels of Bernard Shaw. 1929. $8.50 Hdbd. Folcroft Pr., PA.

Brown, G. E. George Bernard Shaw. (Literary Critiques Ser). 1970. (ISBN 0-668-02364-3); $1.95 pa. (ISBN 0-668-02365-1). Arco Publ. Co., NY.

Carpenter, Charles A. Bernard Shaw & the Art of Destroying Ideals: The Early Plays. 1969. $10.00 Hdbd. (ISBN 0-299-05300-8). Univ. of Wisconsin Pr., WI.

Chappelow, Allan. Shaw, the Chucker-Out: A Biographical Exposition & Critique. (1969) $15.00 Hdbd. (ISBN 0-404-08359-5). AMS Pr., NY.

Chesterton, Gilbert K. George Bernard Shaw. 1956. $1.25 pa. (ISBN 0-8090-0503-4). Hill & Wang, NY.

Clarke, Winifred. George Bernard Shaw. 1949. $5.00 Hdbd. Folcroft Pr., PA.

Cliff's Notes Editors. Arms & the Man Notes. $1.00 pa. (ISBN 0-8220-0192-6). Cliffs Notes, NB.

Cliff's Notes Editors. Caesar & Cleopatra Notes. $1.00 pa. (ISBN 0-8220-0274-4). Cliffs Notes, NB.

Cliff's Notes Editors. Pygmalion Notes. $1.00 pa. (ISBN 0-8220-1102-6). Cliffs Notes, NB.

Collis, John S. Shaw. 1971. (1925) $8.50 Hdbd. (ISBN 0-8046-1561-6). Kennikat Pr., NY.

Coolidge, Olivia. George Bernard Shaw. (Jr. Hi.). 1968. $3.95 Hdbd. (ISBN 0-395-06723-5). Houghton-Mifflin, NY.

Costello, Donald P. Serpent's Eye: Shaw & the Cinema. 1965. $6.50 Hdbd. (ISBN 0-268-00252-5). Univ. of Notre Dame Pr., IN.

Craig, Edward G. Ellen Terry & Her Secret Self. 1932. $12.50 Hdbd. Benjamin Blom, NY.

Crompton, Louis. Shaw the Dramatist. 1969. $7.95 Hdbd. (ISBN 0-8032-0031-5). Univ. of Nebraska Pr., NB.

Dukore, Bernard F. Bernard Shaw, Director. 1971. $7.95 Hdbd. (ISBN 0-295-95083-8). Univ. of Washington Pr., WA.

Fiske, Irving. Bernard Shaw's Debt to William Blake. 1951. $5.00 Hdbd. Folcroft Pr., PA.

Fromm, Harold. Bernard Shaw & the Theater of the Nineties. 1967. $5.00 Hdbd. (ISBN 0-7006-0020-5). Univ. Pr. of Kansas, KS.

Furlong, William B. Shaw & Chesterton: The Metaphysical Jesters. $7.95 Hdbd. (ISBN 0-271-00110-0). Pennsylvania St. Univ. Pr., PA.

Gupta, S. C. Art of Bernard Shaw. $15.00 Hdbd. Folcroft Pr., PA.

Hamon, Augustin. Technique of Bernard Shaw's Plays. 1912. $10.00 Hdbd. Folcroft Pr., PA.

Hamon, Augustin. Twentieth Century Moliere: Bernard Shaw. 1916. $20.00 Hdbd. Folcroft Pr., PA.

Henderson, Archibald. George Bernard Shaw. (Theater Ser). (1956) price "n.g." Hdbd. (ISBN 0-306-71490-6). Plenum Publ. Corp., NY.

Henderson, Archibald. George Bernard Shaw: A Lecture. 1957. $4.00 Hdbd. Folcroft Pr., PA.

Henderson, Archibald. Is Bernard Shaw a Dramatist. 1929. $6.50 Hdbd. Folcroft Pr., PA.

Holberg, Stanley M. Economic Rogue in the Plays of Bernard Shaw. 1971. (1953) $12.50 Hdbd. Lansdowne Pr., PA.

Howe, Percival P. Bernard Shaw: A Critical Study. 1915. $15.00 Hdbd. Folcroft Pr., PA.

Huang, John. Shaw & Galsworthy. 1932. $10.00 Hdbd. Folcroft Pr., PA.

Huggett, Richard. Truth About Pygmalion. 1970. $6.95 Hdbd. (ISBN 0-394-44977-0). Random House, NY.

Hulse, James W. Revolutionists in London: A Study of Five Unorthodox Socialists. 1970. $6.75 Hdbd. (ISBN 0-19-827175-1). Oxford Univ. Pr., NY.

Irvine, William. Universe of G. B. S. 1968. (1949) $13.00 Hdbd. Russell & Russell Publ., NY.

Jackson, Holbrook. Bernard Shaw. 2nd ed. (Select Bibliographies Ser). (1909) $9.50 Hdbd. (ISBN 0-8369-5247-O). Books for Libraries, NY.

Joad, C. E. Shaw & Society: An Anthology & a Symposium. 1953. $17.50 Hdbd. Folcroft Pr., PA.

Kaufmann, Ralph J., ed. G. B. Shaw: A Collection of Critical Essays. 1965. $1.95 pa. (ISBN 0-13-807776-2). Prentice-Hall, NY.

Lowenstein, F. E. Rehearsal Copies of Bernard Shaw's Play. 1950. $5.50 Hdbd. Folcroft Pr., PA.

Lowers, James K. Man & Superman Notes. $1.00 pa. (ISBN 0-8220-0807-6). Cliffs Notes, NB.

McCabe, Joseph. George Bernard Shaw: A Critical Study. 1914. $15.00 Hdbd. Folcroft Pr., PA.

MacCarthy, Desmond. Shaw. 1951. $12.50 Hdbd. Folcroft Pr., PA.

MacCarthy, Desmond. Shaw's Plays in Review. 1951. $12.50 Hdbd. Folcroft Pr., PA.

Matthews, John F. George Bernard Shaw. (Columbia Essays on Modern Writers, No. 45). 1969. $1.00 pa. (ISBN 0-231-03145-9). Columbia Univ. Pr., NY.

Mayne, Frederick. Wit and Satire of George Bernard Shaw. 1967. $6.95 Hdbd. St. Martin's Pr., NY.

Mencken, Henry L. George Bernard Shaw: His Plays. 1905. $10.00 Hdbd. Folcroft Pr., PA.

Mills, John A. Language & Laughter: Comic Diction in the Plays of Bernard Shaw. 1969. $6.50 Hdbd. (ISBN 0-8165-0182-3). Univ. of Arizona Pr., AZ.

Minney, R. J. Recollections of George Bernard Shaw. Orig. Title: Recollections of Shaw. 1969. $7.95 Hdbd. (ISBN 0-13-767384-1). Prentice-Hall, NY.

Nethercot, Arthur H. Men & Supermen: The Shavian Portrait Gallery. 2nd ed. 1966. $12.50 Hdbd. Benjamin Blom, NY.

Nickson, Richard. Monarch Literature Notes on Shaw's Arms & the Man. $1.00 pa. Monarch Pr., NY.

Nickson, Richard. Monarch Literature Notes on Shaw's Candida. $1.00 pa. Monarch Pr., NY.

Nickson, Richard. Monarch Literature Notes on Shaw's Man & Superman. $1.00 pa. Monarch Pr., NY.

Norwood, Gilbert. Euripides & Shaw. $6.00 Hdbd. Crescendo Publ., MA.

Nourse, Joan T. Monarch Literature

Notes on Shaw's Major Barbara. $1.00 pa. Monarch Pr., NY.

O'Donovan, John. Shaw & the Charlatan Genius. 1966. $4.50 Hdbd. Dufour Editions, PA.

Ohmann, Richard M. Shaw: The Style & the Man. $7.50 Hdbd. (ISBN 0-8195-3029-8). Wesleyan Univ. Pr., CT.

Pearson, Hesketh. George Bernard Shaw: His Life & Personality. 1963. $1.95 pa. (ISBN 0-689-70149-7, 36). Atheneum Publ., NY.

Pilecki, Gerard. Shaw's Geneva: A Critical Study of the Evolution of the Text in Relation to Shaw's Political Thought & Dramatic Practice. 1965. $8.00 pa. Humanities Pr., NY.

Purdom, Charles B. Guide to the Plays of Bernard Shaw. $1.75 pa. Apollo Editions, NY.

Rockman, Robert. Monarch Literature Notes on Shaw's Plays. $1.00 pa. Monarch Pr., NY.

Rosenblood, Norman, ed. Shaw: Seven Critical Essays. $6.00 Hdbd. (ISBN 0-8020-1731-2). Univ. of Toronto Pr., CAN.

Roy, R. N. Bernard Shaw's Philosophy of Life. 1964. $15.00 Hdbd. Folcroft Pr., PA.

Schwartz, Grace H. Monarch Literature Notes on Shaw's Caesar & Cleopatra. $1.00 pa. Monarch Pr., NY.

Schwartz, Grace H. Monarch Literature

Notes on Shaw's Pygmalion. $1.00 pa. Monarch Pr., NY.

Schwartz, Grace H. Monarch Literature Notes on Shaw's Saint Joan. $1.00 pa. Monarch Pr., NY.

Shaw, Bernard. Religious Speeches of Bernard Shaw. Smith, Warren S., ed. 1963. $5.00 Hdbd. (ISBN 0-271-73095-1). Pennsylvania St. Univ. Pr., PA.

Shaw, Bernard. Road to Eternity: Ten Unpublished Lectures and Essays 1884–1918. Crompton, Louis, ed. $7.50 Hdbd. Beacon Pr., NY.

Shaw, George B. G. B. Shaw: A Collection of Critical Essays. Kaufmann, R. J., ed. 1965. $5.95 Hdbd. (ISBN 0-13-807784-3). Prentice-Hall, NY.

Slosson, Edwin E. Six Major Prophets. 1917. $15.00 Hdbd. Folcroft Pr., PA.

Stanton, Stephen, ed. Casebook on Candida. 1962. $3.95 pa. (ISBN 0-690-17212-5). Thomas Y. Crowell, NY.

Strauss, E. Bernard Shaw, Art & Socialism. 1942. $10.00 Hdbd. Folcroft Pr., PA.

Strong, Archibald T. Four Studies. 1932. $10.00 Hdbd. Folcroft Pr., PA.

Ussher, Arland. Three Great Irishmen: Shaw, Yeats, Joyce. 1953. $6.75 Hdbd. (ISBN 0-8196-0222-1). Biblo & Tannen, NY.

Wagenknecht, Edward C. Guide to Bernard Shaw. 1971. (1929) $10.00 Hdbd. Russell & Russell Publ., NY.

Ward, Alfred C. Bernard Shaw. (Writers

& Their Work Ser No. 1). $2.25 Hdbd.; $1.00 pa. British Book Center, NY.

Watson, Barbara B. Shavian Guide to the Intelligent Woman. 1964. $6.00 Hdbd. (ISBN 0-393-04218-9). W. W. Norton, NY.

Weatherford, Richard M. Barron's Simplified Approach to Shaw's Pygmalion. (Hi–Sch.). 1968. $0.95 pa. Barron's Educ. Series, NY.

Weintraub, Stanley. Journey to Heartbreak Crucial Years of Bernard Shaw, 1914–1918. 1971. $8.95 Hdbd. Weybright & Talley, Inc., NY.

Weintraub, Stanley. Private Shaw & Public Shaw. 1962. $5.00 Hdbd. (ISBN 0-8076-0202-7). George Braziller, Inc., NY.

Wells, Geoffrey H. Bibliography of the Books & Pamphlets of George Bernard Shaw. 1925. $6.50 Hdbd. Folcroft Pr., PA.

West, Alick. George Bernard Shaw. 1950. $12.50 Hdbd. Folcroft Pr., PA.

West, Alick. Good Man Fallen Among Fabians. (Select Bibliographies Reprint Ser). 1950. $8.75 Hdbd. (ISBN 0-8369-5350-9). Books for Libraries, NY.

West, Alick. Good Man Fallen Among Fabians: G. B. Shaw. $12.50 Hdbd. Folcroft Pr., PA.

Whitehead, George. Bernard Shaw Explained. 1925. $20.00 Hdbd. Folcroft Pr., PA.

Wilson, Colin. Bernard Shaw: A Re-assessment. 1969. $6.95 Hdbd. (ISBN 0-689-10296-8). Atheneum Publ., NY.

Winsten, Stephen. Days with Bernard Shaw. $3.75 Hdbd. (ISBN 0-8149-0641-9). Vanguard Pr., NY.

Woodbridge, Homer E. G. B. Shaw: Creative Artist. 1963. $4.50 Hdbd. (ISBN 0-8093-0106-7, AB); $1.65 pa. (ISBN 0-8093-0159-8). Southern Illinois Univ. Pr., IL.

Zimbardo, Rose, ed. Twentieth Century Interpretations of Major Barbara. 1970. $4.95 Hdbd. (ISBN 0-13-545632-0). $1.25 pa. (ISBN 0-13-545624-X). Prentice-Hall, NY.

Sheridan, Richard Brinsley

Armstrong, Cecil F. Shakespeare to Shaw. 1913. $8.50 Hdbd. (ISBN 0-404-00383-4). AMS Pr., NY.

Darlington, W. A. Sheridan. (Writers & Their Work Ser No. 18). $2.25 Hdbd. $1.00 pa. British Book Center, NY.

Fiskin, A. M. The Rivals Notes. Incl. School for Scandal Notes. $1.00 pa. (ISBN 0-8220-1156-5). Cliffs Notes, NB.

Foss, Kenelm. Here Lies Richard Brinsley Sheridan. 1940. $22.50 Hdbd. Lansdowne Pr., PA.

Foss, Kenelm. Here Lies Richard Brinsley Sheridan. 1940. $22.50 Hdbd. Folcroft Pr., PA.

Gibbs, Lewis, pseud. Sheridan. 1970. (1947) $10.00 Hdbd. (ISBN 0-8046-0826-1). Kennikat Pr., NY.

LeFanu, William, ed. Betsy Sheridan's Journal: Letters from Sheridan's Sister, 1784–1786 & 1788–1790. 1960. $6.00 Hdbd. (ISBN 0-8135-0350-7). Rutgers Univ. Pr., NJ.

Moore, Thomas. Life of the Rt. Hon. Richard Brinsley Sheridan, 2 Vols. 1826. Set—$26.25 Hdbd. (ISBN 0-403-00072-6). Scholarly Pr., MI.

Moore, Thomas. Memoirs of the Life of the Right Honorable Richard Brinsley Sheridan. 1858. $26.25 Hdbd. (ISBN 0-8371-0573-0). Greenwood Pr., CT.

Oliphant, Margaret O. Sheridan. Morley, John, ed. 1889. $12.50 Hdbd. (ISBN 0-404-51724-2). AMS Pr., NY.

Oliver, Robert T. Four Who Spoke Out. (Biography Index Reprint Ser). 1946. $9.75 Hdbd. (ISBN 0-8369-8005-0). Books for Libraries, NY.

Price, C. J., ed. Sheridan: The School for Scandal. 1971. $1.60 pa. Oxford Univ. Pr., NY.

Rhodes, R. Crompton. Harlequin Sheridan, the Man & the Legend. 1933. $12.50 Hdbd. Benjamin Blom, NY.

Rhodes, R. Crompton. Harlequin Sheridan, the Man & the Legends. 1933. $20.00 Hdbd. Folcroft Pr., PA.

Sadler, Michael T. Political Career of Richard Brinsley Sheridan. 1912. $10.00 Hdbd. Folcroft Pr., PA.

Sheridan, Richard B. Plays & Poems of Richard Brinsley Sheridan, 3 Vols. Rhodes, Raymond C., ed. 1962. (1929) Set—$25.00 Hdbd. Russell & Russell Publ., NY.

Sherwin, Oscar. Uncorking Old Sherry: Richard Brinsley Sheridan. $6.00 Hdbd. Twayne Publ., NY.

Snider, Rose. Satire in the Comedies of Congreve, Sheridan, Wilde & Coward. 1937. $7.50 Hdbd. Folcroft Pr., PA.

Skelton, John

Carpenter, Nan C. Jóhn Skelton. Bowman, Sylvia E., ed. (English Authors Ser., No. 61). 1968. $4.95 Hdbd. Twayne Publ., NY.

Edwards, H. L. Skelton. facs. ed. (Select Bibliographies Reprint Ser). 1949. $12.50 Hdbd. (ISBN 0-8369-5673-7). Books for Libraries, NY.

Gordon, Ian A. John Skelton, Poet Laureate. 1969. (1943) $8.00 Hdbd. (Dist. by NYGS). Octagon Books, NY.

Gordon, Ian A. John Skelton, Poet Laureate. 1943. $12.50 Hdbd. Ridgeway Books, PA.

Graves, Robert. John Skelton, Laureate. $5.00 Hdbd. Ridgeway Books, PA.

Green, Peter. Skelton. (Writers & Their Work Ser No. 128). 1960. $1.75 Hdbd.; $1.00 pa. British Book Center, NY.

Heiserman, A. R. Skelton & Satire. 1961. $6.50 Hdbd. (ISBN 0-226-32570-9). Univ. of Chicago Pr., IL.

Lloyd, Leslie J. John Skelton: A Sketch of His Life & Writings. 1969. (1938) $8.00 Hdbd. Russell & Russell Publ., NY.

Nelson, William. John Skelton, Laureate. 1964. (1939) $8.50 Hdbd. Russell & Russell Publ., NY.

Pollet, Maurice. John Skelton. Warrington, John, tr. $10.00 Hdbd. (ISBN 0-8387-7737-6). Bucknell Univ. Pr., PA.

Skinner, Cornelia Otis

Skinner, Cornelia. Family Circle. $5.95 Hdbd. (ISBN 0-395-08195-5). Houghton-Mifflin, NY.

Sophocles

Adams, Sinclair M. Sophocles the Playwright. 1957. $6.50 Hdbd. (ISBN 0-8020-5048-4). Univ. of Toronto Pr., CAN.

Bates, William N. Sophocles. Poet & Dramatist. (Illus.). 1961. $1.95 pa. (ISBN 0-498-04047-X). A. S. Barnes, NY.

Bates, William N. Sophocles, Poet & Dramatist. 1969. (1940) $10.00 Hdbd. Russell & Russell Publ., NY.

Bowra, C. Maurice. Sophoclean Tragedy. (Hi–Sch.). 1944. $9.75 Hdbd. (ISBN 0-19-814303-6); $2.50 pa. (ISBN 0-19-881096-2). Oxford Univ. Pr., NY.

Cameron, Alister. Identity of Oedipus the King: Five Essays on the Oedipus Tyrannus. 1968. $6.95 text ed. (ISBN 0-8147-0071-3). New York Univ. Pr., NY.

Campbell, Lewis. Tragic Drama in Aeschylus, Sophocles & Shakespeare. 1965. (1904) $8.50 Hdbd. Russell & Russell Publ., NY.

Cook, Albert, ed. Oedipus Rex: A Mirror for Greek Drama. (Guides to Literary Study Ser). 1963. $2.95 pa. Wadsworth Publ. Co., CA.

Ehrenberg, Victor. Sophocles & Pericles. 1954. $5.00 Hdbd. Humanities Pr., NY.

Falk, Eugene H. Renunciation As a Tragic Focus: A Study of Five Plays. 1967. $3.75 pa. (ISBN 0-512-00174-X). Garrett Pr., NY.

Genthe, Hermann F. ⸜Index Commentationum Sophoclearum Ab a 1836 Editarum Triplex. 1967. (1874) $19.50 Hdbd. (ISBN 0-8337-1324-8). Burt Franklin, NY.

Goheen, Robert F. Imagery of Sophocles' Antigone. 1951. $6.00 Hdbd. (ISBN 0-691-06057-6). Princeton Univ. Pr., NJ.

Grene, David. Reality & the Heroic Pattern: Last Plays of Ibsen, Shakespeare & Sophocles. 1967. $1.95 pa. (ISBN 0-226-30789-1, 349). 1967. $6.00 Hdbd. (ISBN 0-226-30788-3). Univ. of Chicago Pr., IL.

Hill, Melvin. Critical Study Guide to Sophocles' Oedipus Rex & Other Plays. abr. ed. 1966. $1.00 pa. Littlefield, Adams & Co., NJ.

Kamerbeek, J. C. The Plays of Sophocles: Commentaries. Incl. Pt. 1. The/ Ajax. 1963. $14.75 Hdbd; Pt. 2. Trachinae. 1970. $14.00 Hdbd; Pt. 3. The/Antigone. price "n.g." Hdbd; Pt. 4. The/Oepidus Tyrannus. $14.75 Hdbd. 1967. Humanities Pr., NY.

Kirkwood, Gordon M. Study of Sophoclean Drama. 1958. $15.00 Hdbd. Johnson Reprint Corp., NY.

Knox, Bernard M. Heroic Temper: Studies in Sophoclean Tragedy. 1965. $7.00 Hdbd. (ISBN 0-520-00661-5). Univ. of Calif. Pr., CA.

Knox, Bernard M. Oedipus at Thebes: Sophocles' Tragic Hero & His Time. 1957. $7.50 Hdbd. (ISBN 0-300-00635-7). Yale Univ. Pr., CT.

Long, A. A. Language & Thought in Sophocles: A Study in Abstract Nouns & Poetic Technique. 1968. $8.80 Hdbd. Oxford Univ. Pr., NY.

Milch, Robert. King Oedipus, Oedipus at Colonus & Antigone: Notes. $1.00 pa. (ISBN 0-8220-0708-8). Cliffs Notes, NB.

Musurillo, Herbert. Light & the Darkness: Studies in the Dramatic Poetry of Sophocles. 1967. $13.25 Hdbd. Humanities Pr., NY.

O'Brien, Michael J., ed. Twentieth Century Interpretations of Oedipus Rex. 1968. $1.25 pa. (ISBN 0-13-530459-1). $4.95 Hdbd. (ISBN 0-13-630467-2). Prentice-Hall, NY.

Parlaviantza-Friedrich, Ursula. Taeuschungsszenen in den Tragoedien des Sophokles. (Ger). $6.05 Hdbd. (ISBN 3-11-002568-X). De Gruyter, Germany.

Patin, Alois. Asthetisch-Kritische Studien Zu Sophokles. 1911. $6.00 pa. Johnson Reprint Corp., NY.

Robinson, Charles A. Sophocles: The Theban Saga. (Jr. Hi.). 1966. $4.50 Hdbd. Franklin Watts, Inc., NY.

Shackford, Martha H. Shakespeare, Sophocles: Dramatic Themes & Modes. 1960. $1.45 pa. College & Univ. Pr., CT.

Sheppard, J. T. Aeschylus & Sophocles (Their Work & Influence. (Our Debt to Greece & Rome Ser). 1930. $3.50 Hdbd. (ISBN 0-8154-0205-8). Cooper Sq. Pr., NY.

Waldock, Arthur J. Sophocles the Dramatist. $4.50 Hdbd.; $2.25 pa. (ISBN 0-521-09374-0, 374) Cambridge Univ. Pr., NY.

Walter, William. Monarch Literature Notes on the Plays of Sophocles. $1.00 pa. Monarch Pr., NY.

Webster, Thomas B. Introduction to Sophocles. 2nd ed. 1969. $5.25 Hdbd. Barnes & Noble, NY.

Whitman, Cedric H. Sophocles: A Study of Heroic Humanism. 1951. $8.00 Hdbd. (ISBN 0-674-82140-8). Harvard Univ. Pr., MA.

Woodard, Thomas M., ed. Sophocles: A Collection of Critical Essays. 1966. $1.95 pa. (ISBN 0-13-822791-8). $5.95 Hdbd. (ISBN 0-13-822809-4). Prentice-Hall, NY.

Synge, John Millington

Bickley, Francis. J. M. Synge & the Irish Dramatic Movement. 1968. Repr. of 1912 ed. $6.50 Hdbd. Russell & Russell Publ., NY.

Bickley, Francis J. J. M. Synge & the Irish Dramatic Movement. 1912. $5.00 Hdbd. Folcroft Pr., PA.

Bourgeois, Maurice. John Millington Synge & the Irish Theatre. (Studies in Irish Literature Ser., No. 16). 1969. (1913) $8.95 Hdbd. (ISBN 0-8383-0511-3). Haskell House Publ., NY.

Bourgeois, Maurice. John Millington Synge & the Irish Theatre. 1913. $10.00 Hdbd. Benjamin Blom, NY.

Corkery, Daniel. Synge & Anglo-Irish Literature. 1965. (1931) $8.00 Hdbd. Russell & Russell Publ., NY.

Corkery, Daniel. Synge & Anglo-Irish Literature. 1971. $2.25 pa. (ISBN 0-8277-0548-4). British Book Center, NY.

Coxhead, Elizabeth. J. M. Synge & Lady Gregory. (Writers & Their Work Ser No. 149). 1962. $2.25 Hdbd.; $1.00 pa. British Book Center, NY.

Estill, Adelaide. Sources of Synge. 1939. $7.50 Hdbd. Folcroft Pr., PA.

Frenzel, Herbert. John Millington Synge's Work As a Contribution to Irish Folk-Lore. 1932. $10.00 Hdbd. Folcroft Pr., PA.

Gerstenberger, Donna. John Millington Synge. (Eng. Authors Ser., No. 12). 1964. $4.95 Hdbd. Twayne Publ., NY.

Howe, Percival P. J. M. Synge: A Critical Study. 1912. $8.50 Hdbd. Folcroft Pr., PA.

Howe, Percival P. J. M. Synge: A Critical Study. (Studies in Irish Literature Ser., No. 16). 1969. (1912) $8.95 Hdbd. (ISBN 0-8383-0202-5). Haskell House Publ., NY.

Howe, Percival P. J. M. Synge, a Critical Study. 1912. $9.25 Hdbd. (ISBN 0-8371-1628-7). Greenwood Pr., CT.

Johnston, Denis. John Millington Synge. 1965. $1.00 pa. (ISBN 0-231-02725-7). Columbia Univ. Pr., NY.

Masefield, John. John M. Synge. 1924. $5.00 Hdbd. Ridgeway Books, PA.

Saddlemyer, Ann. J. M. Synge & Modern Comedy. 1968. $2.50 Hdbd. Dufour Editions, PA.

Shaw, Ruth. John Synge's Aran. $7.50 Hdbd. Devin-Adair Co., NY.

Skelton, Robert. J. M. Synge & His World. 1971. $7.95 Hdbd. (ISBN 0-670-40729-1, Studio). Viking Pr., NY.

Skelton, Robert. J. M. Synge. Carens, James F., ed. (Irish Writers Ser). $4.50 Hdbd. (ISBN 0-8387-7769-4); $1.95 pa. (ISBN 0-8387-7687-6). Bucknell Univ. Pr., PA.

Strong, L. A. John Millington Synge. 1941. $5.50 Hdbd. Folcroft Pr., PA.

Synge, John M. John Millington Synge 1871-1909: A Catalogue of an Exhibition. 1959. $10.00 Hdbd. Folcroft Pr., PA.

Whitaker, Thomas R., ed. Twentieth Century Interpretations of Playboy of the Western World. 1969. $1.25 pa. (ISBN 0-13-682302-5). Prentice-Hall, NY.

Whitaker, Thomas R., ed. Twentieth Century Interpretations of The Playboy of the Western World. 1969. $4.95 Hdbd. (ISBN 0-13-682310-6). Prentice-Hall, NY.

Tagore, Rabindranath, Sir

Appasamy, Jaya. Rabanindranath Tagore & the Art of His Times. 1970. $15.00 Hdbd. International Publ. Service, NY.

Catlin, G. E. Rabindranath Tagore. 1964. $2.00 Hdbd. (ISBN 0-8188-1021-1). Paragon Books, NY.

Chakravarty, B. C. Rabindra Nath Tagore: His Mind & Art. 1971. $6.50 text ed. Fernhill House, NY.

Hay, Stephen N. Asian Ideas of East & West: Tagore & His Critics in Japan, China, & India. (East Asian Ser., No. 40). 1970. $15.00 text ed. (ISBN 0-674-04975-6). Harvard Univ. Pr., MA.

Khanolkar, G. D. Lute & the Plough: Life of Rabindranath Tagore. 1963. $8.00 Hdbd. Hillary House Publ., NY.

Kripalani, Krishna. Rabindranath Tagore: A Biography. 1962. $8.00 Hdbd. (ISBN 0-19-211137-X). Oxford Univ. Pr., NY.

Mukerjee, Himangshir B. Education for Fullness. $16.00 Hdbd. (ISBN 0-210-33845-8). Asia Publ. House, NY.

Radhakrishnan, Sarvepalli, ed. Rabindranath Tagore 1861-1961, a Centenary Vol. 1971. $22.50 Hdbd.- International Publ. Service, NY.

Ray, Benoy G. Philosophy of Rabindranath Tagore. 1970. $3.50 Hdbd. Lawrence Verry, Inc., CT.

Rhys, Ernest. Rabindrath Tagore. (1970) $8.95 Hdbd. (ISBN 0-8383-1185-7). Haskell House Publ., NY.

Singh, B. Tagore & the Romantic Ideology. 1963. $3.50 Hdbd. Lawrence Verry, Inc., CT.

Sinha, Sasadhar. Social Thinking of Rabindranath Tagore. 1962. $4.50 Hdbd. (ISBN 0-210-33998-5). Asia Publ. House, NY.

Tengshe, L. H. Tagore & His View of Art. 1961. $2.50 Hdbd. Lawrence Verry, Inc., CT.

Thomas, Dylan

Brinnin, John M. Dylan Thomas in America. 1971. $2.45 pa. (ISBN 0-316-10825-1). Little, Brown & Co., MA.

Brinnin, John M., ed. Casebook on Dylan Thomas. 1960. $3.50 pa. (ISBN 0-690-17354-7). Thomas Y Crowell, NY.

Cox, Charles B., ed. Dylan Thomas: A Collection of Critical Essays. 1966. $5.95 Hdbd. (ISBN 0-13-919381-2). Prentice-Hall, NY.

Cox, Charles B., ed. Dylan Thomas: A Collection of Critical Essays. 1966. $1.95 pa. (ISBN 0-13-919373-1). Prentice-Hall, NY.

Emery, Clark M. World of Dylan Thomas, 1962. $6.50 Hdbd. (ISBN 0-87024-013-7). Univ. of Miami Pr., FL.

Fitzgibbon. Constantine. Life of Dylan

Thomas. 1965. $8.95 Hdbd. (ISBN 0-316-28445-9, Pub. by Atlantic Monthly Pr); $2.65 pa. (ISBN 0-316-28444-0). Little, Brown & Co., MA.

Fraser, George S. Dylan Thomas. (Writers & Their Work Ser No. 90). $2.25 pa. British Book Center, NY.

Heppenstall, Rayner. Four Absentees: Eric Gill, Dylan Thomas, George Orwell & John Middleton Murry. 1963. $3.50 Hdbd. Dufour Editions, PA.

Korg, Jacob. Dylan Thomas. (Eng. Authors Ser., No. 20). 1964. $4.95 Hdbd. Twayne Publ., NY.

Maud, Ralph & Glover, Albert, eds. Dylan Thomas in Print: A Bibliographical History. 1970. $11.95 Hdbd. (ISBN 0-8229-3201-6). Univ. of Pittsburgh Pr., PA.

Moynihan, William T. Craft & Art of Dylan Thomas. 1966. $8.50 Hdbd. (ISBN 0-8014-0305-7); $1.95 pa. (ISBN 0-8014-9068-5). Cornell Univ. Pr., NY.

Pratt, Annis. Dylan Thomas Early Prose: A Study in Creative Mythology. 1970. $2.95 pa. (ISBN 0-8229-5215-7). Univ. of Pittsburgh Pr., PA.

Read, Bill & McKenna, Rollie. Days of Dylan Thomas. 1964. $1.95 pa. (ISBN 0-07-051281-7). McGraw-Hill, NY.

Thomas, Dylan. Portrait of the Artist As a Young Dog. 1956. $1.35 pa. New Directions Publ., NY.

Tindall, William Y. Reader's Guide to Dylan Thomas. 1962. $2.25 pa. Farrar, Straus & Giroux, NY.

Thomas, Dylan

Michaels, Sidney. Dylan. 1964. $5.50 Hdbd.; $1.65 pa. Random House, NY.

Tolstoi, Lev Nikolaevich, Graf

Aldanov, Mark. Zagadka Tolstogo. 1st U. S. ed. Winner, Thomas G., ed. 1969. $3.00 pa. (ISBN 0-87057-114-1). Brown Univ. Pr., RI.

Arnold, Matthew. Essays in Criticism: Second Series. Littlewood, S. R., ed. 1938. $1.95 Hdbd. St. Martin's Pr., NY.

Berlin, Isaiah. Hedgehog & the Fox: An Essay on Tolstoy's View of History. $1.25 pa. Simon & Schuster, NY.

Bodde, Derk. Tolstoy & China. 1950. $5.00 Hdbd. Johnson Reprint Corp., NY.

Bulgakov, Valentin. Last Year of Leo Tolstoy. Dunnigan, Ann, tr. 1971. $7.95 Hdbd. Dial Pr., NY.

Christian, Reginald F. Tolstoy: A Critical Introduction. 1970. $10.50 Hdbd. (ISBN 0-521-07493-2); $2.95 pa. (ISBN 0-521-09585-9, 585). Cambridge Univ. Pr., NY.

Collis, John S. Marriage & Genius: Stringberg & Tolstoy. 1963. $10.00 Hdbd. Hillary House Publ., NY.

Davis, Helen E. Tolstoy & Nietzsche. (Studies in Comparative Literature, No. 35). 1970. (1929) $5.95 Hdbd. (ISBN 0-8383-1079-6). Haskell House Publ., NY.

Ellis, Havelock. New Spirit. 1969.

(1925) $10.00 Hdbd. Kraus Reprint Co., NY.

Fausset, Hugh L. Tolstoy, the Inner Drama. 1968. (1927) $10.00 Hdbd. Russell & Russell Publ., NY.

Flaccus, Louis W. Artists & Thinkers. (Essay Index Reprint Ser). 1916. $1.75 Hdbd. (ISBN 0-8369-0444-3). Books for Libraries, NY.

Garrod, H. W. Tolstoi's Theory of Art. 1971. (1935) $4.00 Hdbd. Lansdowne Pr., PA.

Gibian, George. Tolstoi & Shakespeare. 1957. $3.00 pa. Humanities Pr., NY.

Gibian, George. Tolstoy & Shakespeare. 1957. $10.00 Hdbd. Folcroft Pr., PA.

Goldenweizer, A. B. Talks with Tolstoy. 1969. (1923) $6.50 Hdbd. (ISBN 0-8180-0208-5); $2.45 pa. (ISBN 0-8180-0209-3). Horizon Pr., NY.

Gorky, Maxim. Reminiscences of Tolstoy, Chekhov & Andreev. 1968. $3.00 Hdbd. Hillary House Publ., NY.

Gorky, Maxim. Reminiscences of Tolstoy, Chekhov & Andreyev. $1.25 pa. (ISBN 0-670-00055-8). Viking Pr., NY.

Gunn, Elizabeth. Daring Coiffeur: Reflections on War & Peace & Anna Karenina. 1971. $5.00 Hdbd. (ISBN 0-87471-031-6). Rowman & Littlefield, Inc., NY.

Hayman, Ronald, Tolstoy. (Profiles in Literature Ser). 1970. $3.50 Hdbd; $1.75 pa. (ISBN 0-391-00050-0) (ISBN 0-391-00051-9). Humanities Pr., NY.

Heller, Otto. Prophets of Dissent: Essays on Maeterlinck, Strindberg, Nietzsche & Tolstoi. 1918. $8.00 Hdbd. (ISBN 0-8046-0200-X). Kennikat Pr., NY.

Kenworthy, L. C. Tolstoy: His Life & Works. (Studies in European Literature Ser., No. 151). 1971. $9.95 Hdbd. (ISBN 0-8383-1287-X). Haskell House Publ., NY.

Lavrin, Janko. Tolstoy, an Approach. 1968. (1946) $7.50 Hdbd. Russell & Russell Publ., NY.

Lednicki, Waclaw. Tolstoy Between War & Peace. 1965. $9.00 Hdbd. Humanities Pr., NY.

Leslie, Shane, 3rd. Salutation to Five: Mrs. Fitzherbert, Edmund Warre, Sir William Butler, Leo Tolstoy, Sir Mark Sykes. (Biography Index Reprint Ser., Vol. 2). 1951. $9.00 Hdbd. (ISBN 0-8369-8027-1). Books for Libraries, NY.

Matlaw, Ralph E., ed. Tolstoy: A Collection of Critical Essays. 1967. $5.95 Hdbd. (ISBN 0-13-934704-1). $1.95 pa. (ISBN 0-13-924704-1). Prentice-Hall, NY.

Merezhkovski, Dmitri. Tolstoi As Man & Artist with an Essay on Dostoievski. 1970. (1902) $13.00 Hdbd. (ISBN 0-403-00350-4). Scholarly Pr., MI.

Merezhkovski, Dmitri S. Tolstoi As Man & Artist. 1902. $11.00 Hdbd. (ISBN 0-8371-4098-6). Greenwood Pr., CT.

Mittal, Sarla. Tolstoy: Social & Political

Ideas. 1966. $7.50 Hdbd. Lawrence Verry, Inc., CT.

Munoz, V. Tolstoy Chronology. $5.95 Hdbd. Herbert C. Roseman, NY.

Noyes, George R. Tolstoy. 1968. $2.50 pa. (ISBN 0-486-21930-5). Dover Publ., NY.

Noyes, George R. Tolstoy. $4.75 Hdbd. Peter Smith Publ., MA.

Philipson, Morris. Count Who Wished He Were a Peasant: A Life of Leo Tolstoy. (Pantheon Portrait Ser). (Jr Hi.). 1967. $5.17 Hdbd. Pantheon Books, Inc., NY.

Reaske, Herbert. Monarch Literature Notes on Tolstoy's Anna Karenina. $1.00 pa. Monarch Pr., NY.

Redpath, Theodore. Tolstoy. 1961. (1960) $2.50 Hdbd. Hillary House Publ., NY.

Rolland, Romain. Tolstoy. Miall, Bernard, tr. 1971. (1911) $10.00 Hdbd. (ISBN 0-8046-1608-6). Kennikat Pr., NY.

Rothkopf, Carol. Leo Tolstoy. (Immortals: Biographies, II). (Jr Hi.). 1968. $4.50 Hdbd. (ISBN 0-531-00926-2). Franklin Watts, Inc., NY.

Schutte, William. Six Novelists: Stendahl, Dostoyevsky, Tolstoy, Hardy, Dreiser, Proust. 1959. $12.50 Hdbd. Ridgeway Books, PA.

Shestov, Lev. Dostoevsky, Tolstoy & Nietzsche. 1969. $10.00 Hdbd. (ISBN 0-8214-0053-3). Ohio Univ. Pr., OH.

Simmons, Ernest J. Introduction to Tolstoy's Writings. 1968. $5.50 Hdbd. (ISBN 0-226-75807-9). 1969. $1.95 pa. (ISBN 0-226-75808-7). Univ. of Chicago Pr., IL.

Simmons, Ernest J. Leo Tolstoy, 2 Vols. Set—$7.00 Hdbd. Peter Smith Publ., MA.

Speirs, Logan. Tolstoy & Chekhov. 1971. $8.00 Hdbd. (ISBN 0-521-07950-0). Cambridge Univ. Pr., NY.

Steiner, Edward A. Tolstoy the Man. (Philosophy Ser., No. 40). 1969. (1909) $11.95 Hdbd. (ISBN 0-8383-1006-0). Haskell House Publ., NY.

Sturman, Marianne. Anna Karenina Notes. $1.00 pa. (ISBN 0-8220-0183-7). Cliffs Notes, NB.

Troyat, Henri. Tolstoy. Amphoux, Nancy, tr. 1967. $7.95 Hdbd. Doubleday & Co., NY.

Troyat, Henri. Tolstoy. 1969. $1.65 pa. Dell Publ. Co., NY.

Weitz, Morris. Philosophy in Literature: Shakespeare, Voltaire, Tolstoy & Proust. 1963. $2.45 pa. (ISBN 0-8143-1201-2). Wayne St. Univ. Pr., MI.

Zweers, Alexander F. Grown-up Narrator & Child-Like Hero: An Analysis of the Literary Devices in Tolstoy's Trilogy-Childhood, Boyhood, & Youth. 1971. $9.00 Hdbd. Humanities Pr., NY.

Vega Carpio, Lope Felix De

Fitzmaurice-Kelly, J. Lope De Vega & Spanish Drama. (Eruopean Literature Ser., No. 151). 1970. (1902) $5.95

(ISBN 0-8383-1073-7). Haskell House Publ., N.Y.

Flores, Angel. Lope De Vega, Monster of Nature. 1930. $10.00 Hdbd. (ISBN 0-8371-2541-3). Greenwood Pr., CT.

Flores, Angel. Lope De Vega: Monster of Nature. 1969. (1930) $9.00 Hdbd. (ISBN 0-8046-0675-7). Kennikat Pr., NY.

Hayes, Francis C. Lope De Vega. (World Authors Ser., No. 28). 1968. $5.50 Hdbd. Twayne Publ., NY.

McCrary, William C. Goldfinch & the Hawk: A Study of Lope De Vega's: El Caballero De Olmedo. (Romance Language & Literature Studies). 1966. $5.00 pa. (ISBN 0-8078-9062-6). Univ. of N.C. Pr., NC.

Morley, S. G. & Bruerton, C. Chronology of Lope De Vega's Comedias. 1940. $17.00 pa. Kraus Reprint Co., NY.

Parker, Jack H. & Fox, Arthur M., eds. Lope De Vega Studies, 1937–62: A Critical Survey & Annotated Bibliography. 1964. $7.50 pa. (ISBN O-8020-1389-9). Univ. of Toronto Pr., CAN.

Peyton, Myron A., ed. Lope De Vega: El Peregrino En Su Patria. (Sp). 1971. $14.00 pa. (ISBN 0-8078-9097-9). Univ. of N.C. Pr., NC.

Rennert, Hugo A. Life of Lope De Vega. 1968. $12.50 Hdbd. Benjamin Blom, NY.

Schevill, Rudolph. The Dramatic Art of Lope De Vega. Incl. La Dama Boba.

(Span.). 1964. (1918) $8.50 Hdbd. Russell & Russell Publ., NY.

Spitzer, Leo. Literarisierung Des Lebens in Lope's Dorotea. 1932. $3.50 pa. Johnson Reprint Corp., NY.

Vega Carpio, Lope Felix De— Bibliography

Parker, Jack H. & Fox, Arthur M., eds. Lope De Vega Studies, 1937–62: A critical Survey & Annotated Bibliography. 1964. $7.50 pa. (ISBN 0-8020-1389-9). Univ. of Toronto Pr., CAN.

Webster, John

Ansari, K. H. John Webster: Image Patterns & Canon. 1969. $7.50 Hdbd. Lawrence Verry, Inc., CT.

Bogard, Travis. Tragic Satire of John Webster. 1965. (1955) $8.00 Hdbd. Russell & Russell Publ., NY.

Boklund, Gunnar. Sources of the White Devil, John Webster. (Studies in Comparative Literature Ser., No. 35). 1969. (1957) $10.95 Hdbd. (ISBN 0-8383-0648-9). Haskell House Publ., NY.

Boklund, K. Gunnar. Duchess of Malfi: Sources, Themes, Characters. 1962. $5.50 Hdbd. (ISBN 0-674-21801-9). Harvard Univ. Pr., MA.

Brooke, Rupert. John Webster & the Elizabethan Drama. 1967. (1916) $8.00 Hdbd. Russell & Russell Publ., NY.

Hunter, G. K. & Hunter, S. K., eds. John Webster. (Critical Anthologies Ser). 1970. $2.25 pa. (ISBN 0-14-080135-9). Penguin Books, MD.

Leech, C. John Webster. (English Biography Ser., No. 31). 1969. (1951) $8.95 Hdbd. (ISBN 0-8383-0690-X). Haskell House Publ., NY.

Leech, Clifford. Duchess of Malfi by Webster: Critical Analysis. Daiches, David, ed. (Studies in English Literature Ser). (Hi-Sch.). 1963. $1.00 pa. Barron's Educ. Series, NY.

Murray, Peter B. Study of John Webster. (Studies in English Literature Ser, No. 50). 1970. $12.00 Hdbd. Humanities Pr., NY.

Rabkin, Norman. Twentieth Century Interpretations of the Duchess of Malfi. 1968. $4.95 Hdbd. (ISBN 0-13-221069-X). $1.25 pa. (ISBN 0-13-221051-7). Prentice-Hall, NY.

Scott-Kilvert, Ian. John Webster. (Writers & Their Work Ser No. 175). 1964. $2.25 Hdbd.; $1.00 pa. British Book Center, NY.

Stoll, Elmer E. John Webster. 1906. $5.00 Hdbd. Folcroft Pr., PA.

Stoll, Elmer E. John Webster, the Periods of His Work As Determined by His Relations to the Drama of His Day. 1967. (1905) $6.00 Hdbd. (ISBN 0-87752-107-7). Gordian Pr., NY.

Tannenbaum, Samuel. John Webster: A Concise Bibliography. 1941. $10.00 Hdbd. Ridgeway Books, PA.

Wells, Herbert George

Belgion, Montgomery. H. G. Wells. (Writers & Their Work Ser No. 40).

$2.25 Hdbd.; $1.00 pa. British Book Center, NY.

Bergonzi, Bernard. Early H. G. Wells: Study of the Scientific Romances. 1962. $6.25 Hdbd. Univ. of Toronto Pr., CAN.

Brome, Vincent. H. G. Wells. 1951. $10.75 Hdbd. (ISBN 0-8371-3827-2). Greenwood Pr., CT.

Brome, Vincent. H. G. Wells. (Select Bibliographies Reprint Ser). 1961. $9.75 Hdbd. (ISBN 0-8369-5547-1). Books for Libraries, NY.

Brooks, Van Wyck. The World of H. G. Wells. $6.95 Hdbd. Haskell House Publ., NY.

Brooks, Van-Wyck. World of H. G. Wells. 1970. (1915) $6.95 Hdbd. (ISBN 0-403-00536-1). Scholarly Pr., MI.

Brooks, Van Wyck. World of H. G. Wells. $6.50 Hdbd. Gordon Publ., NY.

Connes, G. A. Dictionary of the Characters & Scenes in the Novels, Romances & Short Stories of H. G. Wells. 1926. $20.00 Hdbd. Folcroft Pr., PA.

Costa, Richard H. H. G. Wells. (Eng. Authors Ser., No. 43). 1966. $4.95 Hdbd. Twayne Publ., NY.

Cross, Wilbur L. Four Contemporary Novelists. 1930. $5.25 Hdbd. (ISBN 0-404-01867-X). AMS Pr., NY.

Dickson, Lovat. H. G. Wells: His Turbulent Life & Times. (IL). 1969. $10.00 Hdbd. (ISBN 0-689-10067-1); $3.45 pa.

(ISBN 0-689-70274-4). Atheneum Publ., NY.

Hillegas, Mark R. Future As Nightmare: H. G. Wells and the Anti-Utopians. 1967. $6.50 Hdbd. (ISBN 0-19-500575-9). Oxford Univ. Pr., NY.

Hopkins, R. Thurston. H. G. Wells. 1971. (1922) $20.00 Hdbd. Lansdowne Pr., PA.

Hopkins, R. Thurston. H. G. Wells. 1922. $20.00 Hdbd. Folcroft Pr., PA.

Raknem, Ingvald. H. G. Wells & His Critics. 1962. $8.00 Hdbd. Hillary House Publ., NY.

Van Wyck Brooks, F., ed. World of H. G. Wells. (English Biography Ser., No. 31). 1969. $6.95 Hdbd. (ISBN 0-838-0962-3). Haskell House Publ., NY.

West, Geoffrey. H. G. Wells, a Sketch For a Portrait. 1930. $15.00 Hdbd. Folcroft Pr., PA.

Wood, James P. I Told You So: A Life of H. G. Wells. (Portrait Ser). (Hi-Sch.). 1969. $4.50 Hdbd. Pantheon Books, NY.

Wilde, Oscar

Beckson, Karl, ed. Oscar Wilde: The Critical Heritage. (The Critical Heritage Ser). 1970. $15.00 Hdbd. (ISBN 0-389-04059-2). Barnes and Noble, NY.

Bendz, Ernst. Oscar Wild. 1921. $8.50 Hdbd. Folcroft Pr., PA.

Braybrooke, Patrick. Oscar Wilde: A Study. 1929. $12.50 Hdbd. Folcroft Pr., PA.

Douglas, Alfred. Oscar Wilde: A Summing Up. 1940. $5.00 Hdbd. Lawrence Verry Inc., CT.

Ellman, Richard, ed. Oscar Wilde: A Collection of Critical Essays. (Twentieth Century Views Ser). 1969. $5.95 Hdbd. (ISBN 0-13-959486-8) (ISBN 0-13-959478-7). $1.95 pa. (ISBN 0-13-959478-7). Prentice-Hall, NY.

Harris, Frank. Oscar Wilde. 1959. $7.00 Hdbd. (ISBN 0-87013-043-9). Mich State Univ. Pr., MI.

Jullian, Philippe. Oscar Wilde. Wyndham, V., tr. 1969. $7.95 Hdbd. (ISBN 0-670-52906-0). Viking Pr., NY.

Laver, James. Oscar Wilde. (Writers & Their Work Ser No. 53). $2.24 Hdbd.; $1.00 pa. British Bk Ctr., NY.

Lewis, Lloyd & Smith, Henry J. Oscar Wilde Discovers America, Eighteen Eighty-Two. (Illus.). 1967. Repr. $12.50 Hdbd. Benjamin Blom, NY.

Mason, Stuart. Oscar Wilde & the Aesthetic Movement. (English Literature Ser., No. 33). 1970. (1930) $9.95 Hdbd. (ISBN 0-8383-1077-X). Haskell House Publ., NY.

Ojala, Aatos. Aestheticism & Oscar Wilde, Part 1 & 2, Life & Letters. 1955. $17.50 ea. Hdbd. Folcroft Pr., PA.

Partridge, Edward. Oscar Wilde. Carens, James F., ed. (Irish Writers Ser). $4.50 Hdbd. (ISBN 0-8387-7763-5); $1.95 pa. (ISBN 0-8387-7700-7). Bucknell Univ. Pr., PA.

Ransom, Arthur. Oscar Wilde: A Critical Study. (English Literature—General Ser., No. 33). 1971. $9.95 Hdbd. (ISBN 0-8383-1230-6). Haskell House Publ., NY.

Ransome, Arthur. Oscar Wilde: A Critical Study. 1912. $15.00 Hdbd. Folcroft Pr., PA.

Raymond, Jean P. & Ricketts, Charles. Oscar Wilde Recollections. 1932. $10.00 Hdbd. Folcroft Pr., PA.

Roditi, Edouard. Oscar Wilde. $3.00 Hdbd. New Directions, NY.

Ryskamp, Charles, ed. Wilde & the Nineties. 1966. $3.50 Hdbd. (ISBN 0-87811-010-0). Princeton Univ. Lib., NJ.

Saltus, Edgar. Oscar Wilde: An Idler's Impression. 1917. $10.00 Hdbd. (ISBN 0-404-05542-7). AMS Pr., NY.

San Juan, Epitanio, Jr. Art of Oscar Wilde. 1967. $7.50 Hdbd. (ISBN 0-691-06006-1). Princeton Univ. Pr., NJ.

Schwartz, Grace H. Monarch Literature Notes on the Plays of Oscar Wilde. $1.00 pa. Monarch Pr., NY.

Sherard, R. H. Oscar Wilde. (English Biography, No. 31). 1970. (1905) $9.95 Hdbd. (ISBN 0-8383-1181-4). Haskell House Publ., NY.

Snider, Rose. Satire in the Comedies of Congreve, Sheridan, Wilde & Coward. 1937. $7.50 Hdbd. Folcroft Pr., PA.

Symonds, Arthur. Study of Oscar Wilde. 1930. $10.00 Hdbd. Folcroft Pr., PA.

Wit & Wisdom of Oscar Wilde. (Stan-

yan Bks). 1970. $3.00 Hdbd. (46811). Random House, NY.

Williams, Tennessee

Austell, Jan. What's in a Play. (Curriculum-Related Bks). (Hi-Sch.). 1968. $3.50 Hdbd. (ISBN 0-15-295500-3). Harcourt Brace Jovanovich, NY.

Donahue, Francis. Dramatic World of Tennessee Wiliiams. 1964. $6.50 Hdbd. (ISBN 0-8044-2139-0). Frederick Ungar, NY.

Falk, Signi. Tennessee Williams. (U.S. Authors Ser., No. 10). $4.95 Hdbd. Twayne Publ., NY.

Falk, Signi L. Tennessee Williams. (Twayne's United States Authors Ser). 1961. $2.45 pa. (10, T). Coll. & Univ. Pr., NY.

Fedder, Norman. Influence of D. H. Lawrence on Tennessee Williams. 1966. $6.25 pa. Humanities Pr., NY.

Hurrell, John D., ed. Two Modern American Tragedies. (Research Anthology Ser). 1961. $2.95 pa. (ISBN 0-684-41292-6). Charles Scribner's Sons, NY.

Jackson, Esther M. Broken World of Tennessee Williams. 1965. $2.50 pa. (ISBN 0-299-03424-0). Univ. of Wis. Pr., WI.

Nelson, Benjamin. Monarch Literature Notes on the Major Plays of Tennessee Williams. $1.00 pa. (00650). Monarch Pr., NY.

Nelson, Benjamin. Tennessee Williams.

1970. $7.00 Hdbd. (ISBN 0-391-00071-3). Humanities Pr., NY.

Nelson, Benjamin. Tennessee Williams. 1961. $6.50 Hdbd. (ISBN 0-8392-1111-2). Astor-Honor, Inc., NY.

Rathbun, Gilbert. Monarch Literature Notes on Williams' Glass Menagerie. $1.00 pa. (00700). Monarch Pr., NY.

Rathbun, Gilbert. Monarch Literature Notes on Williams' Street Car Named Desire. $1.00 pa. (00701). Monarch Pr., NY.

Roberts, James L. The Glass Menagerie Notes. Incl. A Streetcar Named Desire Notes. $1.00 pa. (ISBN 0-8220-0533-6). Cliffs Notes, NB.

Tischler, Nancy M. Tennessee Williams. (Southern Writers Ser). 1969. $1.00 pa. (ISBN 0-8114-3847-3). Steck-Vaughn Co., TX.

Weales, Gerald. Tennessee Williams. 1965. $0.95 pa. (ISBN 0-8166-0368-5, MPAW53). Univ. of Minn. Pr., MN.

Wodehouse, P. G.

Jasen, David A. Bibliography & Reader's Guide to the First Editions of P. G. Wodehouse. 1970. $9.00 Hdbd. (ISBN 0-208-01030-0). Shoe String Pr., CT.

Voorhees, Richard J. P. G. Wodehouse. (Eng. Authors Ser., No. 44). 1966. $4.95 Hdbd. Twayne Publs., NY.

Yeats, William Butler

Adams, Hazard. Blake & Yeats: The Contrary Vision. 1968. (1955) $11.00 Hdbd. Russell & Russell, NY.

Aldington, Richard. A. E. Housman & W. B. Yeats. 1955. $5.00 Hdbd. Folcroft Pr., PA.

Barker, Dudley. Prominent Edwardians. 1969. $6.50 Hdbd. (ISBN 0-689-10021-3). Atheneum Publ., N.Y.

Berryman, Charles W. Yeats: Design of Opposites. 1967. $6.00 Hdbd. (ISBN 0-682-45715-9). Exposition Pr., NY.

Beum, Robert. Poetic Art of William Butler Yeats. 1968. $5.50 Hdbd. (ISBN 0-8044-2039-4). Frederick Ungar, NY.

Bjersby, B. Interpretation of the Cuchulain Legend in the Works of W. B. Yeats. 1950. $15.00 Hdbd. Folcroft Pr., PA.

Bloom, Harold. Yeats. 1970. $12.50 Hdbd. (ISBN 0-19-500489-2). Oxford Univ. Pr., NY.

Bornstein, George. Yeats & Shelley. 1970. $8.75 Hdbd. (ISBN 0-226-06645-2). Univ. of Chicago Pr., IL.

Bradford, Curtis. Yeats at Work. 1965. $12.50 Hdbd. (ISBN 0-8093-0180-6). S. Ill. Univ. Pr., IL.

Bushrui, S. B. Yeats's Verse-Plays: The Revisions 1900–1910. 1965. $4.50 Hdbd. (ISBN 0-19-811616-0). Oxford Univ. Pr., NY.

Clarke, Auston. Celtic Twilight & the Nineties. 1970. $5.50 Hdbd. Dufour Editions, PA.

Cowell, Raymond. W. B. Yeats. (Arco Literary Critiques Ser). 1970. $3.95 Hdbd. (ISBN 0-668-02180-2); $1.95 pa. (ISBN 0-668-02179-9). Arco Publ. Co., NY.

Cowell, Raymond, ed. Critics on Yeats. $3.95 Hdbd. (ISBN 0-87024-200-8). Univ. of Miami Pr., FL.

Domville, Eric. Concordance to the Plays of W. B. Yeats, 2 Vols. (Concordances). 1971. Vol. 1. price "n.g." Hdbd. (ISBN 0-8014-0663-3); Vol. 2. price "n.g." Hdbd. (ISBN 0-8014-0666-8). Cornell Univ. Pr., NY.

Donoghue, D. Integrity of Yeats. 1971. $1.25 pa. (ISBN 0-8277-0544-1). British Bk. Ctr., NY.

Donoghue, Denis. Integrity of Yeats. 1964. $10.00 Hdbd. Folcroft Pr., PA.

Donoghue, Denis. William Butler Yeats. (Modern Master Ser). 1971. $4.95 Hdbd. Viking Pr., NY.

Dougan, R. O. W. B. Yeats Manuscripts & Printed Books. 1956. $5.00 Hdbd. Folcroft Pr., PA.

Eddins, Dwight. Yeats: The Nineteenth Century Matrix. 1971. $6.75 Hdbd. (ISBN 0-8173-7309-8). Univ. of Ala. Pr., AL.

Ellis-Fermor, Una. Irish Dramatic Movement. 2nd ed. (Orig.). 1967. $2.75 Hdbd. (ISBN 0-416-69740-2, 204). Barnes & Noble, NY.

Ellman, Richard. Yeats: The Man & the Masks. $1.95 pa. (ISBN 0-525-47024-7). E. P. Dutton, NY.

Ellmann, Richard. Eminent Domain: Yeats Among Wilde, Joyce, Pound, Eliot & Auden. 1967. $5.50 Hdbd. (ISBN 0-19-500540-6). 1970. $1.75 pa. Oxford Univ. Pr., NY.

Ellmann, Richard. Identity of Yeats. 2nd ed. 1964. $10.00 Hdbd. (ISBN 0-19-501233-X). $2.45 pa. (ISBN 0-19-500712-3). Oxford Univ. Pr., NY.

Engelberg, Edward. Vast Design: Patterns in W. B. Yeats's Aesthetic. 1964. $7.50 Hdbd. (ISBN 0-8020-5135-9). Univ. of Toronto Pr., CAN.

Fraser, George S. W. B. Yeats. (Writers & Their Work Ser No. 50). $22.25 Hdbd.; $1.00 pa. British Book Center, NY.

Gilbert, Sandra. Monarch Literature Notes on the Poetry of Yeats. $1.00 pa. Monarch Pr., NY.

Gogarty, Oliver S. William Butler Yeats. 1963. $2.25 Hdbd. Dufour Editions, PA.

Green, Martin. Yeats's Blessings on Von Hugel. 1968. $7.95 Hdbd. (ISBN 0-393-04296-0). W. W. Norton, NY.

Gwynn, Stephen. William Butler Yeats. Orig. Title: Scattering Branches. 1940. $8.00 Hdbd. (ISBN 0-8046-0187-9). Kennikat Pt., NY.

Hall, James & Steinmann, Martin. Permanence of Yeats. $4.00 Hdbd. Peter Smith Publ., MA.

Hall, James & Steinmann, Martin, eds. Permanence of Yeats. 1961. $1.50 pa. Macmillan Co., NY.

Hanley, Mary. Thoor Ballylee: Home of William Butler Yeats. Miller, Liam, ed. 1965. $1.50 pa. Dufour Editions, PA.

Hone, Joseph. W. B. Yeats Eighteen Sixty-Five to Nineteen Thirty-Nine. 2nd ed. 1962. $14.00 Hdbd. St. Martin's Pr., NY.

Jeffares, Alexander Norman. Circus Animals: Essays on W. B. Yeats. 1970. $8.50 Hdbd. (ISBN 0-8047-0754-5). Stanford Univ. Pr., CA.

Jeffares, Alexander Norman. W. B. Yeats. (Profiles in Literature Ser). 1971. $3.75 text ed. (ISBN 0-391-00163-9). Humanities Pr., NY.

Jeffares, Alexander Norman. W. B. Yeats: Man & Poet. 1966. $6.50 Hdbd.; $2.50 pa. (ISBN 0-389-02585-2, 421). Barnes & Noble, NY.

Kermode, Frank. Romantic Image. 1964. $1.65 pa. (ISBN 0-394-70260-3). Random House, NY.

Krans, Horatio S. William Butler Yeats & the Irish Literary Revival. (Studies in Irish Literature Ser., No. 16). 1969. (1904) $10.95 Hdbd. (ISBN 0-8383-0691-8). Haskell House Publ., NY.

Lentricchia, Frank. Gaiety of Language: An Essay on the Radical Poetics of W. B. Yeats & Wallace Stevens. 1968. $5.75 Hdbd. (ISBN 0-520-00722-0). Univ. of Cal. Pr., CA.

Levine, Bernard. Dissolving Image: Spiritual-Esthetic Development of W. B. Yeats. 1970. $6.95 Hdbd. (ISBN 0-8143-1414-7). Wayne St. Univ. Pr., MI.

McHugh, Roger, ed. Ah, Sweet Dancer: W. B. Yeats & Margot Ruddock, a Correspondence. 1971. $4.95 Hdbd. Macmillan Co., NY.

Marcus, Phillip L. Yeats & the Beginning of the Irish Renaissance. 1970.

$10.50 Hdbd. (ISBN 0-8014-0591-2). Cornell Univ. Pr., NY.

Misra, B. P. W. B. Yeats. 1962. $10.00 Folcroft Pr., PA.

Mokashi-Punekar, Shankar. Later Phase in the Development of W. B. Yeats. 1966. $20.00 Hdbd. Folcroft Pr., PA.

Moore, John R. Masks of Love & Death: Yeats As Dramatist. 1971. $9.75 Hdbd. (ISBN 0-8014-0608-0). Cornell Univ. Pr., NY.

Nathan, Leonard E. Tragic Drama of William Butler Yeats: Figures in a Dance. 1965. $9.00 Hdbd. (ISBN 0-231-02765-6). Columbia Univ. Pr., NY.

O'Connor, Ulick, ed. Yeats We Knew, 1971. $1.25 pa. (ISBN 0-8277-0603-0). British Book Center, NY.

Pollock, J. H. William Butler Yeats. 1935. $10.00 Hdbd. Folcroft Pr., PA.

Rajan, Balachandra. W. B. Yeats: A Critical Introduction. 2nd ed. (Hutchinson University Library-Literature). 1970. $4.50 Hdbd. Hutchinson Univ. Library, NY.

Reid, Forrest. W. B. Yeats: A Critical Study. 1915. $15.00. Folcroft Pr., PA.

Ronsley, Joseph. Yeats's Autobiography: Life As Symbolic Pattern. 1968. $5.00 Hdbd. (ISBN 0-674-96495-0). Harvard Univ. Pr., MA.

Rudd, Margaret E. Divided Image. (Studies in Blake, No. 3). 1970. (1953)

$9.95 Hdbd. (ISBN 0-8383-1015-X). Haskell House Publ., NY.

Saul, George B. Prolegomena to the Study of Yeats' Plays. (1971) $7.50 Hdbd. 1970. $6.50 Hdbd. Octagon Books, Inc., NY.

Shaw, Priscilla W. Rilke, Valery & Yeats: The Domain of the Self. 1964. $6.00 Hdbd. (ISBN 0-8135-0454-6). Rutgers Univ. Pr., NJ.

Skelton, Robin & Saddlemyer, Ann, eds. World of W. A. Yeats. rev. ed. 1967. $6.95 Hdbd.; $2.95 pa. (ISBN 0-295-97853-8). Univ. of Wash. Pr., WA.

Stoll, John E. Bibliography of W. B. Yeats. 1971. $7.50 Hdbd. (ISBN 0-87875-010-X). Whitston Publ. Co., NY.

Symons, A. J. Bibliography of the First Editions of Books of William Butler Yeats. 1924. $5.00 Hdbd. Folcroft Pr , PA.

Symons, A. J. First Edition Books of William Butler Yeats. 1971. $7.50 Hdbd. Porter, Bern, ME.

Tindall, William Y. W. B. Yeats. 1966. $1.00 pa. (ISBN 0-231-02753-2). Columbia Univ. Pr., NY.

Torchiana, Donald T. W. B. Yeats & Georgian Ireland. 1966. $10.95 Hdbd. (ISBN 0-8101-0238-2). Northwestern Univ. Pr., IL.

Unterecker, John. Reader's Guide to William Butler Yeats. 1971. (1959) $10.00 Hdbd. (ISBN 0-374-98048-9). Octagon Books, Inc., NY.

Unterecker, John. Reader's Guide to William Butler Yeats. 1959. $2.25 pa. Farrar, Straus & Giroux, NY.

Unterecker, John E., ed. Yeats: A Collection of Critical Essays. 1963. $1.95 pa. (ISBN 0-13-971911-3). $5.95 Hdbd. (ISBN 0-13-971929-6). Prentice-Hall, NY.

Ure, Peter. Yeats the Playwright: A Commentary on Character & Design in the Major Plays. 1963. $5.00 Hdbd. Barnes & Noble, NY.

Ussher, Arland. Three Great Irishmen: Shaw, Yeats, Joyce. 1953. $6.75 Hdbd. (ISBN 0-8196-0222-1). Biblo & Tannen, NY.

Veeder, William R. W. B. Yeats—the Rhetoric of Repetition. (U. C. Publ. in English Studies Ser., Vol. 34). 1968. $2.00 pa. (ISBN 0-520-09074-8). Univ. of Cal. Pr., CA.

Vendler, Helen H. Yeat's Vision & the Later Plays. 1963. $8.00 Hdbd. (ISBN 0-674-96541-8). Harvard Univ. Pr., MA.

Verhoeff, Abraham. Practice of Criticism: A Comparative Analysis of W. B. Yeat's Among School Children. 1925. $15.00 Hdbd. Folcroft Pr., PA.

Wade, Allan. Bibliography of the Writings of W. B. Yeats. 3rd ed. Alspach, Russell K., ed. 1968. $10.25 Hdbd. Oxford Univ. Pr., NY.

Whitaker, Thomas R. Swan & Shadow: Yeats's Dialogue with History. 1964. $7.50 Hdbd. (ISBN 0-8078-0916-0). Univ. of N.C. Pr., NC.

Yeats, William B. Autobiography. 1953. $6.95 Hdbd. Macmillan Co., NY.

Zwerdling, Alex. Yeats & the Heroic Ideal. (Gotham Library). (Orig.). $7.50 Hdbd. (ISBN 0-8147-0454-9); $1.95 pa. (ISBN 0-8147-0455-7). New York Univ. Pr., NY.

PLAYWRITING

Burack, A. S. Television Plays for Writers. $6.95 Hdbd. (ISBN 0-87116-003-X); $8.95 text ed. Writer, MA.

Byers, Ruth. Creating Theater. (Paul Baker Studies in Theater, No. 2). 1968. $8.00 Hdbd. (ISBN 0-911536-05-1). Trinity Univ. Pr., TX.

Cole, Toby, ed. Playwrights on Playwriting: The Meaning & Making of Modern Drama. $3.95 Hdbd. (ISBN 0-8090-7700-0, Drama); $1.95 pa. (ISBN 0-8090-0529-8). Hill & Wang, NY.

Couch, William, Jr., ed. New Black Playwrights. $1.65 pa. Avon, NY.

Egri, Lajos. Art of Dramatic Writing. 1965. $1.95 pa. Simon & Schuster, NY.

Grebanier, Bernard. Playwriting. $2.25 pa. Apollo Ed., NY.

Hull, Raymond. Profitable Playwriting. 1968. $5.95 Hdbd. (740320). Funk & Wagnalls., NY.

Kerr, Walter. How Not to Write a Play. 1955. $5.95 text ed. (ISBN 0-87116-035-8). Writer, MA.

Kline, Peter. Playwriting. (Theatre Student Ser). (Hi-Sch.). 1970. $6.96 Hdbd. (ISBN 0-8239-0196-3). Richard Rosen Pr., NY.

Langner, Lawrence. Play's the Thing. (Hi-Sch.). 1960. $6.95 text ed. (ISBN 0-87116-036-6). Writer, MA.

Lawson, John H. Theory & Technique of Playwriting. 1960. $1.95 pa. (ISBN 8090-0525-5). Hill & Wang, NY.

MacGowan, Kenneth. Primer of Playwriting. $5.95 Hdbd. (ISBN 0-394-40680-X). Random House, NY.

Matthews, Brander, ed. Papers on Playmaking. (Essay Index Reprint Ser). $10.75 Hdbd. (ISBN 0-8369-1890-8). Books for Libraries, NY.

Smiley, Sam. Playwriting: The Structure of Action. (Theatre & Drama Ser). 1971. $7.95 Hdbd. (ISBN 0-13-684548-7): $4.50 text ed. (ISBN 0-13-684530-4). Prentice-Hall, NY.

Van Druten, John. Playwright at Work. 1971. (1953) $10.00 Hdbd. (ISBN 0-8371-3847-7, UAPL). Greenwood Pr., CT.

Weales, Gerald. Play & Its Parts. (Culture & Discovery Ser). (Hi-Sch.). 1964. $5.95 text ed. (ISBN 0-465-05783-7). Basic Books, NY.

PSYCHODRAMA

Moreno, J. L. The First Psychodramatic Family. $6.00 Hdbd. Beacon House., NY.

Moreno, J. L. Psychodrama, 3 Vols.

Incl. Vol. 1. Collected Papers. $13.50 Hdbd.; $10.00 pa. Vol. 2. Foundations in Psychotherapy. $12.00 Hdbd. Vol. 3. Action-Therapy & Principles of Practice. $13.00 Hdbd. Beacon House, NY.

Moreno, J. L. Sociometry, Experimental Method & the Science of Society. $12.00 Hdbd. Beacon House, NY.

PUPPETS AND PUPPET-PLAYS

Abbe, Dorothy. Dwiggins Marionettes: A Complete Experimental Theatre in Miniature. 1970. $45.00 Hdbd. (ISBN 0-8109-0090-4). Harry N. Abrams, NY.

Ando, Tsuruo. Bunraku: The Puppet Theatre. (Performing Arts of Japan Ser., Vol. 1). 1970. $5.95 Hdbd. (ISBN 0-8348-1501-X). Weatherhill, John, NY.

Arnott, Peter D. Plays Without People: Puppetry & Serious Drama. 1964. $4.50 Hdbd. (ISBN 0-253-16340-4). Ind. Univ. Pr., IN.

Baird, Bil. Art of the Puppet. (Hi-Sch.). 1966. $19.95 Hdbd. (ISBN 0-8238-0067-9). Plays, MA.

Batchelder, Marjorie & Comer, Virginia L. Puppets & Plays: A Creative Approach. 1956. $5.50 Hdbd. (ISBN 0-06-000300-6). Harper & Row, NY.

Batchelder, Marjorie H. Puppet Theatre Handbook. (Hi-Sch.). 1947. $7.50 Hdbd. (ISBN 0-06-000270-0, HarpT). Harper & Row, NY.

Baumann, Hans. Caspar & His Friends: A Collection of Puppet Plays. Emerson, Joyce, tr. Orig. Title: Kasperle hat viele Freunde. (Elem.). 1969. $5.00 Hdbd. (ISBN 0-8098-2400-0). Henry Z. Walck, NY.

Bohmer, Gunter. Wonderful World of Puppetry. 1971. $8.95 Hdbd. (ISBN 0-8238-0084-9). Plays, MA.

Bramall, Eric & Somerville, Christopher C. Expert Puppet Technique. (Hi-Sch.). 1966. $4.95 Hdbd. (ISBN 0-8238-0068-7). Plays, MA.

Bufano, Remo. Remo Bufano's Book of Puppetry. Richmond, A., ed. 1950. $4.95 Hdbd. Macmillan, NY.

Bussell, Jan. Puppets. Pringle, P., ed. (Pegasus Books Ser., No. 16). 1968. $4.00 Hdbd. Internatl. Publ. Ser., NY.

Creegan, George. Sir Georges' Book of Hand Puppetry. (Elem.). 1966. $1.98 Hdbd. (ISBN 0-695-48003-0). Follett Publ., IL.

Crothers, J. Frances. Puppeteer's Library Guide: A Bibliographic Index to the Literature of the World Puppet Theatre, Vol. 1. 1971. $10.00 Hdbd. (ISBN 0-8108-0319-4). Scarecrow Pr., NJ.

Cummings, Richard. One Hundred & One Hand Puppets. (Elem–Hi-Sch.). 1962. $3.95 Hdbd. McKay, David, NY.

Currell, David. Puppetry for School Children. (Elem.). 1970. $4.25 Hdbd. (ISBN 0-8231-3028-2). Branford, Charles T., MA.

Dietl, Ulla. Evas Dolls & Puppets. 1971. $1.98 pa. Crown Publ., NY.

Dunn, Charles J. Early Japanese Puppet Drama. 1966. $15.00 Hdbd. Lawrence Verry, CT.

Fraser, Peter. Introducing Puppetry. (Introducing Ser). 1968. $7.95 Hdbd. (ISBN 0-8230-6285-6). Watson-Guptill, NY.

French, Susan. Presenting Marionettes. 1964. $6.95 Hdbd. Van Nostrand-Reinhold, NY.

Goaman, Muriel. Judy's & Andrew's Puppet Book. $3.95 Hdbd. (ISBN 0-8238-0069-5). Plays, MA.

Green, Evelyn. Guignol, et Ses Amis. (Fr). 1966. $2.40 pa. (ISBN 0-03-054795-4); Also avail. on tapes dual track 7.5 ips $20.00, full track $3.75 ips $20.00. Holt, Rinehart & Winston, NY.

Green, M. C. & Targett, B. R. Space Age Puppets & Masks. (Elem.-Hi-Sch.). 1969. $5.95 Hdbd. (ISBN 0-8238-0070-9). Plays, MA.

Hironago, Shuzaburo. Bunraku: Japan's Unique Puppet Theatre. $7.25 Hdbd. Japan Pubns., CA.

Hopper, G. H. Puppet Making Through the Grades. (Elem.). $5.60 Hdbd. (ISBN 0-87192-022-0). Davis, MA.

Howard, Vernon. Puppet & Pantomime Plays. (Elem.-Hi-Sch.). 1962. $2.95 Hdbd. Sterling Publ., NY.

Inverarity, Bruce. Manual of Puppetry. (Jr Hi.). 1938. $3.50 Hdbd. (ISBN 0-8323-0168-X). Binfords & Mort., OR.

Jagendorf, Moritz. Penny Puppets.

Penny Theatre & Penny Plays. (Elem-Jr Hi.). 1941. $6.95 Hdbd. (ISBN 0-8238-0071-7). Plays, MA.

Jagendorf, Moritz. Puppets for Beginners. (Elem.). 1952. $3.95 Hdbd. (ISBN 0-8238-0072-5). Plays, MA.

Kampmann, Lothar. Creating with Puppets. 1971. $5.95 Hdbd. Van Nostrand-Reinhold, NY.

Keene, Donald. Battles of Coxinga. (Cambridge Oriental Ser). $9.00 Hdbd. Cambridge Univ. Pr., NY.

Kennard, Joseph S. Masks & Marionettes. 1935. $7.50 Hdbd. (ISBN 0-8046-0247-6). Kennikat Pr., NY.

Lano, David. Wandering Showman I. 1957. $5.75 Hdbd. (ISBN 0-87013-027-7). Mich. St. Univ. Pr., MI.

Lewis, Roger. Puppets & Marionettes. (Elem.). 1952. $3.59 Hdbd. Alfred A. Knopf, NY.

Lewis, Shari. Making Easy Puppets. (Elem-Hi-Sch.). 1967. $4.50 Hdbd. (ISBN 0-525-34484-5). Dutton, NY.

Lewis, Shari & Oppenheimer, Lillian. Folding Paper Puppets. $3.95 Hdbd. (ISBN 0-8128-1062-7). Stein & Day, NY.

McPharlin, Marjorie B. Puppet Theatre in America: A History 1524-1948. 1969. (1949) With suppl. $12.50 Hdbd. (ISBN 0-8238-0073-3). Plays, MA.

Morton, Brende. Needlework Puppets. (Elem.). 1964. $4.95 Hdbd. (ISBN 0-8238-0074-1). Plays, MA.

Mulholland, John. Practical Puppetry. 1962. $4.95 Hdbd. (ISBN 0-668-00880-6). Arco Publ., NY.

Niculescu, Margaret, ed. Puppet Theatre of the Modern World. (Hi-Sch.). 1967. $14.95 Hdbd. (ISBN 0-8238-0100-4). Plays, MA.

Obratzov, Sergei. Chinese Puppet Theatre. $3.95 Hdbd. (ISBN 0-8238-0101-2). Plays, MA.

Pels, Gertrude. Easy Puppets. (Elem.). 1951. $3.95 Hdbd. (ISBN 0-690 25377-X). Thomas Y. Crowell, NY.

Philpott, A. R. Dictionary of Puppetry. $8.95 Hdbd. (ISBN 0-8238-0102-0). Plays, MA.

Philpott, A. R. Modern Puppetry. (Elem–Hi-Sch.). 1967. $3.95 Hdbd. (ISBN 0-8238-0104-7). Plays, MA.

Philpott, A. R. Modern Puppetry. Blishan, Bruce, ed. (Hobbies for Young People Ser). (Hi-Sch.). 1969. $3.25 Hdbd. Intl. Pubns. Serv., NY.

Pratt, Lois H. Puppet Do-It-Yourself Book. 1957. $4.00 Hdbd. (ISBN 0-682-40074-2). Exposition Pr., NY.

Priester, Erich. Puppets. Albrecht, Christian, tr. (Play Crafts Ser). 1969. $1.25 pa. Herder & Herder, NY.

Renfro, Nancy. Puppets for Play Production. (Elem.). 1969. $6.95 Hdbd. (780860). Funk & Wagnalls, NY.

Richter, Dorothy. Fell's Guide to Hand Puppets: How to Make & Use Them.

1970. $5.95 Hdbd. (ISBN 0-8119-0185-8). Fell, Frederick, NY.

Robinson, Stuart & Robinson, Patricia. Exploring Puppetry. 1967. $8.50 Hdbd. (ISBN 0-8008-2575-6). Taplinger Publ., NY.

Ross, Laura. Puppet Shows Using Poems & Stories. (Elem.). 1970. $4.95 Hdbd. Lothrop Lee & Shephard, NY.

Saito, Seijiro, et al, eds. Masterpieces of Japanese Puppetry, Sculptured Heads of the Bunraku Theatre. 1961. $27.50 Hdbd. (ISBN 0-8048-0397-8). C E Tuttle, VT.

Scott, Adolphe C. Puppet Theatre of Japan. 1963. $3.50 Hdbd. (ISBN 0-8048-0494-X). C E Tuttle, VT.

Stockwell, A. Puppetry. Foreman, J. B., ed. (Nutshell Books). (Hi-Sch.). 1966. $1.50 Hdbd. (ISBN 0-00-411551-1). William Collins, NY.

Storch, C. Fun Time Puppets. (Elem.). $2.75 Hdbd. Childrens Pr., IL.

Tichenor, Tom. Folk Plays for Puppets You Can Make. 1959. $2.50 Hdbd. (ISBN 0-687-13239-8). Abingdon Pr., TN.

Tichenor, Tom. Tom Tichenor's Puppets. (Elem.-Hi-Sch.). 1971. $5.95 Hdbd. (ISBN 0-687-42363-5). Abingdon Pr., TN.

Von Boehn, Max. Dolls & Puppets. Nicoll, Josephine, tr. 1932. $17.50 Hdbd. (ISBN 0-8154-0026-8). Cooper Sq. Publ., NY.

Wall, Leonard V., et al. Puppet Book. (Hi-Sch.). 1950. $7.95 Hdbd. (ISBN 0-8238-0107-1). Plays, MA.

Wetzel, Chester M. & Curry, Louise H. Teaching with Puppets. 1966. $3.75 Hdbd. (ISBN 0-8006-0079-7). Fortress Pr., PA.

Wilson, Albert E. Penny Plain Two Pence Coloured: A History of the Juvenile Drama. 1969. $18.75 Hdbd. Benjamin Blom, NY.

RECORDING

Reproducing

Aldred, John. Manual of Sound Recording. $10.95 Hdbd. (Pub. by Fountain). Morgan & Morgan, NY.

Bernstein, Julian L. Audio Systems. 1966. $8.50 Hdbd. (ISBN 0-471-07110-2); $5.95 pa. (ISBN 0-471-07113-7). John Wiley & Sons, NY.

Brown, Clement. Sound Recording Works Like This. (Jr. Hi–Hi. Sch.). $3.25 Hdbd. Roy Publ., NY.

Crabbe, John. Hi-Fi in the Home. 1971. $10.00 Hdbd. Intl. Pubns. Service, NY.

Crowhurst, Norman H. Audio Systems Handbook. 1969. $7.95 Hdbd. (ISBN 0-8306-9494-3). TAB Books, PA.

Gelatt, Roland. Fabulous Phonograph. 1966. $6.95 Hdbd. (ISBN 0-696-59534-6). Hawthorn Books, NY.

Murray, Don M. World of Sound Recording. (Jr. Hi.). 1965. $3.95 Hdbd. J. B. Lippincott Co., PA.

Nisbett, Alec. Technique of the Sound Studio. rev. ed. (Library of Communication Techniques Ser). 1970. $13.50 Hdbd. (ISBN 0-8038-7096-5); $10.00 pa. (ISBN 0-8038-7100-7). Hastings House Publ., NY.

Olson, Harry F. Modern Sound Reproduction. price "n.g." Hdbd. Van Nostrand Reinhold, Co., NY.

Slot, G. Audio Quality. 1971. $5.95 Hdbd. (ISBN 0-87749-006-X). Drake Publs., NY.

Tremaine, Howard M. Audio Cyclopedia. 2nd ed. 1969. $29.95 Hdbd. (20675) Howard W. Sams & Co., IN.

Villchur, Edgar. Reproduction of Sound. 1966. $1.25 pa. (ISBN 0-486-21515-6). Dover Books, NY.

Stereophonic Sound Systems

Boyce, William F. Hi-Fi Stereo Handbook. 3rd ed. Orig. Title: Hi-Fi Handbook, II. $5.50 pa. (20565). Howard W. Sams & Co., IN.

Briggs, Gilbert A. Stereo Handbook. 1959. $3.95 Hdbd. (ISBN 0-8436-9604-4). Cahners Publ. Co., MA.

Cisin, Harry G. How & Why of Hi-Fi & Stereo. $1.00 pa. (ISBN 0-8436-9611-7). Cahners Publ. Co., MA.

Crowhurst, Norman H. Servicing Modern Hi-Fi-Stereo Systems. 1970. $7.95 Hdbd. (ISBN 0-8306-0534-7);

$4.95 pa. (ISBN 0-8063-0534-7). TAB Books, PA.

Earl. How to Choose & Use Tuners & Amplifiers. 1970. $8.95 Hdbd. (Pub. by Fountain). Morgan & Morgan, NY.

Fantel, Hans. A B C's of Hi-Fi & Stereo. 2nd ed. $2.75 pa. (20539). Howard W. Sams & Co., IN.

Feldman, Leonard. F-M Multiplexing for Stereo. 2nd ed. 1962. $3.95 pa. (20199). Howard W. Sams & Co., IN.

Guy, P. J. Encyclopedia of High Fidelity: Disc Recording & Reproduction. Borwick, John, ed. $9.50 Hdbd. (ISBN 0-8038-8912-7). Hastings House Publ., NY.

Henderson, H. Encyclopedia of High Fidelity: Radio Reception. Borwick, John, ed. $9.50 Hdbd. (ISBN 0-8038-8914-3). Hastings House Publ., NY.

Jordan, E. J. Encyclopedia of High Fidelity: Loudspeakers. Borwick, John, ed. $9.50 Hdbd. (ISBN 0-8038-8915-1). Hastings House Publ., NY.

McWilliams, A. A. Encyclopedia of High Fidelity: Tape Recording & Reproduction. Borwick, John, ed. $9.50 Hdbd. (ISBN 0-8038-8913-5). Hastings House Publ., NY.

Middleton, Robert G. Hi-Fi Stereo Serving Guide. 1970. $3.95 pa. Howard W. Sams & Co., IN.

Olney, Ross R. Sound All Around: How Hi-Fi & Stereo Work. (Elem.). 1967.

$4.50 Hdbd. (ISBN 0-13-823005-6). Prentice-Hall, NY.

Rosenthal, Murray P. How to Select & Use Hi-Fi & Stereo Equipment, 2 Vols. 1969. Set—$7.00 pa. (0339); $3.50 pa. (0340, 0341). Hayden Book Co., NY.

Salm, Walter G. Stereo in Your Living Room. 1971. $5.95 Hdbd. (ISBN 0-87769-040-5). Auerbach Pubs., NY.

Schanz, G. W. Stereo Handbook. 1970. $5.95 Hdbd. (ISBN 0-87749-003-1). Drake Publs., NY.

York, H. Encyclopedia of High Fidelity: Amplifiers, Borwick, John, ed. $9.50 Hdbd. (ISBN 0-8038-8910-0). Hastings House Publ., NY.

Tape Recorders

Anderson, Ronald & Mooney, Mark. What You Should Know About Your Tape Recorder. 1965. $1.25 pa. Cahners Publ. Co., MA.

Barsley, Michael. Tape Recording. Blishan, Bruce, ed. (Hobbies for Young People Ser). (Hi-Sch.). 1969. $3.25 Hdbd. Intl. Pubns. Service, NY.

Burstein, Herman. Getting the Most Out of Your Tape Recorder. $4.75 pa. (0251). Hayden Book Co., NY.

Burstein, Herman & Pollak, Henry C. Elements of Tape Recorder Circuits. $7.95 pa. (ISBN 0-8306-7067). TAB Books, PA.

Crowhurst, Norman H. A B C's of Tape Recording. 3rd ed. 1971. $2.95 pa.

(ISBN 0-672-20805-9). Howard W. Sams & Co., IN.

Dubbe, Richard F. & Westcott, Charles G. Tape Recorders, How They Work. 2nd ed. YA. (Hi-Sch.). 1964. $4.50 pa. (20445). Howard W. Sams & Co., IN.

Hellyer. How to Choose & Use Tape Recorders. 1970. $8.95 Hdbd. (Pub. by Fountain). Morgan & Morgan, NY.

Jorgensen, Finn. Handbook of Magnetic Recording. 1970. $7.95 Hdbd. TAB Books, PA.

King, Gordon J. Hi-Fi & Tape Recorder Handbook. (Illus.). 1971. $8.75 Hdbd. Transatlantic Arts Inc., NY.

Mark, David. How to Select & Use Your Tape Recorder. 2nd rev. ed. (Illus.). $3.75 pa. (5735). Hayden Book Co., NY.

Marshall. Tape Recorder Service Manual. $2.50 pa. American Photographic Book Publ. Co. Inc., NY.

Nijsen, C. G. Tape Recorder. 1971. $5.95 Hdbd. (ISBN 0-87749-067-8). Drake Publs., NY.

Pear, C. B., Jr. Magnetic Recording in Science & Industry. 1967. $19.50 Hdbd. Van Nostrand Reinhold Co., NY.

Peters, Ken. Modern Tape Recording & Hi-Fi. 1963. $8.00 Hdbd. Transatlantic Arts Inc., NY.

Peters, Ken. Your Book of Tape Recording. (Jr. Hi-Hi Sch.). Transatlantic Arts Inc., NY.

Quatremaine, Michael L. Magnetic Recording. 1952. $1.50 Hdbd. Wehman Brothers, NJ.

Salm, Walter G. Tape Recording for Fun & Profit. Orig. Title: Tape Recording. 1969. $7.95 Hdbd. (ISBN 0-8306-9497-8). TAB Books, PA.

Schroder, H. Tape Recorder Servicing Mechanics. 1968. $5.50 Hdbd. Van Nostrand Reinhold Co., NY.

Shadrin, V. N. Magnetic Recording in Automation. 1962. $12.25 pa. (6119). CCM Information Corp., NY.

Spratt, Hector G. Magnetic Tape Recording. 2nd ed. 1964. $10.50 Hdbd. Van Nostrand Reinhold, NY.

Staab, Joachim G. Fun with Tape. 1968. $5.95 Hdbd. (ISBN 0-498-06880-3). A S Barnes & Co., NJ.

Stewart, Welby E. Magnetic Recording Techniques. 1958. $12.00 Hdbd. (ISBN 0-07-061300-1). McGraw-Hill Book Co., NY.

Tuthill, Cuyler A. How to Service Tape Recorders. 2nd rev. ed. (Illus.). $4.45 pa. (5736). Hayden Book Co., NY.

Zuckerman, Arthur. Tape Recording for the Hobbyist. 2nd ed. Orig. Title: Magnetic Recording for the Hobbyist, Il. $3.95 pa. (20583). Howard W. Sams & Co., IN.

Video Tape Recorders and Recording

Efrein, Joel. Video Tape Production & Communication Techniques. 1971.

$12.95 Hdbd. (ISBN 0-8306-1541-5). TAB Books, PA.

Ennes, Harold E. Television Tape Fundamentals. 1966. $5.95 pa. Howard W. Sams & Co., IN.

Goodall, George S. Television Tape Recording: Primer. $1.00 pa. (ISBN 0-8436-9402-5). Cahners Publ. Co., MA.

National Education Association – Division of Educational Technology. Portable Videotape Recorder, A Guide for Teachers. 1969. $2.00 pa. National Education Assn., D.C.

Stroh, Thomas F. Uses of Video Tape in Training & Development. 1968. $6.00 Hdbd. (ISBN 0-8144-3093-7). Am Mgmt. Assn., NY.

SHAKESPEARE

Authorship and Forgeries

Acheson, Arthur. Shakespeare, Chapman & Sir Thomas More. 1970. (1931) $11.00 Hdbd. (ISBN 0-404-00278-1). AMS Pr., NY.

Allen, Charles. Notes on the Bacon-Shakespeare Question. 1970. (1900) $12.50 Hdbd. (ISBN 0-404-00326-5). AMS Pr., NY.

Amphlett, Hilda. Who Was Shakespeare. (Illus.). 1970. (1955) $10.00 Hdbd. (ISBN 0-404-00325-7). AMS Pr., NY.

Bacon, Delia S. Philosophy of the Plays of Shakespeare Unfolded. 1970. Repr.

$24.50 Hdbd. (ISBN 0-404-00443-1). AMS Pr., NY.

Baldwin, T. W. Shakespeare's Love's Labor's Won. 1957. $5.00 Hdbd. (ISBN 0-8093-0010-9). Southern Illinois Univ. Pr., IL.

Baxter, James P. Greatest of Literary Problems. 1915. lib. bdg. $32.50 Hdbd. (ISBN 0-404-00694-9). AMS Pr., NY.

Bayley, Harold. Tragedy of Sir Francis Bacon. (English Biography, No. 31). 1970. (1902) $9.95 Hdbd. (ISBN 0-8383-1180-6). Haskell House Publ., NY.

Beach, Elizabeth. Shakespeare & the Tenth Muse. 1969. $6.00 Hdbd. Willoughby Books, NJ.

Beeching, Henry C. William Shakespeare, Player, Playmaker, & Poet. 1908. $8.50 Hdbd. (ISBN 0-404-00724-4). AMS Pr., NY.

Bertram, Paul D. Shakespeare & the Two Noble Kinsmen. 1965. $10.00 Hdbd. (ISBN 0-8135-0499-6). Rutgers Univ. Pr., NJ.

Castle, Edward J. Shakespeare, Bacon, Jonson & Greene. 1970. (1897) $11.00 Hdbd. (ISBN 0-8046-1010-X). Kennikat Pr., NY.

Chalmers, George. Supplemental Apology for the Believers in the Shakespeare-Papers. 1970. (1799) $34.00 Hdbd. Augustus M. Kelley, NY.

Chambers, Edmund K. Disintegration of Shakespeare. 1924. $4.00 Hdbd. Folcroft Pr., PA.

Clark, Eva T. Man Who Was Shakespeare. (Illus.). 1970. (1937) $12.50 Hdbd. (ISBN 0-404-01549-2). AMS Pr., NY.

Coleridge, Samuel T. Seven Lectures on Shakespeare & Milton by the Late Samuel Taylor Coleridge. Collier, J. Payne, ed. 1856. $12.50 Hdbd. (ISBN 0-404-01617-0). AMS Pr., NY.

Coleridge, Samuel T. Seven Lectures on Shakespeare & Milton. (Research & Source Works Ser., No. 276). 1969. (1856) $16.50 Hdbd. (ISBN 0-8337-0618-7). Burt Franklin, NY.

Collier, John Payne. Further Particulars Regarding Shakespeare & His Works. 1839. $5.00 Hdbd. (ISBN 0-404-01607-3). AMS Pr., NY.

Collier, John Payne. New Facts Regarding the Life of Shakespeare. 1970. (1835) $5.00 Hdbd. (ISBN 0-404-01609-X). AMS Pr., NY.

Collier, John Payne. New Particulars Regarding the Works of Shakespeare. 1836. $5.00 Hdbd. (ISBN 0-404-01614-6). AMS Pr., NY.

Collier, John Payne. New Facts Regarding the Life of Shakespeare (in a Letter to Thomas Amyot from J. Payne Collier. 1835. $7.00 Hdbd. Reprint House International, NY.

De Chambrun, Clara L. Essential Documents Never Yet Presented in the Shakespeare Case. 1934. $8.50 Hdbd. Folcroft Pr., PA.

Donnelly, Ignatius. Great Cryptogram. 1888. $42.50 Hdbd. (ISBN 0-404-02144-1). AMS Pr., NY.

Durning-Lawrence, Edwin. Bacon Is Shake-Speare. 1910. $11.50 Hdbd. (ISBN 0-8371-2894-3). Greenwood Pr., CT.

Durning-Lawrence, Edwin. Bacon Is Shakespeare. 1971. (1910) $11.50 Hdbd. (ISBN 0-403-00921-9). Scholarly Pr., MI.

Dyce, Alexander. Few Notes on Shakespeare. 1853. $8.50 Hdbd. (ISBN 0-404-02228-6). AMS Pr., NY.

Elze, Karl. Essays on Shakespeare. Schmitz, L. Dora, tr. 1970. (1874) $12.00 Hdbd. Kennikat Pr., NY.

Evans, Alfred J. Shakespeare's Magic Circle. facs. ed. (Select Bibliographies Reprint Ser). 1956. $8.50 Hdbd. (ISBN 0-8369-5504-8). Books for Libraries, NY.

Everitt, E. B. Young Shakespeare: Studies in Documentary Evidence. Tillotson, G., ed. (Anglistica). 1954. $5.00 pa. Fernhill House, NY.

Feuillerat, Albert. Composition of Shakespeare's Plays. facs. ed. (Select Bibliographies Reprint Ser). 1953. $13.50 Hdbd. (ISBN 0-8369-5505-6). Books for Libraries, NY.

Friedman, William F. & Friedman, Elizabeth S. Shakespearean Ciphers Examined. 1957. $5.50 Hdbd. Cambridge Univ. Pr., NY.

Gallup, Elizabeth W. Bi-Literal Cypher of Sir Francis Bacon. 1901. $18.00

Hdbd. (ISBN 0-404-02669-9). AMS Pr., NY.

Gaw, Allison. Origin & Development of One Henry Sixth in Relation to Shakespeare, Marlowe, Peele & Greene. 1926. $9.50 Hdbd. (ISBN 0-404-02689-3). AMS Pr., NY.

Gibson, H. N. Shakespeare Claimants: A Critical Survey of the Four Principal Theories Concerning the Authorship of the Shakespearean Plays. 1971. (1962) $11.00 Hdbd. (ISBN 0-389-04144-0). Barnes & Noble, NY.

Goldsworthy, W. Lancdown. Ben Jonson & the First Folio. 1939. $8.50 Hdbd. Folcroft Pr., PA.

Greenwood, Granville G. Shakespeare Problem Restated. 1908. $25.00 Hdbd. (ISBN 0-404-02898-5). AMS Pr., NY.

Greenwood, Granville G. Shakespeare Problem Restated. 1908. $17.50 Hdbd. (ISBN 0-8371-3102-2). Greenwood Pr., CT.

Greenwood, Granville G. Vindicators of Shakespeare. (1970) $7.50 Hdbd. (ISBN 0-8046-1018-5). Kennikat Pr., NY.

Halliwell-Phillips, James O. Observations on Some of the Manuscript Emendations of the Text of Shakespeare. 1853. $5.00 Hdbd. (ISBN 0-404-03082-3). AMS Pr., NY.

Hamilton, Nicholas. Inquiry into the Genuineness of the Manuscript Corrections in Mr. J. Payne Collier's Annotated Shakespeare, Folio 1632. 1860.

$10.00 Hdbd. (ISBN 0-404-03090-4). AMS Pr., NY.

Haney, John L. Name of William Shakespeare, Study in Orthography. 1906. $4.50 Hdbd. Folcroft Pr., PA.

Harman, Edwin G. Edmund Spenser & the Impersonations of Francis Bacon. 1914. $27.50 Hdbd. (ISBN 0-404-03119-6). AMS Pr., NY.

Herford, Charles H. Sketch of Recent Shakespearean Investigation, 1893-1923. 1923. $5.00 Hdbd. (ISBN 0-404-03246-X). AMS Pr., NY.

Holland, Laurence G. Shakespeare: Some Essays & Lectures. 1970. (1893) $7.50 Hdbd. (ISBN 0-8046-1021-5). Kennikat Pr., NY.

Holmes, Nathaniel. Authorship of Shakespeare, 2 Vols. 1894. $30.50 Hdbd. (ISBN 0-404-03316-4). AMS Pr., NY.

Huston, Craig Shakespeare. Authorship Question. 1971. $4.00 Hdbd. (ISBN 0-8059-1569-9). Dorrance & Co., PA.

Ingleby, Clement M. Complete View of the Shakespeare Controversy. 1861. $15.00 Hdbd. (ISBN 0-404-03484-5). AMS Pr., NY.

Ingleby, Clement M. Shakespeare Fabrications. 1859. $6.50 Hdbd. (ISBN 0-404-03485-3). AMS Pr., NY.

Ireland, Samuel. Investigation of Mr. Malone's Claim to the Character of Scholar, or Critic. 1970. (1797) $11.50 Hdbd. (ISBN 0-678-05136-4). Augustus M. Kelly, NY.

Ireland, Samuel. Investigation of Mr. Malone's Claim to the Character of Scholar. 1797. $6.50 Hdbd. (ISBN 0-404-03505-1). AMS Pr., NY.

Ireland, W. H. Confessions Containing Particulars of His Fabrication of the Shakespeare Manuscripts. new ed. 1969. $15.00 Hdbd. (ISBN 0-8337-1805-3). Burt Franklin, NY.

Kellner, Leon. Restoring Shakespeare: A Critical Analysis of the Misreadings in Shakespeare's Works. 1969. (1925) $7.50 Hdbd. (ISBN 0-8196-0244-2). Biblo & Tanner, NY.

Lang, Andrew. Shakespeare, Bacon & the Great Unknown. 1912. $10.00 Hdbd. (ISBN 0-404-03871-9). AMS Pr., NY.

McManaway, James G. Authorship of Shakespeare (Folger Booklet on Tudor & Stuart Civilization Set). $1.50 pa. (ISBN 0-8139-0091-3). Univ. Pr. of Virginia, VA.

Madden, Fredric. Observations on an Autograph of Shakespeare. 1837. $5.00 Hdbd. (ISBN 0-404-04147-7). AMS Pr., NY.

Mair, John. Fourth Forger: William Ireland & the Shakespeare Papers. (Select Bibliographies Reprint Ser.). (1938) $11.00 Hdbd. (ISBN 0-8369-5631-1). Books for Libraries, NY.

Malone, Edmond. Inquiry into the Authenticity of Certain Miscellaneous Papers & Legal Instruments. 1970.

(1796) $25.00 Hdbd. (ISBN 0-678-05123-2). Augustus M. Kelley, NY.

Martin, Milward W. Was Shakespeare Shakespeare: A Lawyer Reviews the Evidence. 1965. $4.50 Hdbd. (ISBN 0-8154-0147-7). Cooper Sq. Pr., NY.

Maxwell, Baldwin. Studies in the Shakespeare Apocrypha. 1956. $10.75 Hdbd. (ISBN 0-8371-1857-3). Greenwood Pr., CT.

Morgan, James A. Some Shakespearean Commentators. 1882. $5.00 Hdbd. (ISBN 0-404-04429-8). AMS Pr., NY.

Muir, Kenneth. Shakespeare As Collaborator. 1960. $2.50 Hdbd. Barnes & Noble, NY.

Ogburn, Dorothy & Ogburn, Charlton, Jr. Shake-Speare: The Man Behind the Name. $1.95 pa. Apollo Editions, NY.

Ogburn, Dorothy & Ogburn, Charlton, Jr. Shakespeare: The Man Behind the Name. 1962. $6.00 Hdbd. William Morrow Co., NY.

Pitcher, Seymour. Case for Shakespeare's Authorship of the Famous Victories. 1961. $6.00 Hdbd. (ISBN 0-87395-002-X). State Univ. N.Y. Pr., NY.

Pollard, A. W. Shakespeare's Hand in the Play of Sir Thomas More, & Shakespeare's Fight with the Pirates. 1967. $9.50 Hdbd. Cambridge Univ. Pr., NY.

Pott, Constance M. Francis Bacon & His Secret Society. 1891. $20.00 Hdbd. (ISBN 0-404-05096-4). AMS Pr., NY.

Robertson, John M. Baconian Heresy. (Select Bibliographies Reprint Ser). 1913. $19.50 Hdbd. (ISBN 0-8369-5269-3). Books for Libraries, NY.

Robertson, John M. Did Shakespeare Write Titus Andronicus. 1905. $10.00 Hdbd. (ISBN 0-404-05361-0). AMS Pr., NY.

Robertson, John M. Introduction to the Study of the Shakespeare Canon. (Select Bibliographies Reprint Ser). 1924. $16.50 Hdbd. (ISBN 0-8369-5268-5). Books for Libraries, NY.

Robertson, John M. Introduction to the Study of the Shakespeare Canon, Proceeding on the Problem of Titus Andronicus. 1924. $17.00 Hdbd. (ISBN 0-8371-3744-6). Greenwood Pr., CT.

Robertson, John M. Shakespeare Canon, 5 Pts. in 4 Vols. 1922–32. Set—$30.00 Hdbd. (ISBN 0-404-05370-X). AMS Pr., NY.

Shakespeare, William. Locrine. (1911) $12.50 Hdbd. (ISBN 0-404-53375-2). AMS Pr., NY.

Shakespeare, William. London Prodigal. (1605) $10.00 Hdbd. (ISBN 0-404-53410-4). AMS Pr., NY.

Shakespeare, William. Puritan. (1911) $11.50 Hdbd. (ISBN 0-404-53420-1). AMS Pr., NY.

Shakespeare, William. Shakespeare Apocrypha, Being a Collection of Fourteen Plays Which Have Been Ascribed to Shakespeare. Brooke, C. F. Tucker, ed.

1908. $9.00 Hdbd. Oxford Univ. Pr., NY.

Shakespeare, William. Thomas Lord Cromwell. (1911) $10.00 Hdbd. (ISBN 0-404-53397-3). AMS Pr., NY.

Shakespeare, William. Yorkshire Tragedy. (1910) $10.00 Hdbd. (ISBN 0-404-53425-2). AMS Pr., NY.

Singer, Samuel W. Text of Shakespeare Vindicated from the Interpolations & Corruptions. 1853. $12.50 Hdbd. (ISBN 0-404-06095-1). AMS Pr., NY.

Smart, John S. Shakespeare: Truth & Tradition. 1966. $4.00 pa. (ISBN 0-19-811636-5). Oxford Univ. Pr., NY.

Smithson, E. W. Baconian Essays. 1970. (1922) $8.25 Hdbd. (ISBN 0-8046-1034-7). Kennikat Pr., NY.

Stopes, Charlotte C. Bacon-Shakespeare Question Answered. 1889. $12.50 Hdbd. (ISBN 0-404-06285-7). AMS Pr., NY.

Stotsenburg, John H. Impartial Study of the Shakespeare Title. 1970. (1904) $18.50 Hdbd. (ISBN 0-8046-1036-3). Kennikat Pr., NY.

Sykes, H. Dugdale. Authorship of the Taming of the Shrew. 1919. $6.50 Hdbd. Folcroft Pr., PA.

Tannenbaum, Samuel. Shakespeare Forgeries in the Revels Account. 1928. $10.00 Hdbd. Ridgeway Bks., PA.

Tannenbaum, Samuel A. Shakespeare Forgeries in the Revels Accounts. folio ed. (Illus.). 1928. $17.50 Hdbd. (ISBN 0-8046-0458-4). Kennikat Pr., NY.

Tannenbaum, Samuel A. Shakespearian Scraps & Other Elizabethan Fragments. (Illus.). 1933. $8.00 Hdbd. (ISBN 0-8046-0459-2). Kennikat Pr., NY.

Wadsworth, Frank W. Poacher from Stratford: A Partial Account of the Controversy Over the Authorship of Shakespeare's Plays. 1969. (1958) $7.00 Hdbd. (ISBN 0-520-01311-5). Univ. of Cal. Pr., CA.

Wells, William. Authorship of Julius Caesar. 1923 $15.00 Hdbd. Folcroft Pr., PA.

White, Richard G. Essay on the Authorship of the Three Parts of King Henry the Sixth. 1859. $7.50 Hdbd. (ISBN 0-404-06932-0). AMS Pr., NY.

White, Richard G. Shakespeare's Scholar: Being Historical & Critical Studies of His Text, Characters & Commentators with an Examination of Mr. Collier's Folio of 1632. 1854. $20.00 Hdbd. (ISBN 0-404-06934-7). AMS Pr., NY.

Wright, Ernest H. Authorship of Timon of Athens. 1910. $7.50 Hdbd. (ISBN 0-404-07044-2). AMS Pr., NY.

Wyman, William H. Bibliography of the Shakespeare-Bacon Controversy. 1884. $8.50 Hdbd. (ISBN 0-404-07065-5). AMS Pr., NY.

Background

Anders, Henry R. Shakespeare's Books. 1904. $12.50 Hdbd. (ISBN 0-404-00355-9). AMS Pr., NY.

Andrews, Mark E. Law Versus Equity in the Merchant of Venice: A Legalization of Act 4, Scene 1, with Foreword, Judicial Precedents, & Notes. 1965. $9.50 Hdbd. (ISBN 0-87081-017-0). Colo. Assoc. Univ. Pr., CO.

Baldwin, T. W. William Shakespeare's Small Latine Lesse Greeke, 2 Vols. 1956. $12.50 Hdbd. (ISBN 0-252-72648-0). Univ. of Illinois Pr., IL.

Baynes, Thomas S. Shakespeare Studies & an Essay on English Dictionaries. 1894. $17.50 Hdbd. (ISBN 0-404-00697-3). AMS Pr., NY.

Beisly, Sidney. Shakspere's Garden. 1864. $10.00 Hdbd. (ISBN 0-404-00727-9). AMS Pr., NY.

Bell, William. Shakespeare's Puck & His Folklore, 3 Vols. 1852–64. Set—$32.50 Hdbd. (ISBN 0-404-00740-6). AMS Pr., NY.

Blades, William. Shakespeare: Typography: Being an Attempt to Show Shakespeare's Personal Connection with & Technical Knowledge of the Art of Printing. 1969. (1872) $15.00 Hdbd. (ISBN 0-8337-0303-X). Burt Franklin, NY.

Bristol, Frank M. Shakespeare & America. 1898. $6.50 Hdbd. (ISBN 0-404-01085-7). AMS Pr., NY.

Bucknill, John C. Medical Knowledge of Shakespeare. 1971. (1860) $12.50

Hdbd. (ISBN 0-404-01146-2). AMS Pr., NY.

Bucknill, John C. Medical Knowledge of Shakespeare. 1860. $12.50 Hdbd. (ISBN 0-404-01146-2). AMS Pr., NY.

Burgess, William. Bible in Shakespeare. (Studies in Shakespeare Ser., No. 24). 1969. (1903) $11.95 Hdbd. (ISBN 0-8383-0921-6). Haskell House Publ., NY.

Campbell, John C. Shakespeare's Legal Acquirements Considered. 1859. $8.50 Hdbd. (ISBN 0-404-01369-4). AMS Pr., NY.

Castle, Edward J. Shakespeare, Bacon, Jonson & Greene. 1970. (1897) $11.00 Hdbd. (ISBN 0-8046-1010-X). Kennikat Pr., NY.

Clark, Cumberland. Shakespeare & Science. (Studies in Shakespeare, No. 24). 1970. (1929) $10.95 Hdbd. (ISBN 0-8383-0965-8). Haskell House Publ., NY.

Clarkson, Paul S. & Warren, Clyde T. Law of Property in Shakespeare & the Elizabethan Drama. 1968. $10.00 Hdbd. (ISBN 0-87752-022-4). Gordian Pr., NY.

Collins, J. Churton. Studies in Shakespeare. 1904. $12.50 Hdbd. (ISBN 0-404-01637-5). AMS Pr., NY.

Davis, Cushman K. Law in Shakespeare. 1884. $12.50 Hdbd. (ISBN 0-404-01988-9). AMS Pr., NY.

Develman, W. C. Shakespeare's Legal Acquirements. 1899. $5.00 Hdbd. (ISBN 0-404-02118-2). AMS Pr., NY.

Edgar, Irving I. Shakespeare, Medicine & Psychiatry. 1970. $9.95 Hdbd. (ISBN 0-8022-2343-5). Philosophical Library, Inc., NY.

Ellacombe, Henry N. Plant-Lore & Garden-Craft of Shakespeare. 1878. $12.50 Hdbd. (ISBN 0-404-02277-4). AMS Pr., NY.

Ellacombe, Henry N. Shakespeare As an Angler. 1883. $5.00 Hdbd. (ISBN 0-404-02278-2). AMS Pr., NY.

Ellis, Oliver C. Shakespeare As a Scientist. 1933. $3.00 Hdbd. Folcroft Pr., PA.

Faber, Melvin D., ed. Design Within: Psychoanalytic Approaches to Shakespeare. 1970. $13.50 Hdbd. (ISBN 0-87668-024-4). Science House, NY.

Falconer, Alexander F. Glossary of Shakespeare's Sea & Naval Terms Including Gunnery. 1965. $4.75 Hdbd. (ISBN 0-8044-2192-7). Frederick Ungar, NY.

Falconer, Alexander F. Shakespeare & the Sea. $6.00 Hdbd. (ISBN 0-8044-2195-1). Frederick Ungar, NY.

Farmer, Richard. Essay on the Learning of Shakespeare. 1789. $10.00 Hdbd. (ISBN 0-404-02366-5). AMS Pr., NY.

Farnam, Henry W. Shakespeare's Economics. 1931. $17.50 Hdbd. Folcroft Pr., PA.

Gesner, Carol. Shakespeare & the Greek Romance: A Study of Origins. 1970. $7.00 Hdbd. (ISBN 0-8131-1220-6). Univ. Pr. of Ky., KY.

Grindon, Leo H. Shakespeare, Flora. 1883. $12.50 Hdbd. (ISBN 0-404-02929-9). AMS Pr., NY.

Hazlitt, William C. Shakespeare's Library, 6 Vols. 1875. Set—$80.00 Hdbd. (ISBN 0-404-03250-8); $14.50 pa. (ISBN 0-404-03251-6) (ISBN 0-404-03252-4) (ISBN 0-404-03253-2) (ISBN 0-404-03254-0) (ISBN 0-404-03255-9) (ISBN 0-404-03256-7). AMS Pr., NY.

Heard, F. F. Shakespeare As a Lawyer. 1883. $7.50 Hdbd. (ISBN 0-404-03199-4). AMS Pr., NY.

Herford, Charles H. Shakespeare & the Arts. 1927. $4.00 Hdbd. Folcroft Pr., PA.

Kerr, Jessica. Shakespeare's Flowers. (Jr Hi.). 1969. $5.95 Hdbd. (ISBN 0-690-73163-9). Thomas Y. Crowell, NY.

Knight, George W. Shakespearean Tempest. 3rd ed. 1968. $6.75 Hdbd. Barnes & Noble, NY.

Lathrop, E. Where Shakespeare Set His Stage. (Studies in Shakespeare, No. 24). 1970. (1906) $10.95 Hdbd. (ISBN 0-8383-0907-0). Haskell House Publ., NY.

Lucy, Margaret. Shakespeare & the Supernatural. 1906. $5.00 Hdbd. (ISBN 0-404-04065-9). AMS Pr., NY.

Madden, Dodgson H. Diary of Master William Silence: A Study of Shakespeare & Elizabethan Sport. (Studies in Shakespeare Ser., No. 24). 1970. (1897) $12.95 Hdbd. (ISBN 0-8383-0993-3). Haskell House Publ., NY.

Maginn, William. Shakespeare Papers of the Late William Maginn, L.L.D. 1856. $14.00 Hdbd. (ISBN 0-404-04167-1). AMS Pr., NY.

Mayou, Bessie. Natural History of Shakespeare. 1877. $7.00 Hdbd. (ISBN 0-404-04286-4). AMS Pr., NY.

Milward, Peter. Introduction to Shakespeare Plays. 1971. (1964) $10.00 Hdbd. Lansdowne Pr., PA.

Mutschmann, Heinrich & Wentersdorf, Karl. Shakespeare & Catholicism. 1970. (1952) $10.00 Hdbd. (ISBN 0-404-04547-2). AMS Pr., NY.

Noble, Richmond. Shakespeare's Biblical Knowledge & Use of the Book of Common Prayer. 1970. $9.50 Hdbd. Octagon Books, NY.

Nutt, Alfred T. Fairy Mythology of Shakespeare. 1900. $4.00 Hdbd. Folcroft Pr., PA.

Nutt, Alfred T. Fairy Mythology of Shakespeare. (Studies in Shakespeare Ser., No. 24). 1969. (1900) $3.95 Hdbd. (ISBN 0-8383-0929-1). Haskell House Publ., NY.

Patterson, Robert. Natural History of the Insects Mentioned in Shakespeare's Plays. 1842. $12.50 Hdbd. (ISBN 0-404-04909-5). AMS Pr., NY.

Phipson, Emma. Animal-Lore of Shakespeare's Time. 1883. $16.00 Hdbd. (ISBN 0-404-05044-1). AMS Pr., NY.

Plimpton, George A. Education of Shakespeare. facsimile ed. (Select Bibliographies Reprint Ser). 1933. $10.00

Hdbd. (ISBN 0-8369-5267-7). Bks. for Libraries, NY.

Robertson, John M. Montaigne & Shakespeare & Other Essays on Cognate Questions. (Research & Source Works Ser., No. 411). 1970. (1909) $16.50 Hdbd. (ISBN 0-8337-3022-3). Burt Franklin, NY.

Robertson, John M. Montaigne & Shakespeare & Other Essays on Cognate Questions. (Studies in Comparative Literature Ser., No. 35). 1969. (1897) $15.95 Hdbd. (ISBN 0-8383-0234-3). Haskell House Publ., NY.

Rogers, William H. Shakespeare & English History. 1966. $4.95 Hdbd. (31); $1.75 pa. (31). Littlefield, Adams & Co., NJ.

Rohde, Eleanor S. Shakespeare's Wild Flowers. 1935. $8.50 Hdbd. (ISBN 0-404-05385-8). AMS Pr., NY.

Root, Robert K. Classical Mythology in Shakespeare. 1965. (1903) $6.00 Hdbd. (ISBN 0-87752-096-8). Gordian Pr., NY.

Rothery, Guy C. Heraldry of Shakespeare. 1930. $15.00 Hdbd. Folcroft Pr., PA.

Rushton, William L. Shakespeare a Lawyer. 1858. $5.00 Hdbd. (ISBN 0-404-05452-8). AMS Pr., NY.

Rushton, William L. Shakespeare an Archer. 1897. $6.50 Hdbd. (ISBN 0-404-05453-6). AMS Pr., NY.

Rushton, William L. Shakespeare Illustrated by the Lex Scripta. 1870. $6.50

Hdbd. (ISBN 0-404-05455-2). AMS Pr., NY.

Rushton, William L. Shakespeare's Legal Maxims. 1907. $5.00 Hdbd. (ISBN 0-404-05456-0). AMS Pr., NY.

Rushton, William L. Shakespeare's Testamentary Language. 1869. $5.00 Hdbd. (ISBN 0-404-05457-9). AMS Pr., NY.

Savage, Frederick G. Flora & Folk Lore of Shakespeare. 1923. $17.00 Hdbd. (ISBN 0-404-05566-4). AMS Pr., NY.

Schelling, Felix E. Shakespeare & Demi-Science. 1971. Repr. $9.50 Hdbd. (ISBN 0-404-05585-0). AMS Pr., NY.

Scott-Giles, C. Shakespeare's Heraldry. (Illus.). 1971. Repr. $14.00 Hdbd. AMS Pr., NY.

Seager, Herbert W. Natural History in Shakespeare's Time. 1896. $17.50 Hdbd. (ISBN 0-404-05667-9). AMS Pr., NY.

Simpson, R. R. Shakespeare & Medicine. 1959. $7.00 Hdbd. (683-07708-2). Williams & Wilkins Co., MD.

Sims, James H. Dramatic Uses of Biblical Allusions in Marlowe & Shakespeare. (Humanities Monographs Ser., No. 24) 1966. $2.00 pa. (ISBN 0-8130-0206-0). Univ. of Fla. Pr., FL.

Singleton, Esther. Shakespeare Garden. 1922. $15.00 Hdbd. (ISBN 0-404-06096-X). AMS Pr., NY.

Smith, C. Roach. Rural Life of Shakespeare. 1874. $8.50 Hdbd. Folcroft Pr., PA.

Somerville, H. Madness in Shakespearean Tragedy. 1929. $12.50 Hdbd. Folcroft Pr., PA.

Stapfer, Paul. Shakespeare & Classical Antiquity, Greek & Latin Antiquity As Presented in Shakespeare's Plays. (Research & Source Work, No. 403). 1970. (1880) $12.50 Hdbd. (ISBN 0-8337-3365-6). Burt Franklin, NY.

Stearns, Charles W. Shakespeare's Medical Knowledge. 1865. $5.00 Hdbd. (ISBN 0-404-06224-5). AMS Pr., NY.

Thiselton Dyer, T. F. Folk-Love of Shakespeare. $5.00 Hdbd. Peter Smith Publ., MA.

Thiselton-Dyer, T. F. Folklore of Shakespeare. 1966. $3.25 pa. (ISBN 0-486-21614-4). Dover Publs. Inc., NY.

Thompson, Karl F. Modesty & Cunning: Shakespeare's Use of Literary Tradition. 1971. $6.95 Hdbd. (ISBN 0-472-90990-8). Univ. of Mich. Pr., MI.

Thomson, James A. Shakespeare & the Classics. 1952. $5.00 Hdbd. Barnes & Noble, NY.

Whalley, Peter. Enquiry into the Learning of Shakespeare. 1970. (1748) $5.00 Hdbd. (ISBN 0-404-06911-8). AMS Pr., NY.

Whitaker, Virgil K. Shakespeare's Use of Learning: An Inquiry into the Growth of His Mind & Art. 1953. $7.50 Hdbd. Huntington Library, CA.

Wilson, Frank P. Proverbial Wisdom of Shakespeare. 1961. $4.00 Hdbd. Folcroft Pr., PA.

Wilson, William. Shakespeare & Astrology. 1903. $5.00 Hdbd. (ISBN 0-404-06998-3). AMS Pr., NY.

Bibliography

Arts Council Of Great Britain. Pictorial History of Shakespearean Production in England, 1576-1946. Byrne, M. St. Clare, ed. (Select Bibliographies Reprint Ser). 1948. $6.50 Hdbd. (ISBN 0-8369-5249-9). Books for Libraries, NY.

Baldwin, T. W. On Act & Scene Division in the Shakespeare First Folio. 1965. $5.50 Hdbd. (ISBN 0-8093-0153-9). Southern Ill. Univ. Pr., IL.

Bartlett, Henrietta C. & Pollard, Alfred W. Census of Shakespeare's Plays in Quarto, 1594-1709. 1916. $15.00 Hdbd. (ISBN 0-404-00669-8). AMS Pr., NY.

Bartlett, Henrietta C., ed. Mister William Shakespeare, Original & Early Editions of His Quartos & Folios, His Source Books & Those Containing Contemporary Notices. 1969. (1922) $10.00 Hdbd. Kraus Reprint, NY.

Bate, J. How to Find Out About Shakespeare. $4.00 Hdbd. (ISBN 0-08-013003-8); $2.50 pa. (ISBN 0-08-013002-X). Pergamon Pr., NY.

Bohn, Henry G. Biography & Bibliography of Shakespeare. 1863. $12.50 Hdbd. (ISBN 0-404-00920-4). AMS Pr., NY.

Bryant, Joseph A., Jr. Hippolyta's View:

Some Christian Aspects of Shakespeare's Plays. 1961. $6.50 Hdbd. (ISBN 0-8131-1057-2). Univ. Pr. of Ky., KY.

Craig, Hardin. New Look at Shakespeare's Quartos. 1961. $3.50 Hdbd. (ISBN 0-8047-0065-6). Stanford Univ. Pr., CA.

Ebisch, Walther & Schucking, Levin. Shakespeare Bibliography. 1968. $17.50 Hdbd. Benjamin Blom, NY.

Fennell, James H. Shakespeare Reposi-, tory. 1853. $5.00 Hdbd. (ISBN 0-404-02376-2). AMS Pr., NY.

Ford, Herbert L. Shakespeare Seventeen-Hundred-Seventeen-Forty. 1969. (1935) $12.50 Hdbd. Benjamin Blom, NY.

Gardner, Helen. King Lear. 1967. $0.80 Hdbd. Oxford Univ. Pr., NY.

Goldsworthy, W. Lancdown. Ben Jonson & the first Folio. 1939. $8.50 Hdbd. Folcroft Pr., PA.

Gordan, John D. Bard & the Book: Editions of Shakespeare in the Seventeenth Century: An Exhibition. 1964. $1.25 pa. (ISBN 0-87104-019-0). NY Pub. Library, NY.

Greg, Walter W. Shakespeare First Folio: Its Bibliographical & Textual History. 1955. $11.25 Hdbd. (ISBN 0-19-811546-6). Oxford Univ. Pr., NY.

Guttman, Selma. Foreign Sources of Shakespeare's Works. 1968. $7.50 Hdbd. Octagon Books, NY.

Hall, Henry T. Shakespearean Statistics.

1970. (1874) $7.50 Hdbd. (ISBN 0-404-03044-0). AMS Pr., NY.

Hart, Alfred. Stolen & Surreptitious Copies: A Comparative Study of Shakespeare's Bad Quartos. 1942. $25.00 Hdbd. Folcroft Pr., PA.

Hinman, Charlton. Printing & Proof-Reading of the First Folio of Shakespeare, 2 Vols. 1963. $32.00 Hdbd. (ISBN 0-19-811613-6). Oxford Univ. Pr., NY.

Howard-Hill, T. H. Shakespearian Bibliography & Textual Criticism. 1970. $5.75 text ed. Oxford Univ. Pr., NY.

Ingleby, C. M., et al, eds. Shakespeare Allusion-Book: A Collection of Allusions to Shakespeare from 1591 to 1700, 2 Vols. (Select Bibliographies Reprint Ser). 1932. Set—$36.50 Hdbd. (ISBN 0-8369-5512-9). Books for Libraries, NY.

Lee, Sidney. Life of William Shakespeare. rev. ed. 1969. (1931) $3.75 pa. (ISBN 0-486-21967-4). Dover Publ., NY.

Lewis, Benjamin R. Shakespeare Documents: Facsimiles, Transliterations, Translations & Commentary, 2 Vols. 1968. (1940) Set—$150.00 Hdbd. (ISBN 0-8371-4622-4). Greenwood Pr., CT.

Lucy, Margaret. Shakespeare & the Supernatural. 1906. $5.00 Hdbd. (ISBN 0-404-04065-9). AMS Pr., NY.

Morgan, James A., ed. Digest Shakespeareana. 1888. $12.50 Hdbd. (ISBN 0-404-04419-0). AMS Pr., NY.

Payne, R. Waveny. Shakespeare Bibliography. $1.20 Hdbd. Intl. Scholarly Book Serv., OR.

Pollard, Alfred W. Shakespeare Folios & Quartos: A Study in the Bibliography of Shakespeare's Plays. 1594-1685. 1970. (1909) $10.00 Hdbd. (ISBN 0-8154-0322-4). Cooper Sq. Pr., NY.

Raven, Anton A. Hamlet Bibliography & Reference Guide, 1877-1935. 1966. (1936) $9.00 Hdbd. Russell & Russell Publ., NY.

Rhodes, R. Crompton. Shakespeare's First Folio. 1923. $7.50 Hdbd. Folcroft Pr., PA.

Smith, Gordon R., ed. Classified Shakespeare Bibliography, 1936-1958. 1963. $49.50 Hdbd. (ISBN 0-271-73053-6). Penn. State Univ. Pr., PA.

Westfall, Alfred R. American Shakespearean Criticisms 1607-1865. 1968. $12.50 Hdbd. Benjamin Blom, NY.

Willoughby, E. Printer of Shakespeare. (Studies in Shakespeare Ser., No. 24). 1969. (1934) $11.95 Hdbd. (ISBN 0-8383-1212-8). Haskell House, NY.

Biography

Adams, J. Q. Life of William Shakespeare. 1927. $8.95 Hdbd. Houghton-Mifflin, NY.

Armstrong, Edward A. Shakespeare's Imagination: A Study of the Psychology of Association & Inspiration. YA.

1963. $1.95 pa. (ISBN 0-8032-5005-3). Univ. of Nebr. Pr., NB.

Bagehot, Walter. Shakespeare, the Man. 1971. (1901) $7.50 Hdbd. (ISBN 0-404-00446-6). AMS Pr., NY.

Baynes, Thomas S. Shakespeare Studies & an Essay on English Dictionaries. 1894. $17.50 Hdbd. (ISBN 0-404-00697-3). AMS Pr., NY.

Bentley, Gerald E. Shakespeare: A Biographical Handbook. 1961. $6.50 Hdbd. (ISBN 0-300-00302-1); $2.25 pa. (ISBN 0-300-00021-9). Yale Univ. Pr., CT.

Bohn, Henry G. Biography & Bibliography of Shakespeare. 1863. $12.50 Hdbd. (ISBN 0-404-00920-4). AMS Pr., NY.

Burgess, Anthony. Shakespeare. 1970. $17.50 Hdbd. Alfred Knopf, NY.

Calmour, Alfred C. Fact & Fiction About Shakespeare. 1894. $22.50 Hdbd. (ISBN 0-404-01365-1). AMS Pr., NY.

Carter, Thomas. Shakespeare, Puritan & Recusant. 1970. Repr. $10.00 Hdbd. (ISBN 0-404-01397-X). AMS Pr., NY.

Chambers, E. K. Sources for a Biography of Shakespeare. 1946. $3.50 Hdbd. (ISBN 0-19-811698-5). Oxford Univ. Pr., NY.

Chute, Marchette. Shakespeare of London. $7.95 Hdbd. (ISBN 0-525-20182-3); $1.85 pa. (ISBN 0-525-47001-8). E. P. Dutton, NY.

Collier, John Payne. New Facts Regarding the Life of Shakespeare (in a Letter to Thomas Amyot from J. Payne Collier. AMS Pr., NY.

Collier, John P. New Facts Regarding the Life of Shakespeare (in a Letter to Thomas Amyot from J. Payne Collier). $7.00 Hdbd. Reprint House Intl., NY.

Dawson, Giles E. Life of William Shakespeare. (Hi-Sch.). $1.50 pa. (ISBN 0-8139-0083-2). Univ. Pr. of Va., VA.

De Quincey, Thomas. Biographies of Shakespeare, Pope, Goethe & Schiller & on the Political Parties of Modern England. 1863. $17.50 Hdbd. (ISBN 0-404-02079-8). AMS Pr., NY.

Eckhoff, Lorentz. Shakespeare: Spokesman of the Third Estate. 1954. $17.50 Hdbd. Folcroft Pr., PA.

Elton, Charles I. William Shakespeare, His Family & Friends. Thompson, A. Hamilton, ed. 1904. $22.50 Hdbd. (ISBN 0-404-02324-X). AMS Pr., NY.

Elze, Karl. Essays on Shakespeare. Schmitz, L. Dora, tr. 1970. (1874) $12.00 Hdbd. (ISBN 0-8046-1015-0). Kennikat Pr., NY.

Field, Arthur. Recent Discoveries Relating to the Life & Works of William Shakespeare. 1954. $5.00 Hdbd. (ISBN 0-404-02379-7). AMS Pr., NY.

Forbis, John F. Shakespearean Enigma & an Elizabethan Mania. 1970. (1923) $14.00 Hdbd. (ISBN 0-404-02458-0). AMS Pr., NY.

Fripp, Edgar I. Shakespeare, Man & Artist, 2 Vols. 1938. $22.75 Hdbd.

(ISBN 0-19-212158-8). Oxford Univ. Pr., NY.

Furnivall, Frederick J. & Munro, John, eds. Shakespeare Life & Work. 1908. $12.50 Hdbd. (ISBN 0-404-02664-8). AMS Pr., NY.

Guizot, Francois P., ed. Shakespeare & His Times. 2nd ed. 1852. $13.00 Hdbd. (ISBN 0-404-02948-5). AMS Pr., NY.

Halliday, Frank E. Life of Shakespeare. 1964. $1.25 pa. (ISBN 0-14-020642-6, A642, Pelican). Penguin, MD.

Halliday, Frank E. Shakespeare: A Pictorial Biography. 1964. $6.95 Hdbd. (ISBN 0-670-63906-0). Viking Pr., NY.

Halliwell-Phillips, James O. Life of William Shakespeare. 1848. $15.00 Hdbd. (ISBN 0-404-03065-3). AMS Pr., NY.

Halliwell-Phillips, James O. Outlines of the Life of Shakespeare. 1907. $17.50 Hdbd. (ISBN 0-404-03084-X). AMS Pr., NY.

Halliwell-Phillips, James O. Visits of Shakespeare's Company of Actors to the Provincial Cities & Towns of England. 1887. $5.00 Hdbd. (ISBN 0-404-03087-4). AMS Pr., NY.

Harbage, Alfred B. Conceptions of Shakespeare. 1968. $1.95 pa. (ISBN 0-8052-0145-9). Schocken, NY.

Harbage, Alfred B. Conceptions of Shakespeare. 1966. $4.95 Hdbd. (ISBN 0-674-15650-1). Harvard Univ. Pr., NY.

Harris, Frank. Man Shakespeare. 1969. (1909) $10.00 Hdbd. (ISBN 0-8180-

0206-9); $3.45 pa. (ISBN 0-8180-0207-7). Horizon Pr., NY.

Heraud, John A. Shakespeare, His Inner Life As Intimated in His Works. 1865. $25.00 Hdbd. (ISBN 0-404-03245-1). AMS Pr., NY.

Hudson, N. H. Shakespeare: His Life, Art & Characters. (Studies in Shakespeare, No. 24). 1970. (1872) $29.95 Hdbd. (ISBN 0-8383-1100-8). Haskell House, NY.

Isaac, Jorge. Shakespeare's Earliest Years in the Theatre. 1952. $3.50 Hdbd. Folcroft Pr., PA.

Jaggard, William. Shakespeare & the Tudor Jaggards. 1934. $5.00 Hdbd. Folcroft Pr., PA.

Jordan, J. Original Collections on Shakespeare & Stratford-On-Avon. 1864. $7.50 Hdbd. (ISBN 0-404-03606-6). AMS Pr., NY.

Kenny, T. Life & Genius of Shakespeare. 1864. $17.50 Hdbd. (ISBN 0-404-03657-0). AMS Pr., NY.

Knight, Charles. William Shakespeare, a Biography. 1843. $25.00 Hdbd. (ISBN 0-404-03734-8). AMS Pr., NY.

Langdon-Davies, John. Young Shakespeare. (Jackdaw Ser., No. 9). 1968. $3.95 Hdbd. (ISBN 0-670-79460-0). Grossman Publ. Inc., NY.

Lee, Sidney. Impersonal Aspects of Shakespeare's Art. 1909. $3.00 Hdbd. Folcroft Pr., PA.

Lee, Sidney. Life of William Shakespeare. rev. ed. 1969. (1931) $3.75 pa. (ISBN 0-486-21967-4). Dover Publ., NY.

Macardle, Dorothy. Shakespeare, Man & Boy. 1961. $4.50 Hdbd. Hillary House Publ., NY.

Masson, David. Shakespeare Personally. 1914. $10.00 Hdbd. (ISBN 0-404-04246-5). AMS Pr., NY.

Mutschmann, Heinrich & Wentersdorf, Karl. Shakespeare & Catholicism. 1970. (1952) $10.00 Hdbd. (ISBN 0-404-04547-2). AMS Pr., NY.

Ordish, Thomas F. Shakespeare's London: A Study of London in the Reign of Queen Elizabeth. 1897. $12.50 Hdbd. (ISBN 0-404-07957-1). AMS Pr., NY.

Raleigh, Walter A. Shakespeare. 1907. $7.50 Hdbd. (ISBN 0-404-05206-1). AMS Pr., NY.

Rolfe, William J. Life of William Shakespeare. 1905. $20.00 Hdbd. (ISBN 0-404-05387-4). AMS Pr., NY.

Rolfe, William J. Shakespeare As a Boy. 1964. $4.50 Hdbd. (ISBN 0-8044-2744-5). Frederick Ungar, NY.

Rolfe, William J. Shakespeare the Boy. (Studies in Shakespeare, No. 24). 1970. (1900) $9.95 Hdbd. (ISBN 0-8383-1103-2). Haskell House Publ., NY.

Rowse, Alfred L. William Shakespeare. $0.95 pa. (95014). Pocket Books Inc., NY.

Rowse, Alfred L. William Shakespeare.

A Biography. 1963. $8.95 Hdbd. (ISBN 0-06-013710-X). Harper Row, NY.

Schelling, Felix E. Shakespeare Biography & Other Papers, Chiefly Elizabethan. facs. ed. (Essay Index Reprint Ser). 1968. (1937) $8.00 Hdbd. (ISBN 0-8369-0853-8). Bks for Libraries, NY.

Shakespeare Association. Series of Papers on Shakespeare & the Theatre. 1927. $17.50 Hdbd. Folcroft Pr., PA.

Simon, J. Shakespeare the Englishman. (Studies in Shakespeare Ser., No. 24). 1971. $9.95 Hdbd. (ISBN 0-8383-1288-8). Haskell House Publ., NY.

Sisson, Charles J. Mythical Sorrows of Shakespeare. 1934. $4.00 Hdbd. Folcroft Pr., PA.

Smart, John S. Shakespeare: Truth & Tradition. 1966. $4.00 pa. (ISBN 0-19-811636-5). Oxford Univ. Pr., NY.

Smith, Goldwin. Shakespeare the Man. 1900. $5.00 Hdbd. (ISBN 0-404-06121-4). AMS Pr., NY.

Spencer, Hazelton. Art & Life of William Shakespeare. 1969. (1940) $12.50 Hdbd. (ISBN 0-389-01164-9). Barnes & Noble, NY.

Ward, H. S. & Ward, C. W. Shakespeare's Town & Times. 1905. $8.50 Hdbd. (ISBN 0-404-06837-5). AMS Pr., NY.

White, Richard G. Memoirs of the Life of William Shakespeare. 1865. $22.50 Hdbd. (ISBN 0-404-06933-9). AMS Pr., NY.

Locales

Bellew, John C. Shakespeare's Home at New Place. 1863. $15.00 Hdbd. (ISBN 0-404-00736-8). AMS Pr., NY.

Brassington, William S. Shakespeare's Homeland Sketches of Stratford-Upon-Avon. 1903. $15.00 Hdbd. (ISBN 0-404-01068-7). AMS Pr., NY.

Brown, Ivor & Fearson, George. This Shakespeare Industry. (Studies in Shakespeare, No. 24). 1970. (1939) $11.95 Hdbd. (ISBN 0-8383-1063-X). Haskell House, NY.

Brown, Ivor & Fearon, George. Amazing Monument. 1970. (1939) $11.00 Hdbd. (ISBN 0-8046-1009-6). Kennikat Pr., NY.

Brown, Ivor & Fearon, George. This Shakespeare Industry: Amazing Monument. 1939. $13.00 Hdbd. (ISBN 0-8371-2850-1). Greenwood Pr., CT.

Fripp, Edgar I. Shakespeare Studies: Biographical & Literary. 1930. $8.00 Hdbd. (ISBN 0-404-07882-6). AMS Pr., NY.

Fripp, Edgar I. Shakespeare's Haunts Near Stratford. 1929. $10.00 Hdbd. (ISBN 0-404-02622-2). AMS Pr., NY.

Fripp, Edgar I. Shakespeare's Haunts Near Stratford. 1929. $15.00 Hdbd. Lansdowne Pr., PA.

Fripp, Edgar I. Shakespeare's Stratford. facs. ed. (Select Bibliographies Reprint Ser). 1928. $10.00 Hdbd. (ISBN 0-8369-5506-4). Books for Libraries, NY.

Lee, Sidney. Stratford-On-Avon from the Earliest Times to the Death of Shakespeare. (Select Bibliographies Reprint Ser). 1890. $12.50 Hdbd. (ISBN 0-8369-5263-4). Books for Libraries, NY.

Pascal, Roy. Shakespeare in Germany, 1740–1815. 1971. $8.00 text ed. Octagon, NY.

Walter, James. Shakespeare's Home & Rural Life. 1874. $9.50 Hdbd. (ISBN 0-404-06826-X). AMS Pr., NY.

Ward, H. S. & Ward, C. W. Shakespeare's Town & Times. 1905. $8.50 Hdbd. (ISBN 0-404-06837-5). AMS Pr., NY.

Williams, James L. Home & Haunts of Shakespeare. 1895. $75.00 Hdbd. (ISBN 0-404-06978-9). AMS Pr., NY.

Wise, John R. Shakespeare: His Birthplace & Its Neighborhood. 1861. $7.50 Hdbd. (ISBN 0-404-07003-5). AMS Pr., NY.

Sources

Brooke, Tucker. Shakespeare of Stratford. facs. ed. (Select Bibliographies Reprint Ser). 1926. $9.50 Hdbd. (ISBN 0-8369-5503-X). Books for Libraries, NY.

Butler, Pierce. Materials for the Life of Shakespeare. 1930. $8.50 Hdbd. (ISBN 0-404-01248-5). AMS Pr., NY.

Chambers, Edmund K. & Williams, Charles. Short Life of Shakespeare: With the Sources. 1933. $3.25 Hdbd. (ISBN 0-19-811514-8). Oxford Univ. Pr., NY.

Dowdall, John. Traditionary Anecdotes of Shakespeare. Collier, John P., ed. 1838. $5.00 Hdbd. (ISBN 0-404-02165-4). AMS Pr., NY.

Halliwell-Phillips, James O. Illustrations of the Life of Shakespeare, in a Discursive Series of Essays on a Variety of Subjects. 1874. $12.50 Hdbd. (ISBN 0-404-03059-9). AMS Pr., NY.

Keen, Alan & Lubbock, Roger. Annotator: The Pursuit of an Elizabethan Reader of Hall's Chronicle Involving Some Surmises About the Early Life of Shakespeare. 1954. $11.00 Hdbd. (ISBN 0-404-03641-4). AMS Pr., NY.

Lambert, Daniel H. Cartae Shakespeareanae: Shakespeare Documents. 1904. $8.00 Hdbd. (ISBN 0-404-03804-2). AMS Pr., NY.

Lewis, Benjamin R. Shakespeare Documents: Facsimiles, Transliterations, Translations & Commentary, 2 Vols. 1968. (1940) Set—$150.00 Hdbd. (ISBN 0-8371-4622-4). Greenwood Pr., CT.

Characters

Bell, William. Shakespeare's Puck & His Folklore, 3 Vols. 1852–64. Set—$32.50 Hdbd. (ISBN 0-404-00740-6). AMS Pr., NY.

Brock, James H. Iago & Some Shakespearean Villains. 1937. $5.00 Hdbd. Folcroft Pr., PA.

Brock, James H. Iago & Some Shakespearean Villains. 1937. $5.00 Hdbd. (ISBN 0-404-01088-1). AMS Pr., NY.

Bucknill, John C. Mad Folk of Shakespeare. 2nd ed. (Research & Source Works Ser. 394). 1970. (1867) $16.50 Hdbd. (ISBN 0-8337-0412-5). Burt Franklin, NY.

Bucknill, John C. Mad Folk of Shakespeare. 1867. $15.00 Hdbd. Folcroft Pr., PA.

Burton, Philip. Sole Voice: Character Portraits from Shakespeare. 1970. $8.95 Hdbd. Dial Pr., NY.

Campbell, Lily G. Shakespeare's Tragic Heroes-Slaves of Passion. 1960. $4.00 Hdbd. Peter Smith Publ., MA.

Carlisle, Carol J. Shakespeare from the Greenroom: Actors' Criticisms of Four Major Tragedies. 1969. $12.50 Hdbd. (ISBN 0-8078-1115-7). Univ. of N.C. Pr., NC.

Charlton, H. B. Shakespeare's Jew. 1934. $4.00 Hdbd. Folcroft Pr., PA.

Clarke, Charles C. Shakespeare-Characters. 1863. $22.50 Hdbd. (ISBN 0-404-01567-0). AMS Pr., NY.

Clarke, Mary C. Girlhood of Shakespeare's Heroines, 3 Vols. 1850-1852. Set—$65.00 Hdbd. (ISBN 0-404-01610-3); $22.50 ea. (ISBN 0-404-01611-1) (ISBN 0-404-01612-X) (ISBN 0-404-01613-8). AMS Pr., NY.

Coe, Charles N. Demi-Devils: The Character of Shakespeare's Villains. 1963. $4.00 Hdbd. Twayne Publs., NY.

Coe, Charles N. Shakespeare's Villains. 1957. $6.50 Hdbd. (ISBN 0-404-01585-9). AMS Pr., NY.

Coles, Blanche. Shakespeare's Four Giants. 1957. $4.50 Hdbd. (ISBN 0-87233-809-6). William Bauhan. Inc., NH.

Dawtrey, John. Falstaff Saga. 1970. (1927) $7.75 Hdbd. (ISBN 0-8046-0818-0). Kennikat Pr., NY.

Desjardins, M., ed. She Loveth: Shakespeare's Women Characters. 1965. $3.50 Hdbd. (ISBN 0-87233-813-4). William Bauhan Inc., NH.

Douce, Francis. Illustrations of Shakespeare & of Ancient Manners, 2 Vols. 1807. $20.00 Hdbd. (ISBN 0-404-02156-5). AMS Pr., NY.

Douce, Francis. Illustrations of Shakespeare and of Ancient Manners. (Research & Source Ser., No. 329). 1969. (1839) $20.00 Hdbd. (ISBN 0-8337-0892-9). Burt Franklin, NY.

Draper, John W. Humors & Shakespeare's Characters. 1971. (1945) $10.00 Hdbd. (ISBN 0-404-02178-6). AMS Pr., NY.

Farren, George. Essays on the Varieties in Mania Exhibited by the Characters of Hamlet, Ophelia, Lear & Edgar. 1833. $5.00 Hdbd. (ISBN 0-404-02367-3). AMS Pr., NY.

French, George R. Shakespeareana Genealogica. 1869. $25.00 Hdbd. (ISBN 0-404-02575-7). AMS Pr., NY.

Friedlander, Gerald. Shakespeare & the Jew. 1921. $5.00 Hdbd. (ISBN 0-404-02579-X). AMS Pr., NY.

Goldsmith, Robert H. Wise Fools in

Shakespeare. 1955. $5.50 Hdbd. (ISBN 0-87013-014-5). Mich. State Univ. Pr., MI.

Goll, August. Criminal Types in Shakespeare. (Studies in Shakespeare Ser., No. 24). 1969. (1909) $10.95 Hdbd. (ISBN 0-8383-0558-X). Haskell House Publ., NY.

Halliwell-Phillipps, James O. On the Character of Sir John Falstaff. 1841. $5.00 Hdbd. (ISBN 0-404-03083-1). AMS Pr., NY.

Hazlitt, William. Characters of Shakespeare's Plays. 1929. $2.50 Hdbd. (ISBN 0-19-250205-0). Oxford Univ. Pr., NY.

Hazlitt, William. The Round Table: Characters of Shakespeare's Plays. $2.95 Hdbd. (ISBN 0-460-00065-9). E. P. Dutton, NY.

Holland, Laurence G. Shakespeare: Some Essays & Lectures. 1970. (1893) $7.50 Hdbd. (ISBN 0-8046-102-5). Kennikat Pr., NY.

Hotson, Leslie. Shakespeare Verses Shallow. (Studies in Shakespeare, No. 24). 1970. (1931) $13.95 Hdbd. (ISBN 0-8383-0981-X). Haskell House Publ., NY.

Hotson, Leslie. Shakespeare Verses Shallow. (Select Bibliographies Reprint Ser). 1931. $14.50 Hdbd. (ISBN 0-8369-5261-8). Bks. for Libraries, NY.

Hotson, Leslie. Shakespeare's Motley. (Studies in Shakespeare, No. 24). 1970.

(1952) $7.95 Hdbd. (ISBN 0-8383-1025-7). Haskell House Publ., NY.

Hudson, Henry N. Shakespeare: His Life, Art, & Character, 2 Vols. 1872. Set—$35.00 Hdbd. AMS Pr., NY.

Hudson, Henry N. Shakespeare: His Life, Art & Characters. (Studies in Shakespeare, No. 24). 1970. (1872) $29.95 Hdbd. (ISBN 0-8383-1100-8). Haskell House Publ., NY.

Hyman, Stanley E. Iago: Some Approaches to the Illusion of His Motivation. 1970. $15.95 Hdbd. (ISBN 0-689-10338-7). Atheneum Publ., NY.

James, David G. Dream of Prospero. 1967. $6.50 Hdbd. (ISBN 0-19-811660-8). Oxford Univ. Pr., NY.

Jameson, Anna B. Shakespeare's Heroines. 1889. $15.00 Hdbd. (ISBN 0-404-03554-X). AMS Pr., NY.

Kellogg, Abner O. Shakespeare's Delineations of Insanity, Imbecility & Suicide. 1866. $9.00 Hdbd. (ISBN 0-404-03644-9). AMS Pr., NY.

Kirschbaum, Leo. Character & Characterization in Shakespeare. (Orig.). 1962. $2.25 pa. (ISBN 0-8143-1180-6). Wayne State Univ. Pr., MI.

Lewis, Wyndham. Lion & the Fox: The Role of the Hero in the Plays of Shakespeare. 1966. $2.50 pa. Publ. by Methuen. (ISBN 0-416-69440-3, 68, UP). Barnes & Noble, NY.

Maginn, William. Shakespeare Papers of the Late William Maginn, L.L.D.

1856. $14.00 Hdbd. (ISBN 0-404-04167-1). AMS Pr., NY.

Martin, Helena F. On Some of Shakespeare's Female Characters. 1970. (1893) $12.00 Hdbd. (ISBN 0-404-04194-9). AMS Pr., NY.

Matheson, B. S. Invented Personages in Shakespeare's Plays. 1933. $6.50 Hdbd. (ISBN 0-404-04258-9). AMS Pr., NY.

Matthews, Honor. Character & Symbol in Shakespeare's Plays: A Study of Certain Christian & Pre-Christian Elements in Their Structure & Imagery. 1969. $6.00 Hdbd. (ISBN 0-8052-3031-9). Schocken Books Inc., NY.

Morgann, Maurice. Essay on the Dramatic Character of Sir John Falstaff. Gill, William A., ed. (Select Bibliographies Reprint Ser). 1912. $9.00 Hdbd. (ISBN 0-8369-5266-9). Books for Libraries, NY.

Morgann, Maurice. Essay on the Dramatic Character of Sir John Falstaff. 1970. (1777) $8.50 Hdbd. (ISBN 0-404-04435-2). AMS Pr., NY.

Nutt, Alfred T. Fairy Mythology of Shakespeare. 1900. $4.00 Hdbd. Folcroft Pr., PA.

Nutt, Alfred T. Fairy Mythology of Shakespeare. (Studies in Shakespeare Ser., No. 24). 1969. (1900) $3.95 Hdbd. (ISBN 0-8383-0929-1). Haskell House Publ., NY.

Palmer, John. Political & Comic Characters of Shakespeare. 1967. $5.50 Hdbd. St. Martin's Pr., NY.

Quiller-Couch, Arthur. Paternity in Shakespeare. 1932. $4.00 Hdbd. Folcroft Pr., PA.

Richardson, William. Essays on Shakespeare's Dramatic Characters. 6th ed. $22.50 Hdbd. Augustus Kelley, NY.

Richardson, William. Essays on Shakespeare's Dramatic Characters of Richard Third, King Lear & Timon of Athens. 1784. $7.50 Hdbd. (ISBN 0-404-05308-4). AMS Pr., NY.

Richardson, William. Essays on Shakespeare's Dramatic Character of Sir John Falstaff & on His Female Characters. 1789. $5.00 Hdbd. (ISBN 0-404-05307-6). AMS Pr., NY.

Richardson, William. Philosophical Analysis & Illustration of Some of Shakespeare's Remarkable Characters. 1780. $10.00 Hdbd. (ISBN 0-404-05309-2). AMS Pr., NY.

Rogers, L. Ghosts in Shakespeare. 1925. $20.00 Hdbd. Folcroft Pr., PA.

Schucking, Levin L. Character Problems in Shakespeare's Plays. $4.75 Hdbd. Peter Smith Publ., MA.

Small, Samuel A. Return of Shakespeare: The Historical Realists. 1927. $5.00 Hdbd. (ISBN 0-404-06108-7). AMS Pr., NY.

Small, Samuel A. Shakespearean Character Interpretation: Merchant of Venice. 1927. $7.50 Hdbd. (ISBN 0-404-06109-5). AMS Pr., NY.

Somerville, H. Madness in Shakespearean Tragedy. 1929. $12.50 Hdbd. Folcroft Pr., PA.

Spivack, Bernard. Shakespeare & the Allegory of Evil. 1958. $11.00 Hdbd. (ISBN 0-231-01912-2). Columbia Univ. Pr., NY.

Stewart, John I. Character & Motive in Shakespeare: Some Recent Appraisals Examined. 1959. $4.00 Hdbd. Barnes & Noble, NY.

Stokes, Francis G. Dictionary of the Characters & Proper Names in the Works of Shakespeare. $6.75 Hdbd. Peter Smith Publ., MA.

Stokes, Francis G. Dictionary of the Characters & Proper Names in the Works of Shakespeare. $3.75 pa. (ISBN 0-486-22219-5). Dover Publ., NY.

Stoll, Elmer E. Falstaff. 1914. $4.00. Folcroft Pr., PA.

Stoll, Elmer E. Shakespeare's Young Lovers. 1937. $8.00 Hdbd. (ISBN 0-404-06282-2). AMS Pr., NY.

Terry, Ellen. Four Lectures on Shakespeare. 1932. $9.75 Hdbd. Benjamin Blom, NY.

Tupper, Frederick. Shakespearean Mob. (Studies in Shakespeare, No. 24). 1970. (1938) $2.95 pa. (ISBN 0-8383-0077-4). Haskell House, NY.

Weilgart, Wolfgang J. Shakespeare's Psychognostic. 1952. $11.00 Hdbd. (ISBN 0-404-06897-9). AMS Pr., NY.

Whately, Thomas. Remarks on Some of the Characters of Shakespeare. 3rd ed.

1839. $8.00 Hdbd. (ISBN 0-404-06917-7). AMS Pr., NY.

Whately, Thomas. Remarks on Some of the Characters of Shakespeare. 3rd ed. 1970. Repr. of 1839 ed. $10.00 lib. bdg. (ISBN 0-678-05129-1). Augustus Kelley, NY.

Wilson, John D. Fortunes of Falstaff. 1943. $5.00 Hdbd.; $1.25 pa. (ISBN 0-521-09246-9, 246). Cambridge Univ. Pr., NY.

Winny, James. Player King: A Theme of Shakespeare's Histories. 1968. $4.00 Hdbd. Barnes & Noble, NY.

Yoder, Audrey E. Animal Analogy in Shakespeare's Character Portrayal. 1947. $12.50 Hdbd. Folcroft Pr., PA.

Yoder, Audrey E. Animal Analogy in Shakespeare's Character Portrayal. 1947. $7.00 Hdbd. (ISBN 0-404-07067-1). AMS Pr., NY.

Concordances

Bartlett, John. Complete Concordance to Shakespeare. 1894. $30.00 Hdbd. St. Martin's Pr., NY.

Becket, Andrew. Concordance to Shakespeare. 1970. (1787) $15.00 Hdbd. (ISBN 0-404-00698-1). AMS Pr., NY.

Clarke, Mary C. Complete Concordance to Shakespeare. rev. ed. 1854. $35.00 lib. bdg. (ISBN 0-404-01574-3). AMS Pr., NY.

Cunliffe, Richard J. New Shakespearean Dictionary. 1922. $25.00 Hdbd. Folcroft Pr., PA.

Edwardes, Marian. Pocket Lexicon & Concordance to the Temple Shakespeare. 1909. $10.00 Hdbd. (ISBN 0-404-02261-8). AMS Pr., NY.

Howard-Hill, T. H., ed. Oxford Shakespeare Concordances. 1970. $9.75 text ed. Oxford Univ. Pr., NY.

O'Connor, Evangeline M. Index to the Works of Shakespeare. 1887. $17.50 Hdbd. Folcroft Pr., PA.

O'Connor, Evangeline M. Index to the Works of Shakespeare. 1887. $17.50 IIdbd. (ISBN 0-404-04810-2). AMS Pr., NY.

Shakespeare, William. Comedy of Errors: Concordance to the Text of the First Folio. Howard-Hill, T., ed. $9.75 Hdbd. Oxford Univ. Pr., NY.

Spevack, Marvin. Complete & Systematic Concordance to the Works of Shakespeare, 6 Vols. 1970. Set— $244.20 Hdbd.; $40.70 ea. S-H Service Agency, NY.

Contemporaries

Akrigg, G. P. Shakespeare & the Earl of Southampton. 1970. $8.50 Hdbd. Albert Saifer Publ., NJ.

Bentley, Gerald E. Shakespeare & Johnson, Their Reputations in the Seventeenth Century Compared, 2 Vols in 1. 1945. $10.00 Hdbd. (ISBN 0-226-04269-3). Univ. of Chicago Pr., IL.

Brooke, C. Tucker. Essays on Shakespeare & Other Elizabethans. 1969. (1948) $6.50 Hdbd. (ISBN 0-208-00613-3). Shoe String Pr., CT.

Campbell, Oscar J. Shakespeare's Satire. 1971. (1943) $8.00 text ed. (ISBN 0-87752-150-6). Gordian Pr., NY.

Collier, J. Payne. Memoirs of the Principal Actors in the Plays of Shakespeare. 1846. $15.00 Hdbd. (ISBN 0-404-01599-9). AMS Pr., NY.

Evans, Alfred J. Shakespeare's Magic Circle. facs. ed. (Select Bibliographies Reprint Ser). 1956. $8.50 Hdbd. (ISBN 0-8369-5504-8). Books for Libraries, NY.

Feis, Jacob. Shakespeare & Montaigne. 1970. (1884) $8.50 Hdbd. (ISBN 0-404-02375-4). AMS Pr., NY.

Fripp, Edgar I. Shakespeare Studies: Biographical & Literary. 1930. $8.00 Hdbd. (ISBN 0-404-07882-6). AMS Pr., NY.

Gayley, Charles M. Shakespeare & the Founders of Liberty in America. 1917. $20.00 Hdbd. Folcroft Pr., PA.

Harrison, George B. Shakespeare's Fellows. 1923. $10.00 Hdbd. Folcroft Pr., PA.

Hotson, Leslie I. William Shakespeare Do Appoint Thomas Russell, Esquire. (Select Bibliographies Reprint Ser). 1937. $12.50 Hdbd. (ISBN 0-8369-5260-X). Books for Libraries, NY.

Musgrove, S. Shakespeare & Johnson. 1957. $7.50 Hdbd. Folcroft Pr., PA.

Musgrove, S. Shakespeare & Jonson: The Macmillan Brown Lectures. 1957. $5.00 Hdbd. (ISBN 0-404-04545-6). AMS Pr., NY.

Pollard, A. W. Shakespeare's Hand in the Play of Sir Thomas More. 1923. $7.50 Hdbd. Ridgeway Books, PA.

Robertson, John M. Shakespeare & Chapman. 1971. (1917) $16.00 Hdbd. Scholarly Pr., MI.

Schrick, W. Shakespeare's Early Contemporaries. 1956. $12.00 Hdbd. (ISBN 0-404-05622-9). AMS Pr., NY.

Slater, Gilbert. Seven Shakespeare. 1931. $15.00 Hdbd. Folcroft Pr., PA.

Stopes, Charlotte C. Shakespeare's Warwickshire Contemporaries. 1907. $12.50 Hdbd. (ISBN 0-404-06288-1). AMS Pr., NY.

Swinburne, Algernon C. Contemporaries of Shakespeare. 1919. $20.00 Hdbd. Folcroft Pr., PA.

Thorndike, Ashley H. Influence of Beaumont & Fletcher on Shakespeare. 1965. (1901) $7.50 Hdbd. Russell & Russell Publ., NY.

Thorndike, Ashley H. Influence of Beaumont & Fletcher on Shakespeare. 1901. $5.00 Hdbd. (ISBN 0-404-06428-0). AMS Pr., NY.

Verity, A. W. Influence of Christopher Marlowe on Shakespeare's Earlier Style. 1886. $6.50 Hdbd. Folcroft Pr., Pa.

Wilson, Frank P. Marlowe & the Early Shakespeare. 1953. $4.00 Hdbd. (ISBN 0-19-811585-7). Oxford Univ. Pr., NY.

Contemporary England

Burgess, Anthony. Shakespeare. 1970. $17.50 Hdbd. Alfred A. Knopf, NY.

Cunningham, J. V. In Shakespeare's Day. (Literature & Ideas Ser). 1970. $0.95 pa. Fawcett World Library, CT.

Douce, Francis. Illustrations of Shakespeare & of Ancient Manners, 2 Vols. 1807. $20.00 Hdbd. (ISBN 0-404-02156-5). AMS Pr., NY.

Douce, Francis. Illustrations of Shakespeare and of Ancient Manners. (Research & Source Ser., No. 329). 1969. (1839) $20.00 Hdbd. (ISBN 0-8337-0892-9). Burt Franklin, NY.

Drake, Nathaniel. Shakespeare & His Times, 2 Vols. (Research & Source Ser. No. 332). 1969. (1817) $25.00 Hdbd. (ISBN 0-8337-0901-1). Burt Franklin, NY.

Farnam, Henry W. Shakespeare's Economics. 1931. $17.50 Hdbd. Folcroft Pr., PA.

Frye, Roland M. Shakespeare's Life & Times: A Pictorial Record. 1967. $10.00 Hdbd. (ISBN 0-691-06119-X). Princeton Univ. Pr., NJ.

Goadby, E. Shakespeare's England. 1881. $10.00 Hdbd. (ISBN 0-404-02839-X). AMS Pr., NY.

Halliday, F. E. Shakespeare in His Age. $7.50 Hdbd. (ISBN 0-498-06068-3). A. S. Barnes, NJ.

Halliwell-Phillipps, James O. Visits of Shakespeare's Comedy of Actors to the Provincial Cities & Towns of England. 1887. $5.00 Hdbd. Folcroft Pr., PA.

Halliwell-Phillips, James O. Illustrations of the Life of Shakespeare, in a Discursive Series of Essays on a Variety of Subjects. 1874. $12.50 Hdbd. (ISBN 0-404-03059-9). AMS Pr., NY.

Harrison, George B. England in Shakespeare's Day. 1928. $6.50 Hdbd. Folcroft Pr., PA.

Harrison, George B. Shakespeare at Work, 1592-1603. 1958. $1.95 pa. (ISBN 0-472-06016-3, 16). Univ. of Mich. Pr., MI.

Harrison, George B., ed. England in Shakespeare's Day. facs. ed. (Select Bibliographies Reprint Ser). 1949. $9.50 Hdbd. (ISBN 0-8369-5402-5). Books for Libraries, NY.

Hatcher, Orie L. Book for Shakespeare Plays & Pageants. 1916. $16.50 Hdbd. (ISBN 0-8371-3105-7). Greenwood Pr., CT.

Hatcher, Orie L. Book for Shakespeare Plays & Pageants. (Select Bibliographies Reprint Ser). 1916. $16.50 Hdbd. (ISBN 0-8369-5258-8). Books for Libraries, NY.

Joseph, B. L. Shakespeare's Eden. (History & Literature Ser). 1971. $12.00 Hdbd. (ISBN 0-389-04129-7); $4.50 pa. (ISBN 0-389-04130-0). Barnes & Noble, NY.

Ordish, Thomas F. Shakespeare's London: A Study of London in the Reign of Queen Elizabeth. 1897. $12.50 Hdbd. (ISBN 0-404-07957-1). AMS Pr., NY.

Plimpton, George A. Education of Shakespeare. (Select Bibliographies Reprint Ser). 1933. $10.00 Hdbd. (ISBN 0-8369-5267-7). Books for Libraries, NY.

Raleigh, Walter, et al, eds. Shakespeare's England: An Account of the Life & Manners of His Age, 2 Vols. 1917. $21.00 Hdbd. (ISBN 0-19-821252-6). Oxford Univ. Pr., NY.

Reese, Max M. Shakespeare: His World & His Work. 1953. $10.00 Hdbd. St. Martin's Pr., NY.

Sheavyn, Phoebe. Literary Profession in the Elizabethan Age. (Drama Scr., No. 39). 1969. (1909) $4.95 Hdbd. (ISBN 0-8383-0621-7). Haskell House Publ., NY.

Sheavyn, Phoebe. Literary Profession in the Elizabethan Age. 2nd rev. ed. Saunders, J. W., ed. 1967. $6.00 Hdbd. Barnes & Noble, NY.

Sisson, C. J. Lost Plays of Shakespeare's Age. (English Literature Ser). 1971. (1936) $9.00 Hdbd. (ISBN 0-391-00151-5). Humanities Pr., NY.

Sutherland, James R. & Hurstfield, J., eds. Shakespeare's World. 1964. $5.00 Hdbd. St. Martin's Pr., NY.

Wilson, John D. Life in Shakespeare's England. (Hi-Sch.). 1944. $1.95 pa. (ISBN 0-14-053005-3). Penguin Books, MD.

Wilson, John D., ed. Life in Shakespeare's England: A Book of Elizabethan Prose. 2nd ed. 1969. $10.00 Hdbd. Barnes & Noble, NY.

Winstantley, Lilian. Macbeth, King

Lear, & Contemporary History. 1922. $6.50 Hdbd. Folcroft Pr., PA.

Criticism and Interpretation

Abercrombie, Lascelles. Plea for the Liberty of Interpreting. 1930. $3.00 Hdbd. Folcroft Pr., PA.

Ackerman, Carl. Bible in Shakespeare. $15.00 Hdbd. Folcroft Pr., PA.

Alexander, Peter. Introductions to Shakespeare. 1964. $1.25 pa. (ISBN 0-393-00216-0). W. W. Norton, NY.

Alexander, Peter. Shakespeare's Life & Art. 1961. $7.50 Hdbd. (ISBN 0-8147-0004-7); $2.45 pa. (ISBN 0-8147-0005-5). N.Y. Univ. Pr., NY.

Alexander, Peter, ed. Studies in Shakespeare: British Academy Lectures. 1964. $1.95 pa. (ISBN 0-19-281024-3). Oxford Univ. Pr., NY.

Anderson, Ruth L. Elizabethan Psychology & Shakespeare's Plays. (Studies in Shakespeare Ser., No. 24). 1969. (1927) $5.95 Hdbd. (ISBN 0-8383-0503-2). Haskell House Publ., NY.

Arthos, John. Art of Shakespeare. 1964. $12.50 Hdbd. Ridgeway Bks., PA.

Asimov, Isaac. Asimov's Guide to Shakespeare, Vols. 1-2. 1970. Set—$25.00 Hdbd.; $12.50 ea. Doubleday & Co., NY.

Barnard, Etwell A. New Links with Shakespeare. 1930. $10.00 Hdbd. (ISBN 0-404-00655-8). AMS Pr., NY.

Barroll, J. Leeds. Shakespeare Studies, Vol. 5. 1970. $14.75 Hdbd. (ISBN 0-697-03854-8). William C. Brown, IA.

Berry, Francis. Shakespeare Inset. 1966. $5.75 Hdbd. Theatre Arts Books, NY.

Besterman, Theodore. Shakespeare & Voltaire. 1965. $5.00 pa. (ISBN 0-87598-025-2). Pierpont Morgan Library, NY.

Bethell, S. L. Shakespeare & the Popular Dramatic Tradition. 1970. (1945) $8.00 Hdbd. Octagon Books Inc., NY.

Blistein, Elmer M., ed. Drama of the Renaissance: Essays for Leicester Bradner. 1970. $7.00 Hdbd. (ISBN 0-87057-117-6). Brown Univ. Pr., RI.

Bloom, Edward A., ed. Shakespeare 1564-1964: A Collection of Modern Essays by Various Hands. 1967. (1964) $6.50 Hdbd. (ISBN 0-87057-083-8). Brown Univ. Pr., RI.

Blunden, Edmund. Shakespeare's Significance. 1929. $2.50 Hdbd. Folcroft Pr., PA.

Bond, Richard W. Studia Otiosa. (Essay Index Reprint Ser). 1938. $9.50 Hdbd. (ISBN 0-8369-1341-8). Books for Libraries, NY.

Bradbrook, Muriel C. Elizabethan Stage Conditions: A Study of Their Place in the Interpretation of Shakespeare's Plays. 1968. $4.95 Hdbd.; $1.65 pa. (ISBN 0-521-09539-5, 539). Cambridge Univ. Pr., NY.

Bradbrook, Muriel C. Shakespeare the

Craftsman: The Clark Lectures 1968. 1969. $5.00 Hdbd. (ISBN 0-389-01034-0). Barnes & Noble, NY.

Brewer, Leighton. Shakespeare & the Dark Lady. 1966. $3.00 Hdbd. (ISBN 0-8158-0058-4). Christopher Publ. House, MA.

Bridges, Robert. Influence of the Audience on Shakespeare's Drama. (Studies in Shakespeare, No. 24). (1970) $4.95 pa. (ISBN 0-8383-0085-5). Haskell House Publ., NY.

Bristol, Frank M. Shakespeare & America. 1971. (1898) $6.50 Hdbd. (ISBN 0-404-01085-7). AMS Pr., NY.

Britton, John. Remarks on the Life & Writings of William Shakespeare. 1814. $5.00 Hdbd. (ISBN 0-404-01086-5). AMS Pr., NY.

Brooke, Stopford A. On Ten Plays of Shakespeare. 1905. $12.50 Hdbd. (ISBN 0-404-01109-8). AMS Pr., NY.

Brown, Ivor. Shakespeare & the Actors. 1971. $5.95 Hdbd. Coward-McCann, NY.

Brown, John R. Shakespeare & His Comedies. 2nd ed. (Orig.). 1968. $2.50 pa. (ISBN 0-416-29530-4). $5.00 Hdbd. Barnes & Noble, NY.

Brown, John R. & Harris, Bernard, eds. Early Shakespeare. (Stratford-Upon-Avon Studies, Vol. 3). 1961. $5.75 Hdbd. St. Martin's Pr., NY.

Brown, John R. & Harris, Bernard, eds.

Early Shakespeare: A Reading & Playing Guide. 1966. $1.95 pa. (ISBN 0-8052-0121-1). Schocken Books, Inc., NY.

Brown, John R. & Harris, Bernard, eds. Later Shakespeare. (Stratford-Upon-Avon Studies, Vol. 8). 1967. $6.95 Hdbd. St. Martin's Pr., NY.

Burckhardt, Sigurd. Shakespearean Meanings. 1968. $10.00 Hdbd. (ISBN 0-691-06146-7). Princeton Univ. Pr., NJ.

Calderwood, James L. & Toliver, Harold E. Essays in Shakespearean Criticism. (English Ser). 1970. ref. ed. $8.95 Hdbd. (ISBN 0-13-283655-6); $4.95 pa. (ISBN 0-13-283648-3). Prentice-Hall, NY.

Calderwood, James L. Shakespearean Metadrama: The Argument of the Play in Titus Adronicus, Love's Labour's Lost, Romeo & Juliet, a Midsummer Night's Dream & Richard 2nd. 1971. $7.50 Hdbd. (ISBN 0-8166-0595-5). Univ. of Minn. Pr., MN.

Chambers, Edmund. Shakespeare: A Survey. $1.95 pa. (ISBN 0-8090-0514-X). Hill & Wang, NY.

Chambers, Edmund K. Shakespearean Gleanings. 1944. $7.50 Hdbd. (ISBN 0-404-01444-5). AMS Pr., NY.

Chambers, Edmund K. William Shakespeare: A Study of Facts & Problems, 2 Vols. (Illus.). 1930. Set—$16.00 Hdbd. (ISBN 0-19-811513-X). Oxford Univ. Pr., NY.

Chapman, Gerald W., ed. Essays on Shakespeare. 1965. $6.00 Hdbd. (ISBN 0-691-06042-8). Princeton Univ. Pr., NJ.

Chapman, John J. Glance Toward Shakespeare. (Select Bibliographies Reprint Ser). 1922. $6.50 Hdbd. (ISBN 0-8369-5252-9). Books for Libraries, NY.

Charlton, Henry B. Shakespearean Comedy. 1961. $5.00 Hdbd. $3.00 pa. (ISBN 0-416-69260-5, 156). Barnes & Noble, NY.

Clark, John P. Example of Shakespeare. 1971. $5.25 text ed. (ISBN 0-8101-0340-0); $2.95 pa. (ISBN 0-8101-0341-9). Northwestern Univ. Pr., IL.

Clayton, Thomas. Shakespearean Addition in the Booke of Sir Thomas Moore: Some Aids to Scholarly & Critical Shakespeare Studies: Monograph 1. Barroll, J. Leeds, ed. 1969· $7.00 Hdbd. (ISBN 0-697-03875-0). William C. Brown, IA.

Coleridge, Samuel T. Coleridge on Shakespeare: The Text of the Lectures of 1811-12. Foakes, R. A., ed. (Folger Monographs on Tudor & Stuart Civilization, No. 3). 1971. $5.75 Hdbd. (ISBN 0-8139-0340-8). Univ. Pr. of Virginia, VA.

Coleridge, Samuel T. Shakespearean Criticism, 2 Vols. Raysor, T. M., ed. $2.95 pa. (ISBN 0-460-00162-0). E. P. Dutton, NY.

Collins, J. Churton. Studies in Shake-speare. 1904. $12.50 Hdbd. (ISBN 0-404-01637-5). AMS Pr., NY.

Craig, Hardin, ed. Essays in Dramatic Literature: The Parrott Presentation Volume, by Pupils of Prof. Thomas M. Parrott. 1967. (1935) $12.50 Hdbd. Russell & Russell Publ., NY.

Crane, Milton. Shakespeare's Prose. 1951. $5.50 Hdbd. (ISBN 0-226-11859-2). Univ. of Chicago Pr., IL.

Croce, Benedetto. Ariosto, Shakespeare & Corneille. Ainslie, Douglas, tr. 1966. (1920) $10.00 Hdbd. Russell & Russell Publ., NY.

Cunningham, J. V. In Shakespeare's Day. (Literature & Ideas Ser). 1970. $0.95 pa. Fawcett World Publ., CT.

Cunningham, J. V. Woe or Wonder: The Emotional Effects of Shakespearian Tragedy. $2.00 pa. Swallow Pr., IL.

Cutts, John P. Shattered Glass: A Dramatic Pattern in Shakespeare's Early Plays. 1968. $5.95 Hdbd. (ISBN 0-8143-1358-2). Wayne St. Univ. Pr., MI.

Danby, John F. Shakespeare's Doctrine of Nature: A Study of King Lear. 1966. $6.00 Hdbd.; $2.50 pa. Hillary House Publ., NY.

David, Richard. Janus of Poets (Being an Essay on the Dramatic Value of Shakespeare's Poetry Both Good & Bad. facs. ed. (Select Bibliographies Reprint Ser). 1935. $8.50 Hdbd. (ISBN 0-8369-5253-7). Books for Libraries, NY.

David, Richard. Janus of Poets: Being an Essay on the Dramatic Value of

Shakespeare's Poetry Both Good & Bad. (1935) $8.50 Hdbd. (ISBN 0-404-01939-0). AMS Pr., NY.

Davies, Thomas. Dramatic Miscellanies, 3 Vols. 1784. $27.50 Hdbd. Benjamin Blom, NY.

Davies, Thomas. Dramatic Miscellanies –on Several Plays of Shakespeare, 3 Vols. 1783-84. Set—$27.50 Hdbd. AMS Pr., NY.

Dean, Leonard F., ed. Shakespeare: Modern Essays in Criticism. 2nd ed. (Hi-Sch.). 1967. $2.95 pa. (ISBN 0-19-500688-7). Oxford Univ. Pr., NY.

Dennis, John. The Impartial Critick. Incl. An Essay on the Genius & Writings of Shakespeare. (1712) (1693) $12.50 Hdbd. Augustus M. Kelley, NY.

Douce, Francis. Illustrations of Shakespeare & of Ancient Manners, 2 Vols. 1807. $20.00 Hdbd. (ISBN 0-404-02156-5). AMS Pr., NY.

Douce, Francis. Illustrations of Shakespeare and of Ancient Manners. (Research & Source Ser., No. 329). 1969. (1839) $20.00 Hdbd. (ISBN 0-8337-0892-9). Burt Franklin, NY.

Dowden, Edward. Introduction to Shakespeare. 1970. (1893) $7.50 Hdbd. (ISBN 0-404-02166-2). AMS Pr., NY.

Dowden, Edward. Introduction to Shakespeare. (Select Bibliographies Reprint Ser). 1907. $7.75 Hdbd. (ISBN 0-8369-5254-5). Books for Libraries, NY.

Dowden, Edward. Shakespeare: A Critical Study of His Mind & Art. 3rd ed.

1962. $7.00 Hdbd. Barnes & Noble, NY.

Drake, Nathaniel. Memorials of Shakespeare. 1828. $25.00 Hdbd. (ISBN 0-404-02177-8). AMS Pr., NY.

Drake, Nathaniel. Shakespeare & His Times, 2 Vols. (Research & Source Ser., No. 332). 1969. (1817) $25.00 Hdbd. (ISBN 0-8337-0901-1). Burt Franklin, NY.

Draper, John W. Stratford to Dogberry (Studies in Shakespeare's Earlier Plays. (Select Bibliographies Reprint Ser). 1961. $15.00 Hdbd. (ISBN 0-8369-5255-3). Books for Libraries, NY.

Driver, Tom F. Sense of History in Greek & Shakespearean Drama. 1960. $2.25 pa. (ISBN 0-231-08576-1, 76). Columbia Univ. Pr., NY.

Eagleton, Terence. Shakespeare & Society: Critical Studies in Shakespearean Drama. (1971) $5.50 Hdbd.; $2.75 pa. (ISBN 0-8052-0306-0). Schocken Books, NY.

Eastman, Arthur & Harrison, George B. Shakespeare's Critics: From Jonson to Auden: A Medley of Judgments. 1964. $9.00 Hdbd. (ISBN 0-472-29870-4); $4.50 pa. (ISBN 0-472-08298-1). Univ. of Mich. Pr., MI.

Eckhoff, Lorentz J. William Shakespeare. 1939. $9.80 Hdbd. (ISBN 0-404-02244-8). AMS Pr., NY.

Edwards, Thomas. Canons of Criticism & Glossary. 7th ed. 1970. (1765) $20.00

Hdbd. (ISBN 0-678-05112-7). Augustus M. Kelley, NY.

Egan, Maurice F. Ghost in Hamlet. 1971. (1906) $15.00 Hdbd. (ISBN 0-404-02264-2). AMS Pr., NY.

Elze, Karl. Essays on Shakespeare. Schmitz, L. Dora, tr. 1970. (1874) $12.00 (ISBN 0-8046-1015-0). Kennikat Pr., NY.

Enright, D. J. Shakespeare & the Students. 1970. $6.00 Hdbd. (ISBN 0-8052-3379-2). Schocken Books, NY.

Evans, Bertrand. Shakespeare's Comedies. 1960. $7.20 Hdbd. (ISBN 0-19-811595-4); $2.50 pa. (ISBN 0-19-881128-4). Oxford Univ. Pr., NY.

Ferfusson, Francis. Shakespeare. 1970. $6.95 Hdbd. Delacorte Publ., NY.

Field, Arthur. Recent Discoveries Relating to the Life & Works of William Shakespeare. 1954. $5.00 Hdbd. (ISBN 0-404-02379-7). AMS Pr., NY.

Fluchere, Henri. Shakespeare. $2.75 pa. Fernhill House, NY.

Fluchere, Henri. Shakespeare & the Elizabethans. Hamilton, Guy. $1.35 pa. (ISBN 0-8090-0501-8). Hill & Wang, NY.

Foakes, R. A. Shakespeare, the Dark Comedies to the Last Plays: From Satire to Celebration. 1971. $5.75 text ed. (ISBN 0-8139-0327-0). Univ. Pr. of Virginia, VA.

Fraser, Russell. Shakespeare's Poetics in Relation to King Lear. 1966. $6.50

Hdbd. (ISBN 0-8265-1081-7). Vanderbilt Univ. Pr., TN.

Frost, D. L. School of Shakespeare: The Influence of Shakespeare on English Drama, 1600–42. 1968. $9.50 Hdbd. Cambridge Univ. Pr., NY.

Frye, Roland M. Shakespeare: The Art of the Dramatist. 1970. $3.95 pa. Houghton-Mifflin, NY.

Garrett, John, ed. More Talking of Shakespeare. (Select Bibliographies Reprint Ser). 1959. $9.50 Hdbd. (ISBN 0-8369-5507-2). Books for Libraries, NY.

Gerstner-Hirzel, Arthur. Economy of Action & the Word in Shakespeare's Plays. 1957. $5.40 Hdbd. (ISBN 0-404-02715-6). AMS Pr., NY.

Gervinus, George G. Shakespeare Commentaries. Bunnett, F. E., ed. 1875. $37.50 Hdbd. (ISBN 0-404-02716-4). AMS Pr., NY.

Ghurye, Govind S. Shakespeare on Conscience & Justice. 1965. $5.50 Hdbd. Humanities Pr., NY.

Goddard, Harold C. Meaning of Shakespeare, 2 Vols. Vol. 1. $1.95 pa. (ISBN 0-226-30041-2); Vol. 2. $2.45 pa. (ISBN 0-226-30042-0, P51); $2.45 pa. 1951. $10.00 Hdbd. (ISBN 0-226-30040-4). Univ. of Chicago Pr., IL.

Goldsworth, W. Lancdown. Shakespeare's Heraldic Emblems: Their Origin & Meaning. 1928. $30.00 Hdbd. Folcroft Pr., PA.

Gordon, George S. Shakespearian

Comedy & Other Studies. 1944. $3.50 Hdbd. (ISBN 0-19-811544-X). Oxford Univ. Pr., NY.

Granville-Barker, Harley. Prefaces to Shakespeare, 4 vols. Incl. Vol. 1. Preface to Hamlet (ISBN 0-691-06101-7); Vol. 2. Prefaces to King Lear, Cymbeline & Julius Caesar (ISBN 0-691-06102-5); Vol. 3. Prefaces to Antony & Cleopatra & Coriolanus (ISBN 0-691-06103-3); Vol. 4. Prefaces to Love's Labour's Lost, Romeo & Juliet, The Merchant of Venice & Othello (ISBN 0-691-06104-1). 1965. $5.00 Hdbd. $2.95 pa. Princeton Univ. Pr., NJ.

Granville-Barker, Harley & Harrison, George B. Companion to Shakespeare Studies. 1934. $9.50 Hdbd. Cambridge Univ. Pr., NY.

Granville-Barker, Harley & Harrison, George B., eds. Companion to Shakespeare Studies. 1960. $1.75 pa. Doubleday & Co., NY.

Grene, David. Reality & the Heroic Pattern: Last Plays of Ibsen, Shakespeare & Sophocles. 1967. $1.95 pa. (ISBN 0-226-30789-1, 349). Univ. of Chicago Pr., IL.

Griffith, Elizabeth. Morality of Shakespeare's Drama. 1971. (1775) $24.50 Hdbd. (ISBN 0-404-02917-5). AMS Pr., NY.

Grose, Kenneth H. & Oxley, B. T. Shakespeare. (1969) $3.95 Hdbd. (ISBN 0-668-01891-7); $1.95 pa. (ISBN 0-668-01892-5). Arco Publ. Co., NY.

Gupta, S. Sen. Problem of Duration in Shakespeare's Plays. $3.50 Hdbd. Lawrence Verry, Inc., CT.

Haines, Charles M. Shakespeare in France–Criticism: Voltaire to Victor Hugo. 1925. $8.00 Hdbd. (ISBN 0-404-07883-4). AMS Pr., NY.

Hales, John W. Notes & Essays on Shakespeare. 1884. $12.50 Hdbd. (ISBN 0-404-03027-0). AMS Pr., NY.

Hall, Henry T. Shakespearean Fly-Leaves & Jottings. 1970. (1871) $9.50 Hdbd. (ISBN 0-404-03043-2). AMS Pr., NY.

Halliday, Frank E. Shakespeare & His Critics: From Ben Johnson to T. S. Eliot. 1963. $1.95 pa. (ISBN 0-8052-0041-X). Schocken Books, Inc., NY.

Hamilton, A. C. Early Shakespeare. 1967. $6.50 Hdbd. Huntington Library, CA.

Hanford, James H., et al. Studies in Shakespeare, Milton & Donne. 1970. $7.50 Hdbd. (ISBN 0-87753-020-3). Phaeton Pr., NY.

Harbage, Alfred. Conceptions of Shakespeare. 1968. $1.95 pa. (ISBN 0-8052-0145-9). Schocken Books, Inc., NY.

Harbage, Alfred. Shakespeare & the Rival Traditions. 1968. (1952) $10.00 Hdbd. Barnes & Noble, NY.

Harbage, Alfred. William Shakespeare: A Reader's Guide. 1963. $8.50 Hdbd.; $2.95 pa. Farrar, Straus & Giroux, NY.

Harbage, Alfred B. Conceptions of Shakespeare. 1966. $4.95 Hdbd. (ISBN 0-674-15650-1). Harvard Univ. Pr., MA.

Harrison, George B. Introducing Shakespeare, rev. ed. (Hi-Sch.). 1966. $1.75 pa. (ISBN 0-14-020043-6, A43). Penguin Books, MD.

Harrison, George B. Shakespeare at Work, 1592–1603. 1958. $1.95 pa. (ISBN 0-472-06016-3, 16). Univ. of Mich. Pr., MI.

Hart, Alfred. Shakespeare & the Homilies. 1971. (1934) $10.44 Hdbd. AMS Pr., NY.

Hart, Alfred. Shakespeare & the Homilies. 1970. (1934) $8.50 Hdbd. Octagon Books, Inc., NY.

Hearn, Lafcadio. Lectures on Shakespeare. Inagaki, Iwao, ed. 1928. $15.00 Hdbd. Folcroft Pr., PA.

Heraud, John A. Shakespere, His Inner Life As Intimated in His Works. 1865. $25.00 Hdbd. (ISBN 0-404-03245-1). AMS Pr., NY.

Holland, Norman N. Shakespearean Imagination. 1964. $7.50 Hdbd. Macmillan Co., NY.

Holland, Norman N. Shakespearean Imagination: A Critical Introduction. 1968. $2.95 pa. (253-20114-4). Ind. Univ. Pr., IN.

Holmes, Martin. Shakespeare's Public, the Touchstone of His Genius. (Hi-Sch.). 1960. $7.50 Hdbd. Transatlantic Arts, NY.

Holzknecht, Karl J. Backgrounds of Shakespeare's Plays. 1950. $11.50 text ed. Van Nostrand-Reinhold Books, NY.

Horowitz, David. Shakespeare: An Existential View. 1965. $4.00 Hdbd. (ISBN 0-8090-8610-7). Hill & Wang, NY.

Hosley, Richard, ed. Essays on Shakespeare & Elizabethan Drama in Honor of Hardin Craig. 1962. $9.50 Hdbd. (ISBN 0-8262-0014-1). Univ. of Missouri Pr., MO.

Hotson, Leslie. Shakespeare's Motley. (Studies in Shakespeare, No. 24). 1970. (1952) $7.95 Hdbd. (ISBN 0-8383-1025-7). Haskell House Publ., NY.

Hubbell, Lindley W. Lectures on Shakespeare. 1959. $9.80 Hdbd. (ISBN 0-404-03373-3). AMS Pr., NY.

Hudson, Henry N. Lectures on Shakespeare, 2 Vols. 1848. Set—$27.50 Hdbd. (ISBN 0-404-03375-X). AMS Pr., NY.

Hunter, Edwin R. Shakespere & Common Sense. 1954. $4.00 Hdbd. (ISBN 0-8158-0119-X). Chris Publ., MA.

Hunter, Joseph. New Illustrations of the Life, Studies & Writings of Shakespeare, 2 Vols. 1845. Set—$32.50 Hdbd. (ISBN 0-404-03455-1). AMS Pr., NY.

Ingleby, C. M. Shakespeare Hermeneutics. (Studies in Shakespeare Ser., No. 24). 1971. price "n.g." Hdbd. (ISBN 0-8383-1294-2). Haskell House, NY.

Jha, Amaranatha. Shakespearean Comedy & Other Studies. 1930. $15.00 Hdbd. Folcroft Pr., PA.

Johnson, Samuel. Johnson on Shakespeare, 2 Vols. Sherbo, A., ed. 1968.

Set—$25.00 Hdbd. (ISBN 0-300-00605-5). Yale Univ. Pr., CT.

Johnson, Samuel. Johnson on Shakespeare. Raleigh, Walter, ed. 1908. $3.25 Hdbd. (ISBN 0-19-811567-9). Oxford Univ. Pr., NY.

Kermode, Frank. Shakespeare: Final Plays. (Writers & Their Work Ser No. 155). 1963. $2.25 Hdbd.; $1.00 pa. British Book Center, NY.

Kermode, Frank, ed. Four Centuries of Shakespearian Criticism. 1965. $1.45 pa. Avon Books, NY.

Kernan, Alvin B. Modern Shakespearean Criticism: Essays on Style, Dramaturgy, & the Major Plays. $3.95 pa. (ISBN 0-15-563375-9). Harcourt, Brace Jovanovich, NY.

Knight, Charles. Studies of Shakespeare. 1849. $25.00 Hdbd. (ISBN 0-404-03733-X). AMS Pr., NY.

Knight, George W. Christian Renaissance. 1962. $1.85 pa. (ISBN 0-393-00197-0, Norton Lib). Norton, NY.

Knight, George W. Shakespeare & Tolstoy. (Studies in Comparative Literature, No. 35). 1970. $1.95 pa. (ISBN 0-8383-0050-2). Haskell House, NY.

Knight, George W. Crown of Life: Essays in Interpretation of Shakespeare's Final Plays. 1964. $3.25 pa. (ISBN 0-416-68770-9). $6.50 Hdbd. Barnes & Noble, NY.

Knight, George W. Imperial Theme: Further Interpretations of Shakespeare's Tragedies Including the Roman Plays.

3rd ed. 1963. $2.95 pa. (ISBN 0-416-68740-7). $6.75 Hdbd. Barnes & Noble, NY.

Knight, George W. Shakespearean Tempest: With a Chart of Shakespeare's Dramatic Universe. 3rd ed. 1968. $6.75 Hdbd. Barnes & Noble, NY.

Knight, George W. Sovereign Flower. 1958. $6.75 Hdbd. Barnes & Noble, NY.

Knight, George W. Wheel of Fire: Interpretation of Shakespeare's Tragedies. 4th rev. ed. 1962. $5.50 Hdbd.; $3.25 pa. (ISBN 0-416-67620-0). Barnes & Noble, NY.

Knights, Lionel C. Further Explorations: Essays in Criticism. 1965. $6.50 Hdbd. (ISBN 0-8047-0276-4). Stanford Univ. Pr., CA.

Knights, Lionel C. Some Shakespearean Themes. Incl. Approach to Hamlet. 1966. $2.95 pa. (ISBN 0-8047-0301-9). Stanford Univ. Pr., CA.

Kozintsev, Grigori. Shakespeare: Time & Conscience. 1966. $5.95 Hdbd. (ISBN 0-8090-8630-1). Hill & Wang, NY.

Lanier, Sidney. Shakespeare & His Forerunners, 2 Vols. 1902. $25.00 Hdbd. (ISBN 0-404-03875-1). AMS Pr., NY.

Lawrence, William W. Speeding up Shakespeare. 1968. $12.50 Hdbd. Benjamin Blom, NY.

Lawrence, William W. Shakespeare's Problem Comedies. 1969. $1.45 pa.

(ISBN 0-14-053010-X, SL10). Penguin Pr., MD.

Lawrence, William W. Shakespeare's Problem Comedies. 1959. $5.00 Hdbd. (ISBN 0-8044-2495-0). Frederick Ungar, NY.

Lee, Sidney. Elizabethan & Other Essays. Boas, F. S., ed. 1970. (1929) $14.00 Hdbd. (ISBN 0-404-03928-6). AMS Pr., NY.

Lee, Sidney. Elizabethan & Other Essays. Boas, F. S., ed. (Essay Index Reprint Ser). 1929. $11.50 Hdbd. (ISBN 0-8369-0614-4). Books for Libraries, NY.

Legouis, Emile. Bacchic Element in Shakespeare's Plays. 1962. $4.00 Hdbd. Folcroft Pr., PA.

Lerner, Laurence, ed. Shakespeare's Comedies: An Anthology of Modern Criticism. 1967. $1.65 pa. (ISBN 0-14-053002-9, SL2). Penguin Pr., MD.

Lerner, Laurence, ed. Shakespeare's Tragedies: An Anthology of Modern Criticism. 1964. $1.45 pa. (ISBN 0-14-053008-8, SL8). Penguin Pr., MD.

Lewis, Wyndham. Lion & the Fox: The Role of the Hero in the Plays of Shakespeare. 1966. $2.50 pa. (ISBN 0-416-69440-3, 68, UP). Barnes & Noble, NY.

Lloyd, William W. Essays on the Life & Plays of Shakespeare. 1875. $20.00 Hdbd. (ISBN 0-404-03998-7). AMS Pr., NY.

Lounsbury, Thomas R. Shakespeare & Voltaire. 1902. $12.50 Hdbd. (ISBN 0-404-04029-?). AMS Pr., NY.

Lovett, David. Shakespeare's Characters in Eighteenth Century Criticism. 1935. $3.00 Hdbd. Folcroft Pr., PA.

Lowell, James R. Among My Books. 1970. (1870) $11.50 Hdbd. (ISBN 0-404-04039-X). AMS Pr., NY.

Lyon, Charles R. Shakespeare & the Ambiguity of Love's Triumph. 1971. $11.00 Hdbd. Humanities Pr., NY.

MacCallum, Mungo W. Shakespeare's Roman Plays & Their Background. 1967. (1910) $13.50 Hdbd. Russell & Russell, NY.

MacKail, John W. Approach to Shakespeare. (Select Bibliographies Reprint Ser). 1930. $8.50 Hdbd. (ISBN 0-8369-5264-2). Books for Libraries, NY.

MacKail, John W. Approach to Shakespeare. 2nd ed. 1963. $6.50 Hdbd. (ISBN 0-404-04131-0). AMS Pr., NY.

Masefield, John. William Shakespeare. 1969. (1964) $3.50 Hdbd. Barnes & Noble, NY.

Mason, H. A. Shakespeare's Tragedies of Love. 1970. $7.50 Hdbd. Barnes & Noble, NY.

Mathews, Brander & Thorndike, Ashley H., eds. Shakespearian Studies. (Department of English & Comparative Literature, Columbia University). 1962. (1916) $10.00 Hdbd. Russell & Russell, NY.

Matthews, Arthur D. & Emery, Clark M., eds. Studies in Shakespeare. 1953. $6.25 Hdbd. (ISBN 0-404-04267-8). AMS Pr., NY.

Matthews, Honor. Character & Symbol in Shakespeare's Plays: A Study of Certain Christian & Pre-Christian Elements in Their Structure & Imagery. 1969. $6.00 Hdbd. (ISBN 0-8052-3031-9). Schocken Pr., NY.

Meader, William G. Courtship in Shakespeare. 1970. $8.50 Hdbd. Octagon Books, NY.

Montagu, Elizabeth. Essay on the Writings & Genius of Shakespeare. Compared with the Greek & French Dramatic Poets. 1970. (1769) $16.50 Hdbd. (ISBN 0-678-05139-9). Augustus M. Kelly, NY.

Montagu, Elizabeth. Essay on the Writings & Genius of Shakespeare Compared with the Greek & French Dramatic Poets. 1810. $12.50 Hdbd. (ISBN 0-404-04358-5). AMS Pr., NY.

Muir, Kenneth. Last Periods of Shakespeare, Racine, Ibsen. 1961. $5.00 Hdbd. (ISBN 0-8143-1140-7). Wayne State Univ. Pr., MI.

Muir, Kenneth & O'Loughlin, Sean. Voyage to Illyria: A New Study of Shakespeare. 1970. (1937) $8.50 Hdbd. (ISBN 0-389-04052-5). Barnes & Noble, NY.

Muir, Kenneth, ed. Shakespeare Survey, Vols. 19–22. 1969. $10.00 ea. Hdbd. (ISBN 0-521-07285-9). Cambridge Univ. Pr., NY.

Murry, John M. Shakespeare. 1967. $6.50 Hdbd. $3.00 pa. Hillary House, NY.

Nicoll, Allardyce. Studies in Shakespeare. $10.00 Hdbd. Folcroft Pr., PA.

Nicoll, Allardyce, ed. Shakespeare Survey, Vol. 1–18. $10.00 ea. Hdbd. Cambridge Univ Pr., NY.

Parrott, Thomas M. Shakespearean Comedy. 1962. (1949) $12.50 Hdbd. Russell & Russell, NY.

Pettet, E. C. Shakespeare & the Romance Tradition. 1949. $3.50 Hdbd. Hillary House, NY.

Prouty, Charles T., ed. Shakespeare: Of an Age & for All Time. 1954. $7.50 Hdbd. (ISBN 0-404-05146-4). AMS Pr., NY.

Rabkin, Norman. Shakespeare & the Common Understanding. 1967. $7.95 Hdbd. (92566); $2.95 pa. Free Pr., NY.

Rabkin, Norman, ed. Approaches to Shakespeare. 1964. $2.95 pa. (ISBN 0-07-051096-2). McGraw Hill, NY.

Ralli, Augustus J. Later Critiques. (Essay Index Reprint Ser). 1968. (1933) $7.75 Hdbd. (ISBN 0-8369-0809-0). Books for Libraries, NY.

Ribner, Irving. Patterns in Shakespearian Tragedy. 1960. $5.00 Hdbd. 1970. $2.25 pa. (ISBN 0-416-18180-5, 334). Barnes & Noble, NY.

Richmond, H. M. Shakespeare's Political Plays. $4.00 Hdbd. Peter Smith, MA.

Ridler, Anne B., ed. Shakespeare Criticism, 1919–1935. (W.C.436). $1.75 Hdbd. (ISBN 0-19-250436-3). 1935–

1960. 1963. $2.75 Hdbd. (ISBN 0-19-250590-4). $2.75 pa. (ISBN 0-19-281082-0). Oxford Univ. Pr., NY.

Ridley, M. R. Shakespeare's Plays: A Commentary. 1937. $15.00 Hdbd. Folcroft Pr., PA.

Righter, Anne. Shakespeare & the Idea of the Play. 1963. $5.00 Hdbd. Barnes & Noble, NY.

Robertson, J. M. Introduction to the Study of the Shakespeare Canon: Proceeding on the Problem of Titus Andronicus. 1971. (1924) $16.50 Hdbd. (ISBN 0-403-01182-5). Scholarly, MI.

Robinson, Herbert S. English Shakespearean Criticism in the Eighteenth Century. 1968. (1932) $8.50 Hdbd. (ISBN 0-87752-094-1). Gordian Pr., NY.

Rohrman, Hendrik. Way of Life, Marlowe & Shakespeare. 1952. $5.00 Hdbd. (ISBN 0-404-05386-6). AMS Pr., NY.

Rossiter, Arthur P. Angel with Horns & Other Lectures on Shakespeare. 1961. $6.85 Hdbd. Theatre Arts, NY.

Ruland, Richard. Native Muse: Theories of American Literature. 1971. $7.95 Hdbd. (ISBN 0-525-16420-0). Dutton, NY.

Sack, Maria. Darstellerzahl und Rollenverteilung bei Shakespeare. 1928. $4.00 pa. Johnson Reprint, NY.

Sanders, Wilbur. Dramatist & the Received Idea: Studies in the Plays of Marlowe & Shakespeare. 1968. $9.50 Hdbd. Cambridge Univ. Pr., NY.

Schanzer, Ernest. Problem Plays of Shakespeare: A Study of Julius Caesar, Measure for Measure, Antony & Cleopatra. 1963. $1.95 pa. (ISBN 0-8052-0110-6). Schocken, NY.

Schelling, Felix E. Shakespeare & Demi-Science. (1927) $9.50 Hdbd. (ISBN 0-404-05585-0). AMS Pr., NY.

Sewell, Arthur. Character & Society in Shakespeare. 1951. $5.00 Hdbd. (ISBN 0-19-811571-7). Oxford Univ. Pr., NY.

Sidgwick, Henry. Miscellaneous Essays & Addresses. 1968. (1904) $18.00 Hdbd. Kraus Reprint, NY.

Siegel, Paul N. Shakespeare in His Time & Ours. 1969. (1968) $6.95 Hdbd. (ISBN 0-268-00253-3); $2.95 pa. (ISBN 0-268-00254-1). Univ. of Notre Dame Pr., IN.

Simon, Andre. Wine in Shakespeare's Days & Shakespeare's Plays. 1964. $3.50 pa. Corner Book Shop, NY.

Sisson, Charles J. Mythical Sorrows of Shakespeare. 1934. $4.00 Hdbd. Folcroft Pr., PA.

Smirnov, A. A. Shakespeare: A Marxist Interpretation. 1936. $12.50 Hdbd. Folcroft Pr., PA.

Smith, David N., ed. Shakespeare Criticism: A Selection. $2.50 Hdbd. (ISBN 0-19-250212-3). Oxford Univ. Pr., NY.

Smith, Gordon R., ed. Essays on Shakespeare. 1965. $9.50 Hdbd. (ISBN 0-271-73062-5). Pennsylvania St. Univ. Pr., PA.

Smith, Marion B. Dualities in Shakespeare. 1966. $7.50 Hdbd. (ISBN 0-8020-5171-5). Univ. of Toronto Pr., CAN.

Snider, Denton J. System of Shakespeare's Dramas, 2 Vols. 1877. $27.00 Hdbd. (ISBN 0-404-06139-7). AMS Pr., NY.

Spencer, Hazelton. Art & Life of William Shakespeare. 1969. (1940) $12.50 Hdbd. (ISBN 0-389-01164-9). Barnes & Noble, NY.

Sprague, Arthur C. Shakespeare & the Audience. 1966. (1935) $8.50 Hdbd. Russell & Russell Publ., NY.

Spurgeon, Caroline F. Keats' Shakespeare. 1928. $6.50 Hdbd. (ISBN 0-19-811643-8). Oxford Univ. Pr., NY.

Stapfer, Paul. Shakespeare & Classical Antiquity, Greek & Latin Antiquity As Presented in Shakespeare's Plays. (Research & Source Work, No. 403). 1970. (1880) $12.50 Hdbd. (ISBN 0-8337-3365-6). Burt Franklin, NY.

Stirling, Brents. Unity in Shakespearian Tragedy. 1966. (1956) $6.50 Hdbd. (ISBN 0-87752-105-0). Gordian Pr., NY.

Stoll, Elmer E. Shakespeare & Other Masters. 1962. (1940) $9.50 Hdbd. Russell & Russell Publ., NY.

Stoll, Elmer E. Shakespeare Studies. 1959. $7.50 Hdbd. (ISBN 0-8044-2835-2). Frederick Ungar, NY.

Sutherland, James R. & Hurstfield, J.,

eds. Shakespeare's World. 1964. $5.00 Hdbd. St. Martin's Pr., NY.

Swinburne, Algernon C. Study of Shakespeare. 1880. $10.00 Hdbd. (ISBN 0-404-06315-2). AMS Pr., NY.

Ten Brink, Bernard A. Five Lectures on Shakespeare. Franklin, Julia, tr. 1895. $10.00 Hdbd. (ISBN 0-404-01080-6). AMS Pr., NY.

Terry, Ellen. Four Lectures on Shakespeare. 1932. $9.75 Hdbd. Benjamin Blom, NY.

Thaler, Alwin. Shakespeare & Our World. 1966. $5.95 Hdbd. (ISBN 0-87049-063-X). Univ. of Tennessee Pr., TN.

Thaler, Alwin & Sanders, Norman J., eds. Shakespearean Essays. (Special Issue No. 2). 1964. $3.50 Hdbd. (ISBN 0-87049-050-8). Univ. of Tennessee Pr., TN.

Theobald, Lewis. Shakespeare Restored, or a Specimen of the Many Errors As Well Committed As Unamended by Mr. Pope in His Late Edition of This Poet. 1726. $8.50 Hdbd. (ISBN 0-404-06364-0). AMS Pr., NY.

Theobald, Lewis. Shakespeare Restored, or a Specimen of the Many Errors As Well Committed As Unamended by Mr. Pope in His Late Edition of This Poet. 1726. $18.50 Hdbd. Kelley, NY.

Tillyard, Eustace M. Shakespeare's Last Plays. 6th ed. 1964. $2.00 Hdbd. Barnes & Noble, NY.

Tillyard, Eustace M. Shakespeare's Problem Plays. (Canadian University Paperbooks). 1949. $2.25 pa. (ISBN 0-8020-6026-9). Univ. of Toronto Pr., CAN.

Tolman, Albert H. Falstaff & Other Shakespearean Topics. 1925. $12.50 Hdbd. (ISBN 0-404-06475-2). AMS Pr., NY.

Toole, William B. Shakespeare's Problem Plays: Studies in Form & Meaning. 1966. $10.50 Hdbd. Humanities Pr., NY.

Traversi, Derek A. Approach to Shakespeare, Vol. 1. From Henry Sixth To Twelfth Night. (1969). $1.95 pa.; $4.95 Hdbd. Vol. 2. From Troilus & Cressida To The Tempest. $1.95 pa. Doubleday & Co., NY.

Turner, Frederich. Shakespeare & the Nature of Time: Moral & Philosophical Themes in Some Plays & Poems of William Shakespeare. 1971. $6.25 Hdbd. Oxford Univ. Pr., NY.

Ure, Peter. Shakespeare: The Problem Plays. (Writers & Their Work Ser No. 140). 1962. $2.25 Hdbd.; $1.00 pa. British Book Center, NY.

Van Doren, Mark. Shakespeare. 1953. $1.25 pa. Doubleday & Co., NY.

Velz, John W. Shakespeare & the Classical Tradition: A Critical Guide to Commentary, 1660–1960. 1968. $17.50 Hdbd. (ISBN 0-8166-0475-4). Univ. of Minn. Pr., MN.

Vickers, Brian. Artistry of Shakespeare's Prose. 1968. $12.00 Hdbd. Barnes & Noble, NY.

Wagner, Bernard M., ed. Appreciation of Shakespeare. 1949. $12.50 Hdbd. (ISBN 0-404-06800-6). AMS Pr., NY.

Wain, John. Living World of Shakespeare: Playgoer's Guide. 1964. $5.95 Hdbd. St. Martin's Pr., NY.

Waith, Eugene M. Herculean Hero in Marlowe, Chapman, Shakespeare & Dryden. 1962. $7.00 Hdbd. (ISBN 0-231-02506-8). Columbia Univ. Pr., NY.

Walder, Ernest. Shakespearian Criticism. 1895. $6.50 Hdbd. (ISBN 0-404-06803-0). AMS Pr., NY.

Warner, Beverley, ed. Famous Introductions to Shakespeare's Plays by the Notable Editors of the 18th Century. (Burt Franklin: Biblio. & Ref. Series, No. 171). 1968. (1966) $15.00 Hdbd. (ISBN 0-8337-3687-6). Burt Franklin, NY.

Webster, Margaret. Shakespeare Today. 1957. $4.95 Hdbd. Dufour Editions, PA.

Weiss, Theodore. Breath of Clowns & Kings: A Book on Shakespeare. 1971. $10.00 Hdbd. (ISBN 0-689-10329-8). Atheneum Publ., NY.

Weitz, Morris. Hamlet & the Philosophy of Literary Criticism. 1964. $6.75 Hdbd. (ISBN 0-226-89238-7). Univ. of Chicago Pr., IL.

Wells, Stanley. Literature & Drama with Special Reference to Shakespeare &

His Contemporaries. (Concepts of Literature Ser). 1971. $4.25 Hdbd.; $2.00 pa. Humanities Pr., NY.

Wendell, B. William Shakespeare: A Study in Elizabethan Literature. 1894. $12.50 Hdbd. (ISBN 0-404-06905-3). AMS Pr., NY.

Westfall, Alfred R. American Shakespearean Criticisms 1607-1865. 1968. $12.50 Hdbd. Benjamin Blom, NY.

White, Richard G. Shakespeare's Scholar: Being Historical & Critical Studies of His Text, Characters & Commentators with an Examination of Mr. Collier's Folio of 1632. 1854. $20.00 Hdbd. (ISBN 0-404-06934-7). AMS Pr., NY.

White, Richard G. Studies in Shakespeare. 1886. $17.50 Hdbd. (ISBN 0-404-06935-5). AMS Pr., NY.

Whiter, Walter. Specimen of a Commentary on Shakespeare. 1794. $12.50 Hdbd. (ISBN 0-404-06939-8). AMS Pr., NY.

Wilson, Frank P. Shakespearian & Other Studies. Gardner, Helen, ed. 1969. $13.00 Hdbd. (ISBN 0-19-811677-2). Oxford Univ. Pr., NY.

Wilson, John D. Essential Shakespeare. 1932-1960. $2.95 Hdbd.; $1.25 pa. (ISBN 0-521-09110-1, 110). Cambridge Univ. Pr., NY.

Wilson, John D. Shakespeare's Happy Comedies. 1963. $6.50 Hdbd. (ISBN 0-8101-0244-7). Northwestern Univ. Pr., IL.

Winny, James. Player King: A Theme of Shakespeare's Histories. 1968. $4.00 Hdbd. Barnes & Noble, NY.

Wynkoop, William M. Three Children of the Universe: Emerson's View of Shakespeare, Bacon & Milton. 1966. $7.25 Hdbd. Humanities Pr., NY.

Young, Karl. Samuel Johnson on Shakespeare: One Aspect. 1923. $7.50 Hdbd. Folcroft Pr., PA.

Comedies, Histories, and Tragedies—Comedies

Bonazza, Blaze O. Shakespeare's Early Comedies: A Structural Analysis. 1966. $7.00 Hdbd. Humanities Pr., NY.

Brown, John R. Shakespeare & His Comedies. 2nd ed. 1968. $2.50 Hdbd. (ISBN 0-416-29530-4). Barnes & Noble, NY.

Champion, Larry S. Evolution of Shakespeare's Comedy: A Study in Dramatic Peerspective. 1970. $8.50 Hdbd. (ISBN 0-674-27140-8). Harvard Univ. Pr., MA.

Charlton, Henry B. Dark Comedies. 1937. $3.00 Hdbd. Folcroft Pr., PA.

Charlton, Henry B. Dark Comedies of Shakespeare. (Studies in Shakespeare, No. 24). 1970. (1937) $2.95 pa. (ISBN 0-8383-0106-1). Haskell House Publ., NY.

Charlton, Henry B. Shakespearean Comedy. 1961. $5.00 Hdbd. Barnes & Noble, NY.

Charlton, Henry B. Shakespeare's Comedies: The Consummation. (Studies in Shakespeare, No. 24). 1970. (1937) $1.95 pa. (ISBN 0-8383-0013-8). Haskell House Publ., NY.

Charlton, Henry B. Shakespearian Comedy. 1961. $3.00 pa. (ISBN 0-416-69260-5, 156, UP). Barnes & Noble, NY.

Cody, Richard. Landscape of the Mind: Pastoralism & Platonic Theory in Tasso's Aminta & Shakespeare's Early Comedies. 1969. $9.75 Hdbd. (ISBN 0-19-811680-2). Oxford Univ. Pr., NY.

Desai, Chiatomoni N. Shakespearian Comedy. 1952. $8.50 Hdbd. (ISBN 0-404-02099-2). AMS Pr., NY.

Evans, Bertrand. Shakespeare's Comedies. 1960. $7.20 Hdbd. (ISBN 0-19-811595-4); $2.50 pa. (ISBN 0-19-881128-4). Oxford Univ. Pr., NY.

Frye, Northrop. Natural Perspective: 1969. (1965) ed. $1.95 pa. (ISBN 0-15-665414-8). Harcourt, Brace & World, NY.

Frye, Northrop. Natural Perspective: The Development of Shakespearean Comedy & Romance. 1965. $5.50 Hdbd. (ISBN 0-231-02813-X). Columbia Univ. Pr., NY.

Gordon, George S. Shakespearian Comedy & Other Studies. 1944. $3.50 Hdbd. (ISBN 0-19-811544-X). Oxford Univ. Pr., NY.

Hunter, G. K. Shakespeare: The Late Comedies. (Writers & Their Work Ser No. 143). 1962. $2.25 Hdbd. $1.00 pa. British Book Center, NY.

Hunter, Robert G. Shakespeare & the Comedy of Forgiveness: 1965. $8.00 Hdbd. (ISBN 0-231-02757-5). Columbia Univ. Pr., NY.

Lawrence, William W. Shakespeare's Problem Comedies. 1959. $5.00 Hdbd. (ISBN) 0-8044-2495-0). Frederick Ungar, NY.

Lawrence, William W. Shakespeare's Problem Comedies. 1969. $1.45 pa. (ISBN 0-14-053010-X). Penguin Books, MD.

Lerner, Laurence, ed. Shakespeare's Comedies: An Anthology of Modern Criticism. 1967. $1.65 pa. (ISBN 0-14-053002-9). Penguin Books, MD.

Low, J. T. Shakespeares Folio Comedies. 1971. $12.50 Hdbd. Darby Books, PA.

Martz, William. Shakespeare's Universe of Comedy. $6.00 Hdbd. David Lewis Publ., NY.

Muir, Kenneth, ed. Shakespeare, the Comedies: A Collection of Critical Essays. 1965. $5.95 Hdbd. (ISBN 0-13-807693-6). $1.95 pa. (ISBN 0-13-807685-5, Spec). Prentice-Hall, NY.

Palmer, D. J., ed. Shakespeare's Later Comedies: An Anthology of Modern Criticism. (Shakespeare Library). 1971. $3.75 pa. (ISBN 0-14-053017-7). Penguin Books, MD.

Parrott, Thomas M. Shakespearean Comedy. 1962. (1949) $12.50 Hdbd. Russell & Russell Publ., NY.

Pettet, E. C. Shakespeare & the Romance Tradition. 1949. $3.50 Hdbd. Hillary House Publ., NY.

Phialas, Peter G. Shakespeare's Romantic Comedies: The Development of Their Form & Meaning. 1966. $7.50 Hdbd. (ISBN 0-8078-1005-3); $2.95 pa. (ISBN 0-8078-4043-2). Univ. of N.C. Pr., NC.

Ranald, Margaret. Monarch Literature Notes on Shakespeare: Selected Comedies. $1.00 pa. Monarch Pr., NY.

Richmond, Hugh M. Shakespeare's Sexual Comedy: A Mirror for Lovers. 1971. $7.50 Hdbd. Bobbs-Merrill Co., IN.

Small, Samuel A. Return of Shakespeare: The Historical Realists. 1927. $5.00 Hdbd. (ISBN 0-404-06108-7). AMS Pr., NY.

Stevenson, David L. Love-Game Comedy. 1946. $7.50 Hdbd. (ISBN 0-404-06263-6). AMS Pr., NY.

Tillyard, Eustace M. Nature of Comedy & Shakespeare. 1958. $3.00 Hdbd. Folcroft Pr., PA.

Tillyard, Eustace M. Shakespeare's Early Comedies. Tillyard, Stephen, ed. 1965. $4.50 Hdbd. Barnes & Noble, NY.

Traversi, Derek A. Shakespeare: The Early Comedies: (Writers & Their Work Ser No. 129). 1960. $2.25 Hdbd. $1.00 pa. British Book Center, NY.

Traversi, Derek A. Shakespeare: The Last Phase. 1955. $7.50 Hdbd. (ISBN 0-8047-0508-9). Stanford Univ. Pr., CA.

Vyvyan, John. Shakespeare & Platonic Beauty. 1970. $5.00 Hdbd. (ISBN 0-389-01123-1). Barnes & Noble, NY.

Whiter, Walter. Specimen of a Commentary on Shakespeare. 2nd rev. & enl. ed. Over, Alan & Bell, Mary, eds. 1967. $11.25 Hdbd. Barnes & Noble, NY.

Whiter, Walter. Specimen of a Commentary on Shakespeare. (1794) $12.50 Hdbd. (ISBN 0-404-06939-8). AMS Pr., NY.

Wilson, John D. Shakespeare's Happy Comedies. 1963. $6.50 Hdbd. (ISBN 0-8101-0244-7). Northwestern Univ. Pr., IL.

Comedies, Histories, and Tragedies—Histories

Bromley, John C. Shakespearean Kings. 1970. $7.95 text ed. (ISBN 0-87081-009-X). Colo Assoc. Univ. Pr., CO.

Campbell, Lily B. Shakespeare's Histories: Mirrors of Elizabethan Policy. 1947. $8.50 Hdbd. Huntington Library, CA.

Charney, Maurice, ed. Discussions of Shakespeare's Roman Plays. (Discussions of Literature). 1964. $2.25 pa. (21998). D. C. Heath & Co., IN.

Charney, Maurice M. Shakespeare's Roman Plays: The Function of Imagery in the Drama. 1961. $7.00 Hdbd. (ISBN 0-674-80475-9). Harvard Univ. Pr., MA.

Courtenay, Thomas P. Commentaries on the History Plays of Shakespeare, 2 Vols. 1840. Set—$32.50 Hdbd. (ISBN 0-404-01781-9); $16.50 ea. Hdbd. (ISBN

0-404-01782-7)   (ISBN 0-404-0783-5).
AMS Pr., NY.

Dorius, R. Joel, ed.   Discussions of
Shakespeare's Histories: Richard Second
to Henry Fifth. (Discussions of Literature). (Hi-Sch.). 1964. $2.25 pa. D. C.
Heath & Co., IN.

Kelly, Henry A.   Divine Providence in
the England of Shakespeare's Histories.
1970. $10.00 Hdbd. (ISBN 0-674-21292-
4). Harvard Univ. Pr., MA.

Knights, L. C.   Shakespeare: The Histories. (Writers & Their Work Ser No.
151). 1962. $2.25 Hdbd.; $1.00 pa.
British Bk Ctr., NY.

Leech, Clifford.   Shakespeare: The
Chronicles. (Writers & Their Work Ser
No. 146). 1962. $2.25 Hdbd.; $1.00 pa.
British Bk Ctr., NY.

Marriott, J. English History in Shakespeare. 1919. $12.50 Hdbd. Folcroft
Pr., PA.

Owen, Lewis J.   Lectures on Four of
Shakespeare's History Plays.   1953.
$15.00 Hdbd. Folcroft Pr., PA.

Pierce, Robert B. Shakespeare's History
Plays: The Family & the State. 1971.
$8.75 Hdbd.   (ISBN 0-8142-0152-0).
Ohio State Univ. Pr., OH.

Reed, H.   English History & Tragic
Poetry As Illustrated by Shakespeare.
1855. $18.00 Hdbd. (ISBN 0-404-05234-
7). AMS Pr., NY.

Reese, Max M.   Cease of Majesty: A
Study of Shakespeare's History Plays.
1961. $8.75 Hdbd. St. Martin's Pr., NY.

Richmond, Hugh M.   Shakespeare's
Political Plays. (Orig.). 1967. $2.95 pa.
Random House, NY.

Sen Gupta, S. C. Shakespeare's Historical Plays. 1964. $5.75 Hdbd. (ISBN 0-
19-811621-7). Oxford Univ. Pr., NY.

Shakespeare, William.   Histories. Incl.
Poems. $2.95 Hdbd. (7). Modern Lib.,
MD.

Shakespeare, William.   Shakespeare's
Tragedies of Monarchy. $1.85 pa. Dell
Publ., NY.

Spencer, T. J.   Shakespeare: Roman
Plays. (Writers & Their Work Ser No.
157). 1963. $2.25 Hdbd.; $1.00 pa.
British Bk Ctr., NY.

Tillyard, Eustace M.   Shakespeare's
History Plays. 2nd ed.   1964. $5.50
Hdbd. Barnes & Noble, NY.

Tillyard, Eustace M.   Shakespeare's
History Plays. 1962. $1.50 pa. Mac-
millan, NY.

Traversi, Derek A. Shakespeare: From
Richard Second to Henry Fifth. 1957.
$6.00 Hdbd.   (ISBN 0-8047-0503-8).
Stanford Univ. Pr., CA.

Traversi, Derek A.   Shakespeare: The
Roman Plays. 1963. $7.50 Hdbd.
(ISBN 0-8047-0182-2). Stanford Univ.
Pr., CA.

Vaughn, Henry H.   New Readings &
New Renderings of Shakespeare's Tragedies, 3 Vols. $55.00 Hdbd. (ISBN
0-404-06780-8). AMS Pr., NY.

Waith, Eugene M., ed. Shakespeare, the
Histories: A Collection of Critical Es-

says. 1965. $1.95 pa. (ISBN 0-13-807701-0). $5.95 Hdbd. (ISBN 0-13-807719-3). Prentice-Hall, NY.

Whately, Thomas. Remarks on Some of the Characters of Shakespeare. 3rd ed. 1839. $8.00 Hdbd. (ISBN 0-404-06917-7). AMS Pr., NY.

Wilson, John D. & Worsley, Thomas C. Shakespeare's Histories at Stratford, 1951. (Select Bibliographies Reprint Ser). 1952. $9.50 Hdbd. (ISBN 0-8369-5515-3). Books for Libraries, NY.

Young, David P., ed. Twentieth Century Interpretations of Henry Fourth Pt. 2. 1968. $4.95 Hdbd. (ISBN 0-13-386995-4). Prentice-Hall, NY.

Comedies, Histories and Tragedies—Tragedies

Baker, Howard. Induction to Tragedy. 1965. (1939) $7.50 Hdbd. Russell & Russell, NY.

Battenhouse, Roy W. Shakespearean Tragedy: Its Art & Its Christian Premises. 1969. $15.00 Hdbd. (ISBN 0-253-18090-2). Ind. Univ. Pr., IN.

Bradley, Andrew C. Shakespearean Tragedy. 1971. $1.25 pa. Fawcett World Lib., NY.

Bradley, Andrew C. Shakespearean Tragedy. $1.25 pa. Fawcett World Lib., NY.

Bradley, Andrew C. Shakespearean Tragedy: Lectures on Hamlet, Othello, King Lear & Macbeth. 1956. $1.50 pa. 2nd ed. 1905. $11.50 Hdbd. St. Martin's Pr., NY.

Brooke, Nicholas. Shakespeare's Early Tragedies. 1968. $5.25 Hdbd. Barnes & Noble, NY.

Cairncross, A. Problem of Hamlet: A Solution. 1971. (1936) $12.50 Hdbd. Lansdowne Pr., PA.

Campbell, Lewis. Tragic Drama in Aeschylus, Sophocles & Shakespeare. 1965. (1904) $8.50 Hdbd. Russell & Russell, NY.

Campbell, Lily. Shakespeare's Tragic Heroes. 1960. $4.00 Hdbd.; $1.95 pa. (ISBN 0-389-01758-2, 433). Barnes & Noble, NY.

Campbell, Lily. Shakespeare's Tragic Heroes-Slaves of Passion. 1960. $4.00 Hdbd. Peter Smith, MA.

Carlisle, Carol J. Shakespeare from the Greenroom: Actors' Criticisms of Four Major Tragedies. 1969. $12.50 Hdbd. (ISBN 0-8078-1115-7). Univ. of N.C. Pr., NC.

Charlton, H. B. Shakespearian Tragedy: 1971. $6.00 Hdbd. Cambridge Univ. Pr., NY.

Coles, Blanche. Shakespeare's Four Giants. 1957. $4.50 Hdbd. (ISBN 0-87233-809-6). William Bauhan, NH.

Cunningham, J. V. Tradition & Poetic Structure: Essays in Literary History & Criticism. $4.00 Hdbd. Swallow Pr., IL.

Cunningham, J. V. Woe or Wonder: The Emotional Effects of Shakespearian Tragedy. $2.00 pa. Swallow Pr., IL.

Dickey, Franklin M. Not Wisely but Too Well: Shakespeare's Love Tragedies.

1957. $6.00 Hdbd. Huntington Library, CA.

Duthie, George I. Bad Quarto of Hamlet. 1941. $15.00 Hdbd. Folcroft Pr., PA.

Dyson, H. V. Emergence of Shakespeare's Tragedy. 1950. $1.95 pa. (ISBN 0-8383-0023-5). Haskell House, NY.

Elliot, George R. Scourge & Minister: A Study of Hamlet As Tragedy of Revengefulness & Justice. 1971. $8.00 Hdbd. (ISBN 0-404-02307-X). AMS Pr., NY.

Elliott, George R. Flaming Minister: A Study of Othello As Tragedy of Love & Hate. 1953. $8.50 Hdbd. (ISBN 0-404-02306-1). AMS Pr., NY.

Frye, Northrop. Fools of Time: Studies in Shakespearean Tragedy. 1967. $4.95 Hdbd. (ISBN 0-8020-1440-2). Univ. of Toronto Pr., CAN.

Harbage, Alfred, ed. Shakespeare: The Tragedies: A Collection of Critical Essays. 1964. $5.95 Hdbd. (ISBN 0-13-807743-6). $1.95 pa. (ISBN 0-13-807735-5). Prentice-Hall, NY.

Harrison, George B. Shakespeare's Tragedies. 1952. $7.25 Hdbd. 1969. (1952) $1.85 pa. (ISBN 0-19-500451-5). Oxford Univ. Pr., NY.

Hawkes, Terence. Shakespeare & the Reason. 1964. $6.50 Hdbd. Humanities Pr., NY.

Holloway, John. Story of the Night: Studies in Shakespeare's Major Trage-dies. 1963. $3.50 Hdbd. (ISBN 0-8032-0075-7). $1.25 pa. (ISBN 0-8032-5092-4). Univ. of Nebr. Pr., NB.

James, David G. Dream of Learning: An Essay on the Advancement of Learning, Hamlet, & King Lear. 1951. $4.50 Hdbd. (ISBN 0-19-81155-5). Oxford Univ. Pr., NY.

Kirsch, James. Shakespeare's Royal Self. (Jung Foundation Ser). 1966. $7.95 Hdbd. G. P. Putnam, NY.

Kitto, Humphrey D. Form & Meaning in Drama. 1956. $3.25 pa. (ISBN 0-416-67520-4). Barnes & Noble, NY.

Knight, George W. Imperial Theme. Further Interpretations of Shakespeare's Tragedies Including the Roman Plays. 3rd ed. 1963. $6.75 Hdbd. $2.95 pa. (ISBN 0-416-68740-7). Barnes & Noble, NY.

Knight, George W. Wheel of Fire: Interpretation of Shakespeare's Tragedies. 4th ed. rev. ed. 1962. $5.50 Hdbd. $3.35 pa. (ISBN 0-416-67620-0, 12, UP). Barnes & Noble, NY.

Laurence, W. J. Shakespeare's Workshop. (Studies in Shakespeare Ser., No. 24). 1969. (1928) $8.95 Hdbd. (ISBN 0-8383-0580-6). Haskell House, NY

Levenworth, Russell E. Interpreting Hamlet. 1960. $2.95 pa. (ISBN 0-8102-0150-X). Chandler Pub., PA.

Leech, Clifford, ed. Shakespeare: The Tragedies. 1965. $6.50 Hdbd. (ISBN 0-8020-1336-8); $2.45 pa. (ISBN 0-8020-1337-6). Univ. of Toronto Pr., CAN.

Leech, Clifford, ed. Shakespeare: The Tragedies: A Collection of Critical Essays. 1965. $6.50 Hdbd. (ISBN 0-226-47017-2); $2.45 pa. (ISBN 0-226-47018-0). Univ. of Chicago Pr., IL.

Lerner, Laurence, ed. Shakespeare's Tragedies: An Anthology of Modern Criticism. 1964. $1.45 pa. (ISBN 0-14-053008-8, SL8). Penguin Books, MD.

McFarland, Thomas. Tragic Meanings in Shakespeare. 1966. $2.95 pa. Random House, NY.

Muir, Edwin. Shakespeare & the Tragic Pattern. 1958. $2.50 Hdbd. Folcroft Pr., PA.

Muir, Kenneth. Shakespeare: The Tragedies. (Writers & Their Work Ser No. 113). 1966. $2.25 Hdbd.; $1.00 pa. British Book Ctr., NY.

Proser, M. N. Heroic Image in Five Shakespearean Tragedies. 1965. $8.50 Hdbd.; $2.95 pa. Princeton Univ. Pr., NJ.

Reed, H. English History & Tragic Poetry As Illustrated by Shakespeare. 1855. $18.00 Hdbd. (ISBN 0-404-05234-7). AMS Pr., NY.

Ribner, Irving. Patterns in Shakespearian Tragedy. 1960. $5.00 Hdbd. 1970. $2.25 pa. (ISBN 0-416-18180-5, 334, UP). Barnes & Noble, NY.

Rosen, William. Shakespeare & the Craft of Tragedy. 1960. $6.50 Hdbd. (ISBN 0-674-80341-8). Harvard Univ. Pr., MA.

Rymer, Thomas. Short View of Tragedy. 1968. (1693) $10.00 Hdbd. (ISBN 0-404-05478-1). AMS Pr., NY.

Sharma, Ram B. Essays on Shakespearean Tragedy. 1965. $5.00 Hdbd. Lawrence Verry Inc., CT.

Slampfer, Judah L. Tragic Engagement: A Study of Shakespeare's Classical Tragedies. $6.95 Hdbd. (740300). Funk & Wagnalls, NY.

Spurgeon, Caroline F. Leading Motives in the Imagery of Shakespeare's Tragedies. (Studies in Shakespeare Scr., No. 24). 1970. (1930) $3.95 Hdbd. (ISBN 0-8383-1203-9). Haskell House Publ., NY.

Spurgeon, Caroline F. Leading Motives in the Imagery of Shakespeare's Tragedies. 1930. $3.00 Hdbd. Folcroft Pr., PA.

Stirling, Brents. Unity in Shakespearian Tragedy. 1966. (1956) $6.50 Hdbd. (ISBN 0-87752-105-0). Gordian Pr., NY.

Uhlig, Claus. Traditionelle Denkformen in Shakespeares Tragischer Kunst. (No. 15, Britannica et Americana). (German). 1968. $6.85 pa. De Gruyter, Germany.

Weitz, Morris. Philosophy in Literature: Shakespeare, Voltaire, Tolstoy & Proust. 1963. $2.45 pa. (ISBN 0-8143-1201-?). Wayne State Univ. Pr., MI.

Whately, Thomas. Remarks on Some of the Characters of Shakespeare. 3rd ed. 1839. $8.00 Hdbd. (ISBN 0-404-0691?-7). AMS Pr., NY.

Whitaker, Virgil K. Mirror up to Nature: The Technique of Shakespeare's

Tragedies. 1965. $7.50 Hdbd. Huntington Library, CA.

Wilson, Harold S. On the Design of Shakespearian Tragedy. 1957. $2.25 pa. (ISBN 0-8020-6077-3). Univ. of Toronto Pr., CAN.

Editorial History

Dyce, Alexander. Remarks on Mister J. P. Collier's & Mister C. Knight's Editions of Shakespeare. 1844. $12.50 Hdbd. (ISBN 0-404-02230-8). AMS Pr., NY.

Dyce, Alexander. Strictures on Mister Collier's New Edition of Shakespeare, 1858. 1859. $10.00 Hdbd. (ISBN 0-404-02231-6). AMS Pr., NY.

Lounsbury, Thomas R. First Editors of Shakespeare: Pope & Theobald. 1906. $25.00 Hdbd. (ISBN 0-404-04028-4). AMS Pr., NY.

McKerrow, Ronald B. Prolegomena for the Oxford Shakespeare: A Study in Editorial Method. 1939. $5.00 Hdbd. (ISBN 0-19-811685-3). Oxford Univ. Pr., NY.

McKerrow, Ronald B. Treatment of Shakespeare's Text by His Earlier Editors. 1933. $4.00 Hdbd. Folcroft Pr., PA.

Morgan, James A. Some Shakespearean Commentators. 1882. $5.00 Hdbd. (ISBN 0-404-04429-8). AMS Pr., NY.

History

Babcock, Robert W. Genesis of Shakespeare Idolatry, 1766–1799. 1964. (1931) $8.50 Hdbd. Russell & Russell Publ., NY.

Charney, Maurice. How to Read Shakespeare. 1971. $6.95 Hdbd. (ISBN 0-07-010655-X); $2.95 pa. McGraw-Hill, NY.

Collison-Morley, Lacy. Shakespeare in Italy. 1916. $9.75 Hdbd. Benjamin Blom., NY.

Cushing, Mary G. Pierre Le Tourneur. 1908. $10.00 Hdbd. (ISBN 0-404-50608-9). AMS Pr., NY.

Drake, Nathan. Memorials of Shakespeare. 1828. $25.00 Hdbd. (ISBN 0-404-02177-8). AMS Pr., NY.

Eastman, Arthur M. Short History of Shakespearean Criticism. 1968. $2.95 pa. (ISBN 0-394-30189-7). Random House, NY.

Ellis-Fermor, Una M. Some Recent Research in Shakespeare's Imagery. 1937. $3.00 Hdbd. Folcroft Pr., PA.

Ellis-Fermor, Una M. Some Recent Research in Shakespeare's Imagery. (Studies in Shakespeare, No. 24). 1970. (1937) $2.95 pa. (ISBN 0-8383-0025-1). Haskell House Publ., NY.

Furness, Clifton J. Walt Whitman's Estimate of Shakespeare. (Studies in Walt Whitman, No. 28). 1970. (1932) $2.95 pa. (ISBN 0-8383-0032-4). Haskell House Publ., NY.

Green, Frederick C. Literary Ideas in Eighteenth Century France & England. 1965. $9.50 Hdbd. (ISBN 0-8044-2299-0). Frederick Ungar, NY.

Harbage, Alfred. Shakespeare's Audience. $4.00 Hdbd. Peter Smith Publ., MA.

Harbage, Alfred. Shakespeare's Audience. 1941. $1.95 pa. (ISBN 0-231-08513-3). Columbia Univ. Pr., NY.

Herford, Charles H. Sketch of Recent Shakespearean Investigation 1893–1923. $5.00 Hdbd. Folcroft Pr., PA.

Hughes, Cecil E. Praise of Shakespeare, an English Anthology, 1596–1902. 1904. $12.50 Hdbd. (ISBN 0-404-03381-4). AMS Pr., NY.

Johnson, Charles F. Shakespeare & His Critics. 1909. $15.00 Hdbd. (ISBN 0-404-03569-8). AMS Pr., NY.

LeWinter, Oswald, ed. Shakespeare in Europe. $4.00 Hdbd. Peter Smith Publ., MA.

Lounsbury, Thomas R. Shakespeare & Voltaire. 1902. $12.50 Hdbd. (ISBN 0-404-04029-2). AMS Pr., NY.

Murray, Patrick. Shakesperian Scene: Some Twentieth-Century Perspectives. 1969. $6.50 Hdbd. (ISBN 0-389-01045-6). Barnes & Noble, NY.

Pillai, V. Ayappan. Shakespeare Criticism: From the Beginnings to 1765. 1932. $15.00 Hdbd. Folcroft Pr., PA.

Ralli, Augustus J. History of Shakespearian Criticism, 2 Vols. 1959. $22.50 Hdbd. Humanities Pr., NY.

Ralli, Augustus J. Later Critiques. (Essay Index Reprint Ser). 1968. (1933) $7.75 Hdbd. (ISBN 0-8369-0809-0). Books for Libraries, NY.

Ridler, Anne B., ed. Shakespeare Criticism, 1935–1960. 1963. $2.75 pa. (ISBN 0-19-281082-0). $2.75 Hdbd. (ISBN 0-19-250590-4). Oxford Univ. Pr., NY.

Robinson, Herbert S. English Shakespearean Criticism in the Eighteenth Century. 1968. (1932) $8.50 Hdbd. (ISBN 0-87752-094-1). Gordian Pr., NY.

Schueller, Herbert M., ed. Persistence of Shakespeare Idolatry: Essays in Honor of Robert W. Babcock. 1964. $5.00 Hdbd. (ISBN 0-8143-1237-3). Wayne St. Univ. Pr., MI.

Small, Samuel A. Return of Shakespeare: The Historical Realists. 1927. $5.00 Hdbd. (ISBN 0-404-06108-7). AMS Pr., NY.

Small, Samuel A. Shakespearean Character Interpretation: Merchant of Venice. 1927. $7.50 Hdbd. (ISBN 0-404-06109-5). AMS Pr., NY.

Smith, David N. Shakespeare in the Eighteenth Century. 1928. $4.00 Hdbd. (ISBN 0-19-811646-2). Oxford Univ. Pr., NY.

Smith, David N., ed. Eighteenth Century Essays on Shakespeare. 2nd ed. 1963. $6.75 Hdbd. (ISBN 0-19-811607-1). Oxford Univ. Pr., NY.

Smith, David N., ed. Shakespeare Criticism: A Selection. $2.50 Hdbd. (ISBN 0-19-250212-3). Oxford Univ. Pr., NY.

Stavisky, Aron Y. Shakespeare & the Victorians: Roots of Modern Criticism. 1969. $4.95 Hdbd. (ISBN 0-8061-0822-3). Univ. of Okla. Pr., OK.

Theobald, Lewis. Shakespeare Restored, or a Specimen of the Many Errors As Well Committed As Unamended by Mr. Pope in His Late Edition of This Poet. $18.50 Hdbd. Augustus M. Kelley, NY.

Warner, Beverley, ed. Famous Introductions to Shakespeare's Plays by the Notable Editors of the 18th Century. (Burt Franklin: Biblio. & Ref. Series, No. 171). 1968. (1966) $15.00 Hdbd. (ISBN 0-8337-3687-6). Burt Franklin, NY.

Westfall, Alfred R. American Shakespearean Criticisms 1607-1865. 1968. $12.50 Hdbd. Benjamin Blom., NY.

Woodberry, George F. Shakespeare: An Address. 1916. $4.00 Hdbd. Folcroft Pr., PA.

Plays

ALL'S WELL THAT ENDS WELL
Halliwell-Phillips, James O. Memoranda on All's Well That Ends Well, the Two Gentlemen of Verona, Much Ado About Nothing & on Titus Andronicus. 1879. $6.50 Hdbd. (ISBN 0-404-03066-1). AMS Pr., NY.

Price, Joseph G. Unfortunate Comedy: A Study of All's Well That Ends Well & Its Critics. 1968. $8.50 Hdbd. (ISBN 0-8020-1526-3). Univ. of Toronto Pr., CAN.

Ranald, Margaret L. Monarch Literature Notes on Shakespeare's All's Well That Ends Well. $1.00 pa. Monarch Pr., NY.

Shakespeare, William. All's Well That Ends Well: A Concordance to the Text of the First Folio. 1969. $9.75 Hdbd. (ISBN 0-19-811134-7). Oxford Univ. Pr., NY.

ANTONY AND CLEOPATRA
Cliff's Notes Editors. Antony & Cleopatra Notes. $1.00 pa. (ISBN 0-8220-0002-4). Cliffs Notes, NB.

Granville-Barker, Harley. Prefaces to Shakespeare, Vol. 3, Prefaces to Anthony & Cleopatra, & Coriolanus. 1965. $5.00 Hdbd. (ISBN 0-691-06103-3); $2.95 pa. (ISBN 0-691-01279-2, 25). Princeton Univ. Pr., NJ.

Markels, Julian. Pillar of the World: Antony & Cleopatra in Shakespeare's Development. 1968. $6.00 Hdbd. (ISBN 0-8142-0090-7). Ohio St. Univ. Pr., OH.

Riemer, A. Reading of Shakespeare's Antony & Cleopatra. 1968. $3.05 Hdbd. (ISBN 0-424-05630-5, Pr). Library Assn. London, ENG.

Shakespeare, William. Antony & Cleopatra. Brown, John R., ed. (Casebook Ser). 1970. (1968) $2.50 pa. (ISBN 0-87695-046-2). Aurora Publ., TN.

Traci, Philip J. Love Play of Antony and Cleopatra: A Critical Study of Shakespeare's Play. (Studies in English Literature). 1971. $9.00 Hdbd. Humanities Pr., NY.

Walsh, William. Monarch Literature Notes on Shakespeare's Antony & Cleopatra. $1.00 pa. Monarch Pr., NY.

AS YOU LIKE IT

Cliff's Notes Editors. As You Like It Notes. $1.00 pa. (ISBN 0-8220-0007-5). Cliffs Notes, NB.

Felheim, Marvin. As You Like It. Shakespeare Ser). price "n.g." Hdbd. (ISBN 0-697-03913-7). William C. Brown, NY.

Halio, Jay L., ed. Twentieth Century Interpretations of As You Like It. (Twentieth Century Interpretations Series). 1968. $1.25 pa. (ISBN 0-13-019486-0). $4.95 Hdbd. (ISBN 0-13-049494-1). Prentice-Hall, NY.

Jamieson, Michael. As You Like It by Shakespeare: Critical Analysis. Daiches, David, ed. (Hi-Sch.). 1965. $1.00 pa. Barron's Educ. Series, NY.

Jones. Barron's Simplified Approach to Shakespeare's As You Like It. 1971. $0.95 pa. Barron's Educ. Series, NY.

Rainer, Pineas. Monarch Literature Notes on Shakespeare's As You Like It. $1.00 pa. Monarch Pr., NY.

Shakespeare, William. As You Like It: A Concordance to the Text of the First Folio. 1969. $9.75 Hdbd. (ISBN 0-19-811132-0). Oxford Univ. Pr., NY.

COMEDY OF ERRORS

Baldwin, Thomas W. On the Compositional Gentics of The Comedy of Errors. 1965. $8.75 Hdbd. (ISBN 0-252-72585-9). Univ. of Ill. Pr., IL.

Blackburn, Ruth H. Monarch Literature Notes on Shakespeare's Comedy of Errors. $1.00 pa. Monarch Pr., NY.

Charlton, Henry B. Shakespeare's Recoil from Romanticism. 1931. $4.00 Hdbd. Folcroft Pr., PA.

Rouse, W. H. Menaechni, the Original of Shakespeare's Comedy of Errors; the Latin Text Together with the Elizabethan Translation. (Shakespeare Classics). 1912. $15.00 Hdbd. Folcroft Pr., PA.

CORIOLANUS

Bradley, Andrew C. Coriolanus. 1912. $4.00 Hdbd. Folcroft Pr., PA.

Cliff's Notes Editors. Coriolanus Notes. $1.00 pa. (ISBN 0-8220-0012-1). Cliffs Notes, NB.

Huffman, Clifford. Coriolanus in Context. $8.00 Hdbd. (ISBN 0-8387-1011-5). Bucknell Univ. Pr., PA.

Kitto, Humphrey D. Poiesis: Structure & Thought. 1966. $10.00 Hdbd. (ISBN 0-520-00651-8). Univ. of Cal. Pr., CA.

Phillips, James E., ed. Twentieth Century Interpretations of Coriolanus. 1970. $4.95 Hdbd. (ISBN 0-13-172668-4). $1.25 pa. (ISBN 0-13-172668-4). Prentice-Hall, NY.

Ranald, Margaret L. Monarch Literature Notes on Shakespeare's Coriolanus. $1.00 pa. Monarch Pr., NY.

CYMBELINE

Elze, Karl. Letter to C. M. Ingleby, Esq. 1885. $5.00 Hdbd. (ISBN 0-404-02326-6). AMS Pr., NY.

Granville-Barker, Harley. Prefaces to Shakespeare, Vol. 2, Prefaces To King Lear, Cymbeline & Julius Caesar. 1965. $5.00 Hdbd. (ISBN 0-691-06102-5);

$2.95 pa. (ISBN 0-691-01278-4, 24); 24 pa. Princeton Univ. Pr., NJ.

Marsh, Derek R. Recurring Miracle: A Study of Cymbeline & the Lost Plays. 1969. (1962) $1.95 pa. (ISBN 0-8032-5126-2, 399, Bison). Univ. of Nebr. Pr., NB.

HAMLET

Alexander, Nigel. Poison, Play & Duel: A Study in Hamlet. 1971. $6.50 Hdbd. (ISBN 0-8032-0772-7). Univ. of Nebr. Pr., NB.

Alexander, Peter. Hamlet: Father & Son. 1955. $5.00 Hdbd. (ISBN 0-19-811501-6). Oxford Univ. Pr., NY.

Babcock, Weston. Hamlet, a Tragedy of Errors. 1961. $1.75 pa. (ISBN 0-911198-01-6). Purdue Univ. Studies, IN.

Babcock, Weston. Hamlet: A Tragedy of Errors. 1971. (1962) $10.00 Hdbd. Lansdowne Pr., PA.

Bowers, Fredson T. Hamlet-Shakespeare. 1967. $1.00 pa. (ISBN 0-389-00839-7, 836). Barnes & Noble, NY.

Bradby, Godfrey F. Problems of Hamlet. (Studies in Shakespeare, No. 24). 1970. (1928) $3.95 pa. (ISBN 0-8383-0006-5). Haskell House Publ., NY.

Brock, James H. Dramatic Purpose of Hamlet. 1935. $5.00 Hdbd. Folcroft Pr., PA.

Brock, James H. Dramatic Purpose of Hamlet. 1935. $5.00 Hdbd. (ISBN 0-404-01087-3). AMS Pr., NY.

Brown, John R. & Harris, Bernard, eds. Hamlet. (Stratford-Upon-Avon Studies, Vol. 5). 1963. $8.95 Hdbd. St. Martin's Pr., NY.

Brown, John R. & Harris, Bernard, eds. Hamlet: A Reading & Playing Guide. 1966. $1.95 pa. (ISBN 0-8052-0120-3). Schocken Books, NY.

Buell, William A. Hamlets of the Theater. 1965. $12.50 Hdbd. (ISBN 0-8392-1158-9). Astor-Honor, Inc., NY.

Charlton, Henry B. Hamlet. 1942. $4.00 Hdbd. Folcroft Pr., PA.

Charney, Maurice. Style in Hamlet. 1969. $9.00 Hdbd. (ISBN 0-691-06163-7). Princeton Univ. Pr., NJ.

Cliff's Notes Editors. Hamlet Notes. $1.00 pa. (ISBN 0-8220-0017-2). Cliffs Notes, NB.

Conklin, Paul S. History of Hamlet Criticism 1601–1821. 1967. $6.50 Hdbd. Humanities Pr., NY.

Conolly, John. Study of Hamlet. 1863. $8.50 Hdbd. (ISBN 0-404-01695-2). AMS Pr., NY.

Corbin, John. Elizabethan Hamlet. 1970. (1895) $6.50 Hdbd. (ISBN 0-404-01726-6). AMS Pr., NY.

Davis, Arthur G. Hamlet & the Eternal Problem of Man. $5.00 pa. (ISBN 0-87075-047-X). St. Johns Univ. Pr., NY.

De Madariaga, Salvador. On Hamlet. 2nd ed. 1964. $5.00 Hdbd. Barnes & Noble, NY.

Devlin, Christopher. Hamlet's Divinity. 1963. $8.50 Hdbd. Ridgeway Books, PA.

Draper, John W. Hamlet of Shakespeare's Audience. 1966. $8.50 Hdbd. Octagon Books, NY.

Duthie, George I. Bad Quarto of Hamlet. 1941. $15.00 Hdbd. Folcroft Pr., PA.

Egan, Maurice F. Ghost in Hamlet. 1971. (1906) $15.00 Hdbd. (ISBN 0-404-02264-2). AMS Pr., NY.

Egan, Maurice F. Ghost in Hamlet. (Essay Index Reprint Ser). 1906. $11.50 Hdbd. (ISBN 0-8369-2185-2). Books for Libraries, NY.

Eissler, Kurt R. Discourse on Hamlet & Hamlet, a Psychoanalytic Inquiry. 1971. price "n.g." Hdbd. (ISBN 0-8236-1287-2). International Univ. Pr., NY.

Feis, Jacob. Shakespere & Montaigne. 1970. (1884) $8.50 Hdbd. (ISBN 0-404-02375-4). AMS Pr., NY.

Fisch, Harold. Hamlet & the Word. $7.50 Hdbd. Frederick Ungar, NY.

Freudenstein, Reinhold. Der Bestrafte Brudermord: Shakespeares Hamlet Auf der Wanderbuehne Des Siebzehntes Jahrhunderts. (Britannica et Americana, No. 3). (Ger). 1958. $3.30 pa. (ISBN 3-11-005648-8). De Gruyter, Germany.

Gilbert, Allan H. Principles & Practice of Criticism: Hamlet, the Merry Wives, Othello. 1959. $7.50 Hdbd. (ISBN 0-404-02758-X). AMS Pr., NY.

Granville-Barker, Harley. Prefaces to Shakespeare, Vol. 1, Preface to Hamlet. 1965. $5.00 Hdbd. (ISBN 0-691-06101-7); $2.95 pa. (ISBN 0-691-01277-6, 23). Princeton Univ. Pr., NJ.

Grebanier, Bernard. Heart of Hamlet. $2.95 pa. (A141). Apollo Editions Inc., NY.

Guernsey, Rocellus S. Ecclesiastical Law in Hamlet: The Burial of Ophelia. (1885) $4.50 Hdbd. (ISBN 0-404-54201-8). AMS Pr., NY.

Halliwell-Phillips, James O. Memoranda on the Tragedy of Hamlet. 1879. $6.50 Hdbd. (ISBN 0-404-03081-5). AMS Pr., NY.

Hankins, John E. Character of Hamlet. facsimile ed. (Select Bibliographies Reprint Ser). (1941). $11.50 Hdbd. (ISBN 0-8369-5676-1). Bks for Libraries, NY.

Hanmer, Thomas. Some Remarks on the Tragedy of Hamlet, Prince of Denmark. 1736. $5.00 Hdbd. (ISBN 0-404-03096-3). AMS Pr., NY.

Hansen, George P. Legend of Hamlet, Prince of Denmark. 1887. $5.00 Hdbd. (ISBN 0-404-03105-6). AMS Pr., NY.

Holmes, Martin. Guns of Elsinore. 1964. $4.00 Hdbd. Barnes & Noble, NY.

Jackson, George S. Hamlet: Scene by Scene. (Orig.). $1.00 pa. Bruce Humphries, Publs., MA.

Johnston, W. Preston. Prototype of Hamlet & Other Shakespearian Problems. 1890. $12.50 Hdbd. (ISBN 0-404-03595-7). AMS Pr., NY.

Jones, Ernest. Hamlet & Oedipus. 1954. $1.45 pa. Doubleday & Co., NY.

Joseph, Bertram. Conscience & the

King. 1953. $15.00 Hdbd. Folcroft Pr., PA.

Knights, Lionel C. Some Shakespearean Themes. Incl. Approach to Hamlet. 1966. $2.95 pa. (ISBN 0-8047-0301-9). Stanford Univ. Pr., CA.

Latham, R. G. Two Dissertations of the Hamlet of Saxo Grammaticus & of Shakespeare. 1872. $8.50 Hdbd. (ISBN 0-404-03883-2). AMS Pr., NY.

Levenson, Jacob C., ed. Discussions of Hamlet. (Discussions of Literature). (Hi-Sch.). 1960. $2.25 text ed. (21873). D. C. Heath & Co., IN.

Levin, Harry. Question of Hamlet. 1959. $5.95 Hdbd. (ISBN 0-19-500521-6). 1970. $1.95 pa. (ISBN 0-19-500808-1, 318, GB). Oxford Univ. Pr., NY.

Lewis, Charlton M. Genesis of Hamlet. 1907. $5.00 Hdbd. Ridgeway Bks., PA.

Lokse, Olav. Outrageous Fortune: Critical Studies in Hamlet & King Lear $4.00 pa. Humanities Pr., NY.

McGinn, Donald J. Shakespeare's Influence on the Drama of His Age. 1965. $8.50 Hdbd. Octagon Books Inc., NY.

MacLeish, Archibald. Hamlet of A. MacLeish. 1971. (1928) $6.50 Hdbd. Lansdowne Pr., PA.

Malone, Kemp. Literary History of Hamlet. (Studies in Shakespeare Ser., No. 24). 1969. (1923) $11.95 Hdbd. (ISBN 0-8383-0593-8). Haskell House Publ., NY.

Mander, Raymond & Mitchenson, Joe. Hamlet Through the Ages. facsimile ed.

Marshall, Herbert, ed. (Select Bibliographies Reprint Ser). (1955) $32.50 Hdbd. (ISBN 0-8369-5677-X). Bks for Libraries, NY.

Marsh, D. R. Shakespeare's Hamlet. 1970. $4.00 Hdbd. (ISBN 0-424-06030-2); $0.70 pa. (ISBN 0-424-06040-X). Intl. Schol. Bk. Serv., OR.

Marshall, Frank A. Study of Hamlet. 1875. $10.00 Hdbd. (ISBN 0-404-04191-4). AMS Pr., NY.

Miles, G. H. Review of Hamlet. 1907. $12.50 Hdbd. (ISBN 0-404-04324-0). AMS Pr., NY.

Monarch Literature Notes on Shakespeare's Hamlet. (Orig.). $1.00 pa. (00514). Monarch Pr., NY.

Muir, Kenneth. Hamlet by Shakespeare. Daiches, David, ed. (Studies in Literature Ser). (Critical Analysis). (Hi-Sch.). 1964. $1.00 pa. Barron Ed. Series, NY.

Pilon, F. Essay on the Character of Hamlet. 1777. $6.50 Hdbd. (ISBN 0-404-05048-4). AMS Pr., NY.

Plumptre, James. Observations on Hamlet. 1796–97. $5.00 Hdbd. (ISBN 0-404-05066-2). AMS Pr., NY.

Price, George R. Barron's Simplified Approach to Shakespeare's Hamlet. 1965. $0.95 pa. Barron Ed. Series, NY.

Robertson, John M. Hamlet Once More. 1923. $17.50 Hdbd. Folcroft Pr., PA.

Robertson, John M. Problem of Hamlet. 1919. $12.50 Hdbd. Folcroft Pr., PA.

Rubow, P. V. Shakespeare's Hamlet. 1951. $5.00 Hdbd. (ISBN 0-404-05448-X). AMS Pr., NY.

Sacks, Claire & Whan, Edgar W., eds. Hamlet. Enter Critic. $2.95 pa. (ISBN 0-390-76898-7). Appleton-Century-Crofts, NY.

Sanford, Wendy C. Theater As Metaphor in Hamlet. (LeBaron Russell Briggs Prize Honors Essays in English). 1967. $1.75 pa. (ISBN 0-674-87540-0). Harvard Univ. Pr., MA.

Schucking, Levin L. Meaning of Hamlet. Rawson, Graham, tr. 1966. $4.50 Hdbd. Barnes & Noble, NY.

Scott, Clement W. Some Notable Hamlets of the Present Time. 1900. $9.75 Hdbd. Benjamin Blom, NY.

Shakespeare, William. Hamlet. Jump, John, ed. (Casebook Ser). 1970. (1968) $2.50 pa. (ISBN 0-87695-047-0). Aurora Publs., TN.

Shakespeare, William. Hamlet: Complete Study Edition. Lamb, Sidney, ed. $1.00 pa. (ISBN 0-8220-1415-7). Cliffs Notes, NB.

Shakespeare, William. Hamlet. Arco Notes. (Hi-Sch.). 1969. $0.95 pa. (ISBN 0-668-01978-6). Arco Publ. Co., NY.

Shattuck, Charles H. Hamlet of Edwin Booth. 1969. $10.95 Hdbd. (ISBN 0-252-00019-6). Univ. of Ill. Pr., IL.

Shawcross, John T. Critical Study Guide to Shakespeare's Hamlet. (Pennant Study Guides). 1968. $1.00 pa. (PQ142). Littlefield, Adams & Co., NJ.

Sterne, Richard L. John Gielgud Directs Richard Burton in Hamlet. 1968. $6.95 Hdbd. (ISBN 0-394-43149-9). Random House, NY.

Stoll, Elmer E. Hamlet: A Historical & Comparative Study. 1919. $3.50 Hdbd. Folcroft Pr., PA.

Stoll, Elmer E. Hamlet: Historical & Comparative Study. 1967. (1919) $4.00 Hdbd. (ISBN 0-87752-106-9). Gordian Pr., NY.

Stoll, Elmer E. Hamlet the Man. 1935. $3.50 Hdbd. Folcroft Pr., PA.

Strachey, Edward. Shakespeare's Hamlet. 1848. $5.00 Hdbd. (ISBN 0-404-06294-6). AMS Pr., NY.

Taylor, Marion A. New Look at the Old Sources of Hamlet. (Studies in English Literature Vol, 42). 1969. $5.00 Hdbd. (68-17895). Humanities Pr., NY.

Thomas, Sidney. Antic Hamlet & Richard the Third. 1943. $6.50 Hdbd. Folcroft Pr., NY.

Tolman, Albert H. Views About Hamlet & Other Essays. 1904. $16.00 Hdbd. (ISBN 0-404-06477-9). AMS Pr., NY.

Turnbull, Monica P. Essays: Hamlet, Macbeth, the Fool in Lear, Iago. 1924. $5.00 Hdbd. Folcroft Pr., PA.

Tyler, Thomas. Philosophy of Hamlet. 1874. $5.00 Hdbd. (ISBN 0-404-06565-1). AMS Pr., NY.

Tyler, Thomas. Philosophy of Hamlet. 1874. $8.50 Hdbd. Folcroft Pr., PA.

Venable, Emerson. Hamlet Problem & Its Solution. 1912. $12.50 Hdbd. Folcroft Pr., PA.

Vining, Edward P. Mystery of Hamlet. 1881. $5.50 Hdbd. (ISBN 0-404-06769-7). AMS Pr., NY.

Vining, Edward P. Time in the Play of "Hamlet". Incl. The First Shakespeare Society. Halliwell-Phillipps, J. O; The Once Used Words in Shakespeare. Butler, James D. (1885) $5.00 Hdbd. (ISBN 0-404-54205-0). AMS Pr., NY.

Waldock, Arthur J. Hamlet: A Study in Critical Method. 1931. $5.00 Hdbd. (ISBN 0-404-06804-9). AMS Pr., NY.

Walker, Roy. Time Is Out of Joint: A Study of Hamlet. 1948. $15.00 Hdbd. Folcroft Pr., PA.

Wallace, Charles W. Children of the Chapel at Blackfriars, 1597–1603. 1970. (1908) $10.00 Hdbd. (ISBN 0-404-06808-1). AMS Pr., NY.

Weitz, Morris. Hamlet & the Philosophy of Literary Criticism. 1964. $6.75 Hdbd. (ISBN 0-226-89238-7). Univ. of Chicago Pr., IL.

Wihan, Josef. Hamletfrage, Ein Beitrag Zur Geschichte Der Renaissance in England. 1967. (1921). $4.00 pa. Johnson Reprint Corp., NY.

Williamson, Claude G., ed. Readings on the Character of Hamlet, 1661–1947. 1950. $22.50 Hdbd. (ISBN 0-87752-149-2). Gordian Pr., NY.

Wilson, J. Dover. What Happens in Hamlet. 3rd ed. 1951. $7.00 Hdbd.;

$2.95 pa. (ISBN 0-521-09109-8, 109). Cambridge Univ. Pr., NY.

Winstanley, Lilian. Hamlet & the Scottish Succession. 1970. Repr. $8.00 Hdbd. Octagon Books Inc, NY.

Winstanley, Lilian. Hamlet & the Scottish Succession. facsimile ed. (Select Bibliographies Reprint Ser). 1921. $8.50 Hdbd. (ISBN 0-8369-5270-7). Bks for Libraries, NY.

Winstanley, Lilian. Hamlet & the Scottish Succession. 1921. $6.50 Hdbd. Folcroft Pr., PA.

Wood, William D. Hamlet from a Psychological Point of View. 1870. $5.00 Hdbd. (ISBN 0-404-07025-6). AMS Pr. NY.

Wormhoudt, Arthur. Hamlet's Mouse Trap. 1970. (1956) $8.80 Hdbd. (ISBN 0-404-07043-4). AMS Pr., NY.

JULIUS CAESAR

Arco Editorial Board. Arco Notes: William Shakespeare's Julius Caesar. (Orig.). (Hi-Sch.). 1969. $0.95 pa. (ISBN 0-668-01984-0). Arco Publ., NY.

Boecher, Alexander. Probable Italian Source of Shakespeare's Julius Caesar. 1971. (1913) $7.50 Hdbd. AMS Pr., NY.

Bonjour, Adrien. Structure of Julius Caesar. 1958. $12.50 Hdbd. Folcroft Pr., PA.

Cliff's Notes Editors. Julius Caesar Notes. $1.00 pa. (ISBN 0-8220-0020-2). Cliffs Notes, NB.

Coles, Blanche. Shakespeare Studies:

Julius Caesar. 1940. $12.00 Hdbd. (ISBN 0-404-01597-2). AMS Pr., NY.

Craik, George L. English of Shakespeare. 3rd ed. 1864. $12.50 Hdbd. (ISBN 0-404-01799-1). AMS Pr., NY.

Dean, Leonard F., ed. Twentieth Century Interpretations of Julius Caesar. 1968. $4.95 Hdbd. (ISBN 0-13-512285-6). $1.25 pa. (ISBN 0-13-512277-5). Prentice-Hall, NY.

Granville-Barker, Harley. Prefaces to Shakespeare, Vol. 2, Prefaces To King Lear, Cymbeline & Julius Caesar. 1965. $5.00 Hdbd. (ISBN 0-691-06102-5); $2.95 pa. (ISBN 0-691-01278-4). Princeton Univ. Pr., NJ.

Leeb, David. Critical Study Guide to Shakespeare's Julius Caesar. 1966. $1.00 pa. Littlefield, Adams, NJ.

Markels, Julian, ed. Shakespeare's Julius Caesar. (Research Anthology Ser). (Hi-Sch.). 1961. text ed. $2.95 pa. (ISBN 0-684-41354-X). Scribner, NY.

Monarch Literature Notes on Shakespeare's Julius Caesar. $1.00 pa. Monarch Pr., NY.

Price, George R. Barron's Simplified Approach to Shakespeare's Julius Caesar. 1964. $0.95 pa. Barron's Educ. Ser., NY.

Ribner, Irving. Julius Caesar-Shakespeare. 1967. $1.00 pa. (ISBN 0-389-00835-4). Barnes & Noble, NY.

Trease, G. Word to Caesar. (Jr. Hi.). 1965. $1.80 text ed. St Martin's Pr., NY.

Wells, William. Authorship of Julius

Caesar. 1923. $10.00 Hdbd. (ISBN 0-404-06903-7). AMS Pr., NY.

Wells, William. Authorship of Julius Caesar. 1923. $15.00 Hdbd. Folcroft Pr., PA.

KING HENRY 4TH

Barasch, Frances. Monarch Literature Notes on Shakespeare's King Henry Fourth, Part 2. $1.00 pa. Monarch Pr., NY.

Beck, Richard J. Henry Fourth by Shakespeare. Daiches, David, ed. (Studies in English Literature Ser). (Orig., Critical Analysis Only). (Hi-Sch.). 1965. $1.00 pa. Barron's Educ. Series, NY.

Bowden, William R. Henry Fourth, Part I-Shakespeare. 1969. $1.00 pa. (ISBN 0-389-01220-3, 873). Barnes & Noble, NY.

Coursen, Herbert R., Jr. Henry Fourth, Pt. 2. Barroll, J. Leeds, ed. (Blackfriars Shakespeare Ser). 1971. $1.25 pa. (ISBN 0-697-03918-8). William C. Brown, NY.

Dorius, R. J., ed. Twentieth Century Interpretations of Henry Fourth, Part One. (Twentieth Century Interpretations Ser). 1970. (ISBN 0-13-387043-X, Spec). $1.45 pa. (ISBN 0-13-387035-9). Prentice-Hall, NY.

Grebanier, Bernard. Barron's Simplified Approach to Shakespeare's Henry Fourth, Pt. 1. 1965. $0.95 pa. Barron's Educ. Series, NY.

Hulme, Hilda M. Henry Fourth, Pt. 1.

(Blackfriars Shakespeare Ser). price "n.g." text ed. William C. Brown, NY.

Jenkins, Harold. Structural Problem in Shakespeare's Henry the Fourth. 1956. $5.00 Hdbd. Folcroft Pr., PA.

Lowers, James K. King Henry Fourth, Pt. 2 Notes. $1.00 pa. (ISBN 0-8220-0026-1). Cliffs Notes, NB.

Manheim, Michael. Critical Study Guide to Shakespeare's Henry Fourth, Pt. 1. (Pennant Study Guides). 1968. $1.00 pa. Littlefield, Adams & Co., NJ.

Marsh, D. R. Shakespeare: Henry Fourth, Part One. (Macmillan Critical Commentaries). 1967. $1.00 pa. Fernhill House, NY.

Shakespeare, William. Henry Four, Part One: A Concordance to the Text of the First Folio. 1970. $8.00 Hdbd. (ISBN 0-19-811142-8). 1971. $12.00 Hdbd. (ISBN 0-19-811147-9). 1970. $8.00 Hdbd. (ISBN 0-19-811143-6). Part Two. (Shakespeare Concordance). 1971. $12.00 Hdbd. (ISBN 0-19-811148-7). Oxford Univ. Pr., NY.

Shakespeare, William. Henry Fourth, Pts. 1 & 2. (Shakespeare Ser). (Hi-Sch.). $0.50 pa. Airmont Publ., CT.

Shakespeare, William. King Henry Fourth: Pt. 1, Complete Study Edition. Lamb, Sidney, ed. $1.00 pa. (ISBN 0-8220-1424-6). Cliff's Notes, NB.

Twentieth Century Interpretations of Henry Fourth Part 2. 1970. $4.95 Hdbd. (ISBN 0-13-387043-X). Prentice-Hall, NY.

Young, David P., ed. Twentieth Century Interpretations of Henry Fourth, Part 2. (Twentieth Century Interpretations Ser). 1968. $1.25 pa. (ISBN 0-13-386987-3). Prentice-Hall, NY.

KING HENRY 5TH

Cliff's Notes Editors. King Henry Fifth Notes. $1.00 pa. (ISBN 0-8220-0029-6). Cliffs Notes, NB.

Forker, Charles R. Henry Fifth. Barroll, J. Leeds, ed. (Blackfriars Shakespeare Ser). 1971. $1.25 pa. (ISBN 0-697-03914-5). William C. Brown, NY.

Lippman, Laura. Monarch Literature Notes on Shakespeare's King Henry Fifth. $1.00 pa. Monarch Pr., NY.

O'Brien, M. A., ed. Shakespeare: Henry Fifth. (Macmillan Critical Commentaries). 1967. $1.00 pa. Fernhill House, NY.

Shakespeare, William. Henry Fifth. (Shakespeare Ser). (Hi-Sch.). $0.50 pa. Airmont Publ., CT.

Shakespeare, William. Henry Five (Shakespeare Concordance). 1971. $12.00 Hdbd. (ISBN 0-19-811149-5). Oxford Univ. Pr., NY.

Wilson, John D. Martin Marprelate & Shakespeare's Fluellen. 1912. $10.00 Hdbd. Folcroft Pr., PA.

KING HENRY 6TH

Gaw, Allison. Origin & Development of Henry Sixth. 1926. $7.50 Hdbd. Folcroft Pr., PA.

Gaw, Allison. Origin & Development of One Henry Sixth in Relation to Shakespeare, Marlow, Peele & Greene. 1926. $9.50 Hdbd. (ISBN 0-404-02689-3). AMS Pr., NY.

Shakespeare, William. Henry the Sixth, Pt. 1. (1913) $11.50 Hdbd. (ISBN 0-404-53368-X). AMS Pr., NY.

Shakespeare, William. Henry Six, Part Two. (Shakespeare Concordance). 1971. $12.00 Hdbd. Oxford Univ. Pr., NY.

Shakespeare, William. Henry the Sixth, Pt 2. (1913) $11.50 Hdbd. (ISBN 0-404-53376-0). AMS Pr., NY.

Van Dam, B. Shakespeare Problems Nearing Solution: Henry Sixth & Richard Third. 1930. $3.50 Hdbd. Folcroft Pr., P.A.

White, Richard G. Essay on the Authorship of the Three Parts of King Henry the Sixth. 1859. $7.50 Hdbd. ·(ISBN 0-404-06932-0). AMS Pr., NY.

KING HENRY 8TH

Kemble, Frances A. Notes Upon Some of Shakespeare's Plays. 1882. $8.00 Hdbd. (ISBN 0-404-03645-7). AMS Pr., NY.

Partridge, A. C. Problem of Henry Eighth Reopened: Some Linguistic Criteria for the Two Styles Apparent in the Play. 1949. $3.50 Hdbd. Fernhill House, NY.

Richmond, H. M. King Henry Eighth. Barroll, J. Leeds, ed. (Blackfriars Shakespeare Ser). 1971. $1.25 pa. (ISBN 0-697-03916-6). William C. Brown, NY.

Shakespeare, William. Henry Eight. (Shakespeare Concordance). 1971.

$12.00 Hdbd. (ISBN 0-19-811146-0). Oxford Univ. Pr., NY.

KING JOHN

Furnivall, F. J. & Munro, John. Troublesome Reign of King John Being the Original of Shakespeare's Life & Death of King John. (Shakespeare Classics). 1913. $15.00 Hdbd. Folcroft Pr., PA.

Halliwell-Phillips, James O. Memoranda on Love's Labour's Lost, King John, Othello, & Romeo & Juliet. 1879. $6.50 Hdbd. (ISBN 0-404-03067-X). AMS Pr., NY.

Shakespeare, William. King John. (Shakespeare Ser). (Hi-Sch.). 1968. $0.50 pa. Airmont Publ., CT.

Shakespeare, William. King John: A Concordance to the Text of the First Folio. 1970. $8.00 Hdbd. Oxford Univ. Pr., NY.

KING LEAR

Bonheim, Helmut, ed. King Lear Perplex. (Guides to Literary Study Ser). 1960. $2.95 pa. Wadsworth Publ. Co., CA.

Bransom, James S. Tragedy of King Lear. 1934. $10.50 Hdbd. (ISBN 0-404-01063-6). AMS Pr., NY.

Brooke, Nicholas. King Lear by Shakespeare. (Studies in English Literature Ser). (Orig., Critical Analysis Only). (Hi-Sch.). 1964. $1.00 pa. Barron's Educ. Series, NY.

Chambers, R. W. King Lear. 1940. $5.00 Hdbd. Folcroft Pr., PA.

Danby, John F. Shakespeare's Doctrine of Nature: A Study of King Lear. 1966. $6.00 Hdbd.; $2.50 pa. Hillary House Publ., NY.

Eccles, Mark. King Lear-Shakespeare. 1967. $1.00 pa. (ISBN 0-389-00838-9, 835). Barnes & Noble, NY.

Elliott, George R. Dramatic Providence in Macbeth: A Study of Shakespeare's Tragic Theme of Humanity & Grace, with a Supplementary Essay on King Lear. 1960. $10.50 Hdbd. (ISBN 0-8371-3091-3). Greenwood Pr., CT.

Elton, William R. King Lear. (Blackfriars Shakespeare Ser). 1969. $1.25 pa. (ISBN 0-697-03904-8). William C. Brown, NY.

Elton, William R. King Lear & the Gods. 1966. $8.50 Hdbd. Huntington Library, CA.

Evans, Robert O. Critical Study Guide to Shakespeare's King Lear. abr. ed. 1967. $1.00 pa. Littlefield, Adams & Co., NJ.

Granville-Barker, Harley. Prefaces to Shakespeare, Vol. 2, Prefaces To King Lear, Cymbeline & Julius Caesar. 1965. $5.00 Hdbd. (ISBN 0-691-06102-5); $2.95 pa. (ISBN 0-691-01278-4, 24); Princeton Univ. Pr., NJ.

Greg, W. W. Variants in the First Quarto of King Lear. (Studies in Shakespeare Ser., No. 24). 1969. (1940) $10.95 Hdbd. (ISBN 0-8383-0559-8). Haskell House Publ., NY.

Heilman, Robert B. This Great Stage:

Image & Structure in King Lear. 1966. $2.45 pa. (ISBN 0-295-74013-2). Univ. of Wash. Pr., WA.

Jorgensen, Paul A. Lear's Self-Discovery. 1967. $5.75 Hdbd. (ISBN 0-520-00621-6). Univ. of Cal. Pr., CA.

Kirschbaum, Leo. True Text of King Lear. 1945. $9.00 Hdbd. (ISBN 0-404-03708-9). AMS Pr., NY.

Lee, Sidney. Chronicle History of King Lear, the Original of Shakespeare's King Lear. (Shakespeare Classics). 1909. $15.00 Hdbd. Folcroft Pr., PA.

Lokse, Olav. Outrageous Fortune: Critical Studies in Hamlet & King Lear. $4.00 pa. Humanities Pr., NY.

Lothian, John M. King Lear: A Tragic Reading of Life. 1949. $8.50 Hdbd. Folcroft Pr., PA.

Lower, James K. King Lear Notes. 1968. $1.00 pa. (ISBN 0-8220-0041-5). Cliffs Notes, NB.

Mack, Maynard. King Lear in Our Time. (California Library Reprint Series 17). $7.75 Hdbd. (ISBN 0-520-01922-9). Univ. of Cal. Pr., CA.

Monarch Literature Notes on Shakespeare's King Lear. $1.00 pa. Monarch Pr., NY.

Muir, Edwin. Politics of King Lear. (Studies in Shakespeare, No. 24). 1970. (1947) $3.95 Hdbd. (ISBN 0-8383-0331-5); $1.95 pa. (ISBN 0-8383-0055-3). Haskell House Publ., NY.

Muir, Edwin. Politics of King Lear. $3.75 Hdbd. Gordon Publ., NY.

Muir, Edwin. Politics of King Lear. 1947. $4.00 Hdbd. Folcroft Pr., PA.

Nolan, Edward F. & Byrd. Barron's Simplified Approach to Shakespeare's King Lear. 1968. $0.95 pa. Barron's Educ. Series, NY.

Perrett, Wilfred. Story of King Lear from Geoffrey of Monmouth to Shakespeare. (1904) $19.00 Hdbd.; $17.00 pa. Johnson Reprint Corp., NY.

Shakespeare, William. King Lear. Northcliffe, ed. (Casebook Ser). 1970. (1968) $2.50 pa. (ISBN 0-87695-050-0). Aurora Publ., TN.

Turnbull, Monica P. Essays: Hamlet, Macbeth, the Fool in Lear, Iago. 1924. $5.00 Hdbd. Folcroft Pr., PA.

Walton, J. K. Copy of the Folio Text of Richard Third. 1955. $8.60 Hdbd. (ISBN 0-404-06827-8). AMS Pr., NY.

Winstanley, Lilian. Macbeth, King Lear & Contemporary History. (1970) $8.50 Hdbd. Octagon Books, NY.

Winstantley, Lilian. Macbeth, King Lear, & Contemporary History. 1922. $6.50 Hdbd. Folcroft Pr., PA.

KING RICHARD 2ND
Cliff's Notes Editors. Richard Second Notes. $1.00 pa. (ISBN 0-8220-0068-7). Cliffs Notes, NB.

Grebanier, Bernard. Barron's Simplified Approach to Shakespeare's Richard Second. (Hi-Sch.). 1967. $0.95 pa. Barron's Educ. Series, NY.

Humphreys, Arthur R. Richard Second by Shakespeare. Critical Analysis Only. 1969. $1.00 pa. Barron's Educ. Series, NY.

Sanders, Norman. Richard Second. Barroll, J. Leeds, ed. (Blackfriars Shakespeare Ser). 1971. $1.25 pa. (ISBN 0-697-03917-X). William C. Brown, NY.

Scanlan, Mary H. Monarch Literature Notes on Shakespeare's King Richard Second. $1.00 pa. Monarch Pr., NY.

Shakespeare, William. Richard Second. (Shakespeare Ser). (Hi-Sch.). $0.50 pa. Airmont Publ., CT.

Shakespeare, William. Richard Two. (Shakespeare Concordance). 1971. $12.00 Hdbd. (ISBN 0-19-811145-2). Oxford Univ. Pr., NY.

Thayer, Calvin. Critical Study Guide to Shakespeare's Richard Second. 1969. $1.00 pa. Littlefield, Adams & Co., NJ.

KING RICHARD 3RD
Brereton, John L. Shakespeare's Richard Third. 1948. $5.00 Hdbd. (ISBN 0-404-01071-7). AMS Pr., NY.

Clemen, Wolfgang H. Commentary on Shakespeare's Richard Third. Bonheim, Jean, tr. 1968. $8.75 Hdbd. Barnes & Noble, NY.

Cliff's Notes Editors. Richard Third Notes. $1.00 pa. (ISBN 0-8220-0071-7). Cliffs Notes, NB.

Haeffner, Paul, ed. Shakespeare: Richard Third. (Macmillan Critical Commentaries). 1966. $1.00 pa. Fernhill House, NY.

Kemble, John P. Macbeth & King Richard Third: An Essay. 1970. (1817) $11.50 Hdbd. (ISBN 0-678-05131-3). Augustus M. Kelley, NY.

Manheim, Michael. Critical Study Guide to Shakespeare's Richard Third. abr. ed. 1966. $1.00 pa. Littlefield, Adams & Co., NJ.

Nugent, Elizabeth. Monarch Literature Notes on Shakespeare's King Richard Third. $1.00 pa. Monarch Pr., NY.

Patrick, David L. Textual History of Richard Third. 1936. $10.00 Hdbd. (ISBN 0-404-51810-9). AMS Pr., NY.

Shakespeare, William. Richard the Third. (1911) $14.50 Hdbd. (ISBN 0-404-53379-5). AMS Pr., NY.

Shakespeare, William. Richard Third. (Shakespeare Ser). (Hi-Sch.). $0.50 pa. Airmont Publ., CT.

Shakespeare, William. Richard Three. (Shakespeare Concordance). 1971. $12.00 Hdbd. (ISBN 0-19-811150-9). Oxford Univ. Pr., NY.

Smidt, Kristian. Inurious Imposters & Richard Third. 1964. $6.00 Hdbd. Humanities Pr., NY.

Smidt, Kristian. Memorial Transmission & Quarto Copy in Richard Third. 1971. $6.75 Hdbd. Humanities Pr., NY.

Thomas, Sidney. Antic Hamlet & Richard the Third. 1943. $6.50 Hdbd. Folcroft Pr., PA.

Van Dam, B. Shakespeare Problems Nearing Solution: Henry Sixth & Richard Third. 1930. $3.50 Hdbd. Folcroft Pr., PA.

Whately, Thomas. Remarks on Some of the Characters of Shakespeare. 3rd ed. 1970. (1839) $10.00 Hdbd. (ISBN 0-678-05129-1). Augustus M. Kelley, NY.

LOVE'S LABOUR'S LOST
Granville-Barker, Harley. Prefaces to Shakespeare Vol. 1, Prefaces to Love's Labor's Lost, Romeo & Juliet, the Merchant of Venice & Othello. 1965. $5.00 Hdbd. (ISBN 0-691-06103-3); $2.95 pa. (ISBN 0-691-01280-6, 26). Princeton Univ. Pr., NJ.

Gray, Henry D. Love's Labour's Lost. 1918. $7.50 Hdbd. Folcroft Pr., PA.

Halliwell-Phillips, James O. Memoranda on Love's Labour's Lost, King John, Othello, & Romeo & Juliet. 1879. $6.50 Hdbd. (ISBN 0-404-03067-X). AMS Pr., NY.

Shakespeare, William. Love's Labour's Lost: A Concordance to the Text of the First Quarto of 1598. 1970. $8.00 Hdbd. (ISBN 0-19-811139-8). Oxford Univ. Pr., NY.

Yates, Frances. Study of Love's Labour's Lost. 1936. $12.50 Hdbd. Folcroft Pr., PA.

LOVE'S LABOUR'S WON
Tolman, Albert H. What Has Become of Shakespeare's Play Love's Labours Won. 1902. $6.00 Hdbd. (ISBN 0-404-06478-7). AMS Pr., NY.

MACBETH
Apollo Books Editors, ed. William

Shakespeare's Macbeth. (E-Z Learner Study Text Ser). (Hi-Sch.). 1971. $1.25 pa. (ISBN 0-524-99111-1). Coshad Inc., CT.

Arco Editorial Board. Arco Notes: William Shakespeare's Macbeth. (Hi-Sch.). 1969. $0.95 pa. (ISBN 0-668-01987-5). Arco Publ. Co., NY.

Bartholomeusz, D. Macbeth & the Players. $11.50 Hdbd. Cambridge Univ. Pr., NY.

Brown, John R. Macbeth by Shakespeare. Daiches, David, ed. (Orig., Critical Analysis Only). 1964. $1.00 pa. Barron Educational Series, NY.

Chambers, David L. Metre of Macbeth. 1903. $10.00 Hdbd. Folcroft Pr., PA.

Chambers, David L. Metre of Macbeth. 1903. $5.00 Hdbd. (ISBN 0-404-01443-7). AMS Pr., NY.

Cliff's Notes Editors. Macbeth Notes. $1.00 pa. (ISBN 0-8220-0046-6). Cliffs Notes, NB.

Coles, Blanche. Shakespeare Studies: Macbeth. 1938. $12.00 Hdbd. (ISBN 0-404-01598-0). AMS Pr., NY.

Curry, Walter C. Demonic Metaphysics of Macbeth. (Studies in Shakespeare, No. 24). 1970. (1933) $1.95 pa. (ISBN 0-8383-0020-0). Haskell House Publ., NY.

Dalgleish, Walter S. Shakespeare's Macbeth. 1869. $6.50 Hdbd. (ISBN 0-404-01918-8). AMS Pr., NY.

Elliott, George R. Dramatic Providence in Macbeth: A Study of Shakespeare's Tragic Theme of Humanity & Grace, with a Supplementary Essay on King Lear. 1960. $10.50 Hdbd. (ISBN 0-8371-3091-3). Greenwood Pr., CT.

Halio, Jay L. Approaches to Macbeth. (Guides to Literary Study Ser). 1966. $2.95 pa. Wadsworth Publ. Co., CA.

Halliwell-Phillips, James O. Cursory Memoranda on Shakespeare's Tragedy of Macbeth. 1880. $5.00 Hdbd. (ISBN 0-404-03054-8). AMS Pr., NY.

Johnston, W. Preston. Prototype of Hamlet & Other Shakespearian Problems. 1890. $12.50 Hdbd. (ISBN 0-404-03595-7). AMS Pr., NY.

Jorgensen, Paul A. Our Naked Frailties: Sensational Art & Meaning in Macbeth. 1971. $7.50 Hdbd. (ISBN 0-520-01915-6). Univ. of Cal. Pr., CA.

Kemble, Frances A. Notes Upon Some of Shakespeare's Plays. 1882. $8.00 Hdbd. (ISBN 0-404-03645-7). AMS Pr., NY.

Kemble, John P. Macbeth Reconsidered. 1786. $5.00 Hdbd. (ISBN 0-404-03646-5). AMS Pr., NY.

Kemble, John P. Macbeth & King Richard Third: An Essay. 1970. (1817) $11.50 Hdbd. (ISBN 0-678-05131-3). Augustus M. Kelley Publ., NY.

Knights, L. C. How Many Children Had Lady Macbeth. 1933. $5.00 Hdbd. Folcroft Pr., PA.

McCutchan, J. Wilson. Macbeth-Shakespeare. 1967. $1.00 pa. (ISBN 0-389-

00834-6, 831, BN). Barnes & Noble, NY.

Miles, G. H. Review of Hamlet. 1907. $12.50 Hdbd. (ISBN 0-404-04324-0). AMS Pr., NY.

Monarch Literature Notes on Shakespeare's Macbeth. $1.00 pa. (00516). Monarch Pr., NY.

Price, George M. Barron's Simplified Approach to Shakespeare's Macbeth. 1966. $0.95 pa. Barron Ed. Series, NY.

Roger, H. Double Profit in Macbeth. 1964. $1.35 pa. (ISBN 0-424-05520-1, Pub by Sydney U Pr), Intl. Schol. Bk. Serv., OR.

Sexton, George. Psychology of Macbeth. 1869. $5.00 Hdbd. (ISBN 0-404-05753-5). AMS Pr., NY.

Shakespeare, William. Macbeth. Wain, John, ed. (Casebook Ser). 1970. (1968) $2.50 Hdbd. (ISBN 0-87695-051-9). Aurora Publs., TN.

Shakespeare, William. Macbeth: Complete Study Edition. Lamb, Sidney, ed. $1.00 pa. (ISBN 0-8220-1427-0). Cliffs Notes, NB.

Siegel, Paul N. Critical Study Guide to Shakespeare's Macbeth. (Pennant Study Guides). 1968. $1.00 pa. Littlefield, Adams & Co., NJ.

Turnbull, Monica P. Essays: Hamlet, Macbeth, the Fool in Lear, Iago. 1924. $5.00. Folcroft Pr., PA.

Waldock, Arthur J. James, Joyce & Others. (Essay Index Reprint Ser).

1937. $7.75 Hdbd. (ISBN 0-8369-0963-1). Books for Libraries, NY.

Walker, Roy. Time Is Free: A Study of Macbeth. 1949. $15.00 Hdbd. Folcroft Pr., PA.

Whately, Thomas. Remarks on Some of the Characters of Shakespeare. 3rd ed. 1970. (1839) $10.00 Hdbd. (ISBN 0-678-05129-1). Augustus M. Kelley Publ., NY.

Wilson, John D. First Steps in Shakespeare, 2 pts. Incl. Pt. 2. Scenes from Macbeth. $0.75 text ed. Cambridge Univ. Pr., NY.

Winstanley, Lilian. Macbeth, King Lear & Contemporary History. (1970) $8.50 Hdbd. Octagon Books Inc., NY.

Winstantley, Lilian. Macbeth, King Lear, & Contemporary History. 1922. $6.50 Hdbd. Folcroft Pr., PA.

MEASURE FOR MEASURE
Bache, William B. Measure for Measure As Dialectical Art. 1969. $1.50 pa. (ISBN 0-911198-18-0). Purdue Univ. Studies, IN.

Bennett, Josephine W. Measure for Measure As Royal Entertainment. 1966. $6.00 Hdbd. (ISBN 0-231-02921-7). Columbia Univ. Pr., NY.

Chambers, Raymond W. Jacobean Shakespeare & Measure for Measure. 1937. $4.50 Hdbd. Folcroft Pr., PA.

Chambers, Raymond W. Jacobean Shakespeare & Measure for Measure, Read 21 April 1937—Annual Shakespeare Lecture. (Select Bibliographies

Reprint Ser). 1937. $5.00 Hdbd. (ISBN 0-8369-5250-2). Bks. for Libraries, NY.

Cliff's Notes Editors. Measure for Measure Notes. $1.00 pa. (ISBN 0-8220-0049-0). Cliffs Notes, NB.

Geckle, G., ed. Twentieth Century Interpretations of Measure for Measure. $1.25 pa. (ISBN 0-13-567719-X). Prentice-Hall, NY.

Halliwell-Phillips, James O. Memoranda on Shakespeare's Comedy of Measure for Measure. 1880. $5.00 Hdbd. (ISBN 0-404-03068-8). AMS Pr., NY.

Lascelles, Mary. Shakespeare's Measure for Measure. 1953. $15.00 Hdbd. Folcroft Pr., PA.

Lascelles, Mary. Shakespeare's Measure for Measure. 1970. (1953) $9.00 Hdbd. (ISBN 0-404-03881-6). AMS Pr., NY.

Shakespeare, William. Measure for Measure: Concordance to the Text of the First Folio. Howard-Hill, T., ed. $9.75 Hdbd. Oxford Univ. Pr., NY.

Stevenson, David L. Achievement of Shakespeare's Measure for Measure. 1966. $5.75 Hdbd. (ISBN 0-8014-0411-8). Cornell Univ. Pr., NY.

Violi, Unicio J. Monarch Literature Notes on Shakespeare's Measure for Measure. $1.00 pa. Monarch Pr., NY.

MERCHANT OF VENICE

Andrews, Mark E. Law Versus Equity in the Merchant of Venice: A Legalization of Act 4, Scene 1, with Foreword, Judicial Precedents, & Notes. 1965. $9.50 Hdbd., boxed (ISBN 0-87081-017-0). Colo Assoc. Univ. Pr., CO.

Barnet, Sylvan, ed. Twentieth Century Interpretations of Merchant of Venice. (Twentieth Century Interpretations Ser). 1970. $1.25 pa. (ISBN 0-13-577148-X). Prentice-Hall, NY.

Charlton, H. B. Shakespeare's Jew. 1934. $4.00 Hdbd. Folcroft Pr., PA.

Cliff's Notes Editors. Merchant of Venice Notes. $1.00 pa. (ISBN 0-8220-0052-0). Cliffs Notes, NB.

Friedlander, Gerald. Shakespeare & the Jew. 1921. $5.00 Hdbd. (ISBN 0-404-02579-X). AMS Pr., NY.

Gollancz, Israel. Allegory & Mysticism in Shakespeare. 1931. $10.00 Hdbd. Folcroft Pr., PA.

Granville-Barker, Harley. Prefaces to Shakespeare Vol. 1, Prefaces to Love's Labor's Lost, Romeo & Juliet, the Merchant of Venice & Othello. 1965. $5.00 Hdbd. (ISBN 0-691-06103-3); $2.95 pa. (ISBN 0-691-01280-6, 26). Princeton Univ. Pr., NJ.

Heline, Theodore. Merchant of Venice: Its Inner Structure. $1.50 Hdbd. New Age Pr., CA.

Lelyveld, Toby B. Shylock on the Stage. 1960. $4.95 Hdbd. (ISBN 0-8295-0028-6). Pr. of Case W.R. Univ., OH.

McNeir, Waldo F. Merchant of Venice-Shakespeare. 1967. $1.00 pa. (ISBN 0-

389-00841-9, 838, BN). Barnes & Noble, NY.

Monarch Literature Notes on Shakespeare's Merchant of Venice. $1.00 pa. (00637). Monarch Pr., NY.

Moody, A. D. Merchant of Venice, Shakespeare: Critical Analysis. Daiches, David, ed. (Orig., Critical Analysis Only). 1964. $1.00 pa. Barron Ed. Series, NY.

Shakespeare, William. Merchant of Venice. Wilders, John, ed. (Casebook Ser). 1970. (1968) $2.50 pa. (ISBN 0-87695-052-7). Aurora Publs., TN.

Shakespeare, William. Merchant of Venice: A Concordance to the Text of the First Quarto of 1600. 1969. $9.75 Hdbd. (ISBN 0-19-811129-0). Oxford Univ. Pr., NY.

Shakespeare, William. Merchant of Venice: Complete Study Edition. Lamb, Sidney, ed. $1.00 pa. (ISBN 0-8220-1430-0). Cliffs Notes, NB.

Sinsheimer, Hermann. Shylock: The History of a Character. (Illus.). 1947. $8.50 Hdbd. Benjamin Blom, NY.

Small, Samuel A. Shakespearean Character Interpretation: Merchant of Venice. 1927. $7.50 Hdbd. (ISBN 0-404-06109-5). AMS Pr., NY.

MERRY WIVES OF WINDSOR
Crofts, John E. Shakespeare & the Post Horses: A New Study of the Merry Wives of Windsor. (1937) $10.50 Hdbd. (ISBN 0-404-01856-4). AMS Pr., NY.

Gilbert, Allan H. Principles & Practice

of Criticism: Hamlet, the Merry Wives, Othello. 1959. $7.50 Hdbd. (ISBN 0-404-02758-X). AMS Pr., NY.

Green, William. Shakespeare's Merry Wives of Windsor. 1962. $7.50 Hdbd. (ISBN 0-691-06120-3). Princeton Univ. Pr., NJ.

Halliwell-Phillips, James O. Account of the Only Known Manuscript of Shakespeare's Plays. 1843. $12.00 Hdbd. (ISBN 0-404-03049-1). AMS Pr., NY.

Shakespeare, William. Merry Wives of Windsor. Oliver, H. J., ed. (Arden Shakespeare Ser). 1971. $8.00 Hdbd. (ISBN 0-416-47690-2). Barnes & Noble, NY.

Shakespeare, William. Merry Wives of Windsor: Concordance to the Text of the First Folio. Howard-Hill, T., ed. $9.75 Hdbd. Oxford Univ. Pr., NY.

MIDSUMMER NIGHT'S DREAM
Black, Matthew. Midsummer Night's Dream—Shakespeare. 1967. $1.00 pa. (ISBN 0-389-00840-0, 837, BN). Barnes & Noble, NY.

Charlton, Henry B. Midsummer Night's Dream. 1933. $3.00 Hdbd. Folcroft Pr., PA.

Cliff's Notes Editors. Midsummer Night's Dream Notes. $1.00 pa. (ISBN 0-8220-0057-1). Cliff's Notes, NB.

Fender, Stephen. Midsummer Night's Dream by Shakespeare—Critical Analysis Only. 1969. $1.00 pa. Barron Ed. Series, NY.

Halliwell, James O. Introduction to

Shakespeare's Midsummer Night's Dream. 1841. $5.00 Hdbd. Folcroft Pr., PA.

Halliwell-Phillips, James O. Illustrations of the Fairy Mythology of a Midsummer Night's Dream. 1970. (1841) $14.50 Hdbd. (ISBN 0-404-03058-0). AMS Pr., NY.

Leoff, Eve. Monarch Literature Notes on Shakespeare's A Midsummer Night's Dream. $1.00 pa. (00638). Monarch Pr., NY.

Nolan, Edward F. Barron's Simplified Approach to Shakespeare's A Midsummer Night's Dream. 1971. $0.95 pa. Barron Ed. Series, NY.

Proescholdt, Ludwig. On the Sources of Shakespeare's Midsummer Night's Dream. 1878. $5.00 Hdbd. (ISBN 0-404-05137-5). AMS Pr., NY.

Shakespeare, William. Midsummer Night's Dream: Concordance to the Text of the First Quarto of 1600. 1970. $8.00 Hdbd. (ISBN 0-19-811137-1). Oxford Univ. Pr., NY.

Sidgwick, Frank. Sources & Analogues of a Midsummer Night's Dream. (Shakespeare Classics). 1908. $15.00 Hdbd. Folcroft Pr., PA.

MUCH ADO ABOUT NOTHING
Cliff's Notes Editors. Much Ado About Nothing Notes. $1.00 pa. (ISBN 0-8220-0060-1). Cliff's Notes, NB.

Davis, Walter R., ed. Twentieth Century Interpretations of Much Ado About Nothing. 1969. $4.95 Hdbd. (ISBN 0-13-604736-X). Prentice-Hall, NY.

Davis, Walter R., ed. Twentieth Century Interpretations of Much Ado About Nothing. (Twentieth Century Interpretations Ser). 1969. $1.25 text ed. (ISBN 0-13-604736-X). Prentice-Hall, NY.

Grennen, Joseph. Monarch Literature Notes on Shakespeare's Much Ado About Nothing. $1.00 pa. Monarch Pr., NY.

Halliwell-Phillips, James O. Memoranda on All's Well That Ends Well, the Two Gentlemen of Verona, Much Ado About Nothing & on Titus Andronicus. 1879. $6.50 Hdbd. (ISBN 0-404-03066-1). AMS Pr., NY.

Mulryne, J. R. Much Ado About Nothing by Shakespeare. Daiches, David, ed. (Studies in English Literature Ser). (Orig., Critical Analysis Only). (Hi-Sch.). 1965. $1.00 pa. Barron's Educ. Serv., NY

Prouty, Charles T. The Sources of Much Ado About Nothing. Incl. Ariodanto & Ieneura. Beverly, Peter. (1950) $8.50 Hdbd. (ISBN 0-8369-5513-7). Books for Libraries, NY.

Shakespeare, William. Much Ado About Nothing: Concordance to the Text of the First Quarto of 1600. 1970. $8.00 Hdbd. (ISBN 0-19-811140-1). Oxford Univ. Pr., NY.

OTHELLO
Barroll, J. Leeds. Othello. new ed. (Blackfriars Shakespeare Ser). 1971. $1.25 text ed. (ISBN 0-697-03911-0). Wm. C. Brown, IO.

Chasseriau, Theodore. Illustrations for Othello. $50.00 Hdbd. Walker & Co., NY.

Cliff's Notes Editors. Othello Notes. $1.00 pa. (ISBN 0-8220-0063-6). Cliffs Notes, NB.

Dean, Leonard F., ed. Casebook on Othello. 1966. $3.95 text ed. (ISBN 0-690-17709-7). Thomas Y. Crowell, NY.

Draper, John W. Othello of Shakespeare's Audience. 1967. $8.50 Hdbd. Octagon, NY.

Elliott, George R. Flaming Minister: A Study of Othello As Tragedy of Love & Hate. 1953. $8.50 Hdbd. AMS Pr., NY.

Gardner, Helen. Noble Moor. 1955. $4.00 Hdbd. Folcroft Pr., PA.

Gilbert, Allan H. Principles & Practice of Criticism: Hamlet, the Merry Wives, Othello. 1959. $7.50 Hdbd. (ISBN 0-404-02758-X). AMS Pr., NY.

Given, Welker. New Study of Shakespeare's Othello. Repr. of 1899 ed. $17.50 Hdbd. (ISBN 0-404-54211-5). AMS Pr., NY.

Granville-Barker, Harley. Prefaces to Shakespeare Vol. 1, Prefaces to Love's Labor's Lost, Romeo & Juliet, the Merchant of Venice & Othello. 1965. $5.00 Hdbd. (ISBN 0-691-06103-3); $2.95 pa. (ISBN 0-691-01280-6, 26). Princeton Univ. Pr., NJ.

Halliwell-Phillips, James O. Memoranda on Love's Labour's Lost, King John, Othello, & Romeo & Juliet. 1879. $6.50 Hdbd. (ISBN 0-404-03067-X). AMS Pr., NY.

Heilman, Robert B. Magic in the Web: Action & Language in Othello. 1956. $2.75 pa. (ISBN 0-8131-0122-0). Univ. Pr. of Ky., KY.

Jorgensen, Paul A. Othello-Shakespeare. 1967. $1.00 pa. (ISBN 0-389-00836-2). Barnes & Noble, NY.

Monarch Literature Notes on Shakespeare's Othello. $1.00 pa. Monarch Pr., NY.

Nolan, Edward F. Barron's Simplified Approach to Shakespeare's Othello. (Hi-Sch.). 1967. $0.95 pa. Barron Educ. Serv., NY.

Price, Thomas R. Construction & Types of Shakespeare's Verse As Seen in the Othello. (1888) $5.00 Hdbd. (ISBN 0-404-54208-5). AMS Pr., NY.

Shakespeare, William. Othello. Horwood, F. C. & Houghton, R. E., eds. 1968. $1.30 Hdbd. (ISBN 0-19-831399-3). Oxford Univ. Pr., NY.

Shakespeare, William. Othello. Complete Study Edition. rev. ed. Lowers, James K., ed. 1968. $1.00 text ed. (ISBN 0-8220-1433-5). Cliffs Notes, NB.

Stoll, Elmer E. Othello: An Historical & Comparative Study. (Studies in Shakespeare Ser., No. 24). 1969. (1915) $3.95 Hdbd. (ISBN 0-8383-0630-6). Haskell House, NY.

Stoll, Elmer E. Othello, an Historical & Comparative Study. 1967. (1915) $4.00

Hdbd. (ISBN 0-87752-108-5). Gordian Pr., NY.

Tannenbaum, Samuel. Shakespeare's Othello. 1943. $10.00 Hdbd. Ridgeway Bks., PA.

Turnbull, William R. Othello, a Critical Study. 1892. $15.00 Hdbd. (ISBN 0-404-06529-5). AMS Pr., NY.

William Shakespeare's Othello. (E-Z Learner Study Text Ser). 1971. $1.25 text ed. Apollo Bks & Casyndekan Inc., eds. Coshad, CT.

Winstantley, Lilian. Othello As the Tragedy of Italy. 1924. $10.00 Hdbd. Folcroft Pr., PA.

PERICLES
Smyth, Albert H. Shakespeare's Pericles & Appolonius of Tyre: A Study in Comparative Literature. 1898. $6.50 Hdbd. (ISBN 0-404-06129-X). AMS Pr., NY.

ROMEO AND JULIET
Brooke, Arthur. Brooke's Romeus & Juliet, Being the Original of Shakespeare's Romeo & Juliet. Munro, J. J., ed. 1970. (1908) $6.00 Hdbd. (ISBN 0-404-04539-1). AMS Pr., NY.

Charlton, Henry B. Romeo & Juliet: As an Experimental Tragedy. 1939. $5.00 Hdbd. Folcroft Pr., PA.

Romeo & Juliet Notes. (Cliff's Notes). $1.00 pa. (ISBN 0-8220-0074-1). Cliffs Notes, NB.

Cole, Douglas, ed. Twentieth Century Interpretations of Romeo & Juliet. 1970. $1.25 pa. (ISBN 0-13-782904-3, Spec). Prentice-Hall, NY.

Evans, Robert O. Critical Study Guide to Shakespeare's Romeo & Juliet. abr. ed. 1966. $1.00 pa. Littlefield, Adams & Co., NJ.

Evans, Robert O. Osier Cage: Rhetorical Devices in Romeo & Juliet. 1966. $4.00 Hdbd. (ISBN 0-8131-1123-4). Univ. Pr. of Ky., KY.

Granville-Barker, Harley. Prefaces to Shakespeare Vol. 1, Prefaces to Love's Labor's Lost, Romeo & Juliet, the Merchant of Venice & Othello. 1965. $5.00 Hdbd. (ISBN 0-691-06103-3); $2.95 pa. (ISBN 0-691-01280-6, 26). Princeton Univ. Pr., NJ.

Guenther, Max. Defense of Shakespeare's Romeo & Juliet Against Modern Criticism. 1876. $5.00 Hdbd. (ISBN 0-404-02946-9). AMS Pr., NY.

Halliwell-Phillips, James O. Discursive Notes on Shakespeare's Tragedy of Romeo & Juliet. 1880. $5.00 Hdbd. (ISBN 0-404-03056-4). AMS Pr., NY.

Halliwell-Phillips, James O. Memoranda on Love's Labour's Lost, King John, Othello, & Romeo & Juliet. 1879. $6.50 Hdbd. (ISBN 0-404-03067-X). AMS Pr., NY.

Heline, Theodore. Romeo & Juliet Esoterically Interpreted. $1.50 Hdbd. New Age Pr., CA.

Hosley, Richard. Corrupting Influence of the Bad Quarto on the Received Text of Romeo & Juliet. 1953. $3.50 Hdbd. Folcroft Pr., PA.

Hosley, Richard. Romeo & Juliet—

Shakespeare. 1968. $1.00 pa. (ISBN 0-389-00842-7, 839, BN). Barnes & Noble, NY.

Hosley, Richard. Use of the Upper Stage in Romeo & Juliet. 1954. $3.50 Hdbd. Folcroft Pr., PA.

Kemble, Frances A. Notes Upon Some of Shakespeare's Plays. 1882. $8.00 Hdbd. (ISBN 0-404-03645-7). AMS Pr., NY.

Monarch Literature Notes on Shakespeare's Romeo & Juliet. $1.00 pa. Monarch Pr., NY.

Munroe, J. J. Brooke's Romeus & Juliet Being the Original of Shakespeare's Romeo & Juliet. (Shakespeare Classics). 1908. $15.00 Hdbd. Folcroft Pr., PA.

Nolan, Edward F. Barron's Simplified Approach to Shakespeare's Romeo & Juliet. 1967. $0.95 pa. Barron's Educ. Series, NY.

Shakespeare, William. Romeo & Juliet: Complete Study Edition. Lamb, Sidney, ed. 1968. $1.00 pa. (ISBN 0-8220-1437-8). Cliff's Notes, NB.

William Shakespeare's Romeo & Juliet. (E-Z Learner Study Text Ser). (Hi-Sch.). 1971. $1.25 pa. Apollo Bks. & Casyndekan Inc. Coshad Inc., CT.

TAMING OF THE SHREW
Charlton, H. B. Taming of the Shrew, 1932. $3.50 Hdbd. Folcroft Pr., PA.

Cliff's Notes Editors. Taming of the Shrew Notes. $1.00 pa. (ISBN 0-8220-0080-6). Cliff's Notes, NB.

Ranald, Margaret L. Monarch Literature Notes on Shakespeare's Taming of the Shrew. $1.00 pa. Monarch Pr., PA.

Shakespeare, William. Taming of the Shrew. (1912) $10.00 Hdbd. (ISBN 0-404-53369-8). AMS Pr., NY.

Shakespeare, William. Taming of the Shrew: A Concordance to the Text of the First Folio. 1969. $9.75 Hdbd. (ISBN 0-19-811133-9). Oxford Univ. Pr., NY.

Sykes, H. Dugdale. Authorship of the Taming of the Shrew. 1919. $6.50 Hdbd. Folcroft Pr., PA.

TEMPEST
Chalmers, George. Another Account of the Incidents from Which the Title & Part of Shakespeare's Tempest Were Derived. 1815. $6.00 Hdbd. (ISBN 0-404-01442-9). AMS Pr., NY.

Cliff's Notes Editors. Tempest Notes. $1.00 pa. (ISBN 0-8220-0083-0). Cliffs Notes, NB.

Fouquet, K. Jakob Ayrers Sidea, Shakespeares Tempest und das Maerchen. 1929. $4.50 pa. Johnson Reprint, NY.

Halliwell-Phillips, James O. Selected Notes Upon Shakespeare's Comedy of the Tempest. 1868. $5.00 Hdbd. (ISBN 0-404-03085-8). AMS Pr., NY.

Hunt, John D., ed. Shakespeare: The Tempest. (Macmillan Critical Commentaries). 1968. $1.00 pa. Fernhill House, NY.

James, David G. Dream of Prospero.

1967. $6.50 Hdbd. (ISBN 0-19-811660-8). Oxford Univ. Pr., NY.

Kemble, Frances A. Notes Upon Some of Shakespeare's Plays. 1882. $8.00 Hdbd. (ISBN 0-404-03645-7). AMS Pr., NY.

Kimball, Arthur G. Barron's Simplified Approach to Shakespeare's Tempest. 1967. $0.95 pa. Barron's Educ. Serv., NY.

Knight, George W. Shakespearean Tempest. 3rd ed. 1971. $4.00 pa. Barnes & Noble, NY.

Neilson, Francis. Shakespeare & the Tempest. 1956. $9.50 Hdbd. Greenwood Pr., CT.

Ranald, Ralph A. Monarch Literature Notes on Shakespeare's The Tempest. $1.00 pa. Monarch Pr., NY.

Shakespeare, William. Tempest. Nathanson, Leonard, ed. (Blackfriars Shakespeare Ser). 1969. $0.95 text ed. (ISBN 0-697-03908-0). Wm. C. Brown, IA.

Shakespeare, William. Tempest. Palmer, D. J., ed. (Casebook Ser). 1970. (1968) $2.50 text ed. (ISBN 0-87695-053-5). Aurora Pubs., TN.

Shakespeare, William. Tempest. Brown, John R., ed. (Casebook Ser). 1970. (1968) $2.50 text ed. (ISBN 0-87695-046-2). Aurora Pubs., TN.

Shakespeare, William. Tempest: Complete Study Edition. Lamb, Sidney, ed. $1.00 pa. (ISBN 0-8220-1440-8). Cliffs Notes, NB.

Shakespeare, William. Tempest: Concordance to the Text of the First Folio. Howard-Hill, T., ed. $9.75 Hdbd. Oxford Univ. Pr., NY.

Smith, Hallett D., ed. Twentieth Century Interpretations of The Tempest. 1969. $4.95 Hdbd. (ISBN 0-13-903302-5). Prentice-Hall, NY.

Still, Colin. Shakespeare's Mystery Play. 1921. $15.00 Hdbd. Folcroft Pr., PA.

Still, Colin. Timeless Theme. 1936. $15.00 Hdbd. Folcroft Pr., PA.

Wilson, John D. Meaning of the Tempest. 1936. $4.00 Hdbd. Folcroft Pr., PA.

TIMON OF ATHENS
Bradbrook, Muriel C. Tragic Pageant of Timon of Athens. $1.00 Hdbd. Cambridge Univ. Pr., NY.

Butler, Francelia. Strange Critical Fortunes of Shakespeare's Timon of Athens. 1966. $5.50 Hdbd. (ISBN 0-8138-1706-4). Iowa State Univ. Pr., IA.

White, Howard B. Copp'd Hills Towards Heaven: Shakespeare & the Classical Polity. (International Archives of the History of Ideas Ser., No. 32). 1971. $7.75 text ed. Humanities Pr., NY.

TITUS ANDRONICUS
Halliwell-Phillips, James O. Memoranda on All's Well That Ends Well, the Two Gentlemen of Verona, Much Ado About Nothing & on Titus Andronicus. 1879. $6.50 Hdbd. (ISBN 0-404-03066-1). AMS Pr., NY.

Robertson, John M. Introduction to the Study of the Shakespeare Canon. (Select Bibliographies Reprint Ser). 1924. $16.50 Hdbd. (ISBN 0-8369-5268-5). Books for Libraries, NY.

Robertson, John M. Introduction to the Study of the Shakespeare Canon, Proceeding on Problem of Titus Andronicus. 1924. $17.00 Hdbd. (ISBN 0-8371-3744-6). Greenwood Pr., CT.

Shakespeare, William. Shakespeare's Titus Andronicus: The First Quarto, 1594. Adams, John Q., ed. (Folger Library). 1936. $2.50 Hdbd. (ISBN 0-8139-0349-1). Univ. Pr. of Va., VA.

TROILUS AND CRESSIDA
Colley, John S. Troilus & Cressida. (Blackfriars Shakespeare Ser). 1970. $1.25 pa. (ISBN 0-697-03916-1). William C. Brown, IA.

Halliwell-Phillips, James O. Memoranda or Shakespeare's Tragedy of Troilus & Cressida. 1880. $5.00 Hdbd. (ISBN 0-404-03069-6). AMS Pr., NY.

Kimbrough, Robert. Shakespeare's Troilus & Cressida & Its Setting. 1964. $6.00 Hdbd. (ISBN 0-674-80520-8). Harvard Univ. Pr., MA.

Lowers, James K. Troilus & Cressida Notes. $1.00 pa. (ISBN 0-8220-0091-1). Cliffs Notes, NB.

Nugent, Elizabeth. Monarch Literature Notes on Shakespeare's Troilus & Cressida & Other Tragedies. $1.00 pa. (00655). Monarch Pr., NY.

Presson, Robert K. Shakespeare's

Troilus & Cressida & the Legends of Troy. 1953. $8.00 Hdbd. (ISBN 0-404-05134-0). AMS Pr., NY.

Tannenbaum, Samuel. Shakespeare's Troilus & Cressida. 1943. $10.00 Hdbd. Ridgeway Bks., PA.

TWELFTH NIGHT
Gilbert, Sandra. Monarch Literature Notes on Shakespeare's Twelfth Night. $1.00 pa. (00645). Monarch Pr., NY.

King, Walter N., ed. Twentieth Century Interpretations of Twelfth Night. YA. (Hi-Sch.). 1968. $1.25 pa. (ISBN 0-13-933408-4). $4.95 Hdbd. (ISBN 0-13-933408-4). Prentice-Hall, NY.

Leech, Clifford. Twelfth Night & Shakespearian Comedy. (Canadian University Paperbooks). 1965. $1.50 pa. (ISBN 0-8020-6080-3). Univ. of Toronto Pr., CAN.

Luce, Morton. Rich's Apolonius & Silla, an Original of Shakespeare's Twelfth Night. (Shakespeare Classics). 1912. $15.00 Hdbd. Folcroft Pr., PA.

Shakespeare, William. Twelfth Night: A Concordance to the Text of the First Folio. 1969. $9.75 Hdbd. (ISBN 0-19-811131-2). Oxford Univ. Pr., NY.

Shakespeare, William. Twelfth Night: Complete Study Edition. Lamb, Sidney, ed. $1.00 pa. (ISBN 0-8220-1444-0). Cliffs Notes, NB.

Twelfth Night Notes. Cliff's Notes. $1.00 pa. (ISBN 0-8220-0094-6). Cliffs Notes, NB.

TWO GENTLEMEN OF VERONA
Charlton, Henry B. Romanticism in Shakespearian Comedy. 1930. $4.00 Hdbd. Folcroft Pr., PA.

Ranald, Margaret L. Monarch Literature Notes on Shakespeare's Two Gentlemen of Verona. $1.00 pa. Monarch Pr., NY.

Halliwell-Phillips, James O. Memoranda on All's Well That Ends Well, the Two Gentlemen of Verona, Much Ado About Nothing & on Titus Andronicus. 1879. $6.50 Hdbd. (ISBN 0-404-03066-1). AMS Pr., NY.

Shakespeare, William. Two Gentlemen of Verona: Concordance to the Text of the First Folio. Howard-Hill, T., ed. $9.75 Hdbd. Oxford Univ. Pr., NY.

WINTER'S TALE
Bethell, Samuel L. Winter's Tale: A Study. 1947. $15.00 Hdbd. Folcroft Pr., PA.

Pyle, Fitzroy. Winter's Tale: Commentary on the Structure. 1969. $5.50 Hdbd. Barnes & Noble, NY.

Ranald, Margaret L. Monarch Literature Notes on Shakespeare's Winter's Tale. $1.00 pa. (00656). Monarch Pr., NY.

Shakespeare, William. Winter's Tale. Muir, Kenneth, ed. (Casebook Ser). 1970. (1968) $2.50 pa. (ISBN 0-87695-054-3). Aurora Publs., TN.

Shakespeare, William. Winter's Tale: A Concordance to the Text of the First

Folio. 1969. $9.75 Hdbd. (ISBN 0-19-811130-4). Oxford Univ. Pr., NY.

Williams, John A. Natural Work of Art: The Experience of Romance in Shakespeare's Winter's Tale. (LeBaron Russell Briggs Prize Honors Essays in English, 1966). 1967. $2.00 pa. (ISBN 0-674-60450-4). Harvard Univ. Pr., MA.

Textual

Bayfield, M. A. Study of Shakespeare's Versification. 1920. $25.00 Hdbd. Folcroft Pr., PA.

Black, Matthew W. & Shaaber, M. A. Shakespeare's Seventeenth-Century Editors, 1632-1685. 1937. $18.00 pa. Kraus Reprint Co., NY.

Bowers, Fredson. On Editing Shakespeare. 1966. $4.50 Hdbd. (ISBN 0-8139-0030-1); $2.45 pa. (ISBN 0-8139-0031-X). Univ. Pr of Va., VA.

Bowers, Fredson. Textual & Literary Criticism. 1959. $5.00 Hdbd.; $1.65 pa. (ISBN 0-521-09407-0, 407). Cambridge Univ. Pr., NY.

Bracy, William. Merry Wives of Windsor: The History & Transmission of Shakespeare's Text. 1952. $2.50 pa. (ISBN 0-8262-0529-1). Univ. of Mo. Pr., MO.

Bulloch, John. Studies on the Text of Shakespeare. 1878. $12.50 Hdbd. (ISBN 0-404-01227-2). AMS Pr., NY.

Butt, John E. Pope's Taste in Shakespeare. (English Literature Ser., No. 150). 1970. (1936) $1.95 pa. (ISBN

0-8383-0011-1). Haskell House Publ., NY.

Capell, Edward. Notes and Various Readings to Shakespeare. 1970. (1783) Set—$60.00 text ed. (ISBN 0-8337-0465-6). Burt Franklin, NY.

Capell, Edward. Notes & Various Readings to Shakespeare, 3 Vols. 1779-83. Set—$97.50 Hdbd. (ISBN 0-404-01400-3). AMS Pr., NY.

Chambers, Edmund K. Distintegration of Shakespeare. 1924. $4.00 Hdbd. Folcroft Pr., PA.

Chambers, Edmund K. William Shakespeare: A Study of Facts & Problems, 2 Vols. 1930. Set—$16.00 Hdbd. (ISBN 0-19-811513-X). Oxford Univ. Pr., NY.

Collier, John Payne. Notes Emendations to the Text of Shakespeare's Plays from Early Manuscript Corrections in a Copy of the Folio, 1632. (Research & Source Work, No. 401). 1970. (1853) $19.50 Hdbd. (ISBN 0-8337-0627-6). Burt Franklin, NY.

Collier, John Payne. Reasons for a New Edition of Shakespeare's Works. 1842. $7.00 Hdbd. (ISBN 0-404-01616-2). AMS Pr., NY.

Craig, Hardin. New Look at Shakespeare's Quartos. 1961. $3.50 Hdbd. (ISBN 0-8047-0065-6). Stanford Univ. Pr., CA.

Craig, Hardin. New Look at Shakespeare's Quartos. 1961. $3.50 Hdbd. (ISBN 0-404-01797-5). AMS Pr., NY.

Daniel, Peter A. Notes & Conjectural Emendations of Certain Doubtful Passages in Shakespeare's Plays. 1870. $6.50 Hdbd. (ISBN 0-404-01919-6). AMS Pr., NY.

Doran, Madeleine. Text of King Lear. 1931. $10.00 Hdbd. (ISBN 0-404-51807-9). AMS Pr., NY.

Duthie, George I. Bad Quarto of Hamlet. 1941. $15.00 Hdbd. Folcroft Pr., PA.

Dyce, Alexander. Few Notes on Shakespeare. 1853. $8.50 Hdbd. (ISBN 0-404-02228-6). AMS Pr., NY.

Dyce, Alexander. Remarks on Mister J. P. Collier's & Mister C. Knight's Editions of Shakespeare. 1844. $12.50 Hdbd. (ISBN 0-404-02230-8). AMS Pr., NY.

Everitt, E. B. Young Shakespeare: Studies in Documentary Evidence. Tillotson, G., ed. (Anglistica). 1954. $5.00 pa. Fernhill House, NY.

Feuillerat, Albert. Composition of Shakespeare's Plays. facs. ed. (Select Bibliographies Reprint Ser). 1953. $13.50 Hdbd. (ISBN 0-8369-5505-6). Books for Libraries, NY.

Foakes, R. A. Coleridge on Shakespeare: The Text of the Lectures of 1811-1812. (Folger Monographs on Tudor & Stuart Civilizations). $5.75 Hdbd. (ISBN 0-8139-0340-8). Univ. Pr. of Va., VA.

Furnivall, Frederick J., ed. Succession of Shakespeare's Works. 1874. $5.00

Hdbd. (ISBN 0-404-02663-X). AMS Pr., NY.

Gould, George. Corrigenda & Explanations of the Text of Shakespeare. 1884. $5.00 Hdbd. (ISBN 0-404-02887-X). AMS Pr., NY.

Greg, Walter W. Variants in the First Quarto of King Lear. (Studies in Shakespeare Ser., No. 24). 1969. (1940) $10.95 Hdbd. (ISBN 0-8383-0559-8). Haskell House Publ., NY.

Greg, Walter W. Editorial Problem in Shakespeare: A Survey of the Foundations of the Text. 3rd ed. 1954. $6.50 Hdbd. (ISBN 0-19-811545-8). Oxford Univ. Pr., NY.

Greg, Walter W. Shakespeare First Folio: Its Bibliographical & Textual History. 1955. $11.25 Hdbd. (ISBN 0-19-811546-6). Oxford Univ. Pr., NY.

Grey, Zachary. Answer to Certain Passages in Mr. W's Preface to His Edition of Shakespeare. 1748. $5.00 Hdbd. (ISBN 0-404-02899-3). AMS Pr., NY.

Grey, Zachary. Critical, Historical & Explanatory Notes on Shakespeare with Emendations of the Text & Metre, 2 Vols. 1754. $32.50 Hdbd. AMS Pr., NY.

Halliwell-Phillips, James O. Observations on Some of the Manuscript Emendations of the Text of Shakespeare. 1853. $5.00 Hdbd. (ISBN 0-404-03082-3). AMS Pr., NY.

Hart, Alfred. Stolen & Surreptitious Copies: A Comparative Study of Shakespeare's Bad Quartos. 1942. $25.00 Hdbd. Folcroft Pr., PA.

Heath, B. Revisal of Shakespeare's Text. 1765. $27.50 Hdbd. (ISBN 0-404-03209-5). AMS Pr., NY.

Herr, J. G. Scattered Notes on the Text of Shakespeare. 1879. $7.50 Hdbd. (ISBN 0-404-03248-6). AMS Pr., NY.

Hinman, Charlton. Printing & Proof-Reading of the First Folio of Shakespeare, 2 Vols. 1963. $32.00 Hdbd. (ISBN 0-19-811613-6). Oxford Univ. Pr., NY.

Holt, J. Attempte to Rescue That Aunciente, English Poet & Playwrighte, Maister Williaume Shakespeare. 1749. $5.00 Hdbd. (ISBN 0-404-03318-0). AMS Pr., NY.

Honigmann, E. A. Stability of Shakespeare's Text. 1965. $5.50 Hdbd. (ISBN 0-8032-0076-5). Univ. of Nebr. Pr., NB.

Hunter, Joseph. Few Worlds in Reply to the Animad Versions of the Reverend Mr. Dyce on Mr. Hunter's Disquisition on the Tempest, 1839. 1853. $5.00 Hdbd. (ISBN 0-404-03449-7). AMS Pr., NY.

Kable, William S. Pavier Quartos & the First Folio of Shakespeare. Barroll, J. Leeds, ed. (Shakespeare Studies, No. 2). 1970. $7.00 text ed. (ISBN 0-697-03876-9). William C. Brown, IA.

Kellner, Leon. Restoring Shakespeare: A Critical Analysis of the Misreadings in Shakespeare's Works. 1969. Repr.

of 1925 ed. $7.50 Hdbd. (ISBN 0-8196-0244-2). Biblo & Tannen, NY.

Kenrick, W. Defense of Mr. Kenrick's Review of Dr. Johnson's Shakespeare. 1766. $5.00 Hdbd. (ISBN 0-404-03658-9). AMS Pr., NY.

Kenrick, W. Review of Doctor Johnson's New Edition of Shakespeare. 1765. $6.50 Hdbd. (ISBN 0-404-03659-7). AMS Pr., NY.

Kirschbaum, Leo. True Text of King Lear. 1945. $9.00 Hdbd. (ISBN 0-404-03708-9). AMS Pr., NY.

Leo, Friedrich A. Shakespeare Notes. 1885. $8.50 Hdbd. (ISBN 0-404-03967-7). AMS Pr., NY.

McKerrow, Ronald B. Prolegomena for the Oxford Shakespeare. 1939. $12.50 Hdbd. Folcroft Pr., PA.

McKerrow, Ronald B. Treatment of Shakespeare's Text by His Earlier Editors, 1709–1768. (Select Bibliographies Reprint Ser). 1933. $5.00 Hdbd. (ISBN 0-8369-5265-0). Bks for Libraries, NY.

Mason, John M. Comments on the Last Edition of Shakespeare's Plays. 1785. $17.50 Hdbd. (ISBN 0-404-04225-2). AMS Pr., NY.

Mason, John M. Comments on the Several Editions of Shakespeare's Plays, Extended to Those of Malone & Steevens. 1807. $25.00 Hdbd. (ISBN 0-404-04226-0). AMS Pr., NY.

Mason, John M. Comments on the Several Editions of Shakespeare's Plays.

1970. (1807) $34.00 Hdbd. Augustus M. Kelley, NY.

Nicholson, Brinsley. Relation of the Quarto to the Folio Version of Henry Fifth. 1877. $10.00 Hdbd. (ISBN 0-404-04706-8). AMS Pr., NY.

Noble, Richmond. Shakespeare's Biblical Knowledge & Use of the Book of Common Prayer. 1970. $9.50 Hdbd. Octagon Books Inc., NY.

Peck, F. Explanatory & Critical Notes on Divers Passages of Shakespeare's Plays. 1740. $25.00 Hdbd. (ISBN 0-404-04965-6). AMS Pr., NY.

Pye, Henry J. Comments on the Commentators on Shakespeare. 1807. $15.00 Hdbd. (ISBN 0-404-05177-4). AMS Pr., NY.

Rhodes, R. Crompton. Shakespeare's First Folio. 1923. $7.50 Hdbd. Folcroft Pr., PA.

Ritson, Joseph. Cursory Criticisms on the Editions of Shakespeare. 1792. $8.50 Hdbd. (ISBN 0-404-05338-6). AMS Pr., NY.

Ritson, Joseph. Remarks Critical & Illustrative of the Last Edition of Shakespeare & the Quip Modest. $15.00 Hdbd. Augustus M. Kelley, NY.

Ritson, Joseph. Remarks, Critical & Illustrative, on the Text & Notes of the Last Edition of Shakespeare. 1783. $10.00 Hdbd. (ISBN 0-404-05348-3). AMS Pr., NY.

Ritson, Joseph & Malone, Edmond. Cursory Criticisms on the Edition of

Shakespeare Published by Edmond Malone, & a Letter to the Rev. Richard Farmer. $11.00 Hdbd. (ISBN 0-678-05132-1). Augustus M. Kelley, NY.

Robertson, John M. Shakespeare Canon, 5 Pts. in 4 Vols. 1922-32. Set—$30.00 Hdbd. (ISBN 0-404-05370-X). AMS Pr., NY.

Seymour, E. H. Remarks Critical, Conjectural & Explanatory Upon the Plays of Shakespeare, 2 Vols. 1805. $37.50 Hdbd. (ISBN 0-404-05754-3). AMS Pr., NY.

Smidt, Kristian. Inurious Imposters & Richard Third. 1964. $6.00 Hdbd. Humanities Pr., NY.

Stewart, Charles D. Some Textual Difficulties in Shakespeare. 1914. $8.50 Hdbd. (ISBN 0-404-06264-4). AMS Pr., NY.

Tannenbaum, Samuel A. Shakespearian Scraps & Other Elizabethan Fragments. 1933. $8.00 Hdbd. (ISBN 0-8046-0459-2). Kennikat Pr., NY.

Taylor, Rupert. Date of Love's Labour's Lost. 1932. $7.50 Hdbd. (ISBN 0-404-06356-X). AMS Pr., NY.

Tyrwhitt, Thomas. Observations & Conjectures Upon Some Passages of Shakespeare. 1766. $5.00 Hdbd. (ISBN 0-404-06574-0). AMS Pr., NY.

Upton, John. Critical Observations on Shakespeare. 2nd ed. 1748. $12.50 Hdbd. (ISBN 0-404-06705-0). AMS Pr., NY.

Van Dam, Bastiaan A. & Stoffel,

Cornelius O. William Shakespeare, Prosody & Text. 1900. $15.00 Hdbd. (ISBN 0-404-06752-2). AMS Pr., NY.

Vaughn, Henry H. New Readings & New Renderings of Shakespeare's Tragedies, 3 Vols. $55.00 Hdbd. (ISBN 0-404-06780-8). AMS Pr., NY.

Walder, Ernest. Shakespearian Criticism. 1895. $6.50 Hdbd. (ISBN 0-404-06803-0). AMS Pr., NY.

Walker, Alice. Textual Problems of the First Folio. (Shakespeare Problems). 1953. $6.00 Hdbd. Cambridge Univ. Pr., NY.

Walker, William S. Critical Examination of the Text of Shakespeare, 3 Vols. 1860. Set—$47.50 Hdbd. (ISBN 0-404-06810-3). AMS Pr., NY.

White, Richard G. Shakespeare's Scholar: Being Historical & Critical Studies of His Text, Characters & Commentators with an Examination of Mr. Collier's Folio of 1632. 1854. $20.00 Hdbd. (ISBN 0-404-06934-7). AMS Pr., NY.

Willoughby, Edwin E. Printing of the First Folio of Shakespeare. 1932. $12.50 Hdbd. Folcroft Pr., PA.

Wilson, Frank P. Shakespeare & the New Bibliography. rev. ed. Gardner, Helen, ed. 1970. $5.75 Hdbd. (ISBN 0-19-811695-0). Oxford Univ. Pr., NY.

Dictionaries & Indexes

Ayscough, Samuel. Index to the Remarkable Passages & Words Made Use of by Shakespeare. 1790. $12.50 Hdbd. (ISBN 0-404-00437-7). AMS Pr., NY.

Baker, Arthur E. Shakespeare Commentary, 2 Vols. 1957. $18.50 Hdbd. (ISBN 0-8044-2018-1). Frederick Ungar, NY.

Baynes, Thomas S. Shakespeare Studies & an Essay on English Dictionaries. 1894. $17.50 Hdbd. (ISBN 0-404-00697-3). AMS Pr., NY.

Campbell, Oscar J. & Quinn, Edward G., eds. Reader's Encyclopedia of Shakespeare. 1966. $15.00 Hdbd. (ISBN 0-690-67412-0). Thomas Y. Crowell, NY.

Clarke, Charles & Cowden, Mary. Shakespeare Key. 1961. $15.00 Hdbd. (ISBN 0-8044-2127-7). Frederick Ungar, NY.

Cunliffe, Richard J. New Shakespearean Dictionary. 1922. $25.00 Hdbd. Folcroft Pr., PA.

Dyce, Alexander. Glossary to the Works of William Shakespeare. 1968. (1902) $18.50 Hdbd. (ISBN 0-8337-0984-4). Burt Franklin, NY.

Falconer, Alexander F. Glossary of Shakespeare's Sea & Naval Terms Including Gunnery. 1965. $4.75 Hdbd. (ISBN 0-8044-2192-7). Frederick Ungar, NY.

Halliday, Frank E. Shakespeare Companion: 1564-1964. rev. ed. 1964. $12.00 Hdbd. (ISBN 0-8052-3237-0). Schocken, NY.

Halliday, Frank E. Shakespeare Com-

panion: 1564-1964. YA. 1964. $2.65 pa. (ISBN 0-14-053011-8, SL11). Penguin, MD.

Halliwell-Phillips, James O. Hand-Book Index to Works of Shakespeare. 1886. $25.00 Hdbd. (ISBN 0-404-03057-2). AMS Pr., NY.

Irvine, Theodora U. How to Pronounce the Names in Shakespeare. 1971. (1919) $15.00 Hdbd. Gryphon, MI.

Kokeritz, Helge. Shakespeare's Names: A Pronouncing Dictionary. 1959. $5.00 Hdbd. (ISBN 0-300-00637-3). Yale Univ. Pr., CT.

Nares, Robert. Glossary of Words, Phrases, Names & Allusions in the Works of English Authors. 1966. (1905) $22.50 Hdbd. Gale Research, MI.

O'Connor, Evangeline M. Index to the Works of Shakespeare. 1887. $17.50 Hdbd. Folcroft Pr., PA.

O'Connor, Evangeline M. Index to the Works of Shakespeare. 1887. $17.50 Hdbd. (ISBN 0-404-04810-2). AMS PR., NY.

Onions, Charles T. Shakespeare Glossary. 2nd rev. ed. 1919. $5.00 Hdbd. (ISBN 0-19-811109-6). Oxford Univ. Pr., NY.

Partridge, Eric. Shakespeare's Bawdy: A Literary & Psychological Essay & a Comprehensive Glossary. Rev. ed. 1947. $1.95 pa. (ISBN 0-525-47055-7). Dutton, NY.

Rushton, William L. Shakespeare Illustrated by the Lex Scripta. 1870. $6.50

Hdbd. (ISBN 0-404-05455-2). AMS Pr., NY.

Schmidt, Alexander. . Shakespeare Lexicon: A Complete Dictionary of All the English Words, Phrases & Constructions in the Work of the Poet, 2 Vols. 1968. $45.00 Hdbd. Benjamin Blom, NY.

Stokes, Francis G. Dictionary of the Characters & Proper Names in the Works of Shakespeare. $6.75 Hdbd. Peter Smith, MA.

Stokes, Francis G. Dictionary of the Characters & Proper Names in the Works of Shakespeare. $3.75 pa. (ISBN 0-486-22219-5). Dover, NY.

Sugden, Edward H. Topographical Dictionary to the Works of Shakespeare & His Fellow Dramatists. 1969. (1925) $27.30 Hdbd. Alder's Foreign Books, NY.

Festivals

Brown, Ivor & Fearson, George. This Shakespeare Industry. (Studies in Shakespeare, No. 24). 1970. (1939) $11.95 Hdbd. (ISBN 0-8383-1063-X). Haskell House Publ., NY.

Brown, Ivor & Fearon, George. Amazing Monument. 1970. (1939) $11.00 Hdbd. (ISBN 0-8046-1009-6). Kennikat Pr., NY.

Deelman, Christian. Great Shakespeare Jubilee. 1964. $6.95 Hdbd. (ISBN 0-670-35046-X). Viking Pr., NY.

England, Martha W. Garrick's Jubilee.

1964. $6.25 Hdbd. (ISBN 0-8142-0046-X). Ohio St. Univ. Pr., OH.

McNeir, Waldo F. & Greenfield, Thelma N., eds. Pacific Coast Studies in Shakespeare. 1966. $7.50 Hdbd. Univ. of Oreg. Bks., OR.

Prouty, Charles T., ed. Shakespeare: Of an Age & for All Time. 1954. $7.50 Hdbd. (ISBN 0-404-05146-4). AMS Pr., NY.

Stochholm, Johanne M. Garrick's Folly: The Stratford Jubilee of 1769. 1964. $3.50 Hdbd. Barnes & Noble, NY.

Woodberry, George E. Shakespeare: An Address. 1916. $4.00 Hdbd. Folcroft Pr., PA.

General Studies

Acheson, Arthur. Shakespeare's Lost Years in London. (Studies in Shakespeare Ser., No. 24). (1971) $9.95 Hdbd. (ISBN 0-8383-1235-7). Haskell House Publ., NY.

Acheson, Arthur. Shakespeare, Chapman & Sir Thomas More. 1970. (1931) $11.00 Hdbd. (ISBN 0-404-00278-1). AMS Pr., NY.

Alden, Raymond M., ed. Shakespeare. 1922. $15.75 Hdbd. (ISBN 0-404-00307-9). AMS Pr., NY.

Alexander, Peter. Shakespeare. 1964. $2.50 Hdbd. (ISBN 0-19-889252-7). Oxford Univ. Pr., NY.

Amphlett, Hilda. Who Was Shakespeare. 1970. (1955) $10.00 Hdbd. (ISBN 0-404-00325-7). AMS Pr., NY.

Anderson, Hans. Strindgerg's Master Olof & Shakespeare. 1952. $8.50 Hdbd. Folcroft Pr., PA.

Arbuthnot, George. Vestry Minute Book of Stratford-On-Avon. 1971. (1899) $6.50 Hdbd. (ISBN 0-404-00366-4). AMS Pr., NY.

Armstrong, Cecil F. Shakespeare to Shaw. 1913. $8.50 Hdbd. (ISBN 0-404-00383-4). AMS Pr., NY.

Armstrong, Edward A. Shakespeare's Imagination. $4.25 Hdbd. Peter Smith Publ., MA.

Auchincloss, Louis. Motiveless Malignity. 1969. $5.00 Hdbd. (ISBN 0-395-07356-1). Houghton & Mifflin, NY.

Austell, Jan. What's in a Play· (Curriculum-Related Bks). (Hi-Sch.). 1968. $3.50 Hdbd. (ISBN 0-15-295500-3). Harcourt Brace, NY.

Bach, Walter M. All the World's a Stage. $2.95 Hdbd. (ISBN 0-8158-0021-5). Christopher Publ. House, MA.

Baldwin, Thomas W. William Shakespeare Adapts a Hanging. 1971. (1931) $15.00 Hdbd. Lansdowne Pr., PA.

Ball, Robert H. Shakespeare on Silent Film. 1968. $12.50 Hdbd. Theatre Arts Books, NY.

Bentley, Gerald E. Shakespeare: A Biographical Handbook. 1961. $6.50 Hdbd. (ISBN 0-300-00302-1); $2.25 pa. (ISBN 0-300-00021-9, y63). Yale Univ. Pr., CT.

Berman, Ronald, ed. Twentieth Century Interpretations of Henry Fifth. (Hi-Sch.). 1968. $1.25 pa. (ISBN 0-13-386664-5, Spec). $4.95 Hdbd. (ISBN 0-13-386672-6). Prentice-Hall, NY.

Berry, Francis. Shakespeare Inset: Word & Picture. 1971. $1.95 pa. (ISBN 0-8093-0532-1, Ab). S. Ill. Univ. Pr., IL.

Bevington, S., ed. Twentieth Century Interpretations of Hamlet. 1968. $4.95 Hdbd. (ISBN 0-13-372375-5). (Hi-Sch.). $1.25 pa. (ISBN 0-13-372367-4). Prentice-Hall, NY.

Bhattacherje, M. M. Courtesy in Shakespeare. 1940. $12.50 Hdbd. Folcroft Pr., PA.

Blades, William. Shakespeare & Typography. 1971. (1872) $6.00 Hdbd. (ISBN 0-404-00894-1). AMS Pr., NY.

Bloom, Harvey J. Shakespeare's Garden. (1903) $8.00 Hdbd. Gale Research Co., MI.

Boas, Frederick S. Introduction to the Reading of Shakespeare. 1927. $5.00 Hdbd. Ridgeway Bks., PA.

Boas, Frederick S. Shakespeare & His Predecessors. (Studies in Shakespeare Ser., No. 24). 1969. (1896) $9.95 Hdbd. (ISBN 0-8383-0914-3). Haskell House Publ., NY.

Boas, Frederick S. Shakespeare & His Predecessors. 1968. (1902) $8.50 Hdbd. (ISBN 0-87752-011-9). Gordian Pr., NY.

Boas, Frederick S. Shakespeare & His Predecessors. 1969. $18.50 Hdbd. (ISBN 0-8371-0316-9). Greenwood Pr., CT.

Boas, Frederick S. Shakespeare & the Universities. 1923. $10.00 Hdbd. Ridgeway Bks., PA.

Bodde, Derk. Shakespeare & the Ireland Forgeries. 1971. (1930) $5.50 Hdbd. Lansdowne Pr., PA.

Booth, Stephen. Essay on Shakespeare's Sonnets. 1969. $7.50 Hdbd. (ISBN 0-300-01100-8); $2.45 pa. (ISBN 0-300-01514-3). Yale Univ. Pr., CT.

Boswell-Stone, W. G. Shakespeare's Holinshed: The Chronicle & the Plays Compared. $6.00 Hdbd. Peter Smith Publ., MA.

Braie, A. E. Collier, Coleridge & Shakespeare. 1860. $7.50 Hdbd. (ISBN 0-404-01061-X). AMS Pr., NY.

Brandes, Georg. William Shakespeare: A Critical Study, 2 Vols. 1963. $15.00 Hdbd. (ISBN 0-8044-2074-2). Frederick Ungar Pr., NY.

Briak, Bernhard. Five Lectures on Shakespeare. 1971. (1895) $10.00 Hdbd. (ISBN 0-404-01080-6). AMS Pr., NY.

Britton, John. Remarks on the Life & Writings of William Shakespeare. 1814. $5.00 Hdbd. (ISBN 0-404-01086-5). AMS Pr., NY.

Brooke, Tucker. Shakespeare of Stratford. (Select Bibliographies Reprint Ser). (1926) $9.50 Hdbd. (ISBN 0-8369-5503-X). Books for Libraries, NY.

Brown, Ivor. William Shakespeare. (International Profiles Ser). 1969. $1.95 Hdbd. (ISBN 0-498-07399-8). A. S. Barnes, NJ.

Brown, Ivor & Fearon, George. Amazing Monument. 1970. (1939) $11.00 Hdbd. (ISBN 0-8046-1009-6). Kennikat Pr., NY.

Brown, Ivor. & Fearon, George. This Shakespeare Industry: Amazing Monument. 1939. $13.00 Hdbd. (ISBN 0-8371-2850-1). Greenwood Pr., CT.

Bulman, Joan. Strindberg & Shakespeare. (Studies in Comparative Literature Ser., No. 35). 1971. (1933) $9.95 Hdbd. (ISBN 0-8383-1239-X). Haskell House Publ., NY.

Chambers, Edmund K. Shakespearean Gleanings. 1971. (1944) $10.00 Hdbd. Lansdowne Pr., PA.

Chambers, Edmund K. William Shakespeare: A Study of Facts & Problems, 2 Vols. 1930. Set—$16.00 Hdbd. (ISBN 0-19-811513-X). Oxford Univ. Pr., NY.

Chambrun, Clara. Shakespeare: A Portrait Restored. facsimile ed. (Select Bibliographies Reprint Ser). 1957. $15.00 Hdbd. (ISBN 0-8369-5251-0). Books for Libraries, NY.

Charlton, H. B. Shakespearian Tragedy. 1971. $6.00 Hdbd. Cambridge Univ. Pr., NY.

Chevrillon, Andre. Three Studies in English Literature, Kipling, Galsworthy & Shakespeare. 1923. $8.00 Hdbd. (ISBN 0-8046-0077-5). Kennikat Pr., NY.

Chute, Marchette. Stories from Shakespeare. (Jr. Hi.). (1708) $5.95 Hdbd. World Pub. Co., OH.

Chute, Marchette & Perrie, Ernestine. Worlds of Shakespeare. $3.95 Hdbd. (ISBN 0-525-23803-4); $1.25 pa. (ISBN 0-525-47125-1). E. P. Dutton, NY.

Clard, Cumberland. Shakespeare & Science. $10.75 Hdbd. Gordon Pubs., NY.

Clark, Eva T. Man Who Was Shakespeare. 1970. (1937) $12.50 Hdbd. (ISBN 0-404-01549-2). AMS Pr., NY.

Clarke, David W. William Shakespeare. (1950) $6.00 Hdbd. (ISBN 0-404-01568-9). AMS Pr., NY.

Coleman, Hamilton, Shakespeare & the Bible. 1955. $7.50 Hdbd. Ridgeway Bks., PA.

Coleridge, Samuel T. Coleridge on Shakespeare: The Text of the Lectures of 1811–12. Foakes, R. A., ed. (Folger Monographs on Tudor & Stuart Civilization, No. 3). 1971. $5.75 Hdbd. (ISBN 0-8139-0340-8). Univ. Pr. of Va., VA.

Coleridge, Samuel T. Seven Lectures on Shakespeare & Milton by Samuel Taylor Coleridge. Collier, J. Payne, ed. 1856. $12.50 Hdbd. (ISBN 0-404-01617-0). AMS Pr., NY.

Coleridge, Samuel T. Seven Lectures on Shakespeare & Milton. (Research & Source Works Ser., No. 276). 1969 (1856) $16.50 Hdbd. (ISBN 0-8337-0618-7). Burt Franklin, NY.

Collier, John Payne. New Facts Regard-

ing the Life of Shakespeare. 1970. (1835) $5.00 Hdbd. (ISBN 0-404-01609-X). AMS Pr., NY.

Collier, John Payne. New Facts Regarding the Life of Shakespeare. 1971. (1835) $7.00 Hdbd. Scholarly Pr., MI.

Cox, Roger L. Between Earth & Heaven: Shakespeare, Dostoevsky, & the Meaning of Christian Tragedy. 1969. $5.95 Hdbd. (ISBN 0-03-081842-7). Holt, Rinehart & Winston, NY.

Craig, Hardin. Interpretation of Shakespeare. 1966. $4.50 pa. (ISBN 0-87543-005-8). Lucas. Bros. Publ., MO.

Creizenach, Wilhelm. English Drama in the Age of Shakespeare. (Drama Ser., No. 39). 1969. (1916) $12.50 Hdbd. (ISBN 0-8383-0533-4). Haskell House Publ., NY.

Dobree, Bonamy. Amateur & the Theatre. 1947. $4.00 Hdbd. Folcroft Pr., PA.

Dodd, William. Beauties of Shakespeare, 2 Vols. 1970. (1752) $37.50 Hdbd. Augustus M. Kelley, NY.

Dowden, Edward. Introduction to Shakespeare. 1970. (1893) $7.50 Hdbd. (ISBN 0-404-02166-2). AMS Pr., NY.

Drinkwater, John. Shakespeare. 1956. $2.95 Hdbd. Dufour Editions, PA.

Dyce, Alexander. Glossary of the Works of William Shakespeare. (Library of Literature, Drama & Criticism). 1970. (1902) $25.00 Hdbd. Johnson Reprint Corp., NY.

Eccles, Mark. Shakespeare in Warwickshire. 1961. $6.50 Hdbd. (ISBN 0-299-02330-3); $1.75 pa. (ISBN 0-299-02334-6). Univ. of Wis. Pr., WI.

Elliot, Thomas Stearns: Shakespeare & the Stoicism of Seneca. 1971. $5.00 Hdbd. Lansdowne Pr., PA.

Ellis, Alexander J. On Early English Pronunciation, with Especial Reference to Shakespeare & Chaucer, 5 Vols. (Language Ser., No. 41). 1969. (1889) $69.95 Hdbd. (ISBN 0-8383-0158-4). Haskell House Publ., NY.

Ellis-Fermor, Una. Shakespeare the Dramatist. 1948. $3.00 Hdbd. Folcroft Pr., PA.

Elze, Karl. William Shakespeare. 1888. $25.00 Hdbd. (ISBN 0-404-02328-2). AMS Pr., NY.

England, Martha W. Garrick & Stratford. (Orig.). 1962. $2.50 pa. (ISBN 0-87104-084-0). NY Publs. Library, NY.

English Department Of The University Of Michigan. Studies in Shakespeare, Milton & Donne. (Studies in Poetry Ser., No. 38). 1969. (1925) $11.95 Hdbd. (ISBN 0-8383-0638-1). Haskell House Publ., NY.

Fairchild, Arthur H. Shakespeare & the Arts of Design: Architecture, Sculpture & Painting. 1971. $10.00 Hdbd. (ISBN 0-87696-021-2). Lemma Publ., Co., NY.

Fairchild, Arthur H. Shakespeare & the Tragic Theme. 1944. $15.00 Hdbd. Ridgeway Bks., PA.

Farnham, W. With Shakespeare at Work. (Studies in Shakespeare Ser., No. 24). 1971. price not set. Hdbd. (ISBN 0-8383-1273-X). Haskell House Publ., NY.

Fennell, James H. Shakespeare Repository. 1853. $5.00 Hdbd. (ISBN 0-404-02376-2). AMS Pr., NY.

Fergusson, Francis. Shakespeare: The Pattern in His Carpet. 1971. price "n.g." pa. Dell Publ., NY.

Fergusson, James. Man Behind Macbeth, & Other Studies. 1970. $6.75 Hdbd. Fernhill House, NY.

Fleay, Frederick G. Chronicle History of the Life & Work of Shakespeare. 1970. (1886) $17.50 Hdbd. (ISBN 0-404-02405-X). AMS Pr., NY.

Fleay, Frederick G. Shakespeare Manual. 1970. (1876) $14.00 Hdbd. (ISBN 0-404-02408-4). AMS Pr., NY.

Foakes, R. A. Shakespeare from the Dark Comedies to the Last Plays. 1971. price "n.g." Hdbd. Univ. Pr. of Va., VA.

Forbes, Thomas R. Chronicle from Aldgate: Life & Death in Shakespeare's London. 1971. $10.00 Hdbd. (ISBN 0-300-01386-8). Yale Univ. Pr., CT.

Forbis, John F. Shakesperean Enigma & an Elizabethan Mania. 1970. (1923) $14.00 Hdbd. (ISBN 0-404-02458-0). AMS Pr., NY.

Freden, Gustaf. William Shakespeare. 1858. $5.00 Hdbd. (ISBN 0-404-02549-8). AMS Pr., NY.

Frye, Roland M. Shakespeare's Life & Times: A Pictorial Record. 1967. $10.00 Hdbd. Princeton Univ. Pr., NJ.

Fullom, S. W. History of William Shakespeare, Player & Poet. 1864. $14.50 Hdbd. (ISBN 0-404-02644-3). AMS Pr., NY.

Galloway, David, ed. Elizabethan Theatre 1. 1970. $6.50 Hdbd. (ISBN 0-208-01144-7). 2. 1970. $7.00 Hdbd. (ISBN 0-208-01145-5). Shoe String Pr., CT.

Ghose, Prabodh C. Shakespeare's Mingled Drama. 1966. $15.00 Hdbd. Ridgeway Bks., PA.

Gibian, George. Tolstoi & Shakespeare. (Orig.). 1957. $3.00 pa. Humanities Pr., NY.

Gibian, George. Tolstoy & Shakespeare. 1957. $10.00 Hdbd. Folcroft Pr., PA.

Gittings, Robert, ed. Living Shakespeare. $3.00 Hdbd. Barnes & Noble, NY.

Gordon, George. Shakespeare's English. 1928. $4.00 Hdbd. Ridgeway Bks., PA.

Granville-Barker, Harley & Harrison, George B. Companion to Shakespeare Studies. 1934. $9.50 Hdbd. Cambridge Univ. Pr., NY.

Granville-Barker, Harley & Harrison, George B., eds. Companion to Shakespeare Studies. 1960. $1.75 pa. Doubleday & Co., NY.

Grebanier, Bernard. Truth About Shylock. 1962. $8.95 Hdbd. (ISBN 0-394-44978-9). Random House Publ., NY.

Greg, Walter W. Capell's Shakesperiana. 1903. $12.50 Hdbd. Folcroft Pr., PA.

Greg, Walter W. Principles of Emendation in Shakespeare. 1971. (1928) $7.00 Hdbd. Scholarly Pr., MI.

Grene, David. Reality & the Heroic Pattern: Last Plays of Ibsen, Shakespeare, & Sophocles. 1967. $6.00 Hdbd. (ISBN 0-226-30788-3). Univ. of Chicago Pr., IL.

Guthrie, William & Holt, John. Essay Upon English Tragedy & an Attempt to Rescue That Aunciente, English Poet, & Playwrighte, Maister Willaume Shakespere. 1970. (1749) $10.00 Hdbd. Augustus M. Kelley, NY.

Hall, Henry T. Shakespearean Statistics. 1970. (1874) $7.50 Hdbd. (ISBN 0-404-03044-0). AMS Pr., NY.

Hall, Henry T. Shaksperean Fly-Leaves & Jottings. 1970. (1871) $9.50 Hdbd. (ISBN 0-404-03043-2). AMS Pr., NY.

Halliday, F. E. Shakespeare. $2.95 Hdbd. (ISBN 0-498-08894-4, Encore). A. S. Barnes, NY.

Harbage, Alfred. Shakespeare & the Rival Traditions. 1970. $3.45 pa. (ISBN 0-253-20129-2). Indiana Univ. Pr., IN.

Harrison, George B. Introducing Shakespeare. rev. ed. (Hi-Sch.). 1966. $1.75 pa. (ISBN 0-14-020043-6). Penguin Books, MD.

Hart, Alfred. Shakespeare & the Homilies. 1970. (1934) $8.50 Hdbd. Octagon Books, NY.

Hearn, Lafcadio. Lectures on Shakespeare. Inagaki, Iwao, ed. 1928. $15.00 Hdbd. Folcroft Pr., PA.

Herford, Charles H. Shakespeare. 1912. $5.00 Hdbd. Folcroft Pr., PA.

Hill, Frank E. To Meet Will Shakespeare. (Select Bibliographies Reprint Ser). 1949. $18.50 Hdbd. (ISBN 0-8369-5259-6). Books for Libraries, NY.

Holland, Laurence G. Shakespeare: Some Essays & Lectures. 1970. (1893) $7.50 Hdbd. (ISBN 0-8046-1021-5). Kennikat Pr., NY.

Hookham, George. Will O' the Wisp: Or the Elusive Shakespeare. 1922. $7.50 Hdbd. (ISBN 0-404-03337-7). AMS Pr., NY.

Howarth, Herbert. Tiger's Heart: Eight Essays on Shakespeare. 1970. $5.00 Hdbd. (ISBN 0-19-519035-1). Oxford Univ. Pr., NY.

Hubbell, Lindley W. Lectures on Shakespeare. 1956. $10.00 Hdbd. Folcroft Pr., PA.

Hudson, N. H. Shakespeare: His Life, Art & Characters. (Studies in Shakespeare, No. 24). 1970. (1872) $29.95 Hdbd. (ISBN 0-8383-1100-8). Haskell House Publ., NY.

Hugo, Victor. William Shakespeare. Anderson, Melville B., tr. (Select Bibliographies Ser). (1886) $14.50 Hdbd. (ISBN 0-8369-5508-0). Books for Libraries, NY.

Hugo, Victor. William Shakespeare. Anderson, M. B., tr. 1887. $17.50 Hdbd. (ISBN 0-404-03382-2). AMS Pr., NY.

I'Haler, Alwin. Shakespeare & Sir Philip Sidney. 1947. $5.00 Hdbd. Folcroft Pr., PA.

Ingleby, Clement M. Shakespeare, the Man & the Book, 2 Vols. 1877-81. Set—$11.50 Hdbd. (ISBN 0-404-03486-1). AMS Pr., NY.

Iyengar, K. R. Shakespeare: His World & His Art. $15.75 Hdbd. (ISBN 0-210-31234-3). Asia Publ. House., NY.

Kaiser, Walter. Praisers of Folly: Erasmus, Rabelais, Shakespeare. (Studies in Comparative Literature Ser. No. 25). 1963. $9.00 Hdbd. (ISBN 0-674-69800-2). Harvard Univ. Pr., MA.

Keightley, Thomas. Shakespeare-Expositor. 1867. $17.50 Hdbd. (ISBN 0-404-03642-2). AMS Pr., NY.

Kellett, Ernest E. Suggestions. 1923. $15.00 Hdbd. Folcroft Pr., PA.

Kellett, Ernest E. Suggestions. (Essay Index Reprint Ser). 1923. $9.00 Hdbd. (ISBN 0-8369-1357-4). Books for Libraries, NY.

Kittredge, George L. Shakespeare. 1916. $4.00 Hdbd. Folcroft Pr., PA.

Kittredge, George L. Shakespeare. 1970. (1916) $5.00 Hdbd. (ISBN 0-404-03709-7). AMS Pr., NY.

Kittredge, George L. Shakespeare: An Address. (Select Bibliographies Reprint

Ser). 1916. $5.00 Hdbd. (ISBN 0-8369-5262-6). Books for Libraries, NY.

Klein, David. Living Shakespeare. $5.00 Hdbd. Twayne Publ., NY.

Klein, David. Milestones to Shakespeare. $5.00 Hdbd. Twayne Publ., NY.

Knight, George Wilson. This Sceptred Isle: Shakespeare's Message. 1940. $5.00 Hdbd. Ridgeway Books, PA.

Knight, George Wilson. Byron & Shakespeare. 1966. $7.00 Hdbd. Barnes & Noble, NY.

Landor, Walter S. Citation & Examination of William Shakespeare, Euseby Treen, Joseph Carnaby & Silas Gough Clerk. 1834. $12.50 Hdbd. (ISBN 0-404-03809-3). AMS Pr., NY.

Laurence, W. J. Shakespeare's Workshop. (Studies in Shakespeare Ser., No. 24). 1969. (1928) $8.95 Hdbd. (ISBN 0-8383-0580-6). Haskell House Publ., NY.

Lee, Sidney. Life of William Shakespeare. 1971. (1898) $19.00 Hdbd. Scholarly Pr., MI.

Lee, Sidney. Pepys & Shakespeare. 1906. $4.00 Hdbd. Folcroft Pr., PA.

Lee, Sidney. Shakespeare & the Italian Renaissance. 1915. $3.00 Hdbd. Folcroft Pr., PA.

Lee, Sidney. Shakespeare & the Modern Stage with Other Essays. 1906. $10.00 Hdbd. (ISBN 0-404-03929-4). AMS Pr., NY.

Lounsbury, Thomas R. Shakespeare & Voltaire. 1968. $12.50 Hdbd. Benjamin Blom, NY.

Ludowyk, Evelyn F. Understanding Shakespeare. 1962. $5.50 Hdbd.; $2.45 pa. (ISBN 0-521-09242-6, 242). Cambridge Univ. Pr., NY.

Luethi, Max. Shakespeares Dramen. (Ger). 1966. $6.55 Hdbd. (ISBN 3-11-000192-6). De Gruyter., Germany

MacKail, John W. Approach to Shakespeare. (Select Bibliographies Reprint Ser). 1930. $8.50 Hdbd. (ISBN 0-8369-5264-2). Books for Libraries, NY.

MacKail, John W. Approach to Shakespeare. 2nd ed. 1963. $6.50 Hdbd. (ISBN 0-404-04131-0). AMS Pr., NY.

Madden, Dodgson H. Diary of Master William Silence: A Study of Shakespeare & Elizabethan Sport. (Studies in Shakespeare Ser., No. 24). 1970. (1897) $12.95 Hdbd. (ISBN 0-8383-0993-3). Haskell House Publ., NY.

Madden, Dodgson H. Diary of Master William Silence: A Study of Shakespeare & of Elizabethan Sport. 1897. $13.00 Hdbd. (ISBN 0-8371-2322-4). Greenwood Pr., CT.

Mansinha, M. Kalidasa & Shakespeare. 1968. $4.50 Hdbd. Lawrence Verry, Inc., CT.

Martin, Michael R. & Harrier, Richard C. Concise Encyclopedic Guide to Shakespeare. 1971. $12.95 Hdbd. (ISBN 0-8180-1159-9). Horizon Pr., NY.

Matthews, Brander & Thorndike, Ashley H. Shakespearian Studies. $12.50 Hdbd. Benjamin Blom, NY.

Matthews, W. Shakespeare & the Reporter. 1935. $3.50 Hdbd. Folcroft Pr., PA.

Meader, William G. Courtship in Shakespeare. (1971) $8.50 text ed. Octagon Books, NY.

Mendilow, Adam A. & Shalvi, Alice. World & Art of Shakespeare. 1967. $6.75 Hdbd. (ISBN 0-8088-2602-6). Daniel Davey & Co., CT.

Michel, Laurence. Thing Contained: Theory of the Tragic. 1970. $7.50 Hdbd. (ISBN 0-253-18870-9). Ind. Univ. Pr., IN.

Momeyer, Arline B. & Bach, Walter M. All the World's a Stage. 1969. $2.95 Hdbd. (ISBN 0-8158-0021-5). Christopher Publ. House, MA.

Morse, Herbert. Back to Shakespeare. 1970. (1915) $10.00 Hdbd. (ISBN 0-8046-1027-4). Kennikat Pr., NY.

Muir, K., ed. Shakespeare: Theatre Poet. price "n.g." Hdbd. Cambridge Univ. Pr., NY.

Murry, John M. Keats & Shakespeare: A Study of Keats' Poetic Life from 1816 to 1820. 1924. $9.75 Hdbd. (ISBN 0-19-212127-8). Oxford Univ. Pr., NY.

Nisbet, U. Onlie Begetter. (Studies in Shakespeare, No. 24). 1970. (1936) $6.95 Hdbd. (ISBN 0-8383-1095-8). Haskell House Publ., NY.

Noyes, Robert G. Thespian Mirror:

Shakespeare in the Eighteenth-Century Novel. 1953. $5.50 Hdbd. (ISBN 0-87057-034-X). Brown Univ. Pr., RI.

O'Connor, Frank. Shakespeare's Progress. 1961. $1.50 pa. Macmillan Co., NY.

Ogburn, Dorothy. This Star of England: William Shakespeare, Man of the Renaissance. (1952) $55.00 Hdbd. (ISBN 0-8371-6177-0). Greenwood Pr., CT.

Parrott, Thomas M. William Shakespeare: A Handbook. rev. ed. 1955. $1.65 pa. (ISBN 0-684-71861-8, 42). Charles Scribner's Sons, NY.

Parrott, Thomas M. William Shakespeare: A Handbook. rev. ed. 1955. $3.75 Hdbd. Peter Smith Publ., MA.

Pascal, Roy. Shakespeare in Germany, 1740–1815. (1971) $8.00 text ed. Octagon Books, NY.

Pettet, E. C. Shakespeare & the Romance Tradition. 1949. buckram bdg. $5.50 Hdbd. Ridgeway Books, PA.

Poel, William. Shakespeare in the Theatre. 1968. $9.75 Hdbd. Benjamin Blom, NY.

Pollard, A. W. Shakespeare's Fight with the Pirates. 1920. $7.50 Hdbd. Ridgeway Books, PA.

Raleigh, Walter. Shakespeare & England. 1918. $3.00 Hdbd. Folcroft Pr., PA.

Raleigh, Walter, et al, eds. Shakespeare's England: An Account of the Life & Manners of His Age, 2 Vols.

1917. $21.00 Hdbd. (ISBN 0-19-821252-6). Oxford Univ. Pr., NY.

Raleigh, Walter. Shakespeare. 1950. pocket ed. $2.50 Hdbd. St. Martin's Pr., NY.

Reese, Max M. Shakespeare: His World & His Work. 1953. $10.00 Hdbd. St. Martin's Pr., NY.

Rhodes, Raymond C. Shakespeare's First Folio. 1923. $7.00 Hdbd. (ISBN 0-404-05287-8). AMS Pr., NY.

Righter, Anne. Shakespeare & the Idea of the Play. (1967) $1.65 pa. (ISBN 0-14-053001-0). Penguin Books, MD.

Ritson, Joseph. Remarks, Critical & Illustrative, on the Text & Notes of the Last Edition of Shakespeare. 1783. $10.00 Hdbd. (ISBN 0-404-05348-3). AMS Pr., NY.

Rohrman, Hendrick. Marlowe & Shakespeare. 1952. $10.00 Hdbd. Folcroft Pr., PA.

Schelling, Felix E. Significance of Shakespeare. 1929. $3.00 Hdbd. Folcroft Pr., PA.

Schlegel, Johann E. Vergleichung Shakespears und Andrus Gryphs. (Orig., Ger). 1970. $1.25 pa. Humanities Pr., NY.

Scott-Giles, Charles W. Shakespeare's Heraldry. 1950. $14.00 Hdbd. (ISBN 0-404-05663-6). AMS Pr., NY.

Shackford, Martha H. Shakespeare, Sophocles: Dramatic Themes & Modes. 1960. $1.45 pa. College & Univ. Pr., CT.

Shakespeare, William. Complete & Systematic Concordance of Works of Shakespeare, 6 Vols. Spevack, Marvon, ed. 1968-70. Set—$275.000 Hdbd. Adler's Foreign Books, NY.

Shakespeare, William. Essays of Shakespeare. Taylor, George C., ed. (Essay Index Reprint Ser). 1947. $7.75 Hdbd. (ISBN 0-8369-2174-7). Books for Libraries, NY.

Shaw, George B. Shaw on Shakespeare. facs. ed. Wilson, Edwin, ed. (Essay Index Reprint Ser). 1961. $11.50 Hdbd. (ISBN 0-8369-2175-5). Books for Libraries, NY.

Sisson, Charles J. Lost Plays in Shakespeare's Age. 1971. (1936) $12.50 Hdbd. Lansdowne Pr., PA.

Sisson, Charles J. Shakespeare, (Writers & Their Work Ser No. 58). $2.25 Hdbd.; $1.00 pa. British Book Center, NY.

Smith, David N., ed. Eighteenth Century Essays on Shakespeare. 2nd ed. 1963. $6.75 Hdbd. (ISBN 0-19-811607-1). Oxford Univ. Pr., NY.

Spencer, T. J., ed. Shakespeare: A Celebration 1564-1964. 1964. $5.00 Hdbd. William Gannon, NM.

Spencer, Theodore. Shakespeare & the Nature of Man. 2nd ed. 1949. $6.00 Hdbd.; $1.95 pa. Macmillan Co., NY.

Spens, Janet. Essay on Shakespeare's Relation to Tradition. 1916. $10.00 Hdbd. Folcroft Pr., PA.

Spielmann, Marion H. Title Page of the First Folio of Shakespeare's Plays: A

Comparative Study of the Droeshout Portrait & the Stratford Monument. 1924. $5.00 Hdbd. (ISBN 0-404-07869-9). AMS Pr., NY.

Spurgeon, Caroline F. Shakespeare's Iterative Imagery. 1931. $4.00 Hdbd. Folcroft Pr., PA.

Stephenson, Henry T. Shakespeare's London. 1905. $14.00 Hdbd. (ISBN 0-404-06258-X). AMS Pr., NY.

Stokes, Henry P. Attempt to Determine the Chronological Order of Shakespeare's Plays. 1878. $10.00 Hdbd. (ISBN 0-404-06281-4). AMS Pr., NY.

Suddard, S. Mary. Keats, Shelley & Shakespeare. 1912. $12.50 Hdbd. Folcroft Pr., PA.

Sykess, H. Dugdale. Sidelights on Shakespeare. 1919. $15.00 Hdbd. Folcroft Pr., PA.

Taylor, George C. Shakespeare's Debt to Montaigne. 1968. (1925) $4.00 (ISBN 0-87753-039-4). Phaeton Pr., NY.

Thaler, Alwin. Shakespeare & Democracy. 1941. $6.50 Hdbd. (ISBN 0-87049-001-X). Univ. of Tenn. Pr., TN.

Thaler, Alwin. Shakespeare & Sir Philip Sidney. 1967. (1947) $6.00 Hdbd. Russell & Russell Publ., NY.

Thaler, Alwin. Shakespeare's Silences. (Shakspere's Silences). 1929. $12.50 Hdbd. (ISBN 0-8369-5514-5). Books for Libraries, NY.

Thomas, William J. Three Notelets on Shakespeare. Incl. Shakespeare in Germany; The Folk-Lore of Shakespeare; Was Shakespeare Ever a Soldier. (1865) $7.50 Hdbd. (ISBN 0-404-06423-X). AMS Pr., NY.

Tolman, Albert H. Views About Hamlet & Other Essays. 1904. $16.00 Hdbd. (ISBN 0-404-06477-9). AMS Pr., NY.

Turnbull, H. G. Shakespeare & Ibsen. (Studies in Comparative Literature, No. 35). 1970. (1926) $6.95 Hdbd. (ISBN 0-8383-1019-2). Haskell House Publ., NY.

Waldron, F. G. Shakespearean Miscellany. 1970. (1802) $5.00 Hdbd. (ISBN 0-404-06805-7). AMS Pr., NY.

Warde, Frederick. Fools of Shakespeare. 1923. $17.50 Hdbd. Folcroft Pr., PA.

Watkins, Walter B. Shakespeare & Spenser. 1956. $2.95 pa. (ISBN 0-691-01282-2, 60). Princeton Univ. Pr., NJ.

Weiss, Theodore. Book on Shakespeare. 1970. price "n.g." Hdbd. Atheneum Publ., NY.

Wendell, Barrett. William Shakespeare. (Studies in Shakespeare Ser., No. 24). 1971. lib. bdg. $13.95 Hdbd. (ISBN 0-8383-1254-3). Haskell House Publ., NY.

Whalley, Peter. Enquiry into the Learning of Shakespeare. 1970. (1748) $5.00 Hdbd. (ISBN 0-404-06911-8). AMS Pr., NY.

Wheler, Robert B. History & Antiquities of Stratford-On-Avon. 1806.

$10.00 Hdbd. (ISBN 0-404-06919-3). AMS Pr., NY.

Wickham, Glynne. Shakespeare's Dramatic Heritage: Collected Studies in Mediaeval Tudor & · Shakespearean Drama. 1969. $7.50 Hdbd. Barnes & Noble, NY.

Wilson, Frank P. Shakespearian & Other Studies. Gardner, Helen, ed. 1969. $13.00 Hdbd. (ISBN 0-19-811677-2). Oxford Univ. Pr., NY.

Wilson, John D. Essential Shakespeare. 1932–1960. $2.95 Hdbd.; $1.25 pa. (ISBN 0-521-09110-1, 110). Cambridge Univ. Pr., NY.

Wiseman, Nicholas P. William Shakespeare: A Lecture. 1865. $6.00 Hdbd. (ISBN 0-404-07004-3). AMS Pr., NY.

Woodberry, George E. Great Writers. facs. ed. (Essay Index Reprint Ser). 1907. $8.00 Hdbd. (ISBN 0-8369-1008-7). Books for Libraries, NY.

Wright, Louis B. Shakespeare for Everyman. (Hi-Sch.). $0.90 pa. Washington Sq. Pr., NY.

Wright, Louis B., ed. Shakespeare Celebrated: Anniversary Lectures Delivered at the Folger Library. 1966. $5.00 Hdbd. (ISBN 0-8139-0352-1). Univ. of Va. Pr., VA.

Young, G. M. Shakespeare & the Termers. 1947. $3.50 Hdbd. Folcroft Pr., PA.

Zukofsky, Louis. Bottom: On Shakespeare, Two Vols. 1964. Set—$15.00 Hdbd. (ISBN 0-292-73621-5). Univ. of Tex. Pr., TX.

Illustrations

Boydell, John, ed. Collection of Prints Illustrating the Dramatic Works of Shakespeare, Boydell Shakespeare Prints. 1968. $28.50 Hdbd. Benjamin Blom, NY.

Bridges, Robert. Influence of the Audience on Shakespeare's Drama. 1927. $4.00 Hdbd. Folcroft Pr., PA.

Hartmann, S. Shakespeare in Art. 1901. $17.50 Hdbd. (ISBN 0-404-03152-8). AMS Pr., NY.

Salamon, Malcolm C. Shakespeare in Pictorial Art. $15.75 Hdbd. Benjamin Blom, NY.

Zaidenberg, Arthur. How to Draw Shakespeare's People. 1967. $3.75 Hdbd. Abelard Schuman, NY.

Language

Abbott, Edwin A. Shakespearian Grammar. 3rd ed. 1870. $3.00 pa. (ISBN 0-486-21582-2). Dover Publs. Inc., NY.

Abbott, Edwin A. Shakespearian Grammar. $5.50 Hdbd. Peter Smith Publ., MA.

Bayfield, M. A Study of Shakespeare's Versification. 1920. $25.00 Hdbd. Folcroft Pr., PA.

Byrne, G. Shakespeare's Use of the Pronoun of Address. (Studies in Shakespeare, No. 24). 1970. (1936) $9.95 Hdbd. (ISBN 0-8383-1097-4). Haskell House Publ., NY.

Canliffe, Richard J. New Shakespearian Dictionary Glossary to Shakespeare's

Language. 1910. $17.00 Hdbd. (ISBN 0-404-01377-5). AMS Pr., NY.

Capell, Edward. Notes and Various Readings to Shakespeare. 1970. (1783) $60.00 Hdbd. (ISBN 0-8337-0465-6). Burt Franklin, NY.

Capell, Edward. Notes & Various Readings to Shakespeare, 3 Vols. 1779-83. Set—$97.50 Hdbd. (ISBN 0-404-01400-3). AMS Pr., NY.

Clarke, Charles & Cowden, Mary. Shakespeare Key. 1961. $15.00 Hdbd. (ISBN 0-8044-2127-7). Frederick Ungar, NY.

Cobden-Sanderson, F. Shakespearian Punctuation. (Bibliography & Reference Ser., No. 301). 1970. (1912) $10.00 Hdbd. (ISBN 0-8337-0609-8). Burt Franklin, NY.

Craik, George L. English of Shakespeare. 3rd ed. 1864. $12.50 Hdbd. (ISBN 0-404-01799-1). AMS Pr., NY.

Dyce, Alexander. Glossary of the Works of William Shakespeare. (Library of Literature, Drama & Criticism). 1970. (1902) $25.00 Hdbd. Johnson Reprint Company, NY.

Ekwall, Eilert. Shakespeare's Vocabulary: Its Etymological Elements. 1903. $8.50 Hdbd. (ISBN 0-404-02269-3). AMS Pr., NY.

Gordon, George S. Shakespeare's English. 1928. $13.50 Hdbd. (ISBN 0-404-02866-7). AMS Pr., NY.

Hart, Alfred. Shakespeare & the Homilies. 1970. (1934) $8.50 Hdbd. Octagon Books Inc., NY.

Hart, Alfred. Shakespeare & the Homilies. 1934. $10.44 Hdbd. (ISBN 0-404-03138-2). AMS Pr., NY.

Jakobson, Roman & Jones, L. G. Shakespeare's Verbal Art in Th'Expence of Spirit. (De Proprietatibus Litterarum, Series Practica, No. 35). 1970. $3.25 pa. Humanities Pr., NY.

Kokeritz, Helge. Shakespeare's Names: A Pronuncing Dictionary. 1959. $5.00 Hdbd. (ISBN 0-300-00637-3). Yale Univ. Pr., CT.

Kokeritz, Helge. Shakespeare's Pronunciation. 1953. $10.00 Hdbd. (ISBN 0-300-00638-1). Yale Univ. Pr., CT.

Lanier, Sidney. Shakespeare & His Forerunners, 2 Vols. fasc. ed. 1902. $25.00 Hdbd. (ISBN 0-404-03875-1). AMS Pr., NY.

Muir, Kenneth, ed. Shakespeare Survey, No. 23 Shakespeare's Language. 1970. $10.00 Hdbd. (ISBN 0-521-07903-9). Cambridge Univ. Pr., NY.

Price, H. T. Construction in Shakespeare. 1951. $5.50 Hdbd. Folcroft Pr., PA.

Rushton, William L. Shakespeare's Euphuism. 1871. $6.50 Hdbd. (ISBN 0-404-05454-4). AMS Pr., NY.

Simpson, Percy. Shakespearian Punctuation. 1911. $5.00 Hdbd. (ISBN 0-19-811135-5). Oxford Univ. Pr., NY.

Vietor, Wilhelm. Shakespeare's Pronunciation, Two. 1906. $9.00 Hdbd. (ISBN 0-404-06765-4). AMS Pr., NY.

Walker, William S. Critical Examination of the Text of Shakespeare, 3 Vols. 1860. Set—$47.50 Hdbd. (ISBN 0-404-06810-3). AMS Pr., NY.

Wilson, Frank P. Shakespeare & the Diction of Common Life. 1941. $3.00 Hdbd. Folcroft Pr., PA.

Windolph, Francis. Reflections of the Law in Literature. (Essay Index Reprint Ser). $6.00 Hdbd. (ISBN 0-8369-1739-1). Books for Libraries, NY.

Literary Influence

Brewer, Wilmon. Shakespeare's Influence on Sir Walter Scott. 1925. $18.50 Hdbd. (ISBN 0-404-01075-X). AMS Pr., NY.

Cohn, Albert. Shakespeare in Germany. (Studies in Shakespeare, No. 24). 1971. $29.95 Hdbd. (ISBN 0-8383-1330-2). Haskell House, NY.

Fleissner, Robert F. Dickens & Shakespeare: A Study in Histrionic Contrasts. (Studies in Comparative Literature Ser., No. 35). 1969. (1965) $10.95 Hdbd. (ISBN 0-8383-0549-0). Haskell House, NY.

Fox, C. A. Notes on William Shakespeare & Robert Tofte. 1957. $4.00 Hdbd. Folcroft Pr., PA.

Frost, D. L. School of Shakespeare: The Influence of Shakespeare on English Drama, 1600–42. 1968. $9.50 Hdbd. Cambridge Univ. Pr., NY.

Herford, Charles H. Post-War Mind of Germany & Other Studies. 1927. $12.50 Hdbd. Folcroft Pr., PA.

Joachimi-Dege, Marie. Deutsche Shakespeare—Probleme im 18. Jahrhundert und im Zeitalter der Romantik. (1907) $16.50 Hdbd. (ISBN 0-8337-4955-2). Burt Franklin, NY.

Jusserand, J. J. Shakespeare in France Under the Ancient Regime. 1899. $20.00 Hdbd. (ISBN 0-8337-4195-0). Burt Franklin, NY.

McGinn, Donald J. Shakespeare's Influence on the Drama of His Age. 1965. $8.50 Hdbd. Octagon, NY.

McKeithan, Daniel M. Debt to Shakespeare in Beaumont & Fletcher Plays. 1970. $7.50 text ed. (ISBN 0-87752-070-4). Gordian Pr., NY.

McKeithan, Daniel M. Debt to Shakespeare in the Beaumont & Fletcher Plays. 1970. Repr. of 1938 ed. $9.50 text ed. (ISBN 0-404-04134-5). AMS Pr., NY.

Music

Boustead, Alan. Music to Shakespeare: A practical Catalogue of Current Incidental Music, Song Settings & Other Related Music. 1964. $3.00 pa. (ISBN 0-19-519115-3). Oxford Univ. Pr., NY.

Bridge, John Frederick. Shakespearean Music in the Plays & Early Operas. (Studies in Shakespeare Ser., No. 24). 1969. (1923) $8.35 Hdbd. (ISBN 0-8383-0513-X). Haskell House, NY.

Bridge, John Frederick. O Mistress Mine: Shakespearean Music in the Plays & Early Operas. 1923. $6.50 Hdbd. (ISBN 0-404-07808-7). AMS Pr., NY.

Brooke, Tucker, ed. Shakespeare Songs. 1929. $12.50 Hdbd. Lansdowne Pr., PA.

Chambers, Henry A. & Hunt, Edgar. Shakespeare Song Book, Recorder Ed. $1.00 Hdbd.; $1.00 pa. (ISBN 0-87597-011-7). Crescendo Publ., MA.

Elson, Louis C. Shakespeare in Music. 1901. $17.50 Hdbd. (ISBN 0-404-02323-1). AMS Pr., NY.

Elson, Louis C. Shakespeare in Music: A Collation of the Chief Musical Allusions in the Plays of Shakespeare, with an Attempt at Their Explanation & Derivation, Together with Much of the Original Music. (Select Bibliographies Reprint Ser). 1900. $14.50 Hdbd. (ISBN 0-8369-5257-X). Books for Libraries, NY.

Harbage, Alfred, ed. Songs from Shakespeare. 1970. $5.95 Hdbd. (ISBN 0-8255-4110-7). Macrae Smith, PA.

Hartnol, Phyllis, ed. Shakespeare in Music. 1964. $10.50 Hdbd. St. Martin's Pr., NY.

Kines, Tom, ed. Songs from Shakespeare's Plays & Popular Songs of Shakespeare's Time. 1964. $2.45 pa. (ISBN 0-8256-0068-5). Oak Publ., NY.

Knight, George W. Shakespearean Tempest. 3rd ed. 1968. $6.75 Hdbd. Barnes & Noble, NY.

Lawrence, William J. Elizabethan Playhouse & Other Studies, 2 Vols. 1963. (1912–13) Set—$15.00 Hdbd. Russell & Russell, NY.

Long, John H. Shakespeare's Use of Music, 3 vols. Incl. Vol. 1. A/Study of the Music & Its Performance in the Original Production of Seven Comedies. 1955. $5.50 Hdbd. (ISBN 0-8130-0145-5); Vol. 2. The/Final Comedies. 1961. $5.50 Hdbd. (ISBN 0-8130-0146-3); Vol. 3. The/Histories & Tragedies. 1971. $11.00 Hdbd. (ISBN 0-8130-0311-3). Univ. of Fla. Pr., FL.

Moncure-Sime, A. H. Shakespeare: His Music & Song. $10.75 Hdbd. Benjamin Blom, NY.

Naylor, Edward W. Shakespeare & Music. 1896. $7.50 Hdbd. (ISBN 0-404-04652-5). AMS Pr., NY.

Naylor, Edward W. Shakespeare & Music. 2nd ed. $7.50 Hdbd. Benjamin Blom, NY.

Naylor, Edward W. Shakespeare & Music. (Music Ser). 1965. $7.50 Hdbd. (ISBN 0-306-70908-2). Plenum Publ., NY.

Noble, Richmond. Shakespeare's Use of Song. 1923. $4.00 Hdbd. Ridgeway Bks., PA.

Noble, Richmond. Shakespeare's Use of Song. 1923. $5.00 Hdbd. (ISBN 0-19-811640-3). Oxford Univ. Pr., NY.

Roberts, W. Wright. Music in Shakespeare. 1923. $4.00 Hdbd. Folcroft Pr., PA.

Seng, Peter J. Vocal Songs in the Plays of Shakespeare: A Critical History. 1967. $8.95 Hdbd. (ISBN 0-674-94155-1). Harvard Univ. Pr., MA.

Sternfeld, F. W. Music in Shakespearean Tragedy. 1963. $10.00 Hdbd. (ISBN 0-486-21130-4). Dover, NY.

Vincent, Charles J., ed. Fifty Shakespearian Songs. 1906. $12.50 Hdbd. (ISBN 0-404-06767-0). AMS Pr., NY.

Philosophy & Psychology

Anderson, Ruth L. Elizabethan Psychology & Shakespeare's Plays. 1966. (1927) $7.50 Hdbd. Russell & Russell, NY.

Bacon, Delia S. Philosophy of the Plays of Shakespeare Unfolded. 1970. $24.50 Hdbd. (ISBN 0-404-00443-1). AMS Pr., NY.

Birch, William J. Inquiry into the Philosophy & Religion of Shakspere. 1848. $25.00 Hdbd. (ISBN 0-404-00868-2). AMS Pr., NY.

Bucknill, John C. Psychology of Shakespeare. 1859. $12.50 Hdbd. (ISBN 0-404-01147-0). AMS Pr., NY.

Campbell, Lily B. Shakespeare's Tragic Heroes. 1960. $4.00 Hdbd.; $1.95 pa. (ISBN 0-389-01758-2, 433). Barnes & Noble, NY.

Curry, Walter C. Shakespeare's Philosophical Patterns. $4.50 Hdbd. Peter Smith, MA.

Feis, Jacob. Shakespere & Montaigne. 1970. (1884) $8.50 Hdbd. (ISBN 0-404-02375-4). AMS Pr., NY.

Herford, Charles H. Normality of Shakespeare: Illustrated in His Treatment of Love & Marriage. 1920. $4.00 Hdbd. Folcroft Pr., PA.

Moulton, Richard G. Moral System of Shakespeare. 1903. $20.00 Hdbd. Folcroft Pr., PA.

Robertson, John M. Montaigne & Shakespeare & Other Essays on Cognate Questions. (Studies in Comparative Literature Ser., No. 35). 1969. (1897) $15.95 Hdbd. (ISBN 0-8383-0234-3). Haskell House, NY.

Robertson, John M. Montaigne & Shakespeare & Other Essays on Cognate Questions. (Research & Source Works Ser., No. 411). 1970. (1909) $16.50 Hdbd. (ISBN 0-8337-3022-3). Burt Franklin, NY.

Snider, Denton J. System of Shakespeare's Dramas, 2 Vols. 1877. $27.00 Hdbd. (ISBN 0-404-06139-7). AMS Pr., NY.

Vyvyan, John. Shakespeare & Platonic Beauty. 1970. $5.00 Hdbd. (ISBN 0-389-01123-1). Barnes & Noble, NY.

Political and Social Views

Bloom, Allan D. & Jaffa, Harry V. Shakespeare's Politics. 1964. $5.95 Hdbd. (ISBN 0-465-07762-5). Basic, NY.

Charlton, Henry B. Shakespeare: Politics & Politicians. 1929. $4.00 Hdbd. Folcroft Pr., NY.

De Selincourt, Ernest. English Poets & the National Ideal. 1915. $8.50 Hdbd. Folcroft Pr., PA.

Farnam, Henry W. Shakespeare's Economics. 1931. $17.50 Hdbd. Folcroft Pr., PA.

Gayley, Charles M. Shakespeare & the Founders of Liberty in America. 1917. $20.00 Hdbd. Folcroft Pr., PA.

Jameson, Thomas H. Hidden Shakespeare: A Study of the Poet's Undercover Dramatic Activity in the Theatre. 1967. $4.95 Hdbd. $2.95 pa. Funk & Wagnalls, NY.

Knights, L. C. Shakespeare's Politics. 1957. $3.50 Hdbd. Folcroft Pr., PA.

Muir, Edwin. Politics of King Lear. 1947. $4.00 Hdbd. Folcroft Pr., PA.

Phillips, James E., Jr. State in Shakespeare's Greek & Roman Plays. 1971. (1940) $9.75 Hdbd. (ISBN 0-374-96427-0). Octagon Books, NY.

Phillips, James E., Jr. State in Shakespeare's Greek & Roman Plays. 1940. $20.00 Hdbd. Ridgeway Books, PA.

Raleigh, Walter. Shakespeare & England. 1918. $3.00 Hdbd. Folcroft Pr., PA.

Stirling, Brents. Populace in Shakespeare. 1949. $10.00 Hdbd. (ISBN 0-404-06277-6). AMS Pr., NY.

Talbert, Ernest W. Problem of Order. 1962. $7.50 Hdbd. (ISBN 0-8078-0856-3). Univ. of N.C. Pr., NC.

Prosody

Bathhurst, Charles. Remarks on the Differences in Shakespeare's Versifica-

tion in Different Periods of His Life. 1970. (1857) $10.00 Hdbd. (ISBN 0-404-00692-2). AMS Pr., NY.

Bayfield, Matthew A. Study of Shakespeare's Versification. 1920. $25.00 Hdbd. Folcroft Pr., PA.

Bayfield, Matthew A. Study of Shakespeare's Versification, with an Inquiry into the Trustworthiness of the Early Texts. 1920. $20.00 Hdbd. (ISBN 0-404-00695-7). AMS Pr., NY.

Brown, George H. Notes on Shakespeare's Versification. 2nd ed. 1886. $5.00 Hdbd. (ISBN 0-404-01138-1). AMS Pr., NY.

Chambers, David L. Metre of Macbeth. 1903. $5.00 Hdbd. (ISBN 0-404-01443-7). AMS Pr., NY and $10.00 Hdbd. Folcroft Pr., PA.

David, Richard. Janus of Poets (Being an Essay on the Dramatic Value of Shakspere's Poetry Both Good & Bad. (Select Bibliographies Reprint Ser). 1935. $8.50 Hdbd. (ISBN 0-8369-5253-7). Books for Libraries, NY.

David, Richard. Janus of Poets: Being an Essay on the Dramatic Value of Shakespeare's Poetry Both Good & Bad. (1935) $8.50 Hdbd. (ISBN 0-404-01939-0). AMS Pr., NY.

Furnivall, Frederick J., ed. Succession of Shakespeare's Works. 1874. $5.00 Hdbd. (ISBN 0-404-02663-X). AMS Pr., NY.

Halliday, Frank E. Poetry of Shakespeare's Plays. 1964. $1.50 pa. (ISBN

0-389-02353-1, 51, UP). Barnes & Noble, NY.

Ness, Frederic W. Use of Rhyme in Shakespeare's Plays. (Yale Studies in English No. 95). 1969. (1941) $5.00 Hdbd. Shoe String Pr., CT.

Sipe, Dorothy L. Shakespeare's Metrics. (Studies in English No. 167). 1968. $8.50 Hdbd. (ISBN 0-300-00955-0). Yale Univ. Pr., CT.

Van Dam, Bastiaan A. & Stoffel, Cornelius O. William Shakespeare, Prosody & Text. 1900. $15.00 Hdbd. (ISBN 0-404-06752-2). AMS Pr., NY.

Quotations

Baten, Anderson M. Slang from Shakespeare. 1931. $10.00 Hdbd. Folcroft Pr., PA.

Lewis, William D. Shakespeare Said It: Topical Quotations from the Works of Shakespeare, Selected & Annotated. 1961. $6.50 Hdbd. (ISBN 0-8156-8000-7). Syracuse Univ. Pr., NY.

McGovern, Ann, ed. Shakespearean Sallies, Sullies & Slanders: Insults for All Occasions. (Jr Hi.). 1969. $3.95 Hdbd. (ISBN 0-690-73092-6). Thomas Y. Crowell, NY.

Quennell, Peter. Shakespeare Quotations. 1971. $8.95 Hdbd. (ISBN 0-8238-0098-9). Plays, Inc., MA.

Schmidt, Alexander. Shakespeare Lexicon & Quotation Dictionary, 2 Vols. 1902. $6.25 pa. (ISBN 0-486-22726-X) (ISBN 0-486-22727-8). Dover Publ., NY.

Stevenson's Book of Shakespeare Quotations. 1971. $35.00 Hdbd. (ISBN 0-8277-0539-5). British Book Center, NY.

Religion and Philosophy

Battenhouse, Roy W. Shakespearean Tragedy: Its Art & Its Christian Premises. 1969. $15.00 Hdbd. (ISBN 0-253-18090-2). Ind. Univ. Pr., IN.

Birch, William J. Inquiry into the Philosophy & Religion of Shakespeare 1848. $25.00 Hdbd. (ISBN 0-404-00868-2). AMS Pr., NY.

Brown, James B. Bible Truths with Shakespearian Parallels. 4th ed. 1879. $10.00 Hdbd. (ISBN 0-404-01136-5). AMS Pr., NY.

Bryant, Joseph A., Jr. Hippolyta's View: Some Christian Aspects of Shakespeare's Plays. 1961. $6.50 Hdbd. (ISBN 0-8131-1057-2). Univ. Pr. of Ky., KY.

Bullock, Charles. Shakespeare's Debt to the Bible. 1870. $6.50 Hdbd. Folcroft Pr., PA.

Burgess, William. Bible in Shakespeare. $10.00 Hdbd. Gordon Publ., NY.

Carter, Thomas. Shakespeare & Holy Scripture. 1970. (1905) $22.50 Hdbd. (ISBN 0-404-01398-8). AMS Pr., NY.

Carter, Thomas. Shakespeare, Puritan & Recusant. (1970) $10.00 Hdbd. (ISBN 0-404-01397-X). AMS Pr., NY.

Clark, C. Shakespeare & the Supernatural. (Studies in Shakespeare Ser., No. 24). 1970. (1931) $11.95 Hdbd.

(ISBN 0-8383-0966-6). Haskell House Publ., NY.

De Groot, John H. Shakespeare & the Old Faith. (Essay Index Reprint Ser). 1946. $9.75 Hdbd. (ISBN 0-8369-0368-4). Books for Libraries, NY.

Eaton, Thomas R. Shakespeare & the Bible. 1860. $10.00 Hdbd. (ISBN 0-404-02237-5). AMS Pr., NY.

Fitch, Robert E. Shakespeare: The Perspective of Value. 1969. $6.95 Hdbd. (ISBN 0-664-20864-9); $3.50 pa. (ISBN 0-664-24853-5). Westminster Pr., PA.

Frye, Roland M. Shakespeare & Christian Doctrine. 1963. $2.95 pa. (ISBN 0-691-06117-3) (ISBN 0-691-01283-0). Princeton Univ. Pr., NJ.

Griffith, Elizabeth. Morality of Shakespeare's Drama. 1971. (1775) $24.50 Hdbd. (ISBN 0-404-02917-5). AMS Pr., NY.

Griffith, Elizabeth. Morality of Shakespeare's Drama Illustrated, 1970. (1775) $34.00 Hdbd. Augustus M. Kelley, NY.

Harbage, Alfred. As They Liked It: A Study of Shakespeare's Moral Artistry. $5.00 Hdbd. Peter Smith Publ., MA.

Howse, Ernest M. Spiritual Values in Shakespeare. (Series S). 1965. $1.25 pa. (ISBN 0-687-39253-5, Apex). Abingdon Pr., NY.

Kelly, Henry A. Divine Providence in the England of Shakespeare's Histories. 1970. $10.00 Hdbd. (ISBN 0-674-21292-4). Harvard Univ. Pr., MA.

Knight, George Wilson. Shakespeare & Religion: Essays of Forty Years. 1968. $2.95 pa. Simon & Schuster, NY.

Knight, George Wilson. Shakespeare & Religion. 1967. $8.50 Hdbd. Barnes & Noble, NY.

Masefield, John. Shakespeare & Spiritual Life. 1924. $4.00 Hdbd. Ridgeway Books, PA.

Moulton, Richard G. Moral System of Shakespeare. 1903. $20.00 Hdbd. Folcroft Pr., PA·

Mutschmann, Heinrich & Wentersdorf, Karl. Shakespeare & Catholicism. 1970. (1952) $10.00 Hdbd. (ISBN 0-404-04547-2). AMS Pr., NY.

Noble, Richmond. Shakespeare's Biblical Knowledge. 1935. $8.50 Hdbd. Ridgeway Books, PA.

Rees, J. Shakespeare & the Bible. 1876. $10.00 Hdbd. (ISBN 0-404-05235-5). AMS Pr., NY.

Sharp, F. Shakespeare's Portrayal of Moral Life. (Studies in Shakespeare, No. 24). 1970. (1902) $9.95 Hdbd. (ISBN 0-8383-1069-9). Haskell House Publ., NY.

Simpson, Richard. Religion of Shakespeare. Bowden, Henry S., ed. 1899. $17.50 Hdbd. (ISBN 0-404-00961-1). AMS Pr., NY.

Stauffer, Donald A. Shakespeare's World of Images: The Development of His Moral Ideas. 1966. $2.95 pa. (ISBN 0-253-20087-3). Ind. Univ. Pr., IN.

Vyvyan, John. Shakespearean Ethic.

1968. $4.00 Hdbd. Barnes & Noble, NY.

West, Robert H. Shakespeare & the Outer Mystery. 1968. $6.50 Hdbd. (ISBN 0-8131-1166-8). Univ. Pr. of Ky., KY.

Whitaker, Virgil K. Mirror up to Nature: The Technique of Shakespeare's Tragedies. 1965. $7.50 Hdbd. Huntington Library, CA.

Wordsworth, Charles. Shakespeare's Knowledge & Use of the Bible. 1880. $18.00 Hdbd. (ISBN 0-404-07039-6). AMS Pr., NY.

Sources

Alden, Raymond M. Shakespeare Handbook. Campbell, Oscar J., ed. (Select Bibliographies Reprint Ser). 1932. $11.00 Hdbd. (ISBN 0-8369-5248-0). Books for Libraries, NY.

Anders, Henry R. Shakespeare's Books. 1904. $12.50 Hdbd. (ISBN 0-404-00355-9). AMS Pr., NY.

Baldwin, Thomas W. On the Literary Genetics of Shakspere's Plays, 1592–1594. 1959. $10.50 Hdbd. (ISBN 0-252-72587-5). Univ. of Ill. Pr., IL.

Boecker, Alexander. Probable Italian Source of Shakespeare's Julius Caesar. 1913. $7.50 Hdbd. (ISBN 0-404-00918-2). AMS Pr., NY.

Boswell-Stone, W. G. Shakespeare's Holinshed. 1967. $8.75 Hdbd. Benjamin Blom, NY.

Broke, Arthur. Brooke's Romeus & Juliet, Being the Original of Shakespeare's Romeo & Juliet. Munro, J. J., ed. 1970. (1908) $6.00 Hdbd. (ISBN 0-404-04539-1). AMS Pr., NY.

Bullough, Geoffrey, ed. Narrative & Dramatic Sources of Shakespeare, 6 vols. Incl. Vol. 1. Early Comedies, Poems, Romeo & Juliet. 1957. (ISBN 0-231-08891-4); Vol. 2. The Comedies, 1597–1603. 1958. (ISBN 0-231-08892-2); Vol. 3. Earlier English History Plays: Henry Fifth, Richard Third, Richard Second. 1960. (ISBN 0-231-08893-0); Vol. 4. Later English History Plays: King John, Henry Fourth, Henry Fifth, Henry Eighth. 1962. (ISBN 0-231-08894-9); Vol. 5. The Roman Plays: Julius Caesar, Antony & Cleopatra, Coriolanus. 1964. (ISBN 0-231-08895-7); Vol. 6. Other Classical Plays: Titus Adronicus, Troilus & Cressida, Timon of Athens, Pericles, Prince of Tyre. 1966. (ISBN 0-231-08896-5). $12.50 Hdbd. Columbia Univ. Pr., NY.

Campbell, Lily B. Mirror for Magistrates. (1970) $15.00 Hdbd. (ISBN 0-389-01755-8). Barnes & Noble, NY.

Capell, Edward. Notes and Various Readings to Shakespeare. 1970. (1783) Set—$60.00 text ed. (ISBN 0-8337-0465-6). Burt Franklin, NY.

Capell, Edward. Notes & Various Readings to Shakespeare, 3 Vols. 1779–83. Set—$97.50 Hdbd. (ISBN 0-404-01400-3). AMS Pr., NY.

Chalmers, George. Another Account of the Incidents from Which the Title &

Part of Shakespeare's Tempest Were Derived. 1815. $6.00 Hdbd. (ISBN 0-404-01442-9). AMS Pr., NY.

Chambers, E. K. Sources for a Biography of Shakespeare. 1946. $3.50 Hdbd. (ISBN 0-19-811698-5). Oxford Univ. Pr., NY.

Charlton, Henry B. Romeo & Juliet: As an Experimental Tragedy. 1939. $5.00 Hdbd. Folcroft Pr., PA.

Collier, John Payne. Shakespeare's Library: A Collection of the Romances, Novels, Poems & Histories Used by Shakespeare As The Foundations Of His Dramas. (1971) price "n.g." Hdbd. (ISBN 0-87817-062-6). Hacker Art Books, NY.

Evans, G. Blakemore, ed. Smock Alley Macbeth, Vol. 5. (Shakespearean Prompt-Books of the Seventeenth Century). 1970 (ISBN 0-8139-0301-7). $25.00 pa. Univ. Pr. of Va., VA.

Gollancz, Israel, ed. Sources of Hamlet, with an Essay on Legend. 1967. $9.50 Hdbd. Octagon Books, NY.

Green, Henry. Shakespeare & the Emblem Writers. 1967. (1817) $19.50 Hdbd. (ISBN 0-8337-1440-6). Burt Franklin, NY.

Griffin, Alice V., ed. Sources of Ten Shakespearean Plays. 1966. $4.95 pa. (ISBN 0-690-75506-6). Thomas Y. Crowell, NY.

Halliwell-Phillips, James O. Memoranda on the Tragedy of Hamlet. 1879.

$6.50 Hdbd. (ISBN 0-404-03081-5). AMS Pr., NY.

Hankins, John E. Shakespeare's Derived Imagery. (1967) $8.50 Hdbd. Octagon Books, NY.

Hansen, George P. Legend of Hamlet, Prince of Denmark. 1887. $5.00 Hdbd. (ISBN 0-404-03105-6). AMS Pr., NY.

Hart, Alfred. Shakespeare & the Homilies. 1934. $10.44 Hdbd. (ISBN 0-404-03138-2). AMS Pr., NY.

Hart, Alfred. Shakespeare & the Homilies. 1970. (1934) $8.50 Hdbd. Octagon Books, NY.

Hazlitt, William C., ed. Shakespeare Jest Books, 3 Vols. 1964. $35.00 Hdbd. (ISBN 0-8337-1634-4). Burt Franklin, NY.

Holinshed, Raphael. Shakespeare's Holinshed: The Chronicle & Plays Compared. Boswell-Stone, W. G., ed. $2.95 pa. (ISBN 0-846-21941-0). Dover Publ., NY.

Holinshed, Raphael. Holinshed's Chronicle As Used in Shakespeare's Plays. $2.95 Hdbd. (ISBN 0-460-00800-5, Evman). E. P. Dutton, NY.

Hosley, Richard, ed. Shakespeare's Holinshed. (Illus.). 1969. (1968) $2.45 pa. G. P. Putnam's Sons, NY.

Lawson, W. A. Shakespeare's Wit & Humor. 1912. $17.50 Hdbd. Folcroft Pr., PA.

Lennox, C. Shakespeare Illustrated, 3 Vols. 1753–54. Set—$42.50 Hdbd. (ISBN 0-404-03970-7). AMS Pr., NY.

Lewis, Charlton M. Genesis of Hamlet. (1967) $6.00 Hdbd. (ISBN 0-8046-0272-7). Kennikat Pr., NY.

Muir, Kenneth. Shakespeare As Collaborator. 1960. $2.50 Hdbd. Barnes & Noble, NY.

Noble, Richmond. Shakespeare's Biblical Knowledge & Use of the Book of Common Prayer. (1970) $9.50 Hdbd. Octagon Books, NY.

Oesterley, Hermann, ed. Shakespeare's Jest Book, 1866: An Edition of a Hundred Mery Talys, 1529. 1970. $10.00 Hdbd. (ISBN 0-8201-1083-3). Scholars Facsimiles & Reprints, FL.

Ovid. Shakespeare's Ovid: A Translation of the Metamorphoses. Rouse, W. H., ed. Golding, Arthur, tr. 1962. $19.50 Hdbd. (ISBN 0-8093-0062-1, Centaur). Southern Ill. Univ. Pr., IL.

Perrett, Wilfred. Story of King Lear from Geoffrey of Monmouth to Shakespeare. (1904) $19.00 Hdbd.; $17.00 pa. Johnson Reprint Corp., NY.

Pollard, A. W. Foundations of Shakespeare's Text. 1923. $4.00 Hdbd. Ridgeway Books, PA.

Potts, Abbie F. Shakespeare & the Faerie Queene. 1958. $12.00 Hdbd. (ISBN 0-8371-1156-0). Greenwood Pr., CT.

Proescholdt, Ludwig. On the Sources of Shakespeare's Midsummer Night's Dream. 1878. $5.00 Hdbd. (ISBN 0-404-05137-5). AMS Pr., NY.

Robertson, John M. Montaigne & Shakespeare & Other Essays on Cognate Questions. (Research & Source Works Ser., No. 411). 1970. (1909) $16.50 Hdbd. (ISBN 0-8337-3022-3). Burt Franklin, NY.

Robertson, John M. Montaigne & Shakespeare & Other Essays on Cognate Questions. (Studies in Comparative Literature Ser., No. 35). 1969. (1897) $15.95 Hdbd. (ISBN 0-8383-0234-3). Haskell House Publ., NY.

Rogers, William H. Shakespeare & English History. 1966. $4.95 Hdbd.; $1.75 pa. Rowman and Littlefield, NY.

Satin, Joseph. Shakespeare & His Sources. 1967. $5.50 pa. Houghton-Mifflin, NY.

Sidgwick, Frank. Sources & Analogues of a Midsummer Night's Dream. 1908. $10.00 Hdbd. (ISBN 0-404-05994-5). AMS Pr., NY.

Singer, S. W. Shakespeare's Jest Book. 1814. $10.00 Hdbd. (ISBN 0-404-06094-3). AMS Pr., NY.

Skeat, Walter W. Shakespeare's Plutarch. 1904. $15.00 Hdbd. (ISBN 0-404-06097-8). AMS Pr., NY.

Spencer, T. J., ed. Shakespeare's Plutarch. 1968. $1.75 pa. (ISBN 0-14-053004-5, SL4). Penguin Books, MD.

Taylor, George C. Shakespeare's Debt to Montaigne. 1925. $7.50 Hdbd. Folcroft Pr., PA.

Taylor, John E. Moor of Venice: Cinthio's Tale & Shakespeare's Tragedy.

1855. $5.00 Hdbd. (ISBN 0-404-06355-1). AMS Pr., NY.

Taylor, Marion A. New Look at the Old Sources of Hamlet. (Studies in English Literature Vol, 42). 1969. $5.00 Hdbd. (68-17895). Humanities Pr., NY.

Tuckerbrooke, C. F. Shakespeare's Plutarch: Study of the Sources of Julius Caesar, Anthony & Cleopatra, & Coriolanus. (Studies in Shakespeare Ser., No. 24). 1969. (1909) $19.95 Hdbd. (ISBN 0-8383-0516-4). Haskell House Publ., NY.

Whitaker, Virgil K. Shakespeare's Use of Learning: An Inquiry into the Growth of His Mind & Art. 1953. $7.50 Hdbd. Huntington Library, CA.

Stagecraft

Beckerman, B. Shakespeare at the Globe, 1599-1609. 1962. $5.95 Hdbd.; $1.95 pa. Macmillan, NY.

Brown, John R. Shakespeare's Plays in Performance. 1967. $8.50 Hdbd. St. Martin's Pr., NY.

Brown, John R. Shakespeare's Plays in Performance. (Orig.). 1969. $1.75 pa. (ISBN 0-14-053007-X). Penguin, MD.

Hosley, Richard. Use of the Upper Stage in Romeo & Juliet. 1954. $3.50 Hdbd. Folcroft Pr., PA.

Joseph, Bertram. Acting Shakespeare. 1969. (1960) $2.25 pa. Theatre Arts, NY.

Kelly, F. M. Shakespearian Costume 2nd rev. ed. Mansfield, A., ed. 1970.

$8.75 Hdbd. (ISBN 0-87830-117-8). Theatre Arts, NY.

Matthews, Brander. Shakespeare as a Playwright. 1970. (1913) $12.50 Hdbd. (ISBN 0-404-04269-4). AMS Pr., NY.

Rannie, David W. Scenery in Shakespeare's Plays & Other Studies. 1926. $32.00 Hdbd. (ISBN 0-404-05225-8). AMS Pr., NY.

Shattuck, Charles H. Shakespeare Promptbooks: A Descriptive Catalogue. 1965. $15.00 Hdbd. (ISBN 0-252-72646-4). Univ. of Ill. Pr., IL.

Sprague, Arthur C. Shakespeare & the Actors, 1660-1905. 1963. (1944) $11.50 Hdbd. Russell & Russell, NY.

Sprague, Arthur C. Stage Business in Shakespeare's Plays. 1954. $3.00 Hdbd. Folcroft Pr., PA.

Squire, John. Shakespeare As a Dramatist. (Studies in Shakespeare Ser., No. 24). 1971. $9.95 Hdbd. (ISBN 0-8383-1221-7). Haskell House Publ., NY.

Styan, J. L. Shakespeare's Stagecraft. 1967. $8.50 Hdbd.; $2.65 pa. (ISBN 0-521-09435-6, 435). Cambridge Univ. Pr., NY.

Webster, Margaret. Shakespeare Today. 1957. $4.95 Hdbd. Dufour Eds., PA.

Stage History

Albright, Victor E. Shakesperian Stage. 1926. $9.00 Hdbd. (ISBN 0-404-00304-4). AMS Pr., NY.

Alleyn, Edward. Alleyn Pa rs: Illustrative of the Early English Stage. 1970. (1843) $6.00 Hdbd. (ISBN 0-404-00329-X). AMS Pr., NY.

Baker, George P. Development of Shakespeare as a Dramatist. 1907. $15.00 Hdbd. (ISBN 0-404-00467-9). AMS Pr., NY.

Baldwin, Thomas W. Organization & Personnel of the Shakespearean Company. 1961. (1927) $15.00 Hdbd. Russell & Russell Publ., NY.

Bartholomeusz, Dennis S. Macbeth & the Players. 1969. $11.50 Hdbd. Cambridge Univ. Pr., NY.

Beckerman, B. Shakespeare at the Globe, 1599–1609. 1962. $5.95 Hdbd.; $1.95 pa. Macmillan Co., NY.

Boas, Frederick S. Shakespeare & the Universities. 1923. $12.50 Hdbd. Benjamin Blom, NY.

Bradbrook, Muriel C. Elizabethan Stage Conditions: A Study of Their Place in the Interpretation of Shakespeare's Plays. 1968. $4.95 Hdbd.; $1.65 pa. (ISBN 0-521-09539-5, 539). Cambridge Univ. Pr., NY.

Brennecke, Ernest & Brennecke, Henry. Shakespeare in Germany, 1590–1700, with Translations of Five Early Plays. 1964. $7.50 Hdbd. (ISBN 0-226-07381-5). Univ. of Chicago Pr., IL.

Brown, John R. Shakespeare's Plays in Performance. 1967. $8.50 Hdbd. St. Martin's Pr., NY.

Brown, John R. Shakespeare's Plays in Performance. 1969. $1.75 pa. (ISBN 0-14-053007-X, SL7). Penguin, MD.

Buell, William A. Hamlets of the Theater. 1965. $12.50 Hdbd. (ISBN 0-8392-1158-9). Astor-Honor, NY.

Burnim, Kalman A. David Garrick, Director. 1961. $5.95 Hdbd. (ISBN 0-8229-3013-7). Univ. of Pittsburgh Pr., PA.

Calmour, Alfred C. Fact & Fiction About Shakespeare. 1894. $22.50 Hdbd. (ISBN 0-404-01365-1). AMS Pr., NY.

Chambers, Edmund K. Elizabethan Stage, 4 Vols. 1923. Set--$38.50 Hdbd. (ISBN 0-19-811511-3). Oxford Univ. Pr., NY.

Chambers, Edmund K. William Shakespeare: A Study of Facts & problems, 2 Vols. 1930. Set—$16.00 Hdbd. (ISBN 0-19-811513-X). Oxford Univ. Pr., NY.

Child, Harold H. Shakespearian Productions of John Philip Kemble. 1935. $5.00 Hdbd. (ISBN 0-404-07847-8). AMS Pr., NY.

Collier, John Payne. Memoirs of the Principal Actors in the Plays of Shakespeare. 1846. $15.00 Hdbd. (ISBN 0-404-01599-9). AMS Pr., NY.

Creizenach, Wilhelm. English Drama in the Age of Shakespeare. rev ed. Schuster, Alfred, ed. Hugon, Cecile, tr. 1967. (1916) $15.00 Hdbd. Russell & Russell, NY.

David, Richard. Shakespeare & the

Players. 1961. $3.50 Hdbd. Folcroft Pr., PA.

Davies, Thomas. Dramatic Miscellanies; on several plays of Shakespeare. 3 Vols. 1784. $27.50 Hdbd. Benjamin Blom, NY.

Davies, Thomas. Dramatic Miscellanies—on Several Plays of Shakespeare, 3 Vols. 1783-84. Set—$27.50 Hdbd. AMS Pr., NY.

Dunn, Esther C. Shakespeare in America. 1968. $12.50 Hdbd. Benjamin Blom, NY.

Gaw, Allison. Origin & Development of One Henry Sixth in Relation to Shakespeare, Marlowe, Peele & Greene. 1926. $9.50 Hdbd. (ISBN 0-404-02689-3). AMS Pr., NY.

Graves, Thornton S. Court & the London Theatres During the Reign of Elizabeth. 1967. (1913) $6.00 Hdbd. Russell & Russell, NY.

Guizot, Francois P., ed. Shakespeare & His Times. 2nd ed. 1852. $13.00 Hdbd. (ISBN 0-404-02948-5). AMS Pr., NY.

Hackett, James H. Notes, Criticisms, & Correspondence Upon Shakespeare's Plays & Actors. 1968. $12.50 Hdbd. Benjamin Blom, NY.

Halliwell-Phillips, James O. Illustrations of the Life of Shakespeare, in a Discursive Series of Essays on a Variety of Subjects. 1874. $12.50 Hdbd. (ISBN 0-404-03059-9). AMS Pr., NY.

Halliwell-Phillips, James O. Visits of Shakespeare's Company of Actors to the Provincial Cities & Towns of England, 1887. $5.00 Hdbd. (ISBN 0-404-03087-4). AMS Pr., NY.

Harbage, Alfred. Shakespeare's Audience. $4.00 Hdbd. Peter Smith, MA.

Harbage, Alfred. Shakespeare's Audience. 1941. $1.95 pa. (ISBN 0-231-08513-3, 13). Columbia Univ. Pr., NY.

Hatcher, Orie L. Book for Shakespeare Plays & Pageants. 1916. $16.50 Hdbd. (ISBN 0-8371-3105-7). Greenwood Pr., CT.

Hatcher, Orie L. Book for Shakespeare Plays & Pageants. (Select Bibliographies Reprint Ser). 1916. $16.50 Hdbd. (ISBN 0-8369-5258-8). Books for Libraries, NY.

Holmes, Martin. Shakespeare's Public, the Touchstone of His Genius. (Hi-Sch.). 1960. $7.50 Hdbd. Transatlantic, NY.

Hotson, Leslie. Shakespeare's Wooden O. 2nd ed. 1960. $6.00 Hdbd. Hillary House, NY.

Jonas, Maurice. Shakespeare & the Stage. 1918. $20.00 Hdbd. Folcroft Pr., PA.

Knight, George Wilson. Shakespearian Production. 3rd ed. 1964. $8.50 Hdbd. (ISBN 0-8101-0137-8). Northwestern Univ. Pr., IL.

Lamborn, Edmund A. & Harrison, George B. Shakespeare: The Man & His Stage. 1923. $6.00 Hdbd. (ISBN 0-404-03805-0). AMS Pr., NY.

Lawrence, William J. Elizabethan Playhouse & Other Studies, 2 Vols. 1963.

(1912–13) Set—$15.00 Hdbd. Russell & Russell, NY.

Lawrence, William J. Physical Conditions of the Elizabethan Public Playhouse. 1968. $4.50 Hdbd. (ISBN 0-8154-0135-3). Cooper Sq. Pr., NY.

Lee, Sidney. Shakespeare & the Modern Stage with Other Essays. 1906. $10.00 Hdbd. (ISBN 0-404-03929-4). AMS Pr., NY

Lelyveld, Toby B. Shylock on the Stage. 1960. $4.95 Hdbd. (ISBN 0-8295-0028-6). Pr of Case Western Reserves, OH.

Long, John H. Shakespeare's Use of Music, 3 vols. Incl. Vol. 1. A Study of the Music & Its Performance in the Original Production of Seven Comedies. 1955. $5.50 Hdbd. (ISBN 0-8130-0145-5); Vol. 2. The Final Comedies. 1961. $5.50 Hdbd. (ISBN 0-8130-0146-3); Vol. 3. The Histories & Tragedies. 1971. $11.00 Hdbd. (ISBN 0-8130-0311-3). Univ. of Fla. Pr., FL.

MacReady, William C. William Charles Macready's King John: Facsimile Prompt-Book. Shattuck, Charles H., ed. 1958. $6.95 Hdbd. (ISBN 0-252-72708-8). Univ. of Ill. Pr., IL.

McSpadden, J. Walker. Shakespeare's Plays in Digest Form. $1.25 pa. (A4). Apollo, NY.

Nagler, Alois M. Shakespeare's Stage. 1958. $5.00 Hdbd. (ISBN 0-300-00784-1); $1.45 pa. (ISBN 0-300-00174-6, Y108). Yale Univ. Pr., CT.

Noyes, Robert G. Thespian Mirror:

Shakespeare in the Eighteenth-Century Novel. 1953. $5.50 Hdbd. (ISBN 0-87057-034-X). Brown Univ. Pr., RI.

Odell, George C. Shakespeare from Betterton to Irving, 2 Vol. $4.75 ea. Hdbd. Peter Smith, MA.

Odell, George C. Shakespeare-from Betterton to Irving, 2 Vols. $18.50 Hdbd. Benjamin Blom, NY.

Odell, George C. Shakespeare from Betterton to Irving, 2 Vols. 1966. $3.00 pa. ea. (ISBN 0-486-21606-3) (ISBN 0-486-21607-1). Dover Publ., NY.

Pascal, Roy. Shakespeare in Germany, 1740–1815. 1971. $8.00 text ed. Octagon Books, NY.

Poel, William. Shakespeare in the Theatre. 1968. $9.75 Hdbd. Benjamin Blom, NY.

Poel, William. Shakespeare in the Theatre. 1913. $9.75 Hdbd. (ISBN 0-404-05067-0). AMS Pr., NY.

Reynolds, George F. Some Principles of Elizabethan Staging. 1905. $5.00 Hdbd. (ISBN 0-404-05286-X). AMS Pr., NY.

Reynolds, George F. On Shakespeare's Stage. Knaub, Richard K., ed. 1967. $3.95 text ed. (ISBN 0-87081-020-0) Colo. Assoc. Univ. Pr., CO.

Scott, Clement W. Some Notable Hamlets of the Present Time. 1900. $9.75 Hdbd. Benjamin Blom, NY.

Shakespeare Association. Series of Papers on Shakespeare & the Theatre. 1927. $17.50 Hdbd. Folcroft Pr., PA.

Shakespeare, William. Stanislavski Produces Othello. Stanislavski, Constantin, ed. $5.95 Hdbd. Theatre Arts, NY.

Sharpe, Robert B. Real War of the Theatres: Shakespeare's Fellows in Rivalry with the Admiral's Men. 1935. $10.00 pa. Kraus Reprint, NY.

Shattuck, Charles H. Shakespeare Promptbooks: A Descriptive Catalogue. 1965. $15.00 Hdbd. (ISBN 0-252-72646-4). Univ. of Ill. Pr., IL.

Shirley, Frances A. Shakespeare's Use of Off-Stage Sounds. 1963. $5.95 Hdbd. (ISBN 0-8032-0174-5). Univ. of Nebr. Pr., NB.

Smith, Irwin. Shakespeare's Blackfriars Playhouse: Its History & Design. 1970. $15.00 Hdbd. (ISBN 0-8147-0391-7); $4.95 pa. (ISBN 0-8147-0483-2). New York Univ. Pr., NY.

Speaight, Robert. William Poel & the Elizabethan Revival. 1954. $3.50 Hdbd. Hillary House, NY.

Spencer, Hazelton. Art & Life of William Shakespeare. 1969. (1940) $12.50 Hdbd. (ISBN 0-389-01164-9). Barnes & Noble, NY.

Spencer, Hazleton. Shakespeare Improved. 1963. $7.00 Hdbd. (ISBN 0-8044-2827-1). Frederick Ungar, NY.

Sprague, Arthur C. Shakespeare & the Actors, 1660–1905. 1963. (1944) $11.50 Hdbd. Russell & Russell, NY.

Sprague, Arthur C. Shakespearian Players & Performances. 1953. $12.75 Hdbd. (ISBN 0-8371-0664-8). Greenwood Pr., CT.

Sprague, Arthur C. Stage Business in Shakespeare's Plays. 1954. $3.00 Hdbd. Folcroft Pr., PA.

Sprague, Arthur C. & Trewin, J. C. Shakespeare's Plays Today: Customs & Conventions of the Stage. 1971. $4.95 Hdbd. (ISBN 0-87249-205-2). Univ. of S.C. Pr., SC.

Sterne, Richard L. John Gielgud Directs Richard Burton in Hamlet. 1968. $6.95 Hdbd. (ISBN 0-394-43149-9). Random House, NY.

Sternfeld, F. W. Music in Shakespearean Tragedy. 1963. $10.00 Hdbd. (ISBN 0-486-21130-4). Dover Publ., NY.

Stopes, C. Burbage & Shakespeare's Stage. (Studies in Shakespeare, No. 24). 1970. (1913) $9.95 Hdbd. (ISBN 0-8383-1020-6). Haskell House, NY.

Thorndike, Ashley. Shakespeare's Theater. $6.95 Hdbd. (61838). Macmillan, NY.

Trewin, J. C. Benson & the Bensonians. 1960. $7.50 Hdbd. Fernhill House, NY.

Venezky, Alice S. Pageantry on the Shakespearian Stage. 1951. $9.50 Hdbd. (ISBN 0-404-06756-5). AMS Pr., NY.

Wallace, Charles W. First London Theatre. 1969. (1913) $12.50 Hdbd. Benjamin Blom, NY.

Watkins, Ronald. On Producing Shakespeare. $12.50 Hdbd. Benjamin Blom, NY.

Webster, Margaret. Shakespeare & the Modern Theatre. 1944. $3.50 Hdbd. Folcroft Pr., PA.

Webster, Margaret. Shakespeare Today. 1957. $4.95 Hdbd. Dufour Ed., PA.

Wilson, John D. & Worsley, Thomas C. Shakespeare's Histories at Stratford, 1951. (Select Bibliographies Reprint Ser). 1952. $9.50 Hdbd. (ISBN 0-8369-5515-3). Books for Libraries, NY.

Winter, William. Shakespeare on the Stage, 3 Series. 1911–1916. $12.50 Hdbd. ea. Benjamin Blom, NY.

Wood, Alice I. Stage History of Shakespeare's King Richard the Third. 1909. $8.00 Hdbd. (ISBN 0-404-07024-8). AMS Pr., NY.

Study

American Heritage Editors. Shakespeare: His Life, His Times, His Works. 1970. $4.95 Hdbd. (ISBN 0-07-001211-3). Am. Heritage Pr., NY.

Asimov, Isaac. Asimov's Guide to Shakespeare, Vols. 1–2. 1970. Set—$25.00 Hdbd.; $12.50 Hdbd. ea. Doubleday, NY.

Beeching, H. C. Character of Shakespeare. 1971. $2.50 Hdbd. Folcroft Pr., PA.

Bennett, H. S. Shakespeare's Audience. 1944. $3.00 Hdbd. Folcroft Pr., PA.

Bluestone, M. & Robkin, N. Shakespeare's Contemporaries: Modern Studies in English Renaissance Drama. 1961.

$4.95 pa. (ISBN 0-13-807727-4) Prentice-Hall, NY.

Burton, Harry M. Shakespeare & His Plays. $3.95 Hdbd. Roy Publ., NY.

Clark, Cumberland. Shakespeare & Science: A Study of Shakespeare's Interest in Literary & Dramatic Use of Natural Phenomena. 1971. (1929) $12.00 Hdbd. Scholarly Pr., MI.

Corson, Hiram. Introduction to the Study of Shakespeare. 1889. $15.00 Hdbd. (ISBN 0-404-01735-5). AMS Pr., NY.

Deveemon, William. Shakespeare's Legal Acquirements. (1899) $5.00 Hdbd. (ISBN 0-404-54212-3). AMS Pr., NY.

Eckhoff, Lorentz. Shakespeare: Spokesman of the Third Estate. 1954. $17.50 Hdbd. Folcroft Pr., PA.

Ellis-Fermor, Una. Study of Shakespeare. 1947. $3.00 Hdbd. Folcroft Pr., PA.

Fleay, Frederick G. Chronicle History of the Life & Work of Shakespeare. 1970. (1886) $17.50 Hdbd. (ISBN 0-404-02405-X). AMS Pr., NY.

Fleay, Frederick G. Introduction to Shakespearian Study. 1970. (1877) $7.50 Hdbd. (ISBN 0-404-02407-6). AMS Pr., NY.

Fleay, Frederick G. Shakespeare Manual. 1970. (1876) $14.00 Hdbd. (ISBN 0-404-02408-4). AMS Pr., NY.

Fleming, William H. How to Study

Shakespeare. 1898. $17.50 Hdbd. (ISBN 0-404-02436-X). AMS Pr., NY.

Ford, H. L. Shakespeare: A Collection of the Editions & Separate Plays with Some Account of T. Johnson & R. Walker. 1935. $12.50 Hdbd. Folcroft Pr., PA.

Frey, Albert R. William Shakespeare & Alleged Spanish Prototypes. (1886) $5.00 Hdbd. (ISBN 0-404-54203-4). AMS Pr., NY.

Herford, Charles H. Sketch of Recent Shakespearean Investigation 1893–1923. $5.00 Hdbd. Folcroft Pr., PA.

Irvine, Theodora U. How to Pronounce the Names in Shakespeare. $15.00 Hdbd. Gale Research, MI.

Jusserand, Jean J. What to Expect of Shakespeare. (Select Bibliographies Ser). (1911) $5.00 Hdbd. (ISBN 0-8369-5509-9). Books for Libraries. NY.

Knight, George Wilson. Myth & Miracle: An Essay on the Mystic Symbolism of Shakespeare. 1929. $5.00 Hdbd. Ridgeway Bks., PA.

Lings, Martin. Shakespeare in the Light of Sacred Art. 1966. $5.00 Hdbd. Fernhill House, NY.

Luce, Morton. Handbook to the Works of William Shakespeare. 07. $22.00 Hdbd. (ISBN 0-404-040 -0). AMS Pr., NY.

Mendl, R. W. Revelation in Shakespeare: A Study of the Supernatural, Religious & Spiritual Elements in His

Art. 1964. $6.00 Hdbd.; $2.75 pa. Fernhill House, NY.

Mizener, Arthur, ed. Teaching Shakespeare. 1969. $1.95 pa. New American Library, NY.

Mroz, Sr. M. Divine Vengeance: Shakespeare. 1941. $8.50 Hdbd. Folcroft Pr., PA.

Muir, Kenneth & Schoenbaum, S. New Companion to Shakespearean Studies. 1971. $12.50 Hdbd. (ISBN 0-521-07941-1); $3.95 pa. (ISBN 0-521-09645-6). Cambridge Univ. Pr., NY.

Muir, Kenneth & O'Loughlin, Sean. The Voyage to Illyria: A New Study of Shakespeare. (1937) $9.00 Hdbd. (ISBN 0-8369-5511-0). Books for Libraries, NY.

O'Connor, F. Shakespeare's Progress, 1961. $1.50 pa. Macmillan, NY.

Price, George R. Reading Shakespeare's Plays: A Guide for College Students. (Hi-Sch.). 1962. $4.00 Hdbd.; $1.25 pa. Barron's Educ. Serv., NY.

Ridley, Maurice R. On Reading Shakespeare. 1940. $3.00 Hdbd. Folcroft Pr., PA.

Rohde, Eleanour S. Shakespeare's Wild Flowers: Fairy Lore, Gardens. Herbs. (1935) $11.00 Hdbd. Gale Research, MI.

Sanders, Gerald D. Shakespeare Primer. 1950. $9.00 Hdbd. (ISBN 0-404-05560-5). AMS Pr., NY.

Trewin, J. C. Shakespeare on the English Stage 1900-1964: A Survey of Productions Illustrated from the Raymond Mander & Jose Mitchenson Theatre Collection. 1964. $8.50 Hdbd. Fernhill House, NY.

Usherwood, Stephen. Shakespeare Play by Play. (Hi-Sch.). 1968. $5.95 Hdbd. (ISBN 0-8090-8620-4). Hill & Wang, NY.

Victor, Wilhelm. Shakespeare Phonology. $5.50 Hdbd. (2945-6). Frederick Ungar, NY.

Victor, Wilhelm. Shakespeare Reader. $5.00 Hdbd. (2947-2). Frederick Ungar, NY.

Watt, Homer A., et al. Outlines of Shakespeare's Plays. rev. ed. 1962. $1.50 pa. (ISBN 0-389-00113-9). Barnes & Noble, NY.

Whalley, Peter & Farmer, Richard. Enquiry into the Learning of Shakespeare & an Essay on the Learning of Shakespeare. 2nd ed. $12.50 Hdbd. Augustus M. Kelly, NY.

Wright, Louis B. & LaMar, Virginia A. Folger Guide to Shakespeare. 1969. $0.90 pa. (ISBN 0-671-47793-5). Washington Square Pr., NY.

Plots

Deutsch, Babette. Reader's Shakespeare. (Jr Hi-Hi-Sch.). 1947. $6.95 Hdbd. Julian Messner, NY.

Fleming, William H. Shakespeare's Plots. 1971. (1902) $22.50 Hdbd. (ISBN 0-404-02437-8). AMS Pr., NY.

McCutchan, J. Wilson. Plot Outlines of Shakespeare's Histories. 1965. $1.50 pa. (ISBN 0-389-00112-0). Barnes & Noble, NY.

McCutchan, J. Wilson. Plot Outlines of Shakespeare's Tragedies. 1965. $3.25 text ed.; $1.25 pa. Barnes & Noble, NY.

McSpadden, J. Walker. Shakespeare's Plays in Digest Form. $1.25 pa. Apollo Eds., NY.

Magill, M. & Ault, Katherine. Synopses of Shakespeare's Plays. 1952. $1.50 pa. Littlefield Adams, NJ.

Style

Brown, John R. Shakespeare's Dramatic Style. 1971. $7.25 Hdbd. (ISBN 0-389-04064-9). Barnes & Noble, NY.

Clemen, Wolfgang H. Development of Shakespeare's Imagery. 1951. $6.00 Hdbd. (ISBN 0-674-20150-7). Harvard Univ. Pr., MA.

Clemen, Wolfgang H. Development of Shakespeare's Imagery. 1962. $1.75 pa. (ISBN 0-8090-0531-X). Hill & Wang, NY.

Ellis-Fermor, Una M. Some Recent Research in Shakespeare's Imagery. 1937. $3.00 Hdbd. Folcroft Pr., PA.

Ellis-Fermor, Una M. Some Recent Research in Shakespeare's Imagery. (Studies in Shakespeare, No. 24). 1970. (1937) $2.95 pa. (ISBN 0-8383-0025-1). Haskell House, NY.

Joseph, Miriam. Rhetoric in Shakespeare's Time. $2.65 pa. (ISBN 0-15-

677094-6, H012, Hbgr). Harcourt Brace Jovanovich, NY.

Joseph, Miriam. Shakespeare's Use of the Arts of Language. 1966. (1947) $7.95 Hdbd.; $3.95 pa. Hafner Publ., NY.

Lounsbury, Thomas. Text of Shakespeare. q/reprint. 1906 ed. 1971. (1906) $10.00 Hdbd. (ISBN 0-404-04035-7). AMS Pr., NY.

Mahood, M. M. Shakespeare's Wordplay. (Orig.). 1967. $2.00 pa. (ISBN 0-416-29560-6, 242, UP). Barnes & Noble, NY.

Rylands, G. W. Words & Poetry. 1928. $10.00 Hdbd. (ISBN 0-404-05477-3). AMS Pr., NY.

Simpson, Percy. Shakespearian Punctuation. 1911. $3.00 Hdbd. Ridgeway Bks., PA.

Smith, Charles G. Shakespeare's Proverb Lore: His Use of the Sententiae of Leonard Culman & Publilius Syrus. 1963. $6.00 Hdbd. (ISBN 0-674-80430-9). Harvard Univ. Pr., MA.

Spurgeon, Caroline F. Leading Motives in the Imagery of Shakespeare's Tragedies. (Studies in Shakespeare Ser., No. 24). 1970. (1930) $3.95 Hdbd. (ISBN 0-8383-1203-9). Haskell House, NY.

Spurgeon, Caroline F. Shakespeare's Imagery & What It Tells Us. 1952. $8.50 Hdbd.; $2.95 pa. Cambridge Univ. Pr., NY.

Spurgeon, Caroline F. Leading Motives in the Imagery of Shakespear's Trag-

edies. 1930. $3.00 Hdbd. Folcroft Pr., PA.

Verity, A. W. Influence of Christopher Marlowe on Shakespeare's Earlier Style. 1886. $6.50 Hdbd. Folcroft Pr., PA.

Wurth, Leopold. Wortspiel Bei Shakspere. 1965. (1895) $13.50 pa. Johnson Reprint, NY.

Supernatural Element

Clark, C. Shakespeare & the Supernatural. (Studies in Shakespeare Ser., No. 24). 1970. (1931) $11.95 Hdbd. (ISBN 0-8383-0966-6). Haskell House, NY.

Gibson, J. Paul. Shakespeare's Use of the Supernatural. 1908. $6.50 Hdbd. (ISBN 0-404-02719-9). AMS Pr., NY.

Lanier, Sidney. Shakespeare & His Forerunners, 2 Vols. 1902. $25.00 Hdbd. (ISBN 0-404-03875-1). AMS Pr., NY.

Lucy, Margaret. Shakespeare & the Supernatural. 1906. $5.00 Hdbd. (ISBN 0-404-04065-9). AMS Pr., NY.

Lucy, Margaret. Shakespeare & the Supernatural. 1906. $5.00 Hdbd. Folcroft Pr., PA.

Nutt, Alfred T. Fairy Mythology of Shakespeare. (1900) $5.50 Hdbd. (ISBN 0-404-53506-2). AMS Pr., NY.

Stewart, Helen H. Supernatural in Shakespeare. 1908. $15.00 Hdbd. Folcroft Pr., PA.

West, Robert H. Shakespeare & the Outer Mystery. 1968. $6.50 Hdbd.

(ISBN 0-8131-1166-8). Univ. Pr. of Ky., KY.

Wiley, Edwin. Study of the Supernatural in Three Plays of Shakespeare. 1913. $6.50 Hdbd. Folcroft Pr., PA.

Technique

Arnold, Morris L. Soliloquies of Shakespeare. 1911. $8.00 Hdbd. (ISBN 0-404-00389-3). AMS Pr., NY.

Baker, George P. Development of Shakespeare As a Dramatist. 1907. $15.00 Hdbd. (ISBN 0-404-00467-9). AMS Pr., NY.

Baldwin, Thomas W. On Act & Scene Division in the Shakespeare First Folio. 1965. $5.50 Hdbd. (ISBN 0-8093-0153-9). Southern Ill. Univ. Pr., IL.

Baldwin, Thomas W. On the Literary Genetics of Shakespeare's Plays, 1592–1594. 1959. $10.50 Hdbd. (ISBN 0-252-72587-5). Univ. of Ill. Pr., IL.

Baldwin, Thomas W. Shakespeare's Five-Act Structure. 1947. $10.00 Hdbd. (ISBN 0-252-72647-2). Univ. of Ill. Pr., IL.

Bradbrook, Muriel C. Elizabethan Stage Conditions; A Study of Their Place in the Interpretation of Shakespeare's Plays. 1968. $4.95 Hdbd.; $1.65 pa. (ISBN 0-521-09539-5, 539). Cambridge Univ. Pr., MA.

Charlton, Henry B. Romeo & Juliet: As an Experimental Tragedy. 1939. $5.00 Hdbd. Folcroft Pr., PA.

Clarke, Charles & Cowden, Mary.

Shakespeare Key. 1961. $15.00 Hdbd. (ISBN 0-8044-2127-7). Frederick Ungar, NY.

Coghill, Nevill. Shakespeare's Professional Skills. $8.50 Hdbd. Cambridge Univ. Pr., NY.

Edwards, Philip. Shakespeare & the Confines of Art. 1968. $5.00 Hdbd. Barnes & Noble, NY.

Flatter, Richard. Shakespeare's Producing Hand. 1948. $9.00 Hdbd. (ISBN 0-8371-2454-9). Greenwood Pr., CT.

Fleming, William H. Shakespeare's Plots. 1971. (1902) $22.50 Hdbd. (ISBN 0-404-02437-8). AMS Pr., NY.

Matthews, Brander. Shakespeare As a Playwright. 1970. (1913) $12.50 Hdbd. AMS Pr., NY.

Moulton, Richard G. Shakespeare As a Dramatic Artist. $5.00 Hdbd. Peter Smith, MA.

Moulton, Richard G. Shakespeare As a Dramatic Artist: A Popular Illustration of the Principles of Scientific Criticism. rev. & enl. ed. 1966. $3.00 pa. Dover, NY.

Moulton, Richard G. Shakespeare As a Dramatic Thinker. 1907. $20.00 Hdbd. Folcroft Pr., PA.

Rymer, Thomas. Short View of Tragedy. 1968. (1693) $10.00 Hdbd. (ISBN 0-404-05478-1). AMS Pr., NY.

Sengupta, S. C. Whirligig of Time. 1961. $4.00 Hdbd. Lawrence Verry, CT.

Snider, Denton J. System of Shakespeare's Dramas, 2 Vols. 1877. $27.00 Hdbd. (ISBN 0-404-06139-7). AMS Pr., NY.

Sprague, Arthur C. Shakespeare & the Audience. 1966. (1935) $8.50 Hdbd. Russell & Russell, NY.

Ten Brink, Bernard A. Five Lectures on Shakespeare. Franklin, Julia, tr. 1895. $10.00 Hdbd. AMS Pr., NY.

Watkins, Ronald. On Producing Shakespeare. $12.50 Hdbd. Benjamin Blom, NY.

STAGE CONSTRUCTION & DESIGN

Adix, Vern. Theatre Scenecraft. 1957. $7.00 Hdbd. Anchorage Pr., TN.

Albright, Victor E. Shakespearian Stage. 1926. $9.00 Hdbd. (ISBN 0-404-00304-4). AMS Pr., NY.

Appia, Adolphe. Music & the Art of the Theatre. Hewitt, Barnard, ed. (Books of the Theatre, No. 3). 1963. $6.50 Hdbd. (ISBN 0-87024-018-8). Univ. of Miami Pr., FL.

Bablet, Denis. Edward Gordon Craig. Woodward, D., tr. 1966. $7.75 Hdbd. Theater Arts Books, NY.

Baker, Hendrik. Stage Management & Theatre Craft. 1968. $9.95 Hdbd. Theatre Arts Books, NY.

Basoli, Antonio. Collezione Di Varie Scene Teatrali. 1968. $18.50 Hdbd. Benjamin Blom, NY.

Bax, Peter. Stage Management. $10.75 Hdbd. Benjamin Blom, NY.

Bibiena, Giuseppe. Architectural & Perspective Designs. 1740. $2.50 pa. (ISBN 0-486-21263-7). Dover Publ., NY.

Bruder, Karl. Properties & Dressing the Stage. Kozelka, Paul, ed. (Theatre Student Ser). (Hi-Sch.). 1969. $6.96 Hdbd. (ISBN 0-8239-0150-5). Rosen Richards Pr., NY.

Buerki, Frederick A. Stagecraft for Nonprofessionals. 2nd ed. 1955. $2.50 pa. (ISBN 0-299-01294-8). Univ. of Wis. Pr., WI.

Burian, Jarka. Scenography of Josef Svoboda. 1971. $25.00 Hdbd. Wesleyan Univ. Pr., CT.

Burris-Meyer, Harold & Cole, Edward C. Scenery for the Theatre. 1971. $32.50 Hdbd. (ISBN 0-316-11754-4). Little, Brown & Co., MA.

Campbell, Lily B. Scenes & Machines on the English Stage During the Renaissance: A Classical Revival. 1970. (1923) $10.00 Hdbd. (ISBN 0-389-01756-6). Barnes & Noble, NY.

Cheney, Sheldon. New Movement in the Theatre. $12.50 Hdbd. Benjamin Blom, NY.

Cheney, Sheldon. Stage Decoration. 1967. $12.50 Hdbd. Benjamin Blom, NY.

Chilver, Peter & Jones, Eric. Designing a School Play. 1970. $6.95 Hdbd. (ISBN 0-8008-2171-8). Taplinger Publ. Co., NY.

Christout, Marie-Francoise. Merveilleux et le Theatre Du Silence En France a Partir Du Dix-Sept Siecle. 1965. $14.50 Hdbd. Humanities Pr., NY.

Cooper, Douglas. Picasso: Theatre. 1968. $25.00 Hdbd. (ISBN 0-8109-0396-2). Harry Abrams, NY.

Corey, Irene. Mask of Reality: An Approach to Design for Theatre. 1968. $20.00 Hdbd. Anchorage Pr., TN.

Cornberg, Sol & Gebauer, Emanuel L. Stage Crew Handbook. rev. ed. 1957. $5.95 Hdbd. (ISBN 0-06-031560-1). Harper & Row, NY.

Craig, Edward G. Scene. 1968. $12.50 Hdbd. Benjamin Blom, NY.

Craig, Edward G. Toward a New Theatre, Forty Designs for Stage Scenes. 1913. $27.50 Hdbd. Benjamin Blom, NY.

Dow, Marguerite R. Magic Mask: A Basic Textbook of Theatre Arts. (Hi-Sch.). 1968. $5.00 text ed. St. Martin's Pr., NY.

Fuerst, Walter Rene & Hume, Samuel J. Twentieth Century Stage Decoration, 2 Vols. 1968. $18.50 Hdbd. Benjamin Blom, NY.

Fuerst, Walter Rene & Hume, Samuel J. Twentieth Century Stage Decoration, 2 Vols. 1967. Repr. $3.00 pa. (ISBN 0-486-21863-5) (ISBN 0-486-21864-3). Dover Publ., NY.

Galliari, Gaspare. Numero Vente Quatro Invenzioni Teatrali. 1969. $18.50 Hdbd. Benjamin Blom, NY.

Gassner, John & Barber, P. Producing the Play. rev. ed. Incl. New Scene Technician's Handbook. 1953. $11.50 text ed. (ISBN 0-03-005565-2). Holt, Rinehart & Winston, NY.

Gillette, Arnold S. Introduction to Scenic Design. 1967. $11.50 text ed. (ISBN 0-06-042324-2). Harper & Row, NY.

Gillette, Arnold S. Stage Scenery. YA. (Hi-Sch.). 1960. $11.50 text ed. (ISBN 0-06-042330-7). Harper & Row, NY.

Gorelik, Mordecai. New Theatres for Old. (Illus.). $2.45 pa. (ISBN 0-525-47102-2, D102, D102). E. P. Dutton, NY.

Gruver, Bert. Stage Manager's Handbook. 1968. $4.50 Hdbd. DBS Pubns., NY.

Hainaux, Rene & Yves-Bonnat. Stage Design Throughout the World Since 1950. 1963. $32.50 Hdbd. Theatre Arts Books, NY.

Hake, Herbert V. Here's How. rev. ed. 1958. $3.95 Hdbd. Samuel French, NY.

Hewitt, Barnard. Renaissance Stage: Documents of Serlio, Sabbattini & Furttenbach. Nicoll, Allardycee, et al, trans. (Books of the Theatre, No. 1). 1959. $6.50 Hdbd. (ISBN 0-87024-004-8). Univ. of Miami Pr., Coral Gables, FL.

Jones, Eric. Stage Constructions for School Plays. (Jr Hi-Hi-Sch.). 1969. $5.95 Hdbd. (ISBN 0-8231-1012-5). Charles T. Branford, MA.

Jones, Inigo. Designs by Inigo Jones for

Masques & Plays at Court. Simpson, Percy & Bell, C. F., eds. 1966. (1924) $35.00 Hdbd. Russell & Russell Publ., NY.

Jones, Robert E. Drawings for the Theatre. $13.50 Hdbd. Theatre Arts Books, NY.

Joseph, Stephen. New Theatre Forms. 1968. $6.25 Hdbd. Theatre Arts Books, NY.

Kernodle, George R. From Art to Theatre: Form & Convention in the Renaissance. 1944. $11.75 Hdbd. (ISBN 0-226-43188-6). Univ. of Chicago Pr., IL.

Komisarjevsky, Theodore & Simonson, Lee. Settings & Costumes of the Modern Stage). 1933. $15.00 Hdbd. Benjamin Blom, NY.

Larson, Orville K., ed. Scene Design for Stage & Screen. 1961. $5.00 Hdbd. (ISBN 0-87013-063-3). Mich. St. Univ. Pr., MI.

Lawrence, William J. Elizabethan Playhouse & Other Studies, 2 Vols. 1963. (1912–13). Set—$15.00 Hdbd. Russell & Russell Publ., NY.

Lawrence, William J. Pre-Restoration Stage Studies. 1967. (Repr.) $12.50 Hdbd. Benjamin Blom, NY.

Leclercq, Louis. Decors, Costumes et Mise En Scene Au Dix-Septieme Siecle. 1968. (1869) $16.50 Hdbd. (ISBN 0-8337-2041-4). Burt Franklin, NY.

MacGowan, Kenneth & Jones, Robert E. Continental Stagecraft. 1922. $12.50 Hdbd. Benjamin Blom, NY.

Melvill, Harald. Designing & Painting Scenery for the Theatre. 1963. (1948) $4.95 Hdbd. Dufour Editions, PA.

Moussinac, Leon. New Movement in the Theatre. 1967. Repr. $35.00 Hdbd. Benjamin Blom, NY.

Nelms, Henning. Scene Design: A Primer of Stagecraft. (Jr Hi.). 1970. $6.95 Hdbd. (ISBN 0-8069-7014-6); (ISBN 0-8069-7015-4). Sterling Publ. Co., NY.

Nicoll, Allardyce. Stuart Masques & the Renaissance Stage. 1938. $17.50 Hdbd. Benjamin Blom, NY.

Oenslager, Donald. Scenery, Then & Now. 1966. (1936) $15.00 Hdbd. Russell & Russell Publ., NY.

Parker, W. Oren & Smith, Harvey K. Scene Design & Stage Lighting. (Rinehart Editions). 1968. $11.95 text ed. (ISBN 0-03-067550-2). 2nd ed. 1968. $13.95 Hdbd. (ISBN 0-03-072215-2); $9.50. Holt, Rinehart & Winston, NY.

Philippi, Herbert. Stagecraft & Scene Design. 1953. $9.50 Hdbd. Houghton-Mifflin, MA.

Reynolds, George F. Some Principles of Elizabethan Staging. 1905. $5.00 Hdbd. (ISBN 0-404-05286-X). AMS Pr., NY.

Reynolds, George F. Staging of Elizabethan Plays at the Red Bull Theatre. 1605–1625. 1940. $9.00 pa. Kraus Reprint Co., NY.

Rischbieter, Henning, ed. Art & the Stage in the Twentieth Century: Painters & Sculptors Work for the Theater.

1969. $35.00 Hdbd. (ISBN 0-8212-0352-5). New York Graphic Society, CT.

Robertson, Joseph, ed. Stage Decoration in France in the Middle Ages. 1910. $10.50 Hdbd. (ISBN 0-404-50609-7). AMS Pr., NY.

Rowell, Kenneth. Stage Design. 1968. $2.75 pa. Van Nostrand-Reinhold Books, NY.

Sayler, Oliver M., ed. Max Reinhardt & His Theatre. 1968. $17.50 Hdbd. Benjamin Blom, NY.

Schlemmer, Oskar, et al. Theatre of the Bauhaus. Gropius, Walter, ed. Wensinger, Arthur S., trans. 1961. $7.50 Hdbd. (ISBN 0-8195-3022-0); $4.95 pa. (ISBN 0-8195-6020-0). Wesleyan Univ. Pr., CT.

Selden, Samuel & Sellman, Hunton D. Stage Scenery & Lighting. 3rd ed. 1959. $7.50 text ed. (ISBN 0-390-79436-8). Appleton-Century-Crofts, NY.

Sheringham, George & Laver, James. Design in the Theatre. $15.00 Hdbd. Benjamin Blom, NY.

Simonson, Lee. Stage Is Set. (Orig.). 1962. $3.95 pa. Theatre Arts Books, NY.

Simonson, Lee, ed. Theatre Art. 1969. (1934) $7.50 Hdbd. (ISBN 0-8154-0289-9). Cooper Sq. Publ., NY.

Southern, Richard. Proscenium & Sight Lines. $7.45 Hdbd. Theatre Arts Books, NY.

Southern, Richard. Stage Setting for

Amateurs & Professionals. $5.95 Hdbd. Theatre Arts Books, NY.

Stell, W. Joseph. Scenery. (Theatre Student Ser). (Hi-Sch.). 1970. $5.97 Hdbd. (ISBN 0-8239-0152-1). Rosen, Richards Pr., NY.

Warre, Michael. Designing & Making Stage Scenery. 1966. $8.95 Hdbd. Van Nostrand-Reinhold Books, NY.

Welker, David. Theatrical Set Design: The Basic Techniques. 1969. $9.95 text ed. Allyn Inc., NJ.

Wickham, Glynne W. Early English Stages: 1300 to 1660, 2 vols. Incl. Vol. 1. 1300 to 1576 (ISBN 0-231-08935-X); Vol. 2, Pt. 1. 1576 to 1660 (ISBN 0-231-08936-8). 1959. $15.00 Hdbd. Columbia Univ. Pr., NY.

Wilfred, Thomas. Projected Scenery: A Technical Manual. 1965. $3.95 spiral bdg. DBS Publ., NY.

TELEVISION

Cameras

Ennes, Harold E. Television Broadcasting: Camera Chains. 1971. $12.95 Hdbd. (ISBN 0-672-20833-4). Sams, IN.

Jones, Peter. Technique of the Television Cameraman. (Library of Communication Techniques Ser). 1965. $10.00 Hdbd. (ISBN 0-8038-7033-7). Hastings House, NY.

Pittaro, Ernest. T. V. & Film Production Data Book. 1959. $2.95 Hdbd. (ISBN 0-87100-067-9). Morgan, NY.

Rudman, Jack. Civil Service Examination Passbook: Television Cameraman. $8.00 Hdbd.; $5.00 pa. Natl. Learning, NY.

Tsukerman, Ilia I. Electron Optics in Television. 1961. $8.50 Hdbd. (ISBN 0-08-009388-4). Pergamon, NY.

Production

Bretz, Rudy. Techniques of Television Production. 2nd ed. 1962. $12.50 text ed. (ISBN 0-07-007664-2). McGraw-Hill, NY.

Cantor, Muriel G. Hollywood TV Producer. 1971. $7.95 Hdbd. (ISBN 0-465-03037-8). Basic Books, NY.

Coombs, Charles I. Window on the World: The Story of Television Production. 1965. $4.50 Hdbd. (2608). World Pub., NY.

Harris, Leon. People Who Make a Television Show. 1971. price n.g. Hdbd. Lippincott Pub., PA.

Jones, Peter. Technique of the Television Cameraman. (Library of Communication Techniques Ser). 1965. $10.00 Hdbd. (ISBN 0-8038-7033-7). Hastings House, NY.

Kingson, Walter K. & Cowgill, Rome. Television Acting & Directing: A Handbook. (Rinehart Editions). 1965. $8.95 text ed. (ISBN 0-03-049810-4, HoltC). Holt, Rinehart & Winston, NY.

Kinross, Felicity. Television for the

Teacher. (Illus.). 1968. $6.95 Hdbd. (ISBN 0-241-91293-8). Dufour Publ., PA.

Lewis, Colby. Television Director Interpreter. (Communication Arts Books Ser). (Illus.). 1968. $8.95 Hdbd. (ISBN 0-8038-7042-6); $5.95 text ed. (ISBN 0-8038-7041-8). Hastings House, NY.

Millerson, Gerald. Technique of Television Production. rev. ed. (Library of Communication Techniques Ser). (Illus.). 1968. $13.50 Hdbd. (ISBN 0-8038-7035-3); $7.20 text ed. (ISBN 0-8038-7034-5). Hastings House, NY.

National Education Association—Division Of Educational Technology. Creating Visuals for TV: A Guide for Educators. 1962. $1.25 pa. National Education Assn., DC.

Stasheff, Edward & Bretz, Rudy. Television Program: Its Direction & Production. rev. ed. (Illus.). 1968. $2.95 pa. (ISBN 0-8090-1341-X). Hill & Wang, NY.

Zettl, Herbert. Television Production Handbook. 2nd ed. 1968. $13.25 Hdbd.; $9.95 text ed.; $4.95 workbook. Wadsworth Pub., NY.

THEATER

Albright, Harry D., et al. Principles of Theatre Art. 2nd ed. 1968. $9.95 Hdbd. Houghton Mifflin Co., MA.

Allen, John. Going to the Theatre. 2nd ed. (Excursions Series for Young

People). (Hi-Sch.). 1970. $3.75 Hdbd. International Publ. Serv., NY.

Anderson, Lindsay & Sherwin, Robert. Film Scripts: Modern. 1969. $1.95 pa. Simon & Schuster, NY.

Angels' Bible: Theatre & Film Finance. 1971. $95.00 Hdbd. (ISBN 0-8277-0725-8). British Book Center, NY.

Appia, Adolphe. Work of Living Art, & Man Is the Measure of All Things. Hewitt, Barnard, ed. (Books of the Theatre, No. 2). 1969. $6.50 Hdbd. (ISBN 0-87024-007-2). Univ. of Miami Pr., FL.

Archer, William. About the Theatre. $8.50 Hdbd. Benjamin Blom, NY.

Archer, William & Barker, H. Granville, eds. National Theatre: Scheme & Estimates. 1970. (1907) $9.50 Hdbd. (ISBN 0-8046-0749-4). Kennikat Pr., Port Washington, NY.

Bakshy, Alexander. Theatre Unbound. 1968. (1923) $6.75 Hdbd. Benjamin Blom, NY.

Bauland, Peter & Ingram, William. Tradition of the Theatre. 1971. $6.25 pa. Allyn Inc., NJ.

Beckerman, Bernard. Dynamics of Drama: Theories & Methods of Analysis. 1970. $3.50 pa. (30043). Alfred A. Knopf, NY.

Beerbohm, Max. Last Theatres. Hart-Davis, Rupert, ed. 1970. $15.00 Hdbd. (ISBN 0-8008-4564-1). Taplinger Publ., NY.

Bentley, Eric. Theatre of Commitment. 1967. $5.00 Hdbd. (ISBN 0-689-10034-5). Atheneum Publ., NY.

Bernheim, Alfred L. Business of the Theatre. 1932. $17.50 Hdbd. Benjamin Blom, NY.

Biner, Pierre. Living Theater. 1971. $7.50 Hdbd. (ISBN 0-8180-0501-7). Horizon Pr., NY.

Bricker, Herschel L., ed. Our Theatre Today. facs. ed. (Essay Index Reprint Ser). 1936. $16.50 Hdbd. (ISBN 0-8369-1823-1). Books for Libraries, NY.

Brook, Peter. Empty Space. 1969. (1967) $1.65 pa. Avon Books, NY.

Brook, Peter. Empty Space: A Book About the Theatre: Deadly, Holy, Rough, Immediate. 1968. $5.00 Hdbd. (ISBN 0-689-10049-3). Atheneum Publ., NY.

Brown, John R. Drama. (Concept Books, No. 5). 1969. $1.25 pa. Humanities Pr., NY.

Burleigh, Louise. Community Theater in Theory & Practice. (1917) $12.50 Hdbd. (ISBN 0-8337-5269-3). Burt Franklin, NY.

Cameron, Kenneth M. & Hoffman, Theodore J. Theatrical Response. 1969. $8.50 text ed. Macmillan, NY.

Cheney, Sheldon. Art Theater. rev. ed. (1925) $12.00 Hdbd. Kraus Reprint, NY.

Cheney, Sheldon. Art Theatre. rev. ed. $12.50 Hdbd. Benjamin Blom, NY.

Cheney, Sheldon. New Movement in the Theatre. $12.50 Hdbd. Benjamin Blom, NY.

Cheney, Sheldon. New Movement in the Theatre. 1914. $12.00 Hdbd. (ISBN 0-8371-3081-6). Greenwood Pr., CT.

Cheney, Sheldon. Open-Air Theatre. (1918) $16.00 Hdbd. Kraus Reprint, NY.

Clark, Brian. Group Theatre. 1971. $6.95 Hdbd. (ISBN 0-87830-052-X). Theatre Arts Books, NY.

Claudel, Paul. My Ideas on the Theatre. Petit, Jacques & Kempf, Jean-Pierre, eds. Trollope, Christine, tr. 1971. $7.95 Hdbd. (ISBN 0-87024-158-3). Univ. of Miami Pr., FL.

Craig, Edward G. Mask, 15 Vols. Guidry, L. F., ed. (Plus index). Set— $285.00 Hdbd.; Vols. individual avail., Benjamin Blom, NY.

Craig, Gordon. On the Art of the Theatre. 1925. $6.50 Hdbd. Theatre Arts Books, NY.

Demuth, Averil, ed. Minack Open-Air Theatre. 1968. $4.50 Hdbd. Fernhill House, NY.

Dobree, Bonamy. Timotheus: The Future of the Theatre. $5.50 Hdbd. Folcroft Pr., PA.

Eaton, Walter P. Actor's Heritage. (Essay Index Reprint Ser). 1924. $10.75 Hdbd. (ISBN 0-8369-1827-4). Books for Libraries, NY.

Esslin, Martin. Reflections: Essays on the Modern Theatre. 1971. $1.95 pa. Doubleday, NY.

Evreinoff, Nicolas. Theatre in Life. 1927. $10.75 Hdbd. Benjamin Blom, NY.

Fitzgerald, Percy. World Behind the Scenes. 1881. $12.50 Hdbd. Benjamin Blom, NY.

Gassner, John. Directions in Modern Theatre & Drama. rev. ed. 1965. $9.95 Hdbd. (ISBN 0-03-051370-7). Holt, Rinehart & Winston, NY.

Gassner, John. Theatre in Our Times. (Orig.). 1954. $7.50 Hdbd.; $2.95 pa. Crown Publ., NY.

Gilder, Rosamond & Freedley, George. Theatre Collections in Libraries & Museums, an International Handbook. (Library of Literature, Drama & Criticism). 1970. (1936) $10.00 Hdbd. Johnson Reprint Corp., NY.

Goldberg, Isaac. Theatre of George Jean Nathan. 1926. $12.50 Hdbd. (ISBN 0-404-02859-4). AMS Pr., NY.

Gorelik, Mordecai. New Theatres for Old. $2.45 pa. (ISBN 0-525-47102-2). E. P. Dutton, NY.

Gottlieb. New Revolutionary Theatre. $7.50 Hdbd. Bobbs-Merrill Co., IN.

Gottlieb, Saul, ed. New Revolutionary Theatre. 1970. $7.50 Hdbd. Bobbs-Merrill Co., IN.

Granville-Barker, Harley G. On Dramatic Method. 1956. $1.50 pa. (ISBN 0-8090-0502-6). Hill & Wang, NY.

Granville-Barker, Harley G. Exemplary Theatre. $9.75 Hdbd. Benjamin Blom, NY.

Green, Abel & Laurie, Joe, Jr. Show Biz: From Vaude to Vido, 2 Vols. 1971. (1951) Vols. 2 $22.50 Hdbd. (ISBN 0-8046-1527-6). Kennikat Pr., NY.

Grey, Elizabeth. Behind the Scenes in the Theatre. (Jr Hi.). 1969. $3.95 Hdbd. Roy Publ., NY.

Griffin, Alice. Living Theatre Study Guide. $0.50 pa. Twayne Publ., NY.

Hatlen, Theodore W. Orientation to the Theater. $3.95 pa. (ISBN 0-390-42301-7). Appleton-Century-Crofts, NY.

Holcroft, Thomas. Theatrical Recorder, 2 Vols. (Research & Source Works Ser, No. 233). 1968. (1806) $36.50 Hdbd. (ISBN 0-8337-1723-5). Burt Franklin, NY.

Hyams, Barry, ed. Theatre, Vol. 2. $3.95 Hdbd. (ISBN 0-8090-9249-2); $1.95 pa. (ISBN 0-8090-0602-2). Hill & Wang, NY.

Jellicoe, Ann. Some Unconscious Influences in the Theatre. 1967. $0.95 Hdbd. Cambridge Univ. Pr., NY.

Kaufman, Julian. Appreciating the Theatre. 1971. $7.95 Hdbd.; $4.00 pa. David McKay Co., NY.

Knight, Joseph. Theatrical Notes. (1893) $15.00 Hdbd. (ISBN 0-404-08839-2). AMS Pr., NY.

Kraft, Hy. On My Way to the Theater. Friede, Eleanor, ed. 1971. $6.95 Hdbd. Macmillan Co., NY.

Lewis, Allan. Contemporary Theatre. rev. ed. 1971. $5.95 Hdbd. Crown Publ., NY.

Lord, W. A. & Webster, H. Theatre. (Enjoying Your Leisure Ser). 1961. $3.25 Hdbd. International Publ. Serv., NY.

Lounsbury, Warren C. Theatre Backstage from A to Z. rev. ed. 1967. $9.00 Hdbd.; $4.95 pa. Univ. of Washington Pr., WA.

Matthews, Brander. Book About the Theater. (1916) $15.00 Hdbd. Kraus Reprint Co., NY.

Matthews, Brander. Book About the Theatre. 1970. (1916) $16.50 Hdbd. (ISBN 0-678-02758-7). Augustus M. Kelley Publ., NY.

Matthews, Brander. Book About the Theatre. 1971. (1916) $18.00 Hdbd. Scholarly Pr., MI.

Matthews, Brander. Playwrights on Playmaking & Other Studies on the Stage. facs. ed. (Essay Index Reprint Ser). 1923. $9.75 Hdbd. (ISBN 0-8369-0698-5). Books for Libraries, NY.

Matthews, Brander. Rip Van Winkle Goes to the Play. 1967. $8.00 Hdbd. (ISBN 0-8046-0303-0). Kennikat Pr., NY.

Mitchell, Roy. Creative Theatre. 1969. (1929) $7.50 Hdbd.; $4.95 pa. DBS Pubns., NY.

Moreno, J. L. Stehgreiftheater. 2nd ed. $6.00 Hdbd. Beacon House, Inc., NY.

Moreno, J. L. The Theater of Spontaneity. $6.00 Hdbd. Beacon House, Inc., NY.

Nathan, George J. Morning After the First Night. $10.00 Hdbd. (ISBN 0-8386-7779-7). Fairleigh Dickinson Univ. Pr., NJ.

Nathan, George J. Popular Theatre. $8.00 Hdbd. (ISBN 0-8386-7945-5). Fairleigh Dickinson Univ. Pr., NJ.

Nathan, George J. The World in Falseface. $10.00 Hdbd. (ISBN 0-8386-7963-3). Fairleigh Dickinson Univ. Pr., NJ.

Passoli, Robert. Book on the Open Theatre. $7.50 Hdbd. Bobbs-Merrill Co., IN.

Poggi, Jack. Theater in America: The Impact of Economic Forces, 1870–1967. 1968. $10.00 Hdbd. (ISBN 0-8014-0340-5). Cornell Univ. Pr., NY.

Rice, Elmer. The Living Theatre. (1959) $13.00 Hdbd. (ISBN 0-8371-4688-7). Greenwood Pr., CT.

Ritter, Charles C. Lively Art of Theatre. 1970. $6.50 text ed. Allyn Inc., NJ.

Roberts, Vera M. Nature of Theatre. 1971. $12.50 Hdbd. (ISBN 0-06-013577-8). $7.95 text ed. (ISBN 0-06-045501-2). Harper & Row, NY.

Roennfeldt, M. J. Drama in Action 2 Vols. 1969. Vol. 1, $2.00 Hdbd. Vol. 2, $2.50 Hdbd. Tri-Ocean, CA.

Roose-Evans, James. Experimental Theater. 1971. $1.65 pa. Avon, NY.

Roose-Evans, James. Experimental Theatre: From Stanislavsky to Today. 1970.

$6.95 Hdbd. (ISBN C-87663-119-7). Universe, NY.

Seldon, Samuel, ed. Theatre Double Game. 1969. $6.00 Hdbd. (ISBN 0-8078-1113-0). Univ. of N.C. Pr., NC.

Shank, Theodore J. Art of Dramatic Art. 1969. $9.25 Hdbd.; $6.95 text ed. Dickenson Publ., CA.

Siks, Geraldine B. & Dunnington, Hazel B., eds. Children's Theatre & Creative Dramatics. (Hi-Sch.). 1961. $6.95 Hdbd.; $3.95 pa. (ISBN 0-295-97875-9, WP29). Univ. of Wash. Pr., WA.

Simonson, Lee. Stage Is Set. 1962. $3.95 pa. Theatre Arts Books, NY.

Steinbeck, Dietrich. Einleitung in Die Theorie und Systematik der Theaterwissenschaft. (Ger). 1970. $10.40 Hdbd. (ISBN 3-11-006389-1). De Gruyter, Germany.

Stubs. The Seating Plan Guide. 1st Western States Ed. 1967. $1.50 Hdbd. Lytton Theatre & Concert Hall Seating Plan (Lond. Engl.). 1967. $2.00 Hdbd. 4th Metropolitan N.Y. Ed. $2.00 Hdbd. Meyer Schattner, ed. Stubs, NY.

Styan, J. L. Elements of Drama. 1960. $6.50 Hdbd.; $2.25 pa. (ISBN 0-521-09201-9, 201). Cambridge Univ. Pr., NY.

Symons, Arthur. Plays, Acting, & Music. rev. ed. $7.00 Hdbd. Benjamin Blom, NY.

Tairov, Alexander. Notes of a Director. Albright, H. D., ed. Kuhlke, William, tr. (Books of the Theatre, No. 7). 1969.

$6.50 Hdbd. (ISBN 0-87024-105-2). Univ. of Miami Pr., FL.

Tennyson, G. B. Introduction to Drama. (Rinehart English Pamphlets). 1967. $1.85 text ed. (ISBN 0-03-060820-1). Holt, Rinehart & Winston, NY.

Tompkins, Dorothy L. Handbook for Theatrical Apprentices. 1962. $1.75 Hdbd. Samuel French, NY.

Waldman, Max. Waldman on Theater. 1971. $8.95 Hdbd. Doubleday, NY.

Weissman, Philip. Creativity in the Theatre. 1966. $1.95 pa. Dell Publ., NY.

Whiting, Frank M. Introduction to the Theatre. 3rd ed. (Auer Ser). 1969. $11.25 text ed. (ISBN 0-06-047091-7). Harper & Row, NY.

Whitworth, Geoffrey. Theatre in Action. $8.50 Hdbd. Benjamin Blom, NY.

Willis, John. Theatre World, Vol. 27. 1971. $8.95 Hdbd. Crown Publ., NY.

Wilson, S. Theatre in the Fifties. $1.70 Hdbd. Library Assoc., ENG.

Wright, Edward A. Understanding Today's Theatre. 1959. $1.95 pa. (ISBN 0-13-936229-0, Spec). Prentice-Hall, NY.

Wright, Edward A. & Downs, Lenthiel H. Primer for Playgoers. 2nd ed. (Speech & Drama Ser). 1969. $8.95 Hdbd.; $6.95 text ed. (ISBN 0-13-700443-5). Prentice-Hall, NY.

Yates, Francis A. Theatre of the World. 1969. $8.50 Hdbd. (ISBN 0-226-95004-2). Univ. of Chicago Pr., IL.

Young, Stark. Theatre. $1.50 pa.

(ISBN 0-8090-0512-3, Drama). Hill & Wang, NY.

Architecture & Construction

Allen, James T. Greek Theatre of Fifth Century Before Christ. (Drama Ser., No. 39). 1969. (1919) $8.95 Hdbd. (ISBN 0-8383-0647-0). Haskell House, NY.

American Theatre Planning Board, ed. Theatre Check List: A Guide to the Planning & Construction of Proscenium & Open Stage Theatres. 1969. $4.95 pa. (ISBN 0-8195-6005-7). Wesleyan Univ. Pr., CT.

Burris-Meyer, Harold & Cole, E. G. Theatres & Auditoriums. 2nd ed. 1964. $25.00 Hdbd. Van Nostrand-Reinhold, NY.

Diderot, Denis & D'Alembert, Jean Le R. Theatre Architecture & Stage Machines: Engravings from the Encyclopedie of Diderot & D'Alembert. 1968. $37.50 Hdbd. Benjamin Blom, NY.

Dumont, Gabriel P. Parallele De Plans Des Plus Bell Salles De Spectacles D'Italie et De France. (Fr.). 1968. $37.50 Hdbd. Benjamin Blom, NY.

Isaacs, Edith J., ed. Architecture for the New Theatre. $8.00 Hdbd.; $0.75 pa. Benjamin Blom, NY.

Joseph, Stephen, ed. Actor & Architect. 1964. $4.25 Hdbd. (ISBN 0-8020-1309-0); $1.95 pa. (ISBN 0-8020-6103-6). Univ. of Toronto Pr., CAN.

McNamara, Brooks. American Playhouse in the Eighteenth Century. 1969. $9.95 Hdbd. (ISBN 0-674-02725-6). Harvard Univ. Pr., MA.

Mielziner, Jo. Shapes of Our Theatres. 1970. $6.95 Hdbd. Clarkson N. Potter, NY.

Mullin, Donald C. Development of the Playhouse: A Survey of Theatre Architecture from the Renaissance to the Present. 1970. $15.00 Hdbd. (ISBN 0-520-01391-3). Univ. of Cal. Pr., CA.

Robinson, Horace. Architecture for the Educational Theatre. 1970. $7.50 Hdbd. Univ. of Ore. Bks., OR.

Sachs, Edwin O. & Woodrow, Ernest A. Modern Opera Houses & Theatres, 3 Vols. 1968. $110.00 Hdbd. Benjamin Blom, NY.

Schubert, Hannelore. Modern Theater Buildings: Architecture, Stage Design, Lighting. 1971. $35.00 Hdbd. Fredrick A. Praeger, NY.

Silverman, Maxwell & Bowman, Ned A. Contemporary Theatre Architecture: An Illustrated Survey & a Checklist of Publications, 1946–1964. 1965. $10.00 Hdbd. (ISBN 0-87104-055-7). NY Public Library, NY.

Southern, Richard. Proscenium & Sight Lines. $7.45 Hdbd. Theatre Arts, NY.

Stubs. The Seating Plan Guide. 1967 1st Western States Ed. $1.50 Hdbd. 1967 Lytton Theatre & Concert Hall Seating Plan (Lond. Engl.) $2.00 Hdbd. 1971 4th Metropolitan NY Ed. $2.00 Hdbd. Meyer Schattner, ed. Stubs, NY.

Yates, Frances A. Theatre of the World. 1969. $8.50 Hdbd. (ISBN 0-226-95004-2). Univ. of Chicago Pr., IL.

Audiences

Hughes, Leo. Drama's Patrons: A Study of the Eighteenth-Century London Audience. 1971. $7.50 Hdbd. (ISBN 0-292-70091-1). Univ. of Tex. Pr., TX.

Jellicoe, Ann. Some Unconscious Influences in the Theatre. 1967. $0.95 Hdbd. Cambridge Univ. Pr., NY.

Lough, John. Paris Theatre Audiences in the Seventeenth & Eighteenth Centuries. 1957. $9.00 Hdbd. (ISBN 0-19-713112-3). Oxford Univ. Pr., NY.

Righter, Anne. Shakespeare & the Idea of the Play. 1967. $1.65 pa. (ISBN 0-14-053001-0, SL1). Penguin, MD.

Seldon, Samuel, ed. Theatre Double Game. 1969. $6.00 Hdbd. (ISBN 0-8078-1113-0). Univ. of N.C. Pr., NC.

Careers

Campbell, Douglas & Devlin, Diana. Looking Forward to a Career: Theater. 1970. $3.95 Hdbd. (ISBN 0-87518-024-8). Dillon Pr., MN.

Dalrymple, Jean. Careers & Opportunities in the Theatre. 1969. $5.95 Hdbd. (ISBN 0-525-07636-0). E. P. Dutton, NY.

Haeberle, Billi. Looking Forward to a Career: Radio & Television. 1970. $3.95 Hdbd. (ISBN 0-87518-025-6). Dillon Pr., MN.

Hirschfeld, Burt. Stagestruck: Your Career in Theatre. (Jr Hi.). 1963. $3.95 Hdbd. Julian Messner, NY.

Censorship

Boas, Frederick S. Shakespeare & the Universities. 1923. $12.50 Hdbd. Benjamin Blom, NY.

Fowell, Frank & Palmer, Frank. Censorship in England. 1967. (1913) $25.00 Hdbd. (ISBN 0-8337-1227-6). Burt Franklin, NY.

Fowell, Frank & Palmer, Frank. Censorship in England. $10.75 Hdbd. Benjamin Blom, NY.

Palmer, John. Censor & the Theatre. $10.75 Hdbd. Benjamin Blom, NY.

Dictionaries & Indexes

Band-Kuzmany, K. R. Glossary of the Theatre. •1970. $9.75 Hdbd. (ISBN 0-444-40716-2). American Elsevier Publ., NY.

Barnet, Sylvan, et al. Aspects of the Drama: A Handbook. (Orig.). $3.50 pa. (ISBN 0-316-08178-7). Little, Brown & Co., MA.

Bowman, Walter P. & Ball, Robert H. Theatre Language, a Dictionary. $7.95 Hdbd. Theatre Arts Books, NY.

Chicorel Index Series. Marietta Chicorel, ed. Vol. 1 Chicorel Theater Index to Plays in Anthologies, Periodicals, Discs & Tapes. 1970. $38.25 Hdbd. (ISBN 87729-001-6). Vol. 2 1971. $42.50 Hdbd. (ISBN 87729-002-3). Vol.

3 1972. $42.50 Hdbd. (ISBN 87729-003-7). Vol. 4 Chicorel Index to Poetry on Discs & Tapes: Poetry-On-Media; Readings by Well Known Actors and Poets. 1972. $42.50 Hdbd. (ISBN 87729-004-9). Chicorel Library Publishing, NY.

Halliday, Frank E. Shakespeare Companion: 1564–1964. (Hi-Sch.). 1964. $2.65 pa. (ISBN 0-14-053011-8). Penguin Books, MD.

Hartnoll, Phyllis, ed. Oxford Companion to the Theatre. 3rd ed. 1967. $15.00 Hdbd. (ISBN 0-19-211531-6). Oxford Univ. Pr., NY.

Lounsbury, Warren C. Theatre Backstage from A to Z. 1967. $9.00 Hdbd.; $4.95 pa. Univ. of Wash. Pr., WA.

Melchinger, Siegfried. Concise Encyclopedia of Modern Drama. Popkin, Henry, ed. Wellworth, George, tr. $15.00 Hdbd. (ISBN 0-8180-0500-9). Horizon Pr., NY.

Rae, Kenneth & Southern, Richard, eds. International Vocabulary of Technical Theatre Terms. $5.25 Hdbd. Theatre Arts Books, NY.

Taylor, John R. Penguin Dictionary of the Theatre. (Orig.). $1.45 pa. (ISBN 0-14-051033-8). Penguin Books, MD.

Directing, Staging, and Producing

Alexander, Martha. Behind the Footlights: From Amateur to Repertory. 1955. $3.00 Hdbd. Transatlantic, NY.

Austell, Jan. What's in a Play. (Curriculum Related Bks.). 1968. $3.50 Hdbd. (ISBN 0-15-095500-3). Harcourt riculum Related Bks). (Hi-Sch.). 1968. $3.50 Hdbd. (ISBN 0-13-095500-3). Harcourt Brace Jovanovich, NY.

Bradbury, Arthur J., et al. Production & Staging of Plays. 1963. $3.50 lib. bdg. (ISBN 0-668-01051-7); $0.95 pa. (ISBN 0-668-01052-5). Arc Bks., NY.

Brown, Andrew. Drama. 1962. $3.50 lib. bdg. (ISBN 0-668-00979-9); $0.95 pa. (979) (ISBN 0-668-00984-5). Arc Bks., NY.

Brown, Gilmor & Garwood, Alice. General Principles of Play Direction. 1936. $2.75 Hdbd. Samuel French, NY.

Burian, Jarka. Scenography of Josef Svoboda. 1971. $25.00 Hdbd. Wesleyan Univ. Pr., CT.

Burton, Ernest J. British Theatre: Its Repertory & Practice, 1100–1900 A.D. 1960. $5.00 Hdbd. Dufour, PA.

Cameron, Ian. Directors for the Seventies. 1971. $6.95 Hdbd.; $2.95 pa. Frederick A. Praeger, NY.

Canfield, C. Craft of Play Directing. (Rinehart Editions). 1963. $8.95 text ed. (ISBN 0-03-041610-8). Holt, Rinehart & Winston, NY.

Clay, James H. & Krempel, D. Theatrical Image. 1967. $7.95 text ed. (ISBN 0-07-011286-X). McGraw-Hill, NY.

Cole, Toby & Chinoy, Helen K., eds. Directors on Directing. rev. ed. Orig. Title: Directing the Play. 1963. $5.00 Hdbd.; $3.50 pa. Bobbs-Merrill, IN.

Cristini, C. M. Styles & Techniques of Scenic Design. price n.g. Hdbd. (ISBN 0-910482-35-7). DBS Publications, NY.

Cullman, Marguerite. Occupation: Angel. 1963. $3.95 Hdbd. (ISBN 0-393-07440-4). W. W. Norton, NY.

Dean, Alexander & Carra, L. Fundamentals of Play Directing. rev. ed. 1965. $9.50 Hdbd. (ISBN 0-03-049815-5) Holt, Rinehart & Winston, NY.

Dietrich, John E. Play Direction. 1953. $8.95 Hdbd. (ISBN 0-13-683342-X). Prentice-Hall, NY.

Donohue, Joseph W., Jr., ed. Theatrical Manager in England & America: Players of a Perilous Game. 1971. $8.50 text ed. (ISBN 0-691-06188-2). Princeton Univ. Pr., NJ.

Farber, Donald C. From Option to Opening: A Guide for the off Broadway Producer. rev. 2nd ed. 1970. $7.50 Hdbd. (ISBN 0-910482-24-1). DBS Publications, NY.

Farber, Donald C. Producing on Broadway: A Comprehensive Guide. 1969. $15.00 Hdbd. DBS Publications, NY.

Fedyszyn, Stan. Scenes: For Actors. 1971. $5.25 pa.; $3.95 text ed. Wadsworth Publ., CA.

Fernald, John. Sense of Direction. 1969. $6.95 Hdbd. (ISBN 0-8128-1162-3); $1.95 pa. (ISBN 0-8128-1261-1). Stein & Day, NY.

Gassner, John & Barber, P. Producing the Play. rev. ed. Incl. New Scene Technician's Handbook. 1953. $11.50

text ed. (ISBN 0-03-005565-2). Holt, Rinehart & Winston, NY.

Gibson, William. Seesaw Log: A Chronicle of the Stage Production, with the Text of Two for a Seesaw. 1959. $5.95 Hdbd. Alfred A. Knopf, NY.

Gregory, W. A. Director: A Guide to Modern Theater Practice. 1968. $6.95 Hdbd. Funk & Wagnalls, NY.

Gross, Edwin & Gross, Nathalie. Teen Theatre: A Guide to Play Production & Six Comedies. (Jr Hi–Hi-Sch.). 1953. $3.50 Hdbd. (ISBN 0-07-024975-X). McGraw-Hill, NY.

Heffner, Hubert C., et al. Modern Theatre Practice: A Handbook of Play Production. 4th ed. 1959. $7.95 text ed. (ISBN 0-390-43101-X). Appleton-Century-Croft, NY.

Hodge, Francis. Play Directing: Analysis, Communication & Style. (Theatre & Drama Ser). 1971. ref. ed. $8.95 Hdbd. (ISBN 0-13-682815-9). Prentice-Hall, NY.

Johnson, Albert & Johnson, Bertha. Directing Methods. 1970. $9.50 Hdbd. (ISBN 0-498-07351-3). A. S. Barnes, NJ.

Kozelka. Directing. (Theatre Student Ser). (Jr Hi.). $6.96 Hdbd. Rosen Richards Pr., NY.

Lewis, Jerry. Total Filmmaker. 1971. $6.95 Hdbd. Random House, NY.

Little, E. J. & Gassner, J. Reading & Staging the Play: An Anthology. (Hi-Sch.). 1967. $4.92 Hdbd. (ISBN 0-03-

052985-9); $1.20 pa. (ISBN 0-03-064590-5). Holt, Rinehart & Winston, NY.

Lubimiv, Alexius. How to Direct Stage Plays. 1969. $1.50 pa. Campus Publ., MI.

McCalmon, George & Moe, Christian. Creating Historical Drama: A Guide for the Community & the Interested Individual. 1965. $12.50 Hdbd. (ISBN 0-8093-0189-X). Southern Ill. Univ. Pr., IL.

Marowitz, Charles & Trussler, Simon, eds. Theatre at Work: Playwrights & Productions in the Modern British Theatre. 1968. $5.00 Hdbd. (ISBN 0-8090-9270-0). Hill & Wang, NY.

Nelms, Henning. Play Production. rev. ed. 1958. $2.25 pa. (ISBN 0-389-00096-5, 73). Barnes & Noble, NY.

Nutall, Kenneth. Your Book of Acting. $3.25 Hdbd. Transatlantic Arts, NY.

Nuttall, Kenneth. Play Production for Young People. (Hi-Sch.). 1963. $4.95 Hdbd. (ISBN 0-8238-0085-7). Plays, Inc., MA.

Ommanney, Katharine A. Stage & the School. 3rd ed. 1960. $7.96 Hdbd. (ISBN 0-07-047669-1). McGraw, Hill Book Co., NY.

Resnik, Muriel. Son of Any Wednesday. 1965. $4.95 Hdbd. (ISBN 0-8128-1169-0). Stein & Day, NY.

Roose-Evans, James. Directing a Play. 1968. $6.95 Hdbd. Theatre Arts Books, NY.

Rossi, Alfred. Minneapolis Rehearsals: Tyrone Guthrie Directs Hamlet. 1971. $12.50 Hdbd. (ISBN 0-520-01719-6). Univ. of Cal. Pr., CA.

Rossiter, H. How to Put on a Minstrel Show. $0.50 pa. Stein Publ. House, IL.

Rowe, Kenneth T. Theater in Your Head. 1967. $6.95 Hdbd. Funk & Wagnalls Co., NY.

Sanders, Sandra. Creating Plays with Children. 1970. $1.25 pa. (ISBN 0-590-09099-2). Scholastic Book Serv., NY.

Selden, Samuel. Stage in Action. 1967. (1941) $2.85 pa. (ISBN 0-8093-0275-6, AB). Southern Ill. Univ. Pr., IL.

Sievers, David W. Directing for the Theater. 2nd ed. 1965. $6.50 Hdbd. (ISBN 0-697-04250-2). William C. Brown, IA.

Smith, Milton M. Play Production. 1948. $7.00 Hdbd. (ISBN 0-390-82499-2). Appleton-Century-Crofts, NY.

Strindberg, August. Open Letters to the Intimate Theater. Johnson, Walter, tr. 1967. $6.95 Hdbd.; $2.95 pa. (ISBN 0-295-97874-0). Univ. of Wash. Pr., WA.

Weales, Gerald. Play & Its Parts. (Culture & Discovery Ser). (Hi-Sch.). 1964. $5.95 Hdbd. (ISBN 0-465-05783-7). Basic Books, NY.

Welker, David. Theatrical Direction. 1971. $9.95 Hdbd. Allyn Inc., NJ.

Young, John W. Directing the Play: From Selection to Opening Night. 1971.

(1958) $8.00 Hdbd. (ISBN 0-8046-1541-1). Kennikat Pr., NY.

Education

Dow, Clyde W., ed. Introduction to Graduate Study in Speech & Theatre. 1961. $6.00 Hdbd. (ISBN 0-87013-060-9). Mich. St. Univ. Pr., MI.

Kernodle, George R. Invitation to the Theatre. abr. ed. 1971. $4.95 pa. (ISBN 0-15-546922-3). Harcourt, Brace & World, NY.

Motter, Charlotte K. Theatre in High School: Planning, Teaching, Directing. (Drama Ser). 1970. $6.95 Hdbd. (ISBN 0-13-913012-8). Prentice-Hall Inc., NY.

Wickham, Glynne. Drama in a World of Science. 1962. $5.00 Hdbd. (ISBN 0-8020-1198-5). Univ. of Toronto Pr., CAN.

England—History

Adams, Joseph Q. Shakespearean Playhouses: A History of English Theatres from the Beginning to the Reformation. 1959. $6.75 Hdbd. Peter Smith Publ., MA.

Adams, William D. Dictionary of the Drama Vol. 1, A–G. 1965. (1904) $28.50 Hdbd. Burt Franklin, NY.

Agate, James. Amazing Theatre. 1939. $12.50 Hdbd. Benjamin Blom, NY.

Agate, James. At Half-Past Eight: Essays on the Theatre 1921–1922. 1923. $10.75 Hdbd. Benjamin Blom, NY.

Agate, James. Contemporary Theatre,

Nineteen Twenty-Three. 1924. $10.75 Hdbd. Benjamin Blom, NY.

Agate, James. Contemporary Theatre, Nineteen Twenty-Four. 1925. $10.75 Hdbd. Benjamin Blom, NY.

Agate, James. Contemporary Theatre, Nineteen Twenty-Five. 1926. $10.75 Hdbd. Benjamin Blom, NY.

Agate, James. Contemporary Theatre, Nineteen Twenty-Six. 1927. $12.50 Hdbd. Benjamin Blom, NY.

Agate, James. First Nights. 1934. $12.50 Hdbd. Benjamin Blom, NY.

Agate, James. Immoment Toys. 1945. $10.75 Hdbd. Benjamin Blom, NY.

Agate, James. James Agate: An Anthology. Thal, Herbert Van, ed. 1961. $6.00 Hdbd. (ISBN 0-8090-2380-6). Hill & Wang, NY.

Agate, James. More First Nights. 1937. $12.50 Hdbd. Benjamin Blom, NY.

Agate, James. My Theatre Talks. 1933. $10.75 Hdbd. Benjamin Blom, NY.

Agate, James. On an English State. 1924. $10.75 Hdbd. Benjamin Blom, NY.

Agate, James. Red Letter Nights. 1944. $12.50 Hdbd. Benjamin Blom, NY.

Agate, James. Their Hour Upon the Stage. 1930. $8.75 Hdbd. Benjamin Blom, NY.

Agate, James. These Were Actors: Extracts from a Newspaper Cutting Book, 1811-1833. 1943. $10.75 Hdbd. Benjamin Blom, NY.

Agate, James. Those Were the Nights. 1947. $10.75 Hdbd. Benjamin Blom, NY.

Agate, James. Thursdays & Fridays. 1941. $10.75 Hdbd. Benjamin Blom, NY.

Agate, James. Short View of the English Stage 1900-1926. 1926. $6.75 Hdbd. Benjamin Blom, NY.

Agate, James. Short View of the English Stage, 1900-1926. (Select Bibliographies Reprint Ser). 1926. $8.00 Hdbd. (ISBN 0-8369-5037-2). Books for Libraries, NY.

Albright, Evelyn M. Dramatic Publications in England: 1580-1640. 1970. $10.00 text ed. (ISBN 0-87752-127-1). Gordian Pr., NY.

Archer, William. Theatrical World of Eighteen Ninety-Three. 1894. $12.50 Hdbd. Benjamin Blom, NY.

Archer, William & Barker, H. Granville, eds. National Theatre: Scheme & Estimates. 1970. (1907) $9.50 Hdbd. (ISBN 0-8046-0749-4). Kennikat Pr., NY.

Armstrong, Cecil F. Century of Great Actors 1750-1850. 1912. $12.50 Hdbd. Benjamin Blom, NY.

Armstrong, William A. Elizabethan Private Theatres: Facts & Problems. 1958. $3.00 Hdbd. Folcroft Pr., PA.

Arnott, James F. English Theatrical Literature, 1559-1900. (1888) $25.50 Hdbd. Johnson Reprint Corp., NY.

Arthur, George C. From Phelps to Gielgud: Reminiscences of the Stage Through Sixty-Five Years. 1936. $12.50 Hdbd. Benjamin Blom, NY.

Arthur, George C. From Phelps to Gielgud: Reminiscences of the Stage Through Sixty-Five Years. facs. ed. (Essay Index Reprint Ser). 1967. (1936) $9.50 Hdbd. (ISBN 0-8369-0160-6). Books for Libraries, NY.

Avery, Emmett L., ed. London Stage, 1660–1800, Pt. 2., 1700–1729, 2 Vols. 1960. $50.00 Hdbd. (ISBN 0-8093-0030-3). $2.25 pa. (ISBN 0-8093-0337-X, AB). Southern Illinois Univ. Pr., IL.

Avery, Emmett L. & Scouten, Arthur H., eds. London Stage, 1600–1800, Pt. 1 1660–1700 A Critical Introduction. 1968. $2.25 pa. (ISBN 0-8093-0336-1, AB). Southern Ill. Univ. Pr., IL.

Baker, Barton. History of the London Stage & Its Famous Players 1576–1903. 1904. $12.50 Hdbd. Benjamin Blom, NY.

Baker, David E., et al. Biographia Dramatica, or Companion to the Playhouse, 3 Vols. 1812. Set—$110.00 Hdbd. (ISBN 0-404-00530-6); $39.50 ea. (ISBN 0-404-00531-4) (ISBN 0-404-00532-2) (ISBN 0-404-00533-0). AMS Pr., NY.

Bakshy, Alexander. Theatre Unbound. 1968. (1923) $6.75 Hdbd. Benjamin Blom, NY.

Baldwin, Thomas W. Organization & Personnel of the Shakespearean Company. 1961. (1927) $15.00 Hdbd. Russell & Russell Publ., NY.

Baring, Maurice. Punch & Judy & Other Essays. facs. ed. (Essay Index Reprint Ser). 1968. (1924) $11.50 Hdbd. (ISBN 0-8369-0172-X). Books for Libraries, NY.

Beerbohm, Max. Around Theatres. Davis, Rupert-Hart, ed. 1969. $6.50 Hdbd. (ISBN 0-8008-0315-9). Taplinger Publ., NY.

Beerbohm, Max. Around Theatres. 1969. Repr. $20.75 Hdbd. (ISBN 0-8371-0303-7). Greenwood Pr., CT.

Beerbohm, Max. More Theatres. Hart-Davis, Rupert, ed. 1969. $15.00 Hdbd. (ISBN 0-8008-5360-1). Taplinger Publ., NY.

Bentley, Gerald E. The Jacobean & Caroline Stage. Incl. Vol. 1–2. Dramatic Companies & Players. 1941. $24.00 Hdbd. (ISBN 0-19-811503-2); Vol. 3–5. Plays & Playwrights. 1956. $38.50 Hdbd. (ISBN 0-19-811504-0); Vol. 6–7. Theatres, Appendixes to Vol. 6 & General Index. 1968. $22.50 Hdbd. (ISBN 0-19-811626-8). Oxford Univ. Pr., NY.

Bentley, Gerald E. Seventeenth-Century Stage: A Collection of Critical Essays. (Patterns of Literary Criticism Ser., No. 6). 1968. $9.75 Hdbd. (ISBN 0-8020-1561-1); $2.95 pa. (ISBN 0-8020-1560-3). Univ. of Toronto Pr., CAN.

Bentley, Gerald E., ed. Seventeenth-Century Stage. 1968. $9.75 Hdbd. (ISBN 0-226-04308-8). $2.95 pa. (ISBN 0-226-04309-6). Univ. of Chicago Pr., IL.

Bernard, John. Retrospections of the

Stage, 2 Vols. in 1. 1830. $25.00 Hdbd. Benjamin Blom, NY.

Bevington, David M. From Mankind to Marlowe: Growth of Structure in the Popular Drama of Tudor England. 1962. $8.50 Hdbd. (ISBN 0-674-32500-1). Harvard Univ. Pr., MA.

Boaden, James. Memoirs of the Life of John Phillip Kemble. 1825. $27.50 Hdbd. Benjamin Blom, NY.

Borgerhoff, Joseph L. Theatre Anglais a Paris Sous La Restauration. (1913) $15.00 Hdbd. (ISBN 0-8337-4961-7). Burt Franklin, NY.

Boswell, Eleanore. Restoration Court Stage, 1660–1702. 1932. $12.50 Hdbd. Benjamin Blom, NY.

Boswell, Eleanore. Restoration Court Stage Sixteen Sixty to Seventeen Two. 1966. $8.50 Hdbd. Barnes & Noble, NY.

Bradbrook, Muriel C. Rise of the Common Player: A Study of Actor & Society in Shakespeare's England. 1962. $8.50 Hdbd. (ISBN 0-674-77235-0). Harvard Univ. Pr., MA.

Bradbrook, Muriel C. Themes & Conventions of Elizabethan Tragedy. 1952–1960. $7.00 Hdbd.; $1.95 pa. (ISBN 0-521-09108-X, 108). Cambridge Univ. Pr., NY.

Broadbent, R. J. Annals of the Liverpool Stage. 1908. $15.75 Hdbd. Benjamin Blom, NY.

Burton, Ernest J. British Theatre: Its Repertory & Practice, 1100–1900 A.D. 1960. $5.00 Hdbd. Dufour Editions, PA.

Burton, Ernest J. Student's Guide to British Theatre & Drama. 1964. $5.25 Hdbd. Intl. Pubns. Serv., NY.

Burton, Hal, ed. Great Acting. 1968. $8.95 Hdbd. (ISBN 0-8090-5110-9). Hill & Wang, NY.

Campbell, Lily B. Scenes & Machines on the English Stage During the Renaissance: A Classical Revival. 1970. (1923) $10.00 Hdbd. (ISBN 0-389-01756-6). Barnes & Noble, NY.

Chambers, Edmund K. Elizabethan Stage, 4 Vols. 1923. Set—$38.50 Hdbd. (ISBN 0-19-811511-3). Oxford Univ. Pr., NY.

Cibber, Colley. Apology for the Life of Colley Cibber Written by Himself, 2 Vols. rev. ed. Lowe, R. W., ed. 1889. $14.50 Hdbd. (ISBN 0-404-01544-1). AMS Pr., NY.

Clunes, Alec. British Theatre. 1965. $12.00 Hdbd. (ISBN 0-498-06263-5). A. S. Barnes, NJ.

Cole, John W. Life & Theatrical Times of Charles Kean, 2 Vols. in 1. 1859. $22.50 Hdbd. Benjamin Blom, NY.

Collier, John Payne. Memoirs of the Principal Actors in the Plays of Shakespeare. 1846. $15.00 Hdbd. (ISBN 0-404-01599-9). AMS Pr., NY.

Collier, Jeremy. Short View of the Immorality, & Profaneness of the English Stage. 1698. $10.00 Hdbd. (ISBN 0-404-01619-7). AMS Pr., NY.

Collier, Jeremy. Short View of the Profaneness & Immorality of the English Stage. 1969. (1730) $20.95 Hdbd. Adler's Foreign Books, NY.

Darbyshire, Alfred. Art of the Victorian Stage. 1907. $10.75 Hdbd. Benjamin Blom, NY.

Darlington, William A. Literature in the Theatre, & Other Essays. facs. ed. (Essay Index Reprint Ser). (1925) $9.00 Hdbd. (ISBN 0-8369-0362-5). Books for Libraries, NY.

Dasent, Arthur I. Nell Gwyn 1650–1687. 1924. $12.50 Hdbd. Benjamin Blom, NY.

David, Richard. Shakespeare & the Players. 1961. $3.50 Hdbd. Folcroft Pr., PA.

Davies, Thomas. Dramatic Miscellanies, on Several Plays of Shakespeare. 3 Vols. (1783-1784) $27.50 Hdbd. Benjamin Blom, NY.

Davies, Thomas. Dramatic Miscellanies on Several Plays of Shakespeare. 3 Vols. 1783-84. Set—$27.50 Hdbd. AMS Pr., NY.

Dibdin, James C. Annals of the Edinburgh Stage. 1888. $17.50 Hdbd. Benjamin Blom, NY.

Doran, John. Their Majesties Servants: Annals of the English Stage. 2 Vols. 1970. (1865) Set—$40.00 Hdbd. (ISBN 0-403-00234-6). Scholarly Pr., MI.

Doran, John Their Majesties' Servants: Or Annals of the English Stage, from Thomas Bettertan to Edmund Kean. 3

Vols. Lowe, R. W., ed. 1888. Set—$36.00 Hdbd. (ISBN 0-404-02170-0). AMS Pr., NY.

Downer, Alan S. Eminent Tragedian: William Charles Macready. 1966. $10.00 Hdbd. (ISBN 0-674-25100-8). Harvard Univ. Pr., MA.

Elsom, John. Theatre: Outside London. 1971. $7.50 text ed. Fernhill House, NY.

Enkvist, Nils E. Caricatures of Americans on the English Stage Prior to 1870. 1968. (1951) $7.50 Hdbd. (ISBN 0-8046-0134-8). Kennikat Pr., NY.

Filon, Augustin. English Stage. Whyte, Frederic, tr. 1970. (1897) $10.00 Hdbd. (ISBN 0-8046-0753-2). Kennikat Pr., NY.

Filon, Pierre M. English Stage. 1897. $10.75 Hdbd. Benjamin Blom, NY.

Fitz-Gerald, S. Adair. Dickens & the Drama. 1910. $12.50 Hdbd. Benjamin Blom, NY.

Fleay, Frederick G. Chronicle History of London Stage, 1559-1642. 1964. (1890) $18.50 Hdbd. (ISBN 0-8337-1152-0). Burt Franklin, NY.

Fleay, Frederick G. Shakespeare Manual. 1970. (1876) $14.00 Hdbd. (ISBN 0-404-02408-4). AMS Pr., NY.

Galloway, David, ed. Elizabethan Theatre 1. 1970. $6.50 Hdbd. (ISBN 0-208-01144-7). Shoe String Pr., CT.

Galloway, David. Elizabethan Theatre 2. 1970. $7.00 Hdbd. (ISBN 0-208-01145-5). Shoe String Pr., CT.

Genest, John. Some Account of the English Stage from the Restoration in 1660 to 1830, 10 Vols. 1965. (1832) Set—$275.00 Hdbd.; $36.50 ea. (ISBN 0-8337-1323-X). Burt Franklin, NY.

Goldstein, Malcolm. Pope & the Augustan Stage. 1958. $10.00 Hdbd. (ISBN 0-404-51827-3). AMS Pr., NY.

Graves, Thornton S. Act Time in Elizabethan Theatres. (Studies in Drama Ser., No. 39). 1970. Repr. $2.95 pa. (ISBN 0-8383-0043-X). Haskell House Publ., NY.

Graves, Thornton S. Court & the London Theatres During the Reign of Elizabeth. 1967. (1913) $6.00 Hdbd. Russell & Russell Publ., NY.

Graves, Thornton S. Court & the London Theatres During the Reign of Elizabeth. 1913. $5.00 Hdbd. Folcroft Pr., PA.

Gray, Charles H. Theatrical Criticism in London to Seventeen Ninety-Five. 1931. $12.50 Hdbd. Benjamin Blom, NY.

Greg, Walter W. Dramatic Documents from Elizabethan Playhouses: Stage Plots: Actors' Parts: Prompt Books, 2 Vols. 1931. $38.40 Hdbd. (ISBN 0-19-811672-1). Oxford Univ. Pr., NY.

Griffin, Alice V. Pageantry on the Shakespearean Stage. 1962. $2.95 pa. College & Univ. Pr., CT.

Gurr, Andrew. Shakespearean Stage, 1574–1642. 1970. $9.50 Hdbd. (ISBN 0-521-07816-4). $2.75 pa. (ISBN 0-521-09632-4). Cambridge Univ. Pr., NY.

Halliwell-Phillips, James O. Illustrations of the Life of Shakespeare, in a Discursive Series of Essays on a Variety of Subjects. 1874. $12.50 Hdbd. (ISBN 0-404-03059-9). AMS Pr., NY.

Harbage, Alfred. Annals of English Drama: 975–1700. rev. ed. Schoenbaum, S., ed. 1964. $18.00 Hdbd. (ISBN 0-8122-7483-0). Univ. of Penna. Pr., PA.

Harbage, Alfred. Shakespeare & the Rival Traditions. 1968. (1952) $10.00 Hdbd. Barnes & Noble, NY.

Harrison, G. B. Elizabethan Plays & Players. 1956. $4.95 Hdbd.; $2.25 pa. (ISBN 0-472-06002-3). (ISBN 0-472-09002-X). Univ. of Mich. Pr., MI.

Harvey, John M. Autobiography of Sir John Martin-Harvey. 1933. $12.50 Hdbd. Benjamin Blom, NY.

Harvey, John M. Book of Martin Harvey. 1928. $12.50 Hdbd. Benjamin Blom, NY.

Hazlitt, William C. Hazlitt on Theatre. Archer, William & Lowe, Robert, eds. (Orig.). 1957. $1.25 pa. (ISBN 0-8090-0507-7). Hill & Wang, NY.

Hazlitt, William C., ed. English Drama & Stage Under the Tudor & Stuart Princes—1543–1663. 1964. (1869) $35.00 Hdbd. (ISBN 0-8337-1618-2). Burt Franklin, NY.

Henslowe, Philip. Henslowe Papers: Being Documents Supplementary to Henslowe's Diary. Walter W. Greg. ed.

(1907) $10.00 Hdbd. (ISBN 0-404-09019-2). AMS Pr., NY.

Herbert, Henry. Dramatic Records of Sir Henry Herbert. Adams, Joseph G., ed. $12.50 Hdbd. Benjamin Blom, NY.

Hill, Aaron & Popple, William. Prompter. Appleton, William W. & Burnim, Kalmann A., eds. $15.00 Hdbd. Benjamin Blom, NY.

Hillebrand, Harold N. Child Actors: A Chapter in Elizabethan Stage History. 1964. (1926) $8.50 Hdbd. Russell & Russell Publ., NY.

Hodges, C. Walter. Shakespeare & the Players. rev. ed. (Hi-Sch.). 1971. $3.00 text ed. Coward-McCann, NY.

Hodges, C. Walter. Shakespeare's Theatre. (Elem.). 1964. $6.50 Hdbd. Coward-McCann, NY.

Hogan, Charles B. London Stage, Pt. 5, Vols. 1-3. 1968. Set—$75.00 Hdbd.; $25.00 Hdbd. (ISBN 0-8093-0437-6). $2.25 pa. (ISBN 0-8093-0340-X, AB). Southern Ill. Univ. Pr., IL.

Hotson, Leslie. Commonwealth & Restoration Stage. 1962. (1928) $12.50 Hdbd. Russell & Russell Publ., NY.

Hotson, Leslie. Shakespeare's Wooden O. 2nd ed. 1960. $6.00 Hdbd. Hillary House Publ., NY.

Hughes, Leo. Drama's Patrons: A Study of the Eighteenth-Century London Audience. 1971. $7.50 Hdbd. (ISBN 0-292-70091-1). Univ. of Tex. Pr., TX.

The Irish University Press Series of the British Parliamentary Papers: Stage & Theatre, 3 vols. 1971. Set—$142.00 Hdbd. Irish Univ. Pr., NY.

Jones, Henry A. Foundations of a National Drama. facs. ed. (Essay Index Reprint Ser). 1967. (1913) $11.50 Hdbd. (ISBN 0-8369-0579-2). Books for Libraries, NY.

Jones, Inigo. Designs by Inigo Jones for Masques & Plays at Court. Simpson, Percy & Bell, C. F., eds. 1966. (1924) $35.00 Hdbd. Russell & Russell Publ., NY.

Joseph, Bertram L. Tragic Actor. 1959. $9.95 Hdbd. Theatre Arts Books, NY.

Joseph, Bertram L. Elizabethan Acting. 2nd ed. 1964. $5.75 Hdbd. (ISBN 0-19-811606-3). Oxford Univ. Pr., NY.

Joseph, Stephen. Story of the Playhouse in England. 1963. $5.00 Hdbd. Fernhill House, NY.

Kinne, Willard A. Revivals & Importations of French Comedies in England, 1749-1800. 1939. $10.00 Hdbd. (ISBN 0-404-03705-4). AMS Pr., NY.

Kitchin, Laurence. Mid-Century Drama. 2nd rev. ed. 1962. $6.50 Hdbd. Humanities Pr., NY.

Knight, Joseph. Theatrical Notes. 1893. $12.50 Hdbd. Benjamin Blom, NY.

Langbaine, Gerard. Account of the English Dramatic Poets. 2nd ed. 1965. (1691) $37.50 Hdbd. (ISBN 0-8337-2003-1). Burt Franklin, NY.

Lanier, Henry W. First English Actresses. 1930. $12.50 Hdbd. Benjamin Blom, NY.

Lawrence, William J. Those Nut-Cracking Elizabethans. (Drama Ser., No. 39). 1970. (1935) $8.95 Hdbd. (ISBN 0-8383-0988-7). Haskell House Publ., NY.

Lawrence, William J. Elizabethan Playhouse & Other Studies, 2 Vols. (Illus., 1963 repr. orig. pub. 1912–13). Set—$15.00 Hdbd. Russell & Russell Publ., NY.

Lawrence, William J. Old Theatre Days & Ways. 1968. $12.50 Hdbd. Benjamin Blom, NY.

Lawrence, William J. Physical Conditions of the Elizabethan Public Playhouse. 1968. $4.50 Hdbd. (ISBN 0-8154-0135-3). Cooper Sq. Publ., NY.

Lawrence, William J. Pre-Restoration Stage Studies. 1967. Repr. $12.50 Hdbd. Benjamin Blom, NY.

Lawrence, William J. Speeding up Shakespeare. 1968. $12.50 Hdbd. Benjamin Blom, NY.

Lawson, Robb. Story of the Scots Stage. 1917. $12.50 Hdbd. Benjamin Blom, NY.

Lynch, James J. Box, Pit & Gallery Stage & Society in Johnson's London. 1971. (1953) $18.00 Hdbd. Russell & Russell Publ., NY.

Marston, Westland. Our Recent Actors, 2 Vols. 1888. $12.75 Hdbd. Benjamin Blom, NY.

Mason, Alfred E. Sir George Alexander & the St. James' Theatre. 1935. $12.50 Hdbd. Benjamin Blom, NY.

Motter, Thomas H. School Drama in England. 1968. Repr. $11.00 Hdbd. (ISBN 0-8046-0325-1). Kennikat Pr., NY.

Murray, John T. English Dramatic Companies, 1558–1642, 2 Vols. 1963. 1910. Set—$20.00 Hdbd. Russell & Russell Publ., NY.

Nagler, Alois M. Shakespeare's Stage. 1958. $5.00 Hdbd. (ISBN 0-300-00784-1); $1.45 pa. (ISBN 0-300-00174-6). Yale Univ. Pr., CT.

Nathan. Costumes: Theatrical Memories. $4.95 Hdbd. Wehman Bros. Hackensack, NJ.

Newton, H. Chance, Crime & the Drama. 1970. (1927) $11.00 Hdbd. (ISBN 0-8046-0761-3). Kennikat Pr., NY.

Nicoll, Allardyce. British Drama: An Historical Survey from the Beginnings to the Present Time. 5th rev. ed. 1963. $6.00 Hdbd. Barnes & Noble, NY.

Nicoll, Allardyce. History of English Drama, 1660–1900, 6 vols. Incl. Vol. 1. The Restoration Drama; Vol. 2. Early Eighteenth Century Drama; Vol. 3. Late Eighteenth Century Drama; Vol. 4. Early Nineteenth Century Drama, 1800–1850; Vol. 5. Late Nineteenth Century Drama; Vol. 6. Alphabetical Catalogue of the Plays. 1959. $14.50 ea. Hdbd. Cambridge Univ. Pr., NY.

Nicoll, Allardyce. Stuart Masques & the

Renaissance Stage. 1938. $17.50 Hdbd. Benjamin Blom, NY.

Noyes. Robert G. Ben Jonson on the English Stage, Sixteen Sixty to Seventeen Seventy-Six. 1935. $12.50 Hdbd. Benjamin Blom, NY.

Nungezer, Edwin. Dictionary of Actors & of Other Persons Associated with the Public Representation of Plays in England Before 1642. 1969. (1929) $15.75 Hdbd. (ISBN 0-8371-0593-5). Greenwood Pr., CT.

Odell, George C. Shakespeare from Betterton to Irving, 2 Vols. $4.75 Hdbd. Peter Smith, MA.

Odell, George C. Shakespeare from Betterton to Irving, 2 Vols. 1966. $3.00 pa. (ISBN 0-486-21606-3). (ISBN 0-486-21607-1). Dover Publ., NY.

Odell, George C. Shakespeare-from Betterton to Irving, 2 Vols. $18.50 Hdbd. Benjamin Blom, NY.

Pascoe, Charles E. Our Actors & Actresses. 2nd rev. & enl. ed. 1880. $12.50 Hdbd. Benjamin Blom, NY.

Pedicord, Harry W. Theatrical Public in the Time of Garrick. 1966. $6.00 Hdbd. (ISBN 0-8093-0221-7, AB); $2.65 pa. (ISBN 0-8093-0222-5). Southern Ill. Univ. Pr., IL.

Penley, Belville S. Bath Stage. 1892. $12.50 Hdbd. Benjamin Blom, NY.

Pepys, Samuel. Pepys on the Restoration Stage. McAfee, Helen, ed. 1916. $10.75 Hdbd. Benjamin Blom, NY.

Poel, William. Shakespeare in the Theatre. 1968. $9.75 Hdbd. Benjamin Blom, NY.

Price, Cecil. English Theatre in Wales. 1948. $3.50 Hdbd. Lawrence Verry, CT.

Purdom, Charles B. Harley Granville Barker, Man of the Theatre, Dramatist & Scholar. (1956) $15.00 Hdbd. (ISBN 0-8371-6155-X). Greenwood Pr., CT.

Ralph, James. Case of Our Present Theatrical Disputes Fairly Stated. 1743. lib. bdg. $12.50 Hdbd. (ISBN 0-404-05208-8). AMS Pr., NY.

Righter, Anne. Shakespeare & the Idea of the Play. 1963. $5.00 Hdbd. Barnes & Noble, NY.

Rollins, Hyder E. Contribution to the History of English Commonwealth Drama. (Studies in Drama, No. 39). 1970. Repr. $3.95 pa. (ISBN 0-8383-0065-0). Haskell House Publ., NY.

Rosenfeld, Sybil. Strolling Players & Drama in the Provinces, 1660–1765. 1970. Repr. $11.00 Hdbd. Octagon Books, NY.

Rosenfield, Sybil. Strolling Players & Drama in the Provinces 1660–1765. 1939. $12.50 Hdbd. Benjamin Blom, NY.

Rosenfeld, Sybil. Theatre of the London Fairs in the 18th Century. 1960. $8.50 Hdbd. Cambridge Univ. Pr., NY.

Rowell, George, ed. Victorian Dramatic Criticism. 1971. $12.75 Hdbd. (ISBN 0-416-12320-1). Barnes & Noble, NY.

Rowell, George. Victorian Theatre: A Survey. 1967. $6.50 Hdbd. (ISBN 0-19-811653-5). Oxford Univ. Pr., NY.

Scouten, Arthur H., ed. London Stage, Pt. 3 1729-1747 A Critical Introduction. 1968. $2.25 pa. (ISBN 0-8093-0338-8, A). $25.00 Hdbd. (ISBN 0-8093-0053-2). Southern Ill. Univ. Pr., IL.

Sharpe, Robert B. Real War of the Theatres: Shakespeare's Fellows in Rivalry with the Admiral's Men. 1935. $10.00 pa. Kraus Reprint Co., NY.

Shattuck, Charles H., ed. Bulwer & Macready: Chronicle of the Early Victorian Theatre. 1958. $6.95 Hdbd. (ISBN 0-252-72330-9). Univ. of Ill. Pr., IL.

Shaw, George B. Dramatic Criticism, 1895-1898: A Selection by John F. Matthews. (1959) $12.75 Hdbd. (ISBN 0-8371-5234-8). Greenwood Pr., CT.

Shaw, George B. Shaw's Dramatic Criticism: 1895-98. John F. Matthews, ed. $1.45 pa. (ISBN 0-8090-0517-4). Hill & Wang, NY.

Shaw, George B. Plays & Players: Essays on the Theatre. 1954. $3.00 Hdbd. (ISBN 0-19-250535-1). Oxford Univ. Pr., NY.

Sherson, Errol. London's Lost Theatres of the Nineteenth Century. 1925. $12.50 Hdbd. Benjamin Blom, NY.

Short, Ernest. Theatrical Cavalcade. 1970. (1942) $8.75 Hdbd. (ISBN 0-8046-8). Kennikat Pr., NY.

Southern, Richard. Victorian Theatre: A Pictorial Survey. 1970. $8.95 Hdbd. (ISBN 0-87830-147-X). Theatre Arts Books, NY.

Speaight, Robert. William Poel & the Elizabethan Revival. 1954. $3.50 Hdbd. Hillary House Publ., NY.

Spencer, Hazelton. Shakespeare Improved. 1963. $7.00 Hdbd. (ISBN 0-8044-2827-1). Frederick Ungar Publ., NY.

Sprague, Arthur C. Beaumont & Fletcher on the Reformation Stage. 1926. $12.50 Hdbd. Benjamin Blom, NY.

Steele, Richard. Theatre, 1720. Loftis, John, ed. 1962. $4.80 Hdbd. (ISBN 0-19-811427-3). Oxford Univ. Pr., NY.

Stone, George W., Jr., ed. London Stage, 1600-1800, Pt. 4 1747-1776, 3 Vols. 1963. $25.00 Hdbd. (ISBN 0-8093-0094-X). $2.25 pa. (ISBN 0-8093-0339-6, AB). Southern Ill. Univ. Pr., IL.

Stopes, C. Burbage & Shakespeare's Stage. (Studies in Shakespeare, No. 24). 1970. (1913) $9.95 Hdbd. (ISBN 0-8383-1020-6). Haskell House Publ., NY.

Stratman, Carl J., ed. Restoration & Eighteenth-Century Theatre Research: Bibliographical Guide, 1900-1968. 1971. $25.00 Hdbd. (ISBN 0-8093-0469-4). Southern Ill. Univ. Pr., IL.

Summers, Montague. Restoration Theater. $13.50 Hdbd. Humanities Pr., Inc., NY.

Taylor, Aline M. Next to Shakespeare. 1950. $17.50 Hdbd. (ISBN 0-404-06351-9). AMS Pr., NY.

Taylor, John R. Angry Theatre: New British Drama. rev. & enl. ed. (il). 1969. $7.50 Hdbd. (ISBN 0-8090-2663-5). Hill & Wang, NY.

Thaler, Alwin. Shakespeare & Democracy. 1941. $6.50 Hdbd. (ISBN 0-87049-001-X). Univ. of Tenn. Pr., TN.

Thaler, Alwin. Shakespeare to Sheridan. 1922. $12.50 Hdbd. Benjamin Blom, NY.

Thompson, Elbert N. Controversy Between the Puritans & the Stage. 1903. $9.00 Hdbd. (ISBN 0-404-06396-9). AMS Pr., NY.

Thompson, Elbert N. Controversy Between the Puritans & the Stage. 1966. (1903) $9.00 Hdbd. Russell & Russell Publ., NY.

Thorndike, Ashley. Shakespeare's Theater. $6.95 Hdbd. Macmillan Co., NY.

Tynan, Kenneth. Curtains. 1961. $10.00 Hdbd. Atheneum Publ., NY.

Van Lennep, William, ed. London Stage, 1660–1800, Pt. 1 1660–1700. 1965. $25.00 Hdbd. (ISBN 0-8093-0901-7). Southern Ill. Univ. Pr., IL.

Victor, Benjamin. History of the Theatre of London & Dublin, 3 Vols. in 1. 1761. $27.50 Hdbd. Benjamin Blom, NY.

Wallace, Charles W. Evolution of the English Drama up to Shakespeare: With a History of the First Blackfriars Theatre. 1968. (1912) $8.50 Hdbd. (ISBN 0-8046-0668-4). Kennikat Pr., NY.

Wallace, Charles W. First London Theatre. 1969. (1913) $12.50 Hdbd. Benjamin Blom, NY.

Watson, Ernest B. Sheridan to Robertson: A Study of the Nineteenth-Century London Stage. 1926. $12.50 Hdbd. Benjamin Blom, NY.

Webster, Margaret. Same Only Different. 1969. $7.95 Hdbd. Alfred A. Knopf, NY.

Whiting, John. On Theatre. 1966. $1.25 Hdbd. Dufour Editions, PA.

Wickham, Glynne W. Drama in a World of Science. 1962. $5.00 Hdbd. (ISBN 0-8020-1198-5). Univ. of Toronto Pr., CAN.

Wickham, Glynne W. Early English Stages: 1300 to 1660, 2 vols. Incl. Vol. 1. 1300 to 1576 (ISBN 0-231-08935-X); Vol. 2, Pt. 1. 1576 to 1660 (ISBN 0-231-08936-8). 1959. $15.00 Hdbd. $17.50 Hdbd. (ISBN 0-231-08937-6). Columbia Univ. Pr., NY.

Wilkinson, Tate. Memoirs of His Own Life, 4 Vols. in 2. rep ed. 1968. $37.50 Hdbd. Benjamin Blom, NY.

Wilkinson, Tate. Wandering Patentee, Or, History of the Yorkshire Theatres from 1770 to the Present Time, 4 Vols. in 2. rep. ed. 1968. $37.50 Hdbd. Benjamin Blom, NY.

Wilson, A. E. Christmas Pantomine: The Story of an English Institution. 1934. $12.50 Hdbd. Benjamin Blom, NY.

Essays

Agate, James. Playgoing: An Essay. 1937. $6.75 Hdbd. Benjamin Blom, NY.

Anderson, Maxwell, ed. Off Broadway Essays About the Theatre. (Theatre Ser). (1947) price "n.g." Hdbd. (ISBN 0-306-71337-3). Plenum Publ. Corp., NY.

Artaud, Antonin. Theater & Its Double. Richards, Mary C., tr. 1958. $1.95 pa. Grove Pr., NY.

Barnet, Sylvan, et al. Aspects of the Drama: A Handbook. (Orig.). $3.50 pa. (ISBN 0-316-08178-7). Little, Brown & Co., MA.

Bentley, Eric. Life of the Drama. 1964. $2.95 pa. (ISBN 0-689-70011-3, 112). Atheneum Publ., NY.

Bentley, Eric, ed. Theory of the Modern Stage: An Introduction to Modern Theatre & Drama. (Hi-Sch.). 1968. $2.45 pa. (ISBN 0-14-020947-6). Penguin Books Inc., MD.

Brecht, Bertolt. Brecht on Theatre. Willett, John, ed. 1964. $6.50 Hdbd. (ISBN 0-8090-3100-0); $2.45 pa. (ISBN 0-8090-0542-5). Hill & Wang, NY.

Carroll, Sidney W. Some Dramatic Opinions. 1968. (1923) $9.50 Hdbd.

(ISBN 0-8046-0069-4). Kennikat Pr., NY.

Corrigan, Robert W. & Rosenberg, James L., eds. Context & Craft of Drama: Critical Essays on the Nature of Drama & Theatre. (Orig.). 1964. $6.25 Hdbd. (ISBN 0-8102-0071-6). Chandler Publ., CA.

Craig, Edward G. Books & Theatres. facs. ed. (Essay Index Reprint Ser). 1925. $11.00 Hdbd. (ISBN 0-8369-0346-3). Books for Libraries, NY.

Craig, Edward G. Theatre Advancing. 1919. $12.50 Hdbd. Benjamin Blom, NY.

Frank, Waldo. Salvos. 1924. $12.50 Hdbd. Benjamin Blom, NY.

Friedman, Maurice, ed. & tr. Martin Buber & the Theater. 1969. $7.95 Hdbd. Funk & Wagnalls, NY.

Gardner, Rufus H. Splintered Stage. 1965. $4.50 Hdbd. Macmillan, NY.

Gassner, John & Allen, Ralph. Theatre & Drama in the Making, 2 Vols. $5.95 pa. Houghton Mifflin, MA.

Irving, Henry. Drama: Addresses. 1893. $6.75 Hdbd. Benjamin Blom, NY.

Isaacs, Edith J., ed. Theatre: Essays on the Arts of the Theatre. (Essay Index Reprint Ser). 1927. $13.75 Hdbd. (ISBN 0-8369-0561-X). Books for Libraries, NY.

James, Henry. Scenic Art: Notes on Acting & the Drama, 1872–1901. Wade,

Allan, ed. 1957. $1.35 pa. (ISBN 0-8090-0505-0, Drama). Hill & Wang, NY.

Jones, Robert E. Dramatic Imagination. $3.95 Hdbd. Theatre Arts, NY.

Kierkegaard, Soren. Crisis in the Life of an Actress & Other Essays on the Drama. 1967. $5.00 Hdbd. Humanities Pr., NY.

Kirby, E. T., ed. Total Theatre: A Critical Anthology. 1969. $6.95 Hdbd. (ISBN 0-525-22137-9); $2.45 pa. (ISBN 0-525-47240-1). E. P. Dutton, NY.

Mackaye, Percy. Playhouse & the Play & Other Addresses Concerning the Theatre & Democracy in America. (Library of Literature, Drama & Criticism). 1970. (1909) $7.00 Hdbd. Johnson Reprint, NY.

Matthews, Brander, ed. Papers on Playmaking. (Essay Index Reprint Ser). $10.75 Hdbd. (ISBN 0-8369-1890-8). Books for Libraries, NY.

Matthews, Brander, ed. Papers on Playmaking. 1957. $1.35 pa. (ISBN 0-8090-0510-7, Drama). Hill & Wang, NY.

Nathan, George Jean. Magic Mirror. 1960. $5.95 Hdbd. Alfred A. Knopf, NY.

Saint-Denis, Michel. Theatre: The Rediscovery of Style. 1969. (1960) $2.85 pa. Theatre Arts, NY.

Schechner, Richard. Public Domain. Essays on the Theatre. 1969. $6.95 Hdbd. Bobbs-Merrill, IN.

Schechner, Richard. Public Domain: Essays on the Theatre. 1970. (1969) $1.65 pa. Avon, NY.

Selden, Samuel. Man in His Theatre. 1957. $4.00 Hdbd. (ISBN 0-8078-0716-8). Univ. of N.C. Pr., NC.

Seltzer, Daniel. Modern Theatre: Readings & Documents. 1967. $5.95 pa. (ISBN 0-316-78108-8). Little, Brown, MA.

Shaw, George B. Shaw on Theatre. West, E. J., ed. 1959. $4.50 Hdbd. (ISBN 0-8090-8650-6); $1.75 pa. (ISBN 0-8090-0518-2). Hill & Wang, NY.

Tulane Drama Review. Theatre in the Twentieth Century. Corrigan, Robert W., ed. (Essay Index Reprint Ser). 1963. $12.50 Hdbd. (ISBN 0-8369-1631-X). Books for Libraries, NY.

Wichelns, Herbert A., et al, eds. Studies in Speech & Drama in Honor of Alexander M. Drummond. 1968. (1944) $13.50 Hdbd. Russell & Russell, NY.

Winter, William. Actor & Other Speeches. (Drama Ser). 1970. (1891) $14.50 Hdbd. (ISBN 0-8337-3822-4). Burt Franklin, NY.

Geographic Locations

Africa

East, N. B. African Theatre: A Checklist of Critical Materials. (Orig., Pap). 1970. $3.75 pa. (ISBN 0-8419-0025-6). Africana, NY.

London, Jack. Daughters of the Rich. (Chronological bibliography of London's plays by James Sissor). 1971.

Wrappers $1.00 Hdbd. (ISBN 0-910740-18-6). Holmes, CA.

Lowe, Robert W. Bibliographical Account of English Theatrical Literature. 1966. Repr. of 1888 ed. $14.00 Hdbd. Gale, MI.

Pence, James H. Magazine & the Drama: An Index. (Drama Ser). 1970. Repr. of 1896 ed. lib. bdg. 14. (ISBN 0-8337-2707-9). Burt Franklin, NY.

Asia

Pronko, Leonard C. Theater East & West: Perspectives Toward a Total Theater. 1967. $8.50 Hdbd. (ISBN 0-520-01041-8). Univ. of Calif. Pr., CA.

Theatre in Southeast Asia. 1967. $12.50 Hdbd. (ISBN 0-674-87585-0). Harvard Univ. Pr., MA.

Australia

Irvin, Eric. Theatre Comes to Australia. 1971. $6.75 Hdbd. (Pub. by Univ. of Queensland Pr.). Library Assoc. ENG.

Austria

Graf-Khittel, Gita, ed. Austria: Music & Theatre. $7.95 Hdbd. Joan Toggitt Ltd., NY.

Griffin, Robert. High Baroque Culture & Theater in Vienna. 1970. $20.00 Hdbd. (ISBN 0-391-00010-1). Humanities Pr. Inc., NY.

Rusack, Hedwig H. Gozzi in Germany. 1930. $11.00 Hdbd. (ISBN 0-404-50434-5). AMS Pr., NY.

Burma

Sein, Kenneth & Withey, Joseph A. Great Po Sein: A Chronicle of the Burmese Theater. 1966. $4.95 Hdbd. (ISBN 0-253-13450-1). Ind. Univ. Pr., IN.

Canada

Edwards, Murray D. Stage in Our Past: English-Speaking Theatre in Eastern Canada from the 1790's to 1914. 1968. $12.50 Hdbd. (ISBN 0-8020-1510-7). Univ. of Toronto Pr., CAN.

Graham, Franklin. Histrionic Monoreal. 1902. $18.75 Hdbd. Benjamin Blom, NY.

Novick, Julius. Beyond Broadway: The Quest for Permanent Theatres. 1969. (1968) $2.95 pa. (ISBN 0-8090-0547-6, Drama). $7.95 Hdbd. (ISBN 0-8090-2950-2). Hill & Wang, NY.

China

Arlington, Lewis C. Chinese Drama. $32.50 Hdbd. Benjamin Blom, NY.

Levenson, Joseph R. Revolution & Cosmopolitanism: The Western Stage & the Chinese Stages. 1971. $5.00 Hdbd. (ISBN 0-520-01737-4). Univ. of Calif. Pr., CA.

Scott, Adolph C. Mei Lan-Fang: Leader of the Pear Garden. 1959. $5.25 Hdbd. (ISBN 0-19-643019-4). Oxford Univ. Pr., NY.

Zucker, Adolph E. Chinese Theatre. $12.00 Hdbd. Benjamin Blom, NY.

Zung, Cecilia S. Secrets of the Chinese

Drama. 1937. $15.00 Hdbd. Benjamin Blom, NY.

East (Far East)

Bowers, Faubion. Theater in the East: A Survey of Ancient Dance & Drama. 1960. $3.95 Hdbd. Grove Pr., NY.

Europe

Dumont, Gabriel P. Parallele De Plans Des Plus Bell Salles De Spectacles D'italie et De France. 1968. Repr. $37.50 Hdbd. Benjamin Blom, NY.

Esslin, Martin, ed. New Theatre of Europe Vol. 4. (Orig.). 1970. $2.75 pa. Dell, NY.

Flanagan, Hallie. Shifting Scenes of the Modern European Theatre. $12.50 Hdbd. Benjamin Blom, NY.

MacGowan, Kenneth & Jones, Robert E. Continental Stagecraft. 1922. $12.50 Hdbd. Benjamin Blom, NY.

Miller, Anne I. Independent Theatre in Europe, Eighteen Eighty-Seven. 1931. $12.50 Hdbd. Benjamin Blom, NY.

Sachs, Edwin O. & Woodrow, Ernest A. Modern Opera Houses & Theatres, 3 Vols. 1968. $110.00 Hdbd. Benjamin Blom, NY.

Smith, Michael. Theatre Trip: A Young American Director-Critic's Personal & Professional Encounter with New Theatre Abroad. 1969. $7.50 Hdbd. Bobbs-Merrill Co. Inc., IN.

Tynan, Kenneth. Curtains. 1961. $10.00 Hdbd. Atheneum Publ., NY.

France

Albert, Maurice. Theatres De la Foire, 1660–1789. (Drama Ser). 1971. (1900) $17.50 Hdbd. (ISBN 0-8337-0030-8). Burt Franklin, NY.

Antoine, Andre. Memories of the Theatre-Libre. Carlson, Marvin, ed. (Books of the Theatre, No. 5). 1964. $6.50 Hdbd. (ISBN 0-87024-034-X). Univ. of Miami Pr., FL.

Bishop, Tom. Avant-Garde Theatrale: French Theater Since 1950. 1970. $8.95 Hdbd. (52316). D. C. Heath & Co., IN.

Brazier, Nicolas. Histoire Des Petits Theatres De Paris. (Research & Source Works Ser., No. 258). 1969. (1838) $19.50 Hdbd. (ISBN 0-8337-0358-7). Burt Franklin, NY.

Brown, Howard M. Music in the French Secular Theater, 1400–1550. 1963. $10.00 Hdbd. (ISBN 0-674-59050-3). Harvard Univ. Pr., MA.

Carlson, Marvin. Theatre of the French Revolution. 1966. $11.50 Hdbd. (ISBN 0-8014-0063-5). Cornell Univ. Pr., NY.

Charden, Henri. Nouveaux Documents Sur les Comediens De Campagne et la Vie De Moliere, 2 Vols. (1886–1905 Reprint 1968). $35.00 Hdbd. (ISBN 0-8337-0536-9). Burt Franklin, NY.

Charden, Henri. Troupe Du Roman Comique Devoilee & Les Comediens De Campagne Au 17e Siecle. (French). 1876. $16.50 Hdbd. (ISBN 0-8337-4032-6). Burt Franklin, NY.

Christout, Marie-Francoise. Merveilleux et le Theatre Du Silence En France a Partir Du Dix-Sept Siecle. 1965. $14.50 Hdbd. Humanities Pr. Inc., NY.

Dorey, Jean. Mime. 1961. $4.95 Hdbd. (ISBN 0-8315-0045-X). Robert Speller & Sons, NY.

Fowlie, Wallace. Dionysus in Paris: A Guide to Contemporary French Theatre. $5.00 Hdbd. Peter Smith Publ. MA.

Gofflot, L. V. Theatre Au College Du Moyen Age a Nos Jours, Avec Bibliographie Et Appendices. 1907. $17.50 Hdbd. (ISBN 0-8337-1365-5). Burt Franklin, NY.

Hallays-Dabot, Victor. Histoire De la Censure Theatrale En France. (Fr). 1862. $17.50 Hdbd. (ISBN 0-8337-4149-7). Burt Franklin, NY.

Hawkins, Frederick W. Annals of the French Stage from Its Origin to the Death of Racine, 2 Vols. (Drama Ser. No. 39). 1969. (1884) $23.95 Hdbd. (ISBN 0-8383-0161-4). Haskell House Publ., NY.

Hawkins, Frederick W. Annals of the French Stage from Its Origin to the Death of Racine. 1968. Repr. of 1884 ed. $23.95 Hdbd. Scholarly Pr., NY.

Hawkins, Fredrick W. Annals of the French Stage from Its Origin to the Death of Racine, 2 Vols. 1969. (1884) $26.75 Hdbd. Greenwood Pr., CT.

Hawkins, Fredrick W. French Stage in the Eighteenth Century, 2 Vols. (Studies in Drama Ser., No. 39). 1969. (1888)

$24.95 Hdbd. (ISBN 0-8383-0162-2). Haskell House Publ., NY.

Hawkins, Fredrick W. French Stage in the Eighteenth Century, 2 Vols. rev. ed. 1968. (1888) $24.95 Hdbd. (ISBN 0-403-00085-8). Scholarly Pr., MI.

Hawkins, Fredrick W. French Stage in the Eighteenth Century, 2 Vols. (Illus.). 1969. (1888) $29.00 Hdbd. (ISBN 0-8371-2746-7). Greenwood Pr., CT.

Hobson, Harold. French Theatre Today. 1953. $8.75 Hdbd. Benjamin Blom, NY.

Leathers, Victor. British Entertainers in France, 1600–1900. 1959. $7.50 Hdbd. (ISBN 0-8020-5077-8). Univ. of Toronto Pr., CAN.

Leclercq, Louis. Decors, Costumes et Mise En Scene Au Dix-Septieme Siecle. 1968. (1869) $16.50 Hdbd. (ISBN 0-8337-2041-4). Burt Franklin, NY.

Lee, Vera G. Quest for a Public: French Popular Theater Since 1945. 1970. $8.95 text ed. (ISBN 0-87073-180-7). Schenkman Publ. Co., MA.

Lough, John. Paris Theatre Audiences in the Seventeenth & Eighteenth Centuries. 1957. $9.00 Hdbd. (ISBN 0-19-713112-3). Oxford Univ. Pr., NY.

Motley. Today's French Theatre. $4.50 pa. Kraus Reprint Co., NY.

Pafaict, F. & Pafaict, C. Historie Du Theatre Francois Depuis Son Origine Jusqu'a Present, 15 Vols. 1966. (1749) $190.00 Hdbd. (ISBN 0-8337-2660-9). Burt Franklin, NY.

Pericaud, Louis. Theatre Des Funam-
bules. 1897. $25.00 Hdbd. Benjamin
Blom, NY.

Quentin, Henri. Theatre Sous la Terreur:
Theatre De la Peur, 1793–1794. (1913)
$28.50 Hdbd. (ISBN 0-8337-4330-9).
Burt Franklin, NY.

Roy, Emile. Etudes Sur le Theatre
Francais Du Quatorzieme et Du Quin-
zieme Siecle. (Research & Source Works
Ser., No. 669). 1971. (1902) $27.50
Hdbd. (ISBN 0-8337-3085-1). Burt
Franklin, NY.

Tavenol, L. & De Noinville, Durey.
Histoire Du Theatre De l'Academie
Royale De Misique En France, Vol.
1–2. 2nd ed. (Fr). 1753. $49.50 Hdbd.
(ISBN 0-8337-4442-9). Burt Franklin,
NY.

Welschinger, Henri. Theatre De la
Revolution, 1789–1799. (1880) $35.00
Hdbd. (ISBN 0-8337-4474-7). Burt
Franklin, NY.

Wicks, C. Beaumont, ed. Parisian Stage,
4 Vols. Vol. 1. $4.00 pa. (ISBN 0-8173-
9502-4); Vol. 2. $2.50 pa. (ISBN 0-
8173-9503-2); Vol. 3. $4.00 pa. (ISBN
0-8173-9504-0); Vol. 4. $6.95 pa. (ISBN
0-8173-9505-9). Univ. of Ala. Pr., AL.

Winter, Marian H. Theatre of Marvels.
$17.50 Hdbd. Benjamin Blom, NY.

Germany

Brecht, Bertolt, et al. Theaterarbeit:
Six Productions of the Berliner En-
semble. $15.00 Hdbd. DBS Pubns., NY.

Carter, Huntly. Theatre of Max Reinhardt. 1914. $12.50 Hdbd. Benjamin
Blom, NY.

Frenzel, Herbert A. & Moser, Hans J.,
eds. Kuerschners Biographisches
Theaterhandbuch: Schauspiel Oper,
Film, Rundfunk (Deutschland, Oester-
reich, Schweiz. (Ger). 1956. $15.90
Hdbd. (ISBN 3-11-002973-1). De
Gruyter, Germany.

Fuchs, Georg. Revolution in the Theatre. Kuhn, Constance C., tr. from Ger.
1971. (1959) $9.50 Hdbd. (ISBN 0-
8046-1524-1). Kennikat Pr., NY.

Ley-Piscator, Maria. Piscator Experiment: The Political Theatre. 1967. $8.50
Hdbd. James H. Heineman, NY.

Moreno, J. L. Stehgreiftheater. 2nd ed.
$6.00 Hdbd. Beacon House, NY.

Robertson, John G. Lessing's Dramatic
Theory. 1939. $15.00 Hdbd. Benjamin
Blom, NY.

Rusack, Hedwig H. Gozzi in Germany.
1930. $11.00 Hdbd. (ISBN 0-404-50434-
5). AMS Pr., NY.

Sayler, Oliver M., ed. Max Reinhardt
& His Theatre. 1968. $17.50 Hdbd.
Benjamin Blom, NY.

Shaw, George B. Shaw's Dramatic Criticism from the Saturday Review 1895–
1898. Matthews, John F., ed. $3.50
Hdbd. Peter Smith Publ., MA.

Shaw, Leroy R., ed. German Theater
Today: A Symposium. (Dept. of Ger-
manic Languages Pubns). 1964. $5.50
Hdbd. (ISBN 0-292-73250-3). Univ. of
Tex. Pr., TX.

Wilson, Albert E. Penny Plain Two Pence Coloured: A History of the Juvenile Drama. 1969. $18.75 Hdbd. Benjamin Blom, NY.

Wilson, John H. Preface to Restoration Drama. 1968. (1965) $6.00 text ed. (ISBN 0-674-69950-5). Harvard Univ. Pr., MA.

Wilson, John H. Preface to Restoration Drama. $3.95 text ed. Houghton Mifflin, MA.

Wright, James. Historica Histrionica. 1968. (1699) $7.50 Hdbd. (ISBN 0-404-07045-0). AMS Pr., NY.

Wright, Louis B. Shakespeare's Theatre & the Dramatic Tradition. (Folger Booklets on Tudor & Stuart Civilization Ser). $1.50 pa. (ISBN 0-8139-0103-0). Univ. Pr. of Va., VA.

Yates, Frances A. Theatre of the World. 1969. $8.50 Hdbd. (ISBN 0-226-95004-2). Univ. of Chicago Pr., IL.

Zoff, .Otto. German Theatre Today. 1960. $0.50 pa. (ISBN 0-87462-417-7). Marquette Univ. Pr., WI.

Greece

Allen, James T. Greek Theatre of Fifth Century Before Christ. (Drama Ser., No. 39). 1969. (1919) $8.95 Hdbd. (ISBN 0-8383-0647-0). Haskell House, NY.

Allen, James T. Stage Antiquities of the Greeks & Romans & Their Influence. (Our Debt to Greece & Rome Ser). $3.50 Hdbd. (ISBN 0-8154-0009-8). Cooper Sq. Pr., NY.

Arnott, Peter. Introduction to the Greek Theatre. 1963. $2.45 pa. (ISBN 0-253-20042-3, MB). Ind. Univ. Pr., IN.

Arnott, Peter D. Ancient Greek & Roman Theatre. 1971. $2.95 pa. Random House, NY.

Bieber, M. History of the Greek & Roman Theater. rev. ed. 1961 $25.00 Hdbd. (ISBN 0-691-03521-0) Princeton Univ. Pr., NJ.

Brown, A. D. Greek Plays As First Productions: An Inaugural Lecture. 1970. $0.75 pa. Humanities Pr., NY.

Flickinger, Roy C. Greek Theater & Its Drama. 4th ed. 1936. $8.50 Hdbd. (ISBN 0-226-25369-4). Univ. of Chicago Pr., IL.

Glen, R. S. Two Muses: An Introduction to Fifth-Century Athens by Way of the Drama. 1968. $4.00 Hdbd. text ed. St. Martin's Pr., NY.

Haigh, A. E. Attic Theatre. 3rd ed. (1907) $13.00 Hdbd. Kraus Reprint, NY.

Haigh, Arthur E. Attic Theatre: A Description of the Stage & Theatre of the Athenians. (Drama Ser., No. 39). 1969. (1898) $12.95 Hdbd. (ISBN 0-8383-0951-8). Haskell House, NY.

O'Connor, John B. Chapters in the History of Actors & Acting in Ancient Greece. (Drama Ser., No. 39). 1969. (1908) $9.95 Hdbd. (ISBN 0-8383-0602-0). Haskell House, NY.

Pickard-Cambridge, Arthur. Dramatic Festivals of Athens. 2nd ed. Lewis,

D. M. & Gould, J. P., eds. 1968. $19.25 Hdbd. (ISBN 0-19-814258-7). Oxford Univ. Pr., NY.

Ridgeway, William. Origin of Tragedy. 1910. $12.50 Hdbd. Benjamin Blom, NY.

Sifakis, Gregory M. Studies in the History of Hellenistic Drama. 1967. $8.80 Hdbd. Oxford Univ. Pr., NY.

Webster, Thomas B. Greek Theatre Production. 2nd ed. 1970. $7.25 Hdbd. (ISBN 0-416-16570-2). Barnes & Noble, NY.

India

Benegal, S. A. Panorama of Theatre in India. 1967. $5.00 Hdbd. Humanities Pr., NY.

Gargi, Balwant. Folk Theatre of India. 1966. $8.95 Hdbd. Univ. of Wash. Pr., WA.

Gargi, Balwant. Theatre in India. $6.95 Hdbd. Theatre Arts, NY.

Mathur, Jagdish C. Drama in Rural India. 1964. $7.50 Hdbd. (ISBN 0-210-22572-6). Asia Society, NY.

Yajnik, R. Indian Theatre. (Drama Ser., No. 39). 1969. (1934) $9.95 Hdbd. (ISBN 0-8383-1214-4). Haskell House, NY.

Yajnik, Ramanlal K. Indian Theatre. $8.00 Hdbd. Benjamin Blom, NY.

Ireland

Bourgeois, Maurice. John Millington Synge & the Irish Theatre. 1913. $10.00 Hdbd. Benjamin Blom, NY.

Bourgeois, Maurice. John Millington Synge & the Irish Theatre. (Studies in Irish Literature Ser., No. 16). 1969. (1913) $8.95 Hdbd. (ISBN 0-8383-0511-3). Haskell House, NY.

Byrne, D. Story of Ireland's National Theatre. (Studies in Drama, No. 39). 1970. (1929) $7.95 Hdbd. (ISBN 0-8383-1089-3). Haskell House, NY.

Byrne, Dawson. Story of Ireland's National Theatre. 1929. $7.95 Hdbd. (ISBN 0-8383-1089-3). Haskell House, NY.

Clark, William S. Early Irish Stage: The Beginnings to 1720. 1955. $7.20 Hdbd. (ISBN 0-19-811519-9). Oxford Univ. Pr., NY.

Clark, William S. Irish Stage in the County Towns, 1720 to 1800. 1965. $11.20 Hdbd. (ISBN 0-19-811618-7). Oxford Univ. Pr., NY.

Eay, J. Frank. Towards a National Theatre. Hogan, Robert, ed. (Irish Theatre Ser). $4.25 Hdbd. Dufour Editions, PA.

Gregory, Augusta. Our Irish Theatre. 1965. $1.95 pa. G. P. Putnam, NY.

Hughes, S. C. Pre-Victorian Drama in Dublin. (Research & Source Works Ser., No. 708). 1970. (1904) $10.00 Hdbd. (ISBN 0-8337-1760-X). Burt Franklin, NY.

O'Driscoll, Robert. Theatre & Nationalism in Twentieth Century Ireland. 1970. $8.50 Hdbd. Univ. of Toronto Pr., CAN.

Slaughter, Howard K. George Fitzmaurice & His Enchanted Land. 1968. $2.95 Hdbd. Dufour Editions, PA.

Stockwell, L. T. Dublin Theatres & Theatre Customs, 1637–1820. 1968. $12.50 Hdbd. Benjamin Blom, NY.

Victor, Benjamin. History of the Theatre of London & Dublin, 3 Vols. in 1. 1761. $27.50 Hdbd. Benjamin Blom, NY.

Weygandt, Cornelius. Irish Plays & Playwrights. 1913. $10.00 Hdbd. (ISBN 0-8046-0498-3). Kennikat Pr., NY.

Israel

Kohansky, Mendel. Hebrew Theatre: Its First Fifty Years. 1969. $10.00 Hdbd. (ISBN 0-87068-072-2). Ktav Publ., NY.

Italy

Craig, Edward G. Books & Theatres. facs. ed. (Essay Index Reprint Ser). 1925. $11.00 Hdbd. (ISBN 0-8369-0346-3). Books for Libraries, NY.

Hewitt, Barnard. Renaissance Stage: Documents of Serlio, Sabbattini & Furttenbach. Nicoll, Allardycee, et al. trs. (Books of the Theatre, No. 1). 1959. $6.50 Hdbd. (ISBN 0-87024-004-8). Univ. of Miami Pr., FL.

Kennard, Joseph S. Italian Theatre, 2 Vols. 1932. $18.50 Hdbd. Benjamin Blom., NY.

McLeod, Addison. Plays & Players in Modern Italy. 1970. (1912) $13.00

Hdbd. (ISBN 0-8046-0758-3). Kennikat Pr., NY.

Smith, Winifred. Italian Actors of the Renaissance. 1968. $12.50 Hdbd. Benjamin Blom, NY.

Japan

Arnott, Peter D. Theatres of Japan. 1969. $12.50 Hdbd. St. Martin's Pr., NY.

Haar, Francis. Japanese Theatre in Highlight: A Pictorial Commentary. 2nd rev. ed. (1954) price "n.g." Hdbd. (ISBN 0-8371-3937-6). Greenwood Pr., CT.

Nakamura, Yasuo. Noh: The Classical Theater. (Performing Arts of Japan Ser., Vol. 4). 1971. $5.95 Hdbd. (ISBN 0-8348-1504-4). John Weatherhill, Inc., NY.

Saito, Seijiro, et al, eds. Masterpieces of Japanese Puppetry, Sculptured Heads of the Bunraku Theatre. 1964. $27.50 Hdbd. (ISBN 0-8048-0397-8). Charles E. Tuttle, VT.

Scott, Adolphe C. Kabuki Theatre of Japan. 1955. $6.75 Hdbd. Barnes & Noble, NY.

Scott, Adolphe C. Kabuki Theatre of Japan. 1966. $2.95 pa. Macmillan Co., NY.

London

Adams, Joseph Q. Conventual Buildings of Blackfriars, London, & the Playhouses Constructed Therein. 1970.

(1917) $6.50 Hdbd. (ISBN 0-404-00289-7). AMS Pr., NY.

Adams, Joseph Q. Shakespearean Playhouses: A History of English Theatres from the Beginning to the Reformation. 1959. $6.75 Hdbd. Peter Smith, MA.

Arundell, Dennis D. Story of Sadler's Wells, 1683-1964. 1966. $6.95 Hdbd. Theatre Arts, NY.

Baker, Barton. History of the London Stage & Its Famous Players 1576-1903. 1904. $12.50 Hdbd. Benjamin Blom, NY.

Boswell, Eleanor. Restoration Court Stage, 1660-1702. 1932. $12.50 Hdbd. Benjamin Blom, NY.

Boswell, Eleanore. Restoration Court Stage Sixteen Sixty to Seventeen Two. 1966. $8.50 Hdbd. Barnes & Noble, NY.

Brereton, Austin. Lyceum & Henry Irving. 1903. $12.50 Hdbd. Benjamin Blom, NY.

Burnim, Kalman A. David Garrick, Director. 1961. $5.95 Hdbd. (ISBN 0-8229-3013-7). Univ. of Pittsburgh Pr., PA.

Chambers, Edmund K. Elizabethan Stage, 4 Vols. 1923. Set—$38.50 Hdbd. (ISBN 0-19-811511-3). Oxford Univ. Pr., NY.

Cole, John W. Life & Theatrical Times of Charles Kean, 2 Vols. in 1. 1859. $22.50 Hdbd. Benjamin Blom, NY.

Duncan, Barry. St. James's Theatre:

Its Strange & Complete History, 1835-1957. 1964. $10.00 Hdbd. Fernhill House, NY.

Ebers, John. Seven Years of the King's Theatre. 1828. $17.50 Hdbd. Benjamin Blom, NY.

Hotson, J. Leslie. Commonwealth & Restoration Stage. 1962. (1928) $12.50 Hdbd. Russell & Russell Publ., NY.

Howard, Diana. London Theaters & Music Halls, 1850-1950. $9.60 Hdbd. Pub. by Library Assoc., ENG.

Howard, Diane. London Theatres & Music Halls 1850-1950. 1971. $15.95 Hdbd. British Book Centre, NY.

Kelly, Michael. Reminiscences of Michael Kelly of the King's Theatre & Theatre Royal Drury Lane 2 Vols. 2nd ed. (Music Ser). 1968. (1826) $32.50 Hdbd. (ISBN 0-306-71094-3). Plenum Publ., NY.

Kelly, Michael. Reminiscences of Micheal Kelly, 2 Vols. in 1. Hook, Theodore E., ed. 1826. $9.50 Hdbd. Benjamin Blom, NY.

MacCarthy, Desmond. Court Theatre, 1904-1907: A Commentary & Criticism. Weintraub, Stanley, ed. (Books of the Theatre, No. 6). 1967. $6.50 Hdbd. (ISBN 0-87024-068-4). Univ. of Miami Pr., FLA.

Mander, Raymond & Mitchenson, Joe. Lost Theatres of London. 1968. $12.00 Hdbd. (ISBN 0-8008-5025-4). Taplinger Publ., NY.

Mason, Alfred E. Sir George Alexander

& the St. James' Theatre. 1935. $12.50 Hdbd. Benjamin Blom, NY.

Nagler, Alois M. Shakespeare's Stage. 1958. $5.00 Hdbd. (ISBN 0-300-00784-1); $1.45 pa. (ISBN 0-300-00174-6, Y108). Yale Univ. Pr., CT.

Nicholson, Watson. Struggle for a Free Stage in London. 1967. Repr. $12.50 Hdbd. Benjamin Blom, NY.

Reynolds, George F. Staging of Elizabethan Plays at the Red Bull Theatre, 1605-1625. 1940. $9.00 pa. Kraus Repr., NY.

Rosenthal, H. Two Centuries at Covent Garden. 1958. $15.00 Hdbd. Dufour Ed., PA.

Royal Shakespeare Theatre Company. 1960-1963. $7.95 Hdbd. Theatre Arts, NY.

Smith, Irwin. Shakespeare's Blackfriars Playhouse: Its History & Design. 1970. $15.00 Hdbd. (ISBN 0-8147-0391-7); $4.95 pa. (ISBN 0-8147-0483-2). New York Univ. Pr., NY.

Thaler, Alwin. Shakespeare to Sheridan. 1922. $12.50 Hdbd. Benjamin Blom, NY.

Van Lennep, William, ed. London Stage, 1660-1800, 1660-1700. 1965. $25.00 Hdbd. (ISBN 0-8093-0901-7). So. Ill. Univ. Pr., IL.

Wallace, Charles W. Children of the Chapel at Blackfriars, 1597-1603. 1970. (1908) $10.00 Hdbd. (ISBN 0-404-06808-1). AMS Pr., NY.

Wallace, Charles W. Evolution of the English Drama up to Shakespeare: With a History of the First Blackfriars Theatre. 1968. (1912) $8.50 Hdbd. (ISBN 0-8046-0668-4). Kennikat Pr., NY.

Watson, Ernest B. Sheridan to Robertson: A Study of the Nineteenth-Century London Stage. 1926. $12.50 Hdbd. Benjamin Blom, NY.

Wright, Louis B. Shakespeare's Theatre & the Dramatic Tradition. (Folger Booklets on Tudor & Stuart Civilization Ser). $1.50 pa. (ISBN 0-8139-0103-0). Univ. Pr. of Va., VA.

Wyndham, Henry S. Annals of the Covent Garden Theatre. 2 Vols. 1906. $27.50 Hdbd. Benjamin Blom, NY.

Middle East

Cocteau, Jean. Maalesh: A Theatrical Tour in the Middle-East. 1956. $5.00 Hdbd. Hillary House, NY.

Landau, Jacob M. Studies in the Arab Theatre & Cinema. 1958. $10.00 Hdbd. (ISBN 0-8122-7188-2). Univ. of Pa. Pr., PA.

Rome

Allen, James T. Stage Antiquities of the Greeks & Romans & Their Influence. (Our Debt to Greece & Rome Ser). $3.50 Hdbd. (ISBN 0-8154-0009-8). Cooper Sq. Pr., NY.

Arnott, Peter D. Ancient Greek & Roman Theatre. 1971. $2.95 pa. text ed. Random House, NY.

Beare, William. Roman Stage: A Short

History of Latin Drama in the Time of the Republic. 3rd ed. Hammond, N. G., ed. 1965. $8.00 Hdbd. Barnes & Noble, NY.

Bieber, M. History of the Greek & Roman Theater. rev. ed. 1961. $25.00 Hdbd. (ISBN 0-691-03521-0). Princeton Univ. Pr., NJ.

Hammon, Nicholsas G., tr. Roman Stage: A Short History of Latin Drama in the Time of the Republic. 3rd ed. 1968. $4.25 Hdbd. (ISBN 0-416-29520-7, 238, UP). Barnes & Noble, NY.

Saunders, Catharine. Costume in Roman Comedy. 1909. $7.50 Hdbd. (ISBN 0-404-05563-X). AMS Pr., NY.

Russia

Carter, Huntley. New Spirit in the Russian Theatre. $10.75 Hdbd. Benjamin Blom, NY.

Carter, Huntly. New Spirit in the Russian Theatre Nineteen Seventeen to Nineteen Twenty-Eight. (Literature of Cinema Ser). 1929. $12.00 Hdbd. (ISBN 0-405-01606-9). Arno Pr., NY.

Carter, Huntly. New Theatre and Cinema of Soviet Russia. (Literature of Cinema Ser). Repr. of 1924 ed. $10.00 Hdbd. (ISBN 0-405-01607-7). Arno Pr., NY.

Chekhov, Anton P. Letters on the Short Story, the Drama & Other Literary Topics. Friedland, Louis S., ed. $4.00 Hdbd. Peter Smith, MA.

Chekhov, Anton P. Letters on the Short

Story, the Drama & Other Literary Topics. Friedland, Louis S., ed. 1966. $2.50 Hdbd. (ISBN 0-486-21635-7). Dover Publ., NY.

Chekhov, Anton P. Chekhov's Letters on the Short Story, the Drama, & Other Literary Topics. Friedland, Louis S., ed. $8.50 Hdbd. Benjamin Blom, NY.

Edwards, Christine. Stanislavsky Heritage: Its Contribution to the Russian & American Theatre. 1965. $10.00 Hdbd. (ISBN 0-8147-0133-7); $3.50 pa. (ISBN 0-8147-0134-5). New York Univ. Pr., NY.

Markov, Pavel A. Soviet Theatre. $10.75 Hdbd. Benjamin Blom, NY.

Miller, Rene Fulop & Gregor, Joseph. Russian Theatre. 1930. $25.00 Hdbd. Benjamin Blom, NY.

Sayler, Oliver M. Inside the Moscow Art Theatre. (Library of Literature, Drama & Criticism). 1970. (1925) $15.00 Hdbd. Johnson Reprint, NY.

Slonim, Marc. Russian Theatre: From the Empire to the Soviets. 1962. $1.50 pa. Macmillan, NY.

Wiener, Leo. Contemporary Drama of Russia. 1924. $10.00 Hdbd. (ISBN 0-404-06943-6). AMS Pr., NY.

Spain

Gregersen, H. Ibsen & Spain: A Study in Comparative Drama. 1936. $10.00 pa. Kraus Reprint, NY.

Rennert, Hugo A. Spanish Stage in the Time of Lope De Vega. 1909. $3.50 pa.

(ISBN 0-486-21110-X). Dover Publ., NY.

Rennert, Hugo A. Spanish Stage in the Time of Lope De Vega. $4.75 Hdbd. Peter Smith, MA.

Rennert, Hugo A. Spanish Stage in the Time of Lope De Vega. 1909. $20.00 Hdbd. Kraus Reprint, NY.

Shergold, N. D. History of the Spanish Stage from Medieval Times Until the End of the Seventeenth Century. 1967. $16.80 Hdbd. (ISBN 0-19-815365-1). Oxford Univ. Pr., NY.

Shoemaker, William H. The Multiple Stage in Spain During the Fifteenth & Sixteenth Centuries. (1935) $8.50 Hdbd. (ISBN 0-8371-5539-8). Greenwood Pr., CT.

Spanish America

Bibliographical Guide to the Spanish American Theatre. (Bibliography & Library Science Ser). 1969. $2.00 Hdbd. Pan American Union, DC.

Cid-Perez, J., et al. Teatro Hispano-americano De Hoy y De Ayer, Vol. 1. price "n.g." Hdbd. (ISBN 0-07-010951-6). McGraw-Hill Book Co., NY.

Jones, Willis K. Behind Spanish American Footlights. 1965. $11.50 Hdbd. (ISBN 0-292-73173-6). Univ. of Tex. Pr., TX.

Lamb, Ruth S. Bibliografia Del Teatro Mexicano Del Siglo Vente. (Span). 1962. $4.00 pa. (ISBN 0-912434-01-5). Ocelot Pr., CA.

Monterde, Francisco, ed. Bibliografia Del Teatro En Mexico. (Bibliography & Reference Ser., No. 369). (Span). 1970. (1934) $25.00 Hdbd. (ISBN 0-8337-2440-1). Burt Franklin, NY.

Woodyard, George, ed. Modern Stage in Latin America: Six Plays. 1971. $2.95 pa. (ISBN 0-525-47296-7). E. P. Dutton, NY.

Turkey

Martinovitch, Nicholas N. Turkish Theatre. 1968. $12.50 Hdbd. Benjamin Blom, NY.

United States

Abramson, Doris E. Negro Playwrights in the American Theatre. Orig. Title: Study of Plays by Negro Playwrights. 1969. $12.50 Hdbd. (ISBN 0-231-03248-X); $2.95 pa. (ISBN 0-231-08593-1). Columbia Univ. Pr., NY.

Adams, William D. Dictionary of the Drama Vol. 1, A-G. 1965. (1904) $28.50 Hdbd. Burt Franklin, NY.

Atkinson, J. Brooks. Broadway Scrapbook. 1947. $12.50 Hdbd. (ISBN 0-8371-3331-9). Greenwood Pr., CT.

Balch, Marston, et al. Theater in America. 1968. $6.50 Hdbd.; $4.95 pa. Theatre Arts Books, NY.

Baral, Robert. Turn West on Twenty-Third. 1966. $5.95 Hdbd. (ISBN 0-8303-0055-4). Fleet Pr. Corp., NY.

Bentley, Eric. Dramatic Event. 1956. $1.25 pa. (ISBN 0-8070-6479-3). Beacon Pr., MA.

Bentley, Eric. What Is Theatre. 1968. $12.50 Hdbd. (ISBN 0-689-10035-3); $4.95 pa. (ISBN 0-689-70012-1, 131). Atheneum Publ., NY.

Bernheim, Alfred L. Business of the Theatre. 1932. $17.50 Hdbd. Benjamin Blom, NY.

Blau, H. Impossible Theatre. 1964. $10.00 Hdbd. Macmillan Co., NY.

Blau, H. Impossible Theater. 1966. $1.95 pa. Macmillan Co., NY.

Blum, Daniel. Pictorial History of the American Theatre: 1860–1970. 3rd enl. ed. Willis, John, ed. 1969. $12.50 Hdbd. Crown Publ., NY.

Blum, Daniel, ed. Theatre World, Vol. 14: Season 1957–58. $15.00 Hdbd. DBS Publ., NY.

Bricker, Herschel L., ed. Our Theatre Today. facs. ed. (Essay Index Reprint Ser). 1936. $16.50 Hdbd. (ISBN 0-8369-1823-1). Books for Libraries, NY.

Brockett, Oscar G. Theatre: An Introduction. 2nd ed. (Rinehart Editions). 1969. $12.95 Hdbd. (ISBN 0-03-082874-0); $10.95 Hdbd. (ISBN 0-03-080270-9). Harcourt Brace Jovanovich, NY.

Brown, John M. Broadway in Review. facsimile ed. (Essay Index Reprint Ser). 1940. $9.00 Hdbd. (ISBN 0-8369-0007-3). Books for Libraries, NY.

Brown, John M. Dramatis Personae: A Retrospective Show. 1963. $2.25 pa. (ISBN 0-670-00171-6). Viking Pr., NY.

Brown, John M. Two on the Aisle. (Es-say & General Literature Index Reprint Ser). (1938) $10.00 Hdbd. (ISBN 0-8046-0546-7). Kennikat Pr., NY.

Brown, John M. Upstage. (Essay & General Literature Index Reprint Ser). 1969. (1930). $10.00 Hdbd. (ISBN 0-8046-0547-5). Kennikat Pr., NY.

Brown, John M. & Moses, Montrose J., eds. American Theatre As Seen by Its Critics, 1752–1934. 1934. $10.00 Hdbd. (ISBN 0-8154-0033-0). Cooper Sq. Publ., NY.

Brustein, Robert. Seasons of Discontent. 1967. $5.95 Hdbd. $1.95 pa. Simon & Schuster, NY.

Brustein, Robert. Third Theatre. 1970. $2.95 pa. Simon & Schuster, NY.

Brustein, Robert. Third Theatre. 1969. $6.95 Hdbd. Alfred A. Knopf, NY.

Buch, Arthur T. Bible on Broadway. 1968. $7.50 Hdbd. Shoe String Pr., CT.

Clapp, J. B. & Edgett, E. Players of the Present, 3 Vols. (Drama Ser). 1968–1970. (1901) $14.50 Hdbd. (ISBN 0-8337-0577-6). Burt Franklin, NY.

Clapp, John B. & Edgett, Edwin F. Players of the Present, 3 Vols. in 1. 1899–1901. $12.50 Hdbd. Benjamin Blom, NY.

Clurman, Harold. Fervent Years. 1957. $1.75 pa. (ISBN 0-8090-0508-5). Hill & Wang, NY.

Coad, Oral S. & Mims, Edwin, Jr. American Stage. (Yale Pageant of

America Ser., Vol. 14). $10.75 Hdbd. United States Publ. Assn., NY.

Coigney, Martha W., et al, eds. Theatre Two: The American Theatre, 1968–69. $4.95 pa. (ISBN 0-87830-539-4). Theatre Arts Books, NY.

Cornyn, Stan. Selective Index to Theatre Magazine. 1964. $6.25 Hdbd. (ISBN 0-8108-0133-7). Scarecrow Pr., NJ.

Crawford, Mary C. Romance of the American Theatre. (1925) $15.00 Hdbd. Gale Research Co., MI.

Crawford, Mary C. Romance of the American Theatre. 1971. (1925) $27.00 Hdbd. Scholarly Pr., MI.

Cullman, Marguerite. Occupation: Angel. 1963. $3.95 Hdbd. (ISBN 0-393-07440-4). W. W. Norton, NY.

Culp, Ralph B. Theatre & Its Drama: Principles & Practices. 1971. $8.50 Hdbd. (ISBN 0-697-04251-0). William C. Brown, IA.

Daly, Charles P. First Theater in America. (Drama Ser). 1970. (1896) $14.50 Hdbd. (ISBN 0-8337-0763-9) Burt Franklin, NY.

Daly, Charles P. First Theatre in America: When Was the Drama First Introduced in America. 1968. (1896) $6.50 Hdbd. (ISBN 0-8046-0095-3). Kennikat Pr., NY.

Daly, Joseph F. Life of Augustin Daly. 1917. $12.50 Hdbd. Benjamin Blom, NY.

Dormon, James H., Jr. Theatre in the Ante Bellum South, 1815–1861. 1967. $8.00 Hdbd. (ISBN 0-8078-1047-9). Univ. of N.C. Pr., NC.

Downer, Alan S., ed. American Theater Today. (Hi-Sch.). 1967. $5.95 Hdbd. (ISBN 0-465-00224-6). Basic Books, NY.

Duffus, Robert L. American Renaissance. 1970. (1928) $10.50 Hdbd. (ISBN 0-404-02214-6). AMS Pr., NY.

Duffus, Robert L. Dunlap Society, Publications Relating to the Drama, Stage & Theatre in Early America, 30 Vols. 1968. (1904) $14.50 ea. pa.; Vols. 1968. (1904) $390.00 pa. $14.50 ea.; (ISBN 0-8337-0958-5). Burt Franklin, NY.

Dunlap, William. History of the American Theatre. (Research & Source Ser., No. 36). 1968. (1797) $23.50 Hdbd. (ISBN 0-8337-0964-X). Burt Franklin, NY.

Dunn, Esther C. Shakespeare in America. 1968. $12.50 Hdbd. Benjamin Blom, NY.

Eaton, Walter P. Actor's Heritage. facs. ed. (Essay Index Reprint Ser). 1924. $10.75 Hdbd. (ISBN 0-8369-1827-4). Books for Libraries, NY.

Edwards, Christine. Stanislavsky Heritage: Its Contribution to the Russian & American Theatre. (Gotham Library). 1965. $10.00 Hdbd. (ISBN 0-8147-0133-7); $3.50 pa. (ISBN 0-8147-0134-5). New York Univ. Pr., NY.

Ellison, Jerome. God on Broadway. (Orig.). 1971. price "n.g." pa. John Knox Pr., VA.

Eustis, Morton. B'way, Inc. the Theatre As a Business. $7.50 Hdbd. Benjamin Blom, NY.

Farber, Donald C. Producing on Broadway: A Comprehensive Guide. 1969. $15.00 Hdbd. DBS Publ., NY.

Flexner, Eleanor. American Playwrights: 1918–1938. (Essay Index Reprint Ser). 1938. $14.50 Hdbd. (ISBN 0-8369-1412-0). Books for Libraries, NY.

Ford, Paul L. Washington & the Theater. (Drama Ser). 1970. (1899) $14.50 Hdbd. (ISBN 0-8337-1204-7). Burt Franklin, NY.

Ford, Paul L. Washington & the Theatre. 1967. Repr. $6.75 Hdbd. Benjamin Blom, NY.

Frohman, Daniel. Encore. (Essay Index Reprint Ser). 1937. $12.50 Hdbd. (ISBN 0-8369-1466-X). Books for Libraries, NY.

Frohman, Daniel. Memories of a Manager. 1911. $9.75 Hdbd. Benjamin Blom, NY.

Gardner, Rufus H. Splintered Stage. 1965 $4.50 Hdbd. Macmillan Co., NY.

Gassner, John. Dramatic Soundings: Evaluations & Retractions Culled from Thirty Years of Dramatic Criticism. 1968. $7.50 Hdbd. Crown Publ., NY.

Gassner, John. Theatre at the Crossroads: Plays & Playwrights on the Mid-Century American Stage. 1960. $5.95 Hdbd. (ISBN 0-03-030290-0). Holt, Rinehart & Winston, NY.

Golden, Joseph. Death of Tinker Bell: The American Theatre in the 20th Century. 1967. $5.00 Hdbd. (ISBN 0-8156-0054-2). Syracuse Univ. Pr., NY.

Goldman, William. Season: A Candid Look at Broadway. 1969. $6.95 Hdbd. (ISBN 0-15-179923-7). Harcourt Brace Jovanovich, Inc., NY.

Gottfried, Martin. Theater Divided: The Postwar American Stage. 1969. $7.50 Hdbd. (ISBN 0-316-32154-0); $2.65 pa. (ISBN 0-316-32155-9). Little, Brown & Co., MA.

Grau, Robert. Stage in the Twentieth Century. 1912. $15.00 Hdbd. Benjamin Blom, NY.

Grimsted, David. Melodrama Unveiled: American Theater & Culture, 1800–1850. 1968. $8.95 Hdbd. (ISBN 0-226-30901-0). Univ. of Chicago Pr., IL.

United States—States and Cities

Alabama

Kendall, John S. Golden Age of the New Orleans Theater. 1968. (1952) $21.50 Hdbd. (ISBN 0-8371-0128 X). Greenwood Pr., CT.

Smither, Nelle. History of the English Theatre at New Orleans, 1806–1842. 1967. Repr. $12.50 Hdbd. Benjamin Blom, NY.

California

Gaer, Joseph, ed. Theatre of the Gold Rush Decade in San Francisco. (Bibliography & Reference Ser., No. 391). 1971. (1935) $10.00 Hdbd. (ISBN 0-8337-1261-6). Burt Franklin, NY.

Gagey, Edmund M. San Francisco Stage, A History. 1950. $12.25 Hdbd. (ISBN 0-8371-3927-9). Greenwood Pr., CT.

MacMinn, George R. Theatre of the Golden Era in California. 1941. $12.50 Hdbd. Benjamin Blom, NY.

District of Columbia

Ford, Paul L. Washington & the Theater. (Drama Ser). 1970. (1899) $14.50 Hdbd. (ISBN 0-8337-1204-7). Burt Franklin, NY.

Kentucky

Hill, West T., Jr. Theatre in Early Kentucky, 1790–1820. 1971. $9.50 Hdbd. (ISBN 0-8131-1240-0). Univ. of Ky., KY.

Massachusetts

Clapp, William W. Record of the Boston Stage. 1853. $16.25 Hdbd. (ISBN 0-8371-0350-9). Greenwood Pr., CT.

Clapp, William W. Record of the Boston 'Stage. (Miscellany of the Theatre Ser). 1969. (1853) $15.00 Hdbd. Johnson Reprint Corp., NY.

Clapp, William Warland. Record of the Boston Stage. 1968. (1853) $12.50 Hdbd. Benjamin Blom, NY.

Clapp, William W. Record of the Boston Stage. 1853. $24.00 Hdbd. (ISBN 0-403-00473-X). Scholarly Pr., MI.

Minnesota

O'Connor, William V., ed. History of the Arts in Minnesota. 1958. $3.00 Hdbd. (ISBN 0-8166-0173). Univ. of Minn. Pr., MN.

Missouri

Bowen, Elbert R. Theatrical Entertainments in Rural Missouri Before the Civil War. 1959. $3.50 Hdbd. (ISBN 0-8262-0541-0). (ISBN 0-8262-0541-0). Univ. of Mo. Pr., MO.

Carson, William G. Managers in Distress: The St. Louis Stage, 1840–1844. 1949. $12.75 Hdbd. Benjamin Blom, NY.

Carson, William G. Theatre on the Frontier: The Early Years of the St. Louis Stage. rev. ed. $12.50 Hdbd. Benjamin Blom, NY.

Nevada

Watson, Margaret G. Silver Theatre: Nevada. 1964. $9.50 Hdbd. (ISBN 0-87062-064-9). Arthur H. Clark, CA.

New Jersey

Moore, Lester L. Outside Broadway: A History of the Professional Theater in Newark, New Jersey from Beginning to 1867. 1970. $5.00 Hdbd. (ISBN 0-8108-0308). Scarecrow Pr., NJ.

New York

Bauland, Peter. Hooded Eagle: Modern German Drama on the New York Stage.

1968. $9.00 Hdbd. (ISBN 0-8156-2119-1). Syracuse Univ. Pr., NY.

Brown, Thomas A. History of the New York Stage, 3 Vols. $55.00 Hdbd. Benjamin Blom, NY.

Ireland, Joseph N. Fifty Years of a Play-Goer's Journal. 1860. $7.50 Hdbd. Benjamin Blom, NY.

Ireland, Joseph N. Records of the New York Stage: Seventeen Fifty to Eighteen Sixty. $32.50 Hdbd. Benjamin Blom, NY.

Ireland, Joseph N. Records of the New York Stage, Seventeen-Fifty to Eighteen-Sixty, 2 Vols. (Bibliography & Reference Ser 226). 1968. (1866) $45.00 Hdbd. (ISBN 0-8337-1810-X). Burt Franklin, NY.

Leuchs, Frederick A. Early German Theatre in New York, 1840–1872. 1928. $10.00 Hdbd. (ISBN 0-404-50432-9). AMS Pr., NY.

Lewis, Allan. American Plays & Playwrights of the Contemporary Theatre. rev. ed. 1970. $5.95 Hdbd. Crown Publ., NY.

Mason, Hamilton. French Theatre in New York. 1940. $12.50 Hdbd. (ISBN 0-404-04224-4). AMS Pr., NY.

Odell, George C. Annals of the New York Stage, 15. 1970. (1927) Set— $695.00 Hdbd. (ISBN 0-404-07830-3); $46.50 ea. AMS Pr., NY.

Phelps, Henry P. Players of a Century: A Record of the Albany Stage. 1880. $15.75 Hdbd. Benjamin Blom, NY.

Philadelphia

James, Reese D. Cradle of Culture: The Philadelphia Stage, 1800–1810. 1957. $9.00 Hdbd. (ISBN 0-8122-7028-7). Univ. of Pa. Pr., PA.

James, Reese D. Old Drury of Philadelphia. (Miscellany of the Theatre Ser). 1969. (1932) $17.50 Hdbd. Johnson Reprint Corp., NY.

James, Reese D. Old Drury of Philadelphia: A History of the Philadelphia Stage, 1800–1835. 1968. (1932) $24.75 Hdbd. (ISBN 0-8371-0115-8). Greenwood Pr., CT.

Wilson, Arthur H. History of the Philadelphia Theatre, 1835 to 1855. 1968. (1935) $27.25 Hdbd. (ISBN 0-8371-0272-3). Greenwood Pr., CT.

Rhode Island

Blake, Charles. Historical Account of the Providence Stage. 1868. $12.50 Hdbd. Benjamin Blom, NY.

Willard, George O. History of the Providence Stage 1762–1891. 1891. $12.50 Hdbd. Benjamin Blom, NY.

South Carolina

Willis, Eola. Charleston Stage in the Eighteenth Century. 1968. $18.50 Hdbd. Benjamin Blom, NY.

Texas

Gallegly, Joseph S. Footlights on the Border: Inc. Galveston & Houston Stage Before 1900. 1962. $10.00 Hdbd. Humanities Pr., NY.

History

Bapst, Germain. Essais Sur L'Histoire Du Theatre, La Mise En Scene, Le Decor, Le Costume, L'Architecture, L'Eclairage L'Hygiene (French). 1893. $28.50 Hdbd. (ISBN 0-8337-3965-4). Burt Franklin, NY.

Beerbohm, Max. Last Theatres. Hart-Davis, Rupert, ed. 1970. $15.00 Hdbd. (ISBN 0-8008-4564-1). Taplinger Publ., NY.

Belli, Angela. Ancient Greek Myths & Modern Drama: A Study in Continuity. (Studies in Comparative Literature). 1969. $8.50 text ed. (ISBN 0-8147-0034-9); $2.50 pa. (ISBN 0-8147-0959-1). NYU Pr., NY.

Bowers, Faubion. Theater in the East: A Survey of Ancient Dance & Drama. 1960. $3.95 Hdbd. Grove Pr., NY.

Brauneck, Martin, ed. Spieltexte der Wanderbuehne, 6 vols. Incl. Vol. 1. Englische Comoedien und Tragoedien. $38.25 Hdbd. (ISBN 3-11-002694-5); Vol. 3. Schau-Buehne Englischer und Franzoesischer Comoedianten: 1670. $38.25 Hdbd. (ISBN 3-11-002695-3). (Ausgaben Deutscher Literatur des Fuenfzehnten bis Achtzehnten Jahrhunderts). (German). 1970. De Gruyter, Germany.

Brockett, Oscar G. History of the Theatre. 1968. $12.50 text ed. (491974). Allyn Inc., NJ.

Brockett, Oscar G. Theatre: An Introduction. 2nd ed. (Rinehart Editions).

1969. $12.95 Hdbd. (ISBN 0-03-082874-0); $10.95 Hdbd. (ISBN 0-03-080270-9). Holt, Rinehart & Winston, NY.

Chambers, Edmund K. Mediaeval Stage, 2 Vols. 1903. Set—$16.00 Hdbd. (ISBN 0-19-811512-1). Oxford Univ. Pr., NY.

Cheney, Sheldon. Theatre. rev. & enl. ed. 1971. $12.95 Hdbd. David McKay, NY.

Downer, Alan S. Art of the Play. 1955. $9.95 text ed. (ISBN 0-03-005310-2). Holt, Rinehart & Winston, NY.

Drew, Elizabeth. Discovering Drama. 1968. (1937) $8.00 Hdbd. (ISBN 0-8046-0116-X). Kennikat Pr., NY.

Dunlap Society. Biennial Reports of the Treasurer & Secretary of the Dunlap Society. (Drama Ser). 1970. Repr. of 1888 ed. $14.50 Hdbd. (ISBN 0-8337-4083-0). Burt Franklin, NY.

Esslin, Martin. Reflections: Essays on Modern Theatre. 1969. $5.95 Hdbd. Doubleday & Co., NY.

Freedley, George & Reeves, John A. History of the Theatre. rev. ed. (Hi-Sch.). 1968. $10.00 Hdbd. Crown Publ., NY.

Fromm, Harold. Bernard Shaw & the Theater of the Nineties. 1967. $5.00 Hdbd. (ISBN 0-7006-0020-5). Univ. Pr. of Kansas, KS.

Galloway, David, ed. Elizabethan Theatre 1. 1970. $6.50 Hdbd. (ISBN 0-208-01144-7). Shoe String Pr., CT.

Galloway, David. Elizabethan Theatre 2. 1970. $7.00 Hdbd. (ISBN 0-208-01145-5). Shoe String Pr., CT.

Gascoigne, Bamber. World Theatre: An Illustrated History. 1968. $15.00 Hdbd. (ISBN 0-316-30500-6). Little, Brown & Co., MA.

Geisinger, Marion. Plays, Players, & Playwrights: An Illustrated History of the Theatre. 1971. $19.95 Hdbd.; pre-Jan. $17.50 Hdbd. Hart Publ. Co., NY.

Gilman, Richard. Common & Uncommon Masks: Writings on Theatre 1960–1970. 1971. $8.95 Hdbd. Random House, NY.

Gottfried, Martin. Opening Nights. 1970. $6.95 Hdbd. G. P. Putnam's Sons, NY.

Gottfried, Martin. Theater Divided: The Postwar American Stage. 1969. $7.50 Hdbd. (ISBN 0-316-32154-0); $2.65 pa. ' (ISBN 0-316-32155-9, LB98). Little, Brown & Co., MA.

Graves, Thornton S. Court & the London Theatres During the Reign of Elizabeth. 1913. $5.00 Hdbd. Folcroft Pr., PA.

Harnoll, Phyllis. Concise History of Theatre. 1968. $7.50 Hdbd. (ISBN 0-8109-0508-6). Harry N. Abrams, NY.

Harnoll, Phyllis. Concise History of Theatre. (Art Paperbacks Ser). (Jr. Hi.). 1968. $7.50 Hdbd. (Pub. by Abrams). Dist. by New American Library, NY.

Hewitt, Barnard. History of the Theatre: From 1800 to the Present. 1970. $3.95 pa. Random House, NY.

Houghton, Norris. Exploding Stage. 1971. $6.95 Hdbd. Weybright, & Talley, Inc., NY.

Hughes, Glenn. Story of the Theatre. 1928. $6.00 Hdbd. Samuel French, Inc., NY.

Hunningher, Benjamin. Origin of the Theater. 1961. $1.35 pa. (ISBN 0-8090-0528-X). Hill & Wang, NY.

Kernodle, George R. From Art to Theatre: Form & Convention in the Renaissance. 1944. $11.75 Hdbd. (ISBN 0-226-43188-6). Univ. of Chicago Pr., IL.

Kernodle, George R. Invitation to the Theatre. 1967. $9.95 Hdbd. (ISBN 0-15-546921-5). Harcourt, Brace & World, NY.

Lawrence, William J. Old Theatre Days & Ways. 1968. $12.50 Hdbd. Benjamin Blom, NY.

MacGowan, Kenneth & Melnitz, W. Golden Ages of the Theater. 1959. $1.95 pa. (ISBN 0-13-357830-5, S8, Spec). Prentice-Hall, NJ.

MacGowan, Kenneth & Melnitz, W. Living Stage: A History of the World Theatre. 1955. $11.95 Hdbd. (ISBN 0-13-538942-9). Prentice-Hall, NJ.

Mantzius, Karl. History of Theatrical Art in Ancient & Modern Times, 6 Vols. Set—$36.00 Hdbd. Peter Smith Publ., MA.

Murdock, James E. Stage. 1880. $12.50 Hdbd. Benjamin Blom, NY.

Nagler, Alois M. Source Book in Theatrical History. $5.50 Hdbd. Peter Smith Publ., MA.

Nagler, Alois M. Source Book in Theatrical History. Orig. Title: Sources of Theatrical History. 1952. $3.50 pa. (ISBN 0-486-20515-0). Dover Publ., NY.

Nicoll, Allardyce. Development of the Theatre. 5th ed. 1967. $15.00 Hdbd. (ISBN 0-15-125327-7). Harcourt Brace Jovanovich, NY.

Nicoll, Allardyce. Masks, Mimes & Miracles. 1931. $17.50 Hdbd. (ISBN 0-8154-0163-9). Cooper Square Publ., NY.

Oenslager, Donald. Scenery, Then & Now. 1966. (1936) $15.00 Hdbd. Russell & Russell Publ., NY.

Ormsbee, Helen. Backstage with Actors. (Essay Index Reprint Ser). $11.75 Hdbd. (ISBN 0-8369-1934-3). Books for Libraries, NY.

Ormsbee, Helen. Backstage with Actors. 1938. $10.75 Hdbd. Benjamin Blom, NY.

Priestley, John B. Wonderful World of Theatre. rev. ed. (Hi-Sch.). 1969. (1959) $3.95 Hdbd. Doubleday & Co., NY.

Riccoboni, Luigi. Historical & Critical Account of the Theatres in Europe. 1738. $28.75 Hdbd. Benjamin Blom, NY.

Roberts, Vera M. On Stage: A History of Theatre. (Hi-Sch.). 1962. $10.00 text ed. (ISBN 0-06-045500-4). Harper & Row Publ., NY.

Rowell, George, ed. Victorian Dramatic Criticism. 1971. $12.75 Hdbd. (ISBN 0-416-12320-1). Barnes & Noble, NY.

Southern, Richard. Seven Ages of the Theatre. 1961. $5.95 Hdbd. (ISBN 0-8090-8550-X, Drama); $2.45 pa. (ISBN 0-8090-0534-4). Hill & Wang, NY.

Stratman, Carl J., ed. Restoration & Eighteenth-Century Theatre Research: Bibliographical Guide, 1900–1968. 1971. $25.00 Hdbd. (ISBN 0-8093-0469-4). Southern Ill. Univ. Pr., IL.

Symons, James M. Meyerhold's Theatre of the Grotesque: The Post-Revolutionary Productions, 1920–1932. $10.00 Hdbd. (ISBN 0-87024-192-3). Univ. of Miami Pr., FL.

Taylor, Karen M. People's Theatre: Twenties to Tomorrow. price "n.g." Hdbd. (ISBN 0-910482-33-0). DBS Pubns., NY.

Tunison, R. S. Dramatic Traditions of the Middle Ages. 1907. $16.50 Hdbd. (ISBN 0-8337-3578-0). Burt Franklin, NY.

Vardac, A. Nicholas. Stage to Screen: Theatrical Method from Garrick to Griffith. 1968. $12.50 Hdbd. Benjamin Blom, NY.

Vargas, Luis. Teach Yourself Guidebook to the Drama. $2.50 Hdbd. (ISBN

0-486-20961-X); $2.00 pa. Dover Publ., NY.

Wells, Staring B., ed. Comparison Between the Two Stages: A Late Restoration Book of the Theatre. 1942. $12.50 Hdbd. Benjamin Blom, NY.

Winter, William. Shadows of the Stage, 3 Series. 1893–1895. $9.75 Hdbd. Benjamin Blom, NY.

Children's Literature

Allen, John P. Great Moments in the Theatre. (Elem.). $2.75 Hdbd. Roy Publ., NY.

Fuller, Edmund. Pageant of the Theatre. (Jr. Hi.). 1965. $5.95 Hdbd. (ISBN 0-690-60809-8). Thomas Y. Crowell, NY.

Leacroft, Helen & Leacroft, Richard. Theatre. (Jr. Hi.). $3.95 Hdbd. Roy Publ., NY.

Male, David. Story of the Theatre. (Jr. Hi.). 1960. $2.95 Hdbd. Dufour Editions Inc., PA.

U.S.

Anderson, John & Fulop-Miller, Rene. American Theater & the Motion Picture in America. (English Literary Reference, House Ser). 1970. (1938) $22.50 Hdbd. Johnson Reprint, NY.

Atkinson, Brooks. Broadway. 1970. $12.50 Hdbd. Macmillan, NY.

Atkinson, Brooks. Broadway: Nineteen Hundred to Nineteen Seventy. Markel, Robert, ed. 1970. $12.50 Hdbd. (Collier). Macmillan, NY.

Balio, Tino & Norvelle, Lee. History of the National Theatre Conference. 1970. $2.95 pa. (ISBN 0-87830-546-7). Theatre Arts, NY.

Bauland, Peter. Hooded Eagle: Modern German Drama on the New York Stage. 1968. $9.00 Hdbd. (ISBN 0-8156-2119-1). Syracuse Univ. Pr., NY.

Bernard, John. Retrospections of America 1797-1811. Brander Matthews & Laurence Hutton, eds. 1887. $12.50 Hdbd. Benjamin Blom, NY.

Blake, Charles. Historical Account of the Providence Stage. 1868. $12.50 Hdbd. Benjamin Blom, NY.

Blum, Daniel. Pictorial History of the American Theatre: 1860–1970. 3rd enl. ed. Willis, John, ed. 1969. $12.50 Hdbd. Crown Publ., NY.

Bowen, Elbert R. Theatrical Entertainments in Rural Missouri Before the Civil War. 1959. $3.50 Hdbd. (ISBN 0-8262-0541-0) (ISBN 0-8262-0541-0). Univ. of Mo. Pr., MO.

Brown, Thomas A. History of the American Stage. 1969. $17.50 Hdbd. (ISBN 0-8337-0387-0). Burt Franklin, NY.

Brown, Thomas A. History of the New York Stage, 3 Vols. $55.00 Hdbd. Benjamin Blom, NY.

Carson, William G. Managers in Distress: The St. Louis Stage, 1840-1844. 1949. $12.75 Hdbd. Benjamin Blom, NY.

Carson, William G. Theatre on the

Frontier: The Early Years of the St. Louis Stage. rev. ed. $12.50 Hdbd. Benjamin Blom, NY.

Case, Victoria & Case, Robert O. We Called It Culture: The Story of Chautauqua. (Biography Index Reprint Ser., Vol. 1). 1948. $11.00 Hdbd. (ISBN 0-8369-8051-4). Books for Libraries, NY.

Clapp, William W. Record of the Boston Stage. 1853. $16.25 Hdbd. (ISBN 0-8371-0350-9). Greenwood Pr., CT.

Clapp, William W. Record of the Boston Stage. (Miscellany of the Theatre Ser.). 1969. (1853) $15.00 Hdbd. Johnson Reprint Corp., NY.

Clapp, William W. Record of the Boston Stage. 1853. $24.00 Hdbd. (ISBN 0-403-00473-X). Scholarly Pr., MI.

Clapp, William Warland. Record of the Boston Stage. 1968. (1853) $12.50 Hdbd. Benjamin Blom, NY.

Coad, Oral S. & Mims, Edwin, Jr. American Stage. (Yale Pageant of America Ser., Vol. 14). $10.75 Hdbd. United States Publ. Assn., NY.

Cowell, Joe. Thirty Years Passed Among the Players in England & America. rep. ed. 1968. $12.50 Hdbd. Benjamin Blom, NY.

Daly, Charles P. First Theater in America. (Drama Ser.). 1970. (1896) $14.50 (ISBN 0-8337-0763-9). Burt Franklin, NY.

Daly, Charles P. First Theatre in America: When Was the Drama First Introduced in America. 1968. (1896) $6.50

Hdbd. (ISBN 0-8046-0095-3). Kennikat Pr., NY.

Dormon, James H., Jr. Theatre in the Ante Bellum South, 1815-1861. 1967. $8.00 Hdbd. (ISBN 0-8078-1047-9). Univ. of N.C. Pr., NC.

Dunlap, William. History of the American Theatre. (Research & Source Ser., No. 36). 1968. (1797) $23.50 Hdbd. (ISBN 0-8337-0964-X). Burt Franklin, NY.

Eaton, Walter P. Theatre Guild, the First Ten Years, with Articles by the Directors. (Select Bibliographies Reprint Ser.). 1929. $13.50 Hdbd. (ISBN 0-8369-5180-8). Books for Libraries, NY.

Eaton, Walter P. Theatre Guild, the First 10 Years. 1971. (1929) $13.00 Hdbd. (ISBN 0-403-00922-7). Scholarly Pr., MI.

Edwards, Christine. Stanislavsky Heritage: Its Contribution to the Russian & American Theatre. (Gotham Library). 1965. $10.00 Hdbd. (ISBN 0-8147-0133-7); $3.50 pa. (ISBN 0-8147-0134-5). N.Y. Univ. Pr., NY.

Felheim, Marvin. Theater of Augustin Daly. 1956. $12.50 Hdbd. (ISBN 0-8371-2209-0). Greenwood Pr., CT.

Ford, Paul L. Washington & the Theater. (Drama Ser.). 1970. (1899) $14.50 Hdbd. (ISBN 0-8337-1204-7). Burt Franklin, NY.

Gaer, Joseph, ed. Theatre of the Gold Rush Decade in San Francisco. (Bibliography & Reference Ser., No. 391). 1971. (1935) $10.00 Hdbd. (ISBN 0-8337-1261-6). Burt Franklin, NY.

Gagey, Edmund M. San Francisco Stage, A History. 1950. $12.25 Hdbd. (ISBN 0-8371-3927-9). Greenwood Pr., CT.

Gallegly, Joseph S. Footlights on the Border: The Galveston & Houston Stage Before 1900. 1962. $10.00 Hdbd. Humanities Pr., NY.

Gottfried, Martin. Theater Divided: The Postwar American Stage. 1969. $7.50 Hdbd. (ISBN 0-316-32154-0); $2.65 pa. (ISBN 0-316-32155-9). Little, Brown & Co., MA.

Gould, Joseph E. Chautauqua Movement. (Illus.). 1961. $1.45 pa. (ISBN 0-87395-004-6). State Univ. N.Y. Pr., NY.

Grimsted, David. Melodrama Unveiled: American Theater & Culture, 1800–1850. 1968. $8.95 Hdbd. (ISBN 0-226-30901-0). Univ. of Chicago Pr., IL.

Hewitt, Barnard W. Theatre U.S.A., 1668 to 1957. 1959. $9.50 text ed. (ISBN 0-07-028585-3). McGraw-Hill, NY.

Hill, West T., Jr. Theatre in Early Kentucky, 1790–1820. 1971. $9.50 Hdbd. (ISBN 0-8131-1240-0). Univ. Pr. of Ky., KY.

Hornblow, Arthur. History of the Theatre in America, 2 Vols. 1919. $25.00 Hdbd. Benjamin Blom, NY.

Hughes, Glenn. History of the American Theatre, 1700–1950. 1951. $6.00 Hdbd. Samuel French, NY.

Hutton, Laurence. Curiosities of the American Stage. 1891. $10.00 Hdbd. (ISBN 0-403-00081-5). Scholarly Pr., MI.

Hutton, Lawrence. Curiosities of the American Stage. (Miscellany of the Theatre Ser.). 1968. (1891) $12.00 Hdbd. Johnson Reprint Corp., NY.

Ireland, Joseph N. Fifty Years of a Play-Goer's Journal. 1860. $7.50 Hdbd. Benjamin Blom, NY.

Ireland, Joseph N. Records of the New York Stage, Seventeen-Fifty to Eighteen-Sixty, 2 Vols. (Bibliography & Reference Ser. 226). 1968. (1866) $45.00 Hdbd. (ISBN 0-8337-1810-X). Burt Franklin, NY.

Ireland, Joseph N. Records of the New York Stage: Seventeen Fifty to Eighteen Sixty. $32.50 Hdbd. Benjamin Blom, NY.

James, Reese D. Old Drury of Philadelphia. (Miscellany of the Theatre Ser.). 1969. (1932) $17.50 Hdbd. Johnson Reprint Corp., NY.

James, Reese D. Old Drury of Philadelphia: A History of the Philadelphia Stage, 1800–1835. 1968. (1932) $24.75 Hdbd. (ISBN 0-8371-0115-8). Greenwood Pr., CT.

James, Reese D. Cradle of Culture: The Philadelphia Stage, 1800–1810. 1957. $9.00 Hdbd. (ISBN 0-8122-7028-2). Univ. of Pa. Pr., PA.

Kendall, John S. Golden Age of the New Orleans Theater. 1968. (1952) $21.50 Hdbd. (ISBN 0-8371-0128-X). Greenwood Pr., CT.

Leuchs, Frederick A. Early German Theatre in New York, 1840–1872. 1928. $10.00 Hdbd. (ISBN 0-404-50432-9). AMS Pr., NY.

Lewis, Allan. American Plays & Playwrights of the Contemporary Theatre. rev. ed. 1970. $5.95 Hdbd. Crown Publ., NY.

Lewis, E. Stages: The Fifty-Year Childhood of the American Theater. $8.50 Hdbd. (ISBN 0-13-840306-6). Prentice-Hall, NY.

Ludlow, Noah M. Dramatic Life As I Found It. $18.50 Hdbd. Benjamin Blom, NY.

MacMinn, George R. Theatre of the Golden Era in California. 1941. $12.50 Hdbd. Benjamin Blom, NY.

McNamara, Brooks. American Playhouse in the Eighteenth Century. 1969. $9.95 Hdbd. (ISBN 0-674-02725-6). Harvard Univ. Pr., MA.

Mason, Hamilton. French Theater in New York. 1940. $12.50 Hdbd. (ISBN 0-404-04224-4). AMS Pr., NY.

Moody, Richard. America Takes the Stage. 1955. $15.00 Hdbd. Kraus Reprint Co., NY.

Moore, Lester L. Outside Broadway: A History of the Professional Theater in Newark, New Jersey from the Beginning to 1867. 1970. $5.00 Hdbd. (ISBN 0-8108-0308-9). Scarecrow Pr., NJ.

Nadel, Norman, et al. Pictorial History of the Theatre Guild. 1969. $10.00 Hdbd. Crown, NY.

O'Connor, William V., ed. History of the Arts in Minnesota. 1958. $3.00 Hdbd. (ISBN 0-8166-0173-9). Univ. of Minn. Pr., MN.

Odell, George C. Annals of the New York Stage, 15 Vols. 1970. (1927) Set—$695.00 Hdbd. (ISBN 0-404-07830-3); $46.50 pa. AMS Pr., NY.

Pence, James H. Magazine & the Drama: An Index. (Drama Ser.). 1970. (1896) $14.50 Hdbd. (ISBN 0-8337-2707-9). Burt Franklin, NY.

Phelps, Henry P. Players of a Century: A Record of the Albany Stage. 1880. $15.75 Hdbd. Benjamin Blom, NY.

Rankin, Hugh F. Theater in Colonial America. 1965. $7.50 Hdbd. (ISBN 0-8078-0950-0). Univ. of N.C. Pr., NC.

Seilhamer, George O. History of the American Theatre, 3 Vols. 1969. (1891) $39.75 Hdbd. (ISBN 0-8371-0653-2). Greenwood Pr., CT.

Seilhamer, George O. History of the American Theatre, 3 Vols. (1968) $37.50 Hdbd. Benjamin Blom, NY.

Seilhamer, George O. History of the American Theatre, 3 Vols. (Studies in Drama Ser., No. 39). 1969. (1891) $39.95 Hdbd. (ISBN 0-8383-0169-X). Haskell House Publ., NY.

Seilhamer, George O. History of the American Theatre 1888-1891, 3 Vols. 1968. $37.50 Hdbd. (ISBN 0-403-00062-9). Scholarly Pr., MI.

Smither, Nelle. History of the English Theatre at New Orleans, 1806-1842. 1967. Repr. $12.50 Hdbd. Benjamin Blom, NY.

Stagg, Jerry. Brothers Shubert. 1969. $1.25 pa. Ballantine Books, NY.

Stagg, Jerry. Brothers Shubert. 1968. $12.50 Hdbd. (ISBN 0-394-41792-5). Random House, NY.

Stone, Henry D. Personal Recollections of the Drama. 1873. $17.50 Hdbd. Benjamin Blom, NY.

Strang, Lewis C. Players & Plays of the Last Quarter Century, 2 Vols. 1903. $10.75 Hdbd. Benjamin Blom, NY.

Taubman, Howard. Making of the American Theatre. rev. ed. 1967. $10.00 Hdbd. Coward-McCann, NY.

Vincent, John H. Chautauqua Movement. facsimile ed. (Select Bibliographies Reprint Ser.). Repr. of 1885 ed. $11.75 Hdbd. (ISBN 0-8369-5664-8). Books for Libraries, NY.

Waldau, Roy S. Vintage Years of the Theatre Guild, 1928-1939. 1971. $12.95 Hdbd. (ISBN 0-8295-0203-3). Pr. of Case Western Reserve, OH.

Watson, Margaret G. Silver Theatre: Nevada. 1964. $9.50 Hdbd. (ISBN 0-87062-064-9). Arthur H. Clark, CA.

Wemyss, Francis C. Wemyss Chro-

nology of the American Stage, from 1752-1852. 1968. $12.50 Hdbd. Benjamin Blom, NY.

Willard, George O. History of the Providence Stage 1762-1891. 1891. $12.50 Hdbd. Benjamin Blom, NY.

Willis, Eola. Charleston Stage in the Eighteenth Century. 1968. $18.50 Hdbd. Benjamin Blom, NY.

Wilson, Arthur H. History of the Philadelphia Theatre, 1835 to 1855. 1968. (1935) $27.25 Hdbd. (ISBN 0-8371-0272-3). Greenwood Pr., CT.

Wood, William B. Personal Recollections of the Stage. 1855. $12.75 Hdbd. Benjamin Blom, NY.

Indigenous

Case, Victoria & Case, Robert O. We Called It Culture: The Story of Chautauqua. (Biography Index Reprint Ser., Vol. 1). 1948. $11.00 Hdbd. (ISBN 0-8369-8051-4). Books for Libraries, NY.

Cheney, Sheldon. Art Theatre: A Discussion of Its Ideals. Its Organization & Its Promise As a Corrective for Present Evils in the Commercial Theatre. 1970. (1917) $12.00 Hdbd. (ISBN 0-403-00550-7). Scholarly Pr., MI.

Gard, Robert. Grassroots Theater: A Search for Regional Arts in America. 1955. $4.00 Hdbd. (ISBN 0-299-01231-X). Univ. of Wis. Pr., WI.

Gould, Joseph E. Chautauqua Movement. (Illus.). 1961. $1.45 pa. (ISBN

0-87395-004-6). State Univ. N.Y. Pr., NY.

Jones, Margo. Theatre in the Round. 1951. $10.00 Hdbd. (ISBN 0-8371-2983-4). Greenwood Pr., CT.

Joseph, Stephen. Theatre in the Round. 1968. $6.50 Hdbd. (ISBN 0-8008-7625-3). Taplinger Publ., NY.

Patten, Marjorie. Arts Workshop of Rural America. 1937. $6.00 Hdbd. (ISBN 0-404-04907-9). AMS Pr., NY.

Vincent, John H. Chautauqua Movement. facsimile ed. (Select Bibliographies Reprint Ser.). Repr. of 1885 ed. $11.75 Hdbd. (ISBN 0-8369-5664-8). Books for Libraries, NY.

Political Aspects

Brustein, Robert. Revolution As Theater: Essays on Radical Style. 1971. $7.95 Hdbd. (ISBN 0-87140-527-X); $1.95 pa. (ISBN 0-87140-045-6). Liveright Publ. Corp., NY.

Himelstein, Morgan Y. Drama Was a Weapon: The Left-Wing Theatre in New York, 1929-1941. 1963. $7.50 Hdbd. (ISBN 0-8135-0420-1). Rutgers Univ. Pr., NJ.

Production and Direction

Alexander, Martha. Behind the Footlights: From Amateur to Repertory. 1955. $3.00 Hdbd. Transatlantic Arts, NY.

Austell, Jan. What's in a Play. (Hi-Sch.). 1968. $3.50 Hdbd. (ISBN 0-15-

295500-3). Harcourt Brace Jovanovich, NY.

Bradbury, Arthur J., et al. Production & Staging of Plays. 1963. $3.50 Hdbd. (ISBN 0-668-01051-7); $0.95 pa. (ISBN 0-668-01052-5). Arc Books, Inc., NY.

Brown, Andrew. Drama. 1962. lib. bdg. $3.50 Hdbd. (ISBN 0-668-00979-9); $0.95 pa. (979) (ISBN 0-668-00984-5). Arc Books, Inc., NY.

Brown, Gilmore & Garwood, Alice. General Principles of Play Direction. 1936. $2.75 Hdbd. Samuel French, NY.

Burian, Jarka. Scenography of Josef Svoboda. 1971. $25.00 Hdbd. Wesleyan Univ. Pr., CT.

Burton, Ernest J. British Theatre: Its Repertory & Practice, 1100-1900 A.D. 1960. $5.00 Hdbd. Dufour Editions, Inc., PA.

Religious Aspects

Baxter, Kay M. Contemporary Theatre & the Christian Faith. 1965. $2.75 Hdbd. (ISBN 0-687-09528-X). Abingdon Pr., TN.

Buch, Arthur T. Bible on Broadway. 1968. $7.50 Hdbd. Shoe String Pr., CT.

Clark, Barrett H. Blush of Shame: A Few Considerations on Verbal Obscenity in the Theatre. 1932. $1.50 pa. Gotham Book Mart, NY.

Collier, Jeremy. Short View of the Immorality, & Profaneness of the English Stage. 1698. $10.00 Hdbd. (ISBN 0-404-01619-7). AMS Pr., NY.

Collier, Jeremy. Short View of the Profaneness & Immorality of the English Stage. 1969. (1730) $20.95 Hdbd. Adler's Foreign Books, NY.

Drake, James. Ancient & Modern Stages Survey'd, or Mr. Collier's View of the Immorality & Profaneness of the English Stage Set in a True Light. 1970. (1699) $12.50 Hdbd. (ISBN 0-404-02176-X). AMS Pr., NY.

Foote, Samuel. Treatise on the Passions, So Far As They Regard the Stage. (1747) $5.00 Hdbd. (ISBN 0-404-02448-3). AMS Pr., NY.

Gosson, Stephen. School of Abuse. Collier, John P., ed. 1841. $4.00 Hdbd. (ISBN 0-404-02886-1). AMS Pr., NY.

Hazlitt, William C., ed. English Drama & Stage Under the Tudor & Stuart Princes—1543–1663. (1869) $35.00 Hdbd. (ISBN 0-8337-1618-2). Burt Franklin, NY.

Krutch, Joseph W. Comedy & Conscience After the Restoration. rev. ed. 1924. $2.75 pa. (ISBN 0-231-08516-8, 16). Columbia Univ. Pr., NY.

Krutch, Joseph W. Comedy & Conscience After the Restoration. (1924, 1949 Repr, 1967). $8.50 Hdbd. Russell & Russell Publ., NY.

Nash, Thomas. Pierce Penilesse, His Supplication to the Divell. 1924. $8.00 Hdbd. (ISBN 0-8371-2919-2). Greenwood, CT.

Northbrooke, John. Treatise Against Dicing, Dancing, Plays & Interludes. 1971. (1843) $7.50 Hdbd. (ISBN 0-404-04793-9). AMS Pr., NY.

Rousseau, Jean-Jacques. Politics & the Arts: Letter to D'Alembert 1960. $4.95 Hdbd. Free Pr., NY

Rousseau, Jean-Jacques. Politics & the Arts: Letter to M. D'Alembert on the Theatre. Bloom, Allan, tr. 1968. 1960. $1.95 pa. (ISBN 0-8014-9071-5). Cornell Univ. Pr., NY.

Thompson, Elbert N. Controversy Between the Puritans & the Stage. 1966. (1903) $9.00 Hdbd. Russell & Russell Publ., NY.

Thompson, Elbert N. Controversy Between the Puritans & the Stage. 1903. $9.00 Hdbd. (ISBN 0-404-06396-9). AMS Pr., NY.

Tunison, R. S. Dramatic Traditions of the Middle Ages. 1907. $16.50 Hdbd. (ISBN 0-8337-3578-0). Burt Franklin, NY.

Reviews

Archer, William. Theatrical World of Eighteen Ninety-Three. 1894. $12.50 Hdbd. Benjamin Blom, NY.

Beerbohm, Max. Around Theatres. Davis, Rupert-Hart, ed. 1969. $6.50 Hdbd. (ISBN 0-8008-0315-9). Taplinger Publ., NY.

Beerbohm, Max. Around Theatres. 1969. $20.75 Hdbd. (ISBN 0-8371-0303-7). Greenwood Pr., CT.

Beerbohm, Max. More Theatres. Hart-Davis, Rupert, ed. 1969. $15.00 Hdbd.

(ISBN 0-8008-5360-1). Taplinger Publ., NY.

Bentley, Eric. What Is Theatre. 1968. $12.50 Hdbd. (ISBN 0-689-10035-3); $4.95 pa. (ISBN 0-689-70012-1, 131). Atheneum Publ., NY.

Cook, Edward D. Nights at the Play. 1883. $12.50 Hdbd. Benjamin Blom, NY.

Gilman, Richard. Common & Uncommon Masks: Writings on Theatre 1960–1970. 1971. $8.95 Hdbd. Random House, NY.

Goldman, William. Season: A Candid Look at Broadway. 1969. $6.95 Hdbd. (ISBN 0-15-179923-7). Harcourt Brace Jovanovich, NY.

Gottfried, Martin. Opening Nights. 1970. $6.95 Hdbd. G. P. Putnam's Sons, NY.

Kerr, Walter. Thirty Plays Hath November. 1969. $6.50 Hdbd. Simon & Schuster, NY.

Phelps, William L. Twentieth Century Theatre. 1968. $6.50 Hdbd. (ISBN 0-8046-0368-5). Kennikat Pr., NY.

Phelps, William L. Twentieth Century Theatre: Observations on the Contemporary English & American Stage. facs. ed. (Essay Index Reprint Ser.). 1918. $7.75 Hdbd. (ISBN 0-8369-0787-6). Books for Libraries, NY.

Stagecraft and Design

Adix, Vern. Theatre Scenecraft. 1957. $7.00 Hdbd. Anchorage Pr., KY.

Albright, Victor E. Shakesperian Stage. 1926. $9.00 Hdbd. (ISBN 0-404-00304-4). AMS Pr., NY.

Aloi, Roberto. Architecture for the Theatre. 1958. $30.00 Hdbd. William S. Heinman, NY.

American Theatre Planning Board, ed. Theatre Check List: A Guide to the Planning & Construction of Proscenium & Open Stage Theatres. 1969. $4.95 pa. (ISBN 0-8195-6005-7). Wesleyan Univ. Pr., NY.

Appia, Adolphe. Music & the Art of the Theatre. Hewitt, Barnard, ed. (Books of the Theatre, No. 3). 1963. $6.50 Hdbd. (ISBN 0-87024-018-8). Univ. of Miami Pr., FL.

Basoli, Antonio. Collezione Di Varie Scene Teatrali. 1968. $18.50 Hdbd. Benjamin Blom, NY.

Bax, Peter. Stage Management. $10.75 Hdbd. Benjamin Blom, NY.

Bibiena, Giuseppe. Architectural & Perspective Designs. 1740. $2.50 pa. (ISBN 0-486-21263-7). Dover Pubns., NY.

Bruder, Karl. Properties & Dressing the Stage. Kozelka, Paul, ed. (Theatre Student Ser.). 1969. $6.96 Hdbd. (ISBN 0-8239-0150-5). Rosen Richards Pr., NY.

Buerki, Frederick A. Stagecraft for Nonprofessionals. 2nd ed. 1955. $2.50 pa. (ISBN 0-299-01294-8). Univ. of Wisc. Pr., WI.

Burian, Jarka. Scenography of Josef

Svoboda. 1971. $25.00 Hdbd. Wesleyan Univ. Pr., CT.

Burris-Meyer, Harold & Cole, Edward C. Scenery for the Theatre. 1971. $32.50 Hdbd. (ISBN 0-316-11754-4). Little, Brown, MA.

Burris-Meyer, Harold & Mallory, Vincent. Sound in the Theatre. 1959. $6.95 Hdbd. Theatre Arts, NY.

Campbell, Lily B. Scenes & Machines on the English Stage During the Renaissance: A Classical Revival. 1970. (1923) $10.00 Hdbd. (ISBN 0-389-01756-6). Barnes & Noble, NY.

Cheney, Sheldon. Stage Decoration. 1967. $12.50 Hdbd. Benjamin Blom, NY.

Chilver, Peter & Jones, Eric. Designing a School Play. 1970. $6.95 Hdbd. (ISBN 0-8008-2171-8). Taplinger Publ., NY.

Contant, Clement & De Fillippi, Joseph. Parallele Des Principaux Theatres Modernes De L'Europe, 2 Vols in One. 1968. Repr. $75.00 Hdbd. Benjamin Blom, NY.

Cooper, Douglas. Picasso: Theatre. 1968. $25.00 Hdbd. (ISBN 0-8109-0396-2). Harry N. Abrams, NY.

Corey, Irene. Mask of Reality: An Approach to Design for Theatre. 1968. $20.00 Hdbd. Anchorage Pr., KY.

Cornberg, Sol & Gebauer, Emanuel L. Stage Crew Handbook. rev. ed. 1957. $5.95 Hdbd. (ISBN 0-06-031560-1). Harper & Row, NY.

Craig, Edward G. Scene. 1968. $12.50 Hdbd. Benjamin Blom, NY.

Craig, Edward G. Toward a New Theatre, Forty Designs for Stage Scenes. 1913. $27.50 Hdbd. Benjamin Blom, NY.

Crowley, Alice L. Neighborhood Playhouse. 1959. $5.00 Hdbd. Theatre Arts, NY.

Dolman, John, Jr. Art of Play Production. rev. ed. 1946. $9.50 text ed. (ISBN 0-06-041680-7). Harper & Row, NY.

Fuerst, Rene & Hume, Samuel J. Twentieth Century Stage Decoration, 2 Vols. 1968. $18.50 Hdbd. Benjamin Blom, NY.

Fuerst, Walter R. & Hume, S. J. Twentieth Century Stage Decoration, 2 Vols. 1967. $3.00 pa. (ISBN 0-486-21863-5) (ISBN 0-486-21864-3) (ISBN 0-486-21863-5) (ISBN 0-486-21864-3). Dover Pubns, NY.

Galliari, Gaspare. Numero Vente Quatro Invenzioni Teatrali. 1969. $18.50 Hdbd. Benjamin Blom, NY.

Gassner, John & Barber, P. Producing the Play. rev. ed. Incl. New Scene Technician's Handbook. 1953. $11.50 text ed. (ISBN 0-03-005565-2). Holt, Rinehart & Winston, NY.

Gillette, Arnold S. Introduction to Scenic Design. 1967. $11.50 text ed. (ISBN 0-06-042324-2). Harper & Row, NY.

Gillett, Arnold S. Stage Scenery. (Hi-Sch.). 1960. (ISBN 0-06-042330-7, Harp C). $11.50 text ed. (ISBN 0-06-042330-7). Harper & Row, NY.

Gorelik, Mordecai. New Theatres for Old. $2.45 pa. (ISBN 0-525-47102-2, E. P. Dutton, NY.

Granville-Barker, Harley. Exemplary Theatre. (Select Bibliographies Reprint Ser.). 1922. $9.50 Hdbd. (ISBN 0-8369-5282-0). Books for Libraries, NY.

Granville-Barker, Harley. On Dramatic Method. 1960. $3.75 Hdbd. Peter Smith, MA.

Langley, Stephen. Theatre Management. price "n.g." Hdbd. (ISBN 0-910482-32-2). DBS Pubns., NY.

Lytton's Theatre Seating Plans: London, England. 1967. $2.00 Hdbd. Stubs Publns., NY.

MacGowan, Kenneth & Jones, Robert E. Continental Stagecraft. 1922. $12.50 Hdbd. Benjamin Blom, NY.

Melling, John K. Lost Theatres. (Discovering Pocket Book Ser.). 1969. $1.00 pa. Intl. Pubns Serv., NY.

Paget, A. H. Elizabethan Play-Houses. 1891. $3.50 Hdbd. Folcroft, PA.

Pride, Leo B., ed. International Theatre Directory. 1971. $35.00 Hdbd. World Trade Academy Pr., NY.

Saunders, George. Treatise on the Theatres. 1968. $25.00 Hdbd. Benjamin Blom, NY.

Simon, Bernard, ed. Simon's Directory of Theatrical Materials, Services & Information. 4th ed. 1970. $5.00 Hdbd. (ISBN 0-911100-01-6). Package Publ., NY.

TRAGEDY

Adamczewski, Zygmunt. Tragic Protest. 1963. $10.00 Hdbd. William S. Heinman, NY.

Aylen, Leo. Greek Tragedy & the Modern World. 1964. $7.25 Hdbd. Methuen Barnes & Noble, NY.

Barnet, Sylvan, et al. eds. Eight Great Tragedies: Prometheus Bound, Oedipus the King, Hippolytus, King Lear, Ghosts, Miss Julie, On Bailles Strand, Desire Under the Elms. $1.25 pa. New American Library, NY.

Bowers, Fredson. Elizabethan Revenge Tragedy. 1958. $4.75 Hdbd. Peter Smith Publ., MA.

Bowers, Fredson. Elizabethan Revenge Tragedy, Fifteen Eighty-Seven–Sixteen Forty-Two. 1940. $2.95 pa. (ISBN 0-691-01259-8, 30). Princeton Univ. Pr., NJ.

Bradbrook, Muriel C. Themes & Conventions of Elizabethan Tragedy. 1952–1960. $7.00 Hdbd. $1.95 pa. (ISBN 0-521-09108-X, 108). Cambridge Univ. Pr., MA.

Brereton, Geoffrey. Principles of Tragedy: A Rational Examination of the Tragic Concept in Life & Literature.

1969. $7.95 Hdbd. (ISBN 0-87024-104-4). Univ. of Miami Pr., FL.

Calarco, N. Joseph. Tragic Being: Apollo & Dionysus in Western Drama. 1969. $6.00 Hdbd. (ISBN 0-8166-0503-3). Univ. of Minn. Pr., MN.

Campbell, Lewis. Tragic Drama in Aeschylus, Sophocles & Shakespeare. 1965. (1904) $8.50 Hdbd. Russell & Russell Publ., NY.

Campbell, Lily B. Shakespeare's Tragic Heroes. 1960. $4.00 Hdbd. $1.95 pa. (ISBN 0-389-01758-2, 433). Barnes & Noble, NY.

Charlton, Henry B. Senecan Tradition in Renaissance Tragedy. 1946. $15.00 Hdbd. Folcroft Pr. Inc., PA.

Corrigan, Robert W., ed. Tragedy: A Critical Anthology. 1971. price "n.g." Hdbd. Houghton Mifflin Co., MA.

Corrigan, Robert W., ed. Tragedy: Vision & Form. 1965. $6.75 Hdbd. (ISBN 0-8102-0072-4). Chandler Publ. Co., CA.

Corrigan, Robert W. & Loney, Glenn M., eds. Tragedy: A Critical Anthology. 1971. price "n.g." Hdbd. Houghton Mifflin Co., MA.

Courtney, William L. Idea of Tragedy in Ancient & Modern Drama. 1967. (1900) $6.00 Hdbd. Russell & Russell Publ., NY.

Demetracopoulos, Elias. Greek Tragedy. 1971. $5.95 Hdbd. Alfred A. Knopf., NY.

Dixon, W. Macneile. Tragedy. 1924. $12.50 Hdbd. Folcroft Pr. Inc., PA.

Falk, Eugene H. Renunciation As A Tragic Focus: A Study of Five Plays. 1967. $3.75 Hdbd. (ISBN 0-512-00174-X). Garrett Pr. Inc., NY.

Farnham, Willard. Medieval Heritage of Elizabethan Tragedy. 1936. $9.50 Hdbd. Barnes & Noble, NY.

Hathorn, Richmond, Y. Tragedy, Myth & Mystery. 1962. $2.65 pa. (ISBN 0-253-20092-X). Ind. Univ. Pr., IN.

Hathorn, Richmond, Y. Tragedy, Myth & Mystery. $4.75 Hdbd. Peter Smith Publ. Inc., MA.

Heilman, Robert B. Tragedy & Melodrama: Versions of Experience. 1968. $8.95 Hdbd. Univ. of Wash. Pr., WA.

Henn, Thomas R. Harvest of Tragedy. 2nd ed. 1966. $2.50 pa. Methuen (ISBN 0-416-69470-5, 70). Barnes & Noble, NY.

Henn, Thomas, R. Harvest of Tragedy. 2nd ed. 1966. $5.75 Hdbd. Methuen. Barnes & Noble, NY.

Hogan, Robert & Molin, Sven E. Drama: The Major Genres, an Introductory Critical Anthology. 1962. $5.95 Hdbd. (ISBN 0-396-06108-7). Dodd, Mead & Co., NY.

Hoy, Cyrus H. Hyacinth Room: An Investigation into the Nature of Comedy, Tragedy, & Tragicomedy. 1964. $6.95 Hdbd. Alfred A. Knopf, NY.

Jepsen, Laura. Ethical Aspects of Tragedy: A Comparison of Certain Tragedies by Aeschylus, Sophocles, Euripides, Seneca & Shakespeare. 1953. $7.50 Hdbd. (ISBN 0-404-03566-3). AMS Pr. Inc., NY.

Kaufmann, Walter. Tragedy & Philosophy. 1969. $1.95 pa. Doubleday & Co., NY.

Krieger, Murray. Tragic Vision. 1966. $1.95 pa. (ISBN 0-226-45298-0). Univ. of Chicago Pr., IL.

Krook, Dorothea. Elements of Tragedy. 1969. $7.50 Hdbd. (ISBN 0-300-01162-8); $2.95 pa. (ISBN 0-300-01513-5). Yale Univ. Pr., CT.

Leaska, Mitchell A. Voice of Tragedy. 1964. $6.00 Hdbd. (ISBN 0-8315-0022-0). Robert Speller & Sons, Publ., NY.

Leech, Clifford. Shakespeare's Tragedies & Other Studies in Seventeenth Century Drama. 1950. $4.25 Hdbd. Oxford Univ. Pr., NY.

Leech, Clifford. Tragedy. (Critical Idiom Ser., Vol. 1). 1969. $2.50 text ed. Methuen; $1.25 pa. Barnes & Noble, NY.

Lucas, Frank L. Tragedy: Serious Drama in Relation to Aristotle's Poetics. 1966. $1.25 pa. Macmillan Co., NY.

Mandel, Oscar. Definition of Tragedy. 1961. $6.95 Hdbd. (ISBN 0-8147-0288-0). $1.95 pa. (ISBN 0-8147-0289-9). New York Univ. Pr., NY.

Miller, Herbert J. Spirit of Tragedy. $0.75 pa. Wash. Square Pr., NY.

Muller, Herbert J. Spirit of Tragedy. 1956. $5.95 pa. Alfred A. Knopf, NY.

Myers, Henry A. Tragedy: A View of Life. 1956. $1.95 pa. (ISBN 0-8014-9007-3). Cornell Univ. Pr., NY.

Nathan, Leonard E. Tragic Drama of William Butler Yeats: Figures in a Dance. 1965. $9.00 Hdbd. (ISBN 0-231-02765-6). Columbia Univ. Pr., NY.

Nicoll, Allardyce. Theory of Drama. 1967. $10.75 Hdbd. Benjamin Blom, NY.

Nietzsche, Friedrich. The Birth of Tragedy. Golffing, Francis, tr. Incl. The Genealogy of Morals. 1956. $1.45 pa. Doubleday & Co., NY.

Nietzsche, Friedrich. The Birth of Tragedy. Kaufman, Walter, tr. Incl. The Case of Wagner. $1.65 pa. Random House, NY.

O'Connor, William V. & O'Connor, Mary A. Climates of Tragedy. 1965. (1943) $7.50 Hdbd. Russell & Russell Publ., NY.

Olson, Elder. Tragedy & the Theory of Drama. 1961. $2.95 pa. (ISBN 0-8143-1149-0). Wayne St. Univ. Pr., MI.

Raphael, D. D. Paradox of Tragedy. $3.50 Hdbd. Peter Smith Publ., MA.

Raphael, D. D. Paradox of Tragedy. 1960. $1.45 pa. (ISBN 0-253-20041-5, MB). Ind. Univ. Pr., IN.

Raphael, David D. Paradox of Tragedy. facs. ed. (Essay Index Reprint Ser). 1960. $6.75 Hdbd. (ISBN 0-8369-2021-X). Books for Libraries, NY.

Russell, Trusten W. Voltaire, Dryden &

Heroic Tragedy. 1946. $9.50 Hdbd. (ISBN 0-404-05467-6). AMS Pr., NY.

Rymer, Thomas. Short View of Tragedy. $13.50 Hdbd. Augustus M. Kelley Publ., NY.

Rymer, Thomas. Short View of Tragedy. 1968. (1693) $10.00 Hdbd. (ISBN 0-404-05478-1). AMS Pr., NY.

Schlesinger, Alfred C. Boundaries of Dionysus: Athenian Foundations for the Theory of Tragedy. (Martin Classical Lecture Ser. No. 17). 1963. $4.50 Hdbd. (ISBN 0-674-08000-9). Harvard Univ. Pr., MA.

Schrade, Leo F. Tragedy in the Art of Music. (Charles Eliot Norton Lecture Ser., 1962–1963). 1964. $3.75 Hdbd. (ISBN 0-674-90195-9). Harvard Univ. Pr., MA.

Sewall, Richard B. Vision of Tragedy. 1959. $5.75 Hdbd. (ISBN 0-300-00895-3); $1.95 pa. (ISBN 0-300-00202-5, Y56). Yale Univ. Pr., CT.

Shearman, Hugh. Purpose of Tragedy. 1954. $1.00 pa. (ISBN 0-8356-7175-5). Theosophical Publ. House, IL.

Simpson, Percy. Theme of Revenge in Elizabethan Tragedy. 1935. $3.50 Hdbd. Folcroft Pr. Inc., PA.

Steiner, George. Death of Tragedy. 1963. $1.95 pa. (ISBN 0-8090-0535-2, Drama). Hill & Wang, N.Y. 1961. $5.95 Hdbd. Alfred A. Knopf, NY.

Swander, Homer D., ed. Man & the Gods: Three Tragedies. Incl. Agamemnon. Aeschylus; The Tragical History of Doctor Faustus. Marlowe, Christopher; Saint Joan. Shaw, George B. $2.75 pa. (ISBN 0-15-554730-5). Harcourt Brace Jovanovich, NY.

Von Fritz, Kurt. Antike und Moderne Tragoedie: Neun Abhandlungen. 1962. $9.58 Hdbd. (ISBN 3-11-005039-0). De Gruyter, Holland.

Williams, Raymond. Modern Tragedy. 1967. $5.50 Hdbd. (ISBN 0-8047-0312-4); $2.25 pa. (ISBN 0-8047-0313-2). Stanford Univ. Pr., CA.

Zebouni, Selma A. Dryden: A Study in Heroic Characterization. 1965. $3.00 Hdbd. (ISBN 0-8071-0843-X). La. State Pr., LA.

Publishers Addresses
in Bibliography

Abelard-Schuman, Ltd.
  257 Park Ave., S., New York, NY 10010
Abingdon Press
  Nashville, TN 37202; New York, NY
  10022
Abrams, Harry N., Inc.
  110 E. 59th St., New York, NY 10022
Adler's Foreign Books, Inc.
  162 Fifth Ave., New York, NY 10010
Airmont Publishing Company, Inc.
  Orders to Associated Booksellers,
  147 McKinley Ave., Bridgeport, CT
  06606
Allyn & Bacon, Inc.
  Rockleigh, NJ 07647
American Elsevier Publishing Company,
  Inc.
  52 Vanderbilt Ave., New York, NY
  10017
AMS Press, Inc.
  56 E. 13th St., New York, NY 10003
Anchorage Press
  Cloverlot, Anchorage, KY 40223
Apollo Editions
  201 Park Ave., S., New York, NY 10003
Appleton-Century-Crofts, Inc.
  440 Park Ave., S., New York, NY 10016
Arc Books
  Orders to Arco Publishing Co., Inc.,
  219 Park Ave., S., New York, NY 10003
Arco Publishing Company, Inc.
  219 Park Ave., S., New York, NY 10003
Argo Book, Inc.
  Rt. 5, Norwich, VT 05055
Arno Press
  330 Madison Ave., New York, NY
  10017
Asia Publishing House
  118 E. 59th St., New York, NY 10022
Astor-Honor, Inc.
  205 E. 42nd St., New York, NY 10017
Atheneum Publishers
  122 E. 42nd St., New York, NY 10017
Aurora Publishers, Inc.
  170 4th Ave., N., Rm. 619, Nashville,
  TN 37219

Avon Books
  959 Eighth Ave., New York, NY 10019

Ballantine Books, Inc.
  101 Fifth Ave., New York, NY 10003
Bantam Books, Inc.
  666 Fifth Ave., New York, NY 10019
Barnes, A. S., & Company, Inc.
  Cranbury, NJ 08512
Barnes & Noble, Inc.
  105 Fifth Ave., New York, NY 10003
Barron's Educational Series, Inc.
  113 Crossways Pk. Dr., Woodbury, NY
  11797
Basic Books, Inc.
  404 Park Ave., S., New York, NY
  10016
Beacon House, Inc.
  Box 311, Beacon, NY 12508
Beacon Press, Inc.
  25 Beacon St., Boston, MA 02108
Bennett, Charles A., Company, Inc.
  809 W. Detweiller Dr., Peoria, IL 61614
Best Books, Inc.
  343 So. Dearborn, Chicago, IL 60605
Bethany Press
  Box 179, St. Louis, MO 63166
Biblo & Tannen Booksellers & Publishers,
  Inc.
  63 4th Ave., New York, NY 10003
Blom, Benjamin, Inc.
  4 W. Mt. Eden Ave., Bronx, NY 10452
Bobbs-Merrill Company, Inc.
  3 W. 57th St., New York, NY 10019
Books for Libraries, Inc.
  50 Liberty Ave., Freeport, NY 11520
Boston Book & Art Shop, Inc.
  655 Boylston St., Boston, MA 02116
Braziller, George, Inc.
  1 Park Ave., New York, NY 10016
Brigham Young University Press
  132 HRCB, Provo, UT 84601
British Book Center
  Maxwell House, Fairview Park,
  Elmsford, NY 10523

Brown University Press
    71 George St., Box 1881, Providence,
    RI 02912
Brown, William C., Co., Publishers
    135 S. Locust St., Dubuque, IA 52001
Bucknell University Press
    c/o Barnes, A. S. & Co., Box 421,
    Cranbury, NJ 08512
Burgess Publishing Company
    426 S. Sixth St., Minneapolis, MN
    55415

Cambridge University Press
    32 E. 57th St., New York, NY 10022
Press of Case Western Reserve University
    Frank Adgate Quail Bldg., Cleveland,
    OH 44106
Chandler Publishing Co.
    Oak St. & Pawnee Ave., Scranton, PA
    18515
Chatham Press Inc.
    15 Wilmont Lane, Riverside, CT 06878
Chicorel Library Publishing Co.
    330 West 58th St., New York, NY 10019
Christopher Publishing House (Mass)
    53 Billings Road, North Quincy, MA
    02171
Citadel Press (NYC)
    222 Park Ave. S., New York, NY 10003
Books published by Cleveland Museum of
    Art. Dist. by Press of Case Western
    Reserve University.
Cliff's Notes, Inc.
    Box 80728, Lincoln, NB 68501
College and University Press
    263 Chapel St., New Haven, CT 06513
Columbia University Press
    440 W. 110th St., New York, NY 10025
Concordia Publishing House
    3558 S. Jefferson Ave., St. Louis, MO
    63118
Cooper Square Publishers Inc.
    59 Fourth Ave., New York, NY 10003
Cornell University Press
    124 Roberts Pl., Ithaca, NY 14850

Corner Book Shop
    102 Fourth Ave., New York, NY 10003
Coshad Inc. (Apollo Bks)
    30 Hazel Terrace, Woodbridge, CT
    06525
Coward-McCann & Geoghegan, Inc.
    200 Madison Ave., New York, NY
    10016
Cowles Book Corporation, Inc.
    Subs. of Henry Regnery Co., 114 W.
    Illinois St., Chicago, IL 60610
Crescendo Publishers
    48-50 Melrose St., Boston, MA 02116
Croner Publications
    211-03 Jamaica Ave., Queens Village,
    NJ
Crowell Thomas Y., Company
    201 Park Ave., S., New York, NY 10003
Crown Publishers, Inc.
    419 Park Ave., S., New York, NY 10016
Croydon House
    1175 N.E. 125th St., Miami, FL 33161

Darby Books
    Darby, PA 19023
Davey, Daniel, & Company, Inc. Pub.
    410 Asylum St., Hartford, CT 06103
Davies, Nina S.
    628 St. Peters St., New Orleans, LA
    70116
Day, oh , Company, Inc.
    Div. of Intext Educational Pubs.,
    275 Park Ave., S., New York, NY 10010
DBS Publications, Inc.
    150 West 52nd St., New York, NY
    10019
De Gruyter, Walter, Inc.
    162 Fifth Ave., New York, NY 10010
Delacorte Press
    Dist. by Dial Press, Inc., 750 Third
    Ave., New York, NY 10017
Dell Publishing Co. Inc.
    750 Third Ave., New York, NY
    10017
Devin-Adair Co., Inc.
    1 Park Ave., Old Greenwich, CT 06870

Dial Press, Inc.
750 Third Ave., New York, N.Y. 10017
Dillon Press, Inc.
106 Washington Ave., N. Minneapolis,
MN 55401
Dodd, Mead & Co.
79 Madison Ave., New York, NY 10016
Dorrance & Co., Inc.
1809 Callowhill St., Philadelphia, PA
19130
Doubleday & Company, Inc.
501 Franklin Ave., Garden City, NY
11530
Dover Publications, Inc.
180 Varick St., New York, NY 10014
Dufour Editions, Inc.
Chester Springs, PA 19425
Duke University Press
6697 College Sta., Durham, NC 27708
Duquesne University Press
600 Forbes Ave., Pittsburgh, PA 15219
Dutton, E.P., & Co., Inc.
201 Park Ave., S., New York, NY 10003

Exposition Press Inc.
50 Jericho Turnpike, Jericho, NY 11753

Fairleigh Dickinson University Press
Box 421, Cranbury, NJ 08512
Farrar, Straus & Giroux, Inc.
19 Union Sq., W., New York, NY 10003
Fawcett World Library
67 W. 44th St., New York, NY 10036
Faxon, F. W. Company, Co. Inc.
15 Southwest Park, Westwood, MA
02090
Fernhill House Ltd.
303 Park Ave., S., New York, NY 10010
Fertig, Howard, Inc.
80 East 11th St., New York, NY 10003
Fides Publishers, Inc.
Box F, Notre Dame, IN 46556
Florida State University Press
Orders to Univ. of Florida Press,
15 N.W. 15th St., Gainesville, FL 32601

Folcroft Press, Inc.
Box 182, Folcroft, PA 19032
Follett Publishing Company
1010 W. Washington Blvd., Chicago, IL
60607
Fortress Press
2900 Queen Lane, Philadelphia, PA
19129
Franklin, Burt, Pub.
Orders to Lenox Hill Publishing &
Distributing Corp.
235 E. 44th St., New York, NY 10017
Free Press
Orders to Macmillan Co., 866 Third
Ave., New York, NY 10022
French, Samuel, Inc.
25 West 45th St., New York, NY 10036
French & European Publications, Inc.
Rockefeller Center, 636 Eleventh Ave.,
New York, NY 10036
Friendship Press
475 Riverside Dr., New York, NY
10027
Funk & Wagnalls Company
Dist. by Thomas Y. Crowell Co.,
201 Park Ave., S., New York, NY 10003

Gale Research Company
Book Tower, Detroit, MI 48226
Garrett Press, Inc.
250 W. 54th St., New York, NY 10019
Gembooks
Box 808, Mentone, CA 92359
Giligia Press
Box 167, Hanover, NH 03755
Gordian Press, Inc.
85 Tompkins St., Staten Island, NY
10304
Gordon Publishers
Box 459, Bowling Green Sta.,
New York, NY 10004
Gotham Book Mart
41 W. 47th St., New York, NY 10036
Greenwood Press, Inc.
51 Riverside Ave., Westport, CT 06880

Gregg Press, Inc.
121 Pleasant Ave., Upper Saddle River, NJ 07458
Grosset & Dunlap, Inc.
51 Madison Ave., New York, NY 10010
Grove Press, Inc.
53 E. 11th St., New York, NY 10003

Hafner Publishing Company, Inc.
866 Third Ave., New York, NY 10022
Orders to Collier-Macmillan Distribution Center, Riverside, NJ 08075
Hall, G. K., & Company
70 Lincoln St., Boston, MA 02111
Harcourt Brace Jovanovich, Inc.
757 Third Ave., New York, NY 10017
Harper & Row Publishers, Inc.
49 E. 33rd St., New York, NY 10016.
Orders to Harper & Row, Scranton, PA 18512
Hart Publishing Company
719 Broadway, New York, NY 10003
Hart's Publishing
Box 42-271, Miami, FL 33142
Harvard University Press
Kittridge Hall, 79 Garden St., Cambridge, MA 02138
Haskell House Publishers, Inc.
280 Lafayette St., New York, NY 10012
Hastings House Publishers, Inc.
10 E. 40th St., New York, NY 10016
Heath, D. C. & Company
2700 North Richardt Ave., Indianapolis, IN 46219
Heineman, James H., Pub.
19 Union Square West, New York, NY 10003
Herald Books
Box 63T, Bronxville, NY 10708
Herder & Herder
232 Madison Ave., New York, NY 10016
Hill & Wang, Inc.
72 Fifth Ave., New York, NY 10011

Hillary House Publishers, Ltd.
Orders to Humanities Press, Inc.
303 Park Ave. S., New York, NY 10010
Hispanic Society of America
Broadway Between 155th & 156th Sts., New York, NY 10032
Holt, Rinehart & Winston, Inc.
383 Madison Ave., New York, NY 10017
Horizon Press, Publishers
156 Fifth Ave., New York, NY 10010
Houghton Mifflin Co.
Educational Div., 110 Tremont St., Boston, MA 02107
Humanities Press, Inc.
303 Park Ave. S., New York, NY 10010
Humphries, Bruce, Inc.
68 Beacon St., Somerville, MA 02143
Huntington, Henry E.
Library & Art Gallery, San Marino, CA 91108
Hutchinson University Library
Orders to Humanities Press, Inc., 303 Park Ave., S., New York, NY 10010

Indiana University Press
Tenth & Morton Sts., Bloomington, IN 47401
International Publications Service
114 E. 32nd St., New York, NY 10016
International Publishers Company, Inc.
381 Park Ave., S., New York, NY 10016
International Scholarly Book Service, Inc., Box 4347, Portland, OR 97208
International Universities Press, Inc.
239 Park Ave., S., New York, NY 10003
Iowa State University Press
Press Bldg., Ames, IA 50010
Irish University Press, Inc.
2 Holland Ave., White Plains, NY 10603

Johns Hopkins Press
Baltimore, MD 21218
Johnson Reprint Corporation, Subs. of Academic Press
111 Fifth Ave., New York, NY 10003

Kelley, Augustus M., Publisher
305 Allwood Rd., Clifton, NJ
Kennikat Press, Inc.
Subs. of Taylor Pub. Co., Dallas,
Port Washington, NY 11050
Kent State University Press
Kent, OH 44240
Knopf, Alfred A., Inc.
Subs. of Random House, Inc., 201 E.
50th St., New York, NY 10022
John Knox Press
801 E. Main St., Box 1176, Richmond,
VA 23209
Kraus Reprint Corporation, A U.S. Div.
of Kraus-Thompson Organization, Ltd.
16 E. 46th St., New York, NY 10017
Ktav Publishing House, Inc.
120 E. Broadway, New York, NY 10002

Lansdowne Press
Box 6471, Philadelphia, PA 19145
Lewis, David, Inc.
216 W. 89th St., New York, NY 10024
Library Press
50 Liberty Ave., Freeport, NY 11520
Lippincott, J. B., Company
E. Washington Sq., Philadelphia, PA
19105
Little, Brown & Company
34 Beacon St., Boston, MA 02106
Littlefield, Adams & Co.
81 Adams Dr., Totowa, NJ 07512
Louisiana State University Press
Baton Rouge, LA 70803

M & S Press
Box 311, Weston, MA 02193
Macfadden Bartell Corporation
205 E. 42nd St., New York, NY 10017
Macmillan Company
Subs. of Crowell Collier & Macmillan,
Inc., 866 Third Ave., New York, NY
10022
McGrath Publishing Company
5932 Westchester Park Dr., College
Park, MD 20740

McGraw-Hill Book Company
330 W. 42 St., New York, NY 10036
McKay, David, Company, Inc.
750 Third Ave., New York, NY 10017
Memphis State University Press
Memphis State University, Memphis,
TN 38111
Messner, Julian, Inc.
Orders to Simon & Schuster, Inc.
1 W. 39th St., New York, NY 10018
Michigan State University Press
Box 550, East Lansing, MI 48823
M.I.T. Press
28 Carleton St., Cambridge, MA 02142
Monarch Press
Orders to Simon & Schuster, Inc.
1 W. 39th St., New York, NY 10018
Morgan & Morgan, Inc.
400 Warburton Ave., Hastings-on-
Hudson, NY 10706

Negro Universities Press
51 Riverside Ave., Westport, CT 06880
New American Library
1301 Ave. of the Americas, New York,
NY 10019
New Directions Publishing Corp.
333 Ave. of the Americas, New York,
NY 10014
New York Graphic Society, Ltd.
140 Greenwich Ave., Greenwich, CT
06830
New York University Press
Washington Sq., New York, NY 10003
Northern Illinois University Press
DeKalb, IL 60115
Northwestern University Press
1735 Benson Ave., Evanston, IL 60201
Norton, W. W. & Company, Inc.
55 Fifth Ave., New York, NY 10003

Octagon Books
19 Union Sq. West, New York, NY
10003

Odyssey Press
    4300 W. 62nd St., Indianapolis, IN
    46268
Ohio State University Press
    2070 Neil Avenue, Columbus, OH
    43210
Oregon State University Press
    Box 689, Corvallis, OR 97330
Organ Literature Foundation
    Braintree, MA 02184
Orientalia Inc.
    61 Fourth Ave., New York, NY 10003
Oxford University Press, Inc.
    16-00 Pollitt Drive, Fair Lawn, NJ
    07410

Pacifica House, Inc., Publishers
    Box 2131, Toluca Lake, North
    Hollywood, CA 91602
Pan American Union
    Publication Div., 19th & Constitution
    Ave., Washington, DC 20006
Pantheon Books
    201 E. 50th St., New York, NY 10022
Paragon Book Reprint Corp.
    14 E. 38th St., New York, NY 10016
Parker Publishing Co.
    Subs. of Prentice-Hall, West Nyack,
    NY 10994
Parnassus Press
    2721 Parker St., Berkeley, CA 94705
Pegasus
    Div. of Western Pub. Co., Inc.,
    850 Third Ave., New York, NY 10022
    Orders to the Book Warehouse,
    Vreeland Ave., Totowa, NJ 07512
Penguin Books, Inc.
    7110 Ambassador Rd., Baltimore, MD
    21207
Pennsylvania State University Press
    215 Wagner Bldg., University Park,
    PA 15801
Pergamon Press, Inc.
    Maxwell House, Fairview Park,
    Elmsford, NY 10523

Peter Smith
    6 Lexington Ave., Gloucester, MA
    01930
Phaeton Press, Inc.
    85 Tompkins St., Staten Island, NY
    10304
Philosophical Library, Inc.
    15 E. 40 St., New York, NY 10016
Philosophical Research Society Inc.
    3910 Los Feliz Blvd., Los Angeles,
    CA 90027
Pinnacle Books
    116 E. 27th St., New York, NY 10016
Playboy Press
    Division of Playboy Enterprises, Inc.,
    919 North Michigan Ave., Chicago,
    IL 60611
Plays, Inc.
    8 Arlington St., Boston, MA 02116
Plenum Publishing Corp.
    114 Fifth Ave., New York, NY 10011,
    Orders to 227 W. 17th St., New York,
    NY 10011
Pocket Books Inc.
    Orders to Simon & Schuster, Inc.,
    1 West 39th St., New York, NY 10018
Porter, Bern
    106 High St., Belfast, ME 04915
Praeger Publishers
    111 Fourth Ave., New York, NY
    10003
Prentice-Hall, Inc.
    Englewood Cliffs, NJ 07632
Princeton University Library
    Princeton, NJ 08540
Princeton University Press
    Princeton, NJ 08540
Purdue University Studies
    South Campus Courts-D, Lafayette,
    IN 47907
G. P. Putnam's Sons
    200 Madison Ave., New York, NY
    10016

Quadrangle Books, Inc.
    Orders to World Publishing Co.,

2231 W. 110th St., Cleveland, OH
44102

Random House, Inc.
Order Dept., Westminster, MD 21157
Random House/Singer School Division
201 E. 50th St., New York, NY 10022
Regent House
108 N. Roselake Ave., Los Angeles,
CA 90026
Regents Publishing Co.
Orders to Simon & Schuster, Inc.,
1 West 39th St., New York, NY 10018
Regnery, Henry, Company
114 West Illinois St., Chicago, IL
60610
Ridgeway Books
Box 6431, Philadelphia, Pa. 19145
Rogers Book Service
Box V, 217 W. 18 St., New York, NY
10011
Roseman, Herbert C.
85 Livingstone St., Brooklyn Heights,
NY 11201
Rosen, Richards, Press, Inc.
29 E. 21 St., New York, NY 10010
Rowman and Littlefield, Inc.
Div. of Littlefield, Adams, & Co.,
87 Adams Dr., Totown, NJ 07512
Roy Publishers, Inc.
30 E. 74th St., New York, NY 10021
Russell & Russell
122 E. 42nd St., New York, NY 10017
Rutgers University Press
30 College Ave., New Brunswick, NJ
08903

S-H Service Agency, Inc.
Div. of the Hafner Publishing Co.,
Collier-Macmillan Distribution Ctr.,
Riverside, NJ 08075
Saifer, Albert, Publisher
Box 56, Town Center, West Orange,
NJ 07052

Sams, Howard W., & Company, Inc
Subs. of ITT, 4300 W. 62nd St.,
Box 558, Indianapolis, IN 46268
San Fernando Valley State College
Northridge, CA 91324
Saunders, W. B., Company
Subs. of Columbia Broadcasting
System, 218 W. Washington Sq.,
Philadelphia, PA 19105
Scarecrow Press, Inc.
Div. of Grolier Educational Corp.,
52 Liberty St., Box 656, Metuchen, NJ
08840
Schocken Books, Inc.
67 Park Ave., New York, NY 10016
Scholarly Press
22929 Industrial Drive, E., St. Clair
Shores, MI 48080
Scholar's Facsmilies & Reprints
1605 N.W. 14th Ave., Gainesville, FL
32601
Scholastic Book Services
Div. of Scholastic Magazines, 50 West
44th St., New York, NY 10036
Science House
59 4th Ave., New York, NY 10003
Science Research Associates
Sub. of IBM, 259 E. Erie St.,
Chicago, IL 60611
Charles Scribner's Sons
597 Fifth Ave., New York, NY 10017
Seabury Press, Inc.
Orders to Feffer & Simon, Inc.,
1 Union Sq., New York, NY 10003
Serina Press
70 Kennedy St., Alexandria, VA 22305
Sheed & Ward, Inc.
64 University Place, New York, NY
10003
Sheridan House, Inc.
Box 254, South Sta., Yonkers, NY
10705
Shoe String Press, Inc.
995 Sherman Ave., Hamden, CT 06514
Simon & Schuster, Inc.
630 Fifth Ave., New York, NY 10021

Soccer Associates
  Box 634, New Rochelle, NY 10802
Southern Illinois University Press
  Carbondale, IL 62901
Spartan Books, Inc.
  432 Park Ave. S., New York, NY
  10016
Speller, Robert, & Sons
  Orders to Box 461, Times Square
  Station, New York, NY 10036
St. Martin's Press, Inc.
  175 Fifth Ave., New York, NY 10010
Stanford University Press
  Stanford, CA 94305
Stanwix House
  3020 Chartiers Ave., Pittsburgh, PA
  15204
State University of New York Press
  Thurlow Terrace, Albany, NY 12201
Steck-Vaughn Company
  Box 2028, Austin, TX 78767
Stein & Day
  7 East 48th St., New York, NY 10017
Sterling Publishing Company, Inc.
  419 Park Ave., S., New York, NY
  10016
Stewart, Henry, Inc.
  249 Bowen Road, East Aurora, NY
  14052
Swallow Press
  1139 S. Wabash Ave., Chicago, IL
  60605
Syracuse University Press
  Box 8 University Sta., Syracuse, NY
  13210

Taplinger Publishing Co., Inc.
  29 E. Tenth St., New York, NY 10003
Templegate Publishers
  Box 963, Springfield, IL 62705
Textile Book Service
  266 Lake Ave., Metuchen, NJ 08890
Theatre Arts Books
  333 Sixth Ave., New York, NY 10014

Theosophical Publishing House
  Box 270, Wheaton, IL 60187
Toggitt, Joan,'Ltd.
  1170 Broadway, New York, NY 10001
Transatlantic Arts, Inc.
  North Village Green, Levittown, NY
  11756
Tri-Ocean, Inc.
  62 Townsend St., San Francisco,
  CA 94107
Trinity University Press
  715 Stadium Dr., San Antonio, TX
  78212
Tudor Publishing Company
  572 Fifth Ave., New York, NY 10036
Tuttle, Charles E., Company, Inc.
  Rutland, VT. 05701
Twayne Publishers
  31 Union Square West, New York,
  NY 10003

Ungar, Frederick, Publishing Company
  Inc.
  250 Park Ave., S., New York, NY
  10003
UNIPUB, Inc.
  Box 433, New York, NY 10016
United Publishing Corp.
  5530 Wisconsin Ave. Washington, D.C.
  20015
United Synagogue Book Service
  218 E. 70th St., New York, NY 10021
United States Publishers Association,
  Inc.
  386 Park Ave. S., New York, NY
  10016
Universitetsforlaget
  Box 142, Boston, MA 02113
University Press
  Drawer N, Wolfe City, TX 75496
United States Publishers Association,
  Inc.
  386 Park Ave. S., New York, NY
  10016

University of Alabama Press
Drawer 2877, University, AL 35486
University of Arizona Press
Box 3398, College Station, Tucson,
AZ 85700
University of California Press
2223 Fulton St., Berkeley, CA 94720
University of Chicago Press
5801 Ellis Ave., Chicago, IL 60637
University of Detroit Press
4001 W. McNichols, Detroit, MI
48221
University of Florida Press
15 NW 15th St., Gainesville, FL 32601
University of Georgia Press
Waddel Hall, Athens, GA 30601
University of Illinois Press
Urbana, IL 61801
University of Iowa Press
Graphic Services Bldg., Iowa City,
IA 52240
University of Massachusetts Press
Amherst, MA 01002
University of Miami Press
Drawer 9088, Coral Gables, FL 33124
University of Michigan Press
615 East University, Ann Arbor,
MI 48106
University of Minnesota Press
2037 University Ave., S.E., Minne-
apolis, MN 55455
University of Missouri Press
103 Swallow Hall, Columbia, MO
65201
University of Nebraska Press
901 N. 17th St., Lincoln, NB 68508
University of New Mexico Press
Albuquerque, NM 87106
University of North Carolina Press
Chapel Hill, NC 27514
University of Notre Dame Press
Notre Dame, IN 46556
University of Oklahoma Press
1005 Asp Ave., Norman, OK 73069
University of Oregon Books
Eugene, OR 97403

University of Pennsylvania Press
3933 Walnut St., Philadelphia, PA
19104
University of Pittsburgh Press
127 North Bellefield Ave., Pittsburgh,
PA 15213
University of Tennessee Press
Communications Bldg., Knoxville,
TN 37916
University of Texas Press
Box 7819, Austin, TX 78712
University of Toronto Press
Toronto 181, Canada; or 33 E. Tupper
St., Buffalo, NY 14208
University of Utah Press
Bldg. 513, Salt Lake City, UT 84112
University of Washington Press
Seattle, WA 98105
University of Wisconsin Press
Box 1379, Madison, WI 53701
University Press
Drawer N, Wolfe City, TX 75496
University Press of Kansas
366 Watson, Lawrence, KS 66044
University Press of Virginia
Box 3608 University Sta.,
Charlottesville, VA 22903
University Press of Washington, D.C.
Suite 321, 1010 Vermont Ave., N.W.,
Washington, D.C. 20005

Vanderbilt University Press
Nashville, TN 37203
Vanguard Press, Inc.
424 Madison Ave., New York, NY
10017
Van Nostrand Reinhold Company
450 West 33rd St., New York, NY
10001
Verry, Lawrence, Inc.
Mystic, CT 06355
Viewpoint Books
Box 9622, San Diego, CA 92109
Viking Press, Inc.
625 Madison Ave., New York, NY
10022

Vision Books. Imprint of Farrar,
Straus & Giroux, Inc.

Wadsworth Publishing Company, Inc.
10 Davis Dr., Belmont, CA 94002
Walck, Henry Z., Inc.
19 Union Square West, New York,
NY 10003
Walden Press
423 S. Franklin Ave., Flint, MI
48503
Washington Square Press, Inc.
Orders to Simon & Schuster, Inc.,
630 5th Ave., New York, NY 10020
Washington State University Press
Pullman, WA 99164
Watts, Franklin, Inc.
845 Third Ave., New York, NY 10022
Wayne State University Press
Detroit, MI 48202
Weatherhill, John, Inc.
Books published by John Weatherhill,
Inc. Distributed by J. B. Lippincott Co
Wehman Brothers
156–158 Main St., Hackensack, NJ
07601
Weiss, Day & Lord, Inc.
7251 Owensmouth St., Canoga Park,
CA 91303
Wesleyan University Press
Middletown, CT 06457
Western Publishing Co., Inc.
850 Third Ave., New York, NY 10022
Westminster Press
Witherspoon Bldg., Philadelphia, PA
19107
Westover Publishing Company
333 E. Grace St., Richmond, VA 23219

Weybright & Talley, Inc.
Orders to McKay, David, Inc.,
750 Third Ave., New York, NY 10017
Whitmore Publishing Company
1809 Callowhill St., Philadelphia, PA
19130
Whitson Publishing Company
Box 322, Troy, NY 12181
Wiley, John, & Sons, Inc.
605 3rd Ave., New York, NY 10016
Williams, Walter M.D.
20 Magnolia Terrace, Springfield, MA
Williams & Wilkins Co.
428 East Preston St., Baltimore, MD
21202
Willoughby Books
14 Hamburg Turnpike, Hamburg, NJ
07419
Wilson, H. W.
950 University Ave., Bronx, NY 10452
Winchester Press
460 Park Ave., New York, NY 10022
World Publishing Co.
110 East 59th St., New York, NY
10022
Writer, Inc.
8 Arlington St., Boston, MA 02116
Writer's Digest
22 E. 12th St., Cincinnati, OH 45210

Xerox College Publishing, Xerox
Education Group
275 Wyman St., Waltham, MA 02154

Yale University Press
92A Yale Station, New Haven, CT
06520